DATE DUE

06 1 1 '96			
NO 1 9 '96			
AP 1 1 '97			
OC 1 7 '97			
AP 1 98			
MY 20			
OC 1 6 '98			
NO 2 '98			
NV 21			
MR 2 3 '06			

The *Mathematica* Handbook

Martha L. Abell

Department of Mathematics and Computer Science
Georgia Southern University
Statesboro, Georgia

James P. Braselton

Department of Mathematics and Computer Science
Georgia Southern University
Statesboro, Georgia

AP PROFESSIONAL
A Division of Harcourt Brace & Company
Boston   San Diego   New York
London   Sydney   Tokyo   Toronto

This book is printed on acid-free paper. ∞

Mathematica is a registered trademark of Wolfram Research, Inc.

Cover design by Peter Altenberg

AP PROFESSIONAL
955 Massachusetts Avenue, Cambridge, MA 02139

An Imprint of ACADEMIC PRESS, INC.
A Division of HARCOURT BRACE & COMPANY

United Kingdom Edition published by
ACADEMIC PRESS LIMITED
24–28 Oval Road, London NW1 7DX

Library of Congress Cataloging-in-Publication Data

Abell, Martha L., date.
     The Mathematica handbook / Martha L. Abell, James P. Braselton.
         p.   cm.
     ISBN 0-12-041536-4
     1. Mathematica (Computer program) 2. Mathematics—Data
processing. I. Braselton, James P., date. II. Title.
QA76.95.A22   1992   92-13599
510'.285'5369—dc20   CIP

Printed in the United States of America
     94 95 96 97 IP 9 8 7 6 5 4 3

Preface

The *Mathematica* Handbook is intended to provide a convenient reference of all built-in *Mathematica* Version 2.0 objects to both beginning and advanced users of *Mathematica* alike. This book arose out of the need to have a convenient reference of all *Mathematica* commands and objects along with typical examples of them. In addition, The *Mathematica* Handbook contains commands and examples of those commands found in the packages contained in the Calculus (beginning on page 584), Statistics (beginning on page 610), and Numerical Math (beginning on page 714) folders (or directories). The commands in these sections are listed within each package, and the packages are listed alphabetically within each folder (or directory) as well. The end of The Handbook includes a list of references (on page 773) and an index (beginning on page 775). The Preface describes how to use the entries of The Handbook and then briefly discusses elementary rules of *Mathematica* syntax, defining functions, and using commands that are contained in the standard *Mathematica* packages

Of course, appreciation must be expressed to those who assisted in this project. In particular, we would like to thank our editor, Charles Glaser, and production editor, Brian Miller, for providing valuable, timely, and pleasant feedback on our work. We would also like to thank the people at Wolfram Research, Inc., particularly Brad Horn, who has been most helpful during this endeavor, for the help they have provided during this project. Finally, we would like to thank those close to us for their patience, kindness, and understanding over the course of this project.

M. L. Abell

J. P. Braselton

March, 1992

How to Use This Handbook

Guide to Entries in The *Mathematica* Handbook

This handbook is divided into two sections. The first section, consisting of Chapters 1 through 26, contains an alphabetical listing of every built-in *Mathematica* object along with a chapter containing examples of graphics commands and options. The *Mathematica* Handbook is cross-referenced with *Mathematica*: A System for Doing Mathematics by Computer, Second Edition, by Stephen Wolfram and published by the Addison-Wesley Publishing Company. A typical entry in the first section of The *Mathematica* Handbook looks similar to the following:

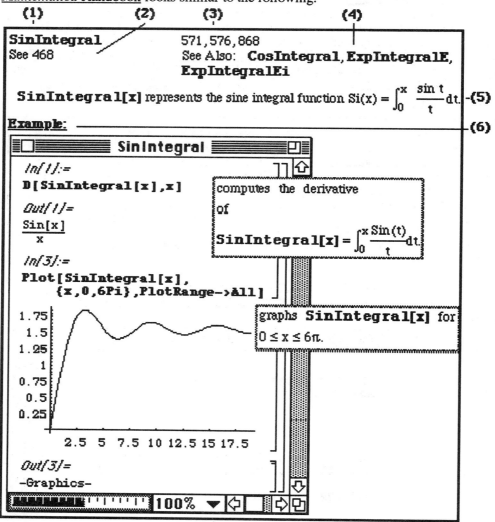

Features of a typical entry in the first section include:
(1) The name of the command or object;
(2) Other pages within The _Mathematica_ Handbook on which the command appears, if
any;
(3) Pages of _Mathematica_: A System for Doing Mathematics by Computer, Second
Edition, on which the command appears, if any;
(4) Related commands;
(5) A description of the command; and
(6) A typical example.

The second section, consisting of Chapter 27: Calculus Packages (see page 584),
Chapter 28: Statistics Packages (see page 610), and Chapter 29: Numerical Math
Packages (see page 714), contains a listing of the commands contained in the frequently
used packages found in the Calculus, Statistics, and Numerical Math folders (or
directories). Brief descriptions of all standard packages shipped with Version 2.0 of
Mathematica are included in the Technical Report: Guide to Standard _Mathematica_
Packages, by Philip Boyland, and published by Wolfram Research, Inc. A typical entry
in the second section of The _Mathematica_ Handbook looks similar to the following:

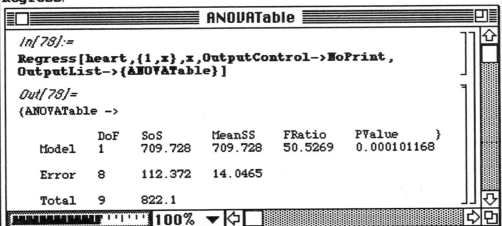

(1)   **(2)**

ANOVATable   Package: **LinearRegression.m**
    ANOVATable is a possible entry in **OutputList** which leads to the
table of the analysis of variance to be included in the list of output of the
functions **Regress** and **DesignedRegress**. This table is computed for   **(3)**
a smaller model by assuming independent samples, normal populations,
and equal population standard deviations. It includes the degrees of
freedom, the sum of the squares, and the mean squares due to the model
and the residuals. It also includes the F-statistic which compares the two
models and the p-value. If the p-value is large, then the null hypothesis is
rejected.
Example:
In the following example, the **ANOVATable** option setting is illustrated.   **(4)**
With the indicated settings, only **ANOVATable** is given as output of
Regress.

ANOVATable

_In[78]:=_
**Regress[heart,{1,x},x,OutputControl->NoPrint,
OutputList->{ANOVATable}]**

Out[78]=
{ANOVATable ->

| | DoF | SoS | MeanSS | FRatio | PValue | }
|--------|-----|---------|---------|---------|-------------|
| Model | 1 | 709.728 | 709.728 | 50.5269 | 0.000101168 |
| Error | 8 | 112.372 | 14.0465 | | |
| Total | 9 | 822.1 | | | |

100%

Features of a typical entry in the second section include:
(1) The name of the command or object;
(2) The package(s) in which the command appears;
(3) A description of the command; and
(4) A typical example.
Pages references to _Mathematica: A System for Doing Mathematics by Computer_,
Second Edition, on which the command appears and related commands are included
when applicable.

For general information regarding _Mathematica_, including purchasing information,
contact
Wolfram Research, Inc.
100 Trade Center Drive
Champaign, Illinois 61820-7237, USA
Telephone: (217) 398-0700
Fax: (217) 398-0747
E-Mail: info@wri.com

Basic Rules of _Mathematica_ Syntax

Mathematica is case-sensitive. Note that every built-in _Mathematica_ object begins with
an upper-case letter.
Example:
Plot   Solve
If a command contains two words or more words, each word in the command begins with
a capital letter:
Example:
ParametricPlot DSolve
Since _Mathematica_ is case-sensitive and every built-in _Mathematica_ object begins with
an upper-case character, this book adopts the convention that every user-defined object
will consist of lower-case characters. As a result, we will be certain to avoid any
possible ambiguity with built-in _Mathematica_ objects.

Arguments of functions are enclosed with square braces, brackets are used to denote lists
and matrices, elements of lists are extracted with double square braces, and parentheses
are used for grouping symbols.
Example:
Entering **f[x]** returns the value of **f** for the variable **x**;
Entering **v={a,b,c}** defines the list **v** to consist of the symbols **a**, **b**, and **c**;
Entering **v[[1]]** returns **a**, **v[[2]]** returns **b**, and **v[[3]]** returns **c** if **v** has been
defined as above; and

Entering **(x + y)/(x − y)** returns $\dfrac{x+y}{x-y}$.

Multiplication of expressions is usually denoted by a space or *****:
Example:
Entering **2 x** (a space between "2" and "x") returns the product of 2 and x;
Entering **2x** (no space between "2" and "x") returns the product of 2 and x;
Entering **2*x** returns the product of 2 and x;
Entering **cat dog** (a space between "**cat**" and "**dog**") returns the product of **cat** and
dog;

Entering **cat*dog** returns the product of **cat** and **dog**; and
Entering **catdog** (no space between "**cat**" and "**dog**") returns the symbol (or variable) **catdog**.

The symbol **%** represents the output of the previous result; the symbol **%%** stands for the output of the next-to-last result; **%%%...%** (k-times) stands for the output of the kth previous result; and **%n** where **n** is a positive integer represents the output of the **n**th command.

Example:
The following example illustrates several uses of the **%** command with basic calculations.

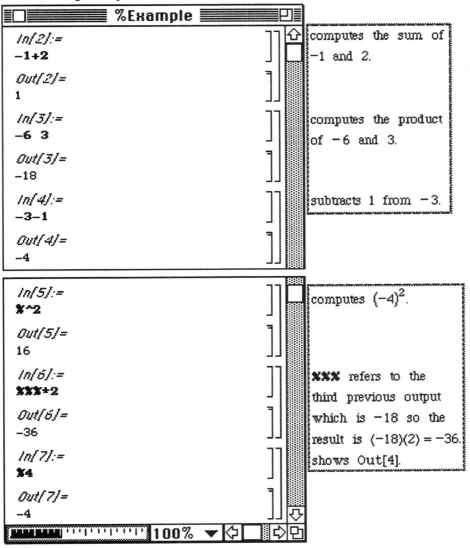

An Introduction to Defining Functions

Since *Mathematica* is case-sensitive, The *Mathematica* Handbook will adopt the convention that every user-defined object will consist of lower-case characters and consequently be certain to avoid any possible ambiguity with built-in *Mathematica* objects. *Mathematica* provides a great deal of flexibility when defining functions so for more specific discussions see the descriptions of **Blank (_)**, **BlankNullSequence (___)**, **BlankSequence (__)**, **Condition (/;)**, **Module**, **RuleDelayed (:>)**, **Set (=)**, **SetDelayed (:=)**, **ReplaceAll (/.)**, **TagSet**, **TagSetDelayed**, and **TagUnset**. When first defining a function, the argument must be enclosed in square brackets and an underline (**Blank**) must be placed after the argument on the left-hand side of the equals sign, but not on the right-hand side, in the definition of the function. Generally, functions may be defined to have any number of arguments and arguments can be any *Mathematica* object. Two ways of defining functions include:

f[arguments]=expression evaluates **expression** for **arguments** when the definition is entered ("immediate assignment"); and

f[arguments]:=expression evaluates **expression** when **f** is called ("delayed assignment"). The following examples illustrate several ways in which functions are defined with *Mathematica*.

Example:

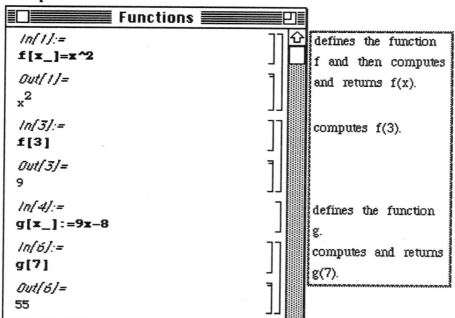

The following example illustrates the difference between using ":=" and "=" by attempting to define the function **h[f,{a,b}]** to graph the function **f** on the interval **[a,b]**. However, since "=" is used, after the definition is entered, *Mathematica* attempts to evaluate **h** for arbitrary **f**, **a**, and **b**.

```
In[8]:=
h[f_,{a_,b_}]=Plot[f[x],{x,a,b}]

      Plot::plln:
          Limiting value a in {x, a, b}
               is not a machine-size real
               number.

Out[8]=
Plot[f[x], {x, a, b}]
```

On the other hand, when ":=" is used, *Mathematica* does not attempt to compute **h** until **h** is called. **h** is used to graph f(x)=x^2, defined above, on the interval [−1,1].

```
In[10]:=
Clear[h]
h[f_,{a_,b_}]:=Plot[f[x],{x,a,b}]

In[11]:=
h[f,{-1,1}]
```

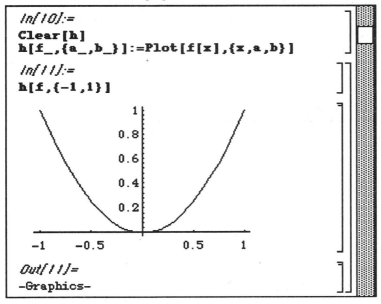

```
Out[11]=
-Graphics-
```

Users can also define functions for specific arguments. In general, entering **f[x]=expression**, without an underline (**Blank**) after the **x** on the left-hand side of the equals sign, defines **f** to have the value **expression** for argument **x**.

```
In[14]:=
a[1]=alpha;
a[2]=beta;
a[3]=gamma;
```

defines the function
a for the values
1, 2, and 3.

```
In[15]:=
?a

        Global`a

        a[1] = alpha

        a[2] = beta

        a[3] = gamma
```

Functions can also be defined recursively and to remember the values computed. The function **f** defined using the pattern **f[x_]:=f[x]=expression** explicitly stores the values computed. This method of defining functions is particularly useful when either the function is recursively defined or when function values are difficult (or time consuming) to compute and will be used more than one time. In the following example, **it[1]=3** and **it[2]=1**. Then **it[n]** is defined to remember the values computed and determined by the relationship

$$it[n] = \frac{it[n-1]}{it[n-2]}.$$

```
In[21]:=
it[1]=3;
it[2]=1;
it[n_]:=it[n]=it[n-1]/it[n-2]
```

A **Do** loop is used to compute the values of **it[n]** for n=3, 4, 5, and 6. Since **it** is defined to remember the values computed, **?it** yields the values of **it[n]** explicitly computed in the **Do** loop and previously defined.

```
In[22]:=
Do[it[n],{n,3,6}]

In[23]:=
?it

      Global`it

      it[1] = 3

      it[2] = 1

      it[3] = 1/3

      it[4] = 1/3

      it[5] = 1

      it[6] = 3

      it[n_] := it[n] = it[n - 1]/it[n - 2]
```

`100%`

Packages

Mathematica packages are identified by package and folder name. *Mathematica*
packages are read in directly with **<<Folder`Package`**, where **Folder** is the folder
(or directory) that contains the package **Package**.
Example:
Below, the package **NLimit** which is contained in the **NumericalMath** folder is
entered, and a limit is determined.

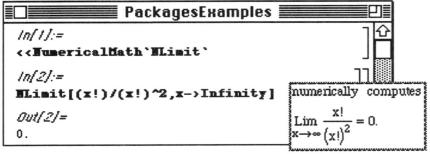

```
PackagesExamples

In[1]:=
<<NumericalMath`NLimit`

In[2]:=
NLimit[(x!)/(x!)^2,x->Infinity]

Out[2]=
0.
```

numerically computes
$$\lim_{x \to \infty} \frac{x!}{(x!)^2} = 0.$$

However, packages can be loaded automatically when needed with
DeclarePackage["Folder`Package`",{"sym1","sym2",...}]. With this
command, **Folder`Package`** is loaded when a command from the list
sym1, sym2, ... is first used.

Example:

In the following example, the **DescriptiveStatistics** package in the
Statistics folder is loaded when either the **Mean** or **Median** symbol is used. In this
case, **Mean** is entered first, so the mean of the list **{2,4,6,8}** is calculated after the
package is loaded.

```
In[3]:=
DeclarePackage[
    "Statistics`DescriptiveStatistics`",
    {"Mean","Median"}]

Out[3]=
Statistics`DescriptiveStatistics`

In[4]:=
Mean[{2,4,6,8}]                 computes  (2+4+6+8)/4 = 5.

Out[4]=
5
```

Occasionally, a symbol from a package is accidentally entered prior to loading the
package. To overcome this problem, the command **Remove** must be employed.
Otherwise, *Mathematica* will not recognize the appropriate definition of the symbol, and
the calculation will not be performed. Of course, the *Mathematica* session can be
terminated and then restarted with the same affect.

Example:

In the following example, the computation of the dot product of the indicated vectors **x**
and **y** is attempted with the command **DotProduct**, which is contained in the package
VectorAnalysis, before the **VectorAnalysis** package is loaded from the
Calculus folder. However, the computation is not performed since the package is not
loaded.

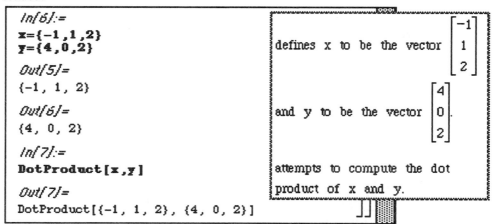

```
In[5]:=
x={-1,1,2}                       defines x to be the vector  ⎡-1⎤
y={4,0,2}                                                    ⎢ 1⎥
                                                             ⎣ 2⎦
Out[5]=
{-1, 1, 2}
                                                             ⎡4⎤
Out[6]=                          and y to be the vector      ⎢0⎥.
{4, 0, 2}                                                    ⎣2⎦

In[7]:=
DotProduct[x,y]                  attempts to compute the dot
                                 product of x and y.
Out[7]=
DotProduct[{-1, 1, 2}, {4, 0, 2}]
```

After **Remove** is used with **DotProduct**, the package is loaded so that the dot product
can be found. Notice the warning messages which accompany the loading of the
VectorAnalysis package. These messages indicate that symbols **x** and **y** appear
within the package and may conflict with prior definitions. *Mathematica* uses more

recently loaded definitions over prior definitions.

```
In[8]:=
Remove[DotProduct]

In[9]:=
<<Calculus`VectorAnalysis`

    x::shdw: Warning: Symbol x
        appears in multiple contexts
        {Calculus`VectorAnalysis`, <<1>>}
        ; definitions in context
        Calculus`VectorAnalysis`
        may shadow other definitions.

    y::shdw: Warning: Symbol y
        appears in multiple contexts
        {Calculus`VectorAnalysis`, <<1>>}
        ; definitions in context
        Calculus`VectorAnalysis`
        may shadow other definitions.

In[10]:=
DotProduct[x,y]        computes the dot product
                       of x and y.
Out[10]=
0
```

The context of symbols in packages must be considered. Because symbols in different packages can have the same name, the context associated with the name of a package is added to the list **$ContextPath** when the package is loaded.

Example:

Below, the current context search path is given.

```
In[11]:=
Context[DotProduct]

Out[11]=
Calculus`VectorAnalysis`

In[12]:=
$ContextPath

Out[12]=
{Calculus`VectorAnalysis`,
  Statistics`DescriptiveStatistics`,
  NumericalMath`NLimit`,
  Graphics`Animation`, Global`, System`}
```

Symbols within packages can possess several types of contexts. These include **Folder`Package`** for symbols which can be used outside of the package, **Folder`Package`Private`** for internal symbols, and **System`** for built-in *Mathematica* commands.

Example:
In the following example, the contexts of several symbols are indicated.

```
In[14]:=
Context[coordsys]

Out[14]=
Global`

In[15]:=
Context[Plot]

Out[15]=
System`
```

$Packages lists the contexts associated with all packages which are loaded.
Example:
The list of contexts associated with the packages that are loaded is given below.

```
In[16]:=
$Packages

Out[16]=
{System`ComplexExpand`,
  Calculus`VectorAnalysis`,
  Statistics`DescriptiveStatistics`,
  NumericalMath`NLimit`, FE`, Global`,
  System`}
```

A

Abort   311, 750
See 44   See Also: **CheckAbort**, **MemoryConstrained**,
                                    Throw, **TimeConstrained**

Use **Abort[]** to interrupt computations.

Example:

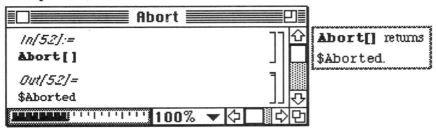

AbortProtect   311, 750
                                    See Also: **CheckAbort**, **MemoryConstrained**,
                                    TimeConstrained

Use **AbortProtect[expression]** to prevent aborts until the evaluation of
expression is complete..

Above   766
                                    See Also: **Below**, **Center**

Above is an option to be used with commands such as **ColumnForm** and
TableForm

Abs   49, 52, 550, 551, 604, 750
See 66, 123, 126, 130, 131   See Also: **Arg**, **ComplexExpand**, **Im**, **Mod**, **Re**
133, 235, 237, 240, 241, 242
411, 541, 568, 583

Abs[z] computes the absolute value of the complex number **z**.

Example:

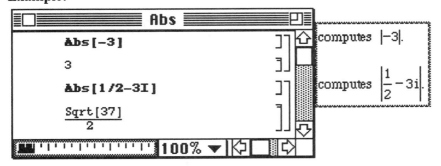

AbsoluteDashing   409, 750, 802, 803
              See Also: **AbsoluteThickness**, **Graphics**,
              Thickness, **GrayLevel**, **Hue**, **RGBColor**
   AbsoluteDashing[{d1,d2,...}] instructs that dashed lines are to be drawn with successive line segments of absolute lengths **d1**, **d2**, ...   These are repeated cyclically.

AbsolutePointSize   408, 750, 802, 803
              See Also: **Graphics**, **PointSize**, **Thickness**
   AbsolutePointSize[r] is a two- and three-dimensional graphics directive used to state that points be plotted as circular regions having absolute radius **r**.

AbsoluteThickness   409, 750, 802, 803
              See Also: **AbsoluteDashing**, **PointSize**, **Dashing**,
              Thickness
   AbsoluteThickness[t] is a two- and three-dimensional graphics directive that indicates that lines be drawn with absolute thickness **t**.

AbsoluteTime   524, 751
              See Also: **Data**, **SessionTime**, **TimeUsed**, **Timing**,
              TimeZone, **ToDate**, **FromData**
   AbsoluteTime[] gives the total number of seconds since the beginning of January 1, 1900 in your current time zone.

AccountingForm   350, 751
              See Also: **PaddedForm**, **NumberForm**,
              ScientificForm
   AccountingForm[number] prints **number** in accounting notation.
AccountingForm only affects the printing of **number**. It does not alter calculations involving it.
Example:

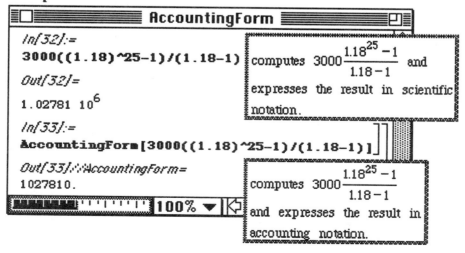

Accumulate   obsolete in Version 2.0
                        superseded by **FoldList**
   Accumulate is not included with Version 2.0; instead it is replaced by **FoldList**.

Accuracy   539, 751
                        See Also: **Precision, N, Chop, SetAccuracy**
   Accuracy[number] computes the number of digits to the right of the decimal place
in **number**.
Example:

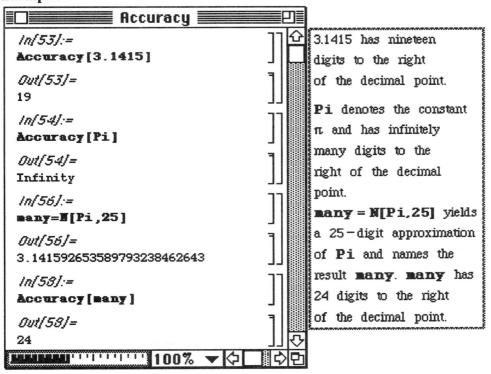

AccuracyGoal   687,690,695,700,751
                          See Also: **PrecisionGoal, WorkingPrecision**
   AccuracyGoal   is an option used with numerical operations such as **NIntegrate**
and **NDSolve** to indicate the number of digits to appear in the result of these functions.
The default setting **AccuracyGoal->Automatic** sets the value of **AccuracyGoal**
to be 10 fewer digits than the setting of **WorkingPrecision** while a setting of
AccuracyGoal->Infinity indicates that **AccuracyGoal** not be used in the
termination criteria for these functions. Note that a setting of **AccuracyGoal->n** often
leads to results with fewer than **n** digits.

AddTo   248, 751
                                                See Also: **Increment**, **PreIncrement**, **PrependTo**,
                                                Set

    AddTo[x,y] computes **x+y** and yields the new value; this operation is also denoted
as **+=**.

Example:

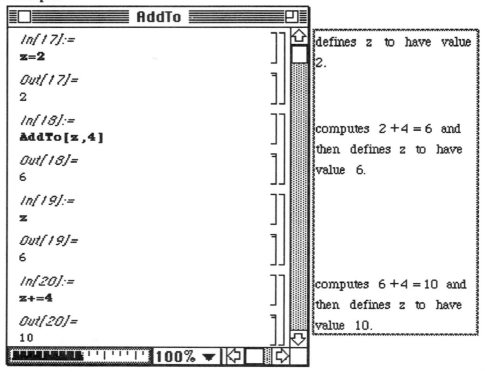

AiryAi[z]   570, 576, 751
                                                See Also: **AiryAiPrime**, **AiryBi**, **AiryBiPrime**, **N**,
                                                Gamma

    AiryAi[z] denotes the Airy function Ai(z) which is a solution of Airy's differential
equation:

$$\frac{d^2y}{dz^2} - zy = 0.$$

Example:

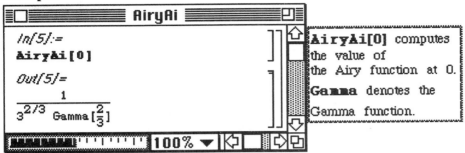

AiryAiPrime[z]   570, 576, 752
                           See Also: **AiryAi**, **AiryBi**, **AiryBiPrime**, **N**, **Gamma**

   AiryAiPrime[z] denotes the derivative Ai$'$(z) of the Airy function.
Example:

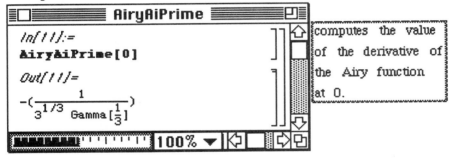

AiryBi[z]   570, 576, 752
                           See Also: **AiryAi**, **AiryAiPrime**, **AiryBiPrime**, **N**,
                           Gamma

   AiryBi[z] represents the Airy function Bi(z) which also solves Airy's equation but
grows exponentially with z.
Example:

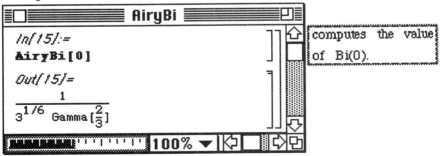

AiryBiPrime[z]   570, 576, 752
                         See Also: **AiryAi**, **AiryAiPrime**, **AiryBi**, **N**, **Gamma**
  AiryBiPrime[z] is the derivative of Bi(z) given above.

Example:

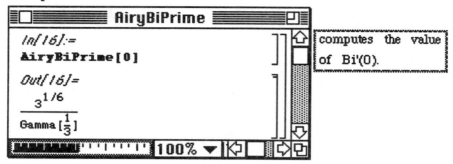

AlgebraicRules   622, 752
                         See Also: **Eliminate**, **Replace**
  AlgebraicRules[equations,variablelist] defines a list of algebraic rules
to replace variables which appear earlier in **variablelist** with those given later in
variablelist. Replacement is done according to **equations**.

Example:

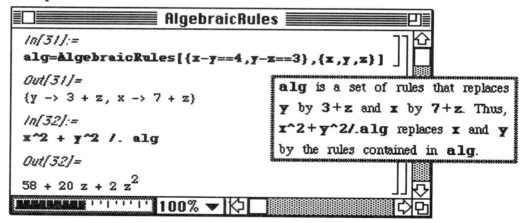

AlgebraicRulesData   622, 752
                         See Also: **AlgebraicRules**
  AlgebraicRulesData is the object generated by **AlgebraicRules** and contains
a representation of the Grobner basis for **equations** defined in
AlgebraicRules[equations,variablelist].

Alias   xix (obsolete in Version 2.0)
                         superseded by **$PreRead**

All   141, 752
                              See Also: **Automatic, None**
   All is a setting for certain options such as **PlotRange** and **FaceGrids**.

Alternatives   229, 752
                              See Also: **Optional**
   Alternatives are used to specify patterns and can be applied to transformation
rules.
Example:

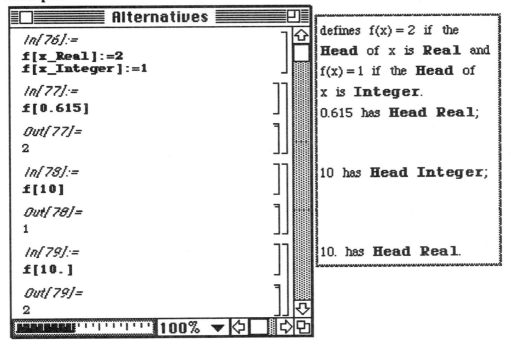

```
defines f(x) = 2 if the
Head of x is Real and
f(x) = 1 if the Head of
x is Integer.
0.615 has Head Real;

10 has Head Integer;

10. has Head Real.
```

AmbientLight   455, 752, 803
See 519   See Also: **GrayLevel, Hue, Lighting, RGBColor,**
                                          LightSources, SurfaceColor
   AmbientLight is a **Graphics3D** option which indicates the level of simulated
ambient light to be used in three-dimensional graphics. These levels are specified with
the directives **RGBColor**, **GrayLevel**, or **Hue**.

Analytic
See 259   See Also: **Limit, Series**
   Analytic is an option for **Limit** and **Series**.

AnchoredSearch   501, 752
   AnchoredSearch is an option used with **Find** and **FindList** to specify whether
the text appears at the beginning of a line.

And   94, 753
See 277, 389, 530, 568,   See Also: **LogicalExpand**
576

And, symbolized by **&&**, represents the logical and function. This function evaluates **exp1&&exp2&&**... by giving a value of **False** if any of the expressions **exp1**, **exp2**, ... are **False** and yielding **True** if they are all **True**.

Example:

In the following example, the command **a==b** tests if a and b are equal. See **Equal**.

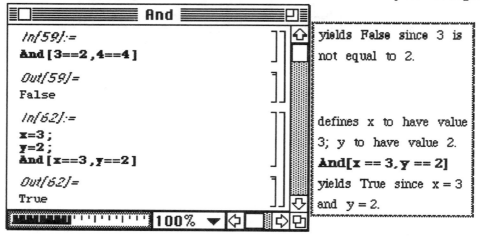

Animate   137, 175
See Also: **ShowAnimation**

Animate[plot,{t,tmin,tmax}] carries out the graphics command **plot** for the sequence of **t**-values from **tmin** to **tmax** and then animates the sequence of frames which results.

Apart   596, 753
See Also: **Cancel**, **PolynomialQuotient**,
Together

Apart[expression] computes the partial fraction decomposition of **expression**.

Example:

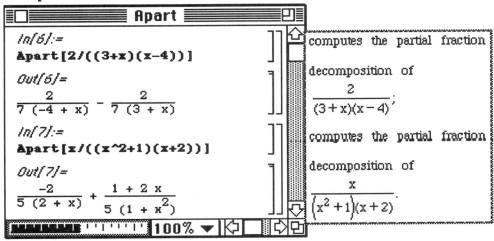

ApartSquareFree

ApartSquareFree[expression,var] writes **expression** as the sum of terms with square-free denominators in the variable **var**.

Append   128, 753
                                   See Also: **AppendTo, Insert, Prepend**
   Append[expression, element] appends **element** to **expression** and gives the expression which results.

Example:

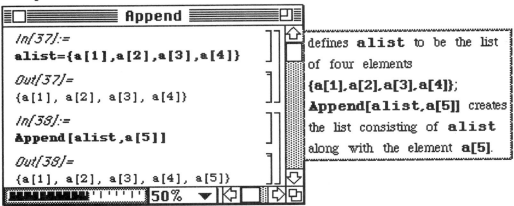

AppendTo   249, 753
                                   See Also: **Append, PrependTo**
   AppendTo[list,element] appends **element** to **list** and names the result **list**.

Example:

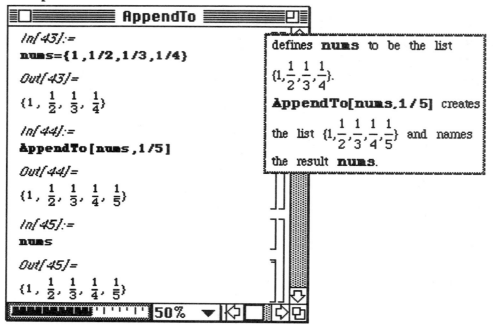

Apply (@@)   203, 753

See 351   See Also: **Map, Scan, Level, Operate, MapThread**

    Apply[f,expression] evaluates **f** at the elements of **expression**. If **list** is a list of numbers, the command **Apply[Plus,list]** adds the elements of list; **Apply[Times,list]** multiplies the elements of **list**. This command can also be denoted by **f@@expression**.

Example:

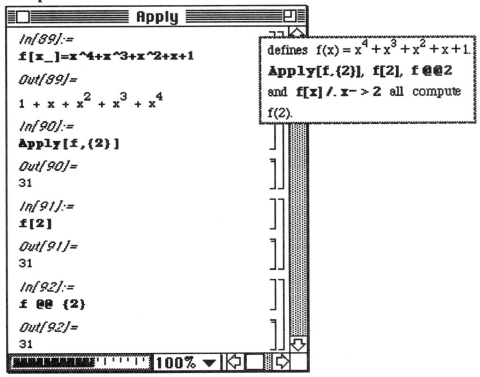

defines $f(x) = x^4 + x^3 + x^2 + x + 1.$ **Apply[f,{2}]**, **f[2]**, **f @@ 2** and **f[x] /. x -> 2** all compute $f(2).$	

ArcCos   562, 753
See 71   See Also: **ArcSin, ArcTan, N**

  ArcCos[z] yields the inverse cosine (in radians) of the complex number **z**. For real numbers between −1 and 1, the result is an exact value between 0 and π. When an exact number is not given, numerical approximations can be computed using the command **N**.

Example:

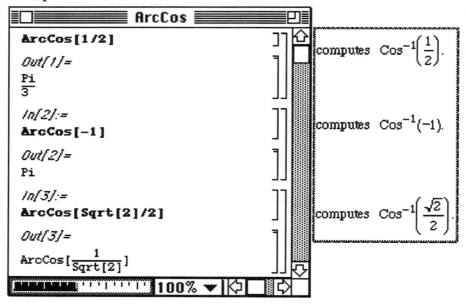

ArcCosh   562, 754
                              See Also: **ArcSech**, **N**

   ArcCosh[z] yields the exact value the inverse hyperbolic cosine of the complex
number **z**.

Example:

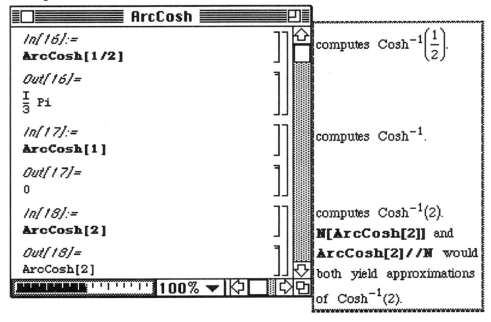

ArcCot   562, 754
See 74   See Also: **ArcTan, N**

    ArcCot[z] gives the inverse cotangent (in radians) of the complex number **z**. If **z** is real, then the result is an exact value on the interval from $-\pi/2$ to $\pi/2$, with the exception of 0.

Example:

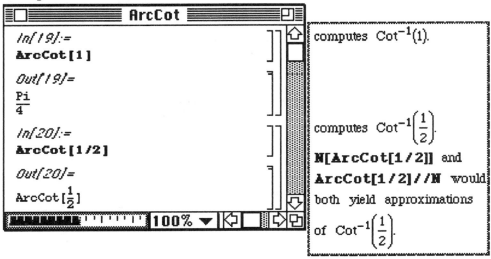

ArcCoth   562, 754
                      See Also: **ArcTanh, N**
  ArcCoth[z] gives the exact value of the inverse hyperbolic cotangent of the complex
number **z**.
Example:

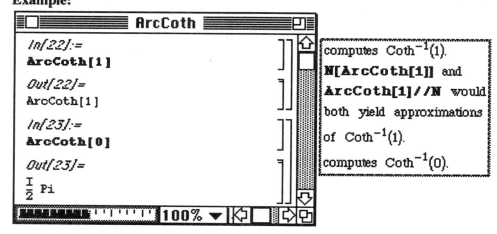

ArcCsc   562, 754
                  See Also: **ArcSec, ArcSin, ArcCos, N**
  ArcCsc[z] yields the inverse cosecant (in radians) of the complex number **z**. For
real values of **z** outside of the interval from −1 to 1, the result is between −π/2 and π/2,
excluding 0.
Example:

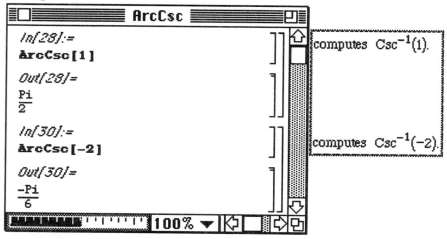

ArcCsch   562, 754
                      See Also: **ArcSech, N**
  ArcCsch[z] gives the exact value of the inverse hyperbolic cosecant of the complex
number **z**.

Example:

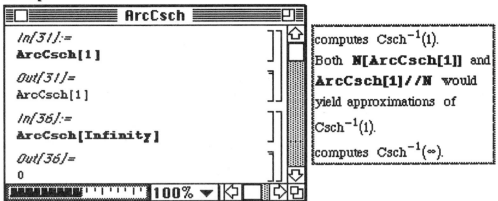

ArcSec   562, 754
                              See Also: **ArcCsc, ArcSin, ArcCos, N**

ArcSec[z] yields the inverse secant (in radians) of the complex number **z**. For real numbers **z** which are outside of the interval $[-1, 1]$, the result is on the range from 0 to π, with the exception of $\pi/2$.

Example:

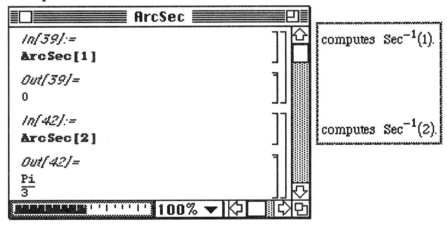

ArcSech   562, 754
                              See Also: **ArcCsch, N**

ArcSech[z] yields the exact value of the inverse hyperbolic secant of the complex number **z**.

Example:

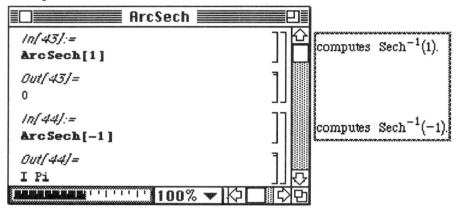

ArcSin   562, 754
See 215   See Also: **ArcCos**, **ArcTan**, **N**

    ArcSin[z] yields the inverse sine (in radians) of the complex number **z**. For real values of **z** between −1 and 1, the result is an exact value between $-\pi/2$ and $\pi/2$.

Example:

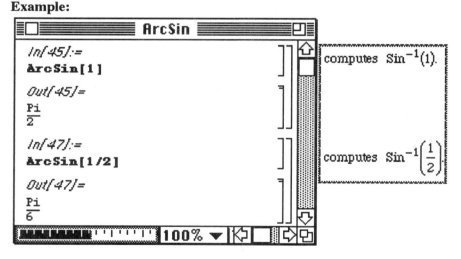

ArcSinh   562, 754
                                See Also: **ArcCsch**, **N**

    ArcSinh[z] gives the exact value of the inverse hyperbolic sine of the complex number **z**.

Example:

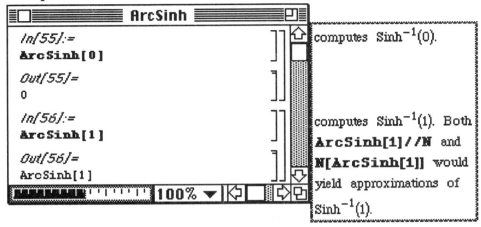

ArcTan   562, 755
See 615   See Also: **ArcCos**, **ArcSin**, **N**, **Arg**

   ArcTan[z] yields the inverse tangent (in radians) of the complex number **z**. The result is an exact value between $\frac{-\pi}{2}$ and $\frac{\pi}{2}$ for real values of **z**. **ArcTan[x,y]** returns the unique angle θ which satisfies $\tan\theta = \frac{y}{x}$ with θ in the same quadrant as the point (x, y).

Example:

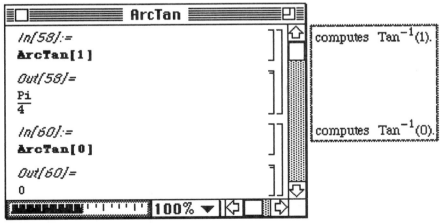

ArcTanh   562, 755
                                   See Also: **ArcCoth**, **N**

   ArcTanh[z] yields the exact value of the inverse hyperbolic tangent of the complex number **z**.

Example:

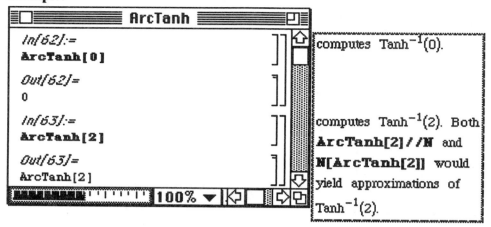

Arg   551, 755

See Also: **ArcTan**, **Sign**, **TargetFunctions**

Arg[z] yields the argument of the complex number **z**.

Example:

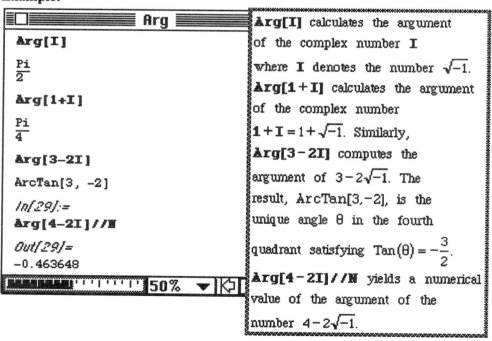

Args

Args is an internal command the attributes of which are protected by the system.

Args$

   Args$** is an internal command. The attribute of **Args$ is Temporary.

ArithmeticGeometricMean 580, 585, 755

                      See Also: **EllipticLog, EllipticExp**

   ArithmeticGeometricMean[x,y] yields the arithmetic-geometric mean of the
numbers **x** and **y**. The arithmetic geometric mean of x and y is obtained by computing

$$x_{n+1} = \frac{1}{2}(x_n + y_n),\ y_{n+1} = \sqrt{x_n\, y_n}\ \text{ until }\ x_n = y_n.$$

Example:

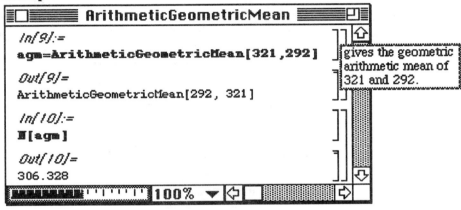

Array   210, 755

See 341, 463   See Also: **ColumnForm, MatrixForm**

                                 Table, TableForm

   Array[function,n] creates a list of length **n** with components **function[i]** for
i=1 to i=n. **Array[function,{m,n}]** forms an **m** × **n** array with
function[i,j] as components.

Example:

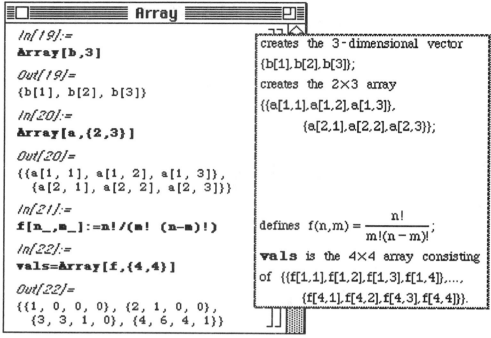

Arrays are viewed in the form of a table (or matrix) with **TableForm**

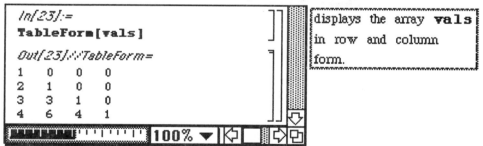

AspectRatio   416, 755, 802, 803
See 512, 515, 516, 519,   See Also: **BoxRatios**, **GoldenRatio**, **Graphics**,
525, 526, 534, 543-546,   **Graphics3D**, **PlotRegion**
548, 552, 553

   AspectRatio is an option used with **Show** to specify the ratio of the height to the
width of a plot. The default value is **AspectRatio->1/GoldenRatio**, where

GoldenRatio is a built - in *Mathematica* constant with value $\dfrac{1+\sqrt{5}}{2} \approx 1.618$

AtomQ   228, 756
                               See Also: **NumberQ**, **Head**, **LeafCount**, **Length**
   AtomQ[expression] gives a value of True if **expression** cannot be divided into
subsections. It gives a value of False otherwise.

Attributes   271, 756
                                  See Also: **SetAttributes**, **ClearAttributes**

  Attributes[symbol] yields the complete list of attributes for **symbol**. These attributes include **Constant**, **Flat**, **HoldAll**, **HoldFirst**, **HoldRest**, **Listable**, **Locked**, **OneIdentity**, **Orderless**, **Protected**, **ReadProtected**, **Stub**, and **Temporary**.

AutoLoad

  AutoLoad is used to automatically load a file necessary for running a command and then execute that command. **AutoLoad** is defined in the following way :
```
AutoLoad[Fn_,File_,Args_]:=
         Block[{},Get[File];Apply[Fn,Args]]
```

Automatic   141, 756
See 127, 513, 514   See Also: **All**, **None**

  Automatic is used as an option with a built-in command to represent the default value automatically chosen by that command.

Auxiliary

  Auxiliary[var] is used by the **Solve** package to indicate that the variable **var** is to be used by **Roots** to determine solutions, but that the values of **var** are not to be included in the final result.

Axes   418, 459, 756, 802, 803
See 513, 517-519, 522, 523,   See Also: **AxesLabel**, **AxesOrigin**, **Frame**,
547, 555, 569, 570, 579   **GridLines**, **Boxed**

  Axes is an option used with graphics commands to specify whether axes are to be drawn or not. **Axes->True** is the default value and requests that axes be drawn while **Axes->False** causes no axes to be drawn. **AxesOrigin** is used with two-dimensional graphics to specify the point at which the axes intersect while in three-dimensions, the axes are drawn along the edges of the bounding box given by the option **AxesEdge**.

AxesEdge   461, 757, 803
See 519   See Also: **Axes**, **AxesLabel**, **Graphics3D**

  AxesEdge is a **Graphics3D** option used to specify along which edges of the boxed region axes are to be drawn. This setting can be made in different forms.
AxesEdge->Automatic causes edges appear in positions determined by an internal algorithm. Also, **AxesEdge->{xsp,ysp,zsp}** indicates different settings for the x, y, and z axes. The three specifications include **None** which causes no edges to appear in the indicated direction and **Automatic** which was described earlier. In addition, each setting can be given with **{dir1,dir2}**. The values of **dir1** and **dir2** are **+1** or **−1** and indicate larger and smaller values of the other two coordinates, respectively.

AxesLabel   419, 462, 757, 802, 803
See 513, 519, 555, 581   See Also: **PlotLabel**, **FrameLabel**
  AxesLabel is an option of graphics functions which is used to label the axes. Settings
can be made in several different forms. **AxesLabel->None** indicates that no labels be
given. **AxesLabel->"label"** prints label on the y-axis.
AxesLabel->{{"labelx","labely"}} assigns labels on the x- and y-axes.

AxesOrigin   419, 757, 802
See 513, 554, 556, 668   See Also: **Axes**, **Graphics**
671, 673
  AxesOrigin is a two-dimensional graphics function option which states the point at
which certain axes should cross. This setting is made in the form
AxesOrigin->{x0,y0}.

AxesStyle   419, 461, 757, 802, 803
See 513, 520   See Also: **Prolog**, **Epilog**, **PlotStyle**, **FrameStyle**
  AxesStyle is an option used with graphics functions to state the style which should
be used in plotting the axes. These styles include **Dashing**, **Hue**, and **Thickness**.
The settings can be made as **AxesStyle->style** which indicates that all axes be
displayed in the indicated style, **AxesStyle->{{stylex},{styley}}** which
specifies styles for the indicated axes.
Example:

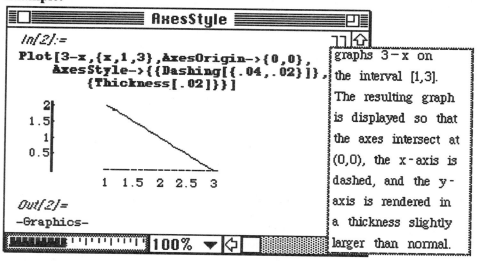

B

Background   412, 757
See 513, 520, 548,   See Also: **DefaultColor, Plot,**
556, 572   **PlotRegion, Prolog**

Background is used as an option for graphics functions to state the background color for the plot. The setting for **BackGround** is made in terms of **Hue, GrayLevel, CMYKColor,** or **RGBColor.**

BaseForm   353, 537, 758
                                 See Also: **IntegerDigits, RealDigits**

BaseForm[expression,n] prints **expression** in base **n**. For **n** >10, the letters a-z are used for the extra digits. The maximum value of **n** is 36.

Example:

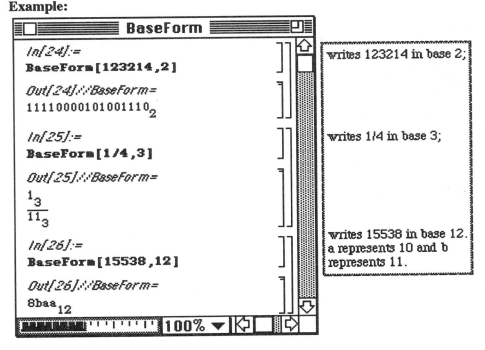

Begin   339, 341, 758
                                 See Also: **BeginPackage, End,**
                                 $ContextPath

Begin["context`"] resets the current context. This affects the parsing of input since symbol interpretation depends on context.

BeginPackage   339, 758
                                 See Also: **EndPackage**

BeginPackage is used at the beginning of packages to reset the values of **$Context** and **$ContextPath.**

Below   766

See Also: **Above**, **Center**

Below is used with commands like **ColumnForm** and **TableForm** to specify the alignment in printforms.

BernoulliB   558, 559, 758

See Also: **Binomial**, **EulerE**, **Multinomial**, **NBernoulliB**, **PartitionsP**, **PartitionsQ**, **Signature**, **StirlingS1**, **StirlingS2**

The Bernoulli polynomials and Bernoulli numbers are obtained from the relation

$$\frac{t e^{xt}}{e^t - 1} = \sum_{n=0}^{\infty} B_n(x) \frac{t^n}{n!},$$ where $B_n(x)$ denotes the nth Bernoulli polynomial and

$B_n(0)$ denotes the nth Bernoulli number. **BernoulliB[n]** yields the nth Bernoulli number while **BernoulliB[n,x]** gives the nth Bernoulli polynomial.

Example:

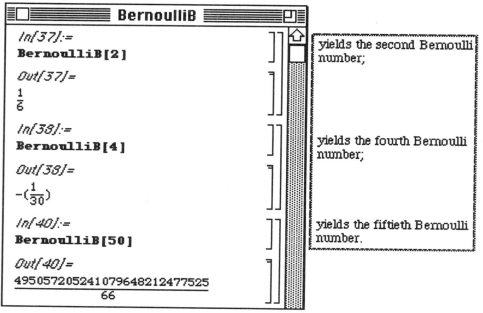

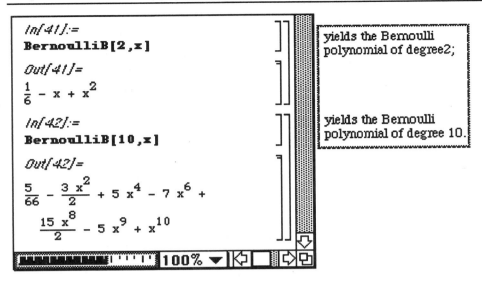

In[41]:=
BernoulliB[2,x]

Out[41]=
$\frac{1}{6} - x + x^2$

yields the Bernoulli polynomial of degree 2;

In[42]:=
BernoulliB[10,x]

Out[42]=
$\frac{5}{66} - \frac{3 x^2}{2} + 5 x^4 - 7 x^6 +$
$\frac{15 x^8}{2} - 5 x^9 + x^{10}$

yields the Bernoulli polynomial of degree 10.

100% ▼

BesselI   570, 576, 758
                              See Also: **BesselJ**, **BesselK**, **BesselY**

Solutions of the differential equation $x^2 \dfrac{d^2 y}{dx^2} + x \dfrac{dy}{dx} - \left(x^2 + n^2\right) y = 0$ are called

modified Bessel functions. **BesselI[n,x]** gives the modified Bessel function of the first kind of order n. **BesselI[n,x]** is regular for x=0.

Example:

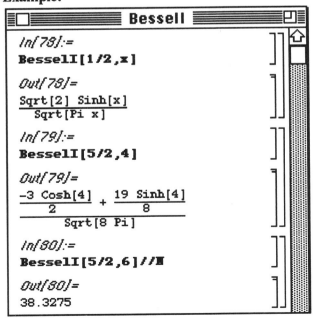

BesselI

In[78]:=
BesselI[1/2,x]

Out[78]=
$\frac{\text{Sqrt[2] Sinh[x]}}{\text{Sqrt[Pi x]}}$

In[79]:=
BesselI[5/2,4]

Out[79]=
$\frac{\frac{-3 \, \text{Cosh[4]}}{2} + \frac{19 \, \text{Sinh[4]}}{8}}{\text{Sqrt[8 Pi]}}$

In[80]:=
BesselI[5/2,6]//N

Out[80]=
38.3275

BesselJ   2, 570, 576, 758
See 749-751   See Also: **BesselI, BesselK, BesselY**

Solutions of the differential equation $x^2 \dfrac{d^2 y}{dx^2} + x\dfrac{dy}{dx} + \left(x^2 - n^2\right)y = 0$ are called Bessel functions.   **BesselJ[n,x]** gives the Bessel function of the first kind of order n, $J_n(x)$, which is regular for x=0 for every value of n. **BesselY[n,x]** gives the Bessel function of the second kind of order n, $Y_n(x)$, which diverges for x=0 for every value of

n. $J_n(x)$ is given by the formula $J_n(x) = \displaystyle\sum_{m=0}^{\infty} \dfrac{(-1)^m \left(\dfrac{x}{2}\right)^{2m+n}}{m!\,\Gamma(m + n + 1)}$ and satisfies

the recurrence relations $\dfrac{d}{dx}\left(x^\alpha J_\alpha(x)\right) = x^\alpha J_{\alpha-1}$, $\dfrac{d}{dx}\left(x^{-\alpha} J_\alpha(x)\right) = -x^{-\alpha}J_{\alpha+1}$,

$J'_\alpha(x) = \dfrac{1}{2}\left[J_{\alpha-1}(x) - J_{\alpha+1}(x)\right]$, and $J_{\alpha+1}(x) = \dfrac{2\alpha}{x}J_\alpha(x) - J_{\alpha-1}(x)$.

Example:

The following example first defines **bessels** to be the table of Bessel functions of the first kind, $J_1(x)$, $J_2(x)$, and $J_3(x)$, and then graphs each for $0 \le x \le 15$. The resulting three graphs are displayed simultaneously; the graph of $J_1(x)$ is the darkest, the graph of $J_3(x)$ the lightest.

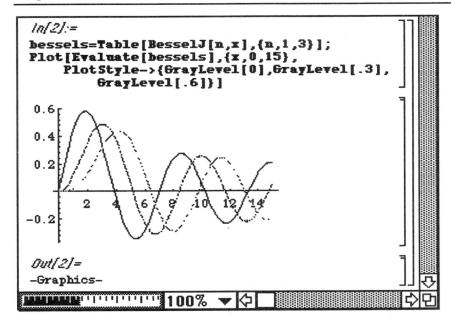

```
In[2]:=
bessels=Table[BesselJ[n,x],{n,1,3}];
Plot[Evaluate[bessels],{x,0,15},
    PlotStyle->{GrayLevel[0],GrayLevel[.3],
        GrayLevel[.6]}]
```

Out[2]=
-Graphics-

BesselK   570, 576, 758

See Also: **BesselI**, **BesselJ**, **BesselY**

BesselK[n,x] gives the modified Bessel function of the second kind of order **n**.

Example:

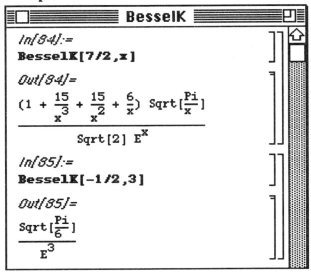

```
In[84]:=
BesselK[7/2,x]
```

Out[84]=

$$\frac{\left(1 + \frac{15}{x^3} + \frac{15}{x^2} + \frac{6}{x}\right) \text{Sqrt}[\frac{Pi}{x}]}{\text{Sqrt}[2]\ E^x}$$

```
In[85]:=
BesselK[-1/2,3]
```

Out[85]=

$$\frac{\text{Sqrt}[\frac{Pi}{6}]}{E^3}$$

BesselY   570, 576, 758
                                     See Also: **BesselI**, **BesselJ**, **BesselK**

BesselY[n,x] gives the Bessel function of the second kind of order **n**.
Example:

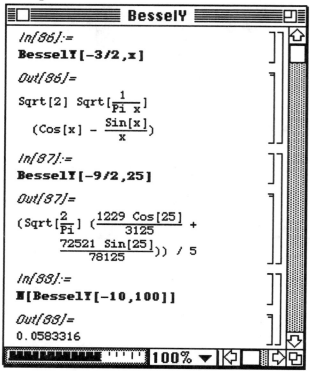

Beta   572, 573, 759
                                    See Also: **BetaRegularized**, **Gamma**,
                                    GammaRegularized

The Gamma function, $\Gamma(z)$, is given by $\Gamma(z) = \underset{n\to\infty}{\text{Lim}} \dfrac{n!\,n^z}{z(z+1)\ldots(z+n)}$

$$= \int_0^\infty e^{-t}t^{z-1}dt.$$

If n is a positive integer, then $\Gamma(n+1) = n!$. The Euler Beta function, $B(a,b)$,

is given by $B(a,b) = \dfrac{\Gamma(a)\Gamma(b)}{\Gamma(a+b)} = \int_0^1 t^{a-1}(1-t)^{b-1}\,dt = \int_0^\infty \dfrac{t^{a-1}}{(1+t)^{a+b}}\,dt$.   The

incomplete Euler Beta function, $B(z,a,b)$, is given by

$B(z,a,b) = \int_0^z t^{a-1}(1-t)^{b-1}\,dt$.   The generalized incomplete Euler Beta function,

$B(w,z,a,b)$, is given by $B(w,z,a,b) = \int_w^z t^{a-1}(1-t)^{b-1}\,dt$.

Beta[a,b] yields the Euler Beta function; **Beta[z,a,b]** gives the incomplete Beta function; and **Beta[w,z,a,b]** gives the generalized incomplete Beta function.
Example:

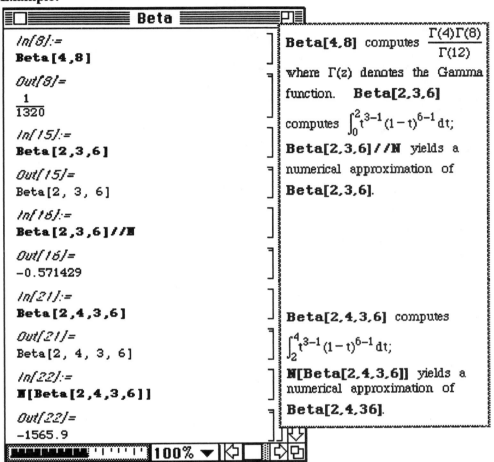

```
In[8]:=
Beta[4,8]

Out[8]=
 1
────
1320

In[15]:=
Beta[2,3,6]

Out[15]=
Beta[2, 3, 6]

In[18]:=
Beta[2,3,6]//N

Out[18]=
-0.571429

In[21]:=
Beta[2,4,3,6]

Out[21]=
Beta[2, 4, 3, 6]

In[22]:=
N[Beta[2,4,3,6]]

Out[22]=
-1565.9
```

Beta[4,8] computes $\dfrac{\Gamma(4)\Gamma(8)}{\Gamma(12)}$ where $\Gamma(z)$ denotes the Gamma function. **Beta[2,3,6]** computes $\int_{0}^{2} t^{3-1}(1-t)^{6-1}\,dt$; **Beta[2,3,6]//N** yields a numerical approximation of **Beta[2,3,6]**.

Beta[2,4,3,6] computes $\int_{2}^{4} t^{3-1}(1-t)^{6-1}\,dt$; **N[Beta[2,4,3,6]]** yields a numerical approximation of **Beta[2,4,36]**.

BetaRegularized   573, 759
See 688, 689   See Also: **Beta, Gamma, GammaRegularized**
   The regularized incomplete Beta function, $I(z,a,b)$, is given by

$I(z,a,b) = \dfrac{B(z,a,b)}{B(a,b)}$.   The generalized regularized incomplete Beta function,

$I(w,z,a,b)$, is given by $I(w,z,a,b) = \dfrac{B(w,z,a,b)}{B(a,b)}$.

BetaRegularized[z,a,b] gives the regularized incomplete Beta function;
BetaRegularized[w,z,a,b] gives the generalized regularized incomplete Beta function.

Example:

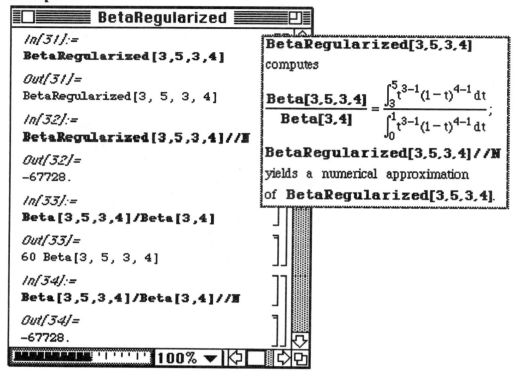

```
╔══════════════ BetaRegularized ══════════════╗
In[31]:=
BetaRegularized[3,5,3,4]

Out[31]=
BetaRegularized[3, 5, 3, 4]

In[32]:=
BetaRegularized[3,5,3,4]//N

Out[32]=
-67728.

In[33]:=
Beta[3,5,3,4]/Beta[3,4]

Out[33]=
60 Beta[3, 5, 3, 4]

In[34]:=
Beta[3,5,3,4]/Beta[3,4]//N

Out[34]=
-67728.
```

BetaRegularized[3,5,3,4]
computes

$$\frac{\text{Beta}[3,5,3,4]}{\text{Beta}[3,4]} = \frac{\int_3^5 t^{3-1}(1-t)^{4-1}\,dt}{\int_0^1 t^{3-1}(1-t)^{4-1}\,dt};$$

BetaRegularized[3,5,3,4]//N
yields a numerical approximation
of BetaRegularized[3,5,3,4].

Binomial   558, 759
                        See Also: **Multinomial**, **Pochhammer**

The Binomial coefficients, $\binom{n}{m}$, are given by the formula

$$\binom{n}{m} = \frac{n!}{(n-m)!\,m!}, \text{ for integers } 0 \le m \le n;\ \binom{n}{0} = \binom{n}{n} = 1.\ \binom{n}{m} \text{ gives the number}$$

of combinations of n distinct objects taken m at a time and

$$(x+c)^n = \sum_{r=0}^{n} \binom{n}{r} x^{n-r} c^r.$$

Binomial[n,m] gives the binomial coefficient "n choose m".

Example:

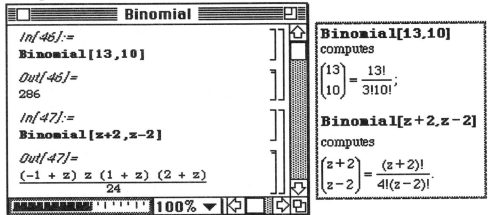

Blank   219, 759
See 32, 37   See Also: **Cases, Pattern, Optional**
   Blank[ ] or _ is the basic *Mathematica* object which is used to represent any expression.

BlankForm
   BlankForm is an internal symbol which is used for formatting and printing.

BlankNullSequence   232, 719, 759
                                   See Also: **Pattern**
   BlankNullSequence[ ] or _ _ _ is a pattern object which can be used to represent any sequence of zero or more *Mathematica* expressions.

Example:

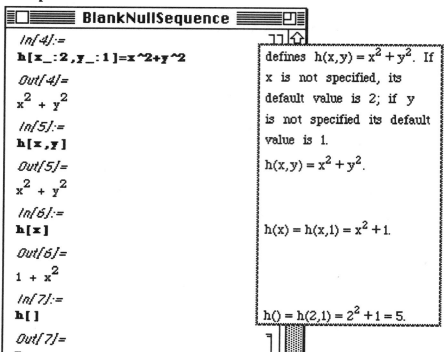

BlankNullSequence

In[4]:=
h[x_:2,y_:1]=x^2+y^2

Out[4]=
$x^2 + y^2$

In[5]:=
h[x,y]

Out[5]=
$x^2 + y^2$

In[6]:=
h[x]

Out[6]=
$1 + x^2$

In[7]:=
h[ ]

Out[7]=
5

defines $h(x,y) = x^2 + y^2$. If x is not specified, its default value is 2; if y is not specified its default value is 1.

$h(x,y) = x^2 + y^2$.

$h(x) = h(x,1) = x^2 + 1$.

$h() = h(2,1) = 2^2 + 1 = 5$.

In[8]:=
g[x_,y___]:=x^2+h[y]

In[10]:=
g[x,y,z]

Out[10]=
$x^2 + y^2 + z^2$

In[11]:=
g[x,y]

Out[11]=
$1 + x^2 + y^2$

In[12]:=
g[x]

Out[12]=
$5 + x^2$

defines $g(x,y) = x^2 + h(y)$. The y – argument in g may consist of zero or more objects.

$g(x,y,z) = x^2 + h(y,z)$
$\qquad = x^2 + y^2 + z^2$.

$g(x,y) = x^2 + h(y) = x^2 + h(y,1)$
$\qquad\qquad = x^2 + y^2 + 1$.

$g(x) = x^2 + h() = x^2 + 5$.

BlankSequence   232, 719, 760
                              See Also: **BlankNullSequence**
    BlankSequence[ ] or _ _   is a pattern object which can be used to represent any
sequence of one or more *Mathematica* expressions.
Example:
The following example uses the function h defined in the previous example.

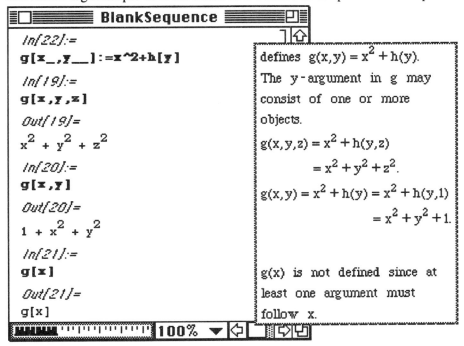

Block   xix, 329, 760
                              See Also: **Module, With, CompoundExpression**
    Block allows for the definition and use of local variables. After the execution of a
block, the original value of each variable is restored.
Example:
In the following example, x is defined to have value −8, y to have value 6, and z to have
value 5. The command **Block** is used to evaluate $x^2+y^2+z^2$ when x has value 1, y has
value 1, and z has value −7. Outside of the block, the orginal values of x, y, and z are
retained so that the value of $x^2+y^2+z^2=(-8)^2+6^2+5^2=125$.

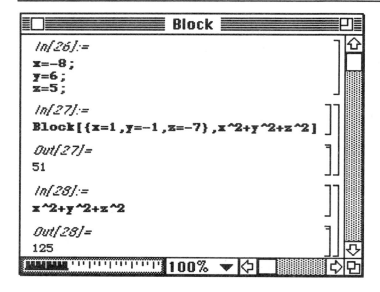

Bottom   357, 879

                               See Also: **Center, TableAlignments, TableForm,**
                               Top
    Bottom is a setting for the **TableAlignments** option used with **TableForm**.

Boxed   156, 459, 760, 803
See 520, 570, 579, 581   See Also: **BoxRatios, BoxStyle, Graphics3D,**
                               SurfaceGraphics
    Boxed is a **Graphics3D** option which states whether or not the edges of the bounding box should be included in a three-dimensional plot.

BoxRatios   441, 760, 803
See 520, 570   See Also: **Boxed, BoxStyle, Graphics3D,**
                               SurfaceGraphics
    BoxRatios is a **Graphics3D** and **SurfaceGraphics** option which gives the ratios of the side lengths of the bounding box drawn in a three-dimensional plot.

BoxStyle   441, 461, 760
See 520   See Also: **Boxed, BoxRatios, AxesStyle, Prolog,**
                               Epilog, DisplayFunction
    BoxStyle is an option for three-dimensional graphics functions which uses graphics directives such as **Dashing, Thickness, GrayLevel,** and **RGBColor** to state how the bounding box should be drawn.

Break   293, 760
                               See Also: **Continue, Return**
    Break[] exits the nearest enclosing **Do, While,** or **For** loop.

Byte   495, 760
    Byte represents a single byte of data and is returned as an integer.

ByteCount   528, 761
                                  See Also: **LeafCount, MemoryInUse,**
                                  MaxMemoryUsed, StringByteCount

    ByteCount[expression] gives the total number of bytes used by *Mathematica* to store **expression**.

Example:

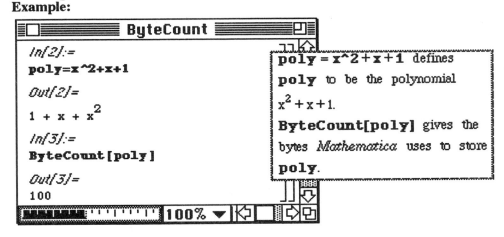

C

C   99, 638, 761
See 112   See Also: **DSolve**, **Unique**

    C[i] is the form in which the ith constant is given in the solution to a differential equation or system of differential equations when solving with **DSolve**. The indices begin with i = 1 and are successive. The default value is C.

CallProcess

    CallProcess[command,f,{x1,x2, ...}] calls the function f in an external process using the arguments **x1, x2, ...** . This command has been superseded by **MathLink**.

Cancel   78, 596, 761
See Also: **Apart**, **Denominator**, **GCD**, **Numerator**, **ComplexExpand**, **Expand**, **Simplify**, **Together**

    Cancel[expression] cancels common factors from the numerator and the denominator of **expression**.

Example:

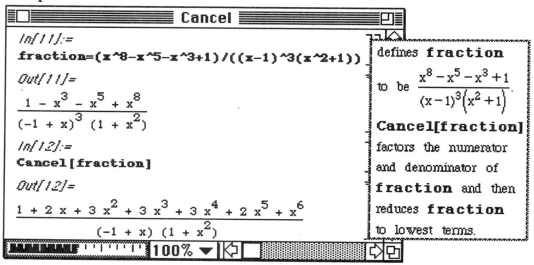

In[11]:=
fraction=(x^8-x^5-x^3+1)/((x-1)^3(x^2+1))

Out[11]=
$$\frac{1 - x^3 - x^5 + x^8}{(-1 + x)^3 (1 + x^2)}$$

In[12]:=
Cancel[fraction]

Out[12]=
$$\frac{1 + 2x + 3x^2 + 3x^3 + 3x^4 + 2x^5 + x^6}{(-1 + x)(1 + x^2)}$$

defines **fraction** to be $\dfrac{x^8 - x^5 - x^3 + 1}{(x-1)^3(x^2+1)}$.

Cancel[fraction] factors the numerator and denominator of **fraction** and then reduces **fraction** to lowest terms.

Cases   221, 222, 725, 761
                                    See Also: **Count**, **DeleteCases**, **Select**, **Position**
  Cases is used to match the elements of a list to a certain pattern.

Example:

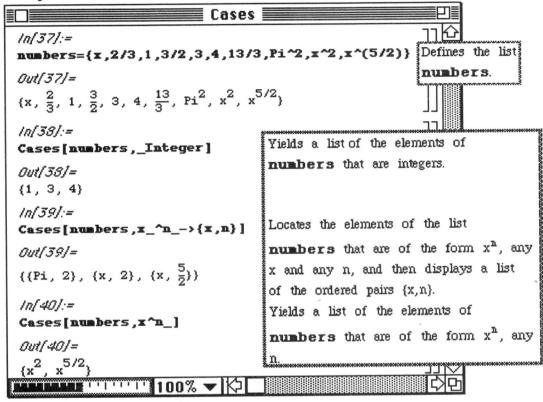

In[37]:=	Defines the list
numbers={x,2/3,1,3/2,3,4,13/3,Pi^2,x^2,x^(5/2)}	**numbers**.

Out[37]=

$\{x, \frac{2}{3}, 1, \frac{3}{2}, 3, 4, \frac{13}{3}, Pi^2, x^2, x^{5/2}\}$

In[38]:=

Cases[numbers,_Integer]

Yields a list of the elements of **numbers** that are integers.

Out[38]=

$\{1, 3, 4\}$

In[39]:=

Cases[numbers,x_^n_->{x,n}]

Locates the elements of the list **numbers** that are of the form x^n, any x and any n, and then displays a list of the ordered pairs {x,n}.

Out[39]=

$\{\{Pi, 2\}, \{x, 2\}, \{x, \frac{5}{2}\}\}$

In[40]:=

Cases[numbers,x^n_]

Yields a list of the elements of **numbers** that are of the form x^n, any n.

Out[40]=

$\{x^2, x^{5/2}\}$

100%

Catalan   566, 761
See 39   See Also: **ComplexInfinity**, **Degree**, **E**, **EulerGamma**,
                                             GoldenRatio, **I**, **Infinity**, **Pi**

   Catalan represents Catalan's constant which has the approximate numerical value of
0.915966.

Example:

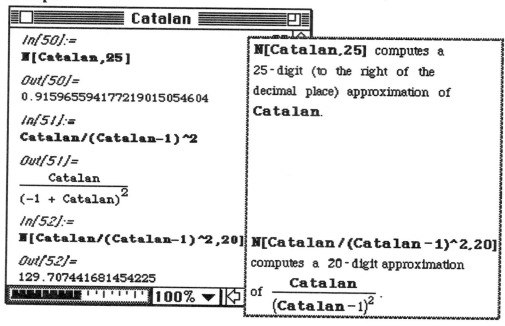

N[Catalan,25] computes a 25-digit (to the right of the decimal place) approximation of **Catalan**.

N[Catalan/(Catalan−1)^2,20] computes a 20-digit approximation of $\dfrac{\text{Catalan}}{(\text{Catalan}-1)^2}$.

Catch   294, 761
                                             See Also: **Break**, **Continue**, **Goto**, **Return**, **Throw**
   Catch[expression] returns the first value of **Throw** generated in the evaluation of
expression. If no **Throw** is produced in the evaluation, then **Catch[expression]**
returns the the value of **expression**.

Ceiling   550, 762
                                See Also: **Floor, Round, Chop**
  Ceiling[x] gives the value of the smallest integer greater than or equal to **x**.

Example:

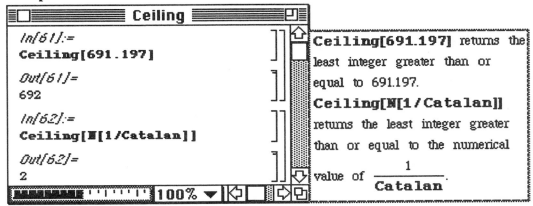

CellArray   xix (obsolete in Version 2.0)
                                superseded by **Raster** and **RasterArray**

Center   357, 766
See 53   See Also: **Above, Below, ColumnForm, TableForm,
                                TableAlignments**
  Center is a setting used with **ColumnForm** and **TableForm** to specify the alignment in printforms.

CForm   182, 762
                                See Also: **FortranForm**
  CForm[expression] prints **expression** in C language.

Example:

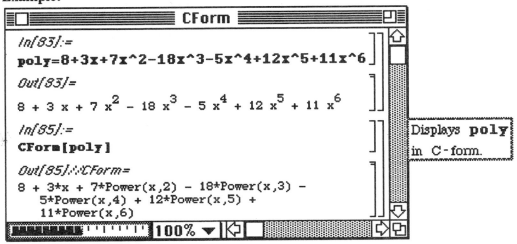

Character   495, 762
                                     See Also: **Byte**, **Expression**, **Hold**, **Real**, **Number**,
                                     Record, **String**, **Word**

    Character represents a single character in **Read** and is returned as a one-character string.

CharacteristicPolynomial

    The **characteristic polynomial** of the $n \times n$ matrix m in terms of the variable x is given by Det(m−xI) where I is the $n \times n$ identity matrix. The command **CharacteristicPolynomial[m,x]** yields the characteristic polynomial of the matrix **m** in terms of the variable **x**.

Example:

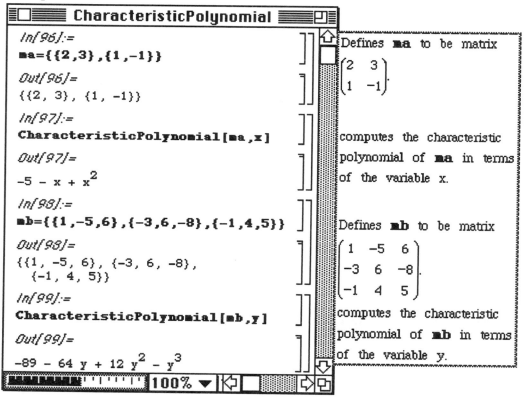

Characters   366, 368, 376, 378, 467, 839, 875
                            See Also: **StringJoin**, **StringLength**,
                            ToCharacterCode,**StringByteCount**,
                            StringToStream

Characters["string"] yields a list of the characters in **string**.

Example:

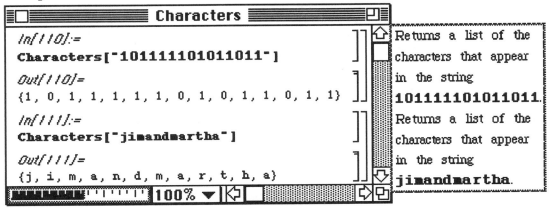

ChebyshevT   567, 568, 762
                            See Also: **ChebyshevU**

ChebyshevT[n,x] yields the nth Chebyshev polynomial of the first kind.

These polynomials are commonly denoted $T_n(x)$ where $T_n(x) = Cos(n\ ArcCos\ (x))$ and

$T_n(x)$ satisfies the differential equation $(1 - x^2)T_n{}'' - xT_n{}' + n^2T_n = 0.$

Example:

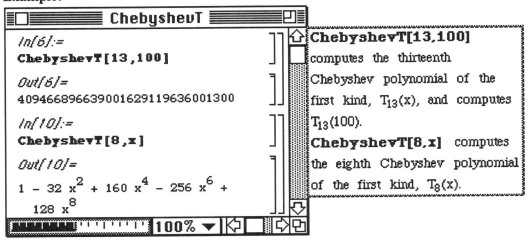

ChebyshevU   567, 568, 762
                                       See Also: **ChebyshevT**

ChebyshevU[n,x] yields the nth Chebyshev polynomial of the second kind.
The Chebyshev polynomials of the second kind, denoted $U_n(x)$, are given by

$$U_n(x) = \frac{\text{Sin}\lfloor (n+1)\ \text{ArcCos}(x) \rfloor}{\sqrt{1-x^2}},\quad n = 0,\ 1,\cdots\ .$$

Example:

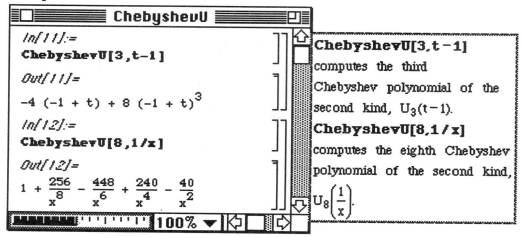

Check   389, 547, 762
                                       See Also: **MessageList**, **$MessageList**, **Message**,
                                       Indeterminant, **TimeConstrained**, **CheckAbort**

Check[expression,error] attempts to evaluate **expression**. If no error message is
produced during the evaluation, then the value of **expression** is returned. Otherwise,
error results.

Example:

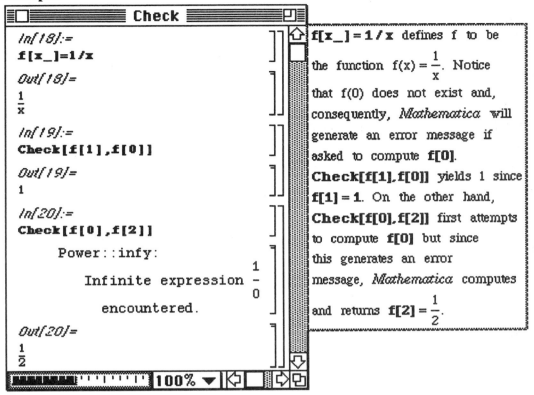

CheckAbort   311, 762

See Also: **Abort**, **AbortProtect**, **Catch**

   CheckAbort[expression,error] evaluates expression. If an abort is encountered, then **error** is returned. However, **CheckAbort** allows calculations which follow an abort to be evaluated.

Example:

In the following example, the first command prints the character "a" and then aborts the command. On the other hand, the second command prints the character "a", aborts the command, and then prints the character "c".

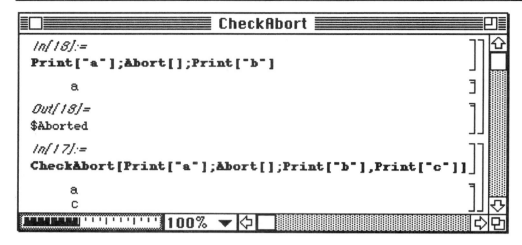

Chop   541, 656, 674, 763
See 163, 170, 224-230,   See Also: **Rationalize, Round**
322, 376, 409

Chop[expression] replaces all real numbers in **expression** which have absolute value less than $10^{\wedge}(-10)$ by zero. **Chop[expression,small]** replaces all real numbers in **expression** which have absolute value less than **small** by **zero**.

Example:

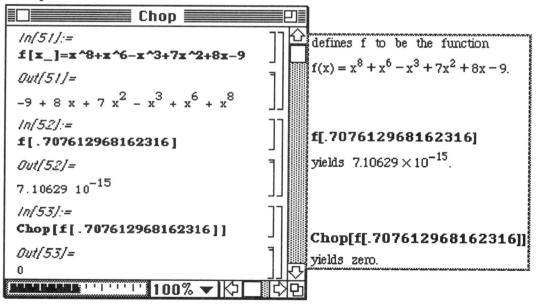

Circle   400, 404, 763
See 512, 525   See Also: **Disk**

Circle[{h,k},r] is a graphics primitive in two-dimensions which represents a circle centered at the point **(h,k)** with radius **r**. **Circle[{h,k},{rx,ry}]** gives an ellipse centered at the point **(h,k)** with semi-axes **rx** and **ry**.

Clear   55, 113, 247, 251, 273, 335, 385, 736, 763
See 568   See Also: **ClearAll**, **Information**, **Remove**
  Clear[symbol] clears all definitions for **symbol**.

Example:

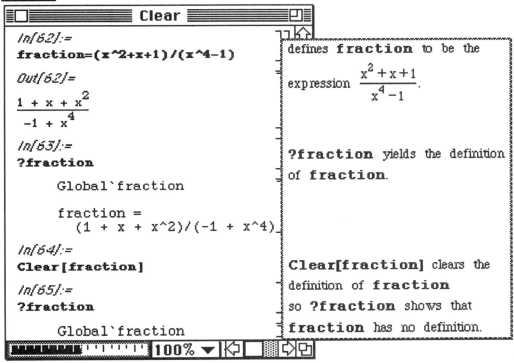

ClearAll   273, 736, 763
                             See Also: **Clear**, **Remove**
  ClearAll[symbol] clears all definitions, values, and attributes of **symbol**, including messages and defaults.

ClearAttributes   230, 271, 763
See 263   See Also: **SetAttributes**, **Unprotect**
  ClearAttributes[symbol,attribute] clears **attribute** from the list of attributes for **symbol**.

ClebschGordan   561, 763
                             See Also: **ThreeJSymbol**, **SixJSymbol**,
                             SphericalHarmonicY
  ClebschGordan[{j1,m1},{j2,m2},{j,m}] yields the Clebsch-Gordan coefficient for the decomposition of the angular momentum vector **{j,m}** in terms of **{j1,m1}** and **{j2,m2}**.

Example:

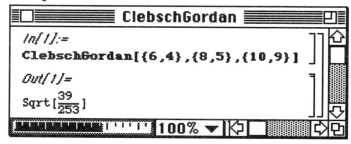

ClipFill   450, 764
See 522, 523, 569, 576,   See Also: **PlotRange**
582

    ClipFill is a **SurfaceGraphics** option to state how portions of the surface which would extend past the bounding box should be shown. **Settings** for this option include **Automatic** and **None**.

Close   485, 499, 502, 764
See 432   See Also: **OpenAppend, SetOptions, Streams**
    Close[stream] closes **stream** where **stream** can either be an **InputStream** or **OutputStream** object.

CMYKColor   472, 764
                                See Also: **RGBColor, ColorOutput**
    CMYKColor[cyan,magenta,yellow,black] specifies that the graphics which follow should be shown in the color levels (between 0 and 1) given by the values in **cyan, magenta, yellow,** and **black**.

Coefficient   82, 593, 764
                                See Also: **CoefficientList, Exponent**
    Coefficient[polynomial,form] yields the coefficient of **form** in **polynomial** while **Coefficient[expression,form,n]** gives the coefficient of **(form)^n** in **expression**.

Example:

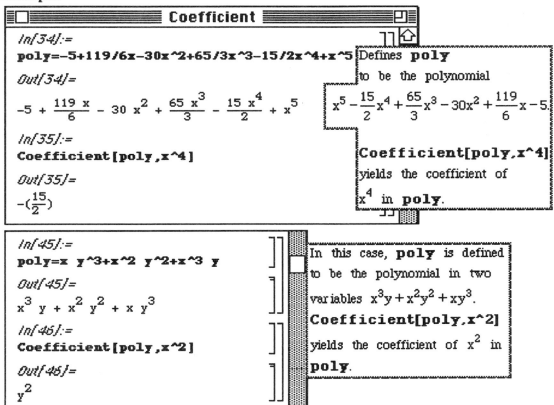

In[34]:=
```
poly=-5+119/6x-30x^2+65/3x^3-15/2x^4+x^5
```

Out[34]=
$$-5 + \frac{119\ x}{6} - 30\ x^2 + \frac{65\ x^3}{3} - \frac{15\ x^4}{2} + x^5$$

In[35]:=
```
Coefficient[poly,x^4]
```

Out[35]=
$$-(\frac{15}{2})$$

Defines **poly** to be the polynomial $x^5 - \frac{15}{2}x^4 + \frac{65}{3}x^3 - 30x^2 + \frac{119}{6}x - 5$.

Coefficient[poly,x^4] yields the coefficient of x^4 in **poly**.

In[45]:=
```
poly=x y^3+x^2 y^2+x^3 y
```

Out[45]=
$$x^3\ y + x^2\ y^2 + x\ y^3$$

In[46]:=
```
Coefficient[poly,x^2]
```

Out[46]=
$$y^2$$

In this case, **poly** is defined to be the polynomial in two variables $x^3y + x^2y^2 + xy^3$. **Coefficient[poly,x^2]** yields the coefficient of x^2 in **poly**.

Coefficient can also be used to obtain the coefficient of terms in expressions that are not polynomials:

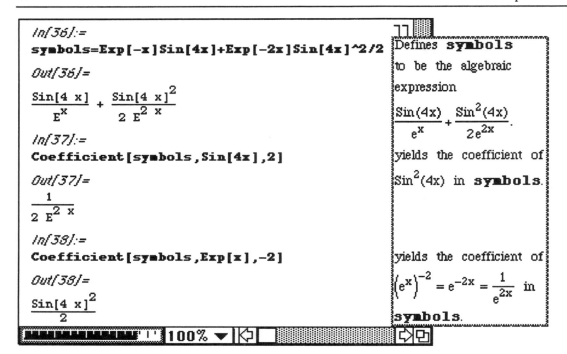

CoefficientList   593, 764

See Also: **Coefficient**, **Series**, **Collect**, **FactorList**

CoefficientList[polynomial,variable] gives a list of the coefficients of each power of **variable** in **polynomial**, starting with **variable^0**.

Example:

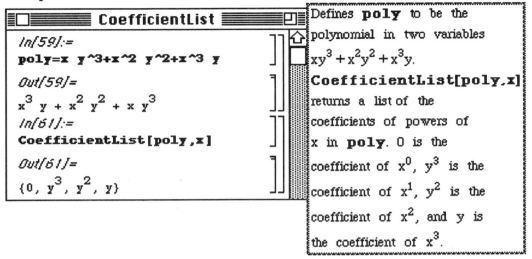

Observe that with *Mathematica*, the symbol **a[i]** can be interpreted as a_i. In the following example, **poly** is defined to be the polynomial in two variables

$a_1 x^2 y^2 + a_2 xy^2 + a_3 y^2 + a_4 x^2 y + a_5 xy + a_6 y + a_7 x^2 + a_8 x + a_9$.

CoefficientList[poly,{y,x}] yields the nested list

$\{\{a_9, a_8, a_7\}, \{a_6, a_5, a_4\}, \{a_3, a_2, a_1\}\}$ which may be interpreted as the matrix

$\begin{pmatrix} a_9 & a_8 & a_7 \\ a_6 & a_5 & a_4 \\ a_3 & a_2 & a_1 \end{pmatrix}$. Notice that the element in the ith row and jth column of

$\begin{pmatrix} a_9 & a_8 & a_7 \\ a_6 & a_5 & a_4 \\ a_3 & a_2 & a_1 \end{pmatrix}$ corresponds to the coefficient of $x^{j-1} y^{i-1}$ in **poly**:

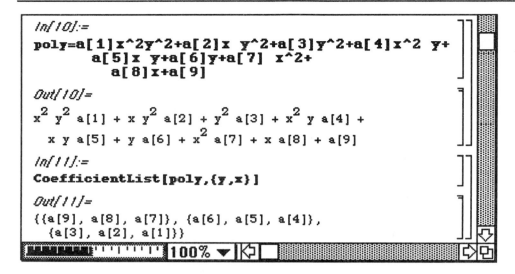

```
In[10]:=
poly=a[1]x^2y^2+a[2]x y^2+a[3]y^2+a[4]x^2 y+
      a[5]x y+a[6]y+a[7] x^2+
      a[8]x+a[9]

Out[10]=
 2  2          2         2        2
x  y  a[1] + x y  a[2] + y  a[3] + x  y a[4] +

           2
   x y a[5] + y a[6] + x  a[7] + x a[8] + a[9]

In[11]:=
CoefficientList[poly,{y,x}]

Out[11]=
{{a[9], a[8], a[7]}, {a[6], a[5], a[4]},
  {a[3], a[2], a[1]}}
```

100% ▼

Collect   80, 591, 765
                                See Also: **Factor, Series, CoefficientList,
                                Together**

   Collect[expression,variable] collects the terms in **expression** involving the
same power of **variable**.

Example:

In the following example, **poly** is defined to be the polynomial
$9+8x+7x^2+6y+5xy+4x^2y+3y^2+2xy^2+x^2y^2$. **Collect[poly,x]** collects the terms of **poly**
involving the same power of **x**; **Collect[poly,y]** collects the terms of **poly** involving the
same power of **y**.

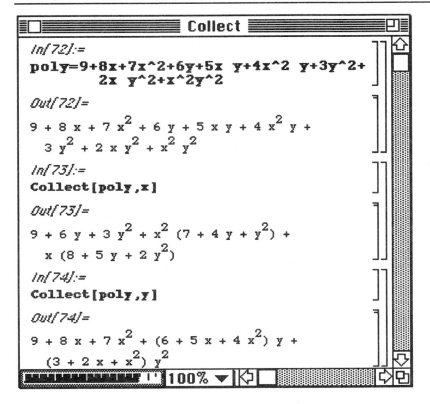

ColonForm

> **ColonForm[a,b]** prints a:b.

Example:

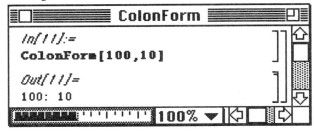

ColorFunction   152, 154, 156, 406, 425, 452, 765
See 516, 522, 523   See Also: **Lighting**, **ColorOutput**

    ColorFunction is an option for **Plot3D**, **ListPlot3D**, **DensityPlot**, **ContourPlot**, and other similar functions used to state a function to apply to z values to determine a color to be used for plotting over particular x,y regions.

ColorOutput   473, 765, 802, 803
See 513, 520

    ColorOutput is a graphics function option with settings such as **CMYKColor**, **GrayLevel**, and **RGBColor** to specify the kind of color output to be given.

Column   356, 357
                                     See Also: **TableDirections**

  Column is a **TableDirections** setting used to state that the dimensions of a table are to be arranged as columns as opposed to rows.

ColumnForm   352, 361, 766
See 122, 592   See Also: **TableForm, MatrixForm, Subscripted,**
                                     SequenceForm

  ColumnForm[list] prints **list** as a column.

Example:

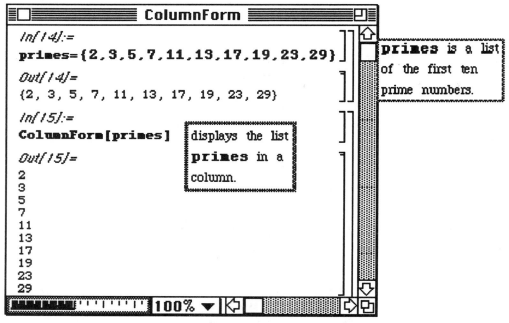

Columns can be right-justified, left-justified or centered:

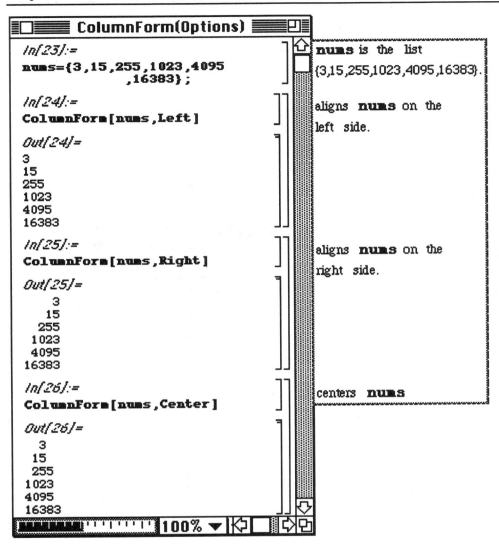

```
≡▣≡≡  ColumnForm(Options)  ≡≡▣
In[23]:=
nums={3,15,255,1023,4095
        ,16383};

In[24]:=
ColumnForm[nums,Left]

Out[24]=
3
15
255
1023
4095
16383

In[25]:=
ColumnForm[nums,Right]

Out[25]=
    3
   15
  255
 1023
 4095
16383

In[26]:=
ColumnForm[nums,Center]

Out[26]=
  3
  15
 255
1023
4095
16383
```

```
nums is the list
{3,15,255,1023,4095,16383}.

aligns nums on the
left side.

aligns nums on the
right side.

centers nums
```

Compile   312, 766

> See Also: **CompiledFunction**, **Dispatch**, **Function**, **InterpolatingFunction**

Compile[{x1,x2, ...},expression] creates a compiled function which evaluates **expression** for the values given in **{x1,x2, ...}**.

Example:

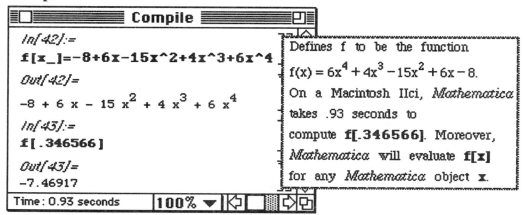

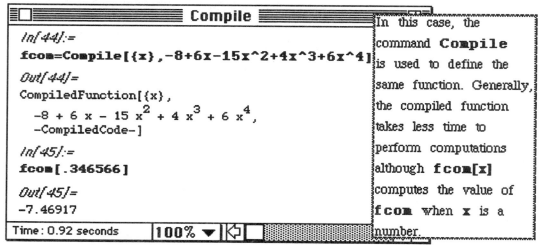

Compiled   143, 152, 154, 313, 688, 690, 695, 700, 766
See 310, 311, 515-518   See Also: **Compile**, **CompiledFunction**

Compiled is an option used with several plotting and numerical functions to specify if the expressions with which they work are to be automatically compiled.

CompiledFunction   212, 316, 475, 767
See Also: **Compile**, **Compiled**

CompiledFunction[{arg1,arg2, ...},{ni,nr,nc,nl},inst,function] represents the compiled code taking arguments from **{arg1,arg2, ...}** and following the list **inst** of actual compiled code instructions. The list **{ni,nr,nc,nl}** gives the number of integer, real, complex, and logical registers required to evaluate the compiled code.

Example:

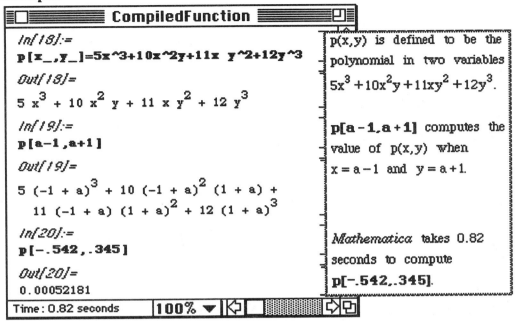

In many cases, compiled functions evaluate more quickly than non-compiled functions.

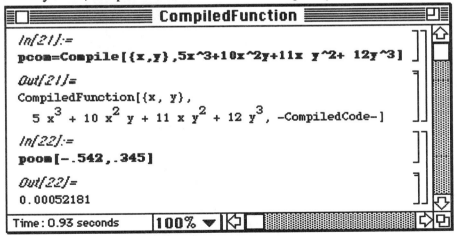

However, arguments of compiled functions can only consist of numbers; not symbols.

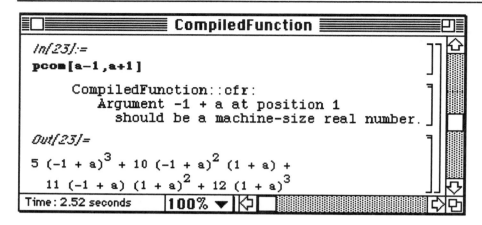

Complement   129, 767
See Also: **Intersection**, **Union**
Complement[universe,list1,list2, ...] lists the elements which are in
universe but not in any of the lists, **list1**, **list2**, ...

Example:

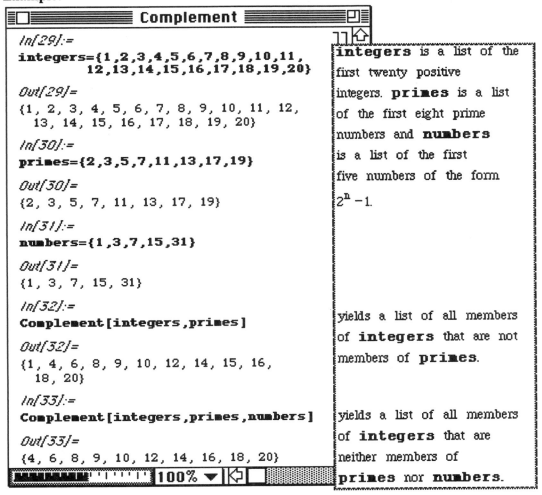

```
In[29]:=
integers={1,2,3,4,5,6,7,8,9,10,11,
         12,13,14,15,16,17,18,19,20}
Out[29]=
{1, 2, 3, 4, 5, 6, 7, 8, 9, 10, 11, 12,
 13, 14, 15, 16, 17, 18, 19, 20}
In[30]:=
primes={2,3,5,7,11,13,17,19}
Out[30]=
{2, 3, 5, 7, 11, 13, 17, 19}
In[31]:=
numbers={1,3,7,15,31}
Out[31]=
{1, 3, 7, 15, 31}
In[32]:=
Complement[integers,primes]
Out[32]=
{1, 4, 6, 8, 9, 10, 12, 14, 15, 16,
 18, 20}
In[33]:=
Complement[integers,primes,numbers]
Out[33]=
{4, 6, 8, 9, 10, 12, 14, 16, 18, 20}
```

integers is a list of the first twenty positive integers. **primes** is a list of the first eight prime numbers and **numbers** is a list of the first five numbers of the form $2^n - 1$.

yields a list of all members of **integers** that are not members of **primes**.

yields a list of all members of **integers** that are neither members of **primes** nor **numbers**.

Complex
See 253, 379, 530, 541, 549

534, 713, 767
See Also: **Head, Real, Re, Im**

Complex is the head used to denote numbers of the form $a+bI$.

Example:

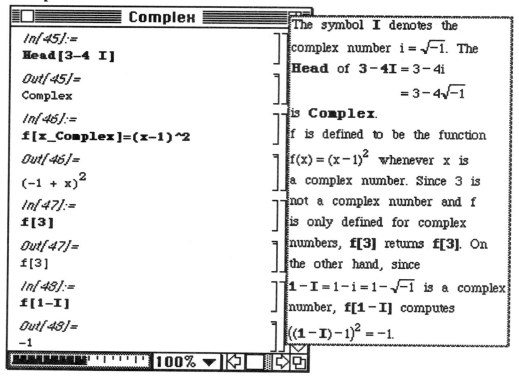

In[45]:=
Head[3-4 I]

Out[45]=
Complex

In[46]:=
f[x_Complex]=(x-1)^2

Out[46]=
$(-1 + x)^2$

In[47]:=
f[3]

Out[47]=
f[3]

In[48]:=
f[1-I]

Out[48]=
-1

The symbol **I** denotes the complex number $i = \sqrt{-1}$. The **Head** of $3 - 4I = 3 - 4i$

$$= 3 - 4\sqrt{-1}$$

is **Complex**. f is defined to be the function $f(x) = (x-1)^2$ whenever x is a complex number. Since 3 is not a complex number and f is only defined for complex numbers, **f[3]** returns **f[3]**. On the other hand, since $1 - I = 1 - i = 1 - \sqrt{-1}$ is a complex number, **f[1-I]** computes $((1-I)-1)^2 = -1$.

100% ▼

ComplexExpand   81, 604, 767
See 113, 202, 459, 586   See Also: **Expand**, **GaussianIntegers**

   ComplexExpand[expr] expands **expr** under the assumption that all of the variables are real. On the other hand, **ComplexExpand[expr,{x1,x2, ...}]** expands **expr** under the assumption that the variables in the list **{x1,x2, ...}** are complex.

Example:

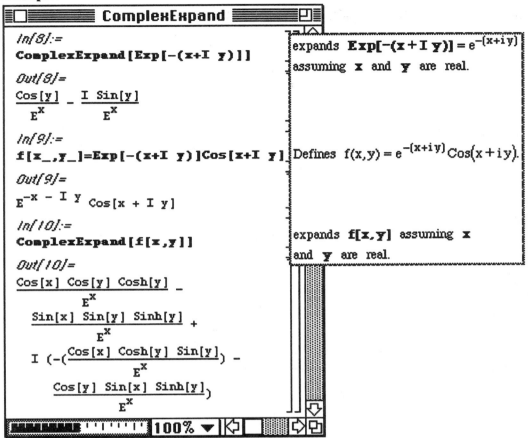

ComplexInfinity   548, 767
See 122, 271   See Also: **ComplexInfinity**, **Infinity**,
                              Indeterminate

ComplexInfinity represents an infinite quantity which also has undetermined direction.

Example:

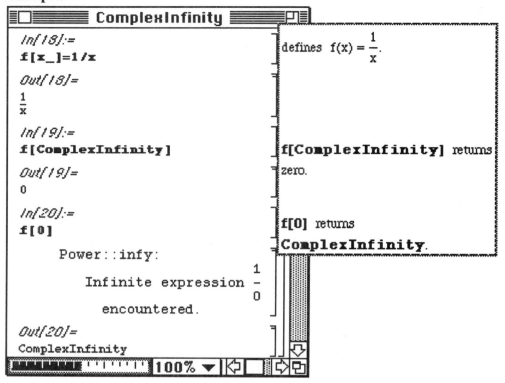

Compose   xix (obsolete in Version 2.0)
                                 superseded by **Composition**

ComposeList   210, 767
                                 See Also: **Composition**, **NestList**, **FoldList**
  ComposeList[{f1,f2,...},x] creates a list of the form
{x,f1[x],f2[f1[x]], ...}.

Example:

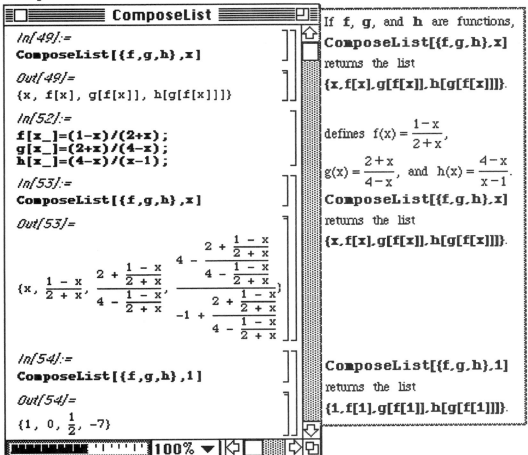

ComposeSeries

See Also: **ComposeList**, **Composition**, **Series**

ComposeSeries[ser1,ser2,ser3,...] composes the power series **ser1**, **ser2**, **ser3**, ... Each series except **ser1** must begin with a positive power of the variable.

Example:

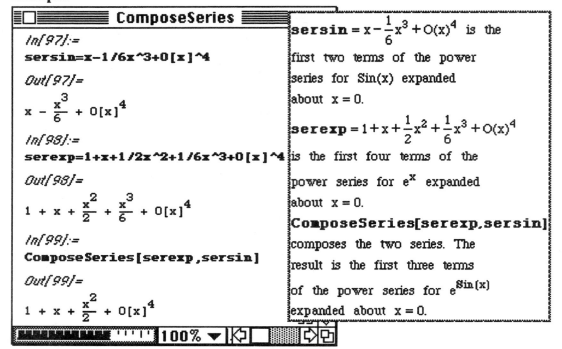

ComposeSeries

In[97]:=

sersin=x-1/6x^3+0[x]^4

Out[97]=

$$x - \frac{x^3}{6} + O[x]^4$$

In[98]:=

serexp=1+x+1/2x^2+1/6x^3+0[x]^4

Out[98]=

$$1 + x + \frac{x^2}{2} + \frac{x^3}{6} + O[x]^4$$

In[99]:=

ComposeSeries[serexp,sersin]

Out[99]=

$$1 + x + \frac{x^2}{2} + O[x]^4$$

$\text{sersin} = x - \frac{1}{6}x^3 + O(x)^4$ is the first two terms of the power series for Sin(x) expanded about $x = 0$.

$\text{serexp} = 1 + x + \frac{1}{2}x^2 + \frac{1}{6}x^3 + O(x)^4$ is the first four terms of the power series for e^x expanded about $x = 0$.

ComposeSeries[serexp,sersin] composes the two series. The result is the first three terms of the power series for $e^{\text{Sin}(x)}$ expanded about $x = 0$.

100% ▼

Composition   213, 278, 768
                               See Also: **Nest, Function**

  Composition[f1,f2,f3,...] yields the composition of the functions **f1**, **f2**, **f3**, ... Compositions are also given with **f1//f2//f3//...** .

Example:

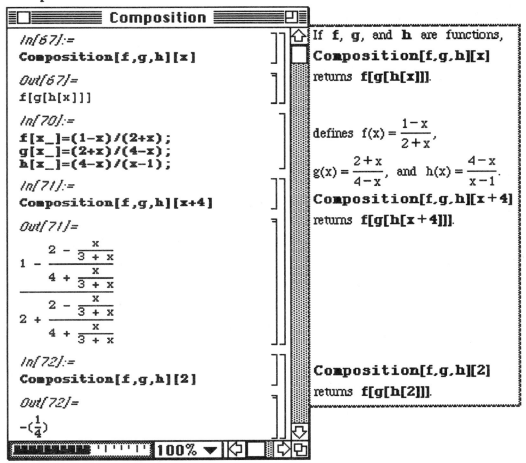

CompoundExpression(;)

59, 718, 768

See 299   See Also: **Block, Condition**

CompoundExpression is a sequence of expressions given in the form
exp1;exp2;exp3;... . When a semicolon (**;**) follows an expression, the output of that expression is not printed even though the expression is evaluated.

Example:

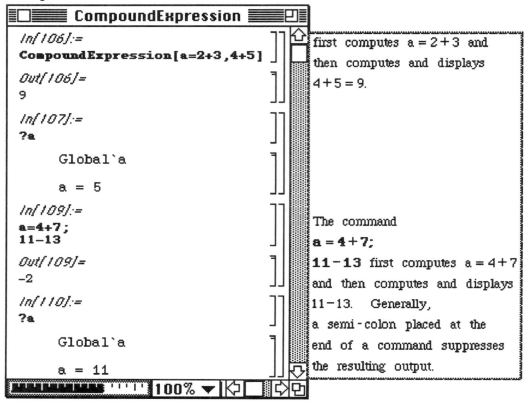

Condition (**/;**)   xix, 224, 287, 320, 768
See 417, 527, 528, 576,   See Also: **If**, **Module**, **Switch**, **Which**, **PatternTest**,
587, 589, 591   **RuleDelayed**, **SetDelayed**

   Condition, represented by the symbols **/;**, specifies a constraint on a certain pattern.

Example:

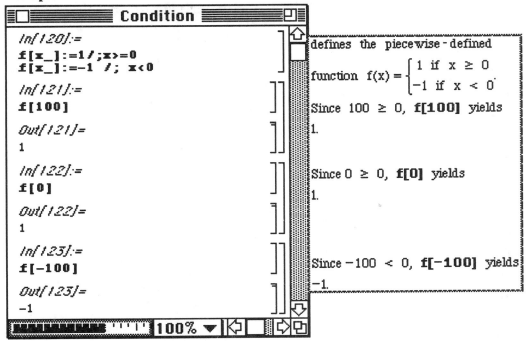

Conjugate   52, 551, 604, 768
                                See Also: **Abs**, **Arg**, **Complex**, **Re**, **Im**
  Conjugate[z] yields the complex conjugate of the complex number **z**.

Example:

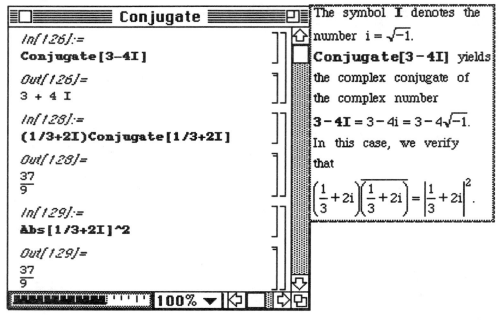

Constant   272, 625, 727, 768

Constant is an attribute of *Mathematica* symbols and indicates that all derivatives of symbols having this attribute are zero.

Constants   625, 768
                                See Also: **D**

Constants is an option of the total derivative command **Dt** and is used to indicate which objects are assumed to be constant. **Constants** can also be defined with **SetAttributes**.

ConstrainedMax   705, 769
                                See Also: **ConstrainedMin**, **LinearProgramming**,
                                FindMinimum

ConstrainedMax[f,ineqlist, varlist}] determines the global maximum of the function, **f**, over the region defined in the list of inequalities, **ineqlist**. All variables in **varlist** are assumed to be greater than or equal to zero. The maximum value of **f** as well as the values of the variables where this maximum occurs are given in the output list.

Example:

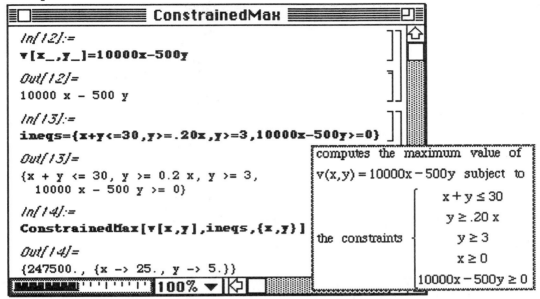

ConstrainedMin   109, 705, 769
                            See Also: **ConstrainedMax**, **LinearProgramming**,
                            FindMinimum

ConstrainedMin[f,ineqlist, varlist}] determines the global minimum of the function, **f**, over the region defined in the list of inequalities, **ineqlist**. All variables in **varlist** are assumed to be greater than or equal to zero.

Example:

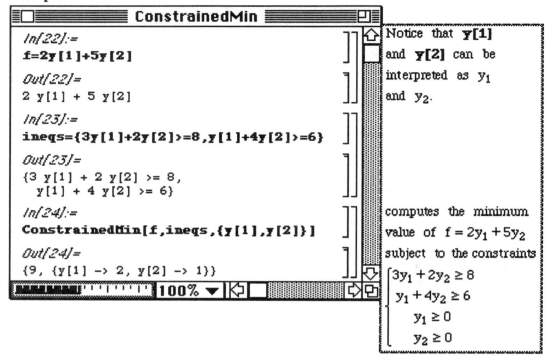

Context   334, 711, 769
                               See Also: **$ContextPath**, **Remove**
    Context[symbol] gives the context of **symbol**.

Contexts   334, 385, 769
                               See Also: **$ContextPath**, **$Packages**
    Contexts[] gives a list of all contexts whereas **Contexts["string"]** gives a list of
those contexts which match **string**.

ContextToFilename   492, 769
    ContextToFilename["context`"]** converts the context name, **context`, to the file
name associated with that particular context on the computer system.

Continuation   517, 769
                               See Also: **StringBreak**, **LineBreak**, **Indent**
    Continuation[n] is the output at the beginning of the nth line of output composed of
more than one line. **Continuation** can be used with **Format** to alter the way output is
printed.

Continue   293, 770
                               See Also: **Break**, **Goto**, **Return**, **Throw**
    Continue[] goes to the next step in the current **Do**, **While**, or **For** loop.

ContourGraphics   395, 425, 770
See 130, 197, 232,   See Also: **ListContourPlot**,
238   **DensityGraphics**

ContourGraphics[array] represents the graphics of a contour plot where **array** is a rectangular array of real numbers. The contour plot produced by **ContourGraphics** is viewed with **Show**. **ContourGraphics** has many options.

ContourLevels   xix (obsolete in Version 2.0); superseded by **Contours**

ContourLines   427, 771
See 515, 535   See Also: **ContourStyle, Contours,**
                           ContourSmoothing

ContourLines is a **ContourGraphics** option used to state whether or not explicit contour lines should be drawn.

ContourPlot   151, 395, 425, 770
See 130, 133, 197, 198,   See Also: **DensityPlot**
232, 238, 515, 534-539

ContourPlot[function,{x,xmin,xmax},{y,ymin,ymax}] produces a plot of numerous contour levels for the two-dimensional function, **function** , over the region [**xmin,xmax**] x [**ymin,ymax**].

Contours   152, 427, 771
See 238, 515, 536

Contours is a **ContourGraphics** option which is used to indicate the number of contour levels as well as the particular levels to be plotted.

ContourShading   152, 427, 428, 771
See 133, 238, 265, 515, 536,
538

ContourShading is an option used with contour plots to specify if the regions between contour lines should be shaded or not.

ContourSmoothing   152, 427, 771
See 515, 537

ContourSmoothing is an option used with contour plots to specify if a smoothing algorithm should be applied to the resulting contours.

ContourSpacing   obsolete in Version 2.0; superseded by **Contours**

ContourStyle   427, 771
See 515, 538   See Also: **PlotStyle**

ContourStyle is an option used with contour plots to indicate a specific style for plotting contour lines. These styles include **Dashing**, **Hue**, and **Thickness**.

CopyDirectory   493, 772
                           See Also: **RenameDirectory, CreateDirectory,**
                           DeleteDirectory

CopyDirectory["dir1","dir2"] copies the directory **dir1** to **dir2** where **dir1** is a previously existing directory and **dir2** is a new directory.

CopyFile   180, 492, 772
                               See Also: **RenameFile**, **DeleteFile**, **CopyDirectory**
  CopyFile["file1","file2"] copies the previously existing file, named **file1**, to the
new file, named **file2**.

Example:

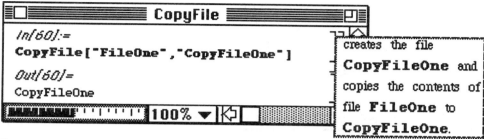

Cos   49, 562, 603, 772
See 26, 431   See Also: **ArcCos**, **Sec**
  Cos[z] gives the cosine of **z** where **z** has radian units.

Example:

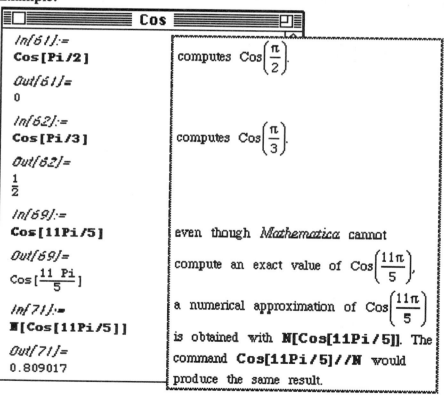

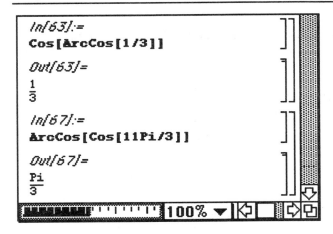

```
In[63]:=
Cos[ArcCos[1/3]]

Out[63]=
1
─
3

In[67]:=
ArcCos[Cos[11Pi/3]]

Out[67]=
Pi
──
3
```

Cosh   562, 772
See 25   See Also: **ArcCosh**, **Sech**

Cosh[z] gives the hyperbolic cosine of **z** where $\cosh(z) = \frac{1}{2}\left(e^z + e^{-z}\right)$.

Example:

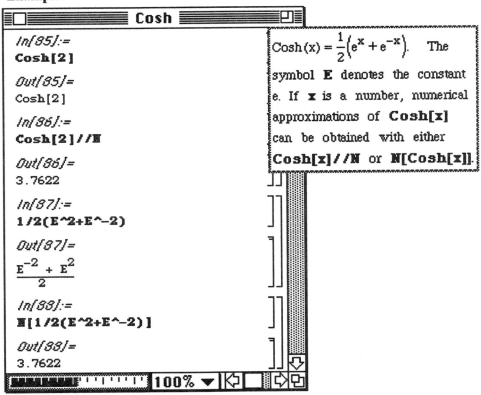

```
In[85]:=
Cosh[2]

Out[85]=
Cosh[2]

In[86]:=
Cosh[2]//N

Out[86]=
3.7622

In[87]:=
1/2(E^2+E^-2)

Out[87]=
 -2    2
E   + E
─────────
    2

In[88]:=
N[1/2(E^2+E^-2)]

Out[88]=
3.7622
```

$\cosh(x) = \frac{1}{2}\left(e^x + e^{-x}\right)$. The symbol **E** denotes the constant e. If **x** is a number, numerical approximations of **Cosh[x]** can be obtained with either **Cosh[x]//N** or **N[Cosh[x]]**.

CoshIntegral
See Also: **SinhIntegral**

CoshIntegral[z] computes the hyperbolic cosine integral function,

$$\gamma + \ln(z) + \int_0^z \frac{\cosh(t) - 1}{t}\, dt, \text{ where}$$

γ = Euler's constant (**EulerGamma**) $\cong 0.577216.$

Example:

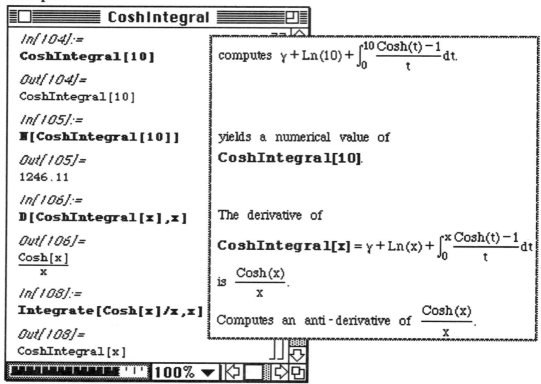

CosIntegral   570, 772
See Also: SinIntegral, ExpIntegralE,
ExpIntegralEi

CosIntegral[z] computes the cosine integral function, Ci(z), where

$$Ci(z) = -\int_z^\infty \frac{\cos(t)}{t}\, dt.$$

Example:

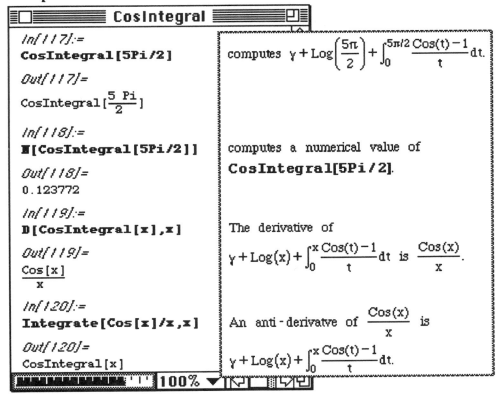

_In[117]:=_
CosIntegral[5Pi/2]

computes $\gamma + \text{Log}\left(\dfrac{5\pi}{2}\right) + \displaystyle\int_0^{5\pi/2} \dfrac{\text{Cos}(t) - 1}{t}\, dt.$

Out[117]=
CosIntegral$[\dfrac{5\ Pi}{2}]$

_In[118]:=_
N[CosIntegral[5Pi/2]]

computes a numerical value of
CosIntegral[5Pi/2].

Out[118]=
0.123772

_In[119]:=_
D[CosIntegral[x],x]

The derivative of

$\gamma + \text{Log}(x) + \displaystyle\int_0^x \dfrac{\text{Cos}(t) - 1}{t}\, dt$ is $\dfrac{\text{Cos}(x)}{x}.$

Out[119]=
$\dfrac{\text{Cos}[x]}{x}$

_In[120]:=_
Integrate[Cos[x]/x,x]

An anti-derivative of $\dfrac{\text{Cos}(x)}{x}$ is

$\gamma + \text{Log}(x) + \displaystyle\int_0^x \dfrac{\text{Cos}(t) - 1}{t}\, dt.$

Out[120]=
CosIntegral[x]

100% ▼

Cot   562, 727, 772

See Also: **ArcCot**

Cot[z] yields the cotangent of **z** where **z** is given in radians.

Example:

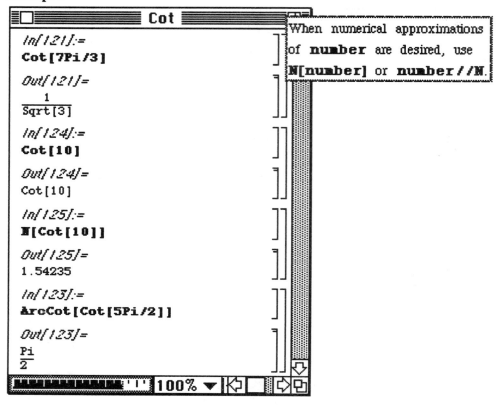

Coth   562, 727, 772
                        See Also: **ArcCoth**

Coth[z] gives the hyperbolic cotangent of z where $\coth(z) = \dfrac{e^z + e^{-z}}{e^z - e^{-z}}$, $z \neq 0$.

Example:

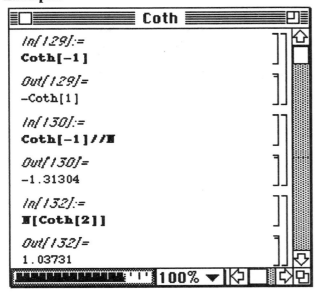

Count   127, 221, 222, 725, 772
                             See Also: **FreeQ**, **MemberQ**, **Cases**, **Select**, **Position**
  Count[list, pattern] yields the number of elements in **list** which match the form
defined by **pattern**.

Example:

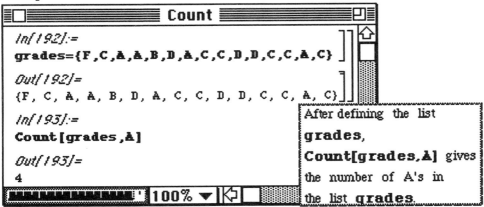

CreateDirectory   493, 773
                             See Also: **DeleteDirectory**, **RenameDirectory**,
                             CopyDirectory
  CreateDirectory["directoryname"] creates the new directory, **directoryname**,
which is initially empty by making a subdirectory of the working directory currently in use.

Csc   562, 727, 773
                                           See Also: **ArcCsc**

    Csc[z] gives the cosecant of **z** where $\text{Csc}(z) = \dfrac{1}{\text{Sin}(z)}$, $z \neq n\pi$, $n = 0, \pm 1, \pm 2 \cdots$.

Example:

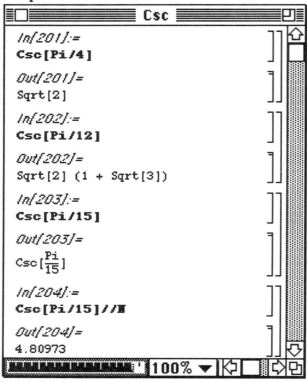

```
In[201]:=
Csc[Pi/4]

Out[201]=
Sqrt[2]

In[202]:=
Csc[Pi/12]

Out[202]=
Sqrt[2] (1 + Sqrt[3])

In[203]:=
Csc[Pi/15]

Out[203]=
Csc[Pi/15]

In[204]:=
Csc[Pi/15]//N

Out[204]=
4.80973
```

Csch   562, 727, 773
                                           See Also: **ArcCsch**

    Csch[z] gives the hyperbolic cosecant of z where $\text{Csch}(z) = \dfrac{2}{e^z - e^{-z}}$, $z \neq 0$.

Example:

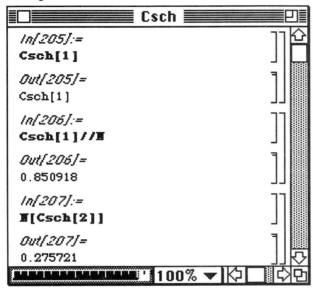

Cubics   773
                              See Also: **Roots, Quartics, NSolve**
   Cubics is an option used with such functions as **Roots** to state whether explicit solutions should be produced for irreducible cubic equations or if they should be left in their original form. **Cubics->False** leaves irreducible cubic equations unsolved.

Cuboid   430, 434, 773
See 519, 562   See Also: **Polygon, Rectangle**
   Cuboid[{x,y,z}] gives the graphics primitive of a unit cube with the points {x,y,z} and {x+1,y+1,z+1} as opposite corners. Also, **Cuboid[{x1,y1,z1},{x2,y2,z2}]** produces the graphics primitive of a rectangular parallelepiped with opposite corners {x1,y1,z1}and {x2,y2,z2}. These graphics primitives are viewed with **Show**.

Cyclotomic   601, 773
See 79   See Also: **Factor, GaussianIntegers**
Cyclotomic[n,x] produces the cyclotomic polynomial of order n,

$$C_n(x) = \prod_k \left(x - e^{2\pi i k/n}\right),$$ where the product ranges over integer values of k which are

relatively prime to n.   The cylcotomic polynomials are irreducible over the integers.

Example:

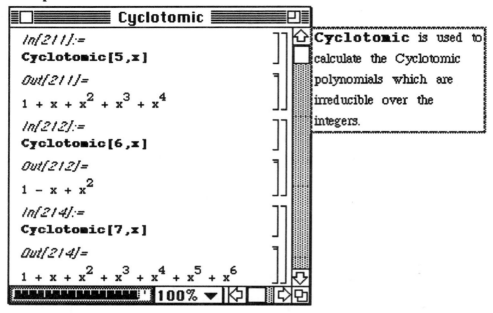

In[211]:=
Cyclotomic[5,x]

Out[211]=
$1 + x + x^2 + x^3 + x^4$

In[212]:=
Cyclotomic[6,x]

Out[212]=
$1 - x + x^2$

In[214]:=
Cyclotomic[7,x]

Out[214]=
$1 + x + x^2 + x^3 + x^4 + x^5 + x^6$

Cyclotomic is used to calculate the Cyclotomic polynomials which are irreducible over the integers.

D

D   88, 624, 774
See 72, 73, 189, 275, 429   See Also: **Dt**, **Derivative**
430

D represents differentiation. This is accomplished in several forms:

D[f,x] gives $\dfrac{df}{dx}$ if f is a function of the single variable x whereas **D[f,x]**

gives the partial derivative $\dfrac{\partial f}{\partial x}$ if f is a function of more than one variable.

D[f,x$_1$,x$_2$, ...] yields the partial derivative $\dfrac{\partial}{\partial x_1}\dfrac{\partial}{\partial x_2}\cdots f$ while **D[f,{x,n}]**

computes $\dfrac{\partial^n f}{\partial x^n}$ if f is a multi–variable function and $\dfrac{d^n f}{dx^n}$ if f is a function of the

single variable x.

Example:

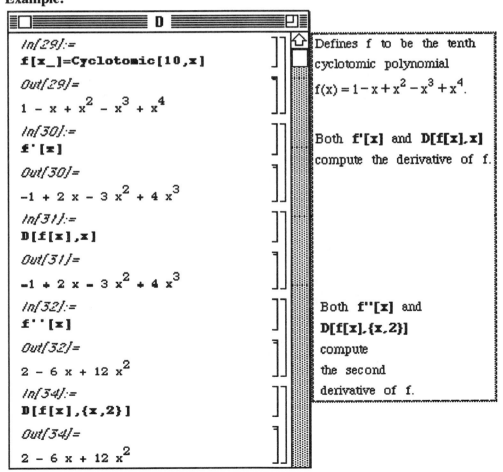

```
In[29]:=
f[x_]=Cyclotomic[10,x]

Out[29]=
         2    3    4
1 - x + x  - x  + x
```
Defines f to be the tenth cyclotomic polynomial $f(x) = 1 - x + x^2 - x^3 + x^4$.

```
In[30]:=
f'[x]

Out[30]=
             2      3
-1 + 2 x - 3 x  + 4 x
```
Both **f'[x]** and **D[f[x],x]** compute the derivative of f.

```
In[31]:=
D[f[x],x]

Out[31]=
             2      3
-1 + 2 x - 3 x  + 4 x
```

```
In[32]:=
f''[x]

Out[32]=
             2
2 - 6 x + 12 x
```
Both **f''[x]** and **D[f[x],{x,2}]** compute the second derivative of f.

```
In[34]:=
D[f[x],{x,2}]

Out[34]=
             2
2 - 6 x + 12 x
```

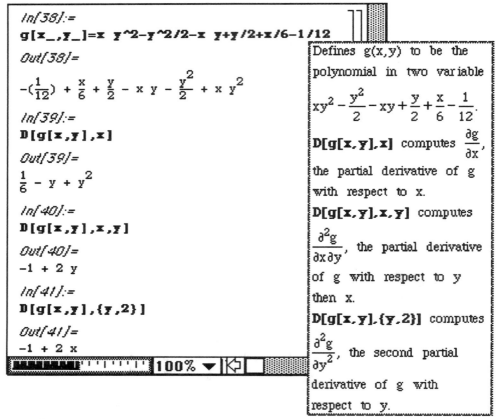

In[38]:=
g[x_,y_]=x y^2-y^2/2-x y+y/2+x/6-1/12

Out[38]=
$$-\left(\frac{1}{12}\right) + \frac{x}{6} + \frac{y}{2} - x\,y - \frac{y^2}{2} + x\,y^2$$

In[39]:=
D[g[x,y],x]

Out[39]=
$$\frac{1}{6} - y + y^2$$

In[40]:=
D[g[x,y],x,y]

Out[40]=
-1 + 2 y

In[41]:=
D[g[x,y],{y,2}]

Out[41]=
-1 + 2 x

Defines g(x,y) to be the polynomial in two variable $xy^2 - \frac{y^2}{2} - xy + \frac{y}{2} + \frac{x}{6} - \frac{1}{12}$.

D[x,y],x] computes $\frac{\partial g}{\partial x}$, the partial derivative of g with respect to x.

D[g[x,y],x,y] computes $\frac{\partial^2 g}{\partial x\,\partial y}$, the partial derivative of g with respect to y then x.

D[g[x,y],{y,2}] computes $\frac{\partial^2 g}{\partial y^2}$, the second partial derivative of g with respect to y.

100%

DampingFactor   794
                     See Also: **FindRoot**
     DampingFactor is a **FindRoot** option which can be used to control the
convergence of Newton's method since each step in this root-finding method is
multiplied by the setting assigned to **DampingFactor**. The default value is 1.

Dashing   409, 774
See 462, 560, 563, 587,   See Also: **AbsoluteDashing**,
589, 591, 596, 597, 712   **AbsoluteThickness**, **Thickness**,
                                 GrayLevel, **Hue**, **RGBColor**
     Dashing is a two- and three-dimensional graphics directive used to indicate that all
lines are to be drawn as a sequence of dashed lines.   The command
Dashing[{r1,r2,...}] specifies that subsequent line segments have lengths **r1**,
r2, ... This sequence repeats itself cyclically.

Date   523, 743, 774
                                            See Also: **AbsoluteTime, TimeZone,**
                                            SessionTime, TimeUsed, ToDate, FromDate,
                                            FileDate, $CreateDate

   Date[] yields the current local date and time according to that which has been set
on the computer system. This information is displayed in the form
{year,month,day,hour,minute,second} where all values are integers except
for second. No corrections are made for time changes or time zones.
Example:

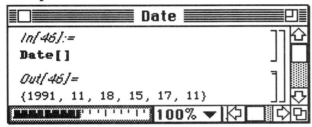

Debug   xix (obsolete in Version 2.0)
                                            superseded by **Trace** and related functions

DeclarePackage   342, 774
                                            See Also: **Needs, $NewSymbol**

   DeclarePackage["package`", {"name1","name2",...}] instructs
Mathematica to automatically load **package** upon encountering a function from
package which is given in the list **{"name1","name2",...}**.

Decompose   601, 608, 774
                                            See Also: **FactorList, Solve**

   Decompose[poly,x] computes the list of polynomials {p1,p2,...} such that
poly equals the composition of functions p1(p2(...(x)...)). This decomposition is not
unique. Polynomials of more than one variable may be considered, but the sequence of
polynomials produced by **Decompose[poly,x]** should be considered as functions of
x only.
Example:
The following example defines **poly** to be the polynomial $16-40x^2+48x^4-28x^6+7x^8$.
Decompose is used to compute a list of polynomials with composition **poly**. The
result is verified using the commands **/.** and **Expand**. Notice that the result of
Decompose is not unique since the list of polynomials {$3+6x^2+7x^4$, x(x+2),x-1} is
also a list with composition **poly**.

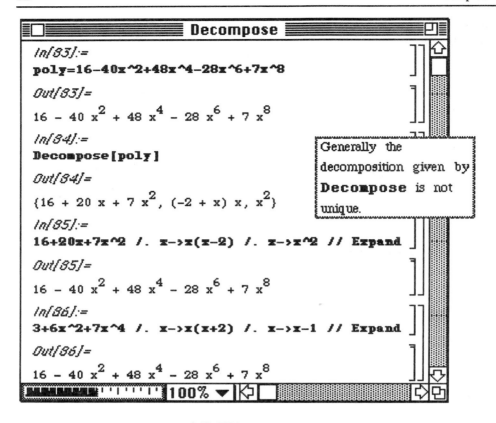

Decrement   248, 774
                                 See Also: **AddTo**, **DivideBy**, **Increment**,
                                 PreDecrement, **PreIncrement**, **SubtractFrom**,
                                 Set, **TimesBy**

   Decrement, symbolized by **i--**, decreases the value of **i** by 1 and returns the value
of **i** before the decrement.

Example:

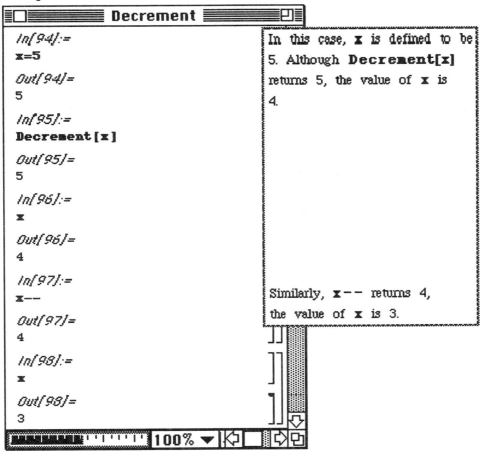

Default   734, 775
See 32   See Also: **Options**

   Default[f] yields the default value of the argument(s) of the function **f** if these values are defined. **Default[f,j]** produces the default value that should be used if **_.** is found as the **j**th argument of **f** where negative **j** counts from the last component. **Default[f,j,n]** determines the default value of the **j**th argument from the list of **n** total arguments.

DefaultColor   412, 775
See 513, 520   See Also: **Prolog, BackGround**

   DefaultColor is a graphics option used to indicate the default color which should be used for the plot. **DefaultColor** must be set using **CMYKColor, GrayLevel, Hue,** or **RGBColor** directives. If not specified, the setting assumed by **DefaultColor** is complimentary to the background setting.

DefaultFont   467, 775
See 513, 520, 574   See Also: **$DefaultFont**
  DefaultFont->{"fontname",fontsize} is a graphics option used to indicate the name and size of the font to be used for text.

DefaultValues   736
  DefaultValues[f] yields the default values for the arguments of **f**.

Definition   479, 775
See 45, 64   See Also: **FullDefinition**, **Information**
  Definition[f1,f2,...] prints the sequence of definitions made for each symbol **f1**, **f2**, ... The *Mathematica* command **?symbol** uses **Definition** to obtain information regarding **symbol**.
  Example:

▤▢▤▤▤▤▤▤▤ **Definition** ▤▤▤▤▤▤▤	Defines **nums** to be a
In[53]:=	list, **symbols** to be an
nums={-1/2,1/6,0,-1/30,0}	algebraic expression, and
symbols=Exp[x^2+y^2]Sin[x^2-y^2]	**omega** to be a number.
omega=5	
Out[51]=	
$\{-(\frac{1}{2}), \frac{1}{6}, 0, -(\frac{1}{30}), 0\}$	
Out[52]=	
$E^{x^2 + y^2} Sin[x^2 - y^2]$	
Out[53]=	
5	yields the definitions of
In[54]:=	the three objects **nums**,
Definition[nums,symbols,omega]	**symbols**, and **omega**.
Out[54]=	
nums = $\{-(\frac{1}{2}), \frac{1}{6}, 0, -(\frac{1}{30}), 0\}$	
symbols = $E^{x^2 + y^2} Sin[x^2 - y^2]$	
omega = 5	
In[55]:=	Similar results can be
?nums	obtained with the command
Global\`nums	**?nums** (**?symbols**
nums = {-1/2, 1/6, 0, -1/30, 0}	or **?omega**, respectively).

100% ▼

Degree   50, 562, 566, 775

   Degree represents **Pi/180**, the number of radians in one degree, and hence, **Degree** can be multiplied by a quantity measured in degrees to convert the quantity to radians.

Example:

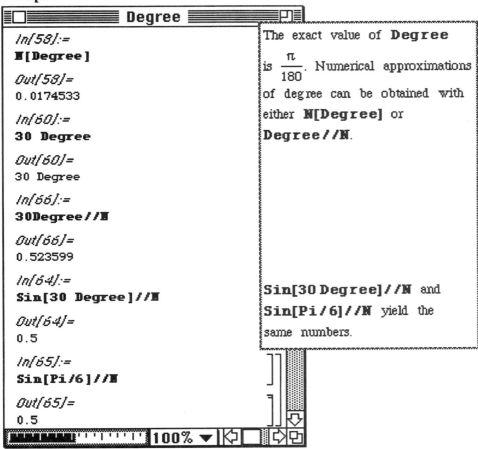

```
In[58]:=
N[Degree]
Out[58]=
0.0174533

In[60]:=
30 Degree
Out[60]=
30 Degree

In[66]:=
30Degree//N
Out[66]=
0.523599

In[64]:=
Sin[30 Degree]//N
Out[64]=
0.5

In[65]:=
Sin[Pi/6]//N
Out[65]=
0.5
```

The exact value of **Degree** is $\frac{\pi}{180}$. Numerical approximations of degree can be obtained with either **N[Degree]** or **Degree//N**.

Sin[30 Degree]//N and **Sin[Pi/6]//N** yield the same numbers.

Delete   128, 775
                                    See Also: **Insert, MapAt, ReplacePart, FlattenAt, DeleteCases**

   Delete is used to delete elements from a list. This can be done in several ways:
Delete[list,j] deletes the **j**th member of **list** and gives the new list as output.
Delete[list,{{j},{k},...}] removes positions **j, k**, ... from **list** and displays the revised list. **Delete[list,{{j1,k1,...},{j2,k2,...},...}]** deletes portions of **list** at the positions {**j1,k1,...**}, {**j2,k2,...**}, ...

Example:

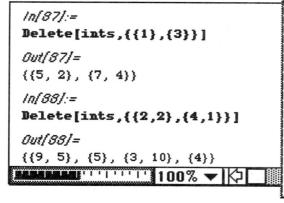

```
In[82]:=
ints={{9,5},{5,2},{3,10},{7,4}}

Out[82]=
{{9, 5}, {5, 2}, {3, 10}, {7, 4}}

In[83]:=
ints[[2]]

Out[83]=
{5, 2}

In[84]:=
ints[[3,1]]

Out[84]=
3

In[85]:=
Delete[ints,1]

Out[85]=
{{5, 2}, {3, 10}, {7, 4}}

In[86]:=
Delete[ints,{2,2}]

Out[86]=
{{9, 5}, {5}, {3, 10}, {7, 4}}
```

ints is defined to be the nested list {{9,5},{5,2},{3,10},{7,4}}.

ints[[2]] yields the second element of **ints**.

ints[[3,1]] yields the first element of the third element of **ints**.

Delete[ints,1] deletes the first element of **ints**.

Delete[ints,{2,2}] deletes the second element of the second element of **ints**.

```
In[87]:=
Delete[ints,{{1},{3}}]

Out[87]=
{{5, 2}, {7, 4}}

In[88]:=
Delete[ints,{{2,2},{4,1}}]

Out[88]=
{{9, 5}, {5}, {3, 10}, {4}}
```

Delete[ints,{{1},{3}}] deletes the first and third elements of **ints**.

Delete[ints,{{2,2},{4,1}}] deletes the second element of the second element and the first element of the fourth element of **ints**.

DeleteCases   222, 725, 776
                                    See Also: **Cases**, **ReplaceAll**, **Delete**,
                                    FlattenAt

DeleteCases[list,pattern] deletes the elements of **list** which match the form defined by **pattern**. In some cases, **DeleteCases** is equivalent to **FlattenAt**.

Example:

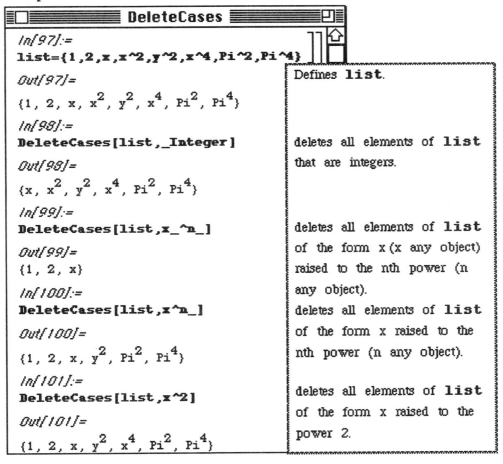

In[97]:= **list={1,2,x,x^2,y^2,x^4,Pi^2,Pi^4}**	Defines **list**.
Out[97]= $\{1, 2, x, x^2, y^2, x^4, Pi^2, Pi^4\}$	
In[98]:= **DeleteCases[list,_Integer]**	deletes all elements of **list** that are integers.
Out[98]= $\{x, x^2, y^2, x^4, Pi^2, Pi^4\}$	
In[99]:= **DeleteCases[list,x_^n_]**	deletes all elements of **list** of the form x (x any object) raised to the nth power (n any object).
Out[99]= $\{1, 2, x\}$	
In[100]:= **DeleteCases[list,x^n_]**	deletes all elements of **list** of the form x raised to the nth power (n any object).
Out[100]= $\{1, 2, x, y^2, Pi^2, Pi^4\}$	
In[101]:= **DeleteCases[list,x^2]**	deletes all elements of **list** of the form x raised to the power 2.
Out[101]= $\{1, 2, x, y^2, x^4, Pi^2, Pi^4\}$	

DeleteContents   493, 776
                                    See Also: **DeleteDirectory**

DeleteContents is a **DeleteDirectory** option which indicates if all directories and files contained in the directory being deleted should also be deleted. If these files and directories are to be deleted, then **DeleteContents->True** is used.

DeleteDirectory   493, 776

> See Also: **CreateDirectory**, **DeleteFile**,
> **DeleteContents**

   DeleteDirectory["dirname"] deletes the directory **dirname** only if it
contains no files. (See **DeleteContents** for deletion of files.) If *Mathematica* is
unable to delete the directory, then $Failed results. Otherwise, Null is displayed.

DeleteFile   180, 492, 776

> See Also: **RenameFile**, **DeleteDirectory**

   DeleteFile["filename"] deletes the file **filename** while
DeleteFile[{"fname1","fname2",...}] deletes the list of files given in
{"fname1","fname2",...}. If the file(s) are deleted, then Null is given as
output while $Failed is given if the command fails.

Example:

The following command deletes the file DeleteCases from the *Mathematica* 2.0
Enhanced folder on a Macintosh IIci.

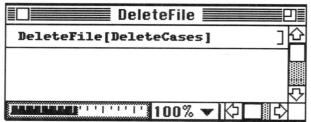

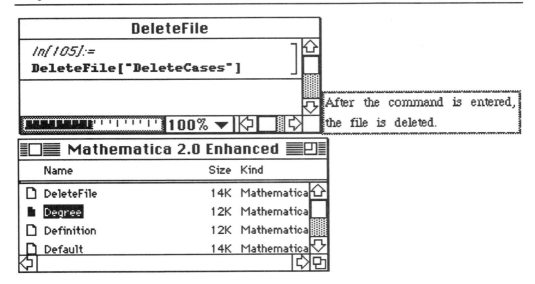

Delimiters
  Delimiters is an internal command, the attributes of which are protected.

Denominator   82, 776
                                   See Also: **Expand**, **ExpandAll**,
                                   ExpandDenominator, **Numerator**
  Denominator[expression] determines the denominator of **expression** by finding the terms of **expression** which have a negative number as a factor in the exponent.
Example:

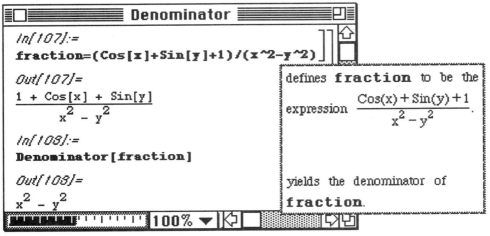

DensityGraphics   395, 425, 777
See 124, 237, 242   See Also: **ListDensityPlot, ContourGraphics,**
                                       Raster, RasterArray

   DensityGraphics[zarray], where **zarray** is a rectangular array of real values
of z, generates an array of values which represents a density plot.
DensityGraphics objects are visualized with **Show**. **DensityGraphics** can also
be used to convert **ContourGraphics** and **SurfaceGraphics** objects to
DensityGraphics. **DensityGraphics** has many available options which include
AspectRatio, Axes, AxesLabel, AxesOrigin, AxesStyle, BackGround,
ColorFunction, ColorOutput, DefaultColor, DefaultFont,
DisplayFunction, Epilog, Frame, FrameLabel, FrameStyle,
FrameTicks, Mesh, MeshRange, MeshStyle, PlotLabel, PlotRange,
PlotRegion, Prolog, RotateLabel, and **Ticks**.

DensityPlot   151, 395, 425, 777
See 124, 237, 242, 411,   See Also: **ContourPlot, ListContourPlot,**
516, 540, 541   **ListDensityPlot, Raster**

   DensityPlot[function,{x,xmin,xmax},{y,ymin,ymax}] produces a
density plot of **function** as a function of x and y over the rectangular region
{xmin,xmax} x **{ymin,ymax}** by displaying higher regions in a lighter color.
Because of the non-standard manner in which **function** is evaluated in
DensityPlot, Evaluate should be used with **function** before applying
DensityPlot. The same options available to **DensityGraphics** can be used with
DensityPlot.

Depth   199, 710, 725, 778
                                       See Also: **TensorRank, Level, LeafCount,**
                                       Length, Nest

   Depth[expression] yields the total number of levels of **expression** by
determining the maximum number of indices necessary to extract any portion of
expression. **Depth[expression]** is this maximum number plus one.
Example:
In the following example, the nested list **lists** is defined. The **Depth** of **lists** is 4.
lists[[1]] yields the first element of **lists** which is a list of three elements;
lists[[2,1]] yields the first element of the second element of **lists** which is a
list of two elements; **lists[[3,2,1]]** yields the first element of the second element
of the third element of **lists**. **lists[[3,2,1]]** is a number.

```
In[116]:=
lists={{{7,5},{6,4},{3,1}},{{9,1},{2,2},{8,3}},
     {{4,6},{8,2},{6,4}},{{2,9},{2,6},{6,9}}}

Out[116]=
{{{7, 5}, {6, 4}, {3, 1}},
   {{9, 1}, {2, 2}, {8, 3}},
   {{4, 6}, {8, 2}, {6, 4}},
   {{2, 9}, {2, 6}, {6, 9}}}

In[117]:=
Depth[lists]

Out[117]=
4

In[118]:=
lists[[1]]

Out[118]=
{{7, 5}, {6, 4}, {3, 1}}

In[119]:=
lists[[2,1]]

Out[119]=
{9, 1}

In[120]:=
lists[[3,2,1]]

Out[120]=
8
```

Derivative   212, 627, 630, 637, 778
                                     See Also: **D**, **Dt**

   The symbol **f'** calculates the first derivative of the function **f** of one variable. More generally, **Derivative[n1,n2,...][f]** computes the derivative of **f** by differentiating **n1** times with respect to the first argument of f, **n2** times with respect to the second argument of **f**, ...

Example:

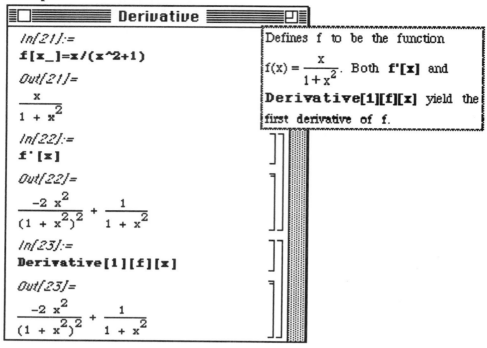

In the following example, note that the **f'[x]** would produce the same results.

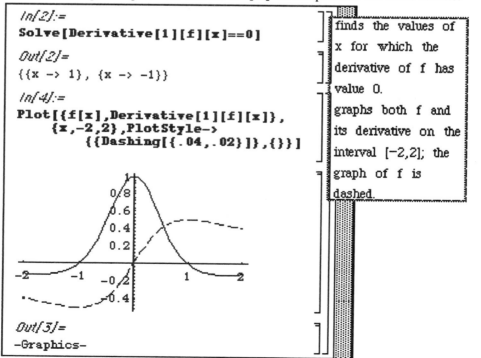

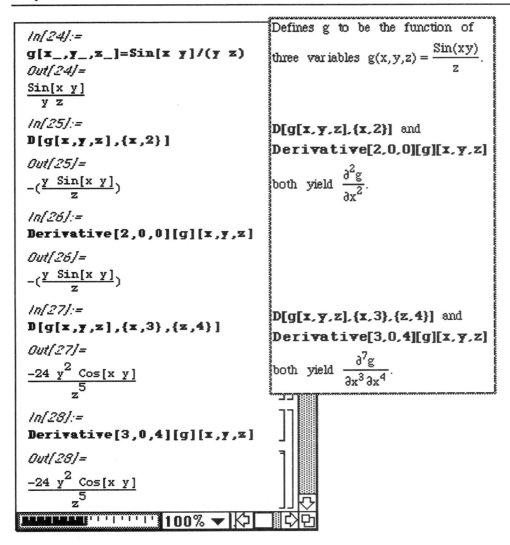

In[24]:=
g[x_,y_,z_]=Sin[x y]/(y z)
Out[24]=
$\frac{Sin[x\ y]}{y\ z}$

In[25]:=
D[g[x,y,z],{x,2}]
Out[25]=
$-(\frac{y\ Sin[x\ y]}{z})$

In[26]:=
Derivative[2,0,0][g][x,y,z]
Out[26]=
$-(\frac{y\ Sin[x\ y]}{z})$

In[27]:=
D[g[x,y,z],{x,3},{z,4}]
Out[27]=
$\frac{-24\ y^2\ Cos[x\ y]}{z^5}$

In[28]:=
Derivative[3,0,4][g][x,y,z]
Out[28]=
$\frac{-24\ y^2\ Cos[x\ y]}{z^5}$

Defines g to be the function of three variables $g(x,y,z) = \frac{Sin(xy)}{z}$.

D[g[x,y,z],{x,2}] and Derivative[2,0,0][g][x,y,z] both yield $\frac{\partial^2 g}{\partial x^2}$.

D[g[x,y,z],{x,3},{z,4}] and Derivative[3,0,4][g][x,y,z] both yield $\frac{\partial^7 g}{\partial x^3\ \partial x^4}$.

100%

Det   123, 657, 778
                           See Also: **CharacteristicPolynomial**, **Minors**,
                           RowReduce, **NullSpace**

Det[mat] computes the determinant of the square matrix, **mat**. **Modulus->p** is an option for **Det[mat]** which calculates the determinant of **mat** modulo **p**.

Example:

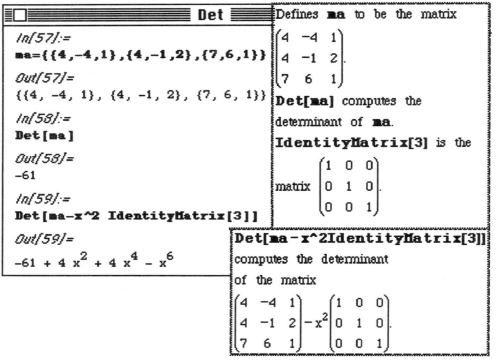

Det[mb] computes the determinant of the matrix

$$mb = \begin{bmatrix} 2 & 5 & -1 & 7 & 0 & -2 \\ -6 & 0 & 7 & -1 & 8 & 9 \\ 4 & 3 & -2 & 6 & -1 & -1 \\ -5 & -3 & -8 & 5 & -10 & 7 \\ -3 & 6 & 10 & 2 & -4 & 9 \\ -6 & -9 & 10 & 8 & 4 & -6 \end{bmatrix}.$$

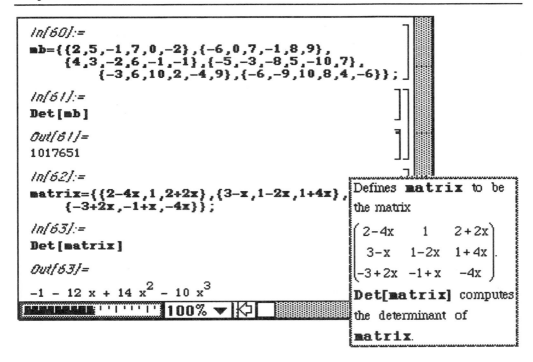

DiagonalMatrix   122, 649, 778
See 427   See Also: **Array**, **IdentityMatrix**, **Table**
   DiagonalMatrix[list] generates a diagonal matrix with the elements of **list** along the diagonal and values of 0 in all other positions of the matrix.

Example:

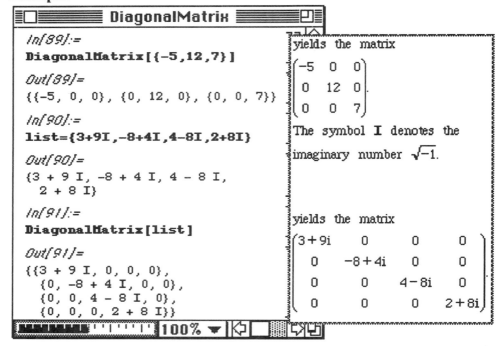

═▭═══ **DiagonalMatrix** ═══▱

In[89]:=
DiagonalMatrix[{-5,12,7}]

Out[89]=
{{-5, 0, 0}, {0, 12, 0}, {0, 0, 7}}

In[90]:=
list={3+9I,-8+4I,4-8I,2+8I}

Out[90]=
{3 + 9 I, -8 + 4 I, 4 - 8 I,
  2 + 8 I}

In[91]:=
DiagonalMatrix[list]

Out[91]=
{{3 + 9 I, 0, 0, 0},
  {0, -8 + 4 I, 0, 0},
  {0, 0, 4 - 8 I, 0},
  {0, 0, 0, 2 + 8 I}}

yields the matrix

$$\begin{pmatrix} -5 & 0 & 0 \\ 0 & 12 & 0 \\ 0 & 0 & 7 \end{pmatrix}.$$

The symbol **I** denotes the imaginary number $\sqrt{-1}$.

yields the matrix

$$\begin{pmatrix} 3+9i & 0 & 0 & 0 \\ 0 & -8+4i & 0 & 0 \\ 0 & 0 & 4-8i & 0 \\ 0 & 0 & 0 & 2+8i \end{pmatrix}$$

100% ▼

Dialog   520, 778

See Also: **TraceDialog**, **Input**, **$Inspector**

In order to create a dialog or "subsession" of a current *Mathematica* session, the command **Dialog** is needed. **Dialog[]** initiates a *Mathematica* dialog and, thus, enables the user to interact with *Mathematica* while it is in the process of performing a calculation.

Example:

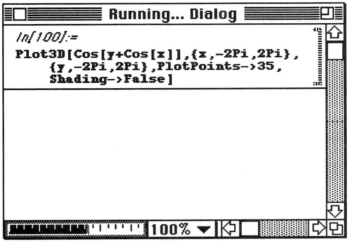

In this case, a twenty-five digit approximation of π is computed during the **Dialog**.
After the **Dialog** is exited, the **Plot3D** command is completed.

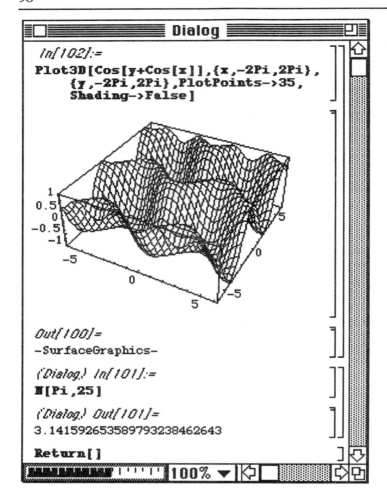

```
In[102]:=
Plot3D[Cos[y+Cos[x]],{x,-2Pi,2Pi},
    {y,-2Pi,2Pi},PlotPoints->35,
    Shading->False]
```

```
Out[100]=
-SurfaceGraphics-

(Dialog) In[101]:=
N[Pi,25]

(Dialog) Out[101]=
3.141592653589793238462643

Return[]
```

DialogIndent   517, 779

                                         See Also: **Indent**

   DialogIndent[d] yields the indentation for the input and output lines of a dialog of depth **d**. The default value is **d** spaces.

DialogProlog   522, 779

                                         See Also: **$Epilog**

   DialogProlog is option used with **Dialog** to state an expression to be evaluated before initiating the dialog. A delayed rule of the form
DialogProlog:>expression must be used to ensure that **expression** is not evaluated prematurely.

Example:

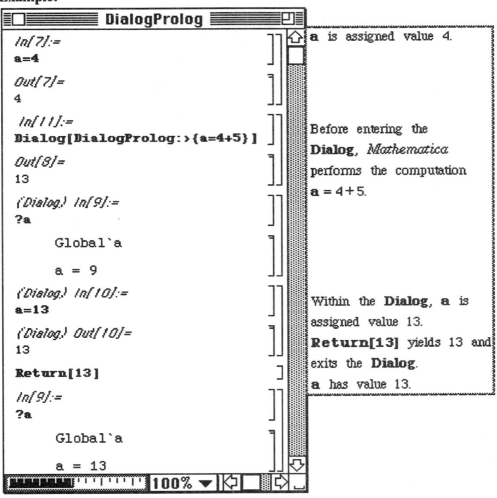

DialogSymbols   522, 779

DialogSymbols is an option used with **Dialog** to give a list of symbols the values of which should be localized in the dialog. This option must be stated in the form **DialogSymbols:>{x,y,...}**. This option can also be used as **DialogSymbols:>{x=x0,y=y0,...}** to define initial values of the variables.

Example:

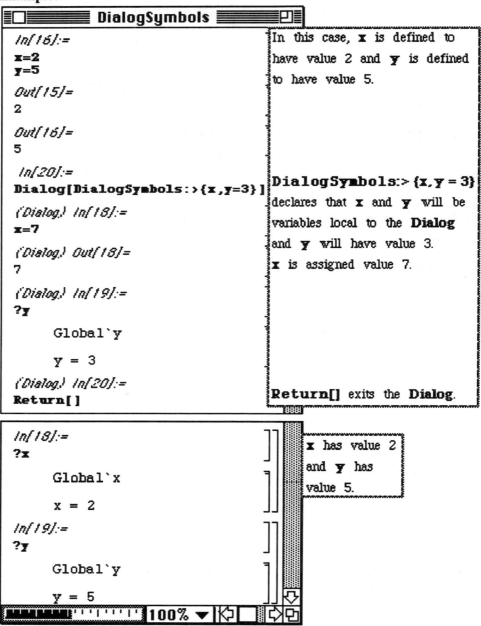

DigitBlock   351, 779

See Also: **NumberForm**

DigitBlock is an option for number formatting functions such as **NumberForm** to indicate the maximum length of blocks of digits between breaks. The default is **DigitBlock->Infinity** which specifies that no breaks be inserted. Otherwise, **DigitBlock->n** indicates that a break be inserted every **n** digits.

DigitQ   378, 779
                                 See Also: **LetterQ**, **Number**

   DigitQ[string] tests whether the characters of **string** are digits.
DigitQ[string] gives a value of **True** if all of the characters of **string** are digits
from 0 to 9. The result is **False**, otherwise.

Example:

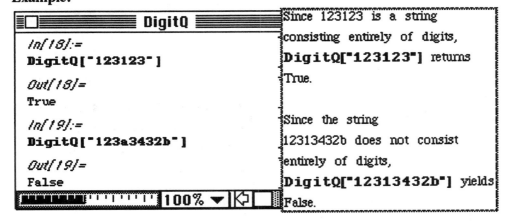

Digits   obsolete in Version 2.0
                                 superseded by **IntegerDigits** and **RealDigits**

Dimensions   122, 210, 652, 755, 779
                                 See Also: **TensorRank**, **VectorQ**, **MatrixQ**

   Dimensions[list] gives the dimensions of the rectangular array **list**. Hence,
list may represent a matrix or a vector.

Example:

In the following example, the dimension of the vector $\begin{bmatrix} -6 \\ 0 \\ -7 \\ 7 \\ -2 \end{bmatrix}$ is 5 and the

dimensions of the matrix $\begin{bmatrix} 3 & 7 & -9 \\ 9 & 2 & 5 \\ -2 & -1 & 9 \\ -10 & 6 & 2 \end{bmatrix}$ are four – by – three.

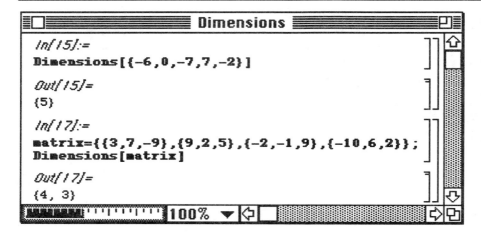

```
In[15]:=
Dimensions[{-6,0,-7,7,-2}]

Out[15]=
{5}

In[17]:=
matrix={{3,7,-9},{9,2,5},{-2,-1,9},{-10,6,2}};
Dimensions[matrix]

Out[17]=
{4, 3}
```

DirectedInfinity   548, 780
                              See Also: **Indeterminate**
  DirectedInfinity is used to represent infinite quantities.
DirectedInfinity[z] represents an infinite quantity in the direction of the
complex number **z**. **DirectedInfinity[]** represents **ComplexInfinity**.

Direction   647, 818
                             See Also: **Limit**
  Direction is an option for **Limit** which is used to indicate the direction for
one-sided limits. The option **Direction->1** specifies that the limit is taken from the
left while **Direction->-1** indicates that the limit is determined from the right.

Directory   180, 489, 780
                             See Also: **$Path**, **SetDirectory**,
                             ResetDirectory, **ParentDirectory**,
                             HomeDirectory, **FileNames**
  Directory[] returns the string which represents the current working directory.

DirectoryStack   489, 780
                             See Also: **ResetDirectory**, **SetDirectory**
  DirectoryStack[] yields the stack of directories maintained by *Mathematica*
during the current session. Directories are added to this stack with **SetDirectory**
and removed with **ResetDirectory**.

Disk   400, 404, 780
See 512, 526   See Also: **Circle, Line, Point, Polygon**
   Disk is a two-dimensional graphics element which represents a filled disk. This command can be used in several forms :
Disk[{x,y},r] gives a circular disk with radius **r** and center **(x,y)**.
Disk[{x,y},{rx,ry}] produces an elliptical disk centered at the point **(x,y)** with semi-axes **rx** and **ry**.
Disk[{x,y},r,{t1,t2}] yields the segment of the disk centered at **(x,y)** of radius **r** for angular values between **t1** and **t2**.
All angles are given in radian measurements and are measured counter-clockwise from the positive x-axis.

Dispatch   246, 780
                             See Also: **ReplaceAll, Compile**
   Dispatch[ruleslist] produces a representation of **ruleslist** which includes dispatch tables. Dispatch tables allows for a much faster application of replacement operations and are particularly useful when **ruleslist** is long.

Display   137, 399, 465, 476, 485, 781
                             See Also: **Write, Show**
   Display[channel,graphics] indicates that **graphics** is to be directed to the specified channel. This output channel may be a single file or pipe, or a list of them.
Graphics, Graphics3D, SurfaceGraphics, ContourGraphics, DensityGraphics, GraphicsArray, and **Sound** can be specified for **graphics**.
Display writes graphics in PostScript form.

DisplayFunction   139, 156, 175, 399, 464, 781
See 127, 131, 165, 312,   See Also: **$DisplayFunction, Show**
513, 520, 534, 536-540,
547, 551, 553, 559, 561,
570, 572, 573, 576-579,
591, 593, 596, 597, 731,
732, 691
   DisplayFunction is an option for graphics functions such as **Show** and **Plot** which indicates the manner in which the graphics primitives produced by these graphics functions should be rendered. The default setting,
DisplayFunction->$DisplayFunction indicates that the graphics objects produced should actually be displayed while the setting
DisplayFunction->Identity generates no display.

Distribute   216, 655, 781
                             See Also: **Expand, Thread**
   Distribute is used to apply the distributive laws. This can be accomplished in many forms : **Distribute[f[x1,x2,...]]** distributes **f** over any **+** sign that appears in the **xi**. **Distribute[expression,g]** distributes over **g**. Distribute differs from **Expand** in that it completely performs the distributive property as opposed to simplifying at each step.

Divide   47, 781

Divide is symbolized by **/**. Hence, **Divide[a,b]** represents **a/b** and is converted to **a b^-1** as input.

Example:

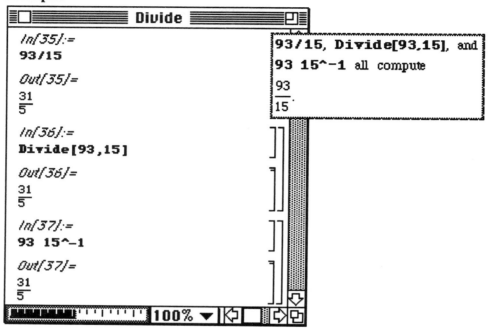

Divide

In[35]:=
93/15

Out[35]=
$\frac{31}{5}$

In[36]:=
Divide[93,15]

Out[36]=
$\frac{31}{5}$

In[37]:=
93 15^-1

Out[37]=
$\frac{31}{5}$

93/15, Divide[93,15], and 93 15^-1 all compute $\frac{93}{15}$.

100% ▼

DivideBy   248, 781
See Also: **AddTo**, **Decrement**, **Increment**, **PreDecement**, **PreIncrement**, **SubtractFrom**, **TimesBy**

DivideBy, represented as **a/=b**, divides **a** by **b** and returns the new value of **a**.

Example:

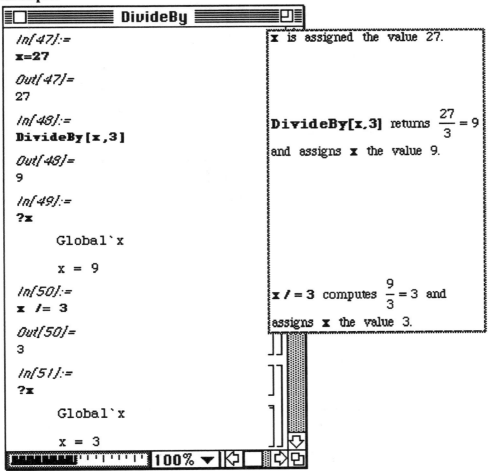

Divisors   554, 781

See Also: **FactorInteger**

Divisors[n] yields a list of the integers, including the integer **n**, which divide **n**. The option **GaussianIntegers->True** specifies that divisors which are Gaussian integers be included in the list of divisors.

Example:

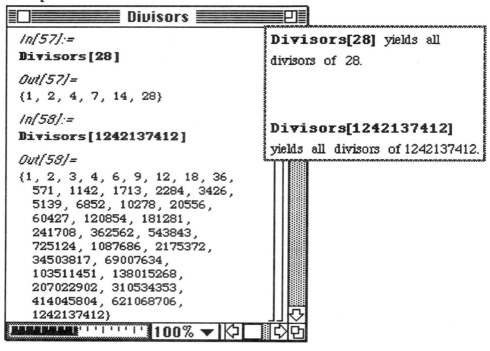

DivisorSigma   556, 782

See Also: **EulerPhi**

    DivisorSigma[k,n] yields the divisor function which represents the sum of the **k**th powers of the divisors of **n**. **DivisorSigma** has the option **GaussianIntegers**. If **GaussianIntegers->True** is used, then divisors which are Gaussian integers are included in the sum.

Example:

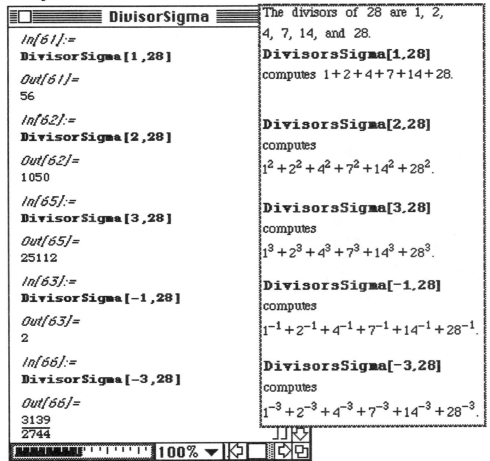

Do   115, 279, 290, 330, 782
See Also: **For, While, Table, Nest, Fold**

Do is used to define repetitive operations in *Mathematica* in a manner similar to programming languages like Fortran. This can be done in numerous ways :

Do[expression,{i}] computes **expression** i times.

Do[expression,{i,imax}] calculates **expression** for values of the variable **i** from $i = 1$ to $i = $ **imax**.

Do[expression,{i,imin,imax}] computes **expression** for values of the variable **i** from $i = $ **imin** to $i = $ **imax**.

Do[expression,{i,imin,imax,step}] determines **expression** for values of the variable **i** from $i = $ **imin** to $i = $ **imax** using a stepsize of **step**.

Do[expression,{i,imin,imax},{j,jmin,jmax},...] calculates **expression** for values of the variable **i** from $i = $ **imin** to $i = $ **imax**, **j** from $j = $ **jmin** to $j = $ **jmax**, ...

Example:

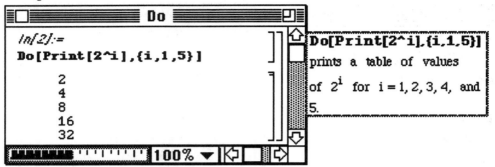

Dot   121, 232, 654, 782
See 287, 376, 408, 409   See Also: **Inner, MatrixPower,
                                NonCommutativeMultiply, Outer

   Dot, represented symbolically as **.** , is used to find the product of vectors, matrices, and tensors. **Dot[{x1,y1},{x2,y2}]** which can also be symbolized with **{x1,y1}.{x2,y2}** determines the scalar product of the vectors **{x1,y1}** and **{x2,y2}**. **Dot[{x1,y1},{{a11,a12},{a21,a22}}]** calculates the product of the vector **{x1,y1}** with the matrix **{{a11,a12},{a21,a22}}**. Also, **Dot[{{a11,a12},{a21,a22}},{{b11,b12},{b21,b22}}]** computes the product of two matrices.

Example:

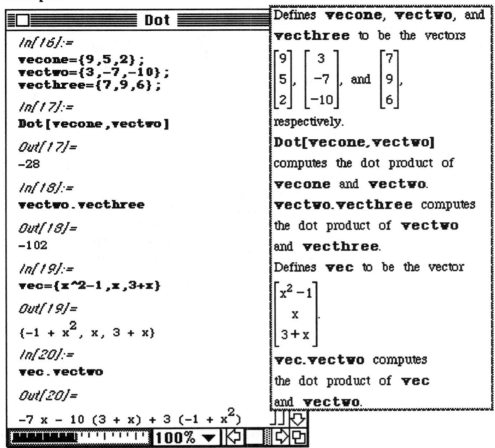

```
≣□≣≣≣≣≣≣≣ Dot ≣≣≣≣≣
In[16]:=
vecone={9,5,2};
vectwo={3,-7,-10};
vecthree={7,9,6};
In[17]:=
Dot[vecone,vectwo]
Out[17]=
-28
In[18]:=
vectwo.vecthree
Out[18]=
-102
In[19]:=
vec={x^2-1,x,3+x}
Out[19]=
{-1 + x , x, 3 + x}
        2
In[20]:=
vec.vectwo
Out[20]=
-7 x - 10 (3 + x) + 3 (-1 + x )
                             2
```

Defines **vecone**, **vectwo**, and **vecthree** to be the vectors

$$\begin{bmatrix} 9 \\ 5 \\ 2 \end{bmatrix}, \begin{bmatrix} 3 \\ -7 \\ -10 \end{bmatrix}, \text{ and } \begin{bmatrix} 7 \\ 9 \\ 6 \end{bmatrix},$$

respectively.

Dot[vecone,vectwo] computes the dot product of **vecone** and **vectwo**.

vectwo.vecthree computes the dot product of **vectwo** and **vecthree**.

Defines **vec** to be the vector

$$\begin{bmatrix} x^2 - 1 \\ x \\ 3+x \end{bmatrix}.$$

vec.vectwo computes the dot product of **vec** and **vectwo**.

DoubleExponential
See Also: **NIntegrate**

DoubleExponential is a setting for the **Method** option for **NIntegrate** whic specifies that **NIntegrate** use an algorithm which is doubly exponentiall convergent.

DoublyInfinite   575
See Also: **LerchPhi**

DoublyInfinite is an option used with the command **LerchPhi** which is a generalization of the zeta and polyalgorithm functions.

LerchPhi[z,s,a,DoublyInfinite-›True] computes the sum

$$\sum_{k=-\infty}^{\infty} \frac{z^k}{(a+k)^s}$$ which is doubly infinite.

DownValues   266, 736, 782
                                        See Also: **Set**, **UpValues**, **Reverse**

   DownValues[function] yields a list of rules corresponding to **function**.
These rules are ordered by *Mathematica* in such a way that more specific rules appear
before those that are more general.   However, this ordering can be altered with
Reverse. The downvalues can also be set with the command
DownValues[function]=rules.
Example:

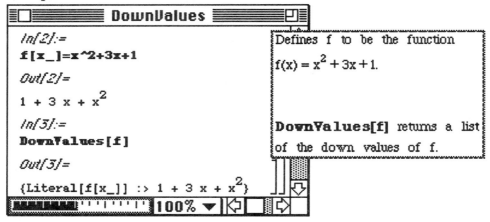

Drop   125, 782
See 566   See Also: **First**, **Last**, **Part**, **Rest**, **StringDrop**,
                                        Take, **Cases**

   Drop is used to remove certain elements of a list. This takes several forms :
Drop[list,n] deletes the first **n** elements of **list** and displays the revised list as
output.
Drop[list,-n] eliminates the last **n** elements of **list** and displays the revised list
as output.
Drop[list,{n}] removes the nth element of **list** and displays the new list.
Drop[list,{m,n}] drops the **m**th through the **n**th elements inclusively from **list**
and gives the altered list as output.

Example:

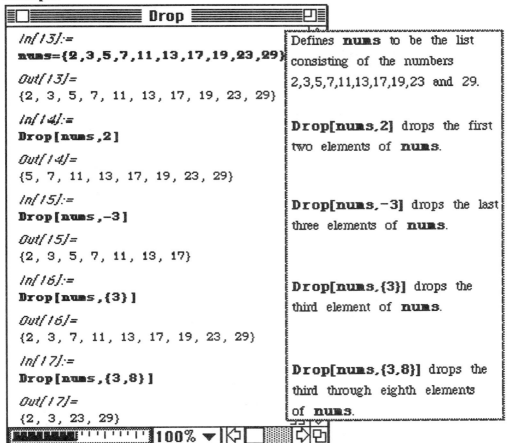

DSolve   99, 637, 683, 783
                         See Also: **NDSolve**, **Solve**

   DSolve is used to solve ordinary differential equations and systems of ordinary differential equations. The command **DSolve[equation,y[x],x]** solves the differential equation given in equation for the dependent variable **y[x]** in terms of the independent variable **x**.
DSolve[{eq1,eq2,...},{y1[x],y2[x],...},x] solves the system of ordinary differential equations defined in the list **{eq1,eq2,...}** for the dependent variables **{y1[x],y2[x],...}** in terms of **x**. **DSolve** is capable of solving linear equations of order 4 or less. Initial conditions can be considered with the command
**DSolve[{eq1,eq2,..,y1[x0]==a,y2[x0]==b,..},{y1[x],y2[x],..}
                       ,x]**
where enough conditions must be stated to uniquely determine the solution.

Example:
The following examples compute the general solution of the differential equation
$x^2y' - 2xy' + 2y = x^4e^x$ and the solution of the initial value problem
$y' - 6y' + 9y = t^2e^{3t}$ subject to $y(0) = 2$ and $y'(0) = 6$.

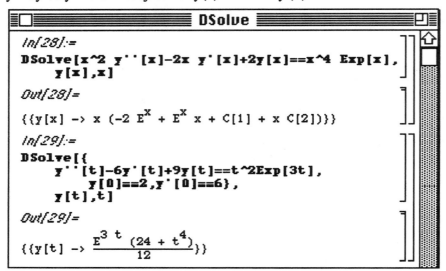

DSolve can also be used to find solutions of some systems. For example, the
following command finds the general solution of the system
$$\begin{cases} x' = 2x + 3y - 7 \\ y' = -x - 2y + 5 \end{cases}.$$

```
In[30]:=
DSolve[{x'[t]==2x[t]+3y[2]-7,
        y'[t]==-x[t]-2y[t]+5},
     {x[t],y[t]},t]

Out[30]=
                  2 t
         7 - 8 E    C[2] - 3 y[2]
{{x[t] -> ----------------------- ,
                   2

              3   C[1]    2 t           3 y[2]
  y[t] -> --- + ---- + E    C[2] + ------}}
              4    2 t                  4
                  E
```

Similarly, the following command computes the solution of the system
$$\begin{cases} x' = 6x - y \\ y' = 5x + 4y \end{cases},$$ subject to $x(0) = -2$ and $y(0) = 8$. The resulting list is named
comp. **comp[[1,1,2]]** yields the first element of **comp** which corresponds to the
solution of x(t).

```
In[44]:=
comp=DSolve[{x'[t]==6x[t]-y[t],
    y'[t]==5x[t]+4y[t],
      x[0]==-2,y[0]==8},{x[t],y[t]},t]

Out[44]=
{{x[t] ->
   I  (5 - 2 I) t
   - E
   2

     (-5 + 2 I + (5 + 2 I) E^4 I t),
  y[t] ->
    E^(5 - 2 I) t (8 - 9 I +

      (8 + 9 I) E^4 I t)
      ------------------
             2
 }}

In[45]:=
comp[[1,1,2]]

Out[45]=
I  (5 - 2 I) t
- E              (-5 + 2 I + (5 + 2 I) E^4 I t)
2
```

To see that the solution is real-valued, use the commands **ComplexExpand** and
Simplify to simplify **comp[[1,1,2]]** and **comp[[1,2,2]]**.

```
In[46]:=
ComplexExpand[comp[[1,1,2]]]//Simplify

Out[46]=
-(E^5 t (2 Cos[2 t] + 5 Sin[2 t]))

In[47]:=
comp[[1,2,2]]

Out[47]=
E^(5 - 2 I) t (8 - 9 I + (8 + 9 I) E^4 I t)
-------------------------------------------
                   2

In[48]:=
ComplexExpand[comp[[1,2,2]]]//Simplify

Out[48]=
E^5 t (8 Cos[2 t] - 9 Sin[2 t])
```

100%

DSolveConstants   783
See Also: **DSolve**

DSolveConstants is a **DSolve** option which is used to specify the function to apply to each index. The default setting for **DSolveConstants** is **C**. Hence, **DSolveConstants->C** gives the constants of integration **C[1]**, **C[2]**, ... whereas the option setting **DSolveConstants->(Module[{C},C]&)** specifies that the constants be unique.

Example:

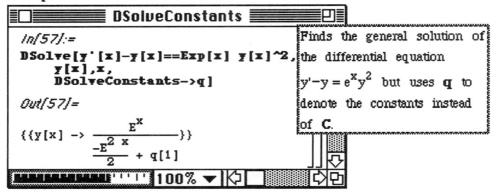

Dt   88, 625, 783
See Also: **D**, **Derivative**

Dt is used to compute the total derivative or the total differential of a function. It can be expresssed in several different ways :

Dt[f,x] computes the total derivative of **f**, $\dfrac{df}{dx}$.

Dt[f] yields the total differential of **f**, df.

Dt[f,{x,n}] calculates the nth derivative of **f**, $\dfrac{d^n f}{dx^n}$.

Dt[f,x 1,x 2,...] produces the multiple derivative $\dfrac{d}{dx_1}\dfrac{d}{dx_2}\cdots f$.

Dt has the option **Constants** which allows for the specification of terms which are assumed to be constant so that the total derivative of these terms is zero.

Example:

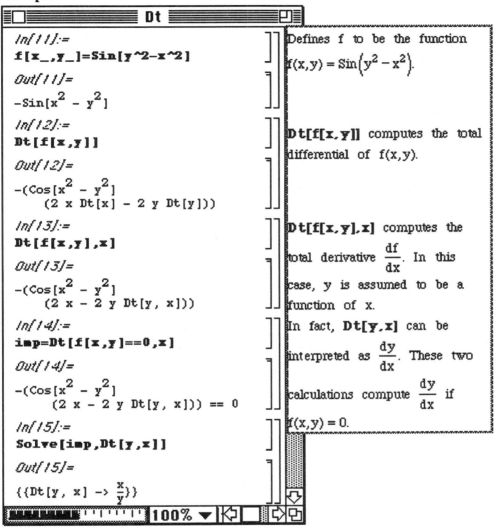

Dt

In[11]:=
`f[x_,y_]=Sin[y^2-x^2]`

Out[11]=
$-Sin[x^2 - y^2]$

In[12]:=
`Dt[f[x,y]]`

Out[12]=
$-(Cos[x^2 - y^2]$
$(2 x Dt[x] - 2 y Dt[y]))$

In[13]:=
`Dt[f[x,y],x]`

Out[13]=
$-(Cos[x^2 - y^2]$
$(2 x - 2 y Dt[y, x]))$

In[14]:=
`imp=Dt[f[x,y]]==0,x]`

Out[14]=
$-(Cos[x^2 - y^2]$
$(2 x - 2 y Dt[y, x])) == 0$

In[15]:=
`Solve[imp,Dt[y,x]]`

Out[15]=
$\{\{Dt[y, x] \rightarrow \frac{x}{y}\}\}$

100%

Defines f to be the function $f(x,y) = Sin(y^2 - x^2)$.

Dt[f[x,y]] computes the total differential of f(x,y).

Dt[f[x,y],x] computes the total derivative $\frac{df}{dx}$. In this case, y is assumed to be a function of x.

In fact, **Dt[y,x]** can be interpreted as $\frac{dy}{dx}$. These two calculations compute $\frac{dy}{dx}$ if $f(x,y) = 0$.

E

E   50, 566, 783
See 27, 270, 303, 737   See Also: **Exp**

E represents the mathematical constant e given by **Exp[1]**. The numerical value of **E** is approximately 2.71828. The command **N[E,n]** yields an **n** digit approximation of **E**.

Example:

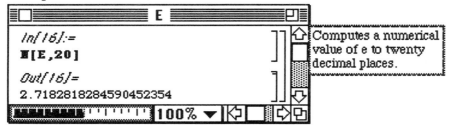

EdgeForm   437, 784
See Also: **FaceForm**, **Line**

EdgeForm is a graphics directive used to indicate the manner in which the edges of polygons are to be drawn. **EdgeForm[]** specifies that no edges be drawn while **EdgeForm[directive]** uses the setting defined by **directive** to display the edges of the polygon. The directives which may be used for **directive** include **RGBColor**, **Hue**, **Thickness**, and **CMYKColor**.

Eigensystem   664, 784
See Also: **NullSpace**, **Eigenvalues**,
Eigenvectors

Eigensystem[mat] yields a list of the eigenvalues and eigenvectors of the n × n matrix **mat**. These lists are given in corresponding order if **mat** has an equal number of eigenvalues as eigenvectors. However, if the number of eigenvalues exceeds the number of eigenvectors, then a zero vector is given in the list of eigenvectors to correspond to each additional eigenvalue. Numerical values for the eigenvalues and eigenvectors are given if **mat** contains approximate real numbers. Output is given the following form : **{{eval1,eval2,...},{evec1,evec2,...}}** where each eigenvector is a list of components.

Example:
In the first example, the exact eigenvalues and eigenvectors of the matrix $\begin{pmatrix} 9 & -1 \\ -1 & 8 \end{pmatrix}$ are computed. In the second example, numerical approximations of the eigenvalues and eigenvectors of the matrix $\begin{pmatrix} 8 & -6 & -1 \\ -3 & -4 & -2 \\ -3 & 4 & -8 \end{pmatrix}$ are computed. Although exact values could be computed (by not using the command **N**), numerical approximations take substantially less computing time.

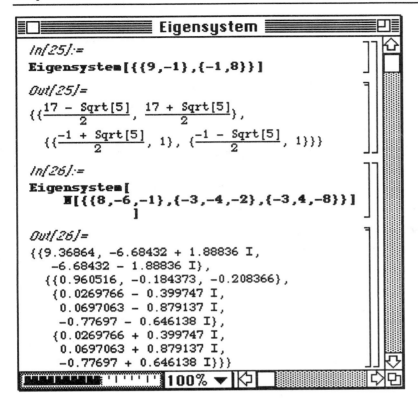

Eigenvalues   9, 123, 664, 665, 784

See Also: **Det**, **Eigenvectors**, **Eigensystem**

Eigenvalues[mat] determines the eigenvalues of the n × n matrix **mat**. An eigenvalue of the n × n matrix A is a number λ such that $Ax = \lambda x$ for a non-zero vector x. If **mat** involves approximate real numbers then the result of **Eigenvalues[mat]** is a list of numerical eigenvalues. If an eigenvalue is repeated, then it appears in the list with the appropriate multiplicity.

Example:

In the first example, the exact eigenvalues of the matrix $\begin{pmatrix} 9 & -1 \\ -1 & 8 \end{pmatrix}$ are computed. In the second example, numerical approximations

of the eigenvalues of the matrix $\begin{pmatrix} 8 & -6 & -1 \\ -3 & -4 & -2 \\ -3 & 4 & -8 \end{pmatrix}$ are computed.

Although exact values could be computed (by not using the command **N**), numerical approximations take substantially less computing time.

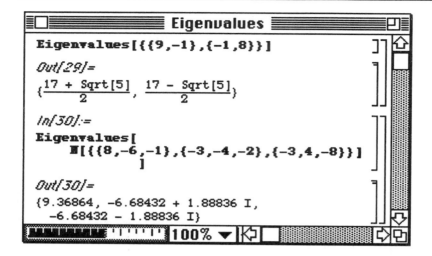

Eigenvectors   123, 664, 665, 784
                              See Also: **NullSpace**, **Eigenvalues**,
                              Eigensystem

   Eigenvectors[mat] computes the eigenvectors of the n × n matrix **mat**. The
output list consists of the linearly independent eigenvectors of **mat** and the correct
number of zero vectors so that the length of the list is n.   An eigenvector of the n × n
matrix A is a non-zero vector x such that Ax=λx for the corresponding eigenvalue λ.
Eigenvectors[mat] yields numerical eigenvectors if **mat** contains approximate
real numbers.
Example:

In the first example, the exact eigenvectors of the matrix $\begin{pmatrix} 9 & -1 \\ -1 & 8 \end{pmatrix}$ are

computed. In the second example, numerical approximations

of the eigenvectors of the matrix $\begin{pmatrix} 8 & -6 & -1 \\ -3 & -4 & -2 \\ -3 & 4 & -8 \end{pmatrix}$ are computed.

Although exact values could be computed (by not using the command **N**), numerical
approximations take substantially less computing time.

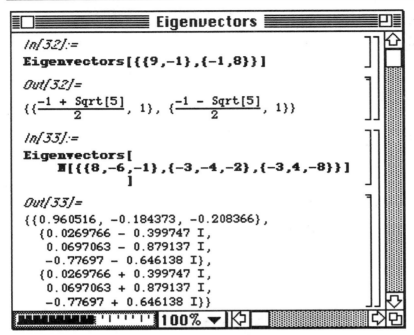

```
▤□▤▤▤▤▤▤▤ Eigenvectors ▤▤▤▤▤▤▤▤▤▤

In[32]:=
Eigenvectors[{{9,-1},{-1,8}}]

Out[32]=
{{-1 + Sqrt[5]       -1 - Sqrt[5]
 {{-----------, 1}, {-----------, 1}}
       2                  2

In[33]:=
Eigenvectors[
    N[{{8,-6,-1},{-3,-4,-2},{-3,4,-8}}]
    ]

Out[33]=
{{0.960516, -0.184373, -0.208366},
  {0.0269766 - 0.399747 I,
   0.0697063 - 0.879137 I,
   -0.77697 - 0.646138 I},
  {0.0269766 + 0.399747 I,
   0.0697063 + 0.879137 I,
   -0.77697 + 0.646138 I}}

▤▤▤▤▤▤▤▤ '''''' 100% ▼ ◁□▨▨▨▨
```

Eliminate   97, 617, 784
                             See Also: **Reduce**, **SolveAlways**, **Solve**,
                             MainSolve, **AlgebraicRules**

   Eliminate[{eq1,eq2,...},{x1,x2,...}] eliminates the variables listed in
{x1,x2,...} from the set of simultaneous equations given in **{eq1,eq2,...}**.
This command can be applied to linear as well as polynomial equations with success.

Example:

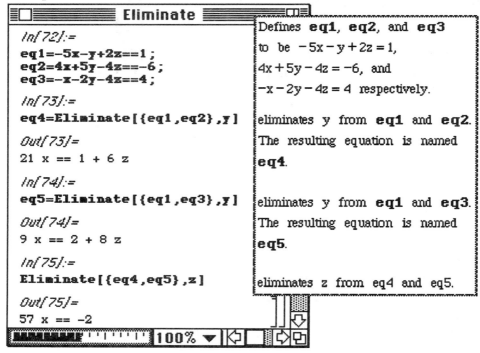

EllipticE   580, 582, 784
                    See Also: **JacobiZeta**

EllipticE[phi,m] denotes the elliptic integral of the second kind. This is

given by the formula $E(\phi|m) = \int_0^\phi \left(1 - m \sin^2\theta\right)^{1/2} d\theta = \int_0^{\sin\phi} \left(1 - m\, t^2\right)^{-1/2} dt.$

Similarly, **Elliptic[m]** represents the complete elliptic integral of the second kind

where $E(m) = E\left(\frac{\pi}{2}\bigg| m\right).$ $E'(m) = E(1-m)$ gives the complementary form of this

function.

Example:

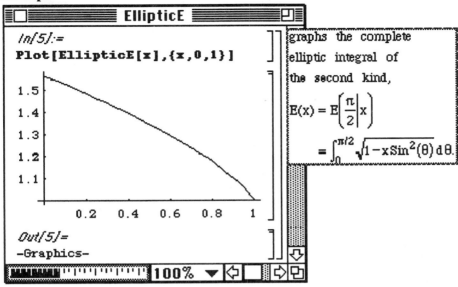

EllipticExp   580, 585, 785
                                   See Also: **EllipticLog**

  EllipticExp[u,{a,b}] yields the generalized exponential associated with the elliptic curve $y^2 = x^3 + ax^2 + bx$. **EllipticExp** is the inverse function of **EllipticLog** and serves as the basis of all built-in elliptic functions. **EllipticExp[u,{a,b}]** produces the list {x,y} which is used in **EllipticLog**.
Example:
The following creates the list {x,**Elliptic[x,{-3,1}]**} for x=0, 1/10, 1/5, 3/10, 2/5, ... , 1/2. Approximations of the result are displayed in column form. Note that the "small" imaginary components can be interpreted as zero and could be removed with the command **Cancel**.

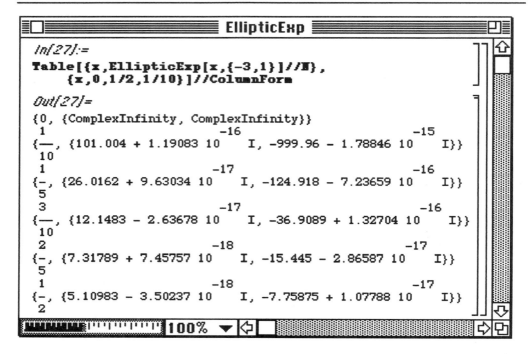

EllipticExpPrime

See Also: **EllipticExp**

EllipticExpPrime[u,{a,b}] yields the derivative of the function **EllipticExp[u,{a,b}]** with respect to the first argument.

EllipticF   580, 581, 785

See Also: **JacobiZeta**

EllipticF[phi,m] gives the elliptic integral of the first kind, denoted $F(\phi|m)$.

The formula for this function is $F(\phi|m) = \int_0^\phi \left(1 - m\sin^2\theta\right)^{-1/2} d\theta$

$$= \int_0^{\sin\phi} \left[(1-t^2)(1-m\,t^2)\right]^{-1/2} dt.$$ This function

is often called the incomplete elliptic integral of the first kind.

Example:

The following graphs the absolute value of the function

$$F(x + i\,y|3) = \int_0^{x+i\,y} \frac{d\theta}{\sqrt{1 - 3\sin^2\theta}}$$ for $-3 \le x \le 3, \ -4 \le y \le 2.$ Since

the option **Shading->False** is included, the resulting graph is not shaded. Twenty-five plotpoints are selected; the default is fifteen.

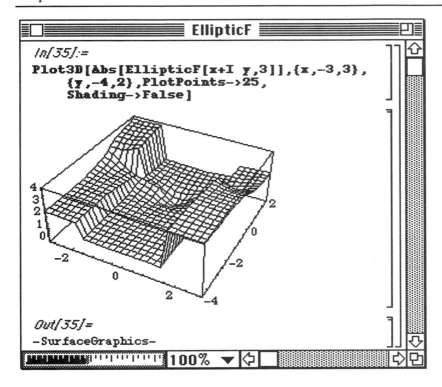

Out[35]=
-SurfaceGraphics-

EllipticK   580, 581, 785
See 232, 235   See Also: **JacobiZeta**

EllipticK[m] represents the complete elliptic integral of the first kind. This is

defined in terms of F(m) as $K(m) = F\left(\frac{\pi}{2}\bigg|m\right)$. The complementary complete elliptic

integral of the first kind is defined by $K'(m) = K(1-m)$.

Example:
The following example creates a density plot of the graph of the absolute value of

$$K(x+iy) = F\left(\frac{\pi}{2}\bigg|x+iy\right) \quad -3 \leq x \leq 3, \quad -4 \leq y \leq 2.$$

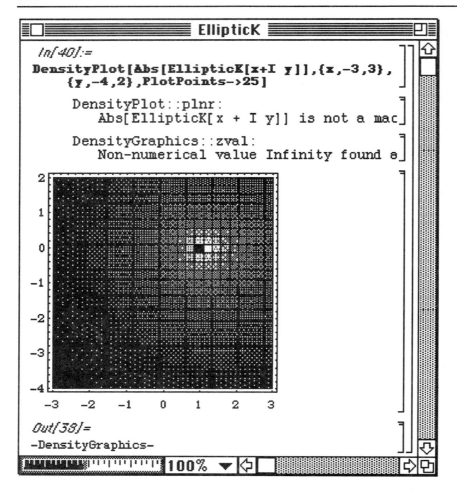

In[40]:=
DensityPlot[Abs[EllipticK[x+I y]],{x,-3,3},
    {y,-4,2},PlotPoints->25]

    DensityPlot::plnr:
        Abs[EllipticK[x + I y]] is not a mac

    DensityGraphics::zval:
        Non-numerical value Infinity found a

Out[38]=
-DensityGraphics-

EllipticLog   580, 585, 785
                          See Also: **EllipticExp**
  EllipticLog[{x,y},{a,b}] yields the generalized logarithm associated with the
elliptic curve $y^2 = x^3 + ax^2 + bx$. This is defined as the value of the integral
$\frac{1}{2}\int_\infty^x \left(t^3 + at^2 + bt\right)^{-1/2}$ dt.   The sign on the square root is assigned by giving the value
of y so that $y = \sqrt{x^3 + ax^2 + bx}$.

EllipticNomeQ   581
                          See Also: **EllipticK**

  EllipticNomeQ[m] determines the nome q, defined by $q(m) = e^{-\pi\frac{K'(m)}{K(m)}}$.
The nome q is an argument in theta functions.

Example:

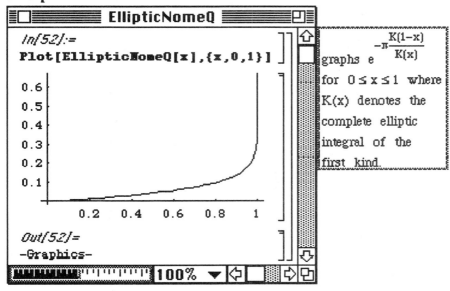

EllipticPi   580, 582, 785

EllipticPi[n,phi,m] yields the (incomplete) elliptic integral of the third kind.

This is given by the formula $\prod(n;\phi|m) = \int_0^\phi \left(1 - n\sin^2\theta\right)^{-1}\left(1 - m\sin^2\theta\right)^{-1/2} d\theta$. The

complete elliptic integral of the third kind, $\prod(n|m) = \prod\left(n;\frac{\pi}{2}|m\right)$, is given by

EllipticPi[n,m].
Example:
The following example graphs the absolute value of the function

$$\prod\left(-3;x + iy|4\right) = \int_0^{x+iy}\left(1 + 3\sin^2\theta\right)^{-1}\left(1 - 4\sin^2\theta\right)^{-1/2} d\theta \text{ for } -1 \le x \le 1, \ -2 \le y \le 2$$

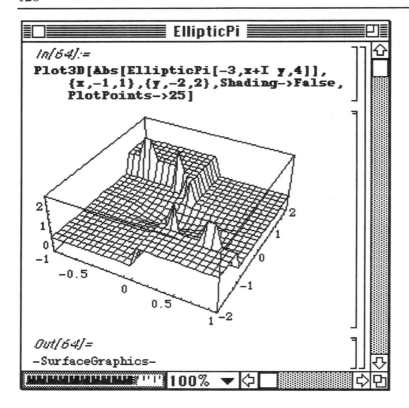

```
In[54]:=
Plot3D[Abs[EllipticPi[-3,x+I y,4]],
     {x,-1,1},{y,-2,2},Shading->False,
     PlotPoints->25]
```

```
Out[54]=
-SurfaceGraphics-
```

EllipticTheta   580, 584, 785

EllipticTheta[a,u,q] represents the elliptic theta function $\theta_a(u|q)$ where $a = 1, 2, 3, 4$.   These are given by

$$\theta_1(u,q) = 2q^{1/4} \sum_{n=0}^{\infty} (-1)^n q^{n(n+1)} \sin((2n+1)u),$$

$$\theta_2(u,q) = 2q^{1/4} \sum_{n=0}^{\infty} (-1)^n q^{n(n+1)} \cos((2n+1)u),$$

$$\theta_3(u,q) = 1 + 2 \sum_{n=0}^{\infty} q^{n^2} \cos(2nu), \ \text{ and } \ \theta_4(u,q) = 1 + 2 \sum_{n=1}^{\infty} (-1)^n q^{n^2} \cos(2nu).$$

All of the theta functions are solutions to the partial differential equation

$$\frac{\partial^2 \theta(u,\tau)}{\partial u^2} = 4\pi i \frac{\partial \theta(u,\tau)}{\partial \tau}.$$

Example:

In the following example, **a[i]** is defined to be a (non-displayed) graph of $\theta_i(x,1/4)$

for

$0 \leq x \leq 2\pi$. **a** is defined using **a[i_]:=a[i]=...** so that *Mathematica* remembers the values of **a[i]** it computes. A table of **a[i]** for i=1,2,3,4 is created with the command **Table** and then partitioned into two element sets with the command **Partition**. The resulting list is named **array**. Notice that **array** is a matrix of graphics objects.

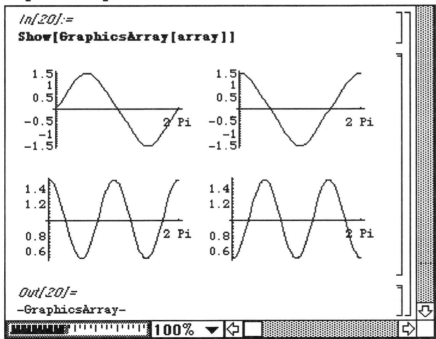

```
In[18]:=
a[i_]:=a[i]=Plot[EllipticTheta[i,x,1/4],
                {x,0,2Pi},
        Ticks->{{0,2Pi},Automatic},
        DisplayFunction->Identity]

In[19]:=
array=Partition[Table[a[i],{i,1,4}],2]

Out[19]=
{{-Graphics-, -Graphics-}, {-Graphics-, -Graphics-}}
```

The resulting four graphics cells are viewed simultaneously with the command **GraphicsArray**:

```
In[20]:=
Show[GraphicsArray[array]]
```

```
Out[20]=
-GraphicsArray-
```

EllipticThetaC   584

See Also: **EllipticTheta**

EllipticThetaC[u,m] describes Neville's elliptic theta function,

$$\theta_c(u) = \frac{\theta_2(u|m)}{\theta_2(0|m)}.$$

Example:

The following example graphs $\theta_c(x)$ with m=2/3 for $-4\pi \le x \le 4\pi$.

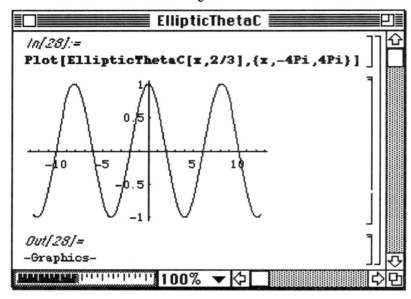

EllipticThetaD   584

See Also: **EllipticTheta**

EllipticThetaD[u,m] describes Neville's elliptic theta function,

$$\theta_d(u) = \frac{\theta_3(u|m)}{\theta_3(0|m)}.$$

Example:

The following example graphs $\theta_d(\pi/3)$ with m=x for $-1 \le x \le 1$.

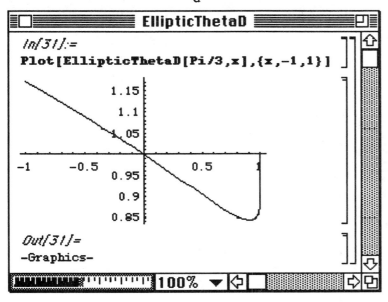

EllipticThetaN   584

See Also: **EllipticTheta**

EllipticThetaN[u,m] describes Neville's elliptic theta function,

$$\theta_n(u) = \frac{\theta_4(u|m)}{\theta_4(0|m)}.$$

Example:

The following graph is a contour plot of $\theta_n(\pi/3)$ with m=x+iy for $-1 \le x \le 2$ and $-1 \le y \le 2$.

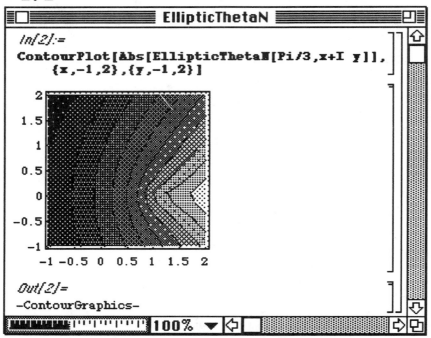

EllipticThetaPrime

See Also: **EllipticTheta**

EllipticThetaPrime[i,z,q] computes the derivative with respect to the second argument of the function $\theta_i(z,q)$ where i = 1, 2, 3, or 4.

Example:

In the following example, **etp[i]** is defined to be a (non-displayed) graph of the absolute value of the derivative of $\theta_i(x+iy, 1/3)$ for $0 \le x \le \pi/2$ and $-\pi/2 \le y \le \pi/2$. **etp** is defined using **etp[i_]:=etp[i]=...** so that *Mathematica* remembers the values of **etp[i]** it computes. A table of **etp[i]** for i=1,2,3,4 is created with the command **Table** and then partitioned into two element sets with the command **Partition**. The resulting list is named **array**. Notice that **array** is a matrix of surface graphics objects. In this case, twenty-five plotpoints are used (the default is fifteen) and the resulting graph is not shaded.

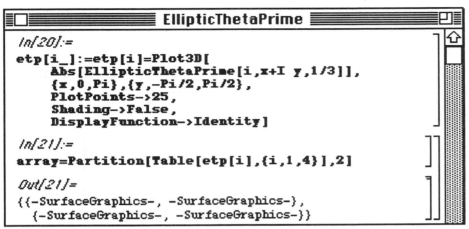

The resulting four graphics cells are viewed simultaneously with the command **GraphicsArray**:

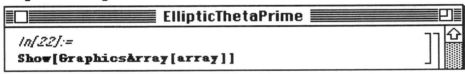

The following shows the resulting graphics object:

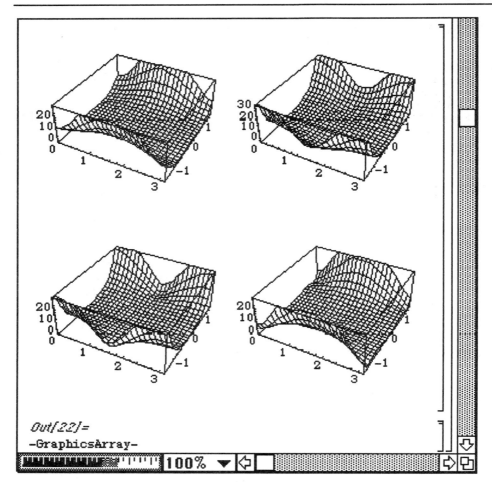

Out[22]=
-GraphicsArray-

100%

EllipticThetaS   584
                            See Also: **EllipticTheta**, **EllipticThetaPrime**,
                            EllipticK
  EllipticThetaS[u,m] describes Neville's elliptic theta function,

$$\theta_s(u) = \frac{2K(m)\,\theta_1(v|m)}{\theta_1'(0|m)}.$$

Example:

The following graph is a contour plot of $\theta_s(\pi/3)$ with m=x+iy for $-1 \le x \le 2$ and

$-1 \le y \le 2$. Since the option **ContourShading->False** is included, the resulting graph is displayed without shading between contour lines.

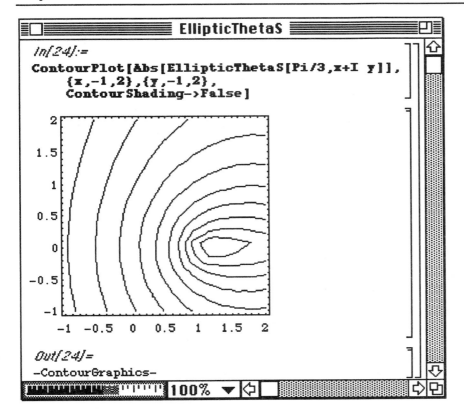

Encode   480, 786
                             See Also: **ReadProtected, $MachineID,**
                             MachineID

Encode is used to encode files in printable ASCII characters only so that they can be read into *Mathematica* but cannot be read or modified as text. This encoding can be done in several ways:

Encode["initialfile","encodefile"] encodes the file **initialfile** and saves it as **encodefile**. This file can be read in with **<<encodefile**.

Encode["initialfile","encodefile","key"] encodes the file **initialfile** and saves it as **encodefile** with **key**. Hence, the file must be read in with **Get["encodefile","key"]**. **Encode** has the option **MachineID** so that files can be read in only by machines of a certain type.

End   339, 341, 786
                             See Also: **$ContextPath**

End[] is used with **Begin["`Private`"]** to return to the context which preceded `Private`. **End[]** resets the value of **$Context** but does not alter **$ContextPath**.

EndAdd
                             See Also: **$ContextPath**

EndAdd[] leaves the present context and returns to the previous one. This command prepends the present context to **$ContextPath**.

EndOfFile   498, 786
                    See Also: **Read, ReadList**

EndOfFile is returned by **Read** when the end of the file is encountered. It appears when using **ReadList** to read a list of objects in the place of the objects which are needed after the end of the file is reached.

EndPackage   339, 786
                    See Also: **$ContextPath, $Context**

EndPackage[] is used with **BeginPackage** to restore the values of **$ContextPath** and **$Context** to their values before the **BeginPackage** command which preceded it. This command is used at the end of most every *Mathematica* package.

EndProcess

EndProcess["command"] is used to terminate external processes which can be called from *Mathematica*. The *MathLink* operations in Version 2.0 have superseded **EndProcess**.

EngineeringForm   350, 786
                    See Also: **BaseForm, NumberForm**

EngineeringForm[expression] prints **expression** in engineering notation where each exponent in scientific notation is arranged to be a multiple of 3. Also, **EngineeringForm[expression, total]** prints **expression** in engineering notation using at most **total** digits. This command only affects the printing of numbers. It does not alter any calculations. **EngineeringForm** uses the same options as **NumberForm**, but the default setting on **ExponentFunction** is given by **ExponentFunction->(3 Quotient[#,3]&)**.

Example:

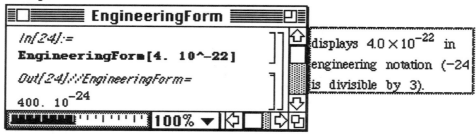

Environment   529, 743, 786
                    See Also: **Run, $CommandLine, $System**

Environment["envar"] returns the value of the operating system environment variable, **envar**. This command gives a string of environment variables if these values are found, but it returns **$Failed** if the value of the requested environment variable is not located.

Epilog   412, 786
                                   See Also: **Prolog**, **AxesStyle**, **PlotStyle**,
                                   DisplayFunction

Epilog is a graphics option used to indicate graphics primitives to be displayed after the completion of the plot.

Equal   92, 94, 606, 787
See 8, 120, 277, 291,   See Also: **SameQ**, **Unequal**, **Order**
307-309, 322, 333, 389,
434, 435, 527, 528

Equal, symbolized by the double equals sign **==**, is used to represent symbolic equations. A value of **True** is given if **lhs==rhs** while **False** is rendered if not. Approximate numbers are considered unequal if they differ in at most their last two decimal places.

Example:

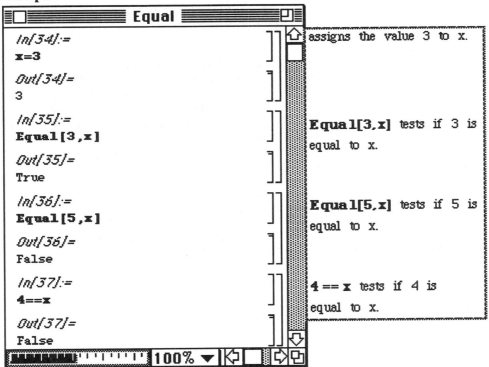

EquatedTo   859
                                   See Also: **Roots**

EquatedTo is an option used with **Roots** to indicate an expression to which the variable to be solved for by **Roots** should be set.

Erf   570, 576, 787
See 216, 621, 624, 625,   See Also: **ExpIntegralE, ExpIntegralEi**
684, 685

Er f[z] represents the error function erf(z) which is the integral of the Gaussian

distribution. The formula for this error function is $\mathrm{erf}(z) = \dfrac{2}{\sqrt{\pi}}\int_0^z e^{-t^2}\, dt$. The

generalized error function, $\mathrm{erf}(z_1) - \mathrm{erf}(z_0)$, is given by

$$\mathbf{Er\,f[z_1,z_0]} = \frac{2}{\sqrt{\pi}}\int_{z_0}^{z_1} e^{-t^2}\, dt.$$

Example:

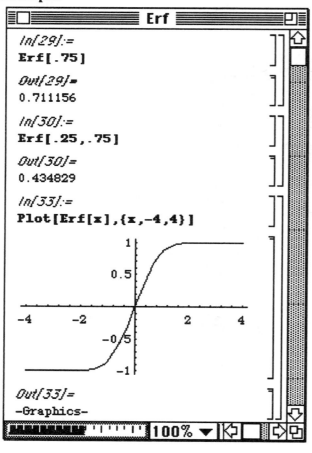

Erfc   570, 576, 787
                                 See Also: **Erf**

    Erfc[z] yields the complementary error function $\text{erfc}(z) = 1 - \text{erf}(z)$.

Example:

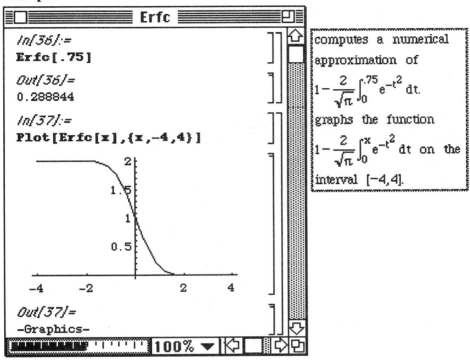

Erfi

                         See Also: **Erf**

    Erfi[z] yields the imaginary error function $\text{erfi}(z) = -i\,\text{erf}(iz)$.

Example:

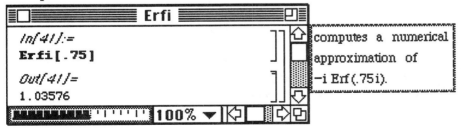

EulerE   558, 787
                                                See Also: **BernoulliB, Binomial, Multinomial,
                                                PartitionsP, PartitionsQ, Signature,
                                                StirlingS1, StirlingS2**

EulerE[x] yields the Euler number E_n while **EulerE[n,x]** calculates the Euler polynomial $E_n(x)$. The Euler polynomials satisfy the relation

$$\frac{2e^{xt}}{e^t + 1} = \sum_{n=0}^{\infty} E_n(x) \, \frac{t^n}{n!}. \quad \text{The Euler numbers are determined by } E_n = 2^n E_n(1/2).$$

Example:

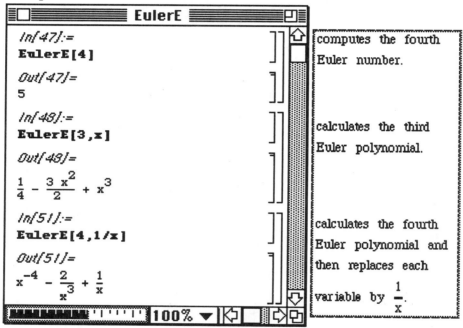

EulerGamma   566, 787
See 72   See Also: **PolyGamma**

EulerGamma represents Euler's constant, γ, which has approximate numerical value 0.577216.

Example:

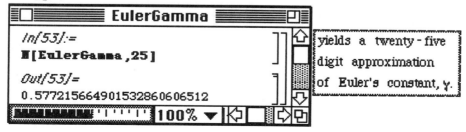

EulerPhi   556, 787
                                See Also: **FactorInteger, Divisors,**
                                DivisorsSigma, MoebiusMu

   EulerPhi[n] determines the number of positive integers less than n which are relatively prime to **n**. This function is called the Euler totient function and denoted $\phi(n)$.

Example:

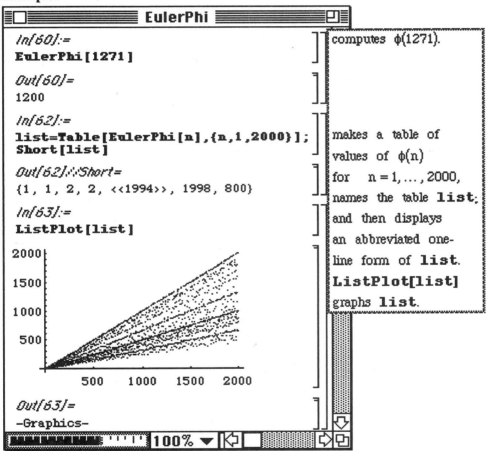

Evaluate   135, 280, 286, 731, 787
See 240, 248, 356, 358,   See Also: **Evaluate**
593, 616-631, 708, 709,
711, 713, 766, 767

   Evaluate[expression] causes *Mathematica* to evaluate **expression** immediately even if the command is the argument of a function the attributes of which indicate that it should be held unevaluated. This command is particularly useful when working with lists of functions.

EvenQ   227, 535, 787
See 527, 528   See Also: **IntegerQ**, **OddQ**, **TrueQ**

   EvenQ[expression] determines if **expression** is an even integer and gives a value of **True** if it is. This command can also be used in the form of a definition to specify that an expression of a particular form such as x^2 should be assumed to be even.
Example:

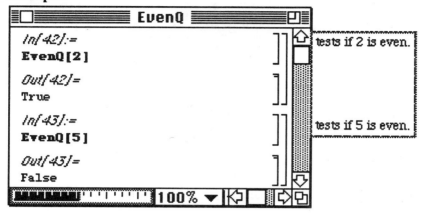

Exit   71, 519, 747, 788
See Also: **Return**, **$IgnoreEOF**

   Exit[] is used to end a current *Mathematica* session. This command can also be used from within a **Dialog** and is equivalent to **Quit**.

Exp   49, 562, 788
                                                     See Also: **Power**, **E**

The exponential function, e^x, is represented as **Exp[x]** in *Mathematica*.

Example:

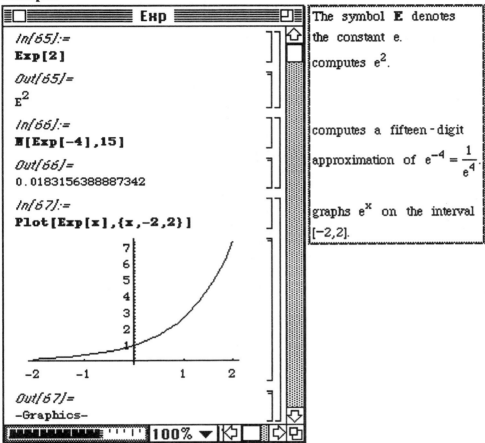

In[55]:=	The symbol **E** denotes
Exp[2]	the constant e.
Out[55]=	computes e^2.
E^2	
In[56]:=	computes a fifteen-digit
N[Exp[-4],15]	approximation of e$^{-4} = \dfrac{1}{e^4}$.
Out[56]=	
0.0183156388887342	
In[57]:=	graphs e^x on the interval
Plot[Exp[x],{x,-2,2}]	[-2,2].
Out[57]=	
-Graphics-	

100%

Expand   76, 78, 591, 595, 603, 788
See 202, 211, 287, 365,   See Also: **ComplexExpand**, **Distribute**,
772   **ExpandAll**, **Apart**, **Series**, **Factor**,
                                            LogicalExpand, **PowerExpand**

Expand is used to expand expressions. This can be accomplished in several ways:
Expand[expression] carries out the multiplication of products and positive integer powers in **expression**. The resulting expression is the sum of terms.
Expand[epression,form] expands only those terms in **expression** which do not match the pattern defined in **form**. When **expression** involves fractions,
Expand[expression] expands the numerator and divides the denominator into each term in **expression**. **Expand** has the option **Trig->True** which causes trigonometric functions to be treated as exponential rational functions so that they can be expanded.

Example:

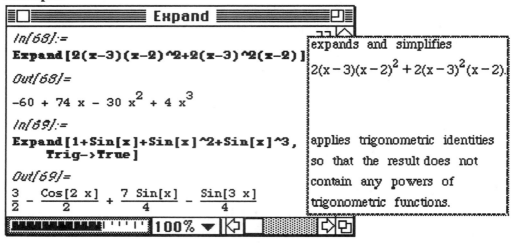

ExpandAll   78, 595, 788
                                 See Also: **Cancel**, **ComplexExpand**, **Expand**,
                                 ExpandDenominator, **ExpandNumerator**,
                                 Simplify

   ExpandAll[expression] completely expands the numerators and denominators
in **expression**. **ExpandAll[expression,form]** does not apply **ExpandAll**
to terms in **expression** which match the pattern defined by **form**. **ExpandAll** also
has the option **Trig->True** as defined above in **Expand**.
Example:
In the following example, **alg** is defined to be the expression
$\dfrac{(x+4)^2}{(x-1)^2}$.   **Expand[alg]** only expands the numerator; **ExpandAll[alg]**

expands both the numerator and denominator.

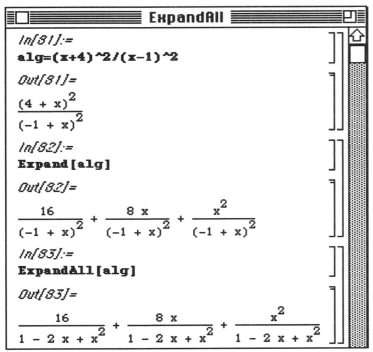

When the option **Trig->True** is included, the numerator and denominator are expanded so that neither contains powers of trigonometric functions.

```
In[91]:=
example=(Cos[x]^2-Cos[x]^4)/(Sin[x]^4-Sin[x]^2)

Out[91]=
Cos[x]^2 - Cos[x]^4
-------------------
-Sin[x]^2 + Sin[x]^4

In[92]:=
ExpandAll[example]

Out[92]=
      Cos[x]^2                Cos[x]^4
------------------- - -------------------
-Sin[x]^2 + Sin[x]^4   -Sin[x]^2 + Sin[x]^4

In[93]:=
ExpandAll[example,Trig->True]

Out[93]=
         1                    Cos[4 x]
------------------- - -------------------
8 (-(1/8) + Cos[4 x]/8)   8 (-(1/8) + Cos[4 x]/8)
```

100% ▼

ExpandDenominator 595, 788

See 424, 470 See'Also: **ComplexExpand**, **Denominator**,
Expand, **ExpandAll**, **ExpandNumerator**,
Together

ExpandDenominator[expression] expands only those terms in **expression** that appear as denominators. Hence, **ExpandDenominator** works only on those terms involving negative integer exponents.

Example:

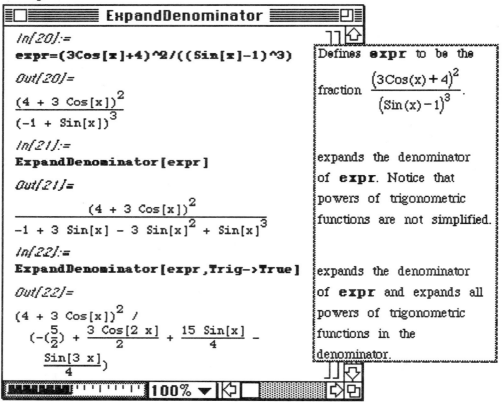

ExpandNumerator 595, 788

See Also: **ComplexExpand**, **Expand**, **ExpandAll**,
ExpandDenominator, **Numerator**, **Together**

ExpandNumerator[expression] multiplies out the terms in **expression** which appear as numerators. Therefore, **ExpandNumerator** applies only to terms having positive integer exponents.

Example:

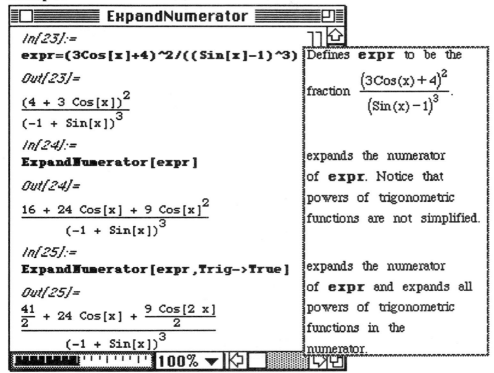

ExpIntegralE   570, 575, 788
                                    See Also: **Erf**, **LogIntegral**, **SinIntegral**,
                                    CosIntegral

ExpIntegralE[n,z] represents the exponential integral function

$$E_n(z) = \int_1^\infty \frac{e^{-zt}}{t^n} dt.$$

Example:

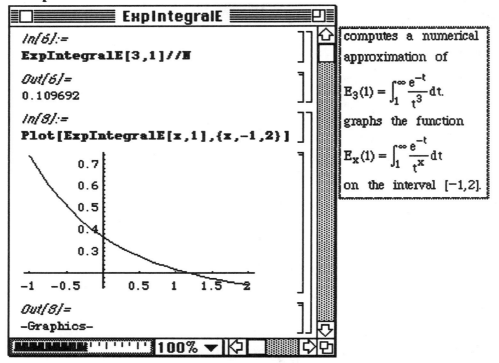

ExpIntegralEi   570, 575, 789

                                  See Also: **Erf**, **LogIntegral**, **SinIntegral**,
                                  CosIntegral

ExpIntegralEi[n,z] represents the second exponential integral function,

$$Ei(z) = \int_{-z}^{\infty} \frac{e^{-t}}{t} dt, \text{ for } z > 0.$$ The principal value of the integral is taken in this case.

Example:

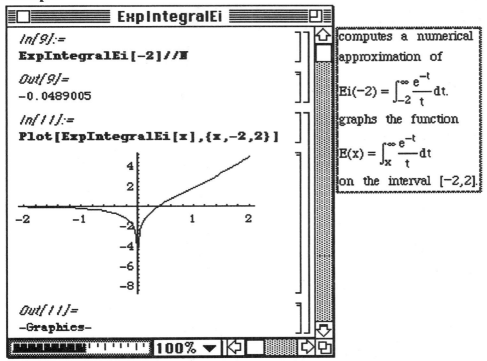

Exponent   82, 593, 789
See Also: **Coefficient, Cases**

Exponent[expression,variable] yields the highest power of **variable** which appears in **expression** where **expression** is a single term or a sum of terms. This command can also be stated in the form
Exponent[expression,variable,function] to apply **function** to the set of exponents which appear in **expression**.

Example:

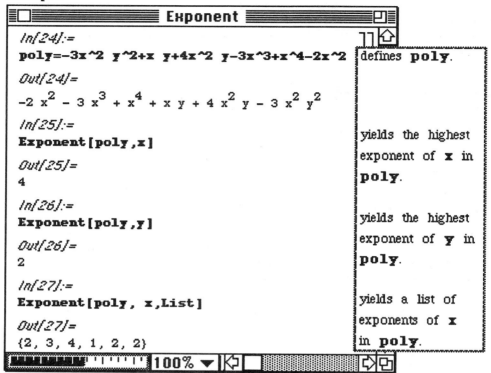

ExponentFunction   351, 789
                          See Also: **NumberFormat**, **EngineeringForm**
    ExponentFunction is an option for commands such as **NumberForm** and **EngineeringForm** used for the formatting of numbers. This option is used to indicate the exponent to be used in the printing of approximate real numbers. The definition of **ExponentFunction** must be entered as a pure function. For example, the setting for **EngineeringForm** in which all exponents are integer multiples of 3 is **ExponentFunction->(3 Quotient[#,3]&)**. Notice that the argument of **ExponentFunction** is always an integer.

ExponentStep   obsolete in Version 2.0
                          superseded by **ExponentFunction**

Expression   495, 789
                          See Also: **ToExpression**
    Expression represents an ordinary *Mathematica* expression in such functions as **ReadList**. **Hold[Expression]** causes *Mathematica* to place **Expression** within **Hold**.

ExtendedGCD   556, 789
                                    See Also: **GCD**

   ExtendedGCD[m,n] produces the output list `{g,{r,s}}` such that `g` is the greatest common divisor of `m` and `n`, and `r` and `s` are integers which satisfy the equation `g = rm + sn`.

Example:

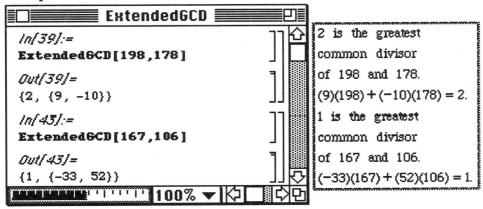

F

FaceForm   438, 789
                                            See Also: **EdgeForm**

FaceForm[front,back] is a three-dimensional graphics directive used to indicate how the front and back faces of a polygon should be drawn. The settings for **front** and **back** must be in the form of **RGBColor**, **Hue**, **GrayLevel**, or **CMYKColor** directives. However, these may also be **SurfaceColor** objects. Faces are ordered in a counter-clockwise manner.

FaceGrids   156, 158, 459, 463, 790
See 520, 583   See Also: **Ticks**, **GridLines**

FaceGrids is a three-dimensional graphics command option which is used to indicate how the grid lines on the bounding box are to be drawn. The settings for this option include **None** which specifies that no lines be drawn, **All** which indicates that lines be drawn on all faces, and **{f1,f2,f3,...}** which instructs lines to be drawn on the faces **f1**, **f2**, **f3**, ... Instructions can be made more specific by using the setting **{{f1,{x1,y1}},...}**.

Factor   76, 78, 591, 596, 598, 602, 603, 608, 790
See 377   See Also: **FactorTerms**, **Solve**, **Expand**,
                                            Simplify, **FactorInteger**

Factor[poly] completely factors the polynomial **poly** over the integers. Factorization can also be accomplished modulo a prime number **p** with **Factor[poly,Modulus->p]**. Other options include **Trig->True** which interprets trigonometric functions as exponential rational functions and factors them correctly, **GaussianIntegers->True** which allows for Gaussian integer coefficients in the factorization, and **Variables->{x1,x2,...}** which indicates an ordering on the variables in **poly**. This ordering may affect the time needed to complete the factorization.

Example:

The following command factors the polynomial

$$162x^5 + 297x^4 + 216x^3 + 78x^2 + 14x + 1:$$

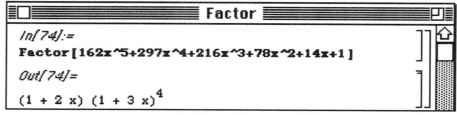

In the following example, the option **Trig->True** is included so that Sin(4x)+Sin(2x) is displayed as a product:

```
In[75]:=
Factor[Sin[4x]+Sin[2x]]

Out[75]=
Sin[2 x] + Sin[4 x]

In[76]:=
Factor[Sin[4x]+Sin[2x],Trig->True]

Out[76]=
2 Cos[x] (1 + 2 Cos[2 x]) Sin[x]
```

The symbol **I** denotes the imaginary number $\sqrt{-1}$. If the option **GaussianIntegers- > True** is included **,** **I** and **- I** are allowed in the factorization **:**

```
In[77]:=
Factor[x^8-1]

Out[77]=
               2        4
(-1 + x) (1 + x) (1 + x ) (1 + x )

In[78]:=
Factor[x^8-1,GaussianIntegers->True]

Out[78]=
                                      2        2
(-1 + x) (-I + x) (I + x) (1 + x) (-I + x ) (I + x )
```

In the following, the first command factors $x^5 + 1$ over the integers; the second command factors $x^5 + 1$ modulo 5.

```
In[79]:=
Factor[x^5+1]

Out[79]=
                    2    3    4
(1 + x) (1 - x + x - x + x )

In[80]:=
Factor[x^5+1,Modulus->5]

Out[80]=
         5
(1 + x)
```

100%

FactorComplete   555, 790
                                          See Also: **FactorInteger**

   FactorComplete is an option used with **FactorInteger** to indicate whether or not the factorization should be complete. The option **FactorComplete->False** causes *Mathematica* to extract at most one factor.

Factorial   49, 558, 790
See 20   See Also: **Gamma**, **Binomial**

   Factorial, symbolized by **n!**, yields the factorial of **n**. If **n** is not an integer, then the value of **n!** is computed by calculating **Gamma[1+n]** where **Gamma[x]** represents the gamma function.

Example:

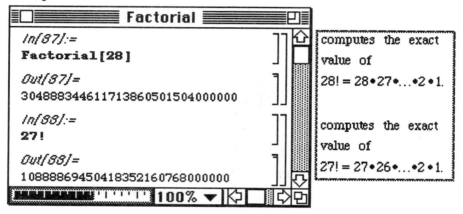

Factorial2   558, 790
                                          See Also: **Gamma**

   Factorial2 represents the double factorial. Hence, **n!! = n(n-2)(n-4)....**

Example:

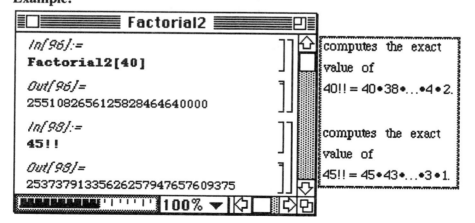

FactorInteger   2, 49, 84, 554, 791
See 301   See Also: **Prime**, **PrimeQ**, **Divisors**

FactorInteger[n] lists the prime factors of **n** along with the exponent of each in the form {pfactor,exponent}. This command has several options. **FactorComplete->False** determines the first factor of **n** only, and **GaussianIntegers->True** determines the factors which are Gaussian integers. Also, the command can be stated as **Factor[n,p]** so that only prime factors of **n** which are less than or equal to **p** are listed. If **n** is negative, then one component in the output list is {-1,1}.

Example:

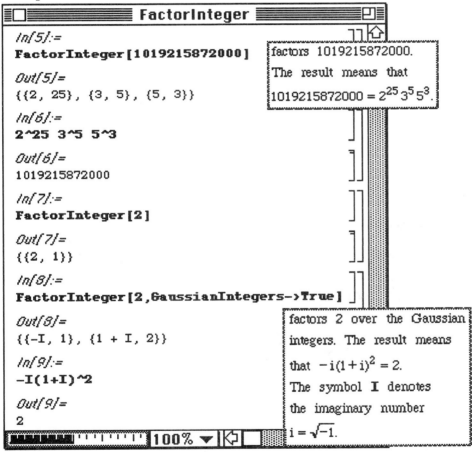

FactorList   598, 791
                                    See Also: **CoefficientList**

FactorList[poly] lists the factors of the polynomial **poly** as well as the exponent of each. The components in the output list are in the form {factor,exponent}. The option **Modulus->p** causes *Mathematica* to find the factors modulo **p** while **GaussianIntegers->True** allows for coefficients which are Gaussian integers.

Example:

The following example first defines **polyone** to be the polynomial $162x^5 + 297x^4 + 216x^3 + 78x^2 + 14x + 1$. The result obtained by **FactorList[polyone]** means

$$(1 + 2x)(1 + 3x)^4 = 162x^5 + 297x^4 + 216x^3 + 78x^2 + 14x + 1.$$

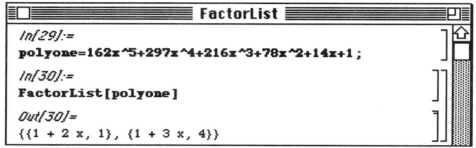

```
In[29]:=
polyone=162x^5+297x^4+216x^3+78x^2+14x+1 ;

In[30]:=
FactorList[polyone]

Out[30]=
{{1 + 2 x, 1}, {1 + 3 x, 4}}
```

In the following example, **polytwo** is defined to be the polynomial $(1 + x)(1 + x + x^2)(1 - x + x^2 - x^3 + x^4) = 1 + x + x^2 + x^5 + x^6 + x^7$. The result of **FactorList[polytwo, Modulus – > 5]** means

$$(1 + x)^5(1 + x + x^2)\,\text{Modulo } 5 = 1 + x + x^2 + x^5 + x^6 + x^7.$$

```
In[31]:=
polytwo=1+x+x^2+x^5+x^6+x^7 ;

In[32]:=
FactorList[polytwo]

Out[32]=
{{1 + x, 1}, {1 + x + x^2, 1}, {1 - x + x^2 - x^3 + x^4, 1}}

In[33]:=
FactorList[polytwo,Modulus->5]

Out[33]=
{{1 + x, 5}, {1 + x + x^2, 1}}
```

Similarly, the result of **FactorList[Sin[2x]^2 Cos[3x]^6,Trig->True]** means $4\,\text{Sin}^2(x)\,\text{Cos}^8(x)\,(2\,\text{Cos}(2x) - 1)^6 = \text{Sin}^2(2x)\,\text{Cos}^6(3x)$.

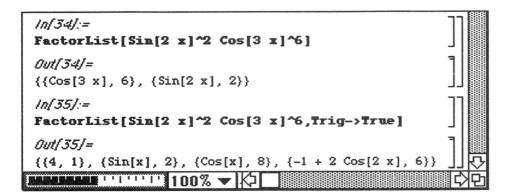

FactorSquareFree   598, 791
                              See Also: **FactorTerms**, **FactorTermsList**,
                              FactorList, **Factor**
   FactorSquareFree[poly] rewrites the polynomial **poly** as a product of factors
each of which is square-free. This is accomplished by factoring out squared factors.
FactorSquareFree has the option **Modulus->p** which factors out squared factors
modulo the prime number **p**.

FactorSquareFreeList 598, 791
                              See Also: **FactorTerms**, **FactorTermsList**,
                              FactorList, **Factor**
   FactorSquareFreeList[poly] lists the square-free factors of the polynomial
poly along with the exponent of each. The components of the output list are of the
form {factor,exponent}.

FactorTerms   80, 591, 598, 791
                              See Also: **Factor**
   FactorTerms[poly] factors out common numerical factors from each term of
poly and factors out any overall common numerical factor. Also, **Factor[poly,x]**
factors out all factors of **poly** which do not depend on **x**. The output is written as a
product of terms.
Example:

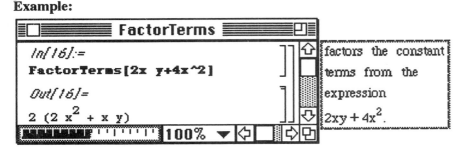

FactorTermsList   598, 791
                                       See Also: **FactorTerms**
FactorTermsList[poly,{x1,x2,x3,...}] lists the factors of the polynomial **poly**. The first component in the list of output is the overall numerical factor while the second is the factor which does not depend on any of the list **{x1,x2,x3,...}**. The third term in the output is a factor that does not depend on any of the list **{x2,x3,...}**. This process continues.

Example:

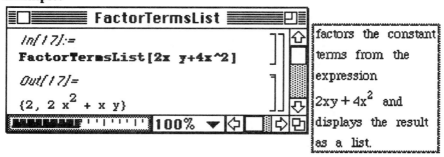

factors the constant terms from the expression $2xy + 4x^2$ and displays the result as a list.

Fail
                                       See Also: **Condition**
Fail is the symbol returned when the command **Condition** is used in an obsolete manner.

False   93, 141, 287, 791
See 123, 126, 131, 133,   See Also: **TrueQ**, **True**
178, 235, 236, 238, 241,
243, 254, 265, 271, 310,
311, 377, 397, 398, 411, 513, 636
False is the symbol used to represent the Boolean value of false.

Example:

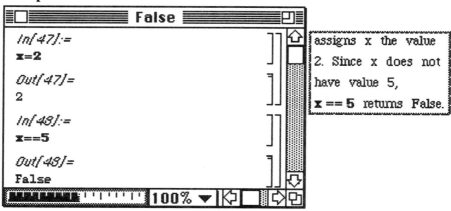

assigns x the value 2. Since x does not have value 5, $x == 5$ returns False.

File   492, 792
                                       See Also: **FileType**
File is a possible value of the command **FileType["filename"]** to denote the type of the file **filename**.

FileByteCount   492, 792

                    See Also: **StringByteCount**, **FileType**

    FileByteCount["filename"] yields the total number of bytes in the file
filename. This number depends on the computer system in use.

Example:

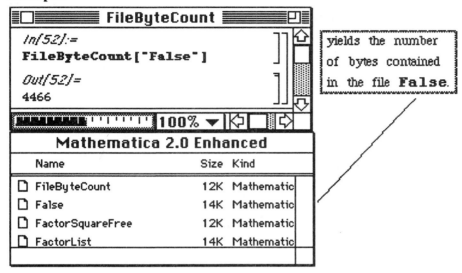

FileDate   492, 792

                    See Also: **SetFileDate**, **FromData**

    FileDate["filename"] returns the date and time of the last modification of the
file **filename**.

Example:

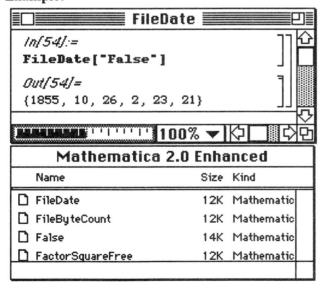

FileInformation

See Also: **FileType**, **FileNames**, **FileDate**,
FileByteCount, **SetFileDate**, **FromData**

FileInformation yields information about files.

Example:

In the following example, **FileInformation** is used to obtain information about the
file **False** (shown below in the *Mathematica* 2.0 Enhanced folder).

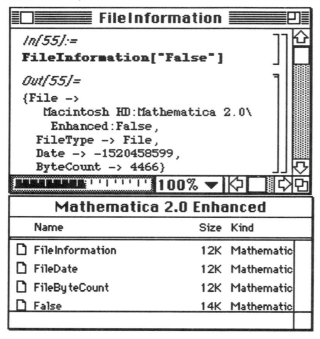

FileNames   180, 491, 792

See Also: **Directory**, **FileType**

FileNames is used to determine the files in the current working directory. This
command can be used in several forms to achieve different results. **FileNames[]**
lists all files in the current working directory. **FileNames["pattern"]** lists all files
with names that are of the form defined by **pattern**.

FileNames["patt1","patt2",...] lists all files with names that are of any of
the forms defined by **patt1**, **patt2**,..... .

FileNames[{"patt1","patt2",...},{direct1,direct2,...}] lists the
files in the directories listed in **{direct1,direct2,...}** which match any of the
patterns given in **{"patt1","patt2",...}**.

FileNames[{"patt1","patt2",...},{direct1,direct2,...},n]
yields the files in the subdirectories of the directories in **{direct1,direct2,...}**
up to **n** levels down which match any of the patterns in **{"patt1","patt2",...}**.

**FileNames[{"patt1","patt2",...},{direct1,direct2,...},Infin-
ity]** gives a list of all subdirectories.

FileNames[{"patt1","patt2",...},$Path,Infinity] lists all files in any subdirectory of directories in **$Path** which match any of the patterns given in **{"patt1","patt2",...}**. This information is listed in the following manner : **:directory:directory:filename.**

FileType   492, 792
                                     See Also: **FileNames, FileByteCount**

   FileType["filename"] yields the type of the file **filename**. The resulting type is usually **File**, **Directory**, or **None**. The value of None is given if the file **filename** does not exist.

Find   502, 505, 793
                                     See Also: **Read, Skip, StreamPosition**

   Find is used to locate certain lines in a stream of input. This can be done in several ways: **Find[strm,"string"]** locates the first line in the input stream **strm** in which the characters given in **string** appear. Also, **Find[strm,{"string1","string2",...}]** locates the first input line which contains any of the text listed in **{"string1","string2",...}**. **EndOfFile** results if the end of the file is reached before any of the specified strings are located. **Find** has several options. **AnchoredSearch** is used to indicate if the text must be at the beginning of a line. **IgnoreCase** is used to instruct *Mathematica* to treat lower- and upper-case letters equally. **RecordSeparators**, **{"\n"}**, is used as record separators just as **WordSeparators**, **{""," \t"}**, is used for separators for words. Finally, **WordSearch** is used to specify whether or not the text must appear as a word in the stream of input.

FindList   16, 181, 500, 505, 793
                                     See Also: **ReadList**

   FindList is used to list the lines of the portion of text which contain a certain string of characters. This can be accomplished in several forms. **FindList["filename","text"]** lists all of the lines in the file **filename** which contain the characters given in **text**. **FindList["filename","text",n]** lists only the first **n** lines of **filename** in which **text** appears. **FindList["filename",{"text1","text2",...}]** lists the lines in **filename** which contain any of the text listed in **{"text1","text2",...}**. The result of **FindList** is a list of lines from the file which contain the specified text. If the text is not found, then the **{}** symbol is given as output.

FindMinimum   109, 703, 794
                                     See Also: **ConstrainedMin, LinearProgramming,**
                                     D, Fit

   FindMinimum is used to search for the local minimum of a function. The command **FindMinimum[function,{x,x0}]** looks for a local minimum of **function** by beginning the search at the value of **x = x0**. If the symbolic derivative of **function** can not be determined, however, the command **FindMinimum[function,{x,{x0,x1}}]** must be used. In this case, the first two values of **x** are given by **x = x0** and **x = x1**. The output of the **FindMinimum** command is of the form **{fmin,{x->xmin}}** where **fmin** is the minimum value of **function** which occurs at **x = xmin**. If **function** is a multivariable function, then **FindMinimum[function,{x,x0},{y,y0},...]** with an initial value for each variable of **function** can be used to locate a local minimum. This command is based on the path of steepest descent algorithm and has numerous options. **AccuracyGoal** is used to indicate the level of desired accuracy of the minimum value of the function, **Compiled** specifies if the function should be compiled before the search is initiated, **Gradient** is used to enter the gradient vector of the function, **MaxIterations** indicates the maximum number of iterations which should be used in the search for the local minimum, **PrecisionGoal** specifies the desired precision of the minimum value of the function, and **WorkPrecision** is used to give the number of digits used during internal computations. The default settings of two of these options are given by **MaxIterations->30** and **WorkingPrecision->Precision[1.0]**. The default settings for **AccuracyGoal** and **PrecisionGoal** are 10 digits fewer than the setting of **WorkingPrecision**.

Example:

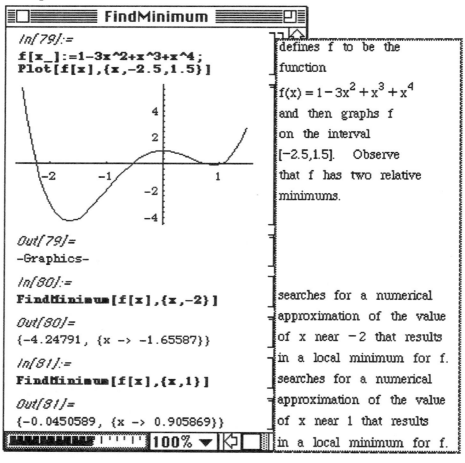

```
In[79]:=
f[x_]:=1-3x^2+x^3+x^4;
Plot[f[x],{x,-2.5,1.5}]
```

defines f to be the function

$$f(x) = 1 - 3x^2 + x^3 + x^4$$

and then graphs f on the interval $[-2.5, 1.5]$. Observe that f has two relative minimums.

```
Out[79]=
-Graphics-
In[80]:=
FindMinimum[f[x],{x,-2}]
Out[80]=
{-4.24791, {x -> -1.65587}}
```

searches for a numerical approximation of the value of x near -2 that results in a local minimum for f.

```
In[81]:=
FindMinimum[f[x],{x,1}]
Out[81]=
{-0.0450589, {x -> 0.905869}}
```

searches for a numerical approximation of the value of x near 1 that results in a local minimum for f.

FindRoot   96, 107, 692, 794
See 749   See Also: **NRoots**, **NSolve**, **Solve**, **FindMinimum**

   FindRoot is used to approximate the numerical solution of an equation or a system of equations. This command is entered as **FindRoot[lhs==rhs,{x,x0}]** where **x0** is the initial guess of the solution to the equation **lhs==rhs**. However, if the derivatives of the equation can not be computed symbolically, then the command **FindRoot[lhs==rhs,{x,x0,x1}]** may be used to find the approximate solution. In this case, the first two values of **x** are taken to be **x0** and **x1**. The **FindRoot** command of the form **FindRoot[lhs==rhs,{x,x0}]** is based on Newton's method while that of **FindRoot[lhs==rhs,{x,x0,x1}]** is a variation of the secant method. Roots of systems of equations can be found with **FindRoot[{eq1,eq2,...},{x,x0},{y,y0},...]**. In this case, an initial guess is supplied for each variable in the system of equations **{eq1,eq2,...}**. The options of **FindRoot** include **AccuracyGoal** to indicate the desired accuracy of the function at the root, **Compiled** to instruct whether or not the function should be compiled, **DampingFactor** to specify the damping factor in Newton's method, **Jacobian** to enter the Jacobian of the system of equations, **MaxIterations** to specify the maximum number of iterations to be taken in the search for the solution, and **WorkingPrecision** to indicate the number of digits to be used in internal computations. Some of the default settings include **DampingFactor->1** and **MaxIterations->15**. The default settings for **AccuracyGoal** is 10 digits fewer than that of **WorkingPrecision**.

Example:

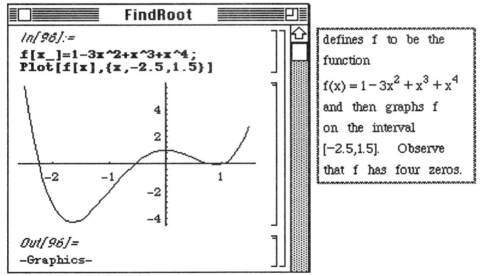

```
In[96]:=
f[x_]=1-3x^2+x^3+x^4;
Plot[f[x],{x,-2.5,1.5}]
```

```
Out[96]=
-Graphics-
```

defines f to be the function
$$f(x) = 1 - 3x^2 + x^3 + x^4$$
and then graphs f on the interval $[-2.5,1.5]$. Observe that f has four zeros.

To use **FindRoot** to locate approximations of the zeros of f(x), observe in the graph that the first three zeros of f are near -2, $-.5$, and $.5$.

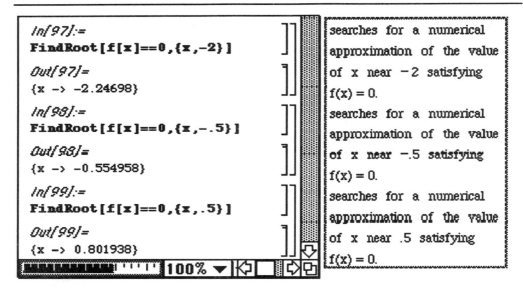

First   125, 794

              See Also: **Drop, Part, Last, Rest, Take, Select**

First[list] yields the first element in **list**. The same result is given with **list[[1]]**.

Example:

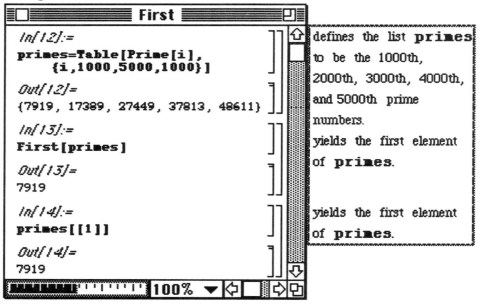

Fit   8, 110, 672, 795
See 758, 760   See Also: **InterpolatingPolynomial**, **Solve**,
                                  PseudoInverse, **QRDecomposition**,
                                  FindMinimum

   Fit[data,basis,variables] produces a function depending on **variables** using the functions listed in **basis** which is the least-squares fit of **data**. The collection of data can be entered in several different ways. It can be listed as **{{x1,y1,...,f1},{x2,y2,...,f2},...}** where the number of coordinates **x**, **y**, ... matches the number of elements in the list **variables**. The data can also be listed as **{f1,f2,...}** when working with a function of one variable. In this case, the first coordinate is assumed to be 1, 2, ... The functions given in **basis** must depend only on the variables listed in **variables**. The least-squares fit is determined by minimizing the sum of the squares of the deviations using the values of **f1**, **f2**, ... The resulting function is a linear combination of the functions given in **basis**.

Example:

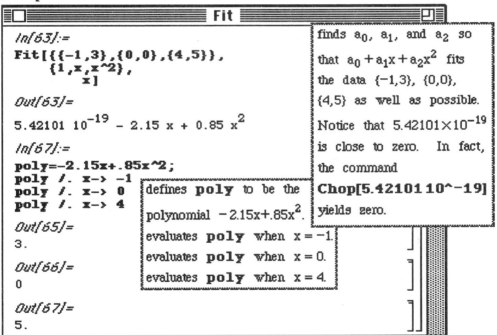

The **Fit** command allows fits consisting of several variables. The following example finds numbers a_0, a_1, and a_2 so that $a_0 + a_1 x + a_2 y$ fits the data $(-1,1,1)$, $(1,2,2)$, $(0,2,1)$ as well as possible.

```
In[68]:=
Fit[{{-1,1,1},{1,2,2},{0,2,1}},
    {1,x,y},
        {x,y}]

Out[68]=
3. + 1. x - 1. y
```

In this case, the result of the fit corresponds to the (unique) plane that passes through the points (-1,1,1), (1,2,2), and (0,2,1).

In fact, **Fit** will find least-squares fits of data using any set of linearly independent functions. The following example finds a_0, a_1, a_2, and a_3 so that the function $a_0 + a_1 \text{Sin}(x) + a_2 \text{Sin}(2x) + a_3 \text{Sin}(3x)$ fits the data points (0,0), (2,11), (4,-7), and (6,1) as well as possible. The resulting function is named f:

```
In[69]:=
Fit[{{0,0},{2,11},{4,-7},{6,1}},
    {1,Sin[x],Sin[2x],Sin[3x]},
        x]

Out[69]=
                 -19
2.97931 10    + 9.52436 Sin[x] -
  1.75407 Sin[2 x] - 3.62199 Sin[3 x]

In[70]:=
f[x_]=9.52Sin[x]-1.75Sin[2x]-3.62Sin[3x]

Out[70]=
9.52 Sin[x] - 1.75 Sin[2 x] - 3.62 Sin[3 x]
```

In this case, the original points along with the fit are graphed using the commands **Plot**, **Graphics**, **Show**, **Map**, and **Point**. The displayed graphics object shows the original data points along with a graph of f. Note that the desired points could have also been displayed using the command **Epilog**.

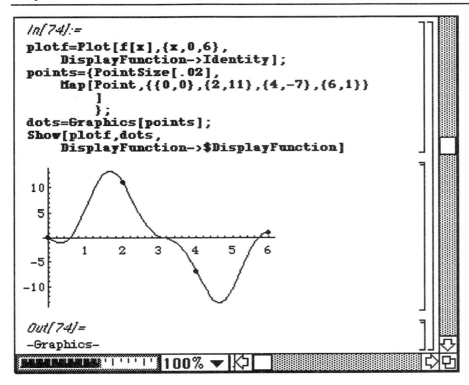

```
In[74]:=
plotf=Plot[f[x],{x,0,6},
    DisplayFunction->Identity];
points={PointSize[.02],
    Map[Point,{{0,0},{2,11},{4,-7},{6,1}}
    ]
    };
dots=Graphics[points];
Show[plotf,dots,
    DisplayFunction->$DisplayFunction]
```

```
Out[74]=
-Graphics-
```

FixedPoint   201, 291, 795
                               See Also: **FixedPointList**, **Nest**,
                               ReplaceRepeated

  FixedPoint[function,x0] finds a fixed point of **function** by repeatedly
evaluating **function** until the value which results does not change. This evaluation
process is initiated with the value **x0**. Also, the command
FixedPoint[function,x0,n] stops the evaluation after at most **n** steps.
FixedPoint has the option **SameTest->comparison** which applies the function
comparison to successive results. When **comparison** yields a value of True, then
FixedPoint returns a value for the fixed point. **FixedPoint** also has the option
MaxIterations to indicate the maximum number of times the function should be
evaluated in search of the fixed point. The default setting for **MaxIterations** is
65536 while a setting of **Infinity** indicates that the number of iterations has no
limit.

FixedPointList   201, 795
                               See Also: **NestList**, **ComposeList**

  FixedPointList[f,x0] lists the values **{x0, f[x0],f[f[x0]],...}**
encountered as **f** is repeatedly evaluated beginning with the value of **x0** until
successive values do not change. The first element in the output list is always **x0**.
FixedPointList has the same options as the **FixedPoint** command.

Flat   230, 272, 275, 734, 795
                                  See Also: **Orderless, OneIdentity**

Flat is a *Mathematica* attribute which when assigned to a function f indicates that all expressions involving nested functions f are flattened out. The *Mathematica* commands **Times**, **Plus** , and **Dot** have the attribute **Flat**. This corresponds to the associative property.

Flatten   11, 132, 215, 250, 796
See 566   See Also: **Partition**

Flatten is used to flatten out nested lists. This command can be entered in several forms to obtain different results. **Flatten[list]** flattens out all levels of **list**. Flattening out unravels all nested lists by omitting the inner braces {}. **Flatten[list,n]** only flattens the first **n** levels in **list**.
Example:

In the following example, **Flatten** is used to flatten various portions of the list **nums**.

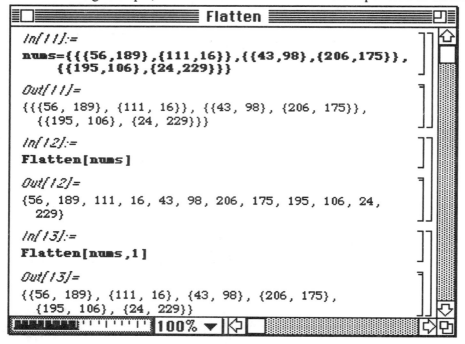

FlattenAt   132, 215, 796
                                  See Also: **DeleteCases**, **Flatten**

FlattenAt is used to flatten specific parts of a list. **FlattenAt[list,n]** flattens the element of **list** at the **n**th position. If **n** is negative, then the **n**th position from the end of **list** is flattened. This command can be entered as **FlattenAt[list,{i,j,...}]** to flatten the member of **list** located at the {i,j,...} position. In order to flatten several terms, the command **FlattenAt[list,{i1,j1,...},{i2,j2,...},...]** is used to flatten the elements of **list** found at the positions {i1,j1,...}, {i2,j2,...}, ...

Floor   550, 796
                        See Also: **Ceiling, Round, Chop**

Floor[x] represents the greatest integer function. Hence, **Floor[x]** yields the greatest integer which is less than or equal to **x**.

Example:

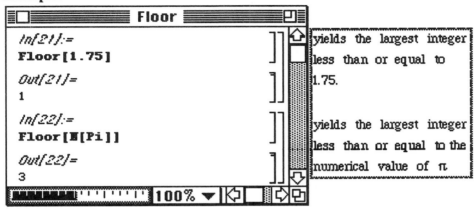

Fn

Fn is an internal system command.

Fold   202, 796
                        See Also: **Nest**

Fold[f,x,{a,b,...}] yields the last member of the list of elements given by the command **FoldList[f,x,{a,b,...}]** where **f** is a function of two variables. The members of this list are {x,f[x,a],f[f[x,a,b]],...}.

Example:

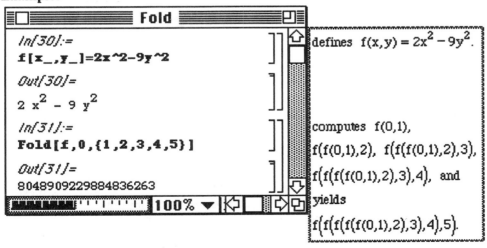

FoldList   11, 202, 210, 796

          See Also: **NestList, ComposeList, Partition, MapIndexed**

   FoldList[f,x,{a,b,...}] repeatedly applies the function **f** of two variables to produce the list {x,f[x,a],f[f[x,a],b],...}.

Example:

In the following example, $f(x,y)=2x^2-9y^2$. The result of the command **FoldLis[f,0,{1,2,3,4,5}]** is the list
{0,f(0,1),f(f(0,1),2),f(f(f(0,1),2),3),f(f(f(f(0,1),2),3), 4),f(f(f(f(0,1),2),3),4),5)}.

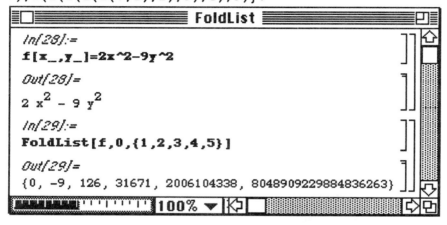

Font

   Font is an internal *Mathematica* command used for printing and formatting.

FontForm   468, 796
See 532   See Also: **Text, DefaultFont, PlotLabel**

   FontForm[expression,{"font",fontsize}] is used to indicate the **font** and **fontsize** that **expression** should be printed. This command is mainly used for the printing of text in a graphics cell. Some of the font settings include **"Courier"**, **"Times"**, and **"Helvetica"**. These may be supplemented with the endings **"Name-Bold"**, **"Name-Oblique"**, and **"Name-BoldOblique"** where **Italic** replaces **Oblique** with **Times** font.

For   292, 797
                                See Also: **If, Do, Switch, Which, While**

   For[initial,condition,increment,body] is a *Mathematica* structure which takes the initial value of **initial**, checks that the test **condition** is satisfied, increments the value stated in **initial** by **increment**, and repeatedly performs the commands given in **body** and **increment** until **condition** fails. This structure is similar to those of other programming languages such as C. However, the roles of the comma and semicolon in *Mathematica* are reversed in C.

Example:

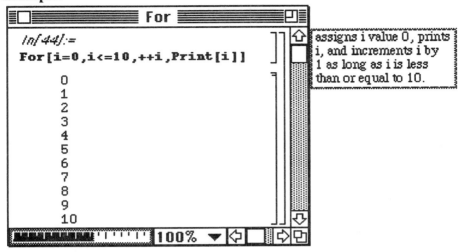

Format   358, 359, 516, 797
                        See Also: **ToString, Short**
    Format is used to define the form in which output is expressed. This can be done in several ways. **Format[expression]:=form** indicates that **expression** is to follow the output pattern given in **form**. This command can also be entered as **Format[expression,type]:=form** in order that the output be given in a form other than the standard *Mathematica* output form (**OutputForm**). Standard format types which can be entered for **type** include **CForm, FortranForm, InputForm, OutputForm, TeXForm**, and **TextForm**.

FormatType   487, 738, 797
                        See Also: **OpenWrite, SetOptions, Format**
    FormatType is an output function option used to indicate the format type to be used for printing expressions. This option is used with **SetOptions** to reset the format type. The default setting for **FormatType** is **InputForm**. However, the format types listed with **Format** are also available settings.

FormatValues   736
                        See Also: **Format**
    FormatValues[f] lists the transformation rules associated with the format used for printing **f**. The transformation rules associated with a symbol are stored in a definite order. In most cases, new transformation rules are added to the end of this list of rules.

FortranForm   16, 182, 344, 739, 797
                        See Also: **CForm**
    FortranForm[expression] converts **expression** to the form required in a Fortran program. Hence, the result can be inserted into a Fortran program. This command affects the printing of **expression**, but it does not alter any of the associated computations.

Fourier   110, 679, 797

See Also: **InverseFourier**, **Fit**

Fourier[{$a_0, a_1, ..., a_n$}] produces the Fourier transform of the list of length n of complex values given in {$a_0, a_1, .., a_n$}. The Fourier transform is determined with $\frac{1}{\sqrt{n}} \sum_{k=1}^{n} a_k \exp[2\pi i (k-1)(s-1)/n]$. Note that this definition is common to the physical sciences. The electrical engineering definition requires a negative sign on the exponent.

Example:

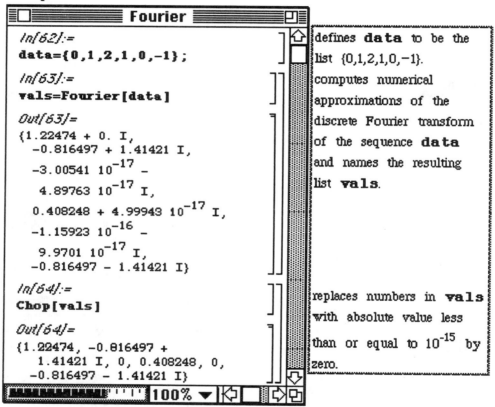

Frame   139, 397, 418, 422, 798
See 411, 513, 515, 516,
539, 541, 543, 544, 553
See Also: **Boxed**, **Ticks**

Frame is an option used with two-dimensional graphics functions to indicate if a frame is placed around the plot. The setting **Frame->True** draws a frame along with a set of axes. However, it removes all tick marks from the axes. In order to include tick marks on the axes, the **Ticks** option must be used as well.

Framed   xix (obsolete in Version 2.0); superseded by **Frame**

FrameLabel   139, 422, 798
See 514   See Also: **AxesLabel, PlotLabel**

FrameLabel is a two-dimensional graphics function option used to label the edges of a framed plot. This option can be entered in several ways to achieve various results. **FrameLabel->None** insures that no labels be included.
FrameLabel->{"xbottom","yleft"} indicates that the labels **xbottom** and **yleft** be placed on the lower edge and the left edge of the frame, respectively. The edges are listed in clockwise order beginning with the lower edge. Hence, all four edges can be labeled with the setting
FrameLabel->{"xbottom","yleft","xtop","yright"}.
Labels on the vertical edges are automatically written vertically unless the option **RotateLabel->False** is used so that they appear horizontally.

FrameStyle   422, 798
See 514, 544   See Also: **Prolog, Epilog, AxesStyle**

FrameStyle is an option used with two-dimensional graphics functions to indicate the manner in which the frame of a plot is drawn. This option can be entered in several forms. **FrameStyle->Style** indicates that all four edges of the frame are drawn using **Style**. **FrameStyle->{{xbstyle},{yleftstyle},...}** is used to give different styles for the edges where the edges are ordered clockwise from the lower horizontal edge. The styles directives which can be used for **Style** include **Dashing**, **Thickness**, and **Hue**.

FrameTicks   139, 422, 798
See 514, 544   See Also: **Ticks, GridLines, FaceGrids**

FrameTicks is a two-dimensional graphics option used to indicate the edges of a plot frame on which ticks are to be drawn. This option can be entered in several ways. **FrameTicks->None** indicates that no ticks be drawn while
FrameTicks->Automatic places tick marks on each edge.
FrameTicks->{{xbticks},{ylticks},...} specifies the edges that should be marked where the edges are ordered clockwise from the lower horizontal edge.

FreeQ   127, 196, 228, 725, 798
                                        See Also: **MemberQ, Count**

FreeQ is a command which allows for the testing of structural properties of expressions. For example, **FreeQ[expression,pattern]** yields True if no portion of **expression** matches the form defined in **pattern**. Similarly, **FreeQ[expression,pattern,level]** tests for matching subexpressions only at the levels indicated in **level**. If a match is found, then False is given as output.

FresnelC   576
See 216   See Also: **Erf**, **FresnelS**

FresnelC[z] defines the Fresnel integral $C(z) = \int_0^z \cos\left(\frac{\pi t^2}{2}\right) dt$. This integral is

used with the Fresnel integral $S(z)$, given below in **FresnelS[z]**, to define the

error function $\text{erf}(z)$. This definition is $C(z) + iS(z) = \frac{i+1}{2}\text{erf}\left(\frac{\sqrt{\pi}}{2}(1-i)\,z\right)$, where

z is real.

Example:

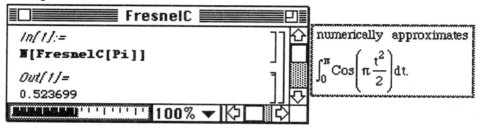

FresnelS   576
                                        See Also: **Erf**, **FresnelC**

FresnelS[z] defines the Fresnel integral $S(z) = \int_0^z \sin\left(\frac{\pi t^2}{2}\right) dt$. This integral is

used with the Fresnel integral $C(z)$, given above in **FresnelC[z]**, to define the

error function $\text{erf}(z)$. This definition is $C(z) + iS(z) = \frac{i+1}{2}\text{erf}\left(\frac{\sqrt{\pi}}{2}(1-i)\,z\right)$,

where z is real.

Example:

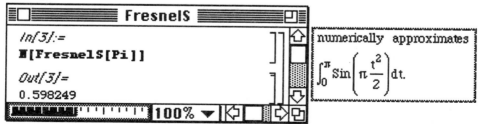

FromASCII   xix (obsolete in Version 2.0)
                                        superseded by **FromCharacterCode**

FromCharacterCode   366, 368, 374, 380, 799
                               See Also: **ToCharacterCode**

FromCharacterCode is used to construct a character or string of characters from a character code. **FromCharacterCode[n]** yields the character which corresponds to the code **n** where **n** is a non-negative integer. The command **FromCharacterCode[{n1,n2,...}]** yields the string which corresponds to the sequence of characters with codes **n1, n2, ...** . An 8-bit character is given if **n** is less than 256, while a 16-bit character results if **n** is between 256 and 65791.

FromDate   524, 799
                               See Also: **ToDate**

FromDate[date] is used to change **date** which is of the form **{year,month,day,hour,minute,second}** to the number of seconds since the beginning of January 1, 1990. Hence, **FromDate** can be applied to the output of the commands **Date** and **AbsoluteTime**.

FullAxes
                               See Also: **Axes**

FullAxes[graphics] lists the axes options of the graphics object, **graphics**.

FullDefinition   479, 799
                               See Also: **Definition**, **Save**, **Information**

FullDefinition[symbol] prints all definitions of **symbol** along with definitions of the objects on which **symbol** depends. These definitions can be written to a file with **FullDefinition[symbol]>>filename**. The definitions of several functions may be obtained with the command **FullDefinition[symbol1,symbol2,...]**.

FullForm   190, 191, 194, 220, 238, 344, 359, 370, 799
                               See Also: **InputForm**, **TreeForm**

FullForm[expression] places **expression** in functional notation without the use of special syntax. Although **FullForm** affects the printing of **expression**, it does not alter any associated calculations.
Example:
The following example expresses $(x-2)^2$ in **FullForm**

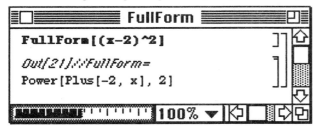

FullGraphics   398, 799

                              See Also: **FullOptions**

   FullGraphics[graphics] creates a new graphics object from the graphics
object **graphics** by giving a list of the graphics primitives for **graphics**. This
command is used with graphics objects found with options such as **FrameTicks**, and
Axes.

FullOptions   150, 398, 799

                              See Also: **Options**, **FullGraphics**

   FullOptions is used to determine the settings of graphics options. The form of
this command can vary. **FullOptions[g]** lists all settings of the options used to
create the graphics primitive **g**. The setting for the particular option, **option**, is found
with **FullOptions[g,option]**. Also, settings for several different options are
given with **FullOptions[g,{option1,option2,...}]**. This command is
useful when working with options such as **PlotRange** since **FullOptions** yields
the actual setting used in the plot even if the setting for **PlotRange** is chosen to be
Automatic or **All** in the **Plot** command.

Function (&)   207, 211, 325, 800

                              See Also: **Apply**, **CompiledFunction**

   Function denotes a pure function in *Mathematica*. These functions can be defined
in several ways. **Function[x,body]** represents a pure function of the single
parameter **x** where **x** can be replaced by any argument provided. A pure function of
several parameters is defined with **Function[{x1,x2,...},body]**.
Function[body] or **body&** also represents a pure function. The parameters in this
case are defined as **#1**, **#2**, ...

Example:

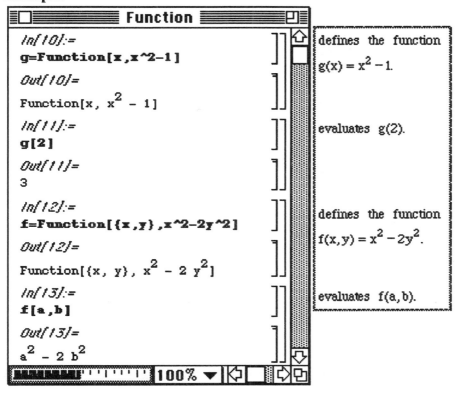

```
≡□≡≡≡≡≡≡ Function ≡≡≡≡≡≡□≡

In[10]:=
g=Function[x,x^2-1]
Out[10]=
Function[x, x^2 - 1]

In[11]:=
g[2]
Out[11]=
3

In[12]:=
f=Function[{x,y},x^2-2y^2]
Out[12]=
Function[{x, y}, x^2 - 2 y^2]

In[13]:=
f[a,b]
Out[13]=
a^2 - 2 b^2

100% ▼
```

defines the function
$g(x) = x^2 - 1.$

evaluates g(2).

defines the function
$f(x,y) = x^2 - 2y^2.$

evaluates f(a,b).

G

Gamma   570, 572, 800
See 5, 766   See Also: **Factorial**, **LogGamma**, **PolyGamma**,
                                RiemannSiegelTheta

   Gamma is used to denote the various forms of the gamma function.
Gamma[z] represents the Euler gamma function given by the formula

$$\Gamma(z) = \int_0^\infty t^{z-1}e^{-t}\, dt\ .$$ The incomplete gamma function, **Gamma[a,z]**, denotes

the function defined by $\Gamma(a,z) = \int_z^\infty t^{a-1}e^{-t}\, dt$. Also, **Gamma[a,z_0,z_1]** represents

the generalized gamma function given by $\Gamma(a,z_0,z_1) = \int_{z_0}^{z_1} t^{a-1}e^{-t}\, dt$.

Example:

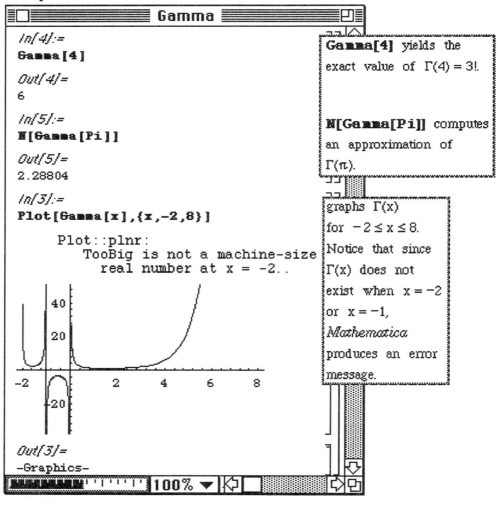

```
In[4]:=
Gamma[4]

Out[4]=
6

In[5]:=
N[Gamma[Pi]]

Out[5]=
2.28804

In[3]:=
Plot[Gamma[x],{x,-2,8}]

        Plot::plnr:
          TooBig is not a machine-size
          real number at x = -2..
```

Gamma[4] yields the exact value of $\Gamma(4) = 3!$.

N[Gamma[Pi]] computes an approximation of $\Gamma(\pi)$.

graphs $\Gamma(x)$ for $-2 \le x \le 8$. Notice that since $\Gamma(x)$ does not exist when $x = -2$ or $x = -1$, *Mathematica* produces an error message.

```
Out[3]=
-Graphics-
```

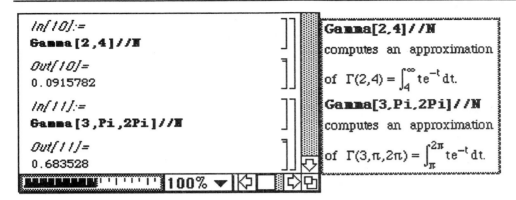

GammaRegularized   573, 800
See 616, 620, 621, 686   See Also: **Gamma**

GammaRegularized[a,z] represents the regularized incomplete gamma

function $Q(a,z) = \dfrac{\Gamma(a,z)}{\Gamma(a)}$ where $\Gamma(z)$ and $\Gamma(a,z)$ are the Euler gamma function

and the incomplete gamma function, respectively, given above under Gamma.

The generalized regularized incomplete gamma function, $Q(a, z_0, z_1)$, is given as

GammaRegularized[a,z$_0$,z$_1$] $= \dfrac{\Gamma(a, z_0, z_1)}{\Gamma(a)}$. Note that $\Gamma(a, z_0, z_1)$ is the

generalized incomplete gamma function described above as **Gamma[a,z$_0$,z$_1$]**.

Example:

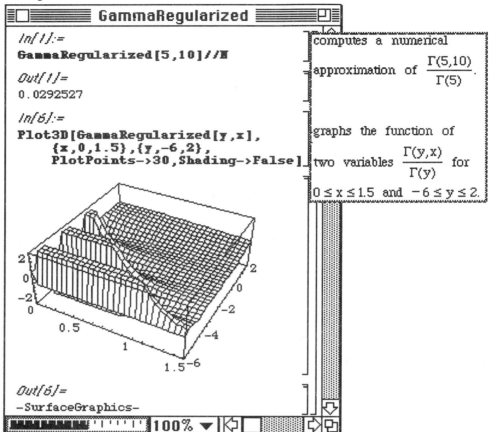

GaussianIntegers   554, 556, 600, 800
See 151, 153   See Also: **ComplexExpand**, **FactorInteger**,
                              Factor, **PrimeQ**

   GaussianIntegers is an option for such *Mathematica* commands as
FactorInteger, **PrimeQ**, and **Factor** which allows for the consideration of
Gaussian integers in the computation process. Note that Gaussian integers are complex
numbers in which the real and imaginary parts are both integers. For example, the
command **FactorInteger[number, GaussianIntegers->True]** computes
the factors of **number** over the field of Gaussian integers as opposed to the field of real
integers used with the setting **GaussianIntegers->False**. When working with
the Gaussian primes, only those integers with positive real part and non-negative
imaginary part are considered by *Mathematica*.

GaussKronrod
See Also: **NIntegrate**

GaussKronrod is a setting for the **Method** option used with the **NIntegrate** command. With the setting **Method->GaussKronrod**, *Mathematica* uses an adaptive Gauss-Kronrod quadrature method for establishing the quadrature rules to be used to approximate the value of the integral under consideration.

GaussPoints   688
See Also: **NIntegrate**

GaussPoints is an option used with **NIntegrate** to indicate the number of sample points which are to be used in the Gaussian portion of the Gauss-Kronrod quadrature for numerical integration. The default setting for this option is **Automatic**.

GCD   8, 553, 602, 800
See Also: **PolynomialGCD**, **Rational**, **LCM**, **ExtendedGCD**

GCD[n1,n2,...] represents the greatest common divisor of the numbers **n1**, **n2**, ..., and, hence, yields the largest integer which divides each of the values **n1**, **n2**, ... exactly. *Mathematica* uses this command during certain calculations to cancel common factors to simplify expressions.

Example:

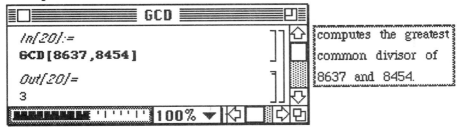

GegenbauerC   567, 568, 801
See Also: **LegendreP**, **ChebyshevT**

GegenbauerC[n,m,x] represents the Gegenbauer, or ultraspherical, polynomials, $C_n^m(x)$, which are generalizations of the Legendre polynomials in systems which have $(m+2)$ - dimensional spherical symmetry. These polynomials are orthogonal with respect to integration over the unit hypersphere using weight function

$$w(x) = \left(1 - x^2\right)^{m-1/2}.$$

Example:
The following example names **polyone** the polynomial
$C_3^8(x) = -144xx + 960x^3$ and **polytwo** the polynomial
$C_5^8(x) = 720x - 10560x^3 + 25344x^5.$

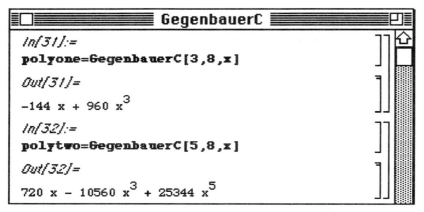

Both **polyone** and **polytwo** are graphed for $-3/4 \le x \le 3/4$:

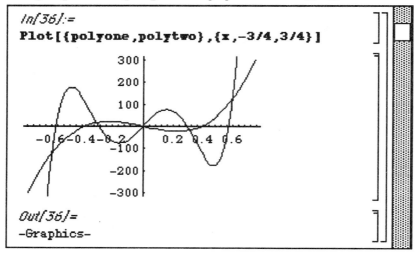

Finally, to see that $C_3^8(x)$ and $C_5^8(x)$ are orthogonal, we compute $\int_{-1}^{1} C_3^8(x) \bullet C_5^8(x) \bullet \left(1 - x^2\right)^{15/2} dx.$ The second calculation computes $\int_{-1}^{1} \left(C_3^8(x)\right)^2 \left(1 - x^2\right)^{15/2} dx.$

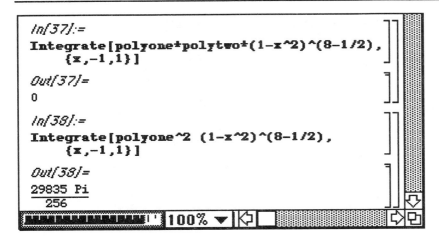

General   388, 801
See 296, 328   See Also: **On, Off**

General is the symbol used to give a general system message. For example, if the incorrect number of arguments is used with the command **Command**, *Mathematica* prints a message such as **Command::argx**. However if the message **Command::argx** cannot be found, then *Mathematica* issues the message **General::argx**. This symbol also appears in the form **General::stop** to indicate that a particular error message was given more than three times during a certain calculation in which there were numerous mistakes. A list of all *Mathematica* warning messages is contained in the technical report *Mathematica* Warning Messages by David Withoff and published by Wolfram Research.

Generic
                                         See Also: **Solve**
    Generic is a setting for the **Mode** option used with the **Solve** command.

Get (<<)   178, 185, 340, 477, 801
See vii-ix, 499, 568   See Also: **Read, Install, RunThrough, Put,**
                                         Splice, Filenames
    Get["filename"] or **<<filename** reads in the *Mathematica* input file **filename**, evaluates all expressions in **filename**, and prints the last expression which appears. If a syntax error is found while *Mathematica* attempts to read **filename**, then the error is reported. Also, the part of **filename** which follows the error is skipped, and a value of **$Failed** is given.

Example:

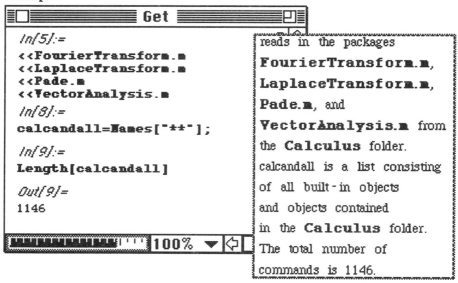

GetContext

See Also: **ContextToFilename**

  GetContext["context`"]** reads in the file which corresponds to **"context`". The file is determined through the use of **ContextToFilename["context`"]**.

GoldenRatio   139, 417, 566, 801
See 20, 303, 512   See Also: **Catalan, Degree, E, EulerGamma, I,**
                                   Infinity, Pi

  GoldenRatio represents the value of the golden ratio or golden mean,

$\frac{1+\sqrt{5}}{2}$, which has numerical value of approximately 1.61803.

Example:

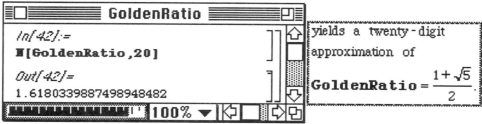

Goto   293, 295, 801
                                   See Also: **Break, Continue, Return, Throw**

  Goto[name] is a control flow command which searches the current procedure for **Label[name]** and transfers control to that location in the procedure.

Gradient   794
                                      See Also: **FindMinimum**

   Gradient is an option used with the **FindMinimum** command in order to list the gradient of the function of which the minimum value is being determined. This option is entered as **Gradient->{D[f,x],D[f,y],...}**.

Graphics   395, 802
See 165, 219, 353, 354,   See Also: **Plot, ListPlot, ParametricPlot**
357, 381, 525-533

      Graphics[primitives,options] denotes the graphical image of a two-dimensional object. These objects are viewed with **Show**. The primitives which may be used include **Circle, Point, Polygon, Rectangle,** and **Line** while the lengthy list of options includes **AspectRatio, Axes, DisplayFunction, Frame, PlotRange,** and **Ticks**. Sound primitives such as **SampledSoundList** and **SampledSoundFunction** can also be considered with **Graphics**. **Graphics** directives such as **GrayLevel, RGBColor,** and **Thickness** may also be included in a **Graphics** command.

GraphicsArray   144, 164, 175, 395, 804
See 127, 131, 312, 527,   See Also: **RasterArray, Rectangle, TableForm**
528, 534, 536-540, 547,
551, 553, 559, 561, 569,
570, 572, 573, 576-578,
593, 596, 597

   GraphicsArray is used to represent an array of graphics objects. This command can be entered in several ways. **GraphicsArray[{graph1,graph2,...}]** represents a row of objects while
GraphicsArray[{{graph11,graph12,...},{graph21,graph22,...}, ...}] yields the array with rows **{graph11,graph12,...}**, **{graph21,graph22,...}**, ... The objects contained within **GraphicsArray** are displayed in identical rectangular regions with **Show**. The same options which are available to **Graphics** can also be used with **GraphicsArray** with the exception of **StringConversion, ColorOutput,** and **DisplayFunction**. Also, with **GraphicsArray**, the default setting for **Ticks** and **FrameTicks** is **None**. In addition to these options, **GraphicsArray** has the option **GraphicsSpacing** which is used to control the spacing between the rectangular display regions. The default setting for **GraphicsSpacing** is **0.1**.

GraphicsSpacing   146, 804
                                      See Also: **GraphicsArray, TableSpacing**

   GraphicsSpacing is a **GraphicsArray** option which is used to indicate the spacing between rectangular display regions for the members of the array. **GraphicsSpacing->0** indicates that no spaces appear between regions while **GraphicsSpacing->{horizontal,vertical}** specify the horizontal spacing as well as the vertical spacing. Also, **GraphicsSpacing->1** is equivalent to **GraphicsSpacing->{1,1}**. The spacing is scaled according to the length and width of the rectangular regions. Horizontal spacing is relative to the width of the region while vertical spacing is relative to the length.

Graphics3D   395, 803
See 519, 562-565   See Also: **Plot3D**, **SurfaceGraphics**,
                                            ParametricPlot3D

    Graphics3D[primitives,options] denotes the graphical image of a
three-dimensional object. These objects are viewed with **Show**. The primitives
available for use with **Graphics3D** include **Cuboid**, **Line**, **Point**, and **Polygon**.
Sound primitives like **SampleSoundList** and **SampleSoundFunction** also may
be used. Directives such as **EdgeForm**, **FaceForm**, **GrayLevel**, **RGBColor**,
SurfaceColor, and **Hue** can be used with **Graphics3D** as can the options
AspectRatio, **Axes**, **Boxed**, **Lighting**, **PlotRange**, **Shading**, and
ViewPoint.

GrayLevel   40, 396, 407, 472, 805
See 240, 248, 318, 356,   See Also: **RGBColor**, **Hue**, **Raster**
358, 462, 519, 529, 531,
548, 550, 556, 557, 560,
563-565, 569, 583, 615,
708, 716, 720, 721, 726,
731, 732, 734

    GrayLevel[intensity] is a directive used with graphics functions to indicate
the level of gray to be used when displaying graphics objects. The value of
intensity is between 0.0 and 1.0 where a level of 0.0 denotes black and 1.0 white.
This directive is most useful when graphing several plots simultaneously.

Greater(>)   94, 805
                                            See Also: **Less**, **Positive**

    Greater represents the relational operation "greater than." Hence, if **a** and **b** are
real numbers, then **a>b** yields a value of **True** if **a** is greater than **b** and gives **False**
otherwise. Sequences of values may be considered as well with **a>b>c>d>**... .

Example:

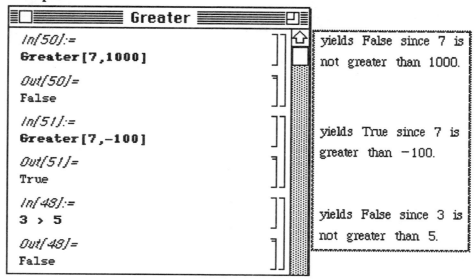

GreaterEqual (>=)   94, 805

           See Also: **Equal**, **LessEqual**, **Unequal**

    GreaterEqual represents the relational operation "greater than or equal to." Hence, if **a** and **b** are real numbers, then **a>=b** yields a value of True if **a** is greater than or equal to **b** and gives False otherwise. Sequences of values may be considered as well with **a>=b>=c>=d>**... .

Example:

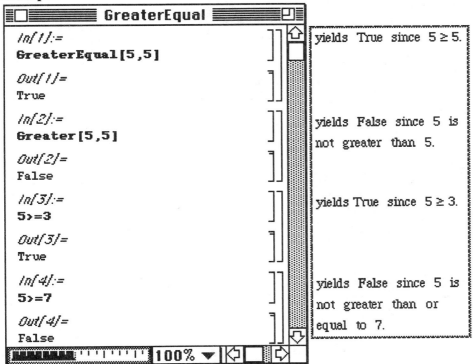

GridLines   139, 418, 423, 805

See 514, 545, 546, 559   See Also: **Ticks**, **FrameTicks**, **FaceGrids**

    GridLines is an option used with two-dimensional graphics functions to indicate the manner in which grid lines are displayed while plotting. The settings for the **GridLines** option include **None** so that no grid lines are drawn and **Automatic** so that grid lines are drawn automatically. In addition, grid lines can be specified in each direction with **{xg,yg}**. The settings for **xg** and **yg** also include **None** and **Automatic**. They also include **{a,b,c,...}** so that grid lines are drawn at the indicated positions, and **{{a,style1},{b,style2},...}** so that the grid lines at the indicated positions are drawn in a particular style such as **Thickness** or **GrayLevel**.

GroebnerBasis   622, 805

See Also: **AlgebraicRules**, **Solve**

GroebnerBasis[{poly1,poly2,...},{x1,x2,...}] creates a Groebner basis for the polynomials listed in **{poly1,poly2,...}** using the list of variables **{x1,x2,...}**. In general, these bases are not unique and may depend on the order in which the variables are listed.

Example:

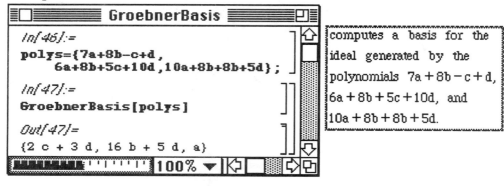

computes a basis for the ideal generated by the polynomials $7a + 8b - c + d$, $6a + 8b + 5c + 10d$, and $10a + 8b + 8b + 5d$.

H

Hash

Hash[expression] yields a hash code in the form of an integer for **expression**.

HashTable

246

See Also: **Dispatch**

HashTable is a component of the output for the **Dispatch** command.

Head

191, 712, 806

See 7, 58, 204, 213, 262, 381, 385, 451

See Also: **Real**, **Integer**, **Symbol**, **Complex**

Head[expression] yields the head of the given expression. The head of an expression can be an operator such as **Plus**, a function name, a type of number such as **Real**, or another *Mathematica* object.

Example:

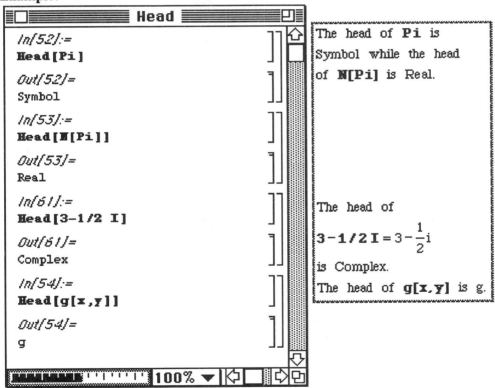

HeadCompose

HeadCompose is a command used to compose several expressions. For example, **HeadCompose[x1,x2,x3,x4]** yields **x1[x2][x3][x4]**.

Headers

Headers is used to indicate if output of a particular channel is to be preceded by notebook headers.

Heads   191, 198, 205, 211, 214, 275, 289, 535, 710, 806
                                                 See Also: **Level**

Heads is an option used with functions such as **TreeForm** and **Position** which rely on level specification to indicate whether or not the heads of expressions are to be included. **Heads->True** includes heads while **Heads->False** does not. The default value of the **Heads** option is **False** for most functions. However, **Position** has **True** for the default setting.

HeldPart   282, 578, 806
                                                 See Also: **ReplaceHeldPart, ReleaseHold, Hold**

HeldPart is used to cause certain parts of an expression to be left unevaluated. This is accomplished by indicating the position or positions of **expression** which are to be kept unevaluated with the command **HeldPart[expression,position]**. These components are placed within a **Hold** command so that they are not evaluated.

HermiteH   567, 806
                                                 See Also: **GegenbauerC**

HermiteH[n,x] represents the Hermite polynomial $H_n(x)$ which satisfies

the ordinary differential equation $\dfrac{d^2y}{dx^2} - 2x\dfrac{dy}{dx} + 2ny = 0$. The Hermite

polynomials are orthogonal with weight function $w(x) = e^{-x^2}$.

Example:

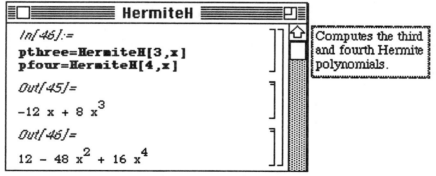

The Hermite polynomial $H_4(x)=12x-48x^2+16x^4$ satisfies the differential equation $y'-2xy'+8y = 0$. The following commands compute and simplify

$H_4''(x) - 2xH_4'(x) + H_4(x)$:

```
In[47]:=
stepone=D[pfour,{x,2}]-2x D[pfour,x]+8pfour

Out[47]=
               2                      3              2       4
-96 + 192 x  - 2 x (-96 x + 64 x ) + 8 (12 - 48 x  + 16 x )

In[48]:=
Simplify[stepone]

Out[48]=
0
```

Both $H_3(x)$ and $H_4(x)$ are graphed for $-2 \le x \le 2$. $H_4(x)$ corresponds to the black graph; $H_3(x)$ corresponds to the dashed graph.

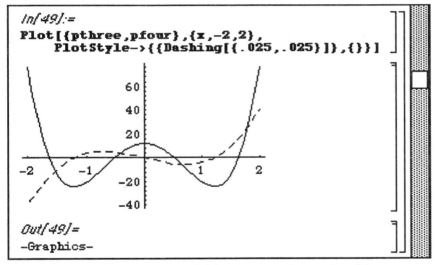

Finally, to see that $H_3(x)$ and $H_4(x)$ are orthogonal, we compute
$$\int_{-1}^{1} H_3(x) \bullet H_4(x) \bullet e^{-x^2}\, dx.$$

```
In[50]:=
Integrate[pthree pfour Exp[-x^2],{x,-1,1}]

Out[50]=
0
```

100% ▼

HiddenSurface   156, 806
See 522, 524   See Also: **Shading**

HiddenSurface is an option used with **Plot3D** and **Show** to indicate whether or not hidden surfaces are to be shown. The setting **HiddenSurface->True** eliminates the hidden surfaces whereas **HiddenSurface->False** causes these surfaces to be drawn as solids.

Hold   281, 308, 498, 732, 806
See 468   See Also: **Literal**, **HoldForm**, **HeldPart**,
                            Unevaluated

Hold[expression] causes **expression** to be left unevaluated by *Mathematica*. This command can be removed by **ReleaseHold**. Several expressions can be kept in an unevaluated form with **Hold[expr1,expr2,...]**.

Example:

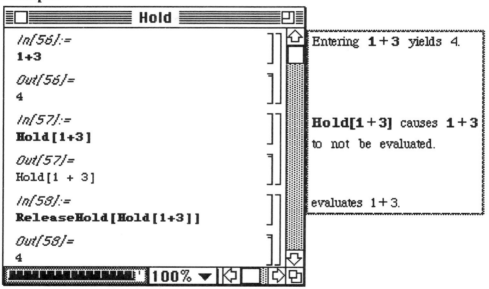

HoldAll   272, 279, 729, 806
                            See Also: **Unevaluated**, **SetAttributes**

HoldAll is an attribute which is used to indicate that all arguments of a function are to be maintained in unevaluated form. The command **Evaluate** can be used to evaluate the arguments of a function which possesses the **HoldAll** attribute.

HoldFirst   272, 279, 806
                            See Also: **HoldAll**, **SetAttributes**

HoldFirst is an attribute which is used to indicate that the first argument of a function is to be left unevaluated.

HoldForm   281, 300, 349, 732, 807
                                  See Also: **ToString, WriteString**

   HoldForm[expression] is similar to **Hold[expression]** in that it leaves
expression unevaluated. However, **HoldForm** does not appear in the output as it
does with **Hold**. **HoldForm** has the attribute **HoldAll** and is removed by
ReleaseHold.

Example:

In the following example, the command
Integrate[x y,{x,-1,5},{x-1,Sqrt[2x+6]}] is not evaluated since the
entire command is enclosed by **HoldForm**; the result is name **integral**. **integral**
is evaluated using the command **ReleaseHold**. Notice that in this case the result
corresponds to the value of the iterated integral

$$\int_{-1}^{5}\int_{x-1}^{\sqrt{2x+6}} xy\, dy\, dx.$$

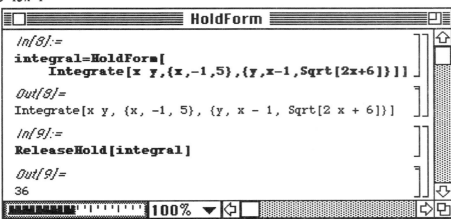

HoldRest   279, 729, 807
                                  See Also: **HoldFirst, HoldAll, SetAttributes**

   HoldRest is an attribute which is used with functions to indicate that all arguments
except the first are to be left unevaluated.

HomeDirectory   490, 807
                                  See Also: **Directory, ParentDirectory**

   HomeDirectory[] yields the name of the home directory.

Example:

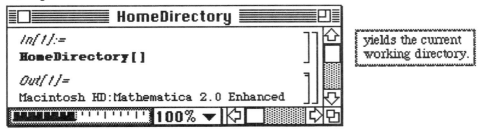

HorizontalForm

See Also: **ColumnForm**, **MatrixForm**, **TableForm**

HorizontalForm is an internal *Mathematica* symbol which is used in printing and formatting.

Hue   40, 162, 407, 472, 807

See Also: **RGBColor**, **GrayLevel**, **CMYKColor**

Hue[hue,sat,bright] is a graphics directive which is used to indicate the levels for hue, saturation, and brightness which are to be used to display the graphics. The values for **hue**, **sat**, and **bright** are each between 0 and 1. The hue index cyclically goes through the sequence of colors red, yellow, green, cyan, blue, magenta, and black. Hence, **hue** values of 0 and 1 both result in the display of the color red. The saturation index indicates the deepness of the colors. A **sat** value of 1 yields the deepest colors while a value of 0 gives very faded colors. The brightness index causes brighter colors to be displayed as the index increases.

HypergeometricPFQ

See Also: **Hypergeometric0F1**,

Hypergeometric1F1, **Hypergeometric2F1**

HypergeometricPFQ[numerator,denominator,z] is the generalized hypergeometric function pFq. In this case, **numerator** represents the list of values which are used in the numerator while **denominator** represents a similar list for the denominator.

Example:

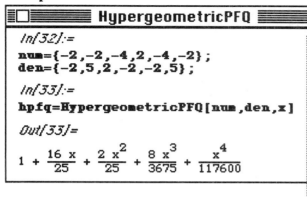

In[32]:=
```
num={-2,-2,-4,2,-4,-2};
den={-2,5,2,-2,-2,5};
```

In[33]:=
```
hpfq=HypergeometricPFQ[num,den,x]
```

Out[33]=

$$1 + \frac{16\ x}{25} + \frac{2\ x^2}{25} + \frac{8\ x^3}{3675} + \frac{x^4}{117600}$$

defines the lists **num** and **den**.

gives the generalized hypergeometric function where **num** is the list of 6 parameters in the numerator and **den** is the list of 6 parameters in the denominator. The resulting polynomial is named **hpfq**.

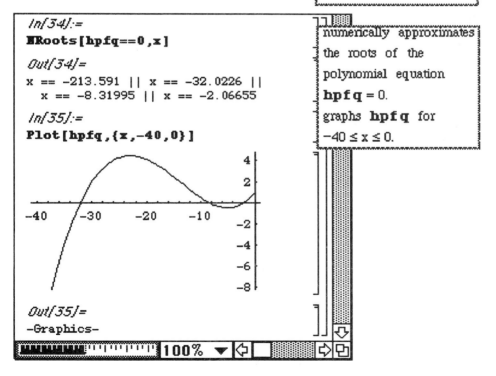

In[34]:=
```
NRoots[hpfq==0,x]
```

Out[34]=
```
x == -213.591 || x == -32.0226 ||
   x == -8.31995 || x == -2.06655
```

In[35]:=
```
Plot[hpfq,{x,-40,0}]
```

Out[35]=
-Graphics-

numerically approximates the roots of the polynomial equation **hpfq** = 0.

graphs **hpfq** for $-40 \le x \le 0$.

HypergeometricPFQRegularized

See Also: **HypergeometricOF1**,
Hypergeometric1F1, Hypergeometric2F1

HypergeometricPFQRegularized[numerator,denominator,z] yields the regularized generalized hypergeometric function pFq. As with **HypergeometricPFQ**, **numerator** represents the list of values which are used in the numerator while **denominator** represents a similar list for the denominator. **HypergeometricPFQRegularized** is related to **HypergeometricPFQ** by **HypergeometricPFQ[numerator,denominator,z]/(Times@@(Gamma/@ denominator))**. However, if an element of **denominator** is a non-positive integer, then analytic continuation must be used to eliminate the indeterminacy.

Example:

The following example computes the regularized generalized hypergeometric function **hpfqr** where **num** is the list of two parameters in the numerator and **den** is the list of three parameters in the denominator.

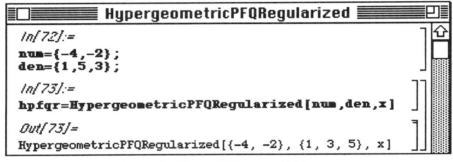

In this case, **hpfqr** is graphed for $-1000 \le x \le 1000$.

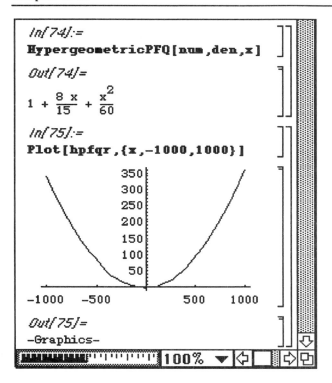

In[74]:=
HypergeometricPFQ[num,den,x]

Out[74]=

$$1 + \frac{8\,x}{15} + \frac{x^2}{60}$$

In[75]:=
Plot[hpfqr,{x,-1000,1000}]

Out[75]=
-Graphics-

HypergeometricU   570, 578, 807

See Also: **Hypergeometric1F1**

HypergeometricU[a,b,z] represents the confluent hypergeometric function

U(a, b, z).   This function is given by the integral formula

$$U(a,b,z) = \frac{1}{\Gamma(a)} \int_0^\infty e^{-zt} t^{a-1} (1+t)^{b-a-1} \, dt.$$ U(a, b, z) is a second linearly independent

solution to Kummer's differential equation $z\dfrac{d^2 y}{dz^2} + (b-z)\dfrac{dy}{dz} - ay = 0$ and is sometimes

called Kummer's function as is **Hypergeometric1F1[a,b,z]**.

Example:

In the following example, the imaginary part of

$$U(5, 2, x + i\,y) = \frac{1}{\Gamma(5)} \int_0^\infty e^{-(x+i\,y)t} t^4 (1+t)^{-4} \, dt$$ is graphed for real

values of x and y, $-2 \le x \le 2$ and $-1 \le y \le 1$.

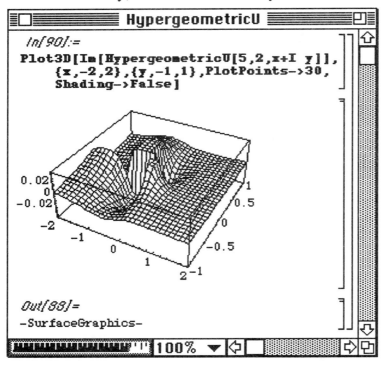

HypergeometricOF1   570, 807
> See Also: **Pochhammer**

Hypergeometric 0 F 1[a ,z] represents the hypergeometric function

$$_0F_1(;a;z) = \sum_{k=0}^{\infty} \frac{z^k}{(a)_k\, k!}$$ where $(a)_k$ is the Pochhammer symbol $\dfrac{\Gamma(a+k)}{\Gamma(a)}$.

Example:

In the following example, a contour plot of the imaginary part of $_0F_1(;3;x+iy)$ is graphed for real values of x and y, $-3 \le x \le 3$ and $-2 \le y \le 2$.

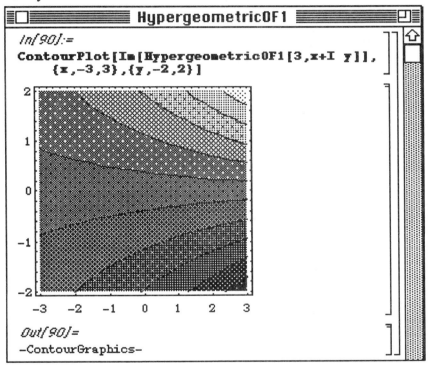

HypergeometricOF1Regularized
> See Also: **HypergeometricOF1**

HypergeometricOF1Regularized[a,z] yields the hypergeometric function **HypergeometricOF1[a,z]/Gamma[a]**.

Example:

In the following example, a contour plot of the imaginary part of $\dfrac{1}{\Gamma(3)} {}_0F_1(;3;x+iy)$ is graphed for real values of x and y, $-3 \le x \le 3$ and $-2 \le y \le 2$.

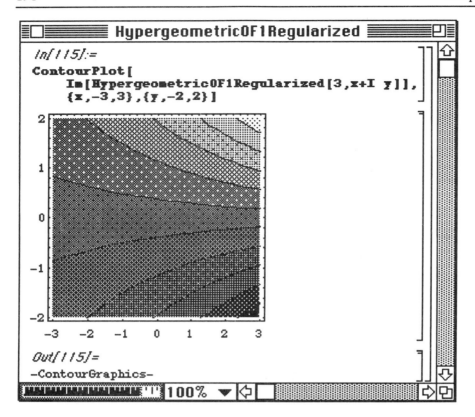

Hypergeometric1F1   570, 578, 807

See Also: Pochhammer

Hypergeometric1F1[a,b,z] represents the Kummer confluent hypergeometric

function $_1F_1(a;b;z) = \sum_{k=0}^{\infty} \frac{(a)_k}{(b)_k} \frac{z^k}{k!}$ where $(a)_k$ and $(b)_k$ are Pochhammer symbols. This

function satisfies Kummer's differential equation $z\frac{d^2y}{dz^2} + (b-z)\frac{dy}{dz} - ay = 0$ with the

boundary conditions $_1F_1(a;b;0) = 1$ and $\frac{\partial}{\partial z} {}_1F_1(a;b;z)|_{z=0} = \frac{a}{b}$. $_1F_1(a;b;z)$ has the

integral representation $_1F_1(a;b;z) = \frac{\Gamma(b)}{\Gamma(b-a)\Gamma(a)} \int_0^1 e^{zt} t^{a-1} (1-t)^{b-a-1} dt$.

Example:

The following two examples compute $_1F_1(-3;4;x)$ and $_1F_1(3;4;x)$.

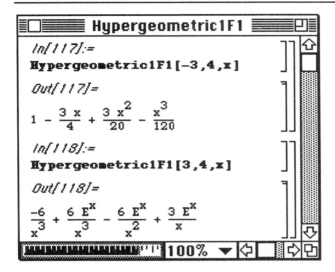

Hypergeometric1F1Regularized

       See Also: **Pochhammer**, **Hypergeometric1F1**

  Hypergeometric1F1Regularized[a,b,z] is the regularized Kummer confluent hypergeometric function given by the formula
Hypergeometric1F1[a,b,z]/Gamma[b].

Example:

The following two examples compute $\dfrac{1}{\Gamma(4)}\,_1F_1(3;4;x)$ and compute and

graph $\dfrac{1}{\Gamma(4)}\,_1F_1(-3;4;x)$.

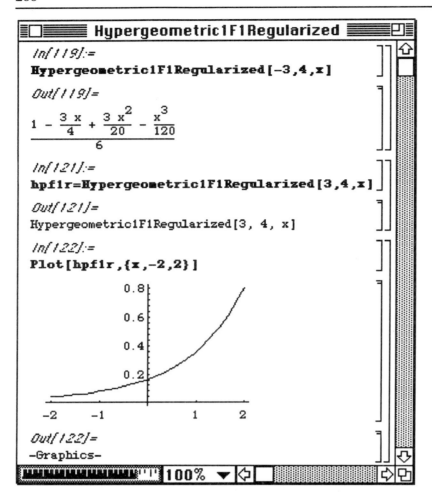

Hypergeometric2F1   570, 579, 807
                        See Also: **Pochhammer**
 Hypergeometric2F1[a,b,c,z] represents the Kummer confluent

hypergeometric function $_2F_1(a;b;z) = \sum_{k=0}^{\infty} \dfrac{(a)_k(b)_k}{(c)_k}\dfrac{z^k}{k!}$ where $(a)_k$ and $(b)_k$ are

Pochhammer symbols. This function satisfies the hypergeometric differential equation

$z(1-z)\dfrac{d^2y}{dz^2} + \lfloor c - (a+b+1)z\rfloor\dfrac{dy}{dz} - aby = 0.$ $_2F_1(a;b;c;z)$ also has the integral

representation $_2F_1(a;b;c;z) = \dfrac{\Gamma(b)}{\Gamma(b)\Gamma(c-b)}\int_0^1 t^{b-1}(1-t)^{c-b-1}(1-tz)^{-a}\,dt.$ Note that the

complete elliptic functions can be written in terms of $_2F_1(a;b;z)$.

Example:

The following example defines $y(x) = {}_2F_1(3,4;2;x)$ and verifies that $y(x) = {}_2F_1(3,4;2;x)$

satisfies the differential equation $x(1-x)y'' + [2 - (3+4+1)x]y' - 12y = 0$.

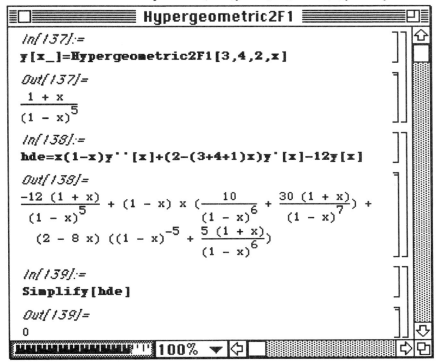

Hypergeometric2F1Regularized

See Also: **Pochhammer**, **Hypergeometric2F1**

Hypergeometric2F1Regularized[a,b,z] is the regularized function given by the formula **Hypergeometric2F1[a,b,c,z]/Gamma[c]**.

Example:

The following example defines $y(x) = \dfrac{1}{\Gamma(3)} \, {}_2F_1(3,4;3;x)$.

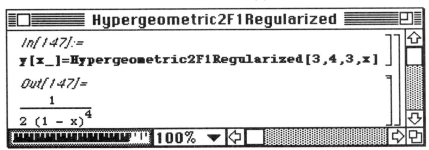

I

I   50, 52, 566, 808
See 13, 18, 58   See Also: **Re**, **Im**, **ComplexExpand**,
                                               GaussianIntegers

   I represents the imaginary number i = $\sqrt{-1}$. Numbers which contain this unit
are classified as Complex.

Example:

The following examples solve the equation $x^2 = -1$ for x, expand the expression $(x+iy)^3$,
expand the expression $e^{iy}Sin(ix)$ assuming x and y are real, and solve the equation
$x^8 = -1$ and yield numerical approximations of the results.

```
In[27]:=
Solve[x^2==-1]

Out[27]=
{{x -> I}, {x -> -I}}

In[28]:=
Expand[(x+I y)^3]

Out[28]=
 3       2          2     3
x  + 3 I x  y - 3 x y  - I y

In[29]:=
ComplexExpand[Exp[I y]Sin[I x]]

Out[29]=
I Cos[y] Sinh[x] - Sin[y] Sinh[x]

In[30]:=
Solve[x^8==-1]//N

Out[30]=
{{x -> 0.92388 + 0.382683 I},
 {x -> 0.382683 + 0.92388 I},
 {x -> -0.382683 + 0.92388 I},
 {x -> -0.92388 + 0.382683 I},
 {x -> -0.92388 - 0.382683 I},
 {x -> -0.382683 - 0.92388 I},
 {x -> 0.382683 - 0.92388 I},
 {x -> 0.92388 - 0.382683 I}}
```

100% ▼

Identity   213, 808
See 127, 131, 165, 312,   See Also: **Composition**, **Through**,
387   **InverseFunction**

Identity[expression] represents the identity operation, and, hence, yields **expression**.

Example:

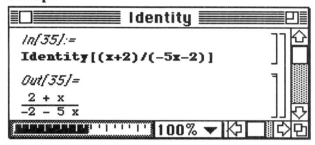

IdentityMatrix   122, 649, 808
See 94, 286   See Also: **DiagonalMatrix**, **Table**

IdentityMatrix[n] yields the **n** × **n** identity matrix.

Example:

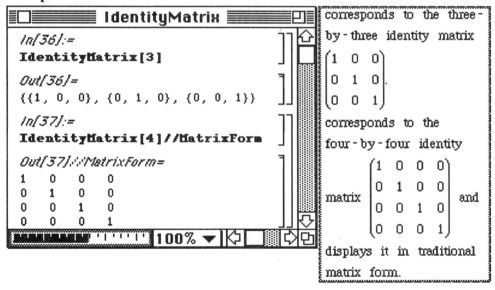

If   94, 279, 287, 808
                                      See Also: **Do**, **Switch**, **Which**, **While**, **Condition**

If is a conditional block similar to those of programming languages. **If[condition,then,else]** performs then if condition is **True** and else if condition is **False**. This block can be entered as

If[condition,then,else,other] if condition is neither **True** nor **False**. In this case, the result is **other**.

Example:
In the following example, g is defined to request a value for x. If x is not an integer, the **If** command is used to print the sentence "x is not an integer" where the symbol x is replaced by the value of x supplied. If x is an integer, the **If** and **PrimeQ** commands are used to determine if x is a prime number. If x is a prime number, the sentence "x is a prime number" is printed; if x is not a prime number, the sentence "x is not a prime number" is printed. In either case, the symbol x is replaced by the value of x supplied.

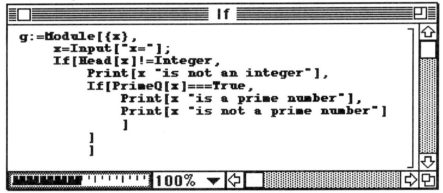

When the command **g** is entered, the following screen appears in a notebook environment:

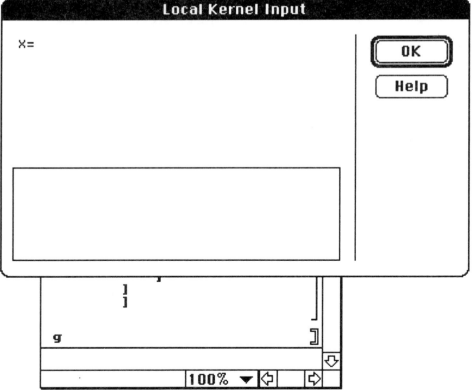

In this case, the number 13 is supplied:

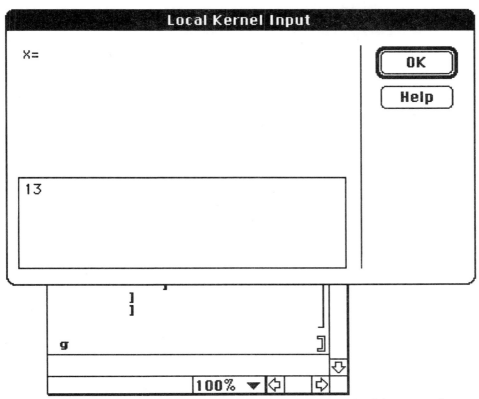

Since 13 is a prime number, the sentence "13 is a prime number" is returned.

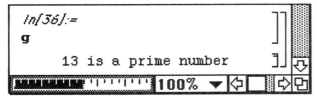

IgnoreCase   379, 384, 501, 808
                                   See Also: **ToUpperCase**, **ToLowerCase**,
                                   SpellingCorrection

   IgnoreCase is an option used with functions such as **StringPosition**, **StringReplace**, **Find**, and **FindList** to indicate whether or not upper- and lower-case letters are to be treated equivalently. The default setting for this option is **IgnoreCase->False**, so cases are treated differently in searches and string manipulation unless otherwise instructed with **IgnoreCase->True**.

Im   52, 551, 604, 808
See 196-198, 254, 271,   See Also: **Re**, **Abs**, **Arg**, **ComplexExpand**
398, 462, 549

   Im[z] yields the imaginary part of the complex number **z**. The argument of this function must be a number. Otherwise, the function is not evaluated.

Example:

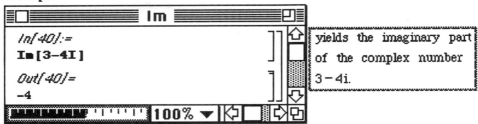

Implies   619, 808
                                          See Also: **LogicalExpand**, **If**
   Implies[p,q] symbolizes the implication **p ⇒ q**. This command can be entered
as **!p||q** as well.

In   54, 61, 62, 513, 514, 743, 808
                                          See Also: **InString**, **Out**, **$Line**
   In[n] represents the information in the nth input line. Entering **In[j]** causes the
input on the **j**th line to be re-evaluated while **In[ ]** yields the input of the previous
line. Also, **In[-m]** yields the input found **m** lines beforehand.

IncludeSingularTerms
                                          See Also: **LerchPhi**, **Zeta**
   IncludeSingularTerms is option used with the commands **LerchPhi** and
Zeta to indicate whether to include terms of the form $(k+a)^2$ where k+a = 0.

Increment (**++**)   248, 808
See 169, 490   See Also: **Decrement**, **DivideBy**, **PreIncrement**,
                                          AddTo, **Set**, **TimesBy**
   The increment of **i**, symbolized as **i++**, adds 1 to the value **i** and returns the
previous value of **i**. **HoldFirst** is an attribute of this function.

Example:

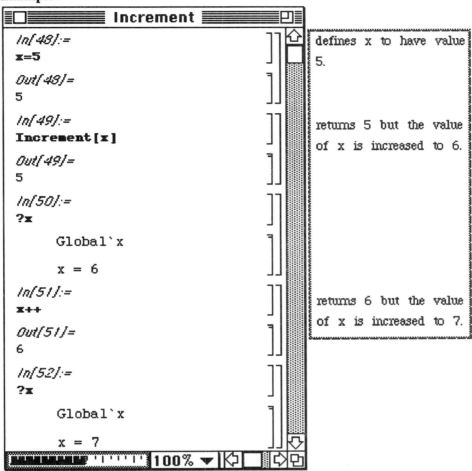

Indent   517, 809
> See Also: **LineBreak**, **Continuation**,
> **StringBreak**, **DialogIndent**

   Indent[d] is used to alter the appearance of output by indenting for a depth **d**
subexpression. The default for this command is **d**.

Indeterminate   547, 809
                                                See Also: **DirectedInfinity**, **Check**
  Indeterminate is the output for computations which yield an indeterminate numerical result such as $0/0$ or $1/0$.
Example:

In the following example, we first define $f(x) = \dfrac{40 + 68x + 24x^2}{5 + 21x + 18x^2}$. $f\left(\dfrac{-5}{6}\right)$

does not exist but $\underset{x \to -5/6}{\text{Lim}} f(x) = \dfrac{-28}{9}$.

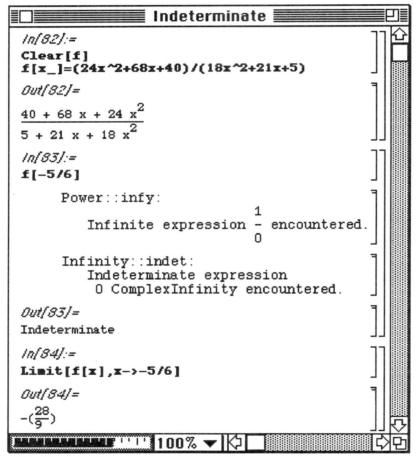

Inequality   721
                                                See Also: **Greater**, **GreaterEqual**, **Unequal**
  Inequality can be used with symbols such as **>** and **>=** to represent inequalities. The advantage of entering an inequality such as **x>=y>z** as
Inequality[x,GreaterEqual,y,Greater,z] is that **Inequality** keeps the agruments from being evaluated twice in the process.

Infinity   50, 198, 548, 566, 809
See 15, 216, 367,   See Also: **ComplexInfinity**, **DirectedInfinity**,
684, 686   **Indeterminate**

   Infinity symbolizes a positive infinite quantity which is internally written as
DirectedInfinity[1].

Example:

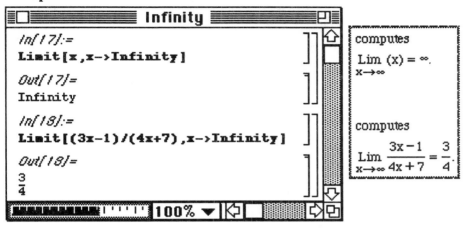

Infix   362, 809
                                See Also: **Postfix**, **Prefix**, **PrecedenceForm**
   Infix[{x,y,...},operator] prints the output using the infix operator as
x operator y operator .... The command can be entered as
Infix[expression,operator,precedence,grouping] to indicate the
manner in which parentheses should be placed in the output. The value for
precedence is an integer while **grouping** can be entered as **NonAssociative**,
None, **Left**, or **Right**.

Information   69, 722, 809
                                See Also: **Definition**, **Names**, **ValueQ**,
                                DownValues, **UpValues**
   Information[symbol] yields the same information concerning **symbol** as the
command **??symbol**. This information can include definitions, options, and
attributes.

Example:

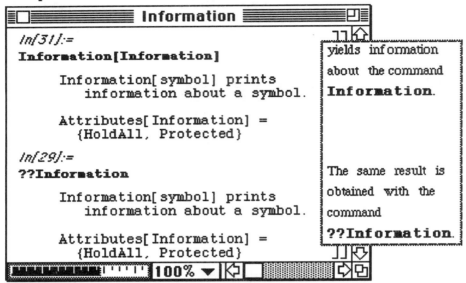

Inner   217, 218, 669, 810
                                               See Also: **Outer, Thread, MapThread**
   Inner[f,list1,list2,g] is a generalized inner product which takes all
possible combinations of the members of **list1** and those of **list2** which have
corresponding positions. This command can be used with tensors as
Inner[f,t1,t2,g] to form the generalized inner product for tensors **t1** and **t2**
with **f** serving as the multiplication operator and **g** as that of addition.

Input   522, 810
See 204   See Also: **InputString, Read, Get, Dialog**
   Input[] is used in order to have *Mathematica* ask for input from the user. The
manner in which this command functions depends on the particular computer system
being used. The command **Input["prompt"]** first displays a prompt and then reads
in the input offered by the user. In many cases the **?** symbol is used as a prompt for
input.

InputForm   16, 144, 343, 371, 396, 739, 810
See 415, 737   See Also: **OutputForm, FullForm**
   InputForm[expression] yields a one-dimensional form of **expression** as
output which can be used for input to *Mathematica*. **InputForm** only affects the
printing of **expression**. It does not alter any evaluations involving **expression**.

Example:

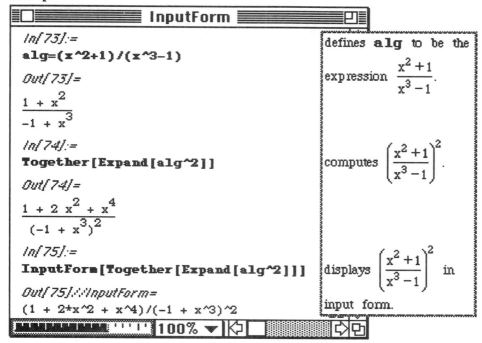

InputStream   484, 738, 810
                    See Also: **\$Input**, **Read**, **Find**, **OpenRead**,
                    StringToStream

InputStream["name",n] is a *Mathematica* object which represents an input stream. This command is used with such commands as **Read** and **Find**. Each input stream has a unique serial number **n**. The commands **OpenRead** and **StringToStream** both return **InputStream** objects.

InputString   522, 810
                    See Also: **Input**

InputString[] is similar to the **Input[]** command in that it allows for interactive input. In this case, the input is read in as a string of characters. Also, **InputString["prompt"]** issues a prompt before the input is entered and read.

Insert   128, 811
                See Also: **Prepend, Append, StringInsert, Take,**
                Drop, Delete, ReplacePart, FlattenAt,
                Position

    Insert is used to insert one or more elements into a list. This command can be
entered in several forms to achieve different results. **Insert[list,member,n]**
inserts **member** at position **n** of **list**. The **n**th position is counted from the end of
list if **n** is a negative integer. Similarly, if the elements of list contain many levels,
then   **Insert[list,member,{i,j,...}]** inserts member at position
{i,j,...}. Also, more than one element can be inserted with
Insert[list,{{i1,j1,...},{i2,j2,...},...}].

Example:

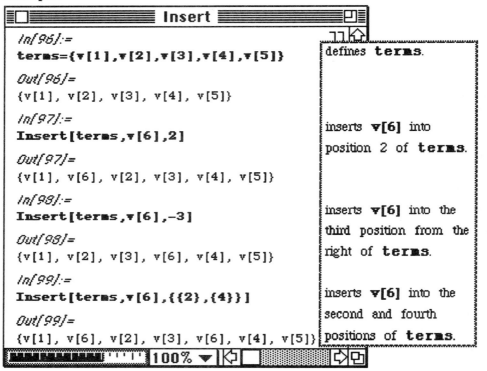

Install   186, 509, 811
                See Also: **Get, Run, RunThrough, Uninstall**
    Install["prog"] initiates the external program **prog** , establishes *MathLink*
communications with it, and installs definitions from *Mathematica* so that functions
from **prog** may be called from *Mathematica*.

InString   62, 513, 743, 811
                See Also: **In, $SyntaxHandler**
    InString[n] yields the input that *Mathematica* read on the **n**th input line. This
input is displayed in textual form. If **n** is a negative integer, then the text from the **n**th
previous line is given. Also, **InString[]** yields the input from the previous line.

Example:

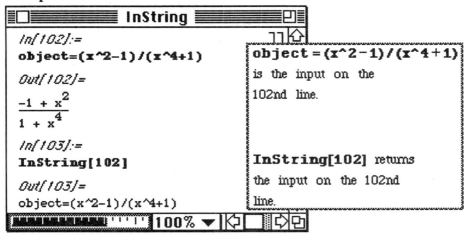

Integer   534, 712, 811
See 7, 37, 87, 204, 379,   See Also: **IntegerDigits**, **BaseForm**
385

Integer represents a type of number in *Mathematica*. Integers can be of any length and can be entered in base **b** with the command **b^^digits**. The largest allowable base is 35.

Example:

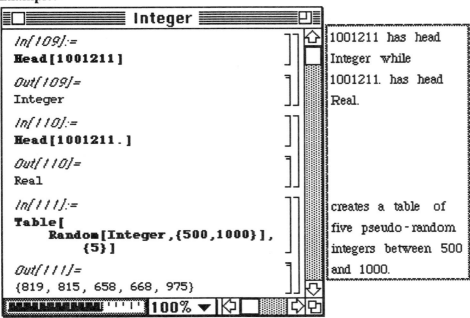

IntegerDigits   537, 553, 811
See 255, 638   See Also: **RealDigits**, **BaseForm**

  IntegerDigits is used to determine the digits of an integer for any base. In base 10, **IntegerDigits[n]** lists the decimal digits of the integer **n** while in base **b**, **IntegerDigits[n,b]** lists the base-**b** digits of **n**.

Example:

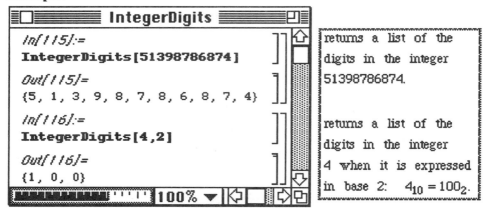

IntegerQ   227, 535, 811
                See Also: **EvenQ**, **OddQ**, **NumberQ**, **TrueQ**

  IntegerQ[expression] yields a value of True if **expression** is an integer and a value of False otherwise. Hence, **IntegerQ[x]=True** can be used to define **x** to be an integer by assigning the head **Integer** to **x**.

Example:

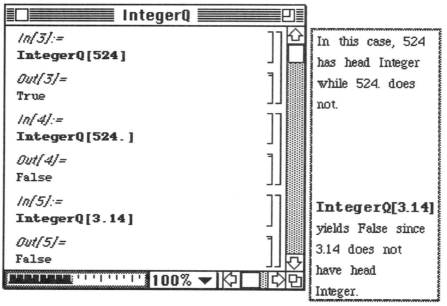

Integrate   77, 90, 630, 635, 683, 812
See 72, 73, 181, 189,   See Also: **NIntegrate, NDSolve, DSolve**
191, 275, 468, 757, 758

Integrate is used to compute the exact value of definite and indefinite integrals. Integrals may be single or multiple. Syntax for these commands is given below.

Integrate[f,x] determines the indefinite integral $\int f \, dx$.

Integrate[f,{x,x1,x2}] evaluates the definite integral $\int_{x1}^{x2} f \, dx$.

For multiple integrals, the command **Integrate[f,{x,x1,x2},{y,y1,y2}]**

calculates $\int_{x1}^{x2} dx \int_{y1}^{y2} dy \, f$. Notice that the first variable listed within the

command is the variable involved in the outermost integral.

Integrate is applicable to those integrals which depend on exponential,

logarithmic, trigonometric, and inverse trigonometric functions if the outcome

also involves these functions.

Example:
In the following example, *Mathematica* computes the indefinite integrals

$$\int \frac{\sqrt{x}}{\left(2-3\sqrt{x}\right)^2} \, dx \quad \text{and} \quad \int x \mathrm{Sin}^{-1}(x) \, dx.$$

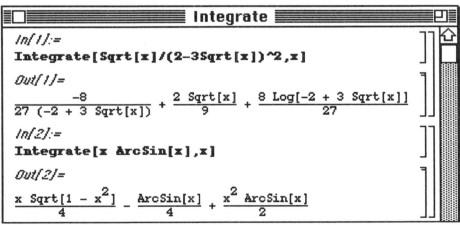

Mathematica also computes the exact value of many proper and improper integrals like

$$\int_{-5/3}^{-1} \sqrt{\frac{x+1}{x-1}} \, dx \quad \text{and} \quad \int_{-\infty}^{+\infty} \frac{1}{x^2+1} \, dx.$$

```
In[3]:=
Integrate[Sqrt[(x+1)/(x-1)],{x,-5/3,-1}]

Out[3]=
4
- - Log[3]
3

In[4]:=
Integrate[1/(x^2+1),{x,-Infinity,Infinity}]

Out[4]=
Pi
```

Sometimes *Mathematica* is able to represent integrals in terms of built-in functions. For example, *Mathematica* contains built-in definitions of

$$\mathbf{Polylog[2,z]} = \int_z^0 \frac{\mathrm{Log}(1-t)}{t}\,dt, \quad \mathbf{FresnelC[z]} = \int_0^z \cos\!\left(\frac{\pi t^2}{2}\right) dt, \quad \text{and}$$

$$\mathbf{Erf[z]} = \frac{2}{\sqrt{\pi}}\int_0^z e^{-t^2}\,dt.$$

```
In[11]:=
Integrate[Log[1-t]/t,{t,z,0}]

Out[11]=
PolyLog[2, z]

In[12]:=
Integrate[Cos[Pi t^2/2],t]

Out[12]=
FresnelC[t]

In[13]:=
Integrate[Exp[-t^2],t]

Out[13]=
Sqrt[Pi] Erf[t]
---------------
       2
```

Since integration is difficult, it is easy to give *Mathematica* integrals it cannot compute. For example, *Mathematica* can neither compute

$$\int \cos(\cos(x))\,dx \quad \text{nor} \quad \int_1^{+\infty} \frac{e^{-zt}}{t^n}.$$

In cases when **Integrate** cannot produce exaxt results and numerical results are adequate, try **NIntegrate**.

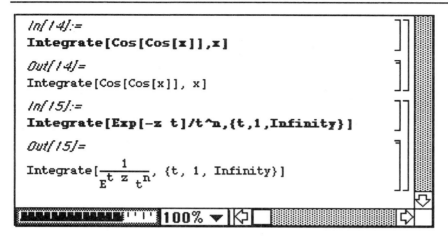

In[14]:=
Integrate[Cos[Cos[x]],x]

Out[14]=
Integrate[Cos[Cos[x]], x]

In[15]:=
Integrate[Exp[-z t]/t^n,{t,1,Infinity}]

Out[15]=
Integrate[$\frac{1}{E^{t\ z}\ t^n}$, {t, 1, Infinity}]

100% ▼

InterpolatingFunction

108, 212, 676, 696, 812
See 307-311   See Also: **CompiledFunction**, **Interpolation**,
                                   InterpolatingPolynomial

   InterpolatingFunction[{x0,x1},<>] is the result of such functions as
Interpolation and **NDSolve** which represents an approximate function obtained
through interpolation. The interval **{x0,x1}** is the range of values over which the
approximation is valid while **<>** represents the table of approximate function values.
The approximate function can be evaluated for a value **x** on the interval **{x0,x1}** with
the command **InterpolatingFunction[{x0,x1},<>][x]**.

Example:

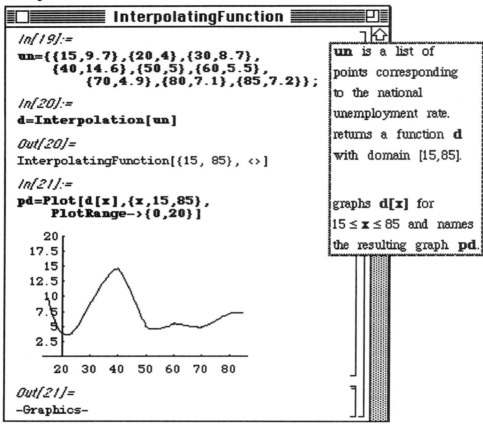

To see that the resulting interpolating function fits the data, we graph d(x) and the unemployment data on the same axes using the commands, **Map**, **Point**, **Show**, **Graphics**, and **PointSize**.

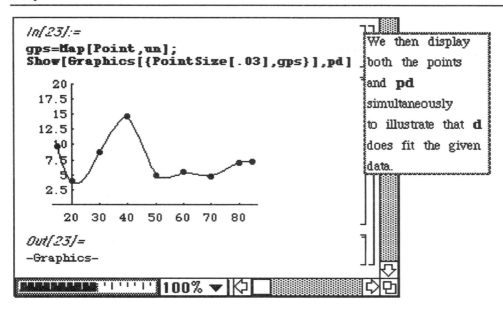

In[23]:=

```
gps=Map[Point,un];
Show[Graphics[{PointSize[.03],gps}],pd]
```

We then display
both the points
and **pd**
simultaneously
to illustrate that **d**
does fit the given
data.

Out[23]=
-Graphics-

100%

InterpolatingPolynomial

602, 675, 812

See Also: **Fit**

InterpolatingPolynomial is used to compute polynomial approximations. This command can appear in several different forms depending on the data. If the data consists of a list of length n of function values, then
InterpolatingPolynomial[{f1,f2,...,fn},x] fits the data with a (n-1) degree polynomial in the variable **x**. However, if the data is a list of data points of the form **{{x1,f1},{x2,f2},...,{xn,fn}}**, then
InterpolatingPolynomial[{{x1,f1},{x2,f2},...,{xn,fn}}},x] is used to obtain the same result. If the value of the function and its derivatives are known, then the **fi** in the previous command is replaced by **{fi,dfi,ddfi,...}**.

Example:

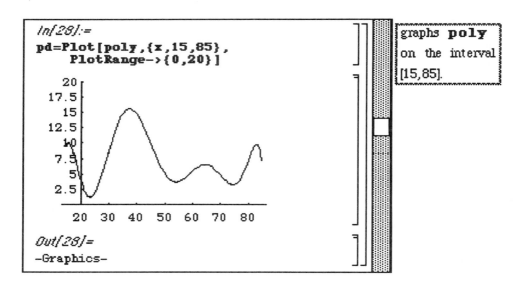

```
≡☐■≡≡≡≡≡     InterpolatingPolynomial     ≡☐≡
In[19]:=
un={{15,9.7},{20,4},{30,8.7},
    {40,14.6},{50,5},{60,5.5},
      {70,4.9},{80,7.1},{85,7.2}};
In[27]:=
poly=InterpolatingPolynomial[un,x]

Out[27]=
9.7 + (-1.14 + (0.107333 +
        (-0.00405333 +
          (0.0000362857 +
            (3.11032 10^-6 +
            (-1.764 10^-7 +
            (5.51299 10^-9 -
            1.46038 10^-10 (-80 + x))
            (-70 + x)) (-60 + x))
            (-50 + x)) (-40 + x))
        (-30 + x)) (-20 + x)) (-15 + x)
```

produces a polynomial in x that fits the data **un** and names it **poly**.

```
In[28]:=
pd=Plot[poly,{x,15,85},
    PlotRange->{0,20}]
```

graphs **poly** on the interval [15,85].

```
Out[28]=
-Graphics-
```

Interpolation   676, 678, 679, 813
                                    See Also: **InterpolatingFunction**,
                                    InterpolatingPolynomial, **Fit**

   Interpolation[data] is used to determine a function which approximates a given collection of data. The result of this command is in the form of **InterpolatingFunction**. The data can assume several forms.
{{x1,f1},{x2,f2},...} is used if both x- and y-values are known.
{f1,f2,...} is used if only the function values are known. In this case, the x-values are automatically taken to have the values 1, 2, ... If the function and derivative values are known, then **data** is entered in the form
{{x1,{f1,df1,ddf1,...},{x2,{f2,df2,ddf2,..},...}. In this case, a different number of derivatives can be given for each x-value. Multivariable approximations may be considered as well with
Interpolation[{{x1,y1,..,f1},{x2,y2,..,f2},..},{x,y,...}] or by specifying derivatives in
**Interpolation[{f1,{dxf1,dyf1,..}},{f2,{dxf2,dyf2,..}},.},
{x,y,...}]**. **Interpolation** has the option **InterpolationOrder** which is 3 by default. A linear interpolation is determined with the setting
InterpolationOrder->1.

InterpolationOrder
                                    See Also: **Interpolation**
   InterpolationOrder is an option used with the **Interpolation** command to indicate the order of interpolating polynomial which is to be found. The default setting for this option is **InterpolationOrder->3**.

Interrupt   311, 813
                                    See Also: **Abort**, **TimeConstrained**,
                                    MemoryConstrained, **$Inspector**

   Interrupt[] causes any calculations to be ceased. This command can be used at any point during a calculation.

Intersection   129, 813
                                    See Also: **Join**, **Union**, **Complement**

   Intersection[set1,set2,...] yields a sorted list of the elements common to the sets **set1**, **set2**, ... Each of the **seti** must have the same head.

Example:

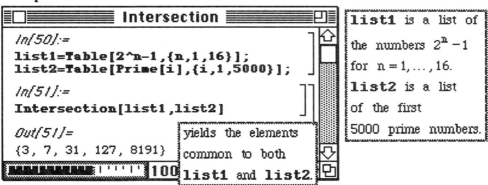

Inverse   9, 123, 655, 657, 662, 813
See 246   See Also: **PseudoInverse**, **LinearSolve**,
                               NullSpace

Inverse[m] computes the inverse of the n × n matrix **m**. *Mathematica* prints a warning message if **m** is not invertible. If the matrix **m** involves approximate real or complex numbers, then the accuracy used in the computation of the inverse can be acquired with **Accuracy**. **Inverse** has the option **ZeroTest->test** which applies **test** to the elements of the matrix to determine whether these elements are zero. The default setting for **ZeroTest** is **ZeroTest->(Together[#]==0)&**. **Inverse** also has the option **Modulus->p** which computes the inverse of the matrix modulo **p**.

Example:

The following commands first define **matrix** to be
$$\begin{pmatrix} -8 & -5 & 4 & 1 \\ -3 & 15 & 15 & -5 \\ -18 & 10 & 8 & 14 \\ 16 & -20 & 12 & -12 \end{pmatrix}$$

and then compute the inverse of **matrix**. The result means that the inverse of **matrix** is the matrix
$$\begin{pmatrix} \dfrac{-97}{781} & \dfrac{-12}{781} & \dfrac{5}{142} & \dfrac{29}{781} \\ \dfrac{-329}{7810} & \dfrac{45}{1562} & \dfrac{-1}{284} & \dfrac{-613}{31240} \\ \dfrac{-17}{781} & \dfrac{14}{781} & \dfrac{3}{71} & \dfrac{125}{3124} \\ \dfrac{-183}{1562} & \dfrac{-79}{1562} & \dfrac{27}{284} & \dfrac{243}{6248} \end{pmatrix}.$$

```
≣▤▢≣▦▦▦▦▦▦▦▦▦▦▦ Inverse ▦▦▦▦▦▦▦▦▦▦▦▦▦▤⊿

In[5]:=
matrix={{-8,-5,4,1},{-3,15,15,-5},
        {-18,10,8,14},{16,-20,12,-12}};

In[6]:=
Inverse[matrix]

Out[6]=
{{-(97/781), -(12/781), 5/142, 29/781},

   {-(329/7810), 45/1562, -(1/284), -(613/31240)},

   {-(17/781), 14/781, 3/71, 125/3124},

   {-(183/1562), -(79/1562), 27/284, 243/6248}}
```

The elements of a matrix need not consist exclusively of numbers. For example, the following calculations first define **matrix** to be the matrix $\begin{pmatrix} -10+10x & -3 \\ 6 & 4 \end{pmatrix}$

and then compute the inverse of **matrix**. The result means that the

inverse of **matrix** is the matrix $\begin{pmatrix} \dfrac{2}{-11+20x} & \dfrac{3}{2(-11+20x)} \\ \dfrac{-3}{-11+20x} & \dfrac{-10+10x}{2(-11+20x)} \end{pmatrix}$.

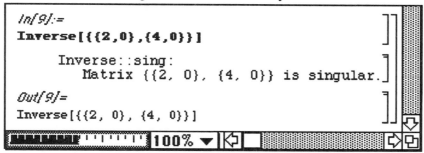

```
In[7]:=
matrix={{-10+10x,-3},{6,4}};
In[8]:=
Inverse[matrix]
Out[8]=
        2                3
{{---------- , -------------- },
  -11 + 20 x   2 (-11 + 20 x)
        -3              -10 + 10 x
  {---------- , -------------- }}
   -11 + 20 x   2 (-11 + 20 x)
```

In fact, if a matrix is singular *Mathematica* tells you so:

```
In[9]:=
Inverse[{{2,0},{4,0}}]

     Inverse::sing:
         Matrix {{2, 0}, {4, 0}} is singular.

Out[9]=
Inverse[{{2, 0}, {4, 0}}]
```
100% ▼

InverseFourier   111, 679, 813
                     See Also: **Fourier**
     InverseFourier[numbers] determines the discrete inverse Fourier
transform for the list of complex numbers given in **numbers**. If b_s
represents a list of numbers having length n, then the inverse Fourier

transform, symbolized by a_r, is given by $\dfrac{1}{\sqrt{n}} \displaystyle\sum_{s=1}^{n} b_s e^{-2\pi i\,(r-1)(s-1)/n}$.

This definition is the standard definition of the inverse Fourier transform
found in the physical sciences. The definition common to electrical
engineering is obtained by reversing the sign of the exponent in the
definition above. The list of complex numbers defined earlier as **numbers**
can be represented as a rectangular array as well.

InverseFunction   200, 213, 613, 814
                                   See Also: **Solve**, **InverseSeries**, **Composition**,
                                   Derivative

InverseFunction[f] yields the inverse function of **f** so that the value of **x** which results from **InverseFunction[f][y]** satisfies the relation **f[x]=y**. This command also can be used with functions of more than one variable. If this is the case, then **InverseFunction[f]** yields the inverse with respect to the first variable. **InverseFunction[f,n]** determines the inverse with respect to the **n**th variable. Also, **InverseFunction[f,n,sum]** represents the inverse with respect to the **n**th variable where the total number of variables is **sum**. The output of this command is given as $f^{(-1)}$. If the inverse is not unique, then **InverseFunction[f]** represents only one of the possible inverses.

InverseFunctions   612, 814
                                   See Also: **FindRoot**, **Solve**

InverseFunctions is an option used with functions such as **Solve** to indicate if inverse functions should be used in determining a solution. The possible settings for **InverseFunctions** are **True** if inverse functions are to be used in all cases, **Automatic** if warning messages are to be printed during faulty calculations, and **False** if no inverse functions are to be used.

InverseJacobiCD
                                   See Also: **JacobiCD**, **InverseJacobiSN**

InverseJacobiCD[v,m] yields the inverse of the Jacobi elliptic function cd at **v** for the parameter **m**. The result is in the parallelogram with sides 2K and 2IK' centered at K. Note that K denotes the complete elliptic integral of the first kind while K' represents the complementary complete elliptic integral of the first kind. These values are related by the formula K' = K(1−m).

Example:

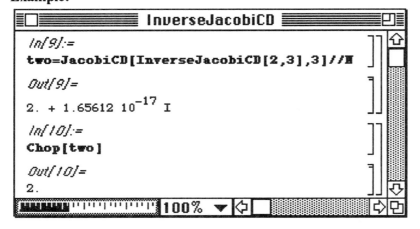

InverseJacobiCN

See Also: **JacobiCN**, **InverseJacobiSN**

InverseJacobiCN[v,m] yields the inverse of the Jacobi elliptic function cn at **v** for the parameter **m**. The result is in the parallelogram with sides 2K and 2IK ' centered at K. Note that K denotes the complete elliptic integral of the first kind while K' represents the complementary complete elliptic integral of the first kind. These values are related by the formula K ' = K(1−m).

Example:

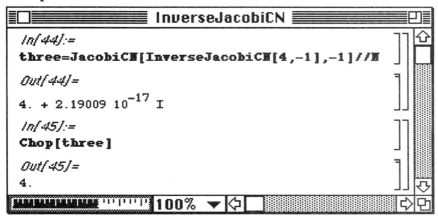

InverseJacobiCS

See Also: **JacobiCS**, **InverseJacobiSN**

InverseJacobiCS[v,m] yields the inverse of the Jacobi elliptic function cs at **v** for the parameter **m**. The result is in the parallelogram with sides 2K and 2IK ' centered at K. Note that K denotes the complete elliptic integral of the first kind while K' represents the complementary complete elliptic integral of the first kind. These values are related by the formula K ' = K(1−m).

Example:

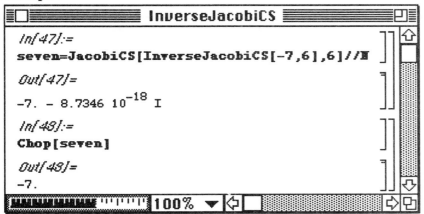

InverseJacobiDC

See Also: **JacobiDC**, **InverseJacobiSN**

InverseJacobiDC[v,m] yields the inverse of the Jacobi elliptic function dc at **v** for the parameter **m**. The result is in the parallelogram with sides 2K and 2IK ′ centered at K + I K′. Note that K denotes the complete elliptic integral of the first kind while K′ represents the complementary complete elliptic integral of the first kind. These values are related by the formula K′ = K(1−m).

Example:

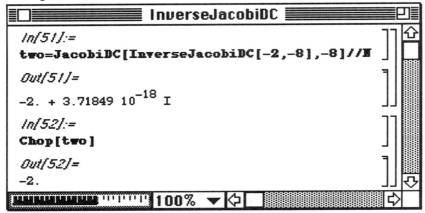

InverseJacobiDN

See Also: **JacobiDN**, **InverseJacobiSN**

InverseJacobiDN[v,m] yields the inverse of the Jacobi elliptic function dn at **v** for the parameter **m**. The result is in the parallelogram with sides 2K and 2IK ′ centered at K + I K′. Note that K denotes the complete elliptic integral of the first kind while K′ represents the complementary complete elliptic integral of the first kind. These values are related by the formula K′ = K(1−m).

Example:

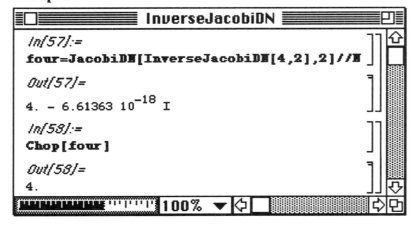

InverseJacobiDS

See Also: **JacobiDS**, **InverseJacobiSN**

InverseJacobiDS[v,m] yields the inverse of the Jacobi elliptic function ds at **v** for the parameter **m**. The result is in the parallelogram with sides 2K and 2IK′ centered at K + I K′. Note that K denotes the complete elliptic integral of the first kind while K′ represents the complementary complete elliptic integral of the first kind. These values are related by the formula K′ = K(1−m).

Example:

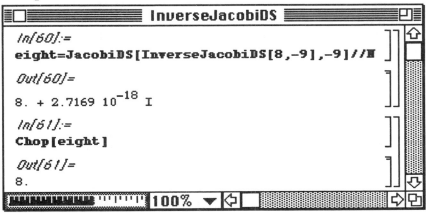

InverseJacobiNC

See Also: **JacobiNC**, **InverseJacobiSN**

InverseJacobiNC[v,m] yields the inverse of the Jacobi elliptic function nc at **v** for the parameter **m**. The result is in the parallelogram with sides 2K and 2IK′ centered at I K′. Note that K denotes the complete elliptic integral of the first kind while K′ represents the complementary complete elliptic integral of the first kind. These values are related by the formula K′ = K(1−m).

Example:

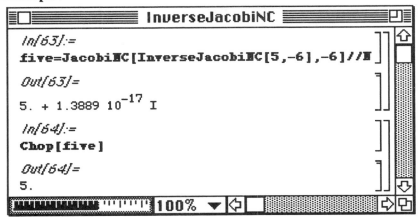

InverseJacobiND

See Also: **JacobiND, InverseJacobiSN**

InverseJacobiND[v,m] yields the inverse of the Jacobi elliptic function nd at **v** for the parameter **m**. The result is in the parallelogram with sides 2K and 2IK ' centered at I K '. Note that K denotes the complete elliptic integral of the first kind while K ' represents the complementary complete elliptic integral of the first kind. These values are related by the formula K ' = K(1−m).

Example:

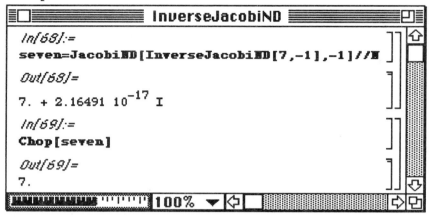

InverseJacobiNS

See Also: **JacobiNS, InverseJacobiSN**

InverseJacobiNS[v,m] yields the inverse of the Jacobi elliptic function ns at **v** for the parameter **m**. The result is in the parallelogram with sides 2K and 2IK ' centered at I K '. Note that K denotes the complete elliptic integral of the first kind while K ' represents the complementary complete elliptic integral of the first kind. These values are related by the formula K ' = K(1−m).

Example:

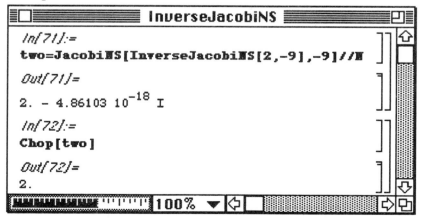

InverseJacobiSC

See Also: **JacobiSC, InverseJacobiSN**

InverseJacobiSC[v,m] yields the inverse of the Jacobi elliptic function sc at **v** for the parameter **m**. The result is in the parallelogram with sides 2K and 2IK ′ centered at 0. Note that K denotes the complete elliptic integral of the first kind while K ′ represents the complementary complete elliptic integral of the first kind. These values are related by the formula K ′ = K(1−m).

Example:

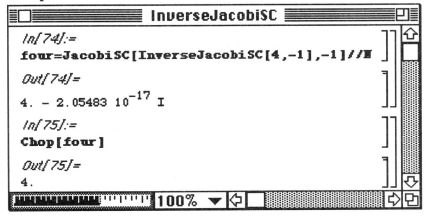

InverseJacobiSD

See Also: **JacobiSD, InverseJacobiSN**

InverseJacobiSD[v,m] yields the inverse of the Jacobi elliptic function sd at **v** for the parameter **m**. The result is in the parallelogram with sides 2K and 2IK ′ centered at 0. Note that K denotes the complete elliptic integral of the first kind while K ′ represents the complementary complete elliptic integral of the first kind. These values are related by the formula K ′ = K(1−m).

Example:

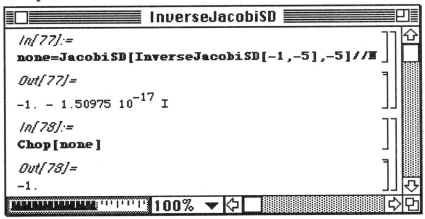

InverseJacobiSN

See Also: **JacobiSN, InverseJacobiSN**

InverseJacobiSN[v,m] yields the inverse of the Jacobi elliptic function sn at **v** for the parameter **m**. The result is in the parallelogram with sides 2K and 2IK′ centered at 0. Note that K denotes the complete elliptic integral of the first kind while K′ represents the complementary complete elliptic integral of the first kind. These values are related by the formula K′ = K(1−m).

Example:

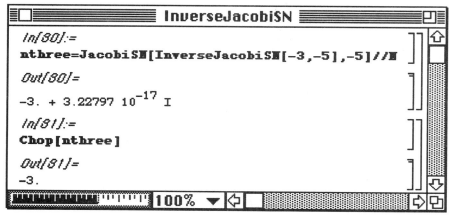

InverseSeries   644, 814

See Also: **Solve, InverseFunction**

InverseSeries[series,x] performs a reversion of the power series given by **series**. Hence, given the power series **ser** the result of **InverseSeries[ser,x]** is a series **y** such that **ser[y]==x**.

InverseWeierstrassP

See Also: **WeierstrassP**

InverseWeierstrassP[{P,P′},g2,g3] yields the value of **u** so that **P=WeierstrassP[u,g2,g3]** and **P′= WeierstrassPPrime[u,g2,g3]**. Note that **WeierstrassPPrime[u,g2,g3]** is the derivative with respect to u of **WeierstrassP[u,g2,g3]**.

J

JacobiAmplitude   580, 583, 815
                                   See Also: **EllipticF**

JacobiAmplitude[u,m] represents the amplitude am(u|m) of the Jacobi elliptic functions. The amplitude is the inverse of the elliptic integral of the first kind, **EllipticF[phi,m]**. Hence, if **u = Elliptic[phi,m]**, then **phi** = am(u|m). Often the parameter m is omitted from list of arguments so that the amplitude is denoted as simply am(u).

Jacobian

                                   See Also: **FindRoot**

Jacobian is an option used with **FindRoot** so that the Jacobian for the system of functions the root of which being sought can be indicated.

JacobiCD   580, 583
                                   See Also: **InverseJacobiCD, JacobiSN,
                                   JacobiCN, JacobiDN**

JacobiCD[u,m] represents the Jacobi elliptic function cd(**u**) = cn(**u**)/dn(**u**) at **u** for the parameter **m**.
Example:

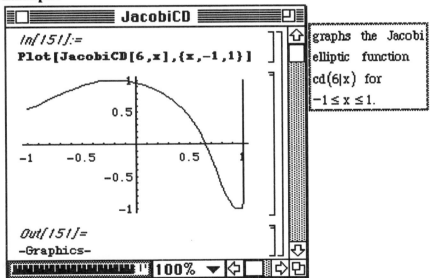

JacobiCN   580, 583
                                   See Also: **InverseJacobiCN, JacobiSN,
                                   JacobiDN**

JacobiCN[u,m] represents the Jacobi elliptic function cn(**u**) at **u** for the parameter **m**. This function satisfies the equation cn(u) = cos(ϕ) where ϕ = am(u|m).
Example:
The following creates a contour graph of the absolute value of the Jacobi elliptic function cn(x+iy|1/10) for $0 \leq x \leq 4$ **EllipticK[1/10]** and
 $0 \leq y \leq 4$ **EllipticK[9/10]** using twenty-five plotpoints (the default is fifteen) where **EllipticK[x]** is the complete elliptic integral of the first kind K(x).

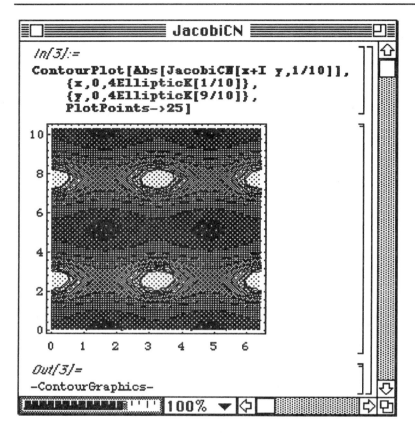

JacobiCS   580, 583
See Also: **EllipticK, InverseJacobiCS,
JacobiSN, JacobiCN, JacobiDN,
JacobiAmplitude**

JacobiCS[u,m] represents the Jacobi elliptic function cs(u) = cn(u)/sn(u) at **u** for the parameter **m**. sn and cn are given by the formulas:

sn(u) = $\mathrm{Sin}(\theta)$ and cn(u) = $\mathrm{Cos}(\theta)$, where $\theta = \mathrm{am}(u|m)$ is the inverse of the elliptic integral of the first kind.

Observe that if $u = F(\theta|m) = \int_0^\theta \dfrac{d\phi}{\sqrt{1 - m\mathrm{Sin}^2(\phi)}}$, then $\theta = \mathrm{am}(u|m)$.

Example:
In the following example, note *Mathematica* generates several error messages (which are not fully displayed); nevertheless, the resulting graph is displayed correctly.

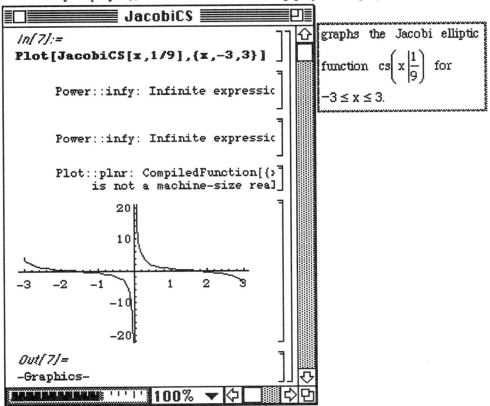

JacobiDC	580, 583
	See Also: **EllipticK**, **InverseJacobiDC**, **JacobiAmplitude**, **JacobiSN**, **JacobiCN**, **JacobiDN**

JacobiDC[u,m] represents the Jacobi elliptic function dc($\mathbf{u}$) = dn($\mathbf{u}$)/cn($\mathbf{u}$) at $\mathbf{u}$ for the parameter **m**. dn and cn are given by the formulas:

$$dn(u) = \sqrt{1 - m\,Sin^2(\theta)} \quad \text{and} \quad cn(u) = Cos(\theta), \quad \text{where } \theta = am\left(u|m\right) \text{ is the inverse of}$$

the elliptic integral of the first kind.

Observe that if $u = F(\theta|m) = \int_0^\theta \dfrac{d\phi}{\sqrt{1 - m\,Sin^2(\phi)}}$, then $\theta = am\left(u|m\right)$.

Example:

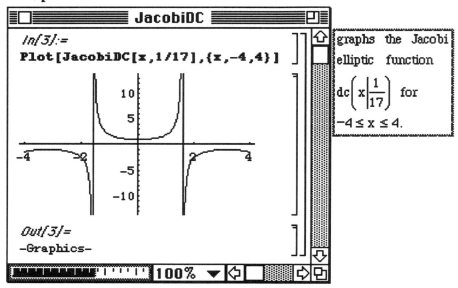

JacobiDN   580, 583
                                  See Also: **InverseJacobiDN**, **JacobiSN**,
                                  JacobiCN

JacobiDN[u,m] represents the Jacobi elliptic function dn(u) where

$dn(u) = \sqrt{1 - m \sin^2 \phi}$, $\phi = am(u|m)$. Note that dn(u|1) = sech(u) and

dn(u|0) = 1.

Example:
The following creates a graph in three-space of the absolute value of the Jacobi elliptic function dn(x+iy|1/20) for $0 \le x \le 2$ **EllipticK[1/20]** and
$0 \le y \le 3$ **EllipticK[19/20]** using twenty plotpoints (the default is fifteen) where **EllipticK[x]** is the complete elliptic integral of the first kind K(x).

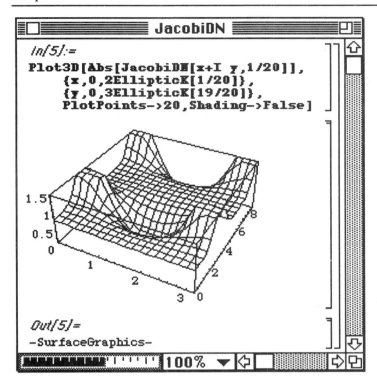

```
In[5]:=
Plot3D[Abs[JacobiDN[x+I y,1/20]],
    {x,0,2EllipticK[1/20]},
    {y,0,3EllipticK[19/20]},
    PlotPoints->20,Shading->False]

Out[5]=
-SurfaceGraphics-
```

JacobiDS   580, 583
                               See Also: **InverseJacobiDS**, **JacobiSN**,
                               JacobiCN, **JacobiDN**

JacobiDS[u,m] represents the Jacobi elliptic function ds(u) = dn(u)/sn(u) at **u** for
the parameter **m**. sn and dn are given by the formulas:

$sn(u) = Sin(\theta)$ and $dn(u) = \sqrt{1-m\sin^2\theta}$, where $\theta = am(u|m)$ is the inverse of
the elliptic integral of the first kind.

Observe that if $u = F(\theta|m) = \int_0^\theta \dfrac{d\phi}{\sqrt{1-mSin^2(\phi)}}$, then $\theta = am(u|m)$.

Example:
The following creates a graph in three-space of the Jacobi elliptic function ds(x|y) for
$-3 \le x \le 3$ and $-4 \le y \le 4$ using thirty plotpoints (the default is fifteen).

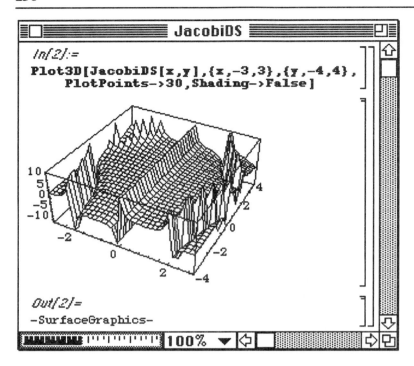

JacobiNC   580, 583
                           See Also: **InverseJacobiNC**, **JacobiSN**,
                           JacobiCN, **JacobiDN**

   JacobiNC[u,m] represents the Jacobi elliptic function $nc(u) = nn(u)/cn(u)$ at **u** for the parameter **m**. Note that $nn(u) = 1$.

Example:

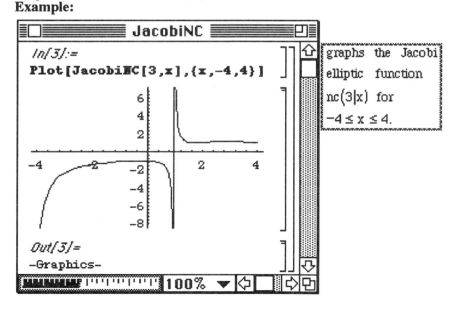

JacobiND   580, 583
                           See Also: **InverseJacobiND**, **JacobiSN**,
                           JacobiCN, **JacobiDN**

  JacobiND[u,m] represents the Jacobi elliptic function nd($\mathbf{u}$) = nn($\mathbf{u}$)/dn($\mathbf{u}$) at $\mathbf{u}$ for the parameter $\mathbf{m}$. Note that nn($\mathbf{u}$) = 1.

Example:
The following creates a density graph of the absolute value of the Jacobi elliptic function nd(x+iy|1/16) for $0 \le x \le 4$ and $0 \le y \le 12$ using thirty plotpoints (the default is fifteen).

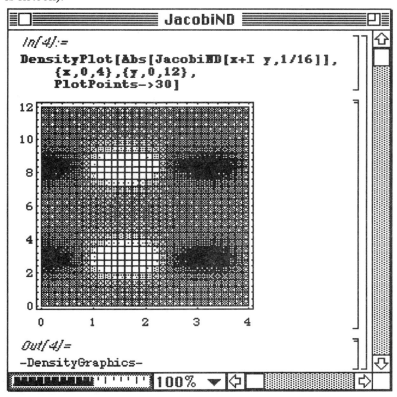

JacobiNS   580, 583
                           See Also: **InverseJacobiNS**, **JacobiSN**,
                           JacobiCN, **JacobiDN**

  JacobiNS[u,m] represents the Jacobi elliptic function ns($\mathbf{u}$) = nn($\mathbf{u}$)/sn($\mathbf{u}$) at $\mathbf{u}$ for the parameter $\mathbf{m}$. Note that nn($\mathbf{u}$) = 1.

Example:
The following creates a contour graph of the absolute value of the Jacobi elliptic function ns(x+iy|1/23) for $0 \le x \le 10$ and $0 \le y \le 20$ using twenty plotpoints (the default is fifteen) and twenty contours (the default is 10). Observe that the resulting graph is not shaded since the **ContourGraphics** option **ContourShading->False** is included.

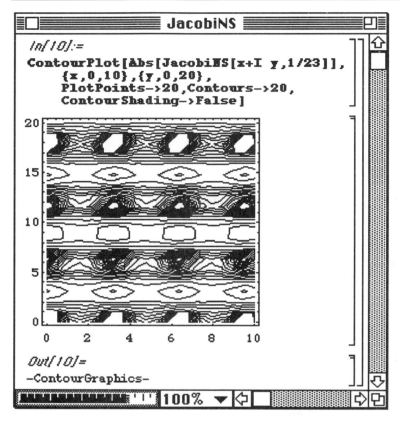

```
=[] ========================== JacobiNS ==========================
In[10]:=
ContourPlot[Abs[JacobiNS[x+I y,1/23]],
    {x,0,10},{y,0,20},
    PlotPoints->20,Contours->20,
    ContourShading->False]
```

Out[10]=
-ContourGraphics-

JacobiP   567, 815
                              See Also: **LegendreP**, **ChebyshevT**, **ChebyshevU**,
                              GegenbaurC

JacobiP[n,a,b,x] yields the Jacobi polynomial $P_n^{(a,b)}(x)$ which arises in
the study of the rotation group in quantum mechanics. These polynomials
satisfy the orthogonality condition $\int_{-1}^{1} P_m^{(a,b)}(x)\ P_n^{(a,b)}(x)\ (1-x)^a(1-x)^b dx = 0$
for $m \neq n$. The Legendre, Chebyshev, and Gegenbaur polynomials are all
special cases of the Jacobi polynomials. An alternate form for the Jacobi
polynomials is $G_n(p,q,x) = \dfrac{n!\ \Gamma(n+p)}{\Gamma(2n+p)} P_n^{(p-q,q-1)}(2x-1)$.

Example:

The following command creates a table of $P_n^{(2,3)}(x)$ for n=1, 2, 3 and names the resulting list **jps**.

```
======================= JacobiP =======================

In[14]:=
jps=Table[JacobiP[n,2,3,x],{n,1,3}]

Out[14]=
{ (-1 + 7 x)/2 , 6 + 16 (-1 + x) + 9 (-1 + x)^2,

    10 + 45 (-1 + x) + (225 (-1 + x)^2)/4 + (165 (-1 + x)^3)/8 }
```

The command **NRoots** is used to find the zeros of each element of the list **jps**. **jps[[1]]** corresponds to the first element of **jps**; **jps[[2]]** the second; and **jps[[3]]** the third.

```
In[15]:=
NRoots[jps[[1]]==0,x]

Out[15]=
x == 0.142857

NRoots[jps[[2]]==0,x]

Out[16]=
x == -0.240253 || x == 0.462475

In[17]:=
NRoots[jps[[3]]==0,x]

Out[17]=
x == -0.461159 || x == 0.104385 || x == 0.629501
```

Finally, the list **jps** is graphed for $-1/2 \leq x \leq 1/2$. In general, when graphing lists, be sure to include the name of the list within the **Evaluate** command.

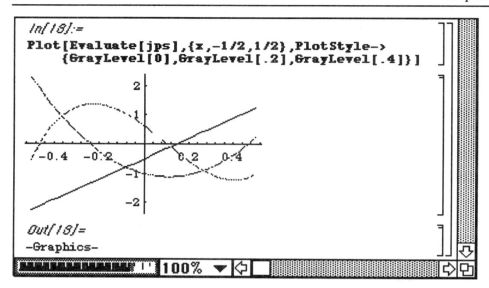

```
In[18]:=
Plot[Evaluate[jps],{x,-1/2,1/2},PlotStyle->
    {GrayLevel[0],GrayLevel[.2],GrayLevel[.4]}]
```

```
Out[18]=
-Graphics-
```

JacobiSC   580, 583
                                      See Also: **InverseJacobiSC**, **JacobiSN**,
                                      JacobiCN, **JacobiDN**

JacobiSC[u,m] represents the Jacobi elliptic function sc($\mathbf{u}$) = sn($\mathbf{u}$)/cn($\mathbf{u}$) at $\mathbf{u}$ for
the parameter $\mathbf{m}$.
Example:
The following example graphs the absolute value of sc(t+it|1/13) for $0 \le t \le 5$.

JacobiSC

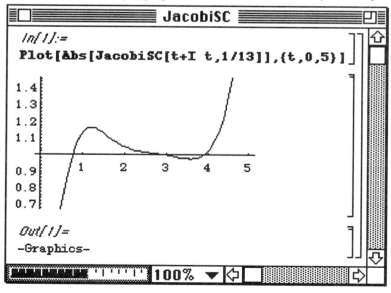

```
In[1]:=
Plot[Abs[JacobiSC[t+I t,1/13]],{t,0,5}]
```

```
Out[1]=
-Graphics-
```

JacobiSD   580, 583
                                     See Also: **InverseJacobiSD, JacobiSN,**
                                     JacobiCN, JacobiDN

  JacobiSD[u,m] represents the Jacobi elliptic function sd($\mathbf{u}$) = sn($\mathbf{u}$)/dn($\mathbf{u}$) at $\mathbf{u}$ for
the parameter $\mathbf{m}$.

Example:
The following creates a graph in three-space of the absolute value of the Jacobi elliptic
function sd(x+iy|1/10) for $0 \leq x \leq 8$ and $0 \leq y \leq 25$ using thirty plotpoints (the default is
fifteen) and does not shade the resulting graph.

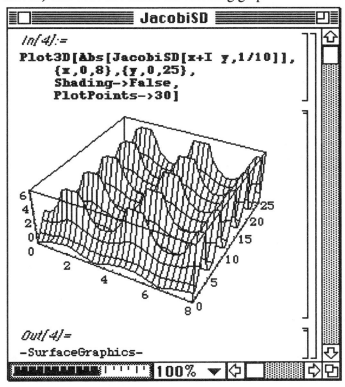

JacobiSN   580, 583, 815
                                     See Also: **InverseJacobiSN, JacobiCN,**
                                     JacobiDN

  JacobiSN[u,m] represents the Jacobi elliptic function sn($\mathbf{u}$) at $\mathbf{u}$ for the parameter
$\mathbf{m}$. This function satisfies the equation sn(u) = sin(ϕ) where ϕ = am(u|m).

Example:
The following creates a density graph of the absolute value of the Jacobi elliptic
function sn(x+iy|1/8) for $0 \leq x \leq 4$ and $0 \leq y \leq 12$ using thirty plotpoints (the default is
fifteen).

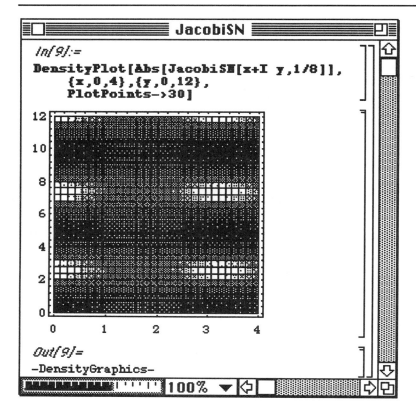

JacobiSymbol   556, 815

JacobiSymbol[n,m] yields the Jacobi symbol, $\left(\frac{n}{m}\right)$, from number theory. If **m** is prime, then the Jacobi symbol is equivalent to the Legendre symbol which is equal to ± 1 depending on whether or not **n** is a quadratic residue of modulo **m**.
Example:
The following example computes a table of values of the Jacobi symbol, $\left(\frac{n}{m}\right)$, for n = 1, 2, 3 and m = 1, 3, 5, 7, 9.

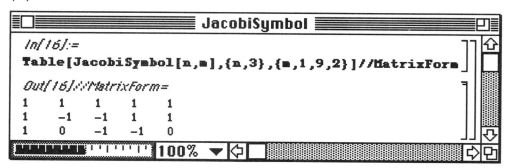

JacobiZeta   580, 815
See Also: EllipticE, EllipticF, EllipticK

JacobiZeta[phi,m] represents the Jacobi zeta function. This function is defined in terms of elliptic integrals as $Z(\phi|m) = E(\phi|m) - E(m)F(\phi|m)/K(m)$ where E is the complete elliptic integral of the second kind, F is the elliptic integral of the first kind, and K is the complete elliptic integral of the first kind.

Example:

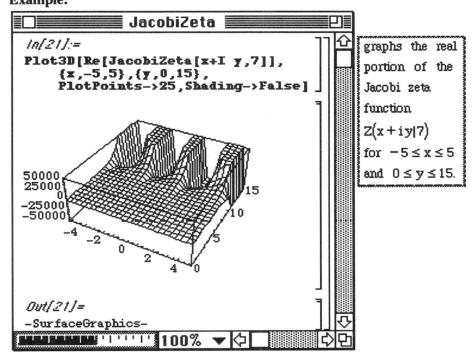

graphs the real portion of the Jacobi zeta function $Z(x+iy|7)$ for $-5 \le x \le 5$ and $0 \le y \le 15$.

Join   129, 815
See Also: Intersection, Union, StringJoin,
Append, Prepend

Join[list1,list2,...] links the lists given in **list1,list2,...** where these lists must have the same head. The result is given in the form of a list.

Example:

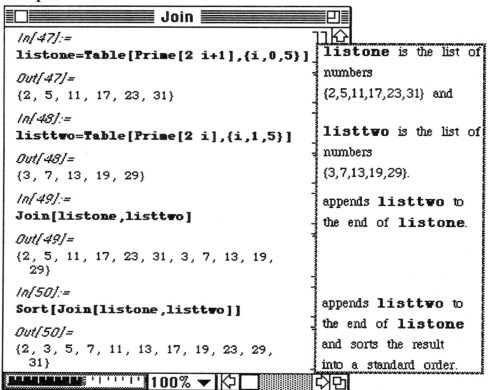

JordanForm

See Also: **CharacteristicPolynomial**,
Inverse, **Eigenvalues**, **Eigenvectors**,
Eigensystem, **QRDecomposition**,
SchurDecomposition

JordanForm[m] yields the list a matrices **{s,j}** such that
m = s.j.Inverse[s] and **j** is the Jordan canonical form of the matrix **m**. In order
to apply this command, all elements of **m** must have infinite precision.

Example:

In the following example, **matrix** is defined to be the 4 × 4 matrix

$$\begin{bmatrix} 2 & 0 & -3 & 0 \\ -4 & 0 & 0 & -1 \\ 3 & 0 & -4 & 0 \\ 0 & -5 & 0 & 0 \end{bmatrix}$$ **JordanForm[matrix]** returns a list of two

matrices and names the resulting list **jfm**.

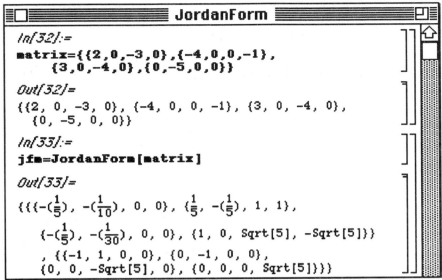

MatrixForm displays matrices in traditional row-and-column form. The following commands display the first and second elements of **jfm** in row-and-column form.

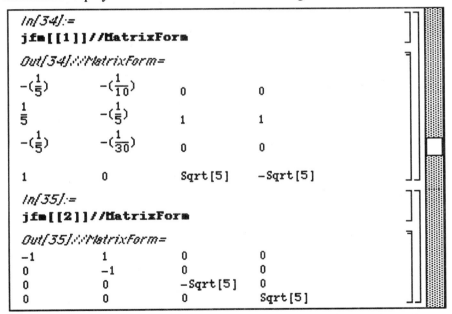

The command **Inverse[matrix]** yields the inverse of **matrix** as long as **matrix** is nonsingular. To verify that **jfm** is indeed the Jordan decomposition of **matrix**, we compute **jfm[[1]].jfm[[2]].Inverse[jfm[[1]]]** and simplify the result.

```
In[36]:=
jfm[[1]].jfm[[2]].Inverse[jfm[[1]]]//Simplify

Out[36]=
{{2, 0, -3, 0}, {-4, 0, 0, -1}, {3, 0, -4, 0},
   {0, -5, 0, 0}}
```

100% ▼

L

Label   295, 815

See Also: **Goto**

Label[marker] is an element in a procedure where control can be transferred with a **Goto**. Notice that **Goto** can be used only when the corresponding **Label** is in the same *Mathematica* procedure. **Label** has the attribute **HoldFirst**.

LaguerreL   567, 578, 815

See 535   See Also: **Hypergeometric1F1**

LaguerreL[n,a,x] represents the Laguerre polynomial which is denoted

$L_n^a(x)$. These polynomials satisfy the ordinary differential equation

$x\dfrac{d^2y}{dx^2} + (a+1-x)\dfrac{dy}{dx} + ny = 0$ and are orthogonal with respect to the weight

function $w(x) = x^a e^{-x}$.

Example:

The following example illustrates that $L_3^4(x)$ satisfies the differential

equation $xy' + (5-x)y' + 3y = 0$.

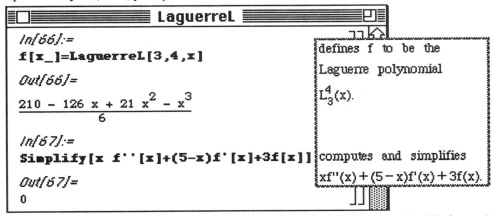

In the following example, a table of Laguerre polynomials is created with the **Table** command and named **t1**.

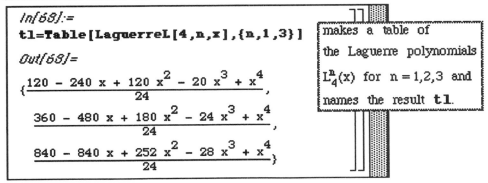

The resulting table of functions is graphed with the **Plot** command. In general, when graphing tables of functions, include the name of the table within the **Evaluate** command as shown:

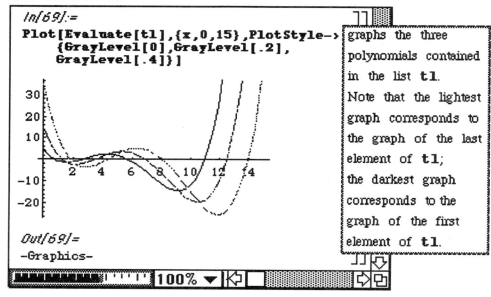

In[69]:=
```
Plot[Evaluate[tl],{x,0,15},PlotStyle->
    {GrayLevel[0],GrayLevel[.2],
    GrayLevel[.4]}]
```
graphs the three polynomials contained in the list **tl**. Note that the lightest graph corresponds to the graph of the last element of **tl**; the darkest graph corresponds to the graph of the first element of **tl**.

Out[69]=
-Graphics-

100% ▼

Last   125, 816
See 703   See Also: **Part, First, Take**

   Last[list] yields the last element of **list**. The same result is obtained with the command **list[[-1]]**.

Example:

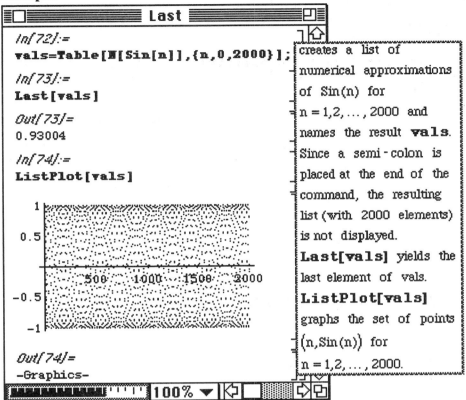

LatticeReduce   556, 816
                         See Also: **RowReduce, Rationalize**

LatticeReduce[{vec1,vec2,...}] represents a lattice reduction function which produces a set of reduced lattice basis vectors for the set of integer vectors given in **{vec1,vec2,...}**. This approach is common in number theory and combinatorics. **LatticeReduce** uses the Lenstra-Lovasz algorithm to determine the reduced basis.

Example:

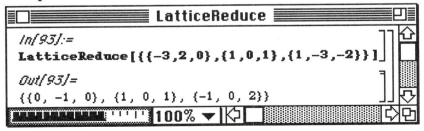

LCM   553, 816
                                          See Also: **ExtendedGCD**, **GCD**

LCM[n1,n2,...] determines the least common multiple of the integers **n1**, **n2**, ...

Example:

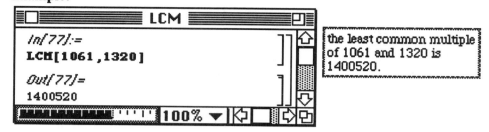

LeafCount   528, 816
                                          See Also: **ByteCount**, **Length**, **Depth**, **AtomQ**,
                                          TreeForm

LeafCount[expression] yields the number of terminal nodes on the tree which results when **expression** is written in expression tree form. This number corresponds to the number of indivisible subexpressions in **expression**.

Example:

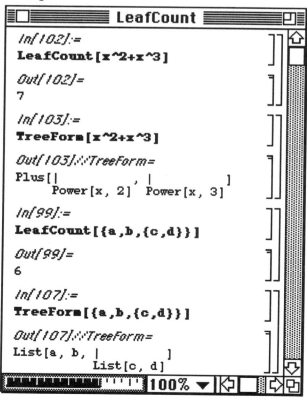

Left   357, 766
See 53   See Also: **Center**, **ColumnForm**, **Right**,
                                          TableForm

   Left is an option setting used with such functions as **ColumnForm** and **TableForm** to indicate alignment in printing.

LegendreP   567, 570, 577, 816
See 253   See Also: **SphericalHarmonicY**

   LegendreP[n,x] represents the Legendre polynomial $P_n(x)$ while

LegendreP[n,m,x] is the associated Legendre polynomial $P_n^m(x)$. The Legendre polynomials are orthogonal with respect to the weight function $w(x) = 1$ and are solutions to the ordinary differential equation

$$\left(1 - x^2\right)\frac{d^2 y}{dx^2} - 2x\frac{dy}{dx} + n(n + 1)y = 0.$$ The associated Legendre polynomials

are given by $P_n^m(x) = (-1)^m (1 - x^2)^{m/2} \frac{d^m}{dx^m} P_n(x)$.

Example:

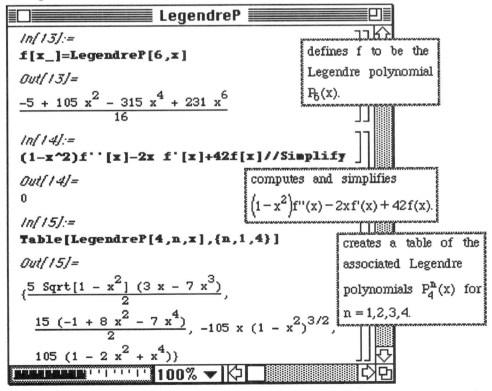

```
In[13]:=
f[x_]=LegendreP[6,x]
```

```
Out[13]=
```
$$\frac{-5 + 105\ x^2 - 315\ x^4 + 231\ x^6}{16}$$

defines f to be the Legendre polynomial $P_6(x)$.

```
In[14]:=
(1-x^2)f''[x]-2x f'[x]+42f[x]//Simplify
```

```
Out[14]=
0
```

computes and simplifies $\left(1 - x^2\right)f''(x) - 2xf'(x) + 42f(x).$

```
In[15]:=
Table[LegendreP[4,n,x],{n,1,4}]
```

```
Out[15]=
```
$$\{\frac{5\ Sqrt[1 - x^2]\ (3\ x - 7\ x^3)}{2},$$

$$\frac{15\ (-1 + 8\ x^2 - 7\ x^4)}{2}, -105\ x\ (1 - x^2)^{3/2},$$

$$105\ (1 - 2\ x^2 + x^4)\}$$

creates a table of the associated Legendre polynomials $P_4^n(x)$ for $n = 1, 2, 3, 4.$

100%

LegendreQ   570, 577, 816
                              See Also: **LegendreP**

LegendreQ[n,z] represents $Q_n(x)$, the Legendre function of the second kind.

LegendreQ[n,m,z] is the associated Legendre function of the ☐¥nd kind which is

denoted $Q_n^m(x)$. These polynomials satisfy the differential equation

$$(1-z^2)\frac{d^2y}{dz^2} - 2z\frac{dy}{dz} + \left[n(n+1) - \frac{m^2}{1-z^2}\right]y = 0.$$ **LegendreType** is an option used to

specify the branch cut to be taken.

Example:

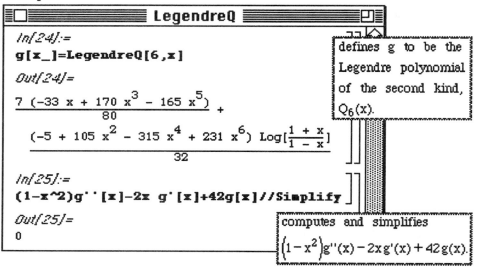

```
In[24]:=
g[x_]=LegendreQ[6,x]

Out[24]=
7 (-33 x + 170 x  - 165 x )
                3          5
─────────────────────────── +
            80

   (-5 + 105 x  - 315 x  + 231 x ) Log[1 + x]
              2          4          6         ─────
                                              1 - x
   ───────────────────────────────────────────────
                       32

In[25]:=
(1-x^2)g''[x]-2x g'[x]+42g[x]//Simplify

Out[25]=
0
```

defines g to be the
Legendre polynomial
of the second kind,
$Q_6(x)$.

computes and simplifies
$\left(1-x^2\right)g''(x) - 2x\,g'(x) + 42\,g(x)$.

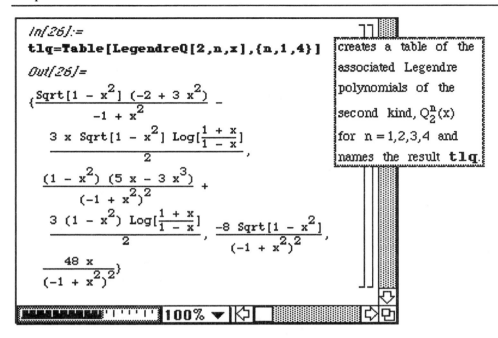

In[26]:=
tlq=Table[LegendreQ[2,n,x],{n,1,4}]

Out[26]=

$$\{\frac{Sqrt[1 - x^2] (-2 + 3 x^2)}{-1 + x^2} -$$

$$\frac{3 x \ Sqrt[1 - x^2] \ Log[\frac{1 + x}{1 - x}]}{2},$$

$$\frac{(1 - x^2) (5 x - 3 x^3)}{(-1 + x^2)^2} +$$

$$\frac{3 (1 - x^2) \ Log[\frac{1 + x}{1 - x}]}{2}, \quad \frac{-8 \ Sqrt[1 - x^2]}{(-1 + x^2)^2},$$

$$\frac{48 x}{(-1 + x^2)^2}\}$$

creates a table of the associated Legendre polynomials of the second kind, $Q_2^n(x)$ for $n = 1,2,3,4$ and names the result **tlq**.

100% ▼

LegendreType   578, 816

See also **LegendreP**, **LegendreQ**

  LegendreType is an option for use with the functions **LegendreP** and **LegendreQ**. The purpose of this option is to indicate the branch cut to be used in the complex plane when using these special functions. The setting **LegendreType->Real** specifies that the branch cuts from **-Infinity** to **-1** and from **+1** to **+Infinity** be taken. On the other hand, **LegendreType->Complex** indicates that there be a branch cut from **-Infinity** to **+1**.

Example:

The following example illustrates how the branch cuts may be chosen with the command **LegendreP**.

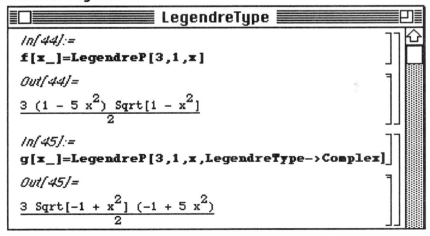

LegendreType

In[44]:=
f[x_]=LegendreP[3,1,x]

Out[44]=

$$\frac{3 (1 - 5 x^2) \ Sqrt[1 - x^2]}{2}$$

In[45]:=
g[x_]=LegendreP[3,1,x,LegendreType->Complex]

Out[45]=

$$\frac{3 \ Sqrt[-1 + x^2] (-1 + 5 x^2)}{2}$$

To visualize that f and g have different branch cuts, we graph the imaginary portion of each:

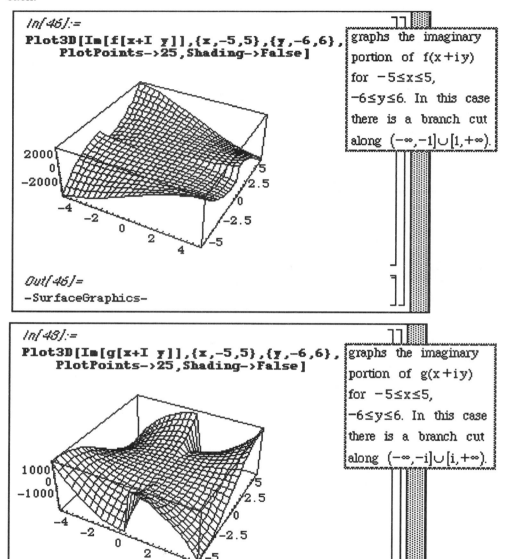

Length   83, 122, 196, 593, 816
See 182, 306   See Also: **LeafCount, ByteCount, Depth**
   Length[list] yields the number of elements in **list**. This command can be used to determine the number of terms in a polynomial as well with **Length[poly]**. If **expression** cannot be divided into subexpressions, then **Length[expression]** = **0**.

Example:

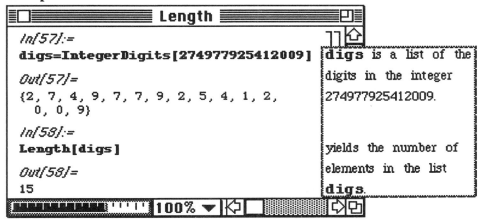

LerchPhi   571, 575, 817
                                    See Also: **Zeta, PolyLog**
   LerchPhi[z,s,a] represents the Lerch transcendent $\phi(z,s,a)$ which is a generalization of the zeta and polylogarithm functions. This function is given by

$$\phi(z,s,a) = \sum_{k=0}^{\infty} \frac{z^k}{(a+k)^s},$$ where terms with $a + k = 0$ are omitted. **LerchPhi** has the

option **DoublyInfinite**. Hence, the command

LerchPhi[z,s,a,DoublyInfinite - > True] yields $\displaystyle\sum_{k=-\infty}^{\infty} \frac{z^k}{(a+k)^s}.$

Example:

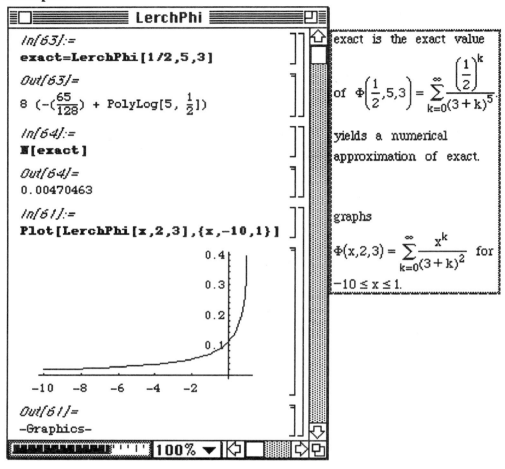

Less (**<**)   94, 817
See 169, 417   See Also: **Greater**, **Positive**

   Less represents the relation "less than". This command results in True or False when used with numbers. Hence, **a<b** yields a value of True if **a** is less than **b**. Also, a sequence of values may be tested with this function to determine if the sequence is strictly increasing. This is accomplished with **x1<x2<x3<...** .

Example:

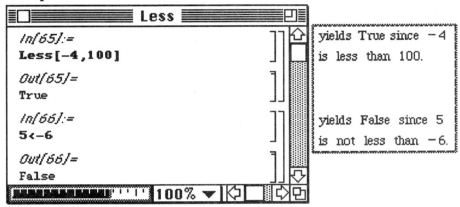

LessEqual (**<=**)   94, 817
See 169, 490   See Also:

   LessEqual represents the relation "less than or equal to". This command results in **True** or **False** when used with numbers. Hence, **a<=b** yields a value of **True** if **a** is less than or equal to **b**. Also, a sequence of values may be tested with this function to determine if the sequence is non-decreasing. This is accomplished with
x1<=x2<x3<=....

Example:

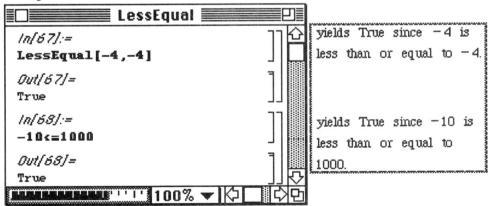

LetterQ   378, 817
          See Also: **DigitQ**, **UpperCaseQ**, **LowerCaseQ**

   LetterQ[string] determines if all of the characters in **string** are letters. If all are letters, then a value of **True** results. Otherwise, a value of **False** is given. By default, a **False** response is printed if **string** contains any spaces or punctuation marks. Only those characters listed with **$Letters** are considered letters by *Mathematica*.

Example:

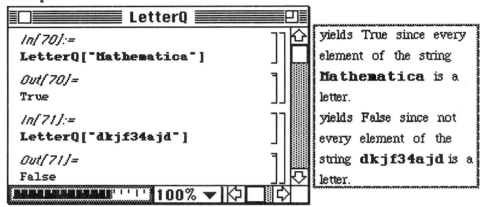

Level   199, 817
See 290   See Also: **Apply**, **Map**, **Scan**

   Level is used to operate on the levels of an expression. This can be done in several ways. **Level[expression,1]** lists all subexpressions of **expression** which are found on level **1** by performing a depth-first search on **expression**. Also, the command **Level[expression,1,func]** applies the function **func** to the list of subexpressions located on level **1**. The atomic portions of **expression** are listed with **Level[expression,{-1}]**.

Lighting   156, 161, 436, 455, 817
See 521, 569   See Also: **Shading**, **ColorFunction**,
                                        SurfaceColor

   Lighting is an option used with **Plot3D** to indicate if simulated illumination is to be used in displaying graphics. The setting **Lighting->True** causes illumination while **Lighting->False** does not. The colors to be used are specified with the **AmbientLight** option, and the position of the light source is indicated by using the **LightSources** option.

LightSources   455, 818
See 521   See Also: **AmbientLight**, **SurfaceColor**

   LightSources is an option used with such commands as **Plot3D** to indicate the position and the color of simulated illumination. This option is of the form **LightSources->{s1,s2,...}** where each source **si** has the form **{direction,color}**. The **direction** setting is in the form of a vector **{x,y,z}**. The x- and y-components correspond to the horizontal and vertical axes in the display while the z-axis is orthogonal to the plane formed by the x and y axes. The positive z-axis is in the front. The **color** setting is made in terms of **Hue**, **GrayLevel**, or **RGBColor**.

Limit   102, 646, 647, 818
See 208, 209, 759   See Also: **Series**, **Residue**

    Limit[expression,x->x0] determines the limit of **expression** as **x** approaches **x0**. An option used with **Limit** is that of **Direction**. **Direction->1** causes *Mathematica* to take the limit as **x** approaches **x0** from below, and **Direction->-1** forces the limit to be evaluated as **x** approaches **x0** from above. In some cases, the result of **Limit** is given in the form RealInterval[{a,b}] when **Limit** encounters an uncertain value which is located on the interval {a,b}. **Limit** leaves expressions which depend on an arbitrary function unevaluated. **Analytic** is an option which can be used with **Limit**.

Example:

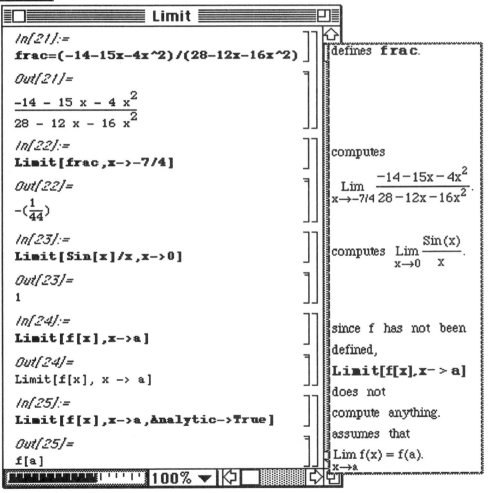

Line   400, 430, 818
See 512, 519, 527, 558, 563   See Also: **Polygon**, **PlotJoined**

   Line[{point1,point2,...}] represents the graphics primitive for a line in two or three dimensions which connects the points listed in **{point1,point2,...}**. Hence, the points can be entered as **{x,y}** or **{x,y,z}**. They can be scaled as well with **Scaled[{x,y}]** and **Scaled[{x,y,z}]**. Several options are available for displaying the line. **Thickness** or **AbsoluteThickness** affects the thickness of the line. **Dashing** or **AbsoluteDashing** controls the dashing of the line. Finally, **CMYKColor**, **GrayLevel**, **Hue**, and **RGBColor** monitor the coloring of the line.

LinearProgramming   707, 818
                        See Also: **ConstrainedMax**, **ConstrainedMin**
   LinearProgramming[c,m,b] determines the vector x which minimizes the value of c.x subject to the constraints given by m.x ≥ b and x ≥ 0. Results of this function are given in terms of rational numbers if c, m, and b are exact.

   Tolerance is an option of **LinearProgramming** for indicating the tolerance level to be used for internal calculations.

Example:

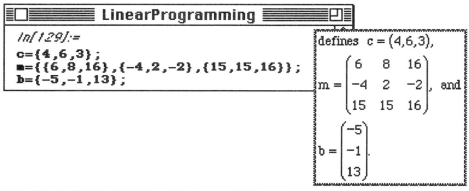

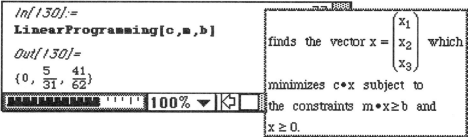

LinearSolve   660, 662, 819
                                   See Also: **Inverse, PseudoInverse, Solve,**
                                   NullSpace

LinearSolve[m,b] computes the solution to the linear system of equations defined in matrix form as **m.x==b**. **LinearSolve** is not restricted to square systems only. The matrix **m** can be rectangular. The options used with **Inverse** are also available for use with **LinearSolve**. The option **Modulus->p** takes the matrix equation to be modulus **p** while **ZeroTest->func** applies the function **func** to the elements of **m** to determine if they are zero.

Example:

In the following example, **m** is defined to be the matrix

$$\begin{bmatrix} 1 & -2 & 0 & -2 & 2 \\ -1 & 0 & 2 & -2 & 0 \\ 1 & -2 & 2 & 2 & -2 \\ 1 & -1 & -2 & -2 & 2 \\ 2 & 1 & -2 & -2 & 1 \end{bmatrix} \text{ and } \mathbf{b} \text{ is defined to be the vector } \begin{bmatrix} 1 \\ 0 \\ 1 \\ -1 \\ 0 \end{bmatrix}.$$

LinearSolve is used to solve the matrix equation **mx=b** for x.

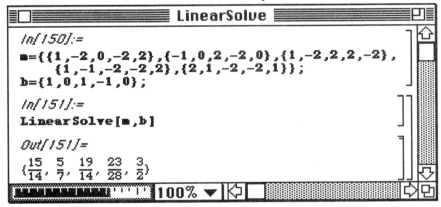

```
In[150]:=
m={{1,-2,0,-2,2},{-1,0,2,-2,0},{1,-2,2,2,-2},
    {1,-1,-2,-2,2},{2,1,-2,-2,1}};
b={1,0,1,-1,0};

In[151]:=
LinearSolve[m,b]

Out[151]=
{15/14, 5/7, 19/14, 23/28, 3/2}
```

LineBreak   517, 819
                                   See Also: **Continuation, StringBreak, Indent,**
                                   Format

LineBreak[n] represents the output given between the **n**th and **(n+1)**st lines of output which exceeds one line. This value is a blank line by default but can be changed with **Format**.

LineForm
                                   See Also: **Graphics**

LineForm[graphic] is a graphics directive for use with three-dimensional graphics functions. The purpose of **LineForm** is to indicate that lines are to be drawn with graphics directive **graphic** or a list of graphics directives given in **graphic**.

List   56, 118, 192, 819
See 148   See Also: **Array**, **Table**

  List, symbolized as **{elem1,elem2,...}**, represents a list of elements. Vectors and matrices are entered as lists with *Mathematica*. For example, {a,b} is a two-dimensional vector while {{a,b},{c,d}} represents a 2 × 2 matrix with row vectors {a,b} and {c,d}. Output is often represented in the form of a list as well, so the ability to extract the elements of a list is quite useful.

Example:

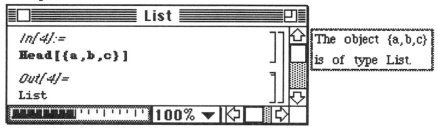

Listable   272, 275, 652, 727, 819
See 280   See Also: **Attributes**, **Thread**, **Map**

  Listable is an attribute of *Mathematica* symbols which indicates that the symbol is automatically "threaded" over any lists which appear as arguments of the symbol. This attribute is assigned to most built-in *Mathematica* functions. Note that all argument lists must have the same length.

Example:

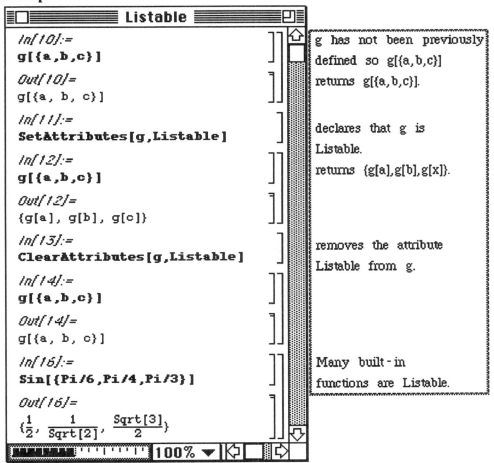

ListContourPlot   164, 395, 819

See 516   See Also: **ContourGraphics**, **ContourPlot**

ListContourPlot[list] creates a contour plot using the values for height given in the array **list**. The plot generated is a **ContourGraphics** object, so **ListContourPlot** has the same options as **ContourGraphics**.

Example:

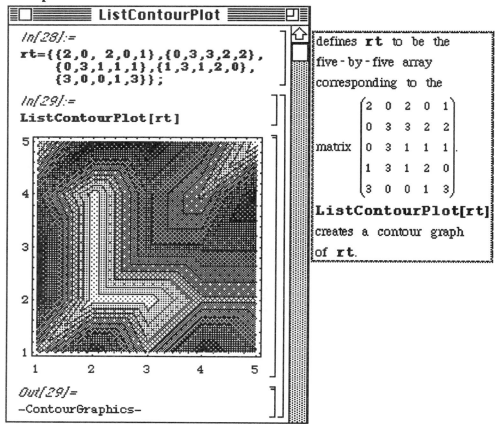

defines **rt** to be the five-by-five array corresponding to the

matrix $\begin{pmatrix} 2 & 0 & 2 & 0 & 1 \\ 0 & 3 & 3 & 2 & 2 \\ 0 & 3 & 1 & 1 & 1 \\ 1 & 3 & 1 & 2 & 0 \\ 3 & 0 & 0 & 1 & 3 \end{pmatrix}$.

ListContourPlot[rt] creates a contour graph of **rt**.

Shading between contours is suppressed if the option **ContourShading->False** is included.

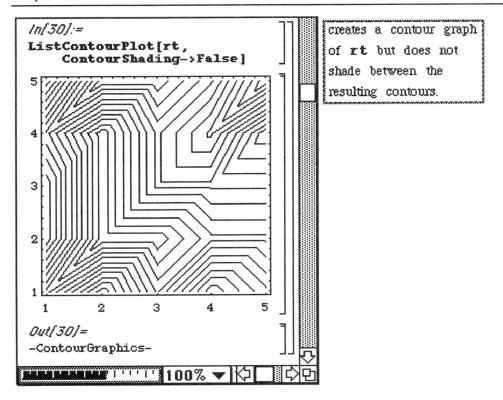

In[30]:=
ListContourPlot[rt,
      ContourShading->False]

creates a contour graph of **rt** but does not shade between the resulting contours.

Out[30]=
-ContourGraphics-

100% ▼

ListDensityPlot   164, 395, 819
See 516   See Also: **DensityGraphics**, **DensityPlot**

   ListDensityPlot[list] creates a density plot using the values for height given in the array **list**. The plot generated is a **DensityGraphics** object, so **ListDensityPlot** has the same options as **DensityGraphics**.

Example:

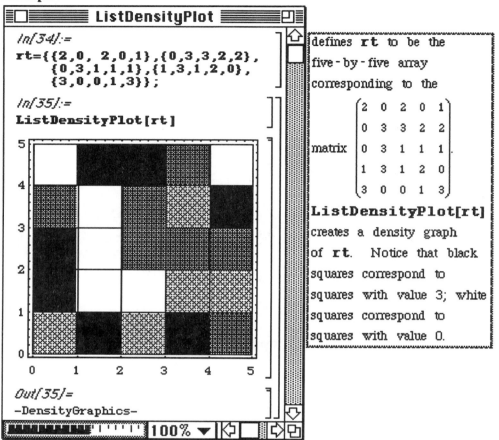

		ListDensityPlot		

In[34]:=
```
rt={{2,0, 2,0,1},{0,3,3,2,2},
    {0,3,1,1,1},{1,3,1,2,0},
    {3,0,0,1,3}};
```

In[35]:=
```
ListDensityPlot[rt]
```

defines **rt** to be the five-by-five array corresponding to the

$$\text{matrix} \begin{pmatrix} 2 & 0 & 2 & 0 & 1 \\ 0 & 3 & 3 & 2 & 2 \\ 0 & 3 & 1 & 1 & 1 \\ 1 & 3 & 1 & 2 & 0 \\ 3 & 0 & 0 & 1 & 3 \end{pmatrix}.$$

ListDensityPlot[rt] creates a density graph of **rt**. Notice that black squares correspond to squares with value 3; white squares correspond to squares with value 0.

Out[35]=
-DensityGraphics-

100%

ListPlay   177, 474, 820
                                    See Also: **Play**, **SampledSoundList**, **Show**
  ListPlay[{a1,a2,...}] plays a sound using the sequence of amplitude levels given in **{a1,a2,...}**. The output is a **Sound** object. The options which are available include **DisplayFunction**, **Epilog**, **PlayRange**, **Prolog**, **SampleDepth**, and **SampleRate**. **ListPlay** can generate a sound in stereo with **ListPlay[{list1,list2}]** and a sound on many channels with **ListPlay[{list1,list2,list3,...}]**. In both cases, silence is inserted if the lists have different lengths.

ListPlot   8, 164, 395, 820
See 139, 249, 425, 517,   See Also: **Plot**, **Fit**, **Prolog**
543-550, 666, 671, 672,
673, 766, 767

   ListPlot is used to plot a list of points. This can be accomplished in one of two ways. **ListPlot[{f1,f2,...}]** plots the list of points {1, **f1**}, {2, **f2**}, ... On the other hand, the points {x,y} in two dimensions to be plotted can be entered within the command using **ListPlot[{x1,y1},{x2,y2},...]**. Since the plot which results is a **Graphics** object, **ListPlot** has the same available options as **Graphics** along with the additional options **PlotJoined** and **PlotStyle**.

Example:

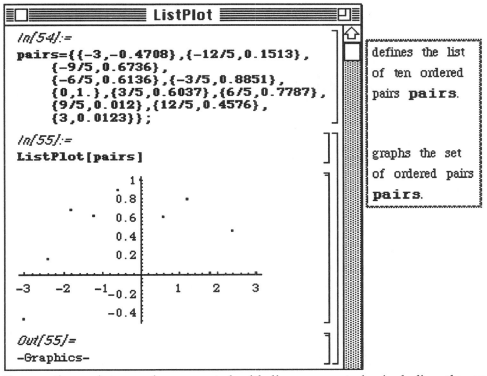

Consecutive points can be connected with line segments by including the option **PlotJoined->True**.

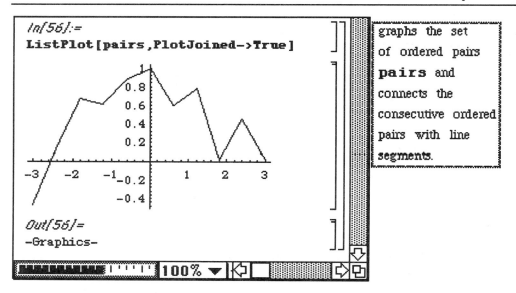

In[56]:=
ListPlot[pairs,PlotJoined->True]

graphs the set of ordered pairs **pairs** and connects the consecutive ordered pairs with line segments.

Out[56]=
-Graphics-

ListPlot3D   164, 395, 447, 452, 820
See 522, 542, 567, 569   See Also: **Plot3D**

ListPlot3D[{{z11,z12,...},{z21,z22,...},...}] creates a plot in three dimensions of the array **{{z11,z12,...},{z21,z22,...},...}** of real-valued heights **zxy**. Note that the x- and y-coordinates correspond to the values x = 1, 2, ... and y = 1, 2, ... These plots can be produced with different shades by using the command

ListPlot3D[{{z11,z12,...},{z21,z22,...},...},shades] where **shades** has the dimensions $(m-1) \times (n-1)$ if

{{z11,z12,...},{z21,z22,...},...} is m × n. The components of **shades** must be **GrayLevel**, **Hue**, **RGBColor**, or **SurfaceColor**.

Example:

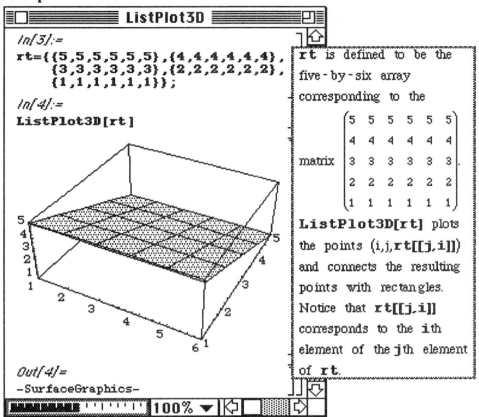

```
                    ListPlot3D
In[3]:=
rt={{5,5,5,5,5,5},{4,4,4,4,4,4},
    {3,3,3,3,3,3},{2,2,2,2,2,2},
    {1,1,1,1,1,1}};
In[4]:=
ListPlot3D[rt]
```

`rt` is defined to be the five-by-six array corresponding to the

matrix
$$\begin{pmatrix} 5 & 5 & 5 & 5 & 5 & 5 \\ 4 & 4 & 4 & 4 & 4 & 4 \\ 3 & 3 & 3 & 3 & 3 & 3 \\ 2 & 2 & 2 & 2 & 2 & 2 \\ 1 & 1 & 1 & 1 & 1 & 1 \end{pmatrix}.$$

`ListPlot3D[rt]` plots the points $(i,j,\texttt{rt[[j,i]]})$ and connects the resulting points with rectangles. Notice that `rt[[j,i]]` corresponds to the ith element of the jth element of `rt`.

```
Out[4]=
-SurfaceGraphics-
100%
```

ListQ

See Also: **List**

ListQ[expression] is used to determine if **expression** is a list by yielding a value of **True** if **expression** is a list and **False** otherwise.

Literal   283, 731, 732, 820
See 296   See Also: **Hold**

Literal is used to prevent evaluation of expressions. For example, **Literal[pattern]** is equivalent to **pattern** in pattern-matching, but **pattern** is kept in an unevaluated form. One application of **Literal** is in the indication of certain patterns which can pertain to unevaluated expressions. **Literal** has the attribute **HoldAll**.

Locked   272, 273, 728, 821
See Also: **Protected, ReadProtected**

Locked is an attribute of *Mathematica* symbols such that other attributes of that symbol cannot be altered once **Locked** is assigned.

Log   49, 562, 821
                            See Also: **Exp, Power**
   Log[z] represents the natural logarithm (base e) of **z** while **Log[b,z]** yields the
logarithm of **z** to base **b**. Exact values result from these functions whenever possible.

Example:

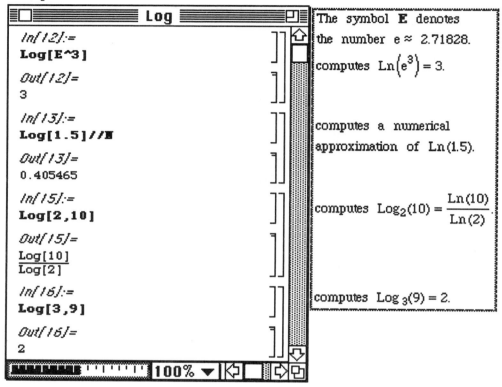

LogGamma   572, 821
                            See Also: **Log**
   LogGamma[z] represents the logarithm of the gamma function, log Γ(z).
LogGamma[z] differs from **Log[Gamma[z]]** in that **LogGamma** is analytic over the
complex plane except for the branch cut along the negative real axis. This function is
useful in number theory.
Example:
In the following example, the imaginary part of the logarithm of the gamma function
logΓ(x+iy) is graphed for $-5 < x < 2$ and $-3 < y < 3$ using twenty-five plotpoints (the
default is fifteen). The final graphics object is not shaded. Notice the branch cut along
the negative real axis in the resulting graph. In fact, *Mathematica* prints several
messages warning that log Γ(x+iy) does not make sense along the negative real axis.

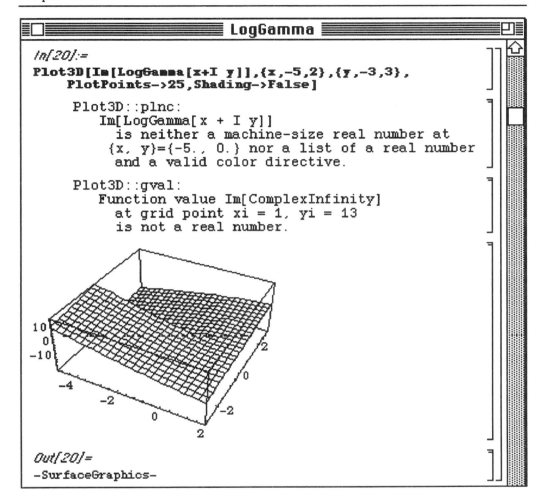

```
≣□▒▒▒▒▒▒▒▒▒▒▒▒ LogGamma ▒▒▒▒▒▒▒▒▒▒▒▒ □≣
In[20]:=
Plot3D[Im[LogGamma[x+I y]],{x,-5,2},{y,-3,3},
     PlotPoints->25,Shading->False]
     Plot3D::plnc:
          Im[LogGamma[x + I y]]
               is neither a machine-size real number at
               {x, y}={-5., 0.} nor a list of a real number
               and a valid color directive.

     Plot3D::gval:
          Function value Im[ComplexInfinity]
               at grid point xi = 1, yi = 13
               is not a real number.
```

Out[20]=
-SurfaceGraphics-

LogicalExpand   94, 95, 98, 606, 612, 645, 821
                         See Also: **Expand**, **SolveAlways**

   LogicalExpand[expression] expands out expressions in **expression** which involve the   logical connectives **&&** and **||** by applying appropriate distributive properties.
Example:

In the following example, $f(x) = \dfrac{a_0 + a_1 x}{b_0 + x}$.   The **Series** command is used to compute the first two terms of the power series for $f(x)$ about $x = 0$; the result is named **serone**.   The term $O[x]^3$ stands for the omitted higher – order terms in the series.

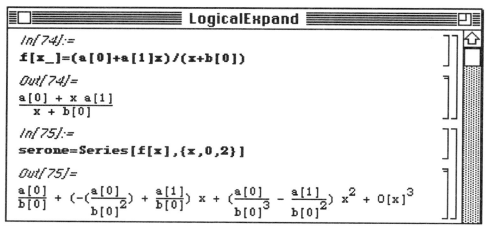

Next, the **Series** command is used to compute the first two terms of

the power series for $\dfrac{1}{1-\mathrm{Sin}(x)}$ about $x = 0$; the result is named **sertwo**.

Since equal power series must have equal coefficients, **LogicalExpand** is used to compute the system of equations that must be satisfied in order that **serone** and **sertwo** are the same as power series. The resulting system of equations is named **eqs**.

In[76]:=
```
sertwo=Series[1/(1-Sin[x]),{x,0,2}]
```
Out[76]=

$$1 + x + x^2 + O[x]^3$$

In[77]:=
```
eqs=LogicalExpand[serone==sertwo]
```
Out[77]=

$$-1 + \frac{a[0]}{b[0]^3} - \frac{a[1]}{b[0]^2} == 0 \ \&\& \ -1 + \frac{a[0]}{b[0]} == 0 \ \&\&$$

$$-1 - \frac{a[0]}{b[0]^2} + \frac{a[1]}{b[0]} == 0$$

The **Solve** command is used to solve for the unknowns in the system of equations **eqs**. The resulting values of a_1, a_0, and b_0 are replaced in the definition of f.

```
In[78]:=
sols=Solve[eqs]
Out[78]=
{{a[1] -> 0, a[0] -> -1, b[0] -> -1}}
In[79]:=
f[x] /. sols[[1]]
Out[79]=
    1
-(-------)
  -1 + x
```

The following compares the graphs of $f(x)$ (in black) and $\dfrac{1}{1-\sin(x)}$ (in gray). Creating these graphs was accomplished with the **Plot** and **GraphicsArray** commands.

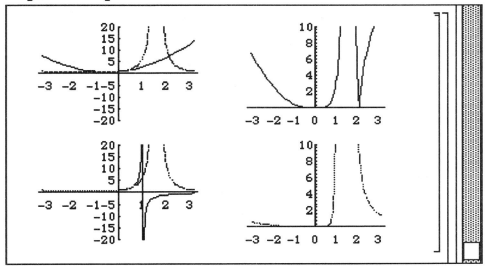

Finally, the comparison is enlarged to illustrate that the rational approximation $f(x)$ is a decent approximation of $\dfrac{1}{1-\sin(x)}$ for some values of x.

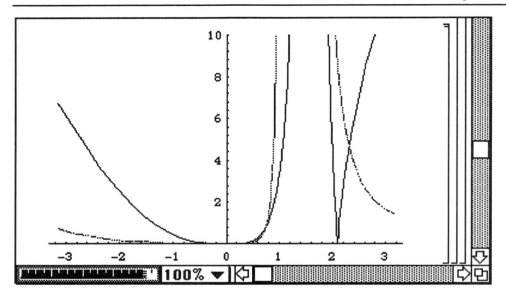

LogIntegral   571, 575, 634, 821
                        See Also: **ExpIntegralE**
   LogIntegral[z] represents the logarithmic integral function

$$\text{li}(z) = \int_0^z \frac{dt}{\log t}, \; z > 1$$ In this case, the principal value of the integral is taken.

This function is important in number theory in the study of the distribution of

primes. Sometimes it is defined as $\int_2^z \dfrac{dt}{\log t}$ so that no principal value is taken.

This definition of li(z) differs from the previous one by a value of li(2).

Example:

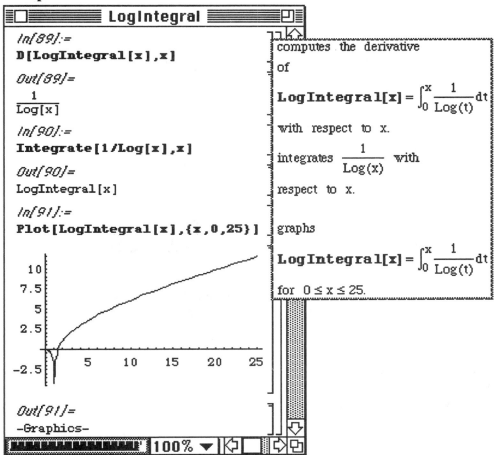

LogIntegral

In[89]:=
D[LogIntegral[x],x]

Out[89]=
$\dfrac{1}{\text{Log}[x]}$

In[90]:=
Integrate[1/Log[x],x]

Out[90]=
LogIntegral[x]

In[91]:=
Plot[LogIntegral[x],{x,0,25}]

Out[91]=
-Graphics-

computes the derivative of

$$\text{LogIntegral[x]} = \int_0^x \frac{1}{\text{Log}(t)} dt$$

with respect to x.

integrates $\dfrac{1}{\text{Log}(x)}$ with respect to x.

graphs

$$\text{LogIntegral[x]} = \int_0^x \frac{1}{\text{Log}(t)} dt$$

for $0 \le x \le 25$.

LowerCaseQ   378, 821
                                     See Also: **UpperCaseQ**, **LetterQ**, **ToLowerCase**,
                                     ToCharacterCode

LowerCaseQ[string] tests **string** to determine if all of the characters are lower-case letters. A value of **True** results if all characters are lower-case while **False** is given otherwise. The lower-case letters are given in the list **$Letters** where the first entry in each sublist of **$Letters** represents the lower-case character.

M

MachineID   480

> See Also: **Encode**, **$MachineID**

MachineID is an option used with **Encode** to indicate the value of **$MachineID** required to read an encoded file. If no specification is made, then any value of **$MachineID** may access the file.

MachineName

> See Also: **Encode**, **$MachineName**

MachineName is an option used with **Encode** to indicate the value of **$MachineName** required to read an encoded file. If no specification is made, then any value of **$MachineName** may access the file.

MachineNumberQ   540, 821

> See Also: **Precision**, **NumberQ**

MachineNumberQ[val] tests **val** to determine if **val** is a machine-precision number. A value of **True** results if **val** passes the test. **False** results otherwise. Note that machine-precision numbers contain a fixed number of digits. The precision of these numbers remains the same throughout all calculations.

Example:

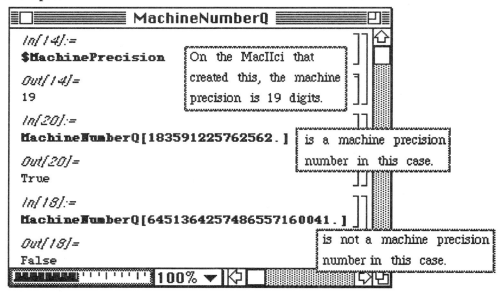

MainSolve   822
                                     See Also: **Solve**, **Eliminate**, **Reduce**,
                                     SolveAlways

  MainSolve[equations] is a function used by **Solve** and **Eliminate** to
transform systems of equations. Each equation listed in **equations** must be of the
from **lhs==rhs** and can be combined with the logical connectives **&&** and **||**. A value
of **False** results from **MainSolve** if no solution exists while **True** is given if all
values of the variables are solutions. This command can be stated as
MainSolve[equations,varsolve,vareliminate,otherorder] to solve
equations for the variables listed in **varsolve** by eliminating those variables listed
in **vareliminate**. The list **otherorder** is included to indicate the order in which
other variables are to be eliminated. **MainSolve** has the options **Mode** and **Method**.
These options indicate the type of solution sought and the intended method of solution,
respectively. **Mode->Rational** is the default setting of the **Mode** option. It indicates
that rational numbers can be introduced. **Mode->Integer** forces the solution to
contain only integers by preventing the introduction of rational numbers.
Mode->Modular implies that equality is modulo an integer. Finally,
Mode->Generic allows both rational numbers and denominators involving
parameters to be introduced. The setting for **Method** are the integers **1**, **2**, and **3**.
Method->1 causes one pass through the elimination variables only, **Method->2**
allows for the possibility of an expression being zero by forming a disjunction of two of
the equations, and **Method->3** determines the roots of the resulting equations. The
algorithm used by **MainSolve** involves the calculation of a Groebner basis for
equations.

Example:

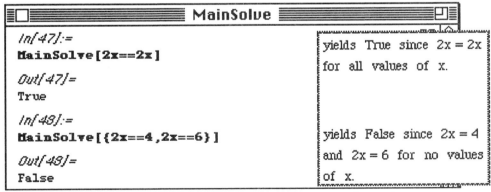

In the following example, **MainSolve** reduces the system of equations

$$\begin{cases} 5x + 2y - z = 4 \\ -4x + 3y = 0 \\ -5x + 4y - 4z = 2 \end{cases}.$$

```
In[49]:=
MainSolve[{5x+2y-z==4,-4x+3y==0,-5x+4y-4z==2}]

Out[49]=
13 x == 6 && 13 y == 8 && 13 z == -6
```

In fact, **MainSolve** will find the solutions of the system

$$\begin{cases} 5x + 2y - z = 4 \\ -4x + 3y = 0 \\ -5x + 4y - 4z = 2 \end{cases} \quad \text{when the option } \texttt{Method->3} \text{ is included.}$$

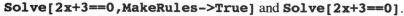

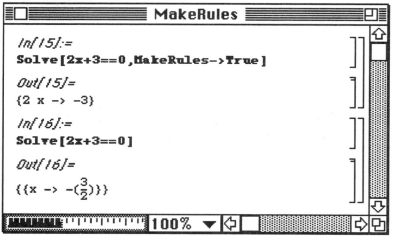

MakeRules

See Also: **Solve**, **FindRoot**

MakeRules is an option used with such functions as **Solve** to indicate whether or not the result is to be given in the form of an **AlgebraicRulesData** object.

Example:

The default value of **MakeRules** in the **Solve** command is False. The following example illustrates the different results obtained with the commands **Solve[2x+3==0,MakeRules->True]** and **Solve[2x+3==0]**.

MantissaExponent   538, 822

See Also: **Log**, **RealDigits**

MantissaExponent[x] separates the mantissa and the exponent of the number **x** and gives the output in the form of the list {mantissa,exponent}.

Example:

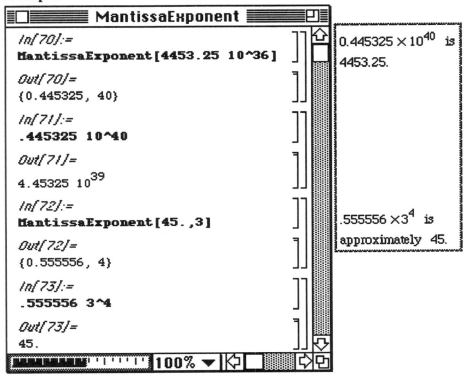

Map (/@)   204, 725, 822
See 165, 219, 353, 354,   See Also: **Apply**, **Scan**, **Level**, **Operate**,
407, 528, 566, 703   **MapThread**, **Listable**

Map is used with functions and expressions to apply a function to particular elements of an expression. This can be done with **Map[f,expression]** to apply the function **f** to each element on the first level of **expression** or with **Map[f,expression,lev]** to apply the function **f** to each element on the level **lev** of **expression**. Note that the command **Map[f,expression]** can be entered as **f/@expression**.

Example:

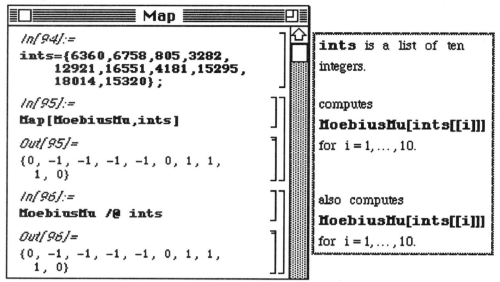

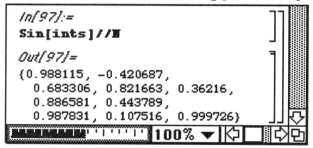

Since the built-in function **Sin** is **Listable**, **Sin[ints]//N** produces the same result as would be obtained with **Map[Sin,ints]//N**.

```
In[97]:=
Sin[ints]//N

Out[97]=
{0.988115, -0.420687,
  0.683306, 0.821663, 0.36216,
  0.886581, 0.443789,
  0.987831, 0.107516, 0.999726}
```

In the following example, h({x,y})=x^2+y^2 is defined to be a function of ordered-pairs and the list of ordered pairs **ops** is defined. **Map[h,ops]** and **h /@ ops** both compute the value of **h** for each ordered pair in **ops**.

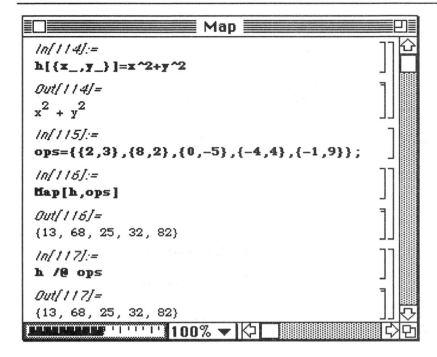

```
================ Map ================
In[114]:=
h[{x_,y_}]=x^2+y^2

Out[114]=
 2    2
x  + y

In[115]:=
ops={{2,3},{8,2},{0,-5},{-4,4},{-1,9}};

In[116]:=
Map[h,ops]

Out[116]=
{13, 68, 25, 32, 82}

In[117]:=
h /@ ops

Out[117]=
{13, 68, 25, 32, 82}
```

MapAll (//@)   204, 214, 822
                    See Also: **ExpandAll**, **ReplaceAll**
   MapAll[f,expression] applies the function **f** to all parts of **expression**.
This command can be entered as **f//@expression** as well.

MapAt   205, 823
                    See Also: **ReplacePart**, **Delete**, **FlattenAt**
   MapAt is used to apply a function to a particular part or to several parts of an
expression. **MapAt[f,expression,n]** applies **f** to the portion of **expression**
located at the **n**th position. Note that if **n** is a negative integer, then the position is
counted from the end of **expression**. **MapAt[f,expression,{i,j,...}]**
applies **f** to the component at position **{i,j,...}**. The function can be applied to
several parts of **expression** with
MapAt[f,expression,{{i1,j1,...},{i2,j2,...},...}]. In this case, **f**
is applied to the components at positions **{i1,j1,...}**, **{i2,j2,...}**,... . If a
particular position of **expression** appears more than once in the list of positions,
then *Mathematica* reapplies **f** to that position each time it is listed.
Example:
In the following example, k({x,y})={y,x} and **ops** is defined to be a list of ordered
pairs. **MapAt[k,ops,3]** applies k to the third element of **ops**;
MapAt[k,ops{{2},{3},{4}}] applies k to the second, third, and fourth elements
of **ops**.

```
┌─────────────────────────────────────────────────────┐
│ ▤□▤▤▤▤▤▤▤▤▤▤▤▤▤▤═ MapAt ═▤▤▤▤▤▤▤▤▤▤▤▤▤▤▤□▤ │
├─────────────────────────────────────────────────────┤
│ In[148]:=                                           ⇧ │
│ k[{x_,y_}]={y,x}                                      │
│ Out[148]=                                             │
│ {y, x}                                                │
│ In[149]:=                                             │
│ ops={{2, 3},{8, 2},{0, -5},{-4, 4},{-1, 9}};          │
│ In[150]:=                                             │
│ MapAt[k,ops,3]                                        │
│ Out[150]=                                             │
│ {{2, 3}, {8, 2}, {-5, 0}, {-4, 4}, {-1, 9}}           │
│ In[151]:=                                             │
│ MapAt[k,ops,{{2},{3},{4}}]                            │
│ Out[151]=                                             │
│ {{2, 3}, {2, 8}, {-5, 0}, {4, -4}, {-1, 9}}         ⇩ │
├─────────────────────────────────────────────────────┤
│ ▤▤▤▤▤▤▤ ʼIʼIʼIʼIʼIʼ 100% ▼ ◁□▤▤▤▤▤▤▤▤▤▤▤▤ ◁▷▫ │
└─────────────────────────────────────────────────────┘
```

MapIndexed   206, 725, 823
                                   See Also: **MapAt**

   MapIndexed is similar to **Map** in that it is used to apply a function to an expression.
However, the position to which the function is applied is listed as a second argument of
the function. **MapIndexed[f,expression]** applies **f** to all parts of **expression**
and includes the part specification of each component as a second argument in each
component of the result. **MapIndexed[f,expression,lev]** applies **f** to the parts
of **expression** at level **lev** and places the index of these components as a second
argument in the resulting expression.

MapThread   206, 823
                                   See Also: **Map**, **Thread**, **Inner**

   MapThread is used to apply a function to several expressions at one time.
MapThread[f,{expression1,expression2,...}] applies **f** to
corresponding parts of each expression listed in
{expression1,expression2,...} while
MapThread[f,{expression1,expression2,...},lev] applies **f** to the
parts of the expressions at level **lev**.
Example:
In the following example, f(a,b,c)=ab-c^2. **MapThread** is used to compute the value of
f for each element of the three elements in the list {{-9,2,9},{0,3,-2},{4,9,6}}.

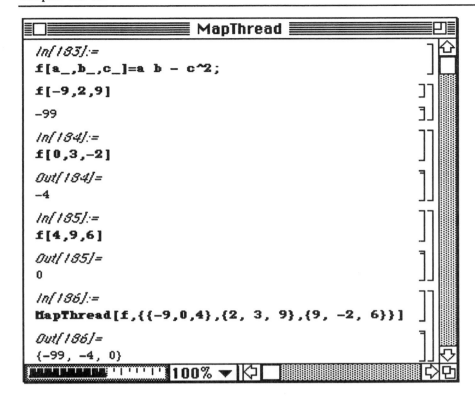

MatchBox

   MatchBox is an internal symbol used by *Mathematica*.

MatchLocalNamesQ

   MatchLocalNamesQ is an internal symbol.

MatchLocalNames   304, 823
                                   See Also: **Trace**

   MatchLocalNames is an option used with **Trace** to prevent the matching of local variables. The default setting is **MatchLocalNames->True** which indicates that a variable x should match local variables of the form x$nnn. If **MatchLocalNames->False** is used, then no replacements for local variable names are allowed.

MatchQ   228, 288, 823
                                   See Also: **StringMatchQ**

   MatchQ[expression,patt] determines if **expression** matches the form defined by **patt**. If a match is confirmed, then True results. Otherwise, False is given.

Example:

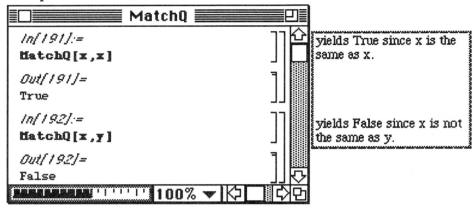

MatrixExp   659, 824

See Also: **MatrixPower**, **Dot**

MatrixExp[a] yields the matrix exponential of the square matrix **a** which

is given by $e^{\mathbf{a}\,t} = I + \mathbf{a}\,t + \dfrac{(\mathbf{a}\,t)^2}{2!} + \dfrac{(\mathbf{a}\,t)^3}{3!} + \cdots$.

Example:

In the following example, **matrix** is defined to be the two-by-two matrix

$\begin{pmatrix} -2 & -2 \\ 0 & -2 \end{pmatrix}$. **em = MatrixExp[matrix]** computes the matrix

$e^{\mathbf{matrix}} = \begin{pmatrix} 1/e^2 & -2/e^2 \\ 0 & 1/e^2 \end{pmatrix}$ and names it **em**.

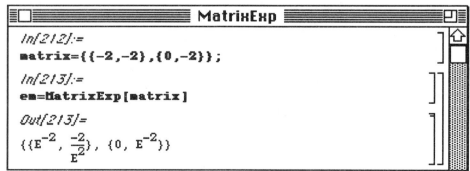

In many situations, numerical results are satisfactory. In the following example,

matrix is defined to be the numerical matrix $\begin{pmatrix} 0. & -3. & 1. \\ -2. & -2. & -1. \\ 1. & -3. & 2. \end{pmatrix}$.

MatrixExp[matrix] yields an approximation of $e^{\mathbf{matrix}}$.

```
In[214]:=
matrix={{0.,-3.,1.},{-2.,-2.,-1.},{1.,-3.,2.}}

Out[214]=
{{0., -3., 1.}, {-2., -2., -1.}, {1., -3., 2.}}

In[215]:=
MatrixExp[matrix]

Out[215]=
{{10.6089, -12.3416, 12.6317},
 {-6.80807, 8.05969, -8.37275},
 {16.8906, -20.8594, 23.0955}}
```

100% ▼

MatrixForm   122, 354, 824
See 242, 245, 287, 408,   See Also: **TableForm, ColumnForm,**
409, 427, 477, 604, 631-   **GraphicsArray**
636

   MatrixForm[{{a11,a12,...},{a21,a22,...},...}] is used to display
the rectangular array given in the usual form of a matrix where each element
{aj1,aj2,...} becomes a row. **MatrixForm** only affects the printing of the
array. It does not alter any calculations. The options used with **TableForm** are used
with **MatrixForm** as well.

Example:

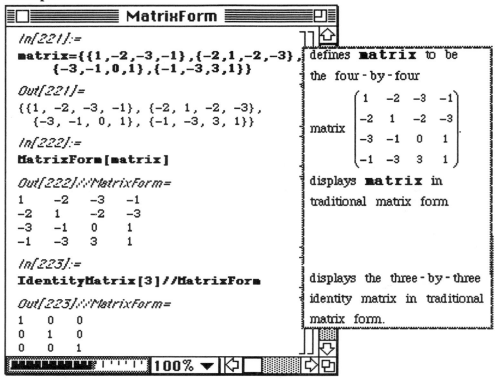

MatrixPower   659, 824

                    See Also: **MatrixExp, MatrixForm, Dot**

MatrixPower[a,n] takes the product of the square matrix **a** with itself **n** times. Note that if **n** is negative, then *Mathematica* computes the powers of the inverse of **a**.

Example:

In the following example, **matrix** is defined to be the matrix

$$\begin{pmatrix} -2 & -1 & -1 \\ 1 & -2 & 1 \\ -2 & -1 & -1 \end{pmatrix}.$$ **MatrixPower[matrix,4]** computes

$$\begin{pmatrix} -2 & -1 & -1 \\ 1 & -2 & 1 \\ -2 & -1 & -1 \end{pmatrix}^4 = \begin{pmatrix} 5 & 45 & -6 \\ -62 & -46 & -28 \\ 5 & 45 & -6 \end{pmatrix}.$$

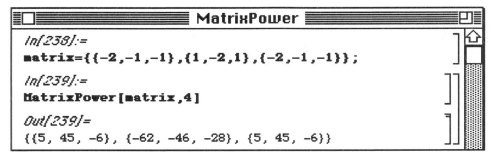

The same result is obtained using the . operator:

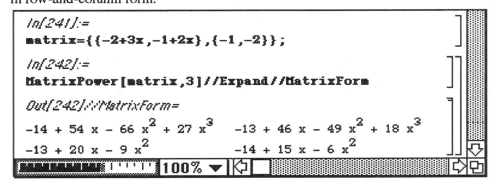

Matrices may contain symbols. The following example defines **matrix** to be the

matrix $\begin{pmatrix} -2+3x & -1+2x \\ -1 & -2 \end{pmatrix}$.

MatrixPower[matrix,3]//Expand//MatrixForm

computes and simplifies $\begin{pmatrix} -2+3x & -1+2x \\ -1 & -2 \end{pmatrix}^3$ and then displays the result

in row-and-column form.

```
In[241]:=
matrix={{-2+3x,-1+2x},{-1,-2}};
In[242]:=
MatrixPower[matrix,3]//Expand//MatrixForm
Out[242]//MatrixForm=
-14 + 54 x - 66 x  + 27 x     -13 + 46 x - 49 x  + 18 x
                 2        3                     2        3
-13 + 20 x - 9 x              -14 + 15 x - 6 x
                2                              2
```

MatrixQ   227, 652, 824

See Also: **ListQ**, **VectorQ**, **TensorRank**

MatrixQ is used to answer certain questions concerning matrices.

MatrixQ[expression] yields True if **expression** is determined to be a matrix, a list of lists having the same length which contain no elements that are lists themselves. **MatrixQ[expression,condition]** applies **condition** to each of the elements of **expression**. If **condition** is True for each of these elements, then **MatrixQ[expression,condition]** also yields True. A value of False is given otherwise. A possible choice for **condition** is **NumberQ** which is used to determine if the expression is a numerical matrix.

Example:

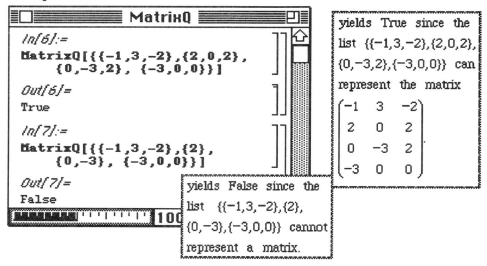

Max   49, 550, 824
See 650   See Also: **FindMinimum**, **Min**, **Order**, **Sort**

Max is used to find the largest numerical value in a list of numbers.
Max[a1,a2,...] gives the largest numerical value of the list {**a1**, **a2**, ...} while
Max[{a1,a2,...},{b1,b2,...},...}] finds the largest value from all of the
lists given. A definite value results in those cases in which all list elements are real
numbers.

Example:

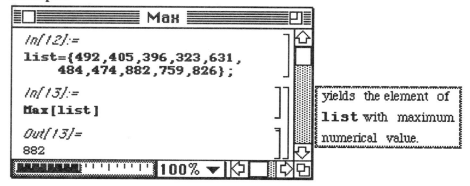

MaxBend   143, 824
See 517, 518   See Also: **Plot**

MaxBend is an option used with **Plot** to indicate the maximum angle allowed
between successive line segments of a curve. *Mathematica* eliminates larger angles by
using a larger number of plot points. However, subdivisions cannot exceed the value of
the **PlotDivision** option. Note that a smaller setting of **MaxBend** causes a
smoother curve to be displayed. **MaxBend** cannot be used with **Show**.

MaxIterations   695
                            See Also: **FindRoot**

    MaxIterations is option used with iterative functions such as **FindRoot** to indicate the maximum number of iterations allowed. For example, with **FindRoot**, **MaxIterations** specifies the maximum number of steps to be taken while seeking a root. If the root is not found within the allotted number of steps, then the most recent value obtained is given as output. This value can then be used as a new starting value.

MaxMemoryUse   526, 743, 824
                            See Also: **MemoryInUse**, **ByteCount**

    MaxMemoryUse[] gives the maximum number of bytes of memory used by *Mathematica* during the current session.

Example:

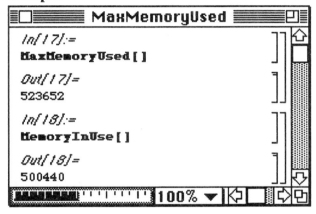

MaxRecursion   688, 830
                            See Also: **NIntegrate**

    MaxRecursion is an option used with recursive functions such as **NIntegrate** to indicate the maximum depth allowed in the procedure before the calculation is ceased even if convergence is not attained. With **NIntegrate**, **MaxRecursion** limits the sample points that *Mathematica* is able to use in the procedure. Hence, increasing the value of **MaxRecursion** slows down the calculation. The default value of **MaxRecursion** with **NIntegrate** is 6.

MaxSteps   700, 702, 829
                            See Also: **NDSolve**

    MaxSteps is an **NDSolve** option which indicates the maximum number of steps in the independent variable to take while seeking a solution. This option eliminates the problem of singularities when applying **NDSolve**. Since **NDSolve** reduces step size until the solution is found, the algorithm could possibly never terminate in the presence of a singularity if a maximum number of steps were not defined with **MaxSteps**. The default setting is **MaxSteps->500**.

MemberQ   127, 228, 825
See Also: **FreeQ**, **Count**, **Cases**

   MemberQ is useful in determining if any elements of a list match a certain pattern.
MemberQ[list,patt] returns **True** if any elements of **list** match the form of
patt. Also, **MemberQ[list,patt,lev]** gives **True** if any elements of **list** at
level **lev** match the form of **patt**. In both cases, **False** is given otherwise.

Example:

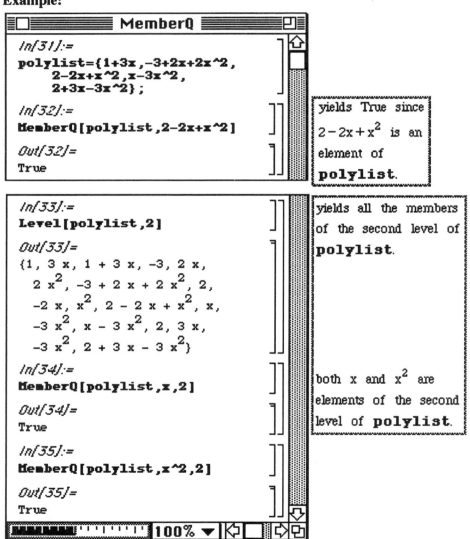

In[31]:=
polylist={1+3x,-3+2x+2x^2,
    2-2x+x^2,x-3x^2,
    2+3x-3x^2};

In[32]:=
MemberQ[polylist,2-2x+x^2]

Out[32]=
True

yields True since $2-2x+x^2$ is an element of **polylist**.

In[33]:=
Level[polylist,2]

Out[33]=
{1, 3 x, 1 + 3 x, -3, 2 x,
  2 x^2, -3 + 2 x + 2 x^2, 2,
  -2 x, x^2, 2 - 2 x + x^2, x,
  -3 x^2, x - 3 x^2, 2, 3 x,
  -3 x^2, 2 + 3 x - 3 x^2}

In[34]:=
MemberQ[polylist,x,2]

Out[34]=
True

In[35]:=
MemberQ[polylist,x^2,2]

Out[35]=
True

yields all the members of the second level of **polylist**.

both x and x^2 are elements of the second level of **polylist**.

MemoryCostrained   527, 825
                          See Also: **TimeConstained, MaxMemoryUsed**,
                          $RecursionLimit

MemoryCostrained allows for memory-constrained calculations.
MemoryConstrained[expression,b] attempts to evaluate **expression** using only **b** bytes of memory. If more bytes are needed, then the calculation is aborted.
MemoryConstrained[expression,b,failure] works similarly except that **failure** is returned if the **b**-byte memory limit is exceeded. **MemoryConstrained** returns **$Aborted** if no failure message is supplied with **failure**. The aborts generated are overruled by **AbortProtect**. **MemoryConstrained** has the attribute **HoldFirst**.
Example:
In the following example, **MemoryConstrained** is used to attempt to solve the equation $5+5x+2x^2=0$ for x using only 2100 bytes of memory. Since more memory is needed, the **Solve** command is aborted. In the second case, **MemoryConstrained** is used to attempt to solve the equation $5+5x+2x^2=0$ for x using only 2200 bytes of memory. In this case, 2200 bytes is sufficient and the values of x that satisfy the equation $5+5x+2x^2=0$ are returned.

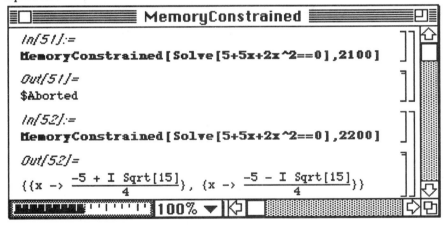

MemoryInUse   526, 743, 825
                          See Also: **MaxMemoryUsed, ByteCount, Dump,**
                          Save

MemoryInUse[] indicates the number of bytes of memory being used in the current *Mathematica* session.
Example:
The following example indicates the number of bytes of memory being used during the *Mathematica* session in which the command was entered.

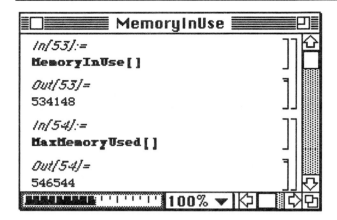

Mesh   154, 156, 425, 449, 825
See 411, 516, 522, 524,   See Also: **FaceGrids, Boxed**
540, 541, 569, 576, 582
   Mesh is a **SurfaceGraphics** and **DensityGraphics** option which indicates
whether a mesh is drawn on the surface. The default value is **True**, so *Mathematica*
automatically draws a rectangular mesh on the surface unless otherwise instructed with
Mesh->False which eliminates the mesh.

MeshRange   449, 825
See 522, 524   See Also: **PlotRange, PlotPoints**
   MeshRange is an option used with **ListPlot3D**, **ListContourPlot**,
ListDensityPlot, and **SurfaceGraphics** to indicate the x- and y-coordinates to
be used for the domain in these three-dimensional plots. The x and y intervals are
specified with the setting **MeshRange->{{x1,x2},{y1,y2}}** while the x and y
values are taken to be the indices from the array of z values with
MeshRange->Automatic. The tick marks placed on the threee-dimensional
surfaces produced by the functions listed above are determined from **MeshRange**.

MeshStyle   411, 425, 449, 825
See 516, 523, 524, 569,   See Also: **Mesh, AxesStyle, Prolog, Epilog,**
583   **DisplayFunction**
   MeshStyle is an option used with **Plot3D**, **ContourPlot**, **DensityPlot**, and
other functions to indicate the manner in which mesh lines are to be displayed. The
setting for **MeshStyle** can include **Dashing**, **Thickness**, **GrayLevel**,
RGBColor, and **Hue**.

Message   390, 486, 826
                                     See Also: **Print**, **Write**, **On**, **Off**, **Check**,
                                     MessageList

Message is used to print messages. **Message[s::tag]** prints the message
s::tag unless it has been turned off. Also,
Message[s::tag,expression1,expression2,...] prints the message with
StringForm[[s::tag,expression1,expression2,...]. If *Mathematica*
cannot find the indicated message, then it searches for a message with the appropriate
tag with the **General** symbol in the place of **s**. A list of all error messages associated
with built-in *Mathematica* objects can be found in the <u>Technical Report:</u> *Mathematica*
<u>Warning Messages by David Withoff</u> published by Wolfram Research, Inc.

MessageList   389, 522, 743, 826, 900
                                     See Also: **$MessageList**

MessageList[n] represents the list of messages generated during the processing
of the **n**th line of input during the current *Mathematica* session. Note that only
messages given as output are considered part of this list. The messages in the list are
each placed within a **HoldForm** command.
Example:
In the following example, a command is entered which results in several error
messages. In this case, portions of the result are not displayed.

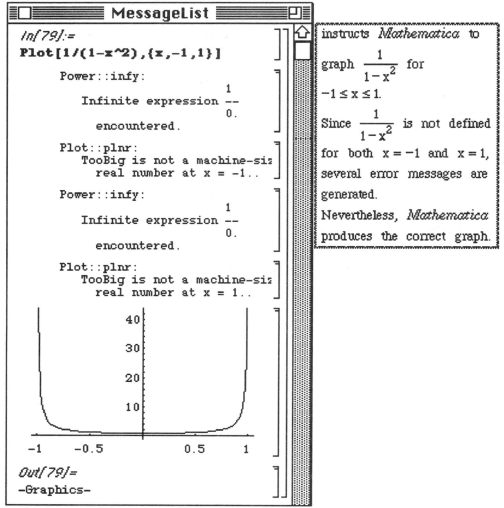

instructs *Mathematica* to graph $\dfrac{1}{1-x^2}$ for $-1 \le x \le 1$.

Since $\dfrac{1}{1-x^2}$ is not defined for both $x = -1$ and $x = 1$, several error messages are generated.

Nevertheless, *Mathematica* produces the correct graph.

A list of all messages generated during the above calculation is obtained with **MessageList**.

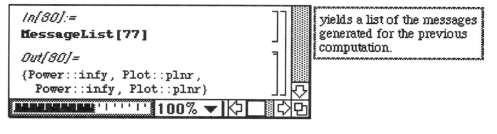

yields a list of the messages generated for the previous computation.

MessageName(: :)   387, 826
See 43   See Also: **Message, MessageList, $MessageList**
   MessageName is symbolized with **symbol::tag** or **symbol::"tag"** in
Mathematica. Using these symbols, messages can be defined. Any characters which
can be used in symbol names can appear in **tag**. An example of a typical message is
f::usage to indicate how the function is used. Messages can be turned on and off
with **On[symbol::tag]** and **Off[symbol::tag]**, respectively.
MessageName[symbol,tag,language] is used to indicate a message in a
particular language.

Messages   387, 736, 826
                                See Also: **Message, MessageList, Off, On**
   Messages[sym] gives all messages associated with the symbol **sym**. If a message
has been turned off, then it is contained within **$Off**. A list of all error messages
associated with built-in *Mathematica* objects can be found in the <u>Technical Report:</u>
<u>*Mathematica* Warning Messages by David Withoff</u> published by Wolfram Research,
Inc.
Example:
The following example displays all messages associated with the symbol **General**.

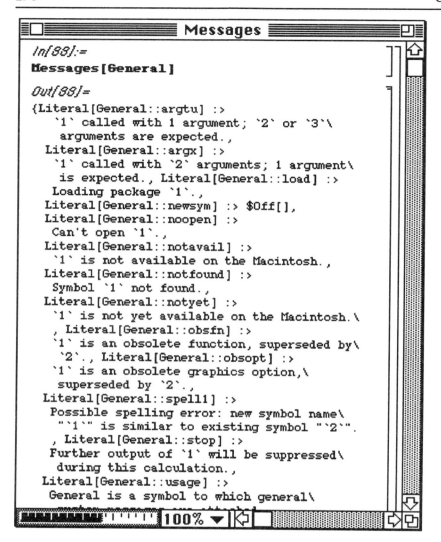

```
In[88]:=
Messages[General]

Out[88]=
{Literal[General::argtu] :>
  `1` called with 1 argument; `2` or `3`\
  arguments are expected.,
 Literal[General::argx] :>
  `1` called with `2` arguments; 1 argument\
  is expected., Literal[General::load] :>
  Loading package `1`.,
 Literal[General::newsym] :> $Off[],
 Literal[General::noopen] :>
  Can't open `1`.,
 Literal[General::notavail] :>
  `1` is not available on the Macintosh.,
 Literal[General::notfound] :>
  Symbol `1` not found.,
 Literal[General::notyet] :>
  `1` is not yet available on the Macintosh.\
  , Literal[General::obsfn] :>
  `1` is an obsolete function, superseded by\
  `2`., Literal[General::obsopt] :>
  `1` is an obsolete graphics option,\
  superseded by `2`.,
 Literal[General::spell1] :>
  Possible spelling error: new symbol name\
  "`1`" is similar to existing symbol "`2`".
  , Literal[General::stop] :>
  Further output of `1` will be suppressed\
  during this calculation.,
 Literal[General::usage] :>
  General is a symbol to which general\
```

MetaCharacters
See Also: **StringPosition**

  MetaCharacters is an option used with **StringPosition** to indicate if certain characters should be assigned special meanings.

Method
See 278, 302, 435, 761   See Also: **Solve**, **NIntegrate**

  Method is an option used with numerical functions such as **Solve** and **NIntegrate** to indicate the algorithm to be used to determine the solution.   Two examples of settings used for this option with **NIntegrate** are **GaussKronrod** and **MultiDimensional**.

Min   49, 550, 826
See 541, 650   See Also: **FindMinimum, Max, Order, Sort**

Min is used to determine the smallest numerical value in a list of numbers.
Min[a1,a2,...] gives the smallest number in the list {**a1, a2**,...} while
Min[{a1,a2,...},{b1,b2,...},...] gives the smallest number from all of
the lists given. If all of the arguments are real-valued, then the output is always a
definite value.

Example:

In the following example, the list of numbers **nums** is defined and the minimum is
found with **Min**.

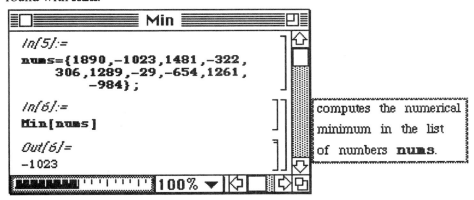

Minors   657, 827
                                See Also: **Det**

Minors[a,k] lists the determinants of all of the **k × k** submatrices of the matrix **a**.
Minors can be applied to rectangular as well as square matrices.

Example:

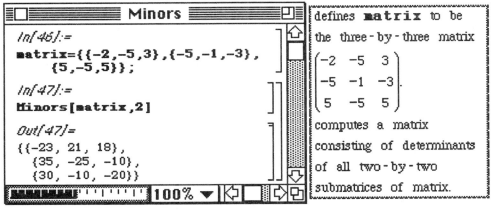

MinRecursion   688, 830
                        See Also: **NIntegrate**

   MinRecursion is an option used with recursive functions such as **NIntegrate** to indicate the minimum depth allowed in the procedure before the calculation is ceased even if convergence is not attained. With **NIntegrate**, **MinRecursion** indicates the minimum number of levels of the recursive subdivision to use. Increasing the setting of **MinRecursion** causes **NIntegrate** to use a larger number of sample points. Hence, increasing the value of **MinRecursion** slows down the calculation. The default value of **MinRecursion** with **NIntegrate** is **0**.

Minus (**-**)   47, 827
                        See Also: **Subtract**, **SubtractFrom**,
                        Decrement, **PreDecrement**

   Minus, symbolized **-**, indictes algebraic negation. The expression **-a** is equivalent to **Times[-1,a]**.

Example:

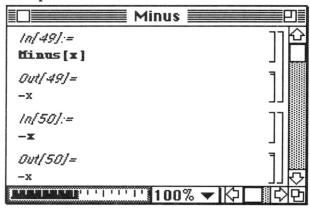

Mod   49, 553, 602, 827
                        See Also: **Modulus**, **PolynomialMod**,
                        PolynomialQuotient, **PolynomialRemainder**,
                        Quotient

   Mod[a,b] represents the remainder generated by **a/b** which is commonly known as **a** mod **b**. The sign of **b** is assigned to the result. The arguments of this command can be **Integer**, **Real**, or **Rational**.

Example:

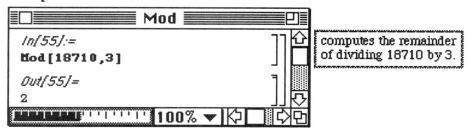

computes the remainder of dividing 18710 by 3.

Mode   620, 822, 869
                             See Also: **Solve**, **MainSolve**
   Mode is an option used with functions such as **Solve** and **MainSolve** to indicate
the manner in which equations are solved. The settings for this option include
Generic, **Integer**, **Modular**, and **Rational**. These settings are described under
MainSolve.

Modular   620, 827
                             See Also: **Modulus**, **Solve**, **MainSolve**, **Mode**
   Modular is a setting for the **Mode** option used with functions like **MainSolve** and
Solve. This setting causes the equality of the two sides of the equation **lhs==rhs** to
be modulo an integer. This weaker form of equality is useful in number theory.

Module   115, 318, 324, 326, 827
See 204, 460, 530, 568   See Also: **With**, **Block**, **Unique**
   Module is a means by which local variables are defined in *Mathematica*.
Module[{x,y,...},body] defines the local variables **{x,y,...}** used in the
commands given in **body**. Even if a variable in the list **{x,y,...}** has the same
name as a global variable, changes in the value of that local variable do not affect the
value of the corresponding global variable. Initial values can be assigned to local
variables with **Module[{x=x0,y=y0,...},body]**. The initial values are
evaluated before the module is executed. **Module** can be used in defining a function
with a condition attached. This is accomplished with
lhs:=Module[variables,rhs/;condition]. This allows for the sharing of
the local variables listed in **variables** with **rhs**. Symbols created within **Module**
have the attribute **Temporary** while **Module** itself carries the attribute **HoldAll**.

Example:

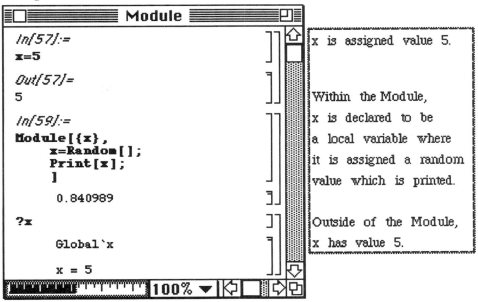

Modulus   602, 620, 663, 827
See 151, 154   See Also: **Mod**, **Modular**, **PolynomialMod**

    Modulus->p is an option used with algebraic functions such as **Factor**, **PolynomialLCM**, **PolynomialGCD**, **Inverse**, **LinearSolve**, and **Det** to indicate that integers are considered modulo the integer **p**. The setting **Modulus->0** specifies that arithmetic is carried out over the full ring of integers.

Example:

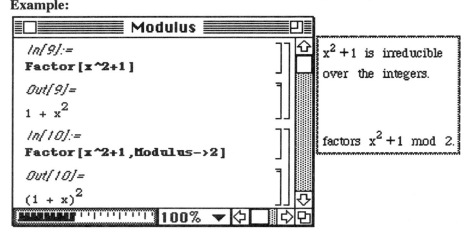

MoebiusMu   556, 828
See 280   See Also: **FactorInteger**

    MoebiusMu[n] represents the Möbius function $\mu(n) = (-1)^k$ if **n** is a product of k distinct primes and 0 if **n** contains a squared factor other than 1. Hence, $\mu(n)$ is 1 if **n** is the product of an even number of primes, − 1 if it is the product of an odd number, and 0 if it has a multiple prime factor.

Example:

```
 In[63]:=
 MoebiusMu[683]

 Out[63]=
 -1

 In[67]:=
 FactorInteger[683]

 Out[67]=
 {{683, 1}}

 In[64]:=
 MoebiusMu[306]

 Out[64]=
 0

 In[68]:=
 FactorInteger[306]

 Out[68]=
 {{2, 1}, {3, 2}, {17, 1}}

 In[66]:=
 MoebiusMu[497]

 Out[66]=
 1

 In[69]:=
 FactorInteger[497]

 Out[69]=
 {{7, 1}, {71, 1}}
```

683 is a prime number and hence the product of an odd number of primes.

306 has a multiple prime factor, 3.

497 is the product of an even number of distinct prime numbers.

MultiDimensional

See Also: **NIntegrate**

MultiDimensional is a setting for the **Method** option used with **NIntegrate**. This setting indicates that **NIntegrate** should use a multi-dimensional algorithm to approximate an integral in two or more dimensions.

Example:

In the following example, **NIntegrate** and the option **Method->MultiDimensional** are used to approximate the integral

$$\int_0^{\pi/2} \int_0^{\pi} \sin\big(\cos(x\sin(y))\big)\, dy\, dx.$$

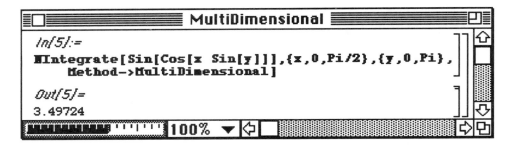

Multinomial   558, 828
                                   See Also: **Binomial**, **Factorial**

   Multinomial[n1,n2,...] yields the multinomial coefficient $\dfrac{(n1+n2+\cdots)!}{n1!\,n2!\cdots}$.

This gives the number of ways of partitioning N distinct objects into m sets of size

ni where $\displaystyle\sum_{i=1}^{m} ni = N$.

Example:

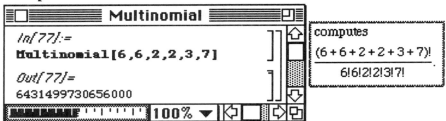

Multiplicity   859
                                   See Also: **Roots**

   Multiplicity is an option used with **Roots** to indicate the multiplicity of each of the roots in the result.

N

N   48, 51, 105, 106, 264, 536, 539, 687, 828
See 3, 38, 249, 345,   See Also: **Chop**, **CompiledFunction**,
770   **Rationalize**, **$MachinePrecision**

N[expression] yields the numerical value of **expression**. The number of digits of precision can be requested with **N[expression,n]**. With this command *Mathematica* performs computations with **n**-digit precision numbers. However, results may involve fewer than **n** digits.

Example:

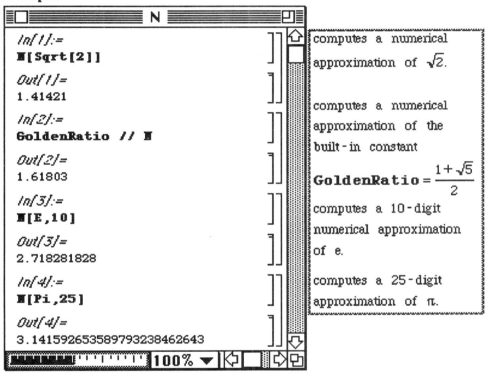

In[1]:=
N[Sqrt[2]]

Out[1]=
1.41421

computes a numerical approximation of $\sqrt{2}$.

In[2]:=
GoldenRatio // N

Out[2]=
1.61803

computes a numerical approximation of the built-in constant

$$\mathbf{GoldenRatio} = \frac{1+\sqrt{5}}{2}$$

In[3]:=
N[E,10]

Out[3]=
2.718281828

computes a 10-digit numerical approximation of e.

In[4]:=
N[Pi,25]

Out[4]=
3.1415926535897932384626443

computes a 25-digit approximation of π.

100%

NameQ   385, 828
                           See Also: **Definition**, **Information**, **Names**

NameQ["form"] yields a value of True if there exist names which match the form defined in **form**. A False value is given otherwise. Metacharacters such as * can be used in form to investigate the existence of more general names.

Example:

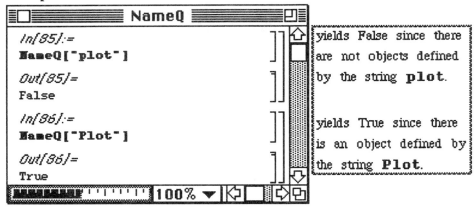

Names   385, 828
See 182   See Also: **Definition**, **Information**, **Contexts**,
                                       Unique, **ValueQ**, **FileNames**, **NameQ**

Names is used to determine symbols with names that match a particular form.
Names["form"] lists all symbols which match the pattern defined in **form**. Patterns
are given using the metacharacters * or @. **Names** also has the option
SpellingCorrection. With the command
Names["form",SpellingCorrection->True], *Mathematica* also finds those
symbols which match **form** after a spelling correction. Hence, names which differ in a
small portion of their characters from those matching **form** are also listed. This
command can be used with the option **IgnoreCase** as well.

Example:

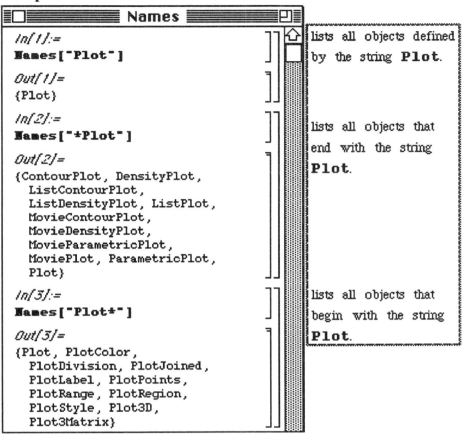

In the following example, the entire result is not displayed since it is several pages long.

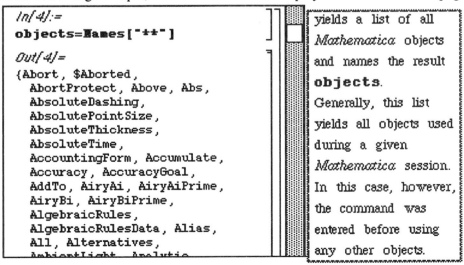

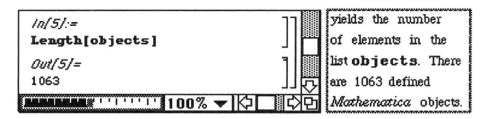

NBernoulliB   559, 828
                                See Also: **BernoulliB**
  NBernoulliB[n] yields the numerical value of the Bernoulli number
BernoulliB[n] directly. Hence, this command achieves the result much more
quickly than **N[BernoulliB[n]]**. Precision to **p** digits can be requested with
NBernoulliB[n,p].

Example:

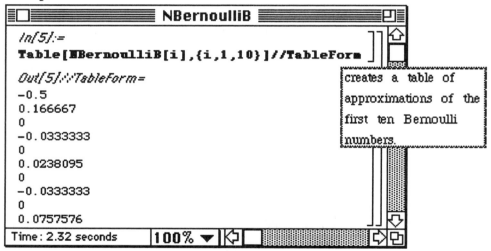

NDSolve   7, 676, 683, 696, 697, 700, 829
                                See Also: **DSolve**, **NIntegrate**,
                                InterpolatingFunction,
                                InterpolatingPolynomial
  NDSolve is used to numerically solve ordinary differential equations (i.e., those
depending on one independent variable). A single equation is solved with
NDSolve[{equation,y[x0]==y0},y,{x,xmin,xmax}] where equation is
solved for **y[x]** and the solution is valid over the interval **{xmin,xmax}**. Systems of
equations can be solved with
NDSolve[{eq1,eq2,...,y1[x0]==a,y2[x0]==b,...},{y1,y2,...},
{x,xmin,xmax}]. Note that enough initial conditions must be given to determine the
solution. Hence, there are no arbitrary variables in the solution which results from
NDSolve. Each component of the result is given in the form
InterpolatingFunction[{xmin,xmax},<>]. These solutions can be plotted
in two dimensions with **ParametricPlot** or in three dimensions with

ParametricPlot3D. The options of **NDSolve** are **AccuracyGoal**, **MaxSteps**, **PrecisionGoal**, **StartingStepSize**, and **WorkingPrecision**. The default setting for **MaxSteps** is 500 while that for **AccuracyGoal** and **PrecisionGoal** are each 10 digits fewer than that of **WorkingPrecision**. The default for

WorkingPrecision is **$WorkingPrecision**.

Example:

In the following example, **NDSolve** is used to a find numerical solution of the differential equation $y'(x) = x^2 + y(x)^2$ subject to $y(0)=1$ for $-.75 \le x \le .75$; the result is named **sol**. The resulting Interpolating Function is graphed with **Plot**.

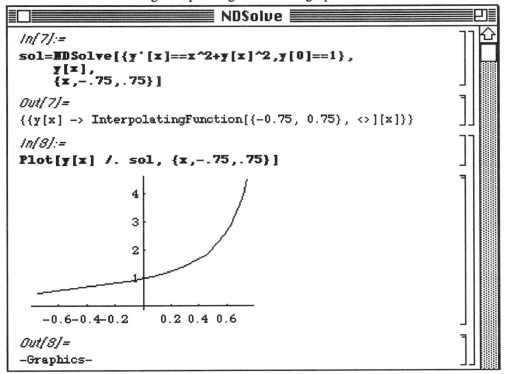

In the following example, **equation** is defined to be the differential equation $x''(t) + .75x'(t) + \sin(x(t)) = 0$. **NDSolve** is used to compute a numerical solution of $x''(t) + .75x'(t) + \sin(x(t)) = 0$ subject to $x(0)=1$ and $x'(0)=0$ for $0 \le t \le 15$; the result is named **sol**.

```
In[32]:=
equation=x''[t]+.75x'[t]+Sin[x[t]]==0
Out[32]=
Sin[x[t]] + 0.75 x'[t] + x''[t] == 0
In[33]:=
sol=NDSolve[{equation,x[0]==1,x'[0]==0},
    x[t],{t,0,15}]
Out[33]=
{{x[t] -> InterpolatingFunction[{0., 15.}, <>][t]}}
```

The following command graphs the resulting Interpolating Function. The option
PlotRange->All is included to guarantee that the entire range is displayed.

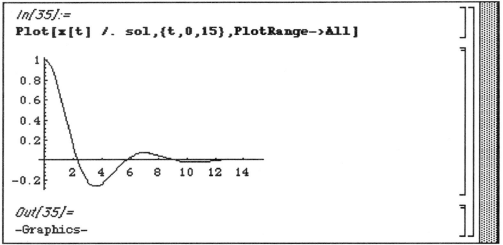

The following defines x(t) to be the Interpolating Function in the list **sol**. The result
can be evaluated for specific numbers.

```
In[39]:=
x[t_]=x[t] /. sol[[1]]
Out[39]=
InterpolatingFunction[{0., 15.}, <>][t]
In[40]:=
x[6]
Out[40]=
0.0334468
```

NDSolve can also be used to compute numerical solutions of systems of differential
equations. In the following example, **NDSolve** is used to compute a numerical

solution of the system $\begin{cases} x'(t) = y(t) \\ y'(t) = .5\left(1 - x(t)^2\right)y(t) - x(t) \\ x(0) = 1 \\ y(0) = 0 \end{cases}$ for $0 \le t \le 15$; the

resulting list of two Interpolating Functions is named **solone**.

```
In[2]:=
eqone=x'[t]==y[t];
eqtwo=y'[t]==.5 (1-x[t]^2)y[t]-x[t];

In[3]:=
solone=NDSolve[{eqone,eqtwo,x[0]==1,y[0]==0},
    {x[t],y[t]},{t,0,15}]

Out[3]=
{{x[t] -> InterpolatingFunction[{0., 15.}, <>][t],
    y[t] -> InterpolatingFunction[{0., 15.}, <>][t]}}
```

ParametricPlot is used to graph the solution. The result is named **plotone**.

```
In[4]:=
plotone=ParametricPlot[{x[t],y[t]} /. solone,
    {t,0,15}]

        ParametricPlot::ppcom:
            Function {x[t], y[t]} /. solone
            cannot be compiled; plotting will proceed with the
            uncompiled function.
```

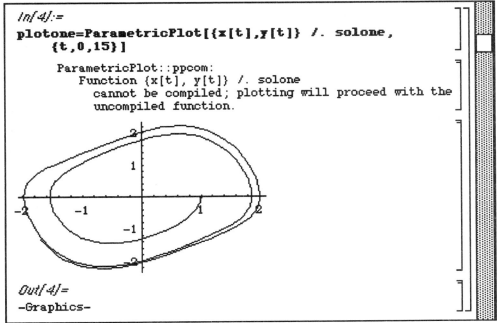

```
Out[4]=
-Graphics-
```

The following solves the same system subject to the conditions that x(0)=0 and y(0)=1 for $0 \le t \le 15$. The resulting solution is named **soltwo** and graphed with **ParametricPlot**.

In[5]:=
soltwo=NDSolve[{eqone,eqtwo,x[0]==0,y[0]==1},
    {x[t],y[t]},{t,0,15}]

Out[5]=
{{x[t] -> InterpolatingFunction[{0., 15.}, <>][t],
    y[t] -> InterpolatingFunction[{0., 15.}, <>][t]}}

In[6]:=
plottwo=ParametricPlot[{x[t],y[t]} /. soltwo,
    {t,0,15},Compiled->False]

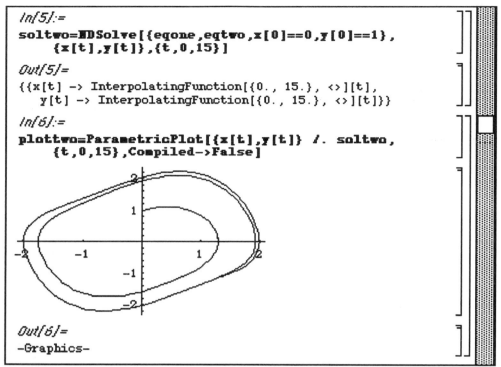

Out[6]=
-Graphics-

The following solves the same system subject to the conditions that x(0)=2 and y(0)=2
for 0 ≤ t ≤ 15. The resulting solution is named **solthree** and graphed with
ParametricPlot.

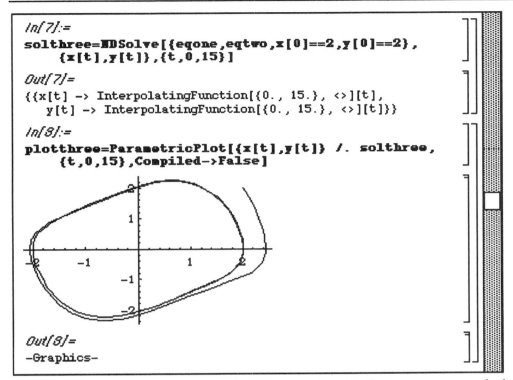

```
In[7]:=
solthree=NDSolve[{eqone,eqtwo,x[0]==2,y[0]==2},
    {x[t],y[t]},{t,0,15}]

Out[7]=
{{x[t] -> InterpolatingFunction[{0., 15.}, <>][t],
    y[t] -> InterpolatingFunction[{0., 15.}, <>][t]}}

In[8]:=
plotthree=ParametricPlot[{x[t],y[t]} /. solthree,
    {t,0,15},Compiled->False]
```

```
Out[8]=
-Graphics-
```

The three above graphs are displayed simultaneously with the **Show** command; the result is named **plotfour**. **plotone**, **plottwo**, **plotthree**, and **plotfour** can be displayed in a single graphics cell with the **GraphicsArray** command.

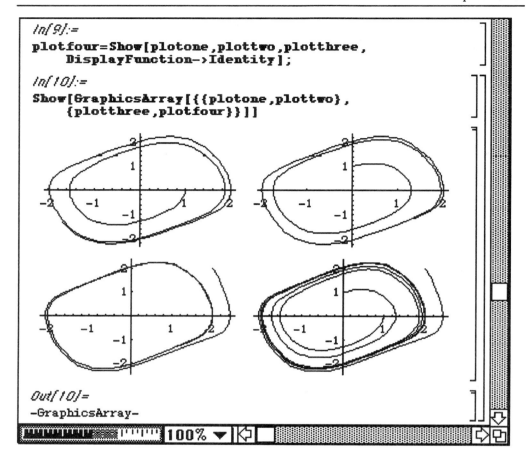

```
In[9]:=
plotfour=Show[plotone,plottwo,plotthree,
    DisplayFunction->Identity];
In[10]:=
Show[GraphicsArray[{{plotone,plottwo},
    {plotthree,plotfour}}]]
```

```
Out[10]=
-GraphicsArray-
```

Needs   340, 829
                                              See Also: **Get, DeclarePackage,**
                                              ContextToFilename, FileNames
   Needs["context`"] reads in the package supplied by
ContextToFilename["context`"] when the specified package is not in
$Packages already. In other words, the package is loaded only if it is needed. Also,
Needs["context`","filename"]** loads **filename** if **context` is not already
in **$Packages**.

Negative   829
                                              See Also: **NonNegative, Positive, Sign**
   Negative[x] yields a value of **True** if **x** is a negative number. If **x** is
non-negative, then a value of **False** is returned. Otherwise, the expression is kept in
unevaluated form. **Negative** can be used in the form **Negative[x]=True** to
define **x** to be a negative number.

Example:

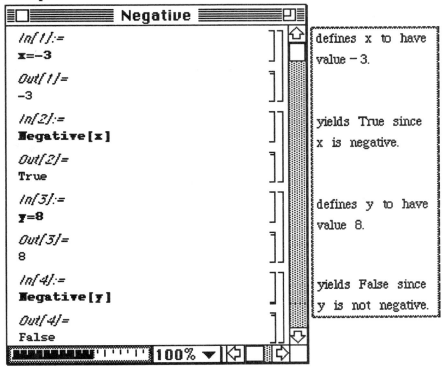

Nest   201, 291, 829
See 478, 541, 549   See Also: **Fold**, **Function**, **FixedPoint**, **Do**
  Nest[fnc,x,n] applies the function **fnc** nested **n** times to the expression **x**.

Example:

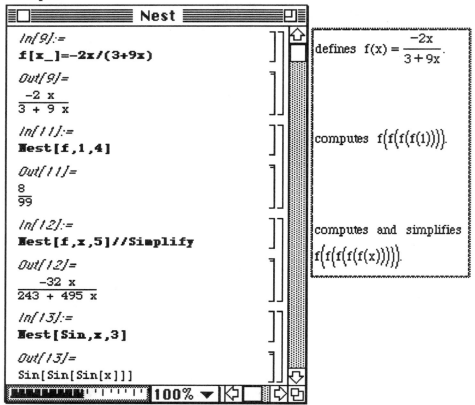

NestList   11, 201, 210, 830
                              See Also: **FoldList**, **ComposeList**, **Nest**
   NestList[f,x,n] yields the list {x,f[x],f[f[x]],...} where **f** is nested
up to **n** times.

Example:

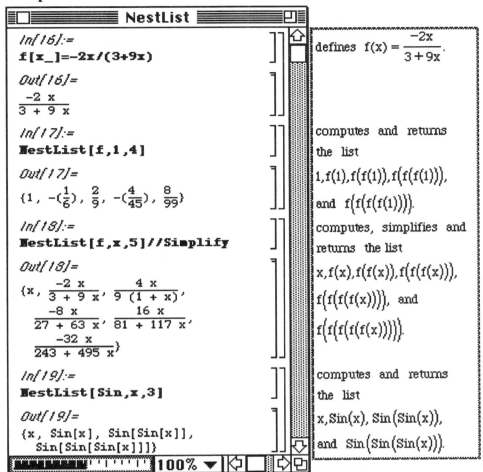

NIntegrate   2, 106, 683, 684, 686, 830
See 302, 478, 748, 749   See Also: **Integrate, NDSolve, NSum**
    NIntegrate[f,{x,xmin,xmax}] numerically computes the definite integral of
f from **x = xmin** to **x = xmax**. Multidimensional integrals can be considered using the
syntax for multidimensional integrals given for **Integrate** and the
Method->MultiDimensional option. The options for **NIntegrate** along with
their default values are **AccuracyGoal->Infinity, Compiled->True,
GaussPoints->Floor[WorkingPrecision/3], MaxRecursion->6,
MinRecursion->0, PrecisionGoal->Automatic, SingularDepth->4**, and
WorkingPrecision->$MachinePrecision. Integrate continues to take
subdivisions until the specified value of **AccuracyGoal** or **PrecisionGoal** is met.
The default setting for **PrecisionGoal** is ten digits fewer than the setting for
WorkingPrecision. NIntegrate has the attribute **HoldAll**.

Example:

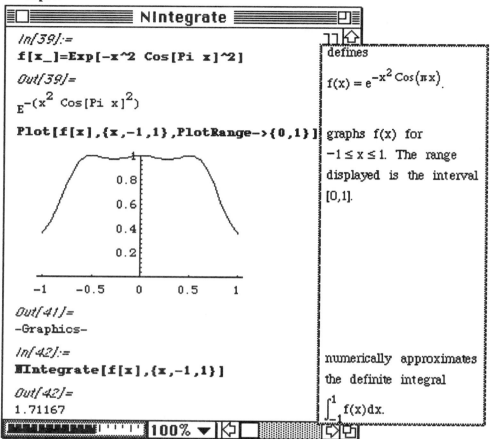

NonAssociative

NonAssociative is a symbol which is used in formatting functions to represent a non-associative operator.

NonCommutativeMultiply (**) 716, 830
                        See Also: **Dot**, **Times**
   NonCommutativeMultiply, symbolized by **a**b**c**, is a form of associative but not commutative multiplication and has the attribute **Flat**. This command is used to generalize multiplication for certain mathematical objects.

NonConstants   624, 830
                        See Also: **D**, **Dt**
   NonConstants is an option used with **D** and **Dt** to indicate which variables depend implicitly on the variable x. The syntax for this option is
NonConstants->{y1,y2,...} where each of the **yi** depends on x.

None   141, 830
See 514   See also: **All**, **Automatic**, **False**, **True**
    None is a setting used with certain options such as the **Graphics** options
ContourSmoothing, **AxesLabel**, and **FaceGrids** to indicate that that particular
option not be included.

NonNegative   831
                                      See Also: **Negative**, **Positive**, **Sign**
    NonNegative[x] yields a value of **True** if **x** is a non-negative number. If **x** is
negative, then a value of **False** is returned. Otherwise, the expression is kept in
unevaluated form. **NonNegative** can be used in the form **NonNegative[x]=True**
to define **x** to be a non-negative number.

Example:

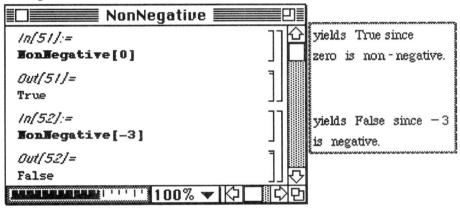

Normal   101, 645, 831
See 595   See Also: **Series**
    Normal[expression] changes **expression** to a normal expression. If
expression is a power series, then this is accomplished by truncating the series by
removing the higher order terms.
Example:
In the following example, $f(x)=\sin(4x)+2\cos(2x)$. The **Series** command is used to
compute the first five terms of the power series for $f(x)$ about $x=0$; the result is named
ser. Observe that the last term of ser contains the term $O[x]^6$ which denotes the
omitted higher-order terms of the series.

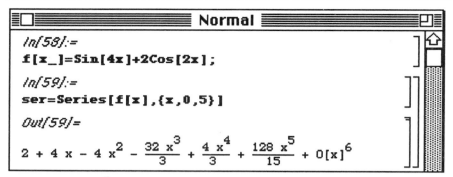

The term $O[x]^6$ is removed from **ser** with the command **Normal**. The resulting polynomial is named **poly**. The **Plot** command is used to graph both **poly** (in black) and **f** (in gray) for $-\pi/2 \le x \le \pi/2$.

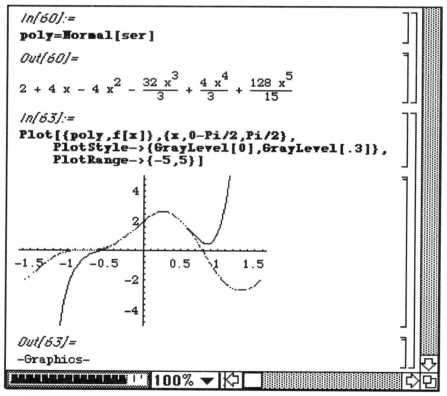

Not (!)   94, 831
See 204   See Also: **LogicalExpand, Unequal**

Not[expression], also symbolized **!expression**, is the logical operation not. It yields **True** if **expression** is **False** and gives **False** if it is **True**. If this command is used to begin a line, then the notation **!expression** cannot be used.

Example:

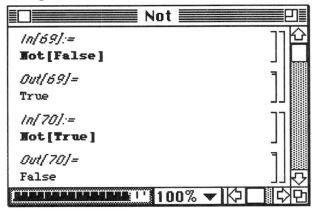

NProduct   106, 683, 689, 831
                        See Also: **NSum**, **Product**, **Sum**
NProduct[f,{i,imin,imax}] numerically approximates the product

 f. Also, the command **NProduct[f,{i,imin,imax},stepsize]**
yields this product by using the increment stepsize. **NProduct** has the same
options as **NSum** except that **NSumTerms** is replaced with **NProductFactors**
and **NSumExtraTerms** is replaced with **NProductExtraFactors**.

Example:

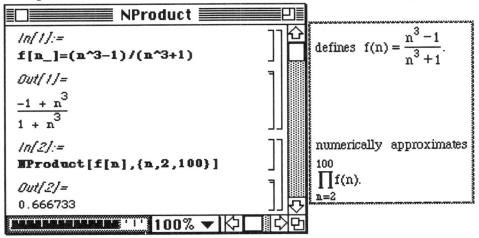

NProductExtraFactors
See Also: **NProduct, WynnDegree**

NProductExtraFactors is an option used with **NProduct** to indicate the number of factors to be used in the extrapolation process. The setting for **NProductExtraFactors** must be greater than two times the value of **WynnDegree**.

NProductFactors
See Also: **NProduct**

NProductFactors is an option used with **NProduct** to indicate the number of factors to be explicitly included in the product before extrapolation.

NProtectedAll
See Also: **N, Set Attributes**

NProtectedAll is an attribute which indicates that none of the arguments of a function should be modified when **N[ ]** is applied to that function.

NProtectedFirst
See Also: **N, Set Attributes**

NProtectedFirst is an attribute which indicates that the first argument of a function should not be modified when **N[ ]** is applied to that function.

NProtectedRest
See Also: **N, Set Attributes**

NProtectedRest is an attribute which indicates that any argument after the first argument of a function should not be modified when **N[ ]** is applied to that function.

NRoots
See 193, 239, 474   See Also: **FindRoot, NSolve, Roots, Solve**

NRoots[eqn,x] lists the numerical approximations of the roots of the polynomial equation **eqn**.

Example:

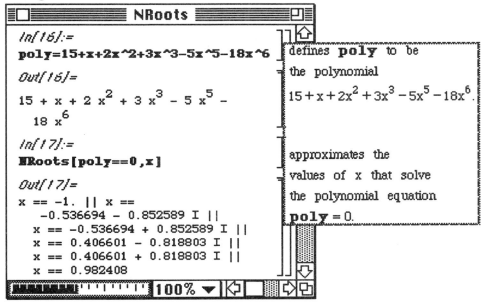

NRoots

In[16]:=
poly=15+x+2x^2+3x^3-5x^5-18x^6

Out[16]=

$15 + x + 2 x^2 + 3 x^3 - 5 x^5 - 18 x^6$

In[17]:=
NRoots[poly==0,x]

Out[17]=
```
x == -1. || x ==
   -0.536694 - 0.852589 I ||
 x == -0.536694 + 0.852589 I ||
 x == 0.406601 - 0.818803 I ||
 x == 0.406601 + 0.818803 I ||
 x == 0.982408
```

defines **poly** to be
the polynomial
$15 + x + 2x^2 + 3x^3 - 5x^5 - 18x^6$.

approximates the
values of x that solve
the polynomial equation
poly $= 0$.

100% ▼

NSolve   107, 609, 683, 691, 831

See Also: **Solve**, **FindRoot**, **NDSolve**, **NRoots**

NSolve is used to compute numerical solutions to polynomial equations.

NSolve[poly==0,x] determines the numerical roots to the polynomial equation in
x. Precision to **d** digits is requested with **NSolve[poly==0,x,d]**. Identical results
are achieved by **N[Solve[poly==0,x]]**.

Example:

In the following example, **NSolve** is used to approximate the solutions of the
polynomial equation $7x - 8x^2 + x^3 - 2x^4 + 4x^5 - x^7 = 0$.

NSolve

In[16]:=
poly=7x-8x^2+x^3-2x^4+4x^5-x^7

Out[16]=

$7 x - 8 x^2 + x^3 - 2 x^4 + 4 x^5 - x^7$

In[17]:=
NSolve[poly==0,x]

Out[17]=
```
{{x -> -2.40575}, {x -> -0.578994 - 1.09613 I},
  {x -> -0.578994 + 1.09613 I}, {x -> 0.},
  {x -> 1.07229 - 0.429382 I},
  {x -> 1.07229 + 0.429382 I}, {x -> 1.41916}}
```

NSolve can also be used to approximate solutions of systems of polynomial equations.

In the following example, **NSolve** is used to approximate the solutions of the system

$$\begin{cases} -2x^5 - 3x^3y^2 - 2xy^4 - 2y^5 = -2 \\ x^5 + 2x^4y + x^3y^2 - 3x^2y^3 + 2xy^4 + 2y^5 = 2 \end{cases}.$$ The command **Chop** is used

to replace numbers with absolute value less than 10^{-10} by the integer 0.

```
In[19]:=

eqone=-2x^5-3x^3y^2-2x y^4-2y^5==-2;
eqtwo=x^5+2x^4y+x^3y^2-3x^2y^3+2x y^4+2y^5==2;

In[22]:=
sols=NSolve[{eqone,eqtwo},{x,y}]//Chop

Out[22]=
{{x -> 0.827198, y -> -1.11338},
 {x -> 0, y -> -0.809017 - 0.587785 I},
 {x -> 0, y -> -0.809017 + 0.587785 I},
 {x -> 0, y -> -0.809017 - 0.587785 I},
 {x -> 0, y -> -0.809017 + 0.587785 I},
 {x -> -0.771293 + 0.650059 I,
  y -> -0.498408 - 0.0597392 I},
 {x -> -0.771293 - 0.650059 I,
  y -> -0.498408 + 0.0597392 I},
 {x -> 0.255618 + 0.786712 I,
  y -> -0.344054 - 1.05889 I},
```

100% ▼

NSum   106, 683, 689, 832
                                    See Also: **NProduct**

NSum[f,{i,imin,imax}] numerically approximates the value of $\displaystyle\sum_{i=imin}^{imax} f$.

A step size other than one unit is used with **NSum[f,{i,imin,imax,istep}]**.
Multidimensional sums are computed with the command
NSum[f,{i,imin,imax},{j,jmin,jmax},...]. The options of **NSum** as well
as their default values are **AccuracyGoal->Infinity**, **Compiled->True**,
Method->Automatic, **NSumExtraTerms->12**, **NSumTerms->15**,
PrecisionGoal->Automatic, **VerifyConvergence->True**, and
WorkingPrecision->$WorkingPrecision. The method used by **NSum** is
either the Euler-Maclaurin (**Integrate**) or Wynn epsilon (**Fit**). **NSum** continues to
perform these algorithms until the error is with **AccuracyGoal** or **PrecisionGoal**
setting. Note, however, that the results obtained may be incorrect and should always be
checked by investigating the sensitivity of the sum to changes in the option setting.
VerifyConvergence is only used when calculating an infinite sum.

Example:

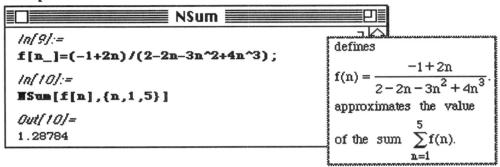

In the following example, **NSum** is used to approximate the sum

$$\sum_{n=1}^{10} \sum_{m=5}^{8} g(n,m) \quad \text{where} \quad g(n,m) = \frac{1}{\left(\sin^4(n) + 1\right)\left(\cos^6(m) + 1\right)^2}.$$

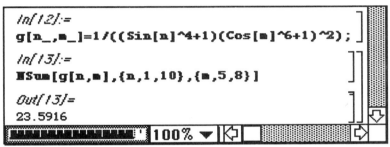

NSumExtraTerms   690
                                        See Also: **NSum, WynnDegree**

   NSumExtraTerms is an option used with **NSum** to indicate the number of terms to be used in the extrapolation process when using the method **SequenceLimit**. The setting for **NSumExtraTerms** must be greater than two times the value of **WynnDegree**.

NSumTerms   690
                                        See Also: **NSum**

   NSumTerms is an option used with **NSum** to indicate the number of terms to be explicitly included in the sum before extrapolation.

Null   516, 746, 832
See 407   See Also: **CompoundExpression, Return**

   Null is a *Mathematica* symbol which represents the absence of a result or an expression. It appears as output when no output is generated by a command. It also represents a blank in a list of expressions such as
{expression1, ,expression2}.

NullRecords   496, 832
                    See Also: **WordSeparators**

NullRecords is an option used with **Read** which indicates whether to keep records of length zero. The default setting is **NullRecords->False** which implies that repeated record separators are considered single record separators.   Otherwise, **NullRecords->True** assumes that a null record occurs between every pair of adjacent separators.

NullSpace   660, 662, 832
                    See Also: **RowReduce, LinearSolve**

NullSpace[m] lists the vectors which form the basis for the null space or kernel of the matrix **m.** These vectors **x** satisfy the matrix equation **m.x==0**. The matrices used with **NullSpace** can be rectangular as well as square. **NullSpace** has the option **Modulus->p** which computes the basis vectors for an integer matrix modulo **p**. Also, the option **ZeroTest** with default **ZeroTest->(#==0)&** determines if the elements of the matrix are zero.

Example:
In the following examples, **NullSpace** is used to first compute a list of vectors that gives a basis for the null space of the matrix $\begin{pmatrix} 1 & 0 & 3 & 0 \\ 2 & 1 & -2 & 0 \\ 0 & 2 & 2 & 2 \end{pmatrix}$ and then compute a list of vectors that gives a basis for the null space of the matrix

$$\begin{pmatrix} 3 & 2 & 1 & 0 \\ 3 & 0 & 2 & 1 \\ -1 & 0 & 1 & -2 \\ -2 & 1 & -1 & -2 \end{pmatrix}.$$

≡ NullSpace ≡

In[52]:=
vecsone={{1,0,3,0},{2,1,-2,0},{0,2,2,2}};
NullSpace[vecsone]

Out[52]=
$\{\{\frac{1}{3}, -(\frac{8}{9}), -(\frac{1}{9}), 1\}\}$

In[54]:=
vecstwo={{3,2,1,0},{3,0,2,1},{-1,0,1,-2},{-2,1,-1,-2}};
NullSpace[vecstwo]

Out[54]=
$\{\{-1, 1, 1, 1\}\}$

100% ▼

NullWords   496, 832
                                       See Also: **TokenWords, RecordSeparators**
   NullWords is an option used with **Read** which indicates whether to keep words of
length zero. The default setting is **NullWords->False** which implies that repeated
word separators are considered single word separators. Otherwise,
NullWords->True assumes that a null word occurs between every pair of adjacent
separators.

Number   181, 495, 833
See 384   See Also: **Real, DigitQ**
   Number represents an integer or approximate real number which is to be read by
Mathematica using **Read**. Approximate real numbers can be in C or Fortran-like form.

NumberForm   350, 352, 833
                                       See Also: **ScientificForm, EngineeringForm,
                                       AccountingForm, BaseForm, PaddedForm, N**
   NumberForm[expression,n] prints **expression** by printing at most **n** digits
of all approximate real numbers which appear in **expression**. The options of
NumberForm including their default values are **DigitBlock->Infinity**,
NumberSeparator->{",",""}, **NumberPoint->"."**,
NumberSigns->{"-",""}, **NumberPadding->{"",""}**,
SignPadding->False, **NumberFormat->Automatic**, and
ExponentFunction->Automatic. All of these options can be applied to real
numbers or integers except **ExponentFunction** which applies only to approximate
real numbers. **NumberForm** only affects the printing of an expression. It does not
alter any calculations involving the expression.

NumberFormat   351, 833
                                       See Also: **ExponentFunction, NumberForm**
   NumberFormat is a **NumberForm** option used to define the function to give the
final format of a number. The specified function contains three argument strings. They
are the mantissa, the base, and the exponent for the number. If there is no exponent,
then *""* is used in the exponent position.

NumberPadding   351, 833
                                       See Also: **SignPadding**
   NumberPadding is a **NumberForm** setting which indicates strings to be used as
padding on the left- and right-hand sides of numbers. These specifications are made
with **NumberPadding->{lside,rside}** where **lside** and **rside** are strings for
padding on the left and right sides, respectively. The default setting in **NumberForm** is
NumberPadding->{"",""} while in **PaddedForm** it is
NumberPadding->{"","0"}.

NumberPoint   351, 833
                                       See Also: **NumberForm**
   NumberPoint is a **NumberForm** option which is used to indicate the string to use
for the decimal point. The default setting is **NumberPoint->"."**.

NumberQ   227, 535, 834
                                             See Also: **IntegerQ**, **TrueQ**

NumberQ[expression] tests **expression** to determine if it is a number. If **expression** is a number, then True is given. Otherwise, False is returned. An expression is a number if it has the head **Real**, **Rational**, **Integer**, or **Complex**. This command can be used as **NumberQ[x]** = **True** to define **x** to be a number.

NumberSeparator   351, 834
                                             See Also: **NumberForm**

NumberSeparator is a **NumberForm** option which is used to indicate the strings to insert on the left- and right-hand sides of a decimal point. **NumberSeparator->"string"** indicates that **string** is to be inserted at every break between digits indicated by **DigitBlock**. Also, **NumberSeparator->{"lside","rside"}** gives different strings, **lside** and **rside**, to be used on the left and right sides of the decimal point, respectively. The default setting is **NumberSeparator->","**.

NumberSigns   351, 834
                                             See Also: **SignPadding**, **NumberForm**

NumberSigns is a **NumberForm** option used to indicate strings to be used as signs for positive and negative numbers. This is accomplished with the setting **NumberSigns->{"nsign","psign"}** where **nsign** is the string for a negative number and **psign** is that of a positive number. The default setting is **NumberSigns->{"","-"}**. Symbols can be placed on both sides of the numbers with **NumberSigns->{{"nlsign","nrsign"},{"plsign","prsign"}}**.

Numerator   82, 834
See 470   See Also: **Denominator**, **ExpandNumerator**

Numerator[expression] yields the numerator of **expression** by selecting the terms of **expression** which do not have exponents having a negative number as a factor. The argument of **Numerator** can be a rational expression.

Example:

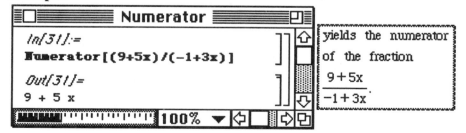

NValues   736
                                             See Also: **Attributes**, **DefaultValues**,
                                             DownValues, **FormatValues**, **Messages**,
                                             Options, **OwnValues**, **UpValues**

NValues[f] lists the transformation rules which correspond to the numerical values defined for the symbol **f**.

O

O   641, 834
See 62, 272, 318,   See Also: **Normal**, **Series**, **SeriesData**
413-415

O is the *Mathematica* symbol used to represent higher order terms in a power series.

$O[x]^n$ appears in the output of a power series and stands for a term of order x^n. This symbol represents the higher order terms that are omitted from the power series.

Likewise, $O[x,x0]^n$ represents the term of order $(x-x0)^n$ and stands for the terms which are omitted from the power series expanded about the point $x = x0$. Higher order terms are removed with **Normal**.

Example:

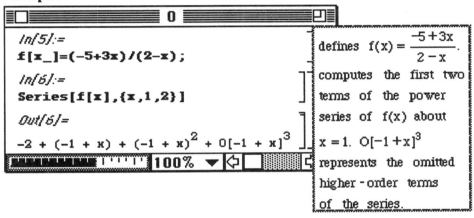

defines $f(x) = \dfrac{-5+3x}{2-x}$.

computes the first two terms of the power series of f(x) about $x = 1$. $O[-1+x]^3$ represents the omitted higher-order terms of the series.

OddQ   227, 535, 834
See 527, 528, 637   See Also: **IntegerQ**, **EvenQ**, **TrueQ**

OddQ is a function used to determine if a number is odd. **OddQ[expression]** yields **True** if **expression** is an odd number. **False** is the result otherwise. This command is also used in the form **OddQ[x]=True** to define **x** to be an odd number. In order for a number to be odd, it must have the head **Integer** and be odd as well.

Example:

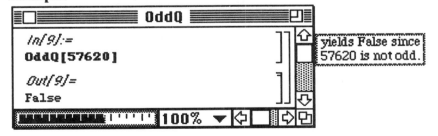

yields False since 57620 is not odd.

Off   70, 386, 387, 835
                                          See Also: **Check, Message, Messages,**
                                          MessageList, On

Off is used to switch off messages. This can be accomplished in several ways.
Off[s::tag] switches off the message **s::tag** so that it is not printed. **Off[s]**
turns off all messages associated with the symbol **s**. Several messages are switched off
with **Off[s1::tag1,s2::tag2,...]**. Also, **Off[]** turns off all tracing
messages. Specific messages may be permanently turned off by inserting the desired
Off command in the **init.m** file.

Example:

Version 2.0 issues an error message when new symbols are defined that are similar in
spelling to existing symbols.

```
In[12]:=
list=Table[i^2,{i,1,7,2}]

        General::spell1:
            Possible spelling error: new symbol name "list"
                is similar to existing symbol "List".

Out[12]=
{1, 9, 25, 49}
```

In the following example, **Off** is used to suppress this message. Thus, even though the
symbol **infinit** is similar to the existing symbol **Infinity**, no error message is
displayed.

```
In[13]:=
Off[General::spell1]

In[14]:=
infinit=10^50

Out[14]=
100000000000000000000000000000000000000000000000000
```

On   70, 386, 387, 835
                                          See Also: **Messages, Off**

On is used to switch on warning or error messages associated with user-defined
functions. **On[s::tag]** switches on the message **s::tag** so that it is printed when
necessary. **On[s]** switches on all tracing messages for the symbol **s**. Several
messages are turned on with **On[s1::tag1,s2::tag2,...]**. Finally, **On[]** turns
on every tracing message associated with any symbol.

Example:

In the previous example, the message **General::spell1** was turned **Off**. In the
following example, it is turned **On**. An error message is displayed since the symbol
off is similar to the existing symbol **Off**.

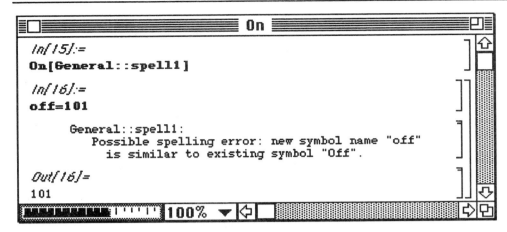

```
In[15]:=
On[General::spell1]

In[16]:=
off=101

    General::spell1:
        Possible spelling error: new symbol name "off"
          is similar to existing symbol "Off".

Out[16]=
101
```

OneIdentity   230, 272, 734, 835
                                 See Also: **Flat**, **Nest**

OneIdentity is an attribute which can be assigned to a function f to imply that the nested function values f[x], f[f[x]],... are equivalent to x in the sense of pattern matching. The built-in operations **Plus** and **Times** have this attribute.

OpenAppend   485, 835
                                 See Also: **Close**, **Put**, **Streams**

OpenAppend["filename"] is an output function which opens an output stream to the file **filename** and appends the output to this file.
OutputStream["filename",n] results from this command where **n** is the unique serial number of the stream for the current *Mathematica* session. Several options can be used with **OpenAppend**. These are as follows including the default setting:
FormatType->InputForm, NameConversion->None, PageHeight->22, PageWidth->78, StringConversion->None, TotalHeight->Infinity, TotalWidth->Infinity. If the file is unsuccessfully opened, then $Failed is returned as output.

OpenRead   499, 502, 836
See 432   See Also: **Close**, **Read**, **ReadList**, **Streams**

OpenRead["filename"] opens the file filename and prepares it to be read by establishing an input stream from the file. The current point in the file is marked by *Mathematica* as the beginning of the file. Also, **OpenRead["!command"]** opens a pipe for the purpose of being read. **OpenRead** returns the object
InputStream["filename",n] where **n** is the unique serial number for the stream for the the current *Mathematica* session. This can then be read with **Read**. If the file is unsuccessfully opened, then $Failed is returned as output.

OpenTemporary   482, 836
                            See Also: **Close, Run**

   OpenTemporary[] is used with functions like **Get** and **Put** in order to prepare data to be exchanged between *Mathematica* and an external program.
OpenTemporary[] opens a temporary file so that output can be written there. The result of this command is an **OutputStream** object. Files of the form **/temporary** are produced with **OpenTemporary** using Unix systems.

OpenWrite   485, 836
                            See Also: **OpenAppend**

   OpenWrite["filename"] opens an output stream to the file **filename** so that output can be written to it. All contents of the file are deleted since *Mathematica* writes the output starting at the beginning of the file. An **OutputStream** object is returned by **OpenWrite**.

Operate   214, 836
                            See Also: **Through, Apply, Heads**

   Operate is used to apply an operator to the head of an expression as opposed to replacing the head. **Operate[p,f[x]]** yields **p[f][x]** while
Operate[p,f[x],n] applies the operator **p** at level **n** in **f**. Operate is a generalization of **Apply**.

Optional(_.)   234, 719, 836
                            See Also: **Alternatives**

   Optional, symbolized by **patt:default**, is used to indicate that if an expression of the form **patt** is not present, then it should be replaced by **default**. This command is useful when working with function arguments. **f[x_:v]** specifies that if the argument **x** is not present, then it is replaced by the default value **v**.
Optional[x_,v] is equivalent to **x_:v**. **Optional[x_]** can be used as a function argument to indicate that if that argument is absent, then it should be replaced by default values which are defined globally by the functions in which they occur.
Optional[x_h] is used to specify that a function can be omitted, but also indicates that if the function is present, then it must have head **h**. Some *Mathematica* commands such as **Power**, **Plus**, and **Times** have built-in default values. Default values for other functions can be defined with **Default[func,..]**. This definition indicates the default arguments to use when **_.** appears as an argument of **func**.

Example:

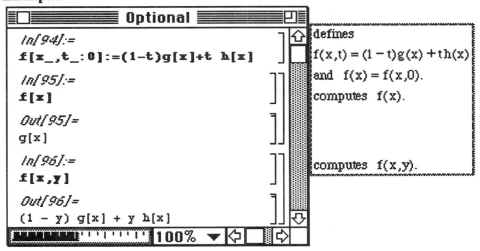

OptionQ

See Also: **Options**

OptionQ[expression] yields True if **expression** is found to be an option for a *Mathematica* command. A value of False is given otherwise.

Options   149, 236, 398, 724, 736, 837
See 418   See Also: **FullOptions**

Options is used to determine the options of *Mathematica* symbols, streams, and expressions. **Options[s]** lists the default options of the symbol **s**.

Options[expression] yields the options indicated in a particular expression.
Options["stm"] yields the options of the stream **stm** Also,
Options[expression,opt] yields the setting of the option with name **opt** which appears in **expression**. For more than one option,
Options[expression,{opt1,op2,...}] is used to list the settings for the options given in **{opt1,op2,...}** which are assigned in **expression**. The default settings for options can be changed with the command
SetOptions[symbol,opt->setting]. This command changes the default setting for the option **opt** of the function **symbol** to **setting**.

Example:

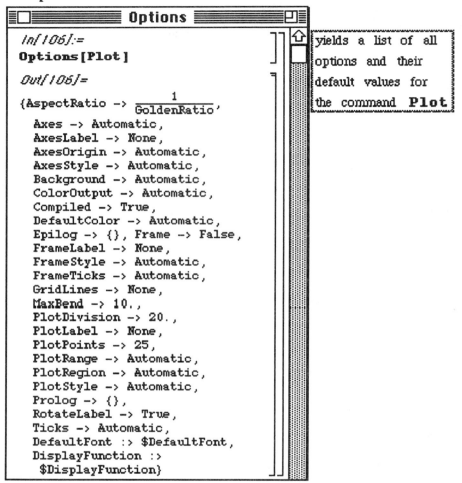

Or (| |)   94, 837, 895
See 576   See Also: **Xor**, **LogicalExpand**

Or, symbolized by | |, represents the logical "or" operator. For the expression **expression1||expression2|| ...**, *Mathematica* evalutes the expressions in order. A value of True results when a True expression is encountered. If all expressions are False, then False results.

Example:

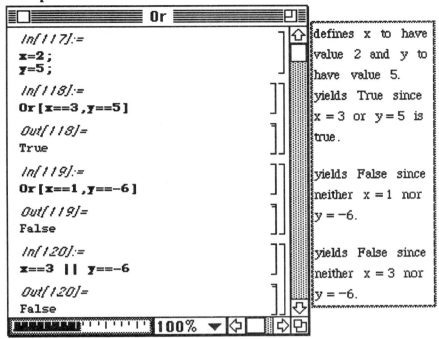

Order   215, 837

See Also: **Equal**, **SameQ**, **Sort**, **$StringOrder**

Order[expression1,expression2] yields a value of 1 if **expression1** appears before **expression2** in standard order. It yields a value of -1 if **expression1** follows **expression2** in standard order. A value of 0 results if **expression1** and **expression2** are identical.

Example:

In the following example, **Order[3,5]** returns 1 since, in a standard order, 3 is before 5; **Order[5,3]** returns -1 since, in a standard order, 5 is not before 3.

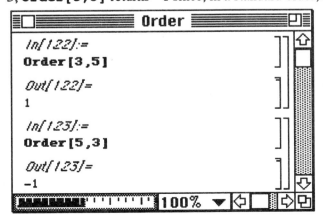

OrderedQ   133, 215, 228, 837
                                     See Also: **Signature**, **Sort**, **$StringOrder**

OrderedQ[list] yields a value of **True** if the elements of **list** occur in standard order. A value of **False** is given otherwise. Note that if identical expressions are listed such as **OrderedQ[{expression,expression}]**, then **True** results. Also, **OrderedQ[list,p]** apples **p** to **list** to determine if the elements are given in standard order.

Example:

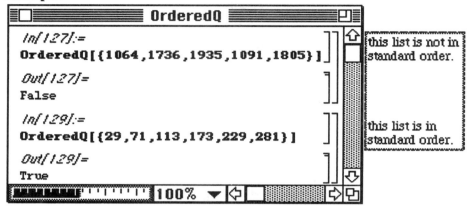

Orderless   230, 272, 275, 734, 837
                                     See Also: **Sort**, **Flat**, **OneIdentity**,
                                     $StringOrder

Orderless is an attribute assigned to orderless, commutative functions which indicates that the arguments should be sorted into standard order. This property is used in pattern matching by trying all possible orderings of the arguments in an attempt to find a match.

Out (%)   54, 61, 346, 513, 514, 743, 838
                                     See Also: **In**, **$Line**, **MessageList**

Out[n] or **%n** represents the value generated on the **n**th line of output. **%** yields the value most recently obtained while **%%** yields the second most recently obtained result. Similarly, **%%...%** (k times) or equivalently, **Out[-k]**, yields the **k**th previous result.

Outer   669, 838
                                     See Also: **Distribute**, **Inner**

Outer[f,list1,list2,...] computes the generalized outer product.

Example:

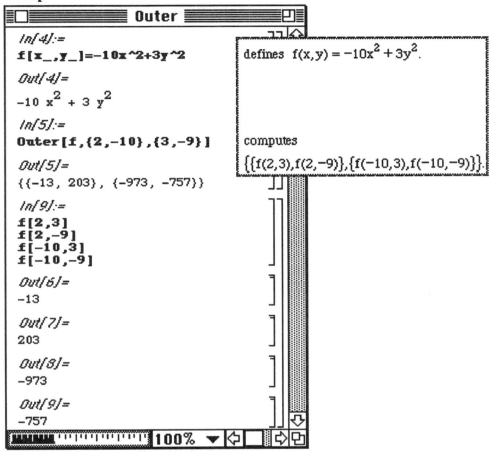

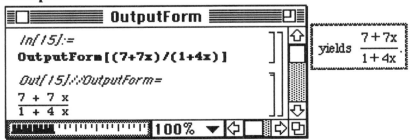

OutputForm   343, 838

See Also: **FullForm, InputForm, Short, TeXForm, TreeForm**

OutputForm[expression] displays expression in the standard *Mathematica* output format.

Example:

OutputStream   484, 838
                  See Also: **InputStream**, **Streams**
  OutputStream objects are returned by **Write**, **OpenWrite**, and **OpenAppend**.

Overflow
                  See Also: **Indeterminate**, **$MaxMachineNumber**,
                  $MaxNumber
  Overflow is the result displayed when the result of a calculation is too large to
represent.

Overlaps
  Overlaps is an option used with StringPosition which determines whether
substrings can overlap.

OwnValues   736
                  See Also: **Attributes**, **DefaultValues**,
                  DownValues, **FormatValues**, **Messages**,
                  NValues, **Options**, **UpValues**,
  OwnValues[f] yields a list corresponding to the values of f.
Example:

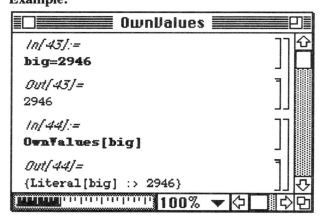

P

PaddedForm   352, 355, 838
See Also: **ColumnForm, TableForm**

   PaddedForm is used to allow for the printing of numbers having a particular number of decimal places. **PaddedForm[expression,sum]** prints **expression** so that all numbers have room for **sum** total digits. Leading spaces are used when needed. Also, **PaddedForm[expression,{sum,part}]** allows for **sum** total digits where **part** digits are to the right of the decimal place. The total number of digits does not include signs or breaks between digits. **PaddedForm** does not affect any calculations done with **expression**. It only alters the manner in which it is printed.

Example:

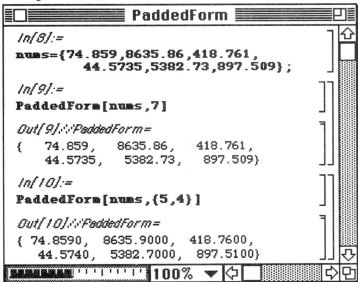

```
In[8]:=
nums={74.859,8635.86,418.761,
       44.5735,5382.73,897.509};

In[9]:=
PaddedForm[nums,7]

Out[9]//PaddedForm=
{   74.859,   8635.86,   418.761,
    44.5735,   5382.73,   897.509}

In[10]:=
PaddedForm[nums,{5,4}]

Out[10]//PaddedForm=
{ 74.8590,  8635.9000,  418.7600,
  44.5740,  5382.7000,  897.5100}
```

PageHeight   838
See Also: **TotalHeight**

   PageHeight is an option used with output streams which indicates the number of lines of text which should be printed between page breaks. The setting **PageHeight->Infinity** indicates that no page breaks occur.

PageWidth   487, 488, 517, 738, 839, 865
See Also: **TotalWidth**

   PageWidth is an option used with output streams to indicate the width of the page. This width is measured in characters. The default setting of this option is **PageWidth->78**. The setting **PageWidth->Infinity** indicates that lines can have arbitrary length. Changes in **PageWidth** are made with **SetOptions[streamname,PageWidth->n]**.

ParametricPlot   167, 395, 839
See 309-311, 517,   See Also: **ContourPlot**, **DensityPlot**, **Plot**
552-554, 731

ParametricPlot is used to plot parametric curves in two dimensions.
ParametricPlot[{x[t],y[t]},{t,tmin,tmax}] plots the curve given by
x=x[t] and **y=y[t]** from **t = tmin** to **t = tmax**. More than one such curve is
generated with **ParametricPlot[{{x1[t],y1[t]},{x2[t],y2[t]},...},**
{t,tmin,tmax}]. The options used with **Plot** are available to
ParametricPlot. The default setting **Axes->True** is different, however. The
result of **ParametricPlot** is a **Graphics** object.

Example:

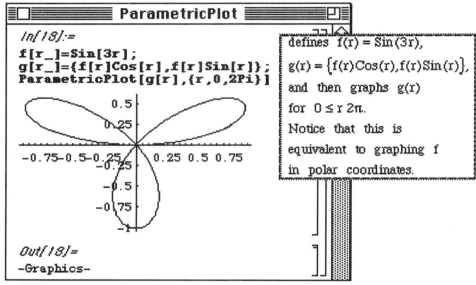

In the following example, the function $\left\{\sqrt{x}\,\mathrm{Cos}(x), \sqrt{x}\,\mathrm{Sin}(x)\right\}$ is graphed

for $0 \le x \le 8\pi$.

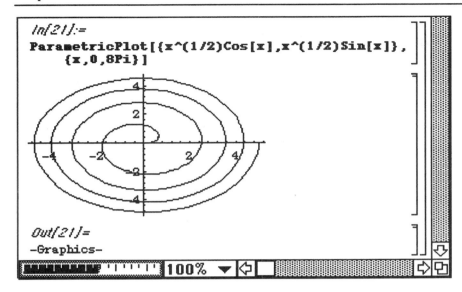

In[21]:=
**ParametricPlot[{x^(1/2)Cos[x],x^(1/2)Sin[x]},
    {x,0,8Pi}]**

Out[21]=
-Graphics-

100%

ParametricPlot3D   168, 395, 703, 839
See 523, 570, 572-574   See Also: **Graphics3D**

   ParametricPlot3D is used to plot parametric curves in three dimensions.
ParametricPlot3D[{x[t],y[t],z[t]},{t,tmin,tmax}] generates the
three-dimensional curve defined by **x = x[t]**, **y = y[t]**, **z = z[t]** for **t=tmin** to
t=tmax. If the coordinates depend on two parameters, then
**ParametricPlot3D[{x[t,u],y[t,u],z[t,u]},{t,tmin,tmax},{u,
umin,umax}]** plots the surface which results. The command
**ParametricPlot3D[{x[t,u],y[t,u],z[t,u],shade},{t,tmin,
tmax},{u,umin,umax}]** shades the surface using the colors defined by **shade**. A
simultaneous plot is generated with
ParametricPlot3D[{x1,y2,z2},{x2,y2,y3},...]. **ParametricPlot3D**
uses the same options as **Graphics3D** with the addition of **Compiled** and
PlotPoints. If the default setting **PlotPoints->Automatic** is used, then the
setting **PlotPoints->75** is used for curves and **PlotPoints->{15,15}** is used
for surfaces.

Example:

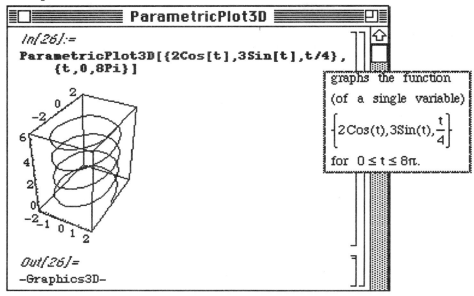

ParametricPlot3D

In[26]:=
```
ParametricPlot3D[{2Cos[t],3Sin[t],t/4},
    {t,0,8Pi}]
```

graphs the function
(of a single variable)

$$\left\{2\,Cos(t), 3\,Sin(t), \frac{t}{4}\right\}$$

for $0 \le t \le 8\pi$.

Out[26]=
-Graphics3D-

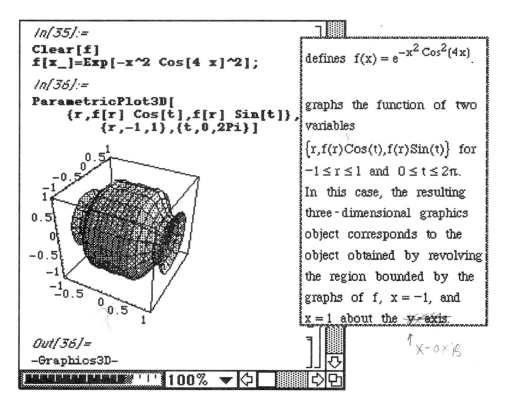

In[35]:=
```
Clear[f]
f[x_]=Exp[-x^2 Cos[4 x]^2];
```

defines $f(x) = e^{-x^2 \, Cos^2(4x)}$.

In[36]:=
```
ParametricPlot3D[
    {r,f[r] Cos[t],f[r] Sin[t]},
        {r,-1,1},{t,0,2Pi}]
```

graphs the function of two variables $\left\{r, f(r)\,Cos(t), f(r)\,Sin(t)\right\}$ for $-1 \le r \le 1$ and $0 \le t \le 2\pi$. In this case, the resulting three-dimensional graphics object corresponds to the object obtained by revolving the region bounded by the graphs of f, $x = -1$, and $x = 1$ about the y-axis.

$\uparrow$ x-axis

Out[36]=
-Graphics3D-

100%

ParentDirectory   490, 839

            See Also: **Directory, HomeDirectory**

    ParentDirectory is used to determine the parent of a directory. **ParentDirectory[]** yields the name of the parent of the current working directory while **ParentDirectory["dname"]** gives the name of the parent of the directory called **dname**.

Example:

Part([[...]])   57, 58, 82, 125, 126, 195, 651, 840

See 91, 113, 162, 245, 246   See Also: **First, Head, Last, HeldPart,**

273, 308, 375, 376, 408,   **Position, ReplacePart, MapAt, Take**

409, 427, 428, 707, 709

    Part is used to extract particular parts of expressions. **Part[expr,i]** or **expr[[i]]** yields the **i**th part of expression. **expr[[-i]]** counts the **i**th part from the end. **expr[[0]]** yields the head of **expr**. **Part[expr,{i,j,..}]** or **expr[[i,j,..]]** yields the part **{i,j,..}** of **expr**. Several parts are given with **Part[expr,i,j,..]**.

Example:

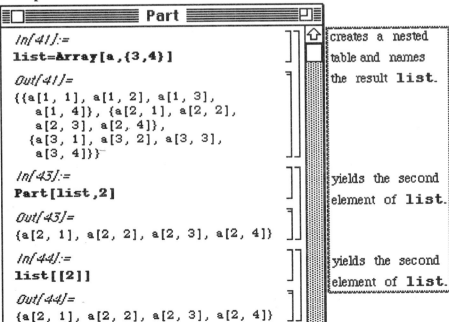

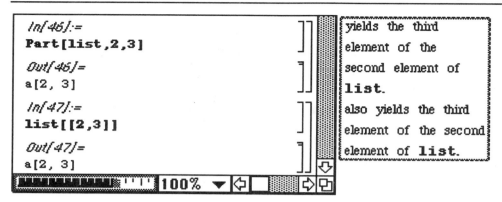

Partition   131, 840
See 127, 131, 566   See Also: **Flatten**, **RotateLeft**

   Partition is used to partition lists into sublists. **Partition[list,n]** forms **n** sublists from **list**. **Partition[list,n,d]** also creates n sublists with each sublist offset by **d** elements. Also, **Partition[list,{n1,n2,...},{d1,d2,...}]** partitions successive levels of list into sublists of length **ni** using offsets **di**.

Example:

In the following example, the set of numbers **nums** is first partitioned into two element subsets and then partitioned into three element subsets using offsets of length two.

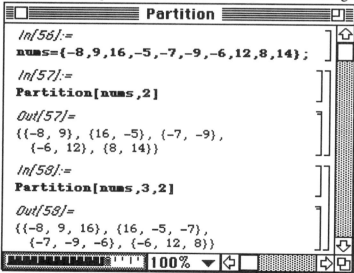

PartitionsP   558, 840
                                  See Also: **StirlingS1**, **StirlingS2**,
                                  PartitionsQ, **Multinomial**

   PartitionP[n] yields the number of unrestricted partitions of the integer **n**, p(**n**).

Example:

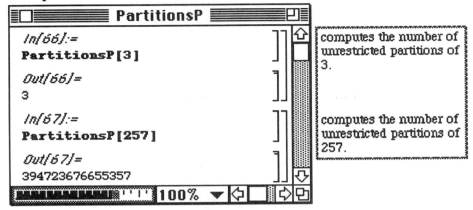

PartitionsQ   558, 840
                           See Also: **PartitionsP, StirlingS1,**
                           StirlingS2, Multinomial

PartitionsQ[n] yields the number of distinct partitions of the integer **n**, q(**n**).

Example:

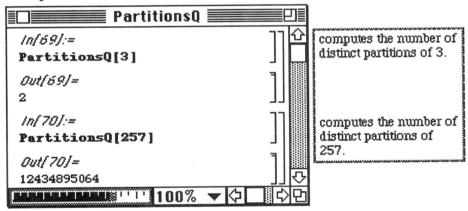

Pattern(:)   223, 719, 840

Pattern, symbolized **sym:obj**, represents the assignment of the pattern object **obj** the name **sym**. This operator has very low precedence.

PatternTest(?)   228, 716, 841
                           See Also: **Condition**

PatternTest, symbolized **patt?test**, represents a pattern **patt** which matches an expression only if the value of **test** is True when it is applied to the expression. Using **PatternTest(?)** instead of **Condition(/;)** applies **test** to the entire expression matched by **patt** to decide if the match exists. With **Condition**, the evaluation of conditions involving pattern names to determine a match is allowed. **PatternTest** has a high precedence level.

Pause   524, 841

See Also: **SessionTime**

Pause[n] causes *Mathematica* to pause for at least **n** seconds. The time elapsed during **Pause[n]** is counted in **SessionTime**. However, it does not count in **TimeUsed**, **Timing**, or **TimeConstrained**.

Example:

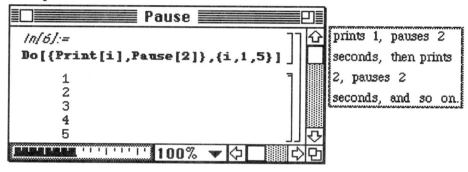

Permutations   11, 133, 841

See Also: **Sort**, **Signature**, **Reverse**,
RotateLeft

Permutations[list] produces all possible orderings of **list**. The output is given in the form of a list. Note that if **list** is of length n, then there are n! possible orderings.

Example:

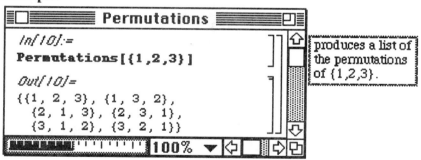

Pi   50, 566, 841

See 3, 303   See Also: **Degree**

Pi is the *Mathematica* symbol for the constant π which has numerical value of approximately 3.14159.

Example:

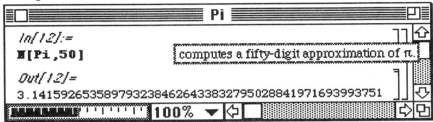

In[12]:=	
N[Pi,50]	computes a fifty-digit approximation of π.
Out[12]=	
3.1415926535897932384626433832795028841971693993751	

Pivoting   667
                          See Also: **QRDecomposition**,
                          SchurDecomposition

Pivoting is an option used with decomposition functions to indicate if column pivoting is to be done. The setting **Pivoting->True** causes *Mathematica* to permute the rows and columns of the matrix M and perhaps rescale before performing the decomposition algorithm. In some cases, this improves the stability of the numerical algorithm. The result of this option setting is the list {Q,R,P} where P is the permutation matrix such that M.P=Conjugate[Transpose[Q]].R

Plain

                          See Also: **TextRendering**

Plain is a setting for the option **TextRendering** which indicates how output on a character-oriented display device is to be rendered. Note that Version 2.0 does not support the **TextRendering** option.

Play   5, 176, 474, 841
                          See Also: **ListPlay**, **SampledSoundFunction**,
                          Show

Play is the command used by *Mathematica* to produce sound. This is accomplished by using a function to define the waveform of a sound. In other words, **Play[func,{t,tmin,tmax}]** causes *Mathematica* to play the sound which has amplitude given by the function of time, **func** over the time period **t** = **tmin** to **t** = **tmax**. Stereo is generated with **Play[{f1,f2},{t,tmin,tmax}]** while sounds over several channels are given with **Play[{f1,f2,...},{t,tmin,tmax}]**. **Play** has many options. They are listed with their default settings as follows: **Compiled->True**, **DisplayFunction->$SoundDisplayFunction**, **Epilog->{}**, **PlayRange->Automatic**, **Prolog->{}**, **SampleDepth->8**, **SampleRate->8192**. The object returned by **Play** is a **Sound** object.

Example:

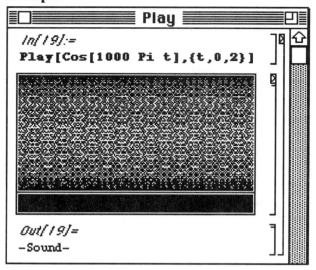

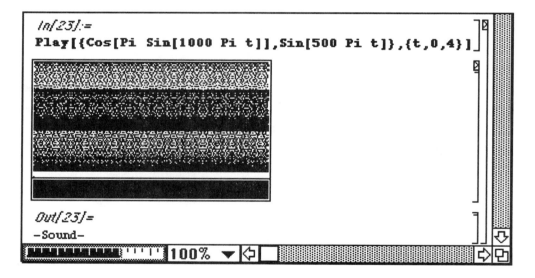

PlayRange   177, 842
                                  See Also: **SampleDepth**

  PlayRange is analogous to the **Graphics** option **PlotRange**. It gives the range of amplitude values allowed for a particular **Play** command. The settings for this option include **Automatic** which internally scale the amplitude values, **All** which specifies that amplitudes should be scaled so that they all fit into the allowed range, and **{ampmin,ampmax}** which places limits on allowable amplitudes. Amplitude values outside of the specified range are clipped.

Plot

See 121, 124, 127-129, 141, 146, 147, 160, 161, 165, 176, 180, 189, 193, 195, 200, 218, 220, 231, 233, 234, 236, 240, 256, 275, 294, 304, 307, 308, 316, 318, 331, 355, 356, 358, 387, 410, 422, 425, 428, 430, 438, 458, 459, 462, 478, 518, 554-557, 559, 560, 587, 589, 591, 593, 596, 597, 614, 615, 617-631, 684, 686, 688, 691, 708, 709, 711, 713, 715-721, 726, 731, 732, 734

134, 139, 279, 285, 395, 411, 842, 844

See Also: **ListPlot, Graphics, ParametricPlot, Plot3D, ParametricPlot3D, DensityPlot, ContourPlot**

Plot is used to plot functions of one variable. **Plot[f[x],{x,xmin,xmax}]** plots the function **f[x]** over the interval **x=xmin** to **x=xmax**.
Plot[{f1[x],f2[x],...},{x,xmin,xmax}] plots several functions simultaneously. The options used with **Graphics** are also available to **Plot** along with the addition of several more. These additional options as well as their default setting are **Complied->True, MaxBend->10, PlotDivision->20, PlotPoints->25**, and **PlotStyle->Automatic**. The setting for **PlotPoints** is used to initially select equally spaced sample points. *Mathematica* then selects other sample points in an attempt to minimize **MaxBend**. The **PlotDivision** setting limits the number of subdivisions taken on any interval. Note that since *Mathematica* samples only a finite number of points, the plot which is produced by **Plot** may be inaccurate. Plot returns a **Graphics** object.

Example:

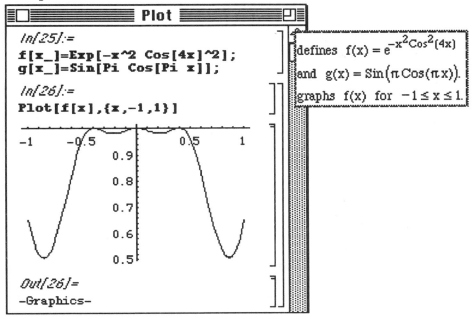

In fact, several functions can be graphed and displayed simultaneously with the **Plot** command.

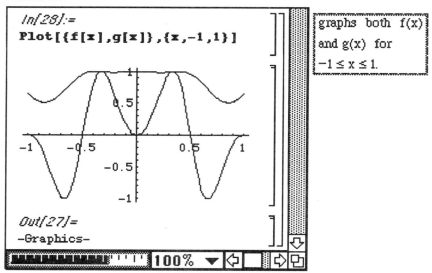

```
In[28]:=
Plot[{f[x],g[x]},{x,-1,1}]
```

graphs both f(x) and g(x) for $-1 \le x \le 1$.

```
Out[27]=
-Graphics-
```

PlotColor   obsolete in Version 2.0
                                                 superseded by **ColorOutput**

PlotDivision   143, 843
See 517, 518   See Also: **MaxBend**

    PlotDivision is an option used with **Plot** to indicate the maximum factor to subdivide an interval in choosing sample points of the function being plotted. *Mathematica* attempts to create a curve which contains no bends greater than **MaxBend**. To do this, it selects more sample points, but this number is limited by value of **PlotDivision**.

PlotJoined   164, 843
See 517, 543-546, 548,   See Also: **Line**
766, 767

    PlotJoined is a **ListPlot** option which indicates if the points that are plotted should be connected with line segments. **PlotJoined->True** specifies that the line segments be drawn. However, the default value is **PlotJoined->False**. Various styles for the line segments can be included with **PlotStyle**.

PlotLabel   139, 418, 459, 843
See 514, 521, 574, 582   See Also: **AxesLabel**

    PlotLabel is a graphics function option which indicates a label for the plot. The default value for this option is **PlotLabel->False**, so a label is not included unless otherwise requested with **PlotLabel->label**. If the label is a mathematical expression, then it is automatically written in **OutputForm**. However, any label containing text should be placed in quotation marks, **PlotLabel->"label"**. If mathematical expressions are placed in quotation marks, then they are printed as they appear in the command.

PlotPoints

See 123, 124, 126, 131, 136, 137, 178, 196, 231, 232, 235-238, 241-243, 248, 254, 271, 397, 398, 411, 515-518, 523, 524, 541, 576, 578, 582, 583

143, 152, 154, 156, 843

See Also: **PlotDivision**

PlotPoints is a plotting function option used to indicate the total number of equally spaced sample points to be used. This setting can be made in several ways. **PlotPoints->n** indicates that **n** points be used while with two variables **PlotPoints->n** implies that **n** points be selected in the direction of both coordinates. If different numbers are to be used in the two directions, then **PlotPoints->{nx,ny}** is used.

PlotRange

See 220, 308, 316, 318, 430, 514, 521, 532, 533, 549, 550, 559, 569, 576, 579, 582, 591, 596, 597, 618-631

139, 142, 152, 156, 414, 450, 843

See Also: **PlotRegion**, **AspectRatio**, **FullOptions**

PlotRange is an option used with graphics functions to indicate the function values to be included in the plot. If the function is one-dimensional, then **PlotRange** limits the y-values. However, if the function is two-dimensional, then the z-coordinate is restricted. The setting **PlotRange->All** indicates that all points are to be included while **PlotRange->Automatic** implies that outlying points be omitted. Also, the setting **PlotRange->{min,max}** places definite limits on the y-values or z-values to be displayed in the plot depending on the number of dimensions present. In addition, this option can be used as **PlotRange->{{xmin,xmax},{ymin,ymax}}** to indicate translation from original to translation coordinates. Note also that **Automatic** can be used as one component of a setting of the form **{min,max}**.

PlotRegion

See 514, 521

414, 843

See Also: **PlotRange**, **AspectRatio**, **Scaled**, **SphericalRegion**, **Background**

PlotRegion is a graphics function option which is used to indicate where the corners of the rectangular region lie within the final display area. The corner positions are scaled values between 0 and 1 across the display area. The default setting is **PlotRegion->{{0,1},{0,1}}** which implies that the rectangular region fill the entire display area. Unfilled portions of the region are displayed according to the setting of the **Background** option.

PlotStyle

See 240, 248, 318, 356, 358, 387, 462, 517, 518, 548, 557, 560, 587, 589, 591, 597

143, 411, 844

See Also: **Graphics**

PlotStyle is an option used with **Plot** and **ListPlot** to indicate the manner in which lines or points be displayed. The setting **PlotStyle->style** implies that all lines or points be drawn using the graphics directive **style**. Such directives include **RGBColor**, **Thickness**, **Hue**, and **GrayLevel**. **PlotStyle** is often useful in multiple plots. The setting **PlotStyle->{{style1,style2,...}}** indicates that successive lines or points be rendered with the listed directives. Styles must be enclosed in lists as they are used cyclically.

Plot3D
See 97, 123, 178, 235, 236, 243, 254, 271, 397, 398, 422, 523, 575, 576, 578, 581-583

154, 156, 162, 285, 395, 447, 452, 842
See Also: **ListPlot3D**, **ContourPlot**, **DensityPlot**, **Graphics3D**

Plot3D is used to plot functions of two variables.

Plot3D[f[x,y],{x,xmin,xmax},{y,ymin,ymax}] yields a three-dimensional plot of the function **f[x,y]** over the region defined by **{xmin,xmax}** × **{ymin,ymax}** in the xy-plane. Also,

Plot3D[{f[x,y],shade},{x,xmin,xmax},{y,ymin,ymax}] yields a three-dimensional plot with shading according to the settings of **shade**. The possible directives used to define shade are **RGBColor**, **GrayLevel**, and **Hue**. The same options which are used with **SurfaceGraphics** are used with **Plot3D** as well, but there are two additional options for use with **Plot3D**. These are **Compiled** and **PlotPoints**. Note that the default setting for these options are **Compiled->True** and **PlotPoints->15**. Hence, *Mathematica* automatically selects 15 sample points in each direction. If no shading option is included and if **Lighting->False**, then shading is done according to height. The object returned by **Plot3D** is a **SurfaceGraphics** object which includes a setting for the **MeshRange** option.

Example:

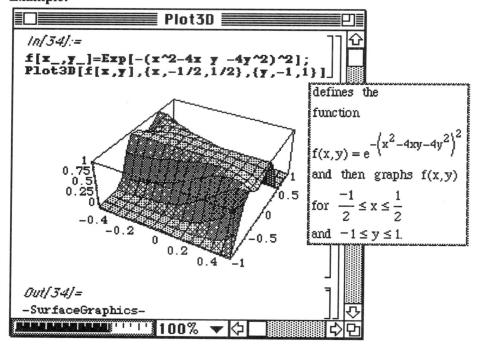

Plot3Matrix

xix (obsolete in Version 2.0)
superseded by **ViewCenter** and **ViewVertical**

Plus (+)   47, 230, 234, 844
See 173, 464   See Also: **Minus**, **Subtract**, **AddTo**, **Increment**

   Plus, symbolized **+**, is used to represent the sum of expressions. The attributes of **Plus** are **Flat**, **Orderless**, and **OneIdentity**. **Plus[]** yields a value of 0 while **Plus[x]** gives **x**.

Example:

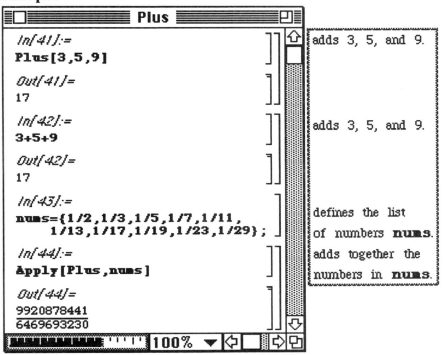

Pochhammer   571, 572, 844
                              See Also: **Beta**, **Binomial**, **Gamma**, **Factorial**, **Hypergeometric0F1**, **Hypergeometric1F1**, **Hypergeometric2F1**

Pochhammer[a,n] represents the Pochhammer symbol $(a)_n = \dfrac{\Gamma(a+n)}{\Gamma(n)}$.

Example:

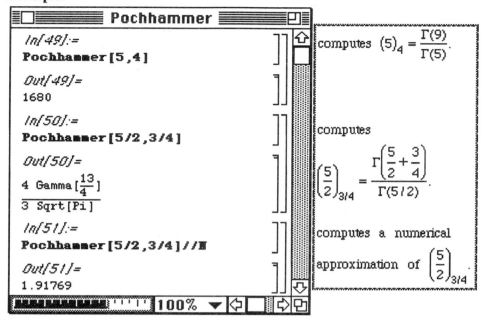

Point   400, 430, 434, 844
See 165, 219, 354, 512,   See Also: **Graphics**, **Text**, **Epilog**, **Prolog**
519, 528, 558, 564

   Point[coords] is the graphics primitive for a point in two or three dimensions. The coordinates given in **coords** can be expressed as **{x,y}** or **{x,y,z}** or they can be scaled with **Scaled[{x,y}]** or **Scaled[{x,y,z}]**. Points are rendered as circular regions and may be shaded or colored using **GrayLevel**, **Hue**, **RGBColor**, or **CMYKColor**. The size of the point is controlled by the option **PointSize**.

Example:

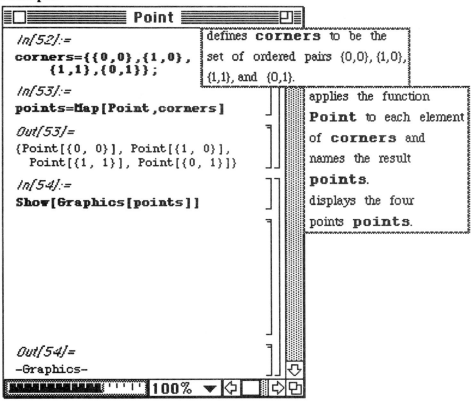

PointForm

See Also: **PointSize**, **Point**

PointForm[direct] is a three-dimensional graphics directive used to indicate that points are to be drawn using the graphics directive **direct**. Also, a list of graphics can be entered for **direct**.

PointSize   408, 435, 844
See 165, 219, 528, 558,   See Also: **AbsolutePointSize**, **Graphics**,
564, 666, 668, 671-673,   **Point**, **Thickness**, **Prolog**, **Epilog**
691

PointSize[r] indicates that all **Point** elements be drawn as circles of radius **r** in the graphics object. The radius **r** is measured as a fraction of the width of the entire plot. The default setting in two dimensions is **PointSize[0.008]** while it is **PointSize[0.01]** for three dimensions.

Example:

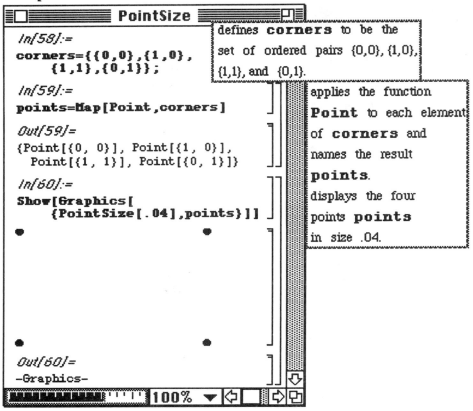

PolyGamma   571, 573, 844
                               See Also: **Gamma**, **LogGamma**, **EulerGamma**

PolyGamma[z] represents the digamma function $\psi(z) = \dfrac{\Gamma'(z)}{\Gamma(z)}$. Also,

PolyGamma[n,z] represents the **n** th derivative of the digamma function

$$\psi^{(n)}(z) \; = \; \frac{d^n}{dz^n}\psi(z).$$

Example:

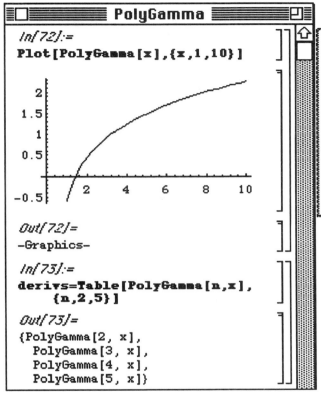

```
In[72]:=
Plot[PolyGamma[x],{x,1,10}]
```

```
Out[72]=
-Graphics-
```

```
In[73]:=
derivs=Table[PolyGamma[n,x],
    {n,2,5}]
```

```
Out[73]=
{PolyGamma[2, x],
  PolyGamma[3, x],
  PolyGamma[4, x],
  PolyGamma[5, x]}
```

graphs the digamma function $\psi(x) = \dfrac{\Gamma'(x)}{\Gamma(x)}$ for $1 \leq x \leq 10$. creates a table of the functions $\psi^{(n)}(x)$ for $n = 2, 3, 4, 5$ and names the result **derivs**.

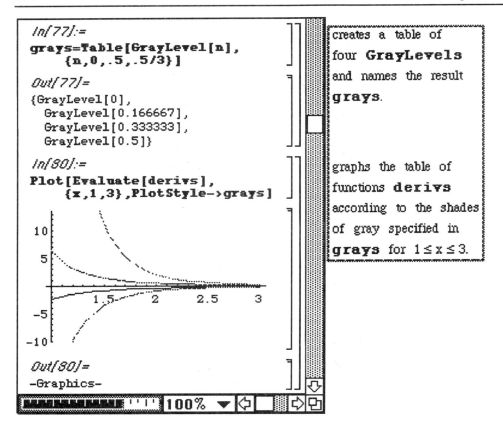

In[77]:=
**grays=Table[GrayLevel[n],
    {n,0,.5,.5/3}]**

Out[77]=
{GrayLevel[0],
   GrayLevel[0.166667],
   GrayLevel[0.333333],
   GrayLevel[0.5]}

In[80]:=
**Plot[Evaluate[derivs],
    {x,1,3},PlotStyle->grays]**

Out[80]=
-Graphics-

creates a table of four **GrayLevels** and names the result **grays**.

graphs the table of functions **derivs** according to the shades of gray specified in **grays** for $1 \leq x \leq 3$.

Polygon   396, 400, 430, 845
See 512, 519, 529, 565   See Also: **Raster**, **Rectangle**, **Cuboid**,
                                SurfaceColor

Polygon is a two- and three-dimensional graphics primitive for a filled polygon.
Polygon[{point1,point2,...}] represents a polygon with corners at the points
listed in **{point1,point2,...}**. These points may be of the form **{x,y}** or
{x,y,z}. Coordinates can be scaled as well with **Scaled[{x,y}]** and
Scaled[{x,y,z}]. Depending on the number of dimensions, **Polygon** can be
used in **Graphics** or **Graphics3D**. Polygons are formed by connecting successive
points. Self-intersecting polygons may occur in two dimensions, However, polygons
which intersect themselves in three dimensions are broken into smaller parts which do
not. Polygons in three dimensions also have a front and a back where faces are ordered
in a counter-clockwise direction from the front of the polygon. Directives such as
EdgeForm and **FaceForm** can be used to render three-dimensional polygons. The
directives **GrayLevel** and **RGBColor** can be used for displaying all polygons.
Polygons are displayed with **Show**.

Example:

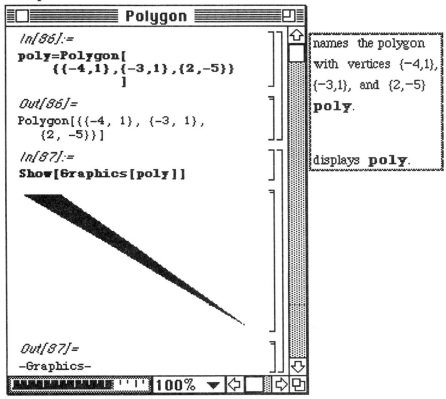

PolygonIntersections 467, 845
See 521   See Also: **RenderAll**

    PolygonIntersections is a **Graphics3D** option which is used to break a polygon which intersects itself into pieces which do not intersect when displayed with **Show**. The setting which accomplishes this is **PolygonIntersections->False**. This option is useful when sending graphics objects to external programs which do not accept self-intersecting polygons. The default setting is
PolygonIntersections->True.

PolyLog   571, 575, 634, 845
See 216   See Also: **Zeta**, **PolyGamma**, **LerchPhi**

    PolyLog[n,z] represents the polylogarithm functions $\text{Li}_n(z) = \sum_{k=1}^{\infty} \frac{z^k}{k^n}$. These

functions are encountered in particle physics and are also called Jonquiere's functions.

Example:

The following example creates the table of functions

$\{Li_{1/2}(x), Li_1(x), Li_{3/2}(x)\}$, names the result **pls**, and graphs **pls** for

$-1 \le x \le \dfrac{3}{4}$. The graph $Li_{1/2}(x)$ is black; the graph of $Li_{3/2}(x)$ is the

lightest.

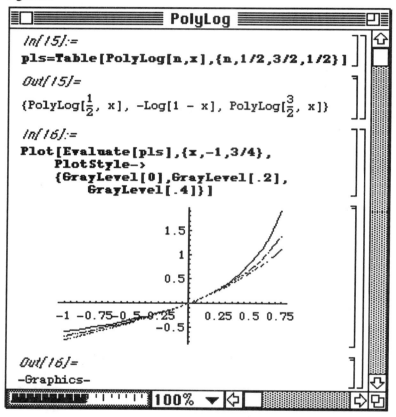

PolynomialDivision

See Also: **Divide, Mod, PolynomialMod, PolynomialQuotient, PolynomialRemainder,**

   PolynomialDivision[p,q,x] lists the quotient and remainder term obtained after division of the polynomial **p** by the poynomial **q**. The functions **p** and **q** as well as the result are functions of the variable **x**.

Example:

The following example defines **polyone** $= -7 - x - 3x^2 - x^3 + 6x^4 + 6x^5$,

polytwo $= 5 + 9x + 2x^2$, and computes

$$5+9x+2x^2\overline{\smash{\big)}-7-x-3x^2-x^3+6x^4+6x^5} = \frac{-1215}{8} + \frac{157}{4}x - \frac{21}{2}x^2 + 3x^3$$

with remainder $\dfrac{6019}{8} + \dfrac{9357}{8}x.$

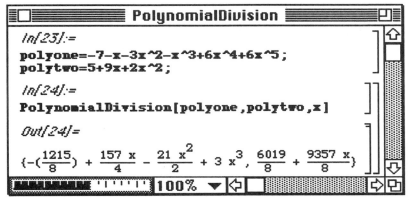

PolynomialGCD   598, 845

See Also: **PolynomialLCM**, **PolynomialQuotient**,
GCD, **Cancel**, **PolynomialMod**

PolynomialGCD[poly1,poly2] yields the greatest common divisor of the two
polynomials, **poly1** and **poly2**. This command has the option **Modulus->p** which
determines the greatest common divisor modulo the integer **p**.

Example:
The following example computes the greatest common divisor of the polynomials
$1024+2048x+640x^2-960x^3-540x^4+108x^5+81x^6$ and
$324-1620x+3321x^2-3564x^3+2106x^4-648x^5+81x^6$.

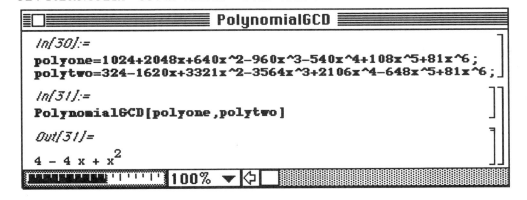

PolynomialLCM   598, 845

See Also: **PolynomialGCD**, **LCM**

PolynomialLCM[poly1,poly2] yields the least common multiple of the two
polynomials, **poly1** and **poly2**. This command has the option **Modulus->p** which
determines the least common multiple modulo the integer **p**.

Example:

The following example computes the least common multiple of the polynomials $243-81x-135x^2+9x^3+24x^4+4x^5$ and $-9+93x-355x^2+603x^3-432x^4+108x^5$.

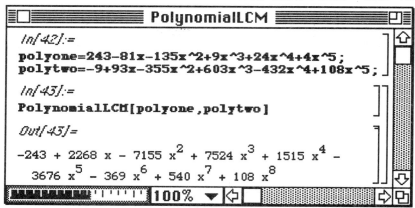

PolynomialMod   598, 846

See Also: **PolynomialGCD, Mod, PolynomialRemainder**

PolynomialMod[poly,m] reduces the polynomial **poly** modulo **m**. If **m** is an integer, then this is done by reducing each of the coefficients modulo **m**. However, if **m** is a polynomial, then *Mathematica* subtracts polynomial multiples of **m** to determine the reduced polynomial having minimal leading coefficient as well as minimal degree. Also, **PolynomialMod[poly,{m1,m2,...}]** reduces **poly** modulo all of the **{m1,m2,...}**.

Example:

The following example reduces the polynomial $10+10x+9x^2+8x^3+8x^4+6x^5$ modulo 2.

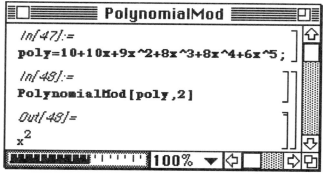

PolynomialQ   227, 593, 846

See Also: **Collect**, **Series**

   Polynomial[expression,var] tests **expression** to determine if it is a polynomial in the variable **var**. A value of True is given if **expression** is a polynomial while a value of **False** is given otherwise. An expression which contains approximate real numbers is not considered a polynomial. This command can be used as **Polynomial[expression,varlist]** to determine if **expression** is a polynomial of the variables listed in **varlist**.

Example:

In the following example, $10 + 10x + 9x^2 + 8x^3 + 8x^4 + 6x^5$ represents

a polynomial object while $\dfrac{-3 - 9x}{4 - 8x}$ does not represent a polynomial

in x.

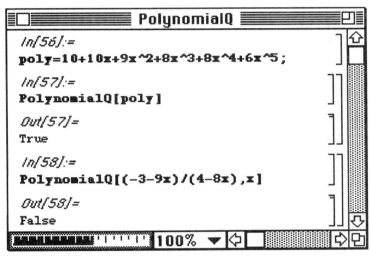

PolynomialQuotient   598, 846

See Also: **PolynomialDivision**,
                PolynomialGCD, **Apart**, **Cancel**, **Quotient**

   PolynomialQuotient[p,q,x] determines the quotient obtained through division of the polynomial **p** by the polynomial **q** where **p** and **q** are both functions of the variable **x**. The remainder is not included in the result.

Example:

The following example shows that the quotient obtained by dividing

$$-7 - x - 3x^2 - x^3 + 6x^4 + 6x^5 \text{ by } 5 + 9x + 2x^2 \text{ is } \frac{-1215}{8} + \frac{157}{4}x - \frac{21}{2}x^2 + 3x^3.$$

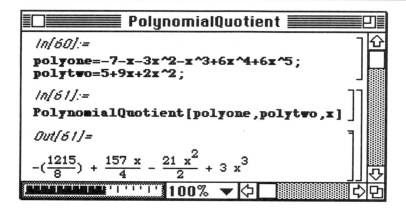

PolynomialRemainder   598, 846
>   See Also: **PolynomialDivision**,
>   **PolynomialMod**, **Apart**, **Cancel**, **Mod**

PolynomialRemainder[p,q,x] determines the remainder obtained through division of the polynomial **p** by the polynomial **q** where **p** and **q** are both functions of the variable **x**. The remainder which results always has order less than that of **q**.

Example:

The following example shows that the remainder obtained by dividing

$$-7 - x - 3x^2 - x^3 + 6x^4 + 6x^5 \quad \text{by} \quad 5 + 9x + 2x^2 \quad \text{is} \quad \frac{6019}{8} + \frac{9357}{8}x.$$

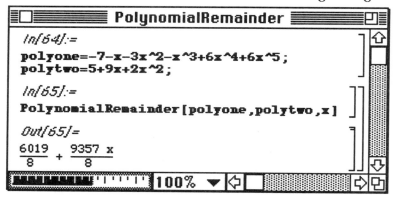

Position   11, 127, 198, 205, 221, 222, 725, 846
>   See Also: **Cases**, **Count**, **Part**, **StringPosition**

Position is used to locate the positions in an expression which match a certain pattern. **Position[expression,patt]** finds the positions in **expression** which match the form defined by **patt**. In this case, *Mathematica* searches all levels of **expression** to find any matches. Also, the command **Position[expression,patt,lev,n]** lists the first **n** positions on level **lev** found in **expression** which match the form of **patt**. However, the command can be entered as **Position[expression,patt,lev]** so that only subexpresssions at level **lev** are searched. The result is given in the form of a list to which **MapAt** can be applied.

Example:
In the following example, the list **vals** is defined. The expression **1+2x** occurs in position {2,1} of **vals**. Hence, entering the command **vals[[2,1]]** would yield 1+2x. Similarly, the expression **2** occurs at positions {2,1,2,1} and {3,2} of **vals** so that the commands **vals[[2,1,2,1]]** and **vals[[3,2]]** would both yield 2.

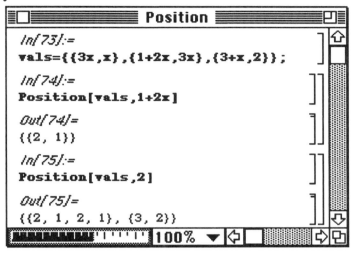

Positive   846
                    See Also: **Negative**, **NonNegative**, **Sign**
   Positive[x] yields a value of **True** if **x** is a positive number. If **x** is zero or negative, then a value of **False** results. If **x** does not fall into any of these classifications, then **Positive[x]** is not evaluated. This command can be used as **Positive[x]=True** to define **x** to be positive.

Example:

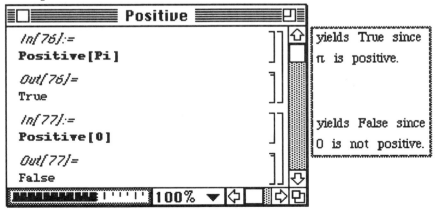

Postfix   362, 847
                          See Also: **Infix**, **Prefix**
   Postfix is used to print expressions in postfix form. **Postfix[f[x],h]** yields **x h** while **Postfix[f[x]]** yields **x//f**.

Example:

PostScript   xx, 465, 847
See 512   See Also: **RGBColor**, **Dashing**, **Thickness**,
                                     PointSize
   PostScript["string1,string2",...] allows for the specification of certain strings to be included verbatim in a two-dimensional graphics primitive. **PostScript** must be used with care. The coordinate system runs from 0 to 1 in the horizontal direction while it goes from 0 to **AspectRatio** in the vertical direction. Also, the **PostScript** stack must be returned to its original form when completed, and the **PostScript** interpreter used to display the graphics must support all inserted graphics primitives.

Power(^)   47, 234, 847
See 173, 279   See Also: **Sqrt**, **Exp**, **PowerExpand**, **PowerMod**,
                                     Log
   Power, symbolized by ^, is used to represent an expression raised to a power. For example, **a^b** means "**a** raised to the power **b**". If the exponent **b** is a fraction, then the result is given as an exact number when possible. When dealing with complex numbers, then **a^b** yields the principal value of exp(**b** log **a**). If **c** is an integer, then **(a^b)^c** automatically becomes **a^(b^c)** and **(a b)^c** automatically becomes **(a^c) (b^c)**.

Example:

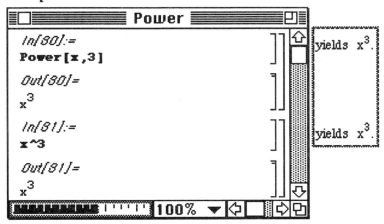

PowerExpand   81, 592, 847

> See Also: **ComplexExpand**, **Expand**, **Distribute**

PowerExpand[expression] expands out terms of the form **(a b)^c** and **(a^b)^c** which appear in **expression**. Unlike **Power**, this expansion is carried out even if **c** is not in the form of an integer.

Example:

The following example illustrates how **PowerExpand** and **Expand** operate differently on the expression $(ab)^{1/3}$.

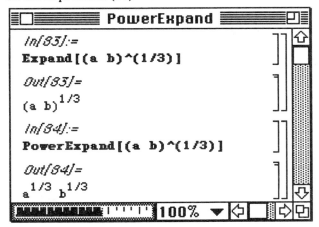

PowerMod   556, 847
                              See Also: **Mod, PolynomialMod**

PowerMod[a,b,n] yields a^b mod **n**. For positive values of **b**, the result is the same as that of **Mod[a^b,n]**, but **PowerMod** yields the result more quickly. Also, for negative values of **b**, the result gives the value of the integer **k** (the modular inverse) such that $ka^{-b} = 1$ mod **n** if such a number exists. Otherwise, the expression is left unevaluated.

Example:

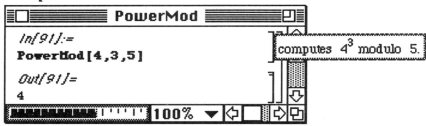

PrecedenceForm   362, 716, 717, 718, 847
                              See Also: **Infix**

PrecedenceForm[expression,n] prints **expression** such that objects are parenthesized with a precedence level of **n**. Precedence levels are integers from 1 to 1000. The higher the precedence level for an operator, the less the need for parentheses. **PrecedenceForm** only affects the printing of an expression. It does not change any calculations.

Precision   539, 848
See 419   See Also: **Accuracy, N, Chop, SetPrecision,**
                              MachineNumberQ

Precision[x] yields the number of significant decimal digits present in the number **x**. If **x** is an expression, then the smallest value of **Precision** for all numbers in the expression is given as the value for **Precision[x]**. Also, if **x** is an integer, then **Precision[x]** yields **Infinity**. In addition, **Precision[x]** gives a value of **$MachinePrecision** if **x** is a machine-precision number.

Example:

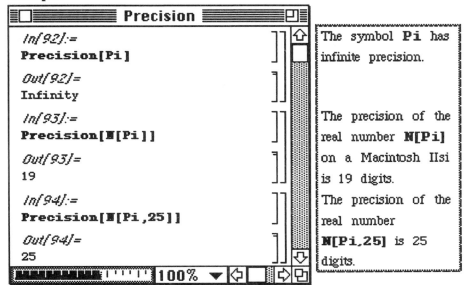

```
In[92]:=
Precision[Pi]

Out[92]=
Infinity

In[93]:=
Precision[N[Pi]]

Out[93]=
19

In[94]:=
Precision[N[Pi,25]]

Out[94]=
25
```

The symbol **Pi** has infinite precision.

The precision of the real number **N[Pi]** on a Macintosh IIsi is 19 digits.

The precision of the real number **N[Pi,25]** is 25 digits.

PrecisionGoal   688, 690, 700, 848
                            See Also: **AccuracyGoal**, **WorkingPrecision**,
                            NIntegrate, **NDSolve**

PrecisionGoal is an option used with numerical functions such as **NIntegrate** and **NDSolve** to indicate the number of digits of precision to attempt to have in the final solution. The default setting for this option is **PrecisionGoal->Automatic** which is 10 digits fewer than the setting for **WorkingPrecision**. The **PrecisionGoal** setting is used as one of the criteria for stopping the recursive algorithm used with **NIntegrate** and **NDSolve** unless **PrecisionGoal->Infinity** is used. In most cases, the setting for **PrecisionGoal** must be less than that of **WorkingPrecision**.

PreDecrement (--)   248, 848
                            See Also: **Decrement**, **Increment**,
                            PreIncrement, **SubtractFrom**, **Set**

PreDecrement, symbolized **--i**, is used to decrease the value of **i** by one unit and return the new value of **i**. In programming languages, this is equivalent to the statement **i=i-1**. **PreDecrement** has the attribute **HoldFirst**.

Example:

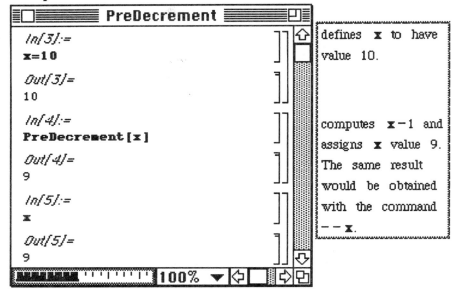

Prefix   362, 848
                                  See Also: `Infix`, `PostFix`
Prefix is used to place expressions in prefix notation. **Prefix[f[x],h]** yields **h
x**. Also, **Prefix[f[x]]** yields **f@x**.

Example:

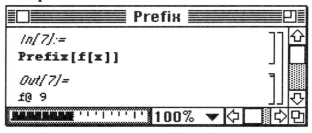

PreIncrement (++)   248, 848
See 530, 568   See Also: **Decrement**, **Increment**, **PreDecrement**,
                                  AddTo, **Set**
   PreIncrement, symbolized **++i**, is used to increase the value of **i** by one unit and
return the new value of **i**. In programming languages, this is equivalent to the
statement **i=i+1**. **PreIncrement** has the attribute **HoldFirst**.

Example:

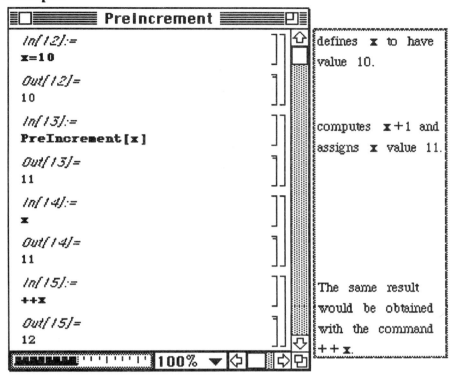

Prepend   128, 848

See Also: **Append**, **Insert**

  Prepend[expression,term] yields **expression** with **term** added to the beginning.

Example:

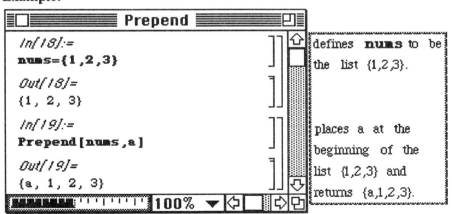

PrependTo   249, 848
                                             See Also: **AppendTo**
  PrependTo[list,element] is equivalent to
list=Prepend[list,element] in that **element** is prepended to **list** and the
value of **list** is reset to the prepended list.

Example:

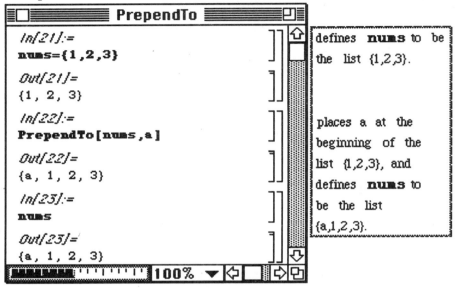

Prime   554, 849
See 44, 108, 169, 204,   See Also: **FactorInteger**, **PrimeQ**, **PrimePi**
299, 407, 460, 490
  Prime[n] yields the value of the **n**th prime number where **Prime[1]=2**. These
values are easily obtained for values of n through 10^8.

Example:

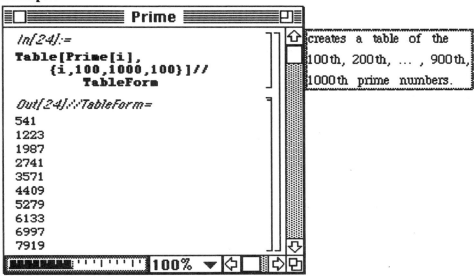

PrimePi   554, 849
                                     See Also: **Prime**, **Zeta**

PrimePi[x] represents the function π(**x**) which yields the number of prime numbers less than or equal to **x**. Note that **x** can be any positive real number, and **PrimePi[1]=0**.

Example:

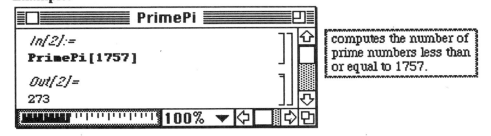

PrimeQ   227, 535, 554, 849
See 412   See Also: **FactorInteger**

PrimeQ[expression] tests **expression** to determine if it is prime. If **expression** is a prime number, then a value of True results. Otherwise, False is given. Note that **PrimeQ[1]** yields False and that **PrimeQ[-n]** yields True if **n** is a prime number. The tests upon which this command is based are the Rabin strong pseudoprime test and the Lucas test. The procedure has been proved for **n** < 2.5 x 10^{10}, but not for larger **n**. For larger values of **n**, the package **NumberTheory`PrimeQ`** can be loaded and used since its procedure is valid for all values of **n**. This procedure is much slower than the built-in command, however.

Example:

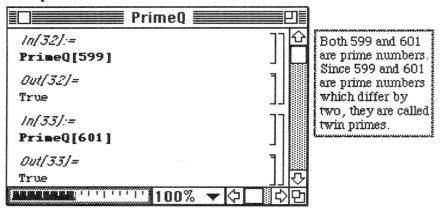

Print   116, 363, 486, 849
See 44, 108, 169, 204,   See Also: **Message**, **Put**, **Write**
299, 407, 460, 490

    Print[expression1,expression2,...] prints the expressions listed with no breaks, but includes a newline at the end. The output is sent to the channel **$Output** and the default format type used with **Print** is **OutputForm**. **ColumnForm** can be used to have expressions printed on several different lines.

PrintForm   344, 849
                                             See Also: **FullForm**, **TreeForm**

    PrintForm[expression] yields the internal representation of the print form for **expression**. The print form is made of the primitives **String** which is a raw character string, **HorizontalForm** which is a horizontal array of print objects, and **VerticalForm** which is a vertical array of print objects. These primitives are nested in the print form of an expression.

Product   90, 683, 849
                                             See Also: **Do**, **Sum**, **Table**, **NProduct**, **NSum**

    Product[f,{i,imax}] computes the product $\prod\limits_{i=1}^{imax} f$ while

Product[f,{i,imin,imax}] calculates the product $\prod\limits_{i=imin}^{imax} f$. If a step

size other than one unit is used, then **Product[f,{i,imin,imax,istep}]** determines the product using increments in **i** of **istep**. Multiple products can be evaluated with **Product[f,{i,imin,imax},{j,jmin,jmax}]**. As is the case with multiple integrals, the range for the outermost variable is given first.

Example:

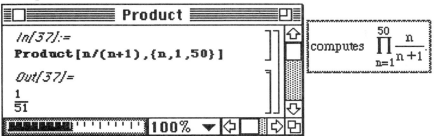

Prolog   412, 850

See 514, 521, 550, 558,   See Also: **Background, DefaultColor, Epilog,**
666, 668, 671, 672, 673,   **AxesStyle, PlotStyle, DisplayFunction**
691, 767

Prolog is a two- and three-dimensional graphics function option which indicates graphics directives to use before a plot is started. The graphics primitives given in Prolog are displayed after axes, boxes, and frames are rendered. Primitives used in two dimensions can also be used for three.

PromptForm

PromptForm[prompt,expression] prints **prompt** as an output prompt and then prints **expression**.

Protect   264, 273, 728, 850

See Also: **Unprotect**

Protect is used to assign the attribute **Protected** to certain symbols. The command **Protect[symbol1,symbol2,...]** assigns this attribute the symbols listed while **Protect["patt1","patt2",...]** assigns **Protected** to all symbols which match the form defined in the patterns listed. Metacharacters such as * can be used in the arguments of **Protect**.

Protected   272, 736, 850

See Also: **Locked, ReadProtected**

Protected is an attribute which when assigned to a symbol does not allow that symbol to be modified. This is an attribute of many built-in *Mathematica* functions.

PseudoInverse   665, 666, 850

See Also: **Inverse, SingularValues, Fit**

PseudoInverse[m] calculates the pseudoinverse or Moore-Penrose inverse for the rectangular matrix **m**. **PseudoInverse** has the option **Tolerance**. With the setting **Tolerance->t**, *Mathematica* removes the singular values of **m** which are smaller than **t** times the maximum singular value. The setting **Tolerance->Automatic**, the value of **t** is taken to be $10^{\wedge}(4-p)$ where p is the numerical precision of the input. The pseudoinverse is equivalent to the inverse for non-singular square matrices.

Put (>>)   178, 185, 371, 478, 850
See 568   See Also: **Save, Definition, Dump, Get**

Put is used to write expressions to files. This can be accomplished in more than one way. **Put[expression1,expression2,...,"namedfile"]** writes the expressions listed in **expression1**, **expression2**, ... to the file called **namedfile**. Also, **expression>>namedfile** writes **expression** to **namedfile**. The format type of these files is **InputForm** by default. Since *Mathematica* writes to the beginning of **namedfile**, previous information in **namedfile** is deleted.

PutAppend (>>>)   178, 478, 850
                                          See Also: **Write**

PutAppend is used to write expressions to files. However, instead of replacing the existing file, **PutAppend** adds output to the end of the file. The command which accomplishes this task is **expression>>>namedfile**. A sequence of expressions may be appended to a file with
PutAppend[expression1,expression2,...,"namedfile"].

Q

QRDecomposition   666, 851
                                    See Also: **SchurDecomposition**,
                                    SingularValues, **Transpose**

 QRDecomposition[m] determines the QR decomposition of the matrix **m**. This decomposition gives the matrix **m** yields the list {q,r} where **m** = q^t r. The matrix q is an orthonormal matrix and r is a triangular matrix. q^t yields the Hermetian conjugate of q. **QRDecomposition** has the option **Pivoting**. With the setting **Pivoting->True**, the list {q,r,p} results where
m.p=**Conjugate[Transpose[q]].r**.
Example:
In the following example, **matrix** is defined to be the numerical matrix
$\begin{bmatrix} 1 & 1 & 2 \\ -4 & 1 & -4 \\ 4 & 3 & 1 \end{bmatrix}$.   The QR decomposition of matrix is named **qrs**. The first

element of qrs is given by **qrs[[1]]**.

```
════════════════ QRDecomposition ════════════════
In[15]:=
matrix=N[{{1,1,2},{-4,1,-4},{4,3,1}}];

In[16]:=
qrs=QRDecomposition[matrix]

Out[16]=
{{{-0.174078, 0.696311, -0.696311},
    {-0.248788, -0.715266, -0.653069},
    {0.952786, -0.0595491, -0.297746}},
  {{-5.74456, -1.5667, -3.82971},
    {0, -2.92326, 1.71042}, {0, 0, 1.84602}}
  }

In[17]:=
qrs[[1]]

Out[17]=
{{-0.174078, 0.696311, -0.696311},
  {-0.248788, -0.715266, -0.653069},
  {0.952786, -0.0595491, -0.297746}}
```

Numerically,

$$\begin{bmatrix} -0.174 & 0.696 & -0.696 \\ -0.248 & -0.715 & -0.653 \\ 0.952 & -0.059 & -0.297 \end{bmatrix} \bullet \begin{bmatrix} -0.174 & 0.696 & -0.696 \\ -0.248 & -0.715 & -0.653 \\ 0.952 & -0.059 & -0.297 \end{bmatrix}^T = \begin{bmatrix} 1 & 0 & 0 \\ 0 & 1 & 0 \\ 0 & 0 & 1 \end{bmatrix}.$$

We illustrate this in the following example by first computing
qrs[[1]].Transpose[qrs[[1]]]:

```
In[18]:=
almost=qrs[[1]].Transpose[qrs[[1]]]

Out[18]=
{{1., 2.71051 10^-20, -1.0842 10^-19},
  {2.71051 10^-20, 1., -1.35525 10^-20},
  {-1.0842 10^-19, -1.35525 10^-20, 1.}}
```

and then using **Chop** to replace those terms with magnitude less than 10^{-10} by 0.

```
In[19]:=
Chop[almost]

Out[19]=
{{1., 0, 0}, {0, 1., 0}, {0, 0, 1.}}
```

qrs[[2]] yields the second element of the list (of two matrices) **qrs**. We illustrate

that $\begin{bmatrix} -0.174 & 0.696 & -0.696 \\ -0.248 & -0.715 & -0.653 \\ 0.952 & -0.059 & -0.297 \end{bmatrix}^{T} \begin{bmatrix} -5.744 & -1.566 & -3.829 \\ 0 & -2.923 & 1.710 \\ 0 & 0 & 1.846 \end{bmatrix} = \begin{bmatrix} 1 & 1 & 2 \\ -4 & 1 & -4 \\ 4 & 3 & 1 \end{bmatrix}$.

```
In[20]:=
qrs[[2]]

Out[20]=
{{-5.74456, -1.5667, -3.82971},
  {0, -2.92326, 1.71042}, {0, 0, 1.84602}}

In[21]:=
Transpose[qrs[[1]]].qrs[[2]]

Out[21]=
{{1., 1., 2.}, {-4., 1., -4.},
  {4., 3., 1.}}
```

100% ▼

Quartics   851
See Also: **Cubics, NSolve, Roots**

Quartics is an option used with functions such as **Roots** and **NSolve** to indicate whether explicit solutions should be found for irreducible quartic equations or if they should be left unsolved. The setting **Quartics->True** causes explicit solutions to be determined while **Quartics->False** causes irreducible fourth-degree equations to be kept in symbolic form.

Example:

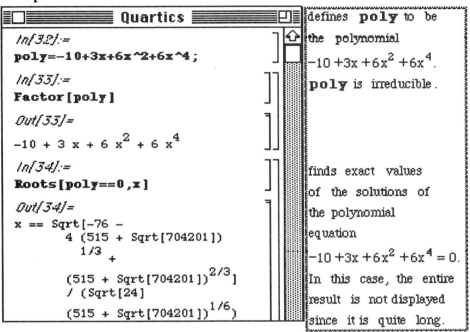

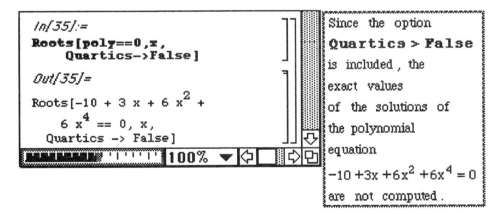

Quit   45, 519, 747, 851

See Also: **Exit, Return, $IgnoreEOF**

Quit[] is used to end a *Mathematica* session and is equivalent to **Exit[]**. If **Quit[n]** is entered, then the integer **n** becomes the exit code for the operating system. The value for the global variable **$Epilog** can be set so that *Mathematica* saves certain objects before exiting the session.

Quotient   553, 851
See Also: **Mod**, **PolynomialQuotient**

Quotient[m,n] yields the integer portion of the quotient **m/n**. This command is equivalent to **Floor[m/n]** for integers **m** and **n**.

Example:

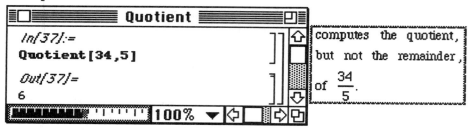

R

Random   49, 552, 588, 851
See 213, 460, 530,   See Also: **SeedRandom**
541, 549, 718

   Random is used to produce pseudorandom numbers. This is done in several ways.
Random[] yields a pseudorandom number between 0 and 1 while
Random[numbertype,{min,max}] gives a pseudorandom number of type
numbertype which is between **min** and **max**. The choices for **numbertype** include
Complex, **Real**, and **Integer**. Also, an **n**-digit precision pseudorandom number is
requested with **Random[numbertype,{min,max},n]**. If an interval **{min,max}**
is not specified, then the default is **{0,1}**. In addition, a single value **max** can be used
to indicate the interval **{0,max}**. When using numbers of type **Complex**, the interval
{min,max} represents the interval defined by **min** and **max**. Finally, note that
Random[Integer] yields 0 or 1 with probability 1/2.

Example:

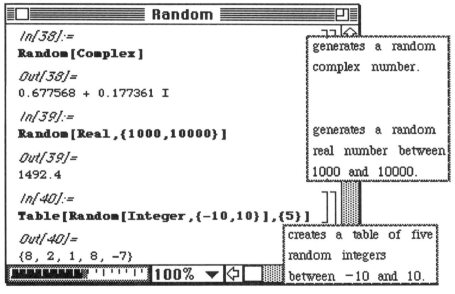

Range   122, 651, 851
See 407   See Also: **Table**

   Range is used to create lists of values. **Range[m]** generates the list {1,2,...m}
while **Range[m1,m2]** gives the list {m1,m1+1,...,m2}. If a step size other than
one unit is desired, then **Range[m1,m2,step]** can be used. In this case, the list
{m1,m1+step,...,m2} results. Note that the arguments of **Range** do not have to
be integers. They may include real numbers as well as other mathematical expressions.

Example:

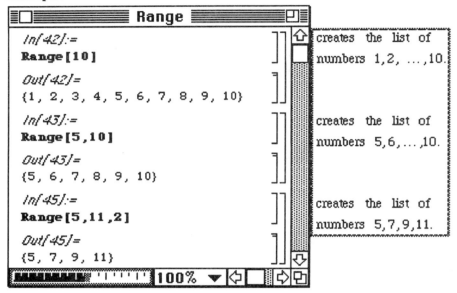

Raster   400, 405, 852
See 512, 530   See Also: **RasterArray**, **DensityGraphics**,
                                    GraphicsArray

   Raster is a two-dimensional graphics primitive used to represent a rectangular array
of gray cells. **Raster[{a11,a12,...},{a21,a22,...},...}]** represents an
array of cells having gray level between 0 and 1 while
**Raster[{a11,a12,...},{a21,a22,...},...},{xmin,xmax},{ymin,
ymax},{glmin,glmax}]** represents an array of gray level values between **glmin**
and **glmax** for cells in the rectangle defined by **{xmin,xmax}** × **{ymin,ymax}**.
Raster has the option **ColorFunction**. The option setting
ColorFunction->func gives a function for which each cell **aij** is evaluated to
determine the coloring of each cell. Also, **ColorFunction->Hue** bases the coloring
on **Hue**.
Example:
In the following example, **shadesone** corresponds to the rectangular array
$\begin{bmatrix} 0 & 1 & 0 \\ .25 & .5 & .25 \\ .5 & .75 & .5 \end{bmatrix}$ and **shadestwo** corresponds to the rectangular array

$\begin{bmatrix} 0 & 1/100 & \cdots & 1 \\ 0 & 1/100 & \cdots & 1 \\ \vdots & \vdots & \vdots & \vdots \\ 0 & 1/100 & \cdots & 1 \end{bmatrix}$ $\left(100 \text{ copies of the list } \left\{0, \frac{1}{100}, \frac{2}{100}, \cdots, \frac{99}{100}, 1\right\}\right)$.

small is a rectangle consisting of nine cells shaded according to **shadesone**; **big** is a rectangle consisting of 100^2 cells shaded according to **shadestwo**. Note that 0 corresponds to black; 1 corresponds to white.

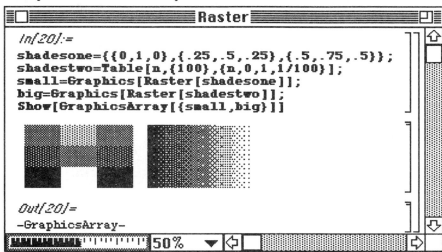

RasterArray   405, 852
See 512   See Also: **Raster, GraphicsArray**

RasterArray is a rectangular array of graphics directives which are used to color a rectangular array of cells.
RasterArray[{{g11,g12,...},{g21,g22,...},...}] colors the corresponding cell **aij** using the graphics directive **gij**. These graphics directives must be **GrayLevel**, **Hue**, or **RGBColor**. If the array of cells is m × n, then the **RasterArray** fills the rectangle **Rectangle[{0,0},{m,n}]**. Using
RasterArray[{{g11,g12,...},{g21,g22,...},...},{xmin,ymin},
{xmax,ymax}] indicates that the rectangle obtained with
Rectangle[{xmin,ymin},{xmax,ymax}] be occupied.

Rational   534, 712, 852
                               See Also: **Integer, Numerator, Denominator,**
                               Real, Head

Rational is the head used to indicate a rational number. Hence, numbers with head **Rational** can be written as a ratio a/b. The commands **Numerator** and **Denominator** are used to extract portions of rational expressions.

Example:

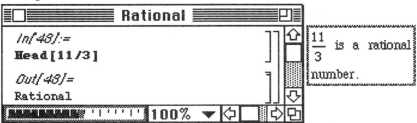

Rationalize   536, 852
See Also: **Chop**, **Round**, **LatticeReduce**

   Rationalize[x] is used to determine a rational number approximation of the approximate real number **x**. This command can be entered as **Rationalize[x,err]** to insure that the approximation is within the desired error **err**. Otherwise, the approximation p/q to **x** is considered acceptable if

$| p/q - \mathbf{x} | < ((10)^{-4})/q^2$. If no acceptable rational approximation exists, then the expression is unevaluated. This problem is avoided with **Rationalize[x,0]** which approximates any value of **x** with a rational number even if the error is larger than desirable.

Example:

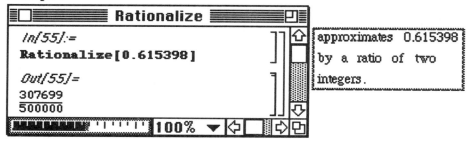

Raw   712, 852
See Also: **Run**

   Raw["head","hexadec"] is used to give raw data contained in some *Mathematica* objects. This data is given in hexadecimal digits which correspond to an array of bytes. **Raw** behaves differently from one implementation to another. Hence, its use is not encouraged. The end result of its use could be crashing the entire *Mathematica* session.

RawMedium

   RawMedium is an internal symbol.

Re   52, 551, 604, 853
See 243, 397, 462, 549   See Also: **Im**, **Arg**, **Abs**, **ComplexExpand**

   Re[z] is a numerical function for use with complex nubers to yield the real part of the complex number **z**. If the argument is not a complex number, then the expression is left unevaluated.

Example:

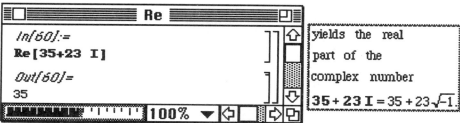

Read   499, 853
See 432   See Also: **Input, StringToStream, Skip, Find**

Read is used to read files in *Mathematica*. **Read[strm]** reads one expression from the input stream **strm** and returns that expression. Also, an object of a particular type from the input stream is read with **Read[strm,type]** as can a sequence of objects with **Read[strm,{type1,type2,...}]**. The types of objects which can be requested are **Byte, Expression, Real, Number, Record, Word, String**, and **Character**. If an object of the desired type is not found, then **$Failed** is returned. The options **WordSeparators, TokenWords, RecordSeparators, NullWords**, and **NullRecords** can be used with **Read** as well. Each time an object is read using **Read**, *Mathematica* sets the current point to be immediately after the object just read. If an attempt is made to read past the end of a file, then **EndOfFile** is returned.

ReadList   16, 181, 185, 493, 854
                                                   See Also: **FindList**

ReadList is used to read a list of data from a file and place them in the form of a *Mathematica* list. **ReadList["namedfile",Number]** reads in a list of numbers from **namedfile** and writes them as a *Mathematica* list. Objects of other types are read with **ReadList["namedfile",type]**. The command **ReadList["namedfile",type,n]** reads at most **n** objects. If no limit is placed on the number of objects, then *Mathematica* reads to the end of the file. Note that the files which are read with **ReadList** do not have to be in input form. Hence, this command is useful when reading files generated by external programs.

Example:
In the following example, **!!data** displays the data file **data**.

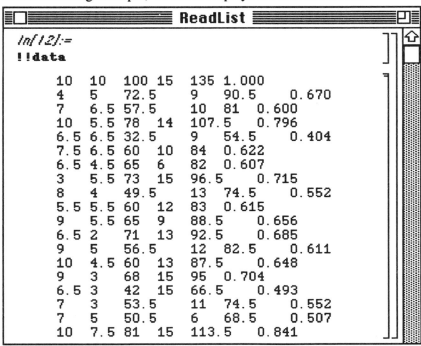

In the following example, **ReadList["data",Number]** reads the sequence of numbers in the file **data** and returns a list.

```
In[13]:=
ReadList["data",Number]

Out[13]=
{10, 10, 100, 15, 135, 1., 4, 5, 72.5, 9, 90.5,
  0.67, 7, 6.5, 57.5, 10, 81, 0.6, 10, 5.5, 78,
  14, 107.5, 0.796, 6.5, 6.5, 32.5, 9, 54.5,
  0.404, 7.5, 6.5, 60, 10, 84, 0.622, 6.5, 4.5,
  65, 6, 82, 0.607, 3, 5.5, 73, 15, 96.5, 0.715,
  8, 4, 49.5, 13, 74.5, 0.552, 5.5, 5.5, 60, 12,
  83, 0.615, 9, 5.5, 65, 9, 88.5, 0.656, 6.5, 2,
  71, 13, 92.5, 0.685, 9, 5, 56.5, 12, 82.5,
  0.611, 10, 4.5, 60, 13, 87.5, 0.648, 9, 3, 68,
  15, 95, 0.704, 6.5, 3, 42, 15, 66.5, 0.493, 7,
  3, 53.5, 11, 74.5, 0.552, 7, 5, 50.5, 6, 68.5,
  0.507, 10, 7.5, 81, 15, 113.5, 0.841}
```

In this case, each successive block of six numbers corresponds to the grades of a student. In the following example, **ReadList["data",Table[Number,{6}]]** reads the file **data** and puts each set of six numbers in a separate list. The result is a nested list.

```
In[14]:=
ReadList["data",Table[Number,{6}]]

Out[14]=
{{10, 10, 100, 15, 135, 1.},
  {4, 5, 72.5, 9, 90.5, 0.67},
  {7, 6.5, 57.5, 10, 81, 0.6},
  {10, 5.5, 78, 14, 107.5, 0.796},
  {6.5, 6.5, 32.5, 9, 54.5, 0.404},
  {7.5, 6.5, 60, 10, 84, 0.622},
  {6.5, 4.5, 65, 6, 82, 0.607},
  {3, 5.5, 73, 15, 96.5, 0.715},
  {8, 4, 49.5, 13, 74.5, 0.552},
  {5.5, 5.5, 60, 12, 83, 0.615},
  {9, 5.5, 65, 9, 88.5, 0.656},
  {6.5, 2, 71, 13, 92.5, 0.685},
  {9, 5, 56.5, 12, 82.5, 0.611},
  {10, 4.5, 60, 13, 87.5, 0.648},
  {9, 3, 68, 15, 95, 0.704},
  {6.5, 3, 42, 15, 66.5, 0.493},
  {7, 3, 53.5, 11, 74.5, 0.552},
  {7, 5, 50.5, 6, 68.5, 0.507},
  {10, 7.5, 81, 15, 113.5, 0.841}}
```

100% ▼

ReadProtected   272, 854
                                 See Also: **Locked, Protected**
   ReadProtected is an attribute such that when it is assigned to a *Mathematica*
symbol prevents any value associated with that symbol from being read. These values
can, however, be used during calculations.

Real   495, 534, 712, 854
See 7, 379, 718   See Also: **Head, Integer, Rational, RealDigits,
                                 BaseForm, Number**
   Real is the head assigned to all approximate real numbers of any precision.
Approximate real numbers can be entered in many ways. These include scientific
notation, **mantissa 10^exponent**; base b notation, **b^^digits**; and directly
entering a floating-point number of any length.

Example:

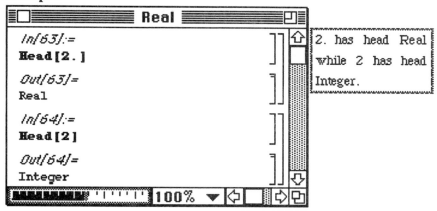

RealDigits   537, 854
                                 See Also: **MantissaExponents, IntegerDigits,
                                 BaseForm**
   RealDigits[x] yields a list of the decimal digits of **x** along with the number of
digits to the left of the decimal. The length of the list returned by RealDigits is equal to
the value of **Precision[x]**. The command can be entered as **RealDigits[x,b]**
to determine the digits of **x** in base **b**. Note that **b** does not have to be an integer. If **b**
is a real number greater than 1, **RealDigits[x,b]** repetitively determines the largest
integer multiples of powers of **b** that can be removed and leave a non-negative
remainder.

Example:

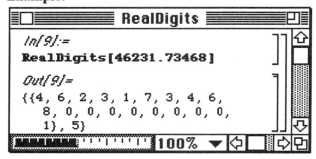

RealInterval   647
                          See Also: **Limit**
    RealInterval[{min,max}] is used to describe an uncertain value which lies somewhere on the interval between **min** and **max**. **RealInterval** objects arise when using **Limit** with functions of bounded variation.

Record   495, 854
                          See Also: **Word, Read, Find**
    Record represents a record in such functions as **Read** and **Find**. A record is a string of characters delimited by record separators.

RecordLists   182, 494, 496, 855
                          See Also: **RecordList**
    RecordLists is an option used with **RecordList** to indicate if objects from separate records should be given in separate sublists. The default setting of **RecordSeparators** is **RecordSeparators->{"\n"}**. With this setting along with **RecordLists->True**, *Mathematica* objects read from different lines are returned in different sublists. With **RecordLists->False** they are all given in the same list.

RecordSeparators   496, 500, 501, 855
                          See Also: **WordSeparators, NullRecords**
    RecordSeparators is an option used with such functions as **Read** and **Find** to indicate the list of strings to interpret as record delimiters. The default setting for this option is **RecordSeparators->{"\n"}**. This specifies that each complete line of input is considered a record. Also, **RecordSeparators->{}** indicates that everything is included in a single record.
RecordSeparators->{{left1,left2,...},{right1,right2,...}} indicates the left and right record separators. If these separators are nested, then the innermost balanced pairs of separators are taken to be delimiters.

Rectangle   400, 423, 855
See 531   See Also: **Poltgon**, **Raster**, **RasterArray**,
                                  Cuboid, **Graphics**, **GraphicsArray**

   Rectangle is a two-dimensional graphics primitive used to represent a rectangle.
Rectangle[{xmin,ymin},{xmax,ymax}] yields a filled rectangle with the
indicated corner coordinates.

Rectangle[{xmin,ymin},{xmax,ymax},graphics] renders the indicated
graphics object within the indicated rectangle. Note that any graphics object can be
displayed within **Rectangle**. The coordinates are simply scaled down so as to fit
within the **Rectangle**. Scaled coordinates, **Scaled[{xmin,ymin}]** and
Scaled[{xmax,ymax}], can be used within **Rectangle** as well.   Graphics
directives such as **RGBColor** and **GrayLevel** can be used to indicate the manner in
which **Rectangle[{xmin,ymin},{xmax,ymax}]** is to be rendered.

Example:

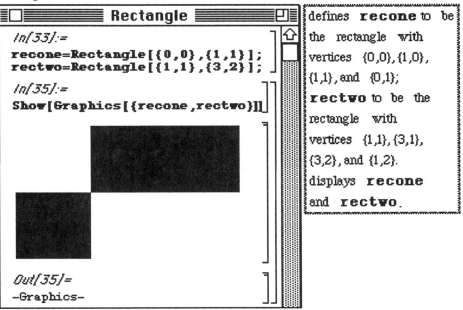

The following example graphs sin(x) for $0 \le x \le 2\pi$ and names the resulting graph
plotone, then graphs cos(x) for $0 \le x \le 2\pi$ and names the resulting graph **plottwo**.
Neither graph is displayed since the option **DisplayFunction->Identity** is
included. **plotthree** is a graphics object consisting of **plotone** and **plottwo**.

```
In[41]:=
plotone=Plot[Sin[x],{x,0,2Pi},
    DisplayFunction->Identity];
plottwo=Plot[Cos[x],{x,0,2Pi},
    PlotStyle->GrayLevel[.3],
    DisplayFunction->Identity];
plotthree=Show[plotone,plottwo];
```

All three graphics objects are displayed in a single graphics cell using the commands
Rectangle, **Show**, and **Graphics**. **plotone** is displayed within the rectangle with
vertices (0,0), (0,1), (1,1), and (1,0); **plottwo** is displayed within the rectangle with

vertices (0,1), (0,2), (1,2), and (1,1); and **plotthree** is displayed within the rectangle with vertices (1,0), (1,2), (2,2) and (2,0).

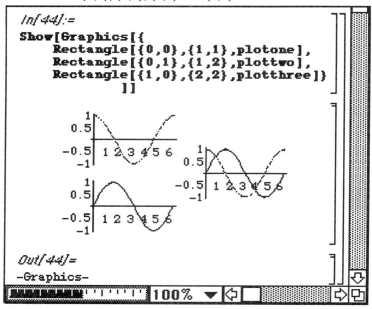

Reduce   98, 614, 615, 855

See Also: **Solve**, **Eliminate**, **LogicalExpand**, **ToRules**

Reduce is used to reduce equations and return all possible solutions.

Reduce[equations,var] reduces **equations** and tries to solve for the variables listed in **var**. **Reduce** returns equations which are equivalent to **equations**. The reduced equations also contain all solutions. Hence, a significant difference between **Reduce** and **Solve** is that **Reduce** determines the conditions necessary for a set of equations to have a solution even if the equations depend on a parameter. **Solve** only yields the generic solution. The command

Reduce[equations,var,eliminate] tries to simplify **equations** by eliminating the variables listed in **eliminate**. The results of **Reduce** appear in the form of equations and nonequalities, symbolized by **==** and **!=**, respectively, that are joined with the logical connectives, **||** and **&&**.

Example:

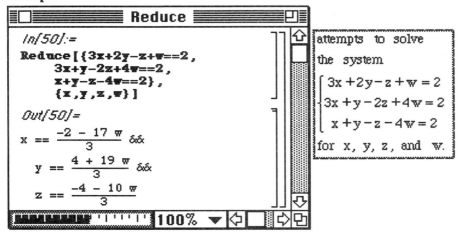

Release   xix (obsolete in Version 2.0)
                                changed to **Evaluate** and **ReleaseHold**

ReleaseHold   282, 308, 856
See 190, 191, 468   See Also: **Evaluate**, **Hold**

   ReleaseHold[expression] removes the attributes of **Hold** and **HoldForm** from **expression**. Note that **ReleaseHold** only removes the outer layer of these attributes. It does not remove those attributes which occur in nested functions.

Remove   68, 335, 338, 385, 736, 856
                                See Also: **Clear**, **ClearAll**

   Remove is used to remove symbols in *Mathematica*. **Remove[symbol]** removes the indicated symbol while **Remove[sym1,sym2,...]** removes all listed symbols. After removal, these symbols are no longer recognized by *Mathematica*. A pattern can be used within **Remove** to remove all symbols which match a certain form. This is done with **Remove["form1","form2",...]**. Metacharacters such as * can be used in defining the pattern. Note that if a symbol has the attribute **Protected**, then it cannot be removed with **Remove**. If an expression is entered which includes a symbol which has been removed, then *Mathematica* returns **Removed["symbolname"]** where **symbolname** is the symbol which was previously removed.

Example:

The following example removes all information about the symbol **z**.

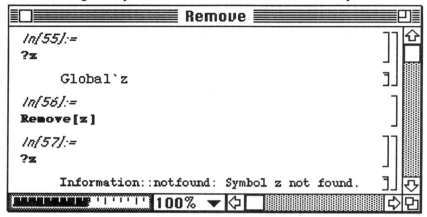

Removed
See Also: Remove

Removed["symbol"] indicates that **symbol** has been removed so that *Mathematica* no longer recognizes it.

RenameDirectory   493, 856
See Also: CopyDirectory, CreateDirectory, DeleteDirectory

RenameDirectory["directory1","directory2"] assigns the name **directory2** to the already existing directory **directory1**. Note that **directory2** must not be a previously existing directory. The modification date for **directory2** becomes that of **directory1**. Also, if **directory1** cannot be renamed, then **$Failed** is returned. Otherwise, the new name is given.

RenameFile   492, 856
See Also: CopyFile, DeleteFile, RenameDirectory

RenameFile["file1","file2"] assigns the name **file2** to the already existing file **file1**. Note that **file2** must not be a previously existing file. The modification date for **file2** becomes that of **file1**. Also, if **file1** cannot be renamed, then **$Failed** is returned. Otherwise, the new name is given.

RenderAll   466, 856
                                  See Also: **PolygonIntersections**

   RenderAll is a **Graphics3D** option used to indicate the form in which PostScript
is rendered. The setting **RenderAll->True** causes all of the polygons which make
up the three-dimensional object to be drawn with those behind being drawn first.
However, only those polygons in the front are visible in the final display. If a graph has
several layers, then even more polygons are left unseen. Therefore, to avoid the
cumbersome PostScript code which accompanies these polygons, the setting
RenderAll->False is used. With this setting, *Mathematica* draws only those
polygons or parts of polygons which can be viewed in the final display. Note, however,
that drawing the object with **RenderAll->False** may take longer and produce a
slightly different image than when using **RenderAll->True**. This is due to
numerical roundoff in PostScript code as well as the rendering system.

Repeated (..)   237, 717, 856
                                  See Also: **BlankSequence**

   Repeated, symbolized by **..**, is used to represent a repeated pattern.
expression.. represents a pattern repeated one or more times. Objects of this form
can be used as the argument of a function to represent a sequence of arguments.

RepeatedNull (...)   237, 717, 857
                                  See Also: **Repeated**

   RepeatedNull, symbolized by **...**, is used to represent a repeated pattern.
expression... represents a pattern which repeats itself zero or more times.

RepeatedString

   RepeatedString is an internal symbol which is used for printing and formatting.

Replace   245, 857
                                  See Also: **Rule**, **StringReplace**, **ReplaceAll**,
                                  ReplacePart, **Set**, **AlgebraicRules**

   Replace is used to apply a rule or list of rules to transform an expression. This is
done with the command **Replace[expression,rules]** where the rules listed in
rules must be entered as **lhs->rhs** or **lhs:>rhs**. If a list of rules is given, then
they are applied in order, and the result obtained after substitution of the first
applicable rule is returned. If the list of rules is nested, then **Replace** is mapped onto
the inner lists.

Example:

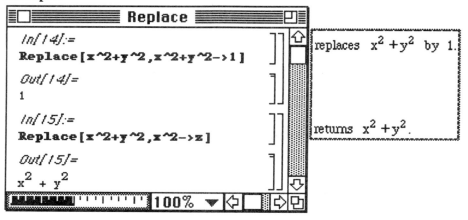

ReplaceAll (**/.**)   243, 622, 857
See 6, 163, 273,   See Also: **Rule**, **Set**
307-311, 403, 727

   ReplaceAll[exp,rules], symbolized by **exp/.rules**, is used to apply a rule or list of rules, **rules**, to every part of an expression **exp**. Each listed rule is applied to every subexpression of **exp**. When a rule applies, then the result that is obtained after the appropriate transformation is returned. If none of the rules apply, then **exp** is returned by *Mathematica*. **ReplaceAll[exp,rules]** is equivalent to **MapAll[Replace[#,rules]&,exp]**.

Example:

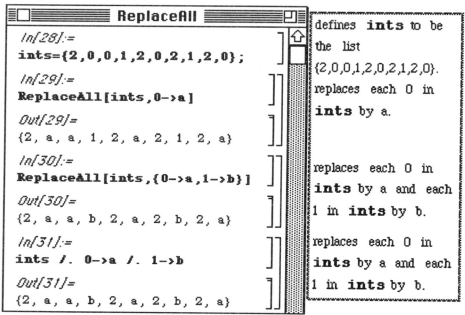

ReplaceAll also offers an alternative for evaluation of some functions:

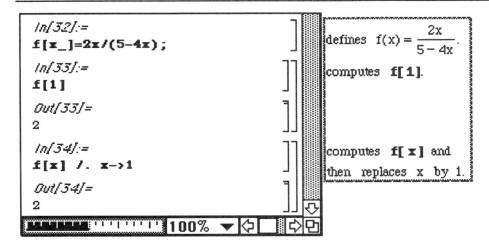

ReplaceHeldPart   282, 857
                           See Also: **HeldPart**, **Unevaluated**

   ReplaceHeldPart is used to replace parts of expressions without evaluating them and to replace parts of functions which do not evaluate their arguments.
ReplaceHeldPart[expression,Hold[newvalue],pos] replaces the element of **expression** at position **pos** with **newvalue** but does not evaluate that part of **expression**. Several parts of **expression** can be replaced with
ReplaceHeldPart[expression,Hold[newvalue],{pos1,pos2,...}].
In this case, each of the listed positions are replaced by the unevaluated value **newvalue**. If **expression** is enclosed in **Hold**, then the command
ReplaceHeldPart[Hold[expression],newvalue,position] replaces the indicated part of **expression** with the evaluated form of **newvalue**.

ReplacePart   128, 195, 857
                           See Also: **Part**, **MapAt**, **Delete**, **Insert**,
                                     FlattenAt

   ReplacePart is used to replace parts of an expression.
ReplacePart[expression,newvalue,pos] replaces the part of **expression** located at position **pos** with **newvalue**. Also, several positions can be replaced with the same value with
ReplacePart[expression,newvalue,{pos1,pos2,...}].
Example:

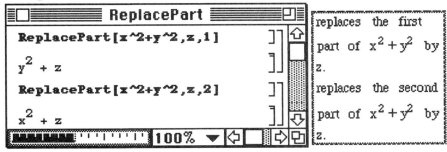

ReplaceRepeated (//.) 244, 858
> See Also: **Set**, **Rule**, **FixedPoint**

ReplaceRepeated[expression,rules], symbolized
expression//.rules, repeatedly applies the rule or list of rules given in **rules** to **expression** until further replacements do not alter **expression**. Special care must be used with **ReplaceRepeated** to avoid an infinite loop. The number of iterations can be limited with the option **MaxIterations**. The default setting is **MaxIterations->65536**.

ResetDirectory   489, 490, 858
> See Also: **SetDirectory**, **Directory**, **$Path**,
> **DirectoryStack**

ResetDirectory[] reverts the current directory back to the previous directory found in the stack given by **DirectoryStack[]**. With every application of **ResetDirectory**, *Mathematica* removes a directory from the stack of directories.

ResetMedium   xix (obsolete in Version 2.0)
> superseded by **SetOptions**

Residue   648, 858
> See Also: **Series**, **Limit**

Residue[expression,{x,x0}] yields the residue of **expression** for the value **x = x0**. This command is useful when **Limit[expression,x->x0]** is

Infinity since the residue gives the coefficient of $(x-x0)^{-1}$ in the Laurent expansion of **expression**.

Example:

In the following example, recall that the symbol **I** denotes the imaginary number $i = \sqrt{-1}$.

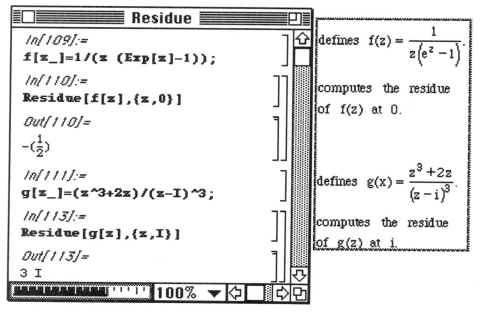

Rest   125, 126, 858, 869
                    See Also: **Drop**, **Take**, **Part**, **First**
   Rest[expression] returns **expression** with the first term removed. This
command has the same results as **Drop[expression,1]**.

Example:

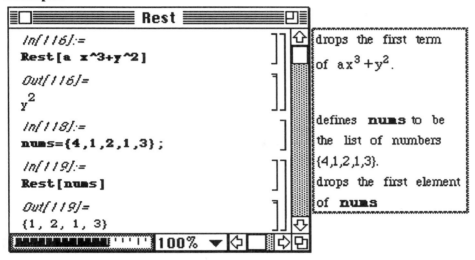

Resultant   598, 858
                    See Also: **Eliminate**, **PolynomialGCD**
   Resultant[polynomial1,polynomial2,var] yields the resultant of the two
polynomials, **polynomial1** and **polynomial2**, in terms of the variable **var**. Note
that the resultant of two polynomials p and q both having leading coefficient 1 is
defined to be the product of all differences $p_i - q_j$ between the roots of the polynomials.

The resultant of any two polynomials is also a polynomial. In addition, the resultant is
zero if and only if the leading coefficients of the polynomials vanish simultaneously or
if they have a common root.

Example:

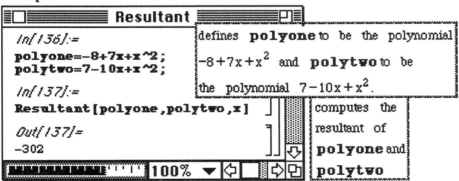

Resultant2
    Resultant2 is a system command and has the attribute **Protected**.

Return	293, 306, 520, 858
See 97, 99, 100, 530, 568	See Also: **Null**, **Throw**, **Break**

    Return[expression] exits any function or control structure and returns the value of **expression**. Also, **Return[]** returns **Null**.

Reverse	130, 196, 858
	See Also: **StringReverse**, **RotateRight**, **RotateLeft**, **Permutations**, **Sort**, **Part**

    Reverse[list] reverses the order of the elements of **list**.

Example:

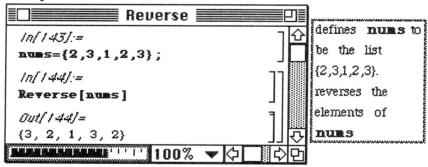

RGBColor	40, 407, 472, 859
	See Also: **Hue**, **ColorOutput**, **CMYKColor**, **GrayLevel**

    RGBColor[redindex,greenindex,blueindex] is a graphics directive used to indicate the colors in which a graphics object should be displayed. Each value of **redindex**, **greenindex**, and **blueindex** is between **0** and **1**, inclusive.

RiemannSiegelTheta	571, 859
	See Also: **Zeta**

    RiemannSiegelTheta[t] represents the Riemann -Siegel theta function

$$\varphi(t) = \operatorname{Im}\, \log\, \Gamma\!\left(\frac{1}{4} + i\frac{t}{2}\right) - t\, \frac{\log \pi}{2},$$ for real values of t. Note that this function is

real for real t. Also, $\varphi(t)$ is analytic except for branch cuts along the imaginary

axis from $\pm \dfrac{i}{2}$ to $\pm i\infty$.

Example:

The following example graphs the real part of $\varphi(x+iy)$ for $-4 \leq x \leq 4$ and $-1 \leq y \leq 1$. Twenty-five plotpoints are used (the default is fifteen) and the resulting graph is not shaded since the option **Shading->False** is included.

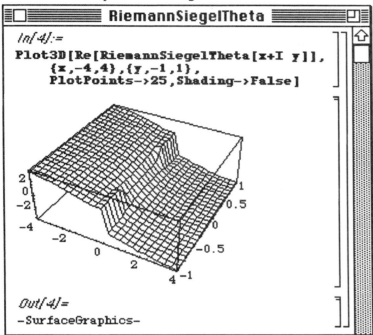

The following example graphs the imaginary part of $\varphi(x+iy)$ for $-4 \leq x \leq 4$ and $-1 \leq y \leq 1$. Twenty-five plotpoints are used (the default is fifteen) and the resulting graph is not shaded since the option **Shading->False** is included.

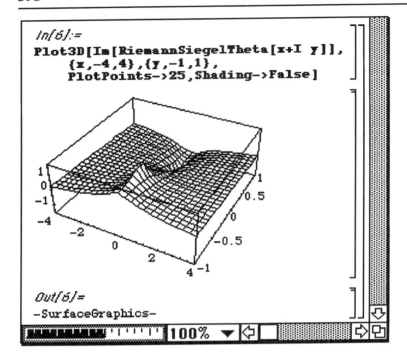

```
In[6]:=
Plot3D[Im[RiemannSiegelTheta[x+I y]],
    {x,-4,4},{y,-1,1},
    PlotPoints->25,Shading->False]

Out[6]=
-SurfaceGraphics-
```

RiemannSiegelZ   571, 859

See Also: **Zeta**

RiemannSiegelZ[t] represents the Riemann - Siegel function

$Z(t) = e^{i\varphi(t)} \zeta\left(\frac{1}{2} + it\right)$, where φ is the Riemann - Siegel theta function and

ζ is the Riemann zeta function. Note that $Z(t)$ is analytic except along the

imaginary axis from $\pm \frac{i}{2}$ to $\pm i\infty$.

Example:

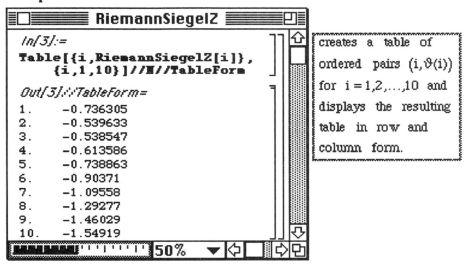

Right   357
See 53

See Also: **ColumnForm**, **TableForm**, **TableAlignments**

Right is a setting used with functions such as **ColumnForm** and **TableForm** to indicate the alignment to be used in printing.

Roots   96, 97, 606, 859
See 377

See Also: **ToRules**, **FindRoot**, **NRoots**, **NSolve**, **Solve**

Roots[lhs==rhs,variable] produces a set of equations of the form **eq1||eq2||...** which represents the solution to the polynomial equation **lhs==rhs**. When such functions as **Solve** cannot determine the solution to an equation, it returns {ToRules[Roots[eqn,var]]} the approximate solutions of which can be determined numerically with **N**. Roots has many options. These include along with their default settings **Cubics->True**, **EquatedTo->Null**, **Modulus->Infinity**, **Multiplicity->1**, **Quartics->True**, and **Using->True**. **Roots** uses **Decompose** and **Factor** in attempting to find the roots.

Example:

The following example first defines **poly** to be the polynomial $32-40x-36x^2+38x^3+23x^4-9x^5-7x^6-x^7$ and then uses **Roots** to find the values of x that satisfy the equation $32-40x-36x^2+38x^3+23x^4-9x^5-7x^6-x^7=0$.

```
============================= Roots =============================
In[15]:=
poly=32-40x-36x^2+38x^3+23x^4-9x^5-7x^6-x^7;

In[16]:=
Roots[poly==0,x]

Out[16]=
x == -2 || x == -2 || x == -2 || x == 1 || x == 1 ||
    x == 1 || x == -4
```

In the following example, the f(x)=-2-4x+4x^2+x^3. **Roots** is used to find the exact values of x that satisfy the equation f(x)=0. In this case, the entire result is not shown since it is very long.

```
In[17]:=
f[x_]=-2-4x+4x^2+x^3;

In[18]:=
Roots[f[x]==0,x]

Out[18]=
```

$$x == -\left(\frac{4}{3}\right) + \frac{28\ (-1)^{11/6}}{3\ (109\ I + \text{Sqrt}[10071])^{1/3}} +$$

$$\frac{(-1)^{1/6}\ (109\ I + \text{Sqrt}[10071])^{1/3}}{3} \quad ||$$

$$x == -\left(\frac{4}{3}\right) + \frac{I}{2}\ \text{Sqrt}[3]$$

$$\left(\frac{28\ (-1)^{5/6}}{3\ (109\ I + \text{Sqrt}[10071])^{1/3}} + \right.$$

$$\left.\frac{(-1)^{1/6}\ (109\ I + \text{Sqrt}[10071])^{1/3}}{3}\right) -$$

$$\left(\frac{28\ (-1)^{11/6}}{\cdots}\right. +$$

```
|||||||||||||||||| ' ' ' | ' ' ' | ' | 50%  ▼ ◁ [ ]                    ◁ ▷
```

RotateLabel   422, 859
See 514   See Also: **Text**
   RotateLabel is an option used with two-dimensional graphics functions which indicates if labels placed on vertical frame axes should be rotated in order that they be horizontal. The default setting for this option is **RotateLabel->False** so that labels are not rotated. These vertical labels are read bottom to top. Hence, the setting **RotateLabel->True** rotates the labels.

RotateLeft   130, 132, 860
                                  See Also: **Reverse**

RotateLeft is used to rotate the elements of a list. **RotateLeft[list]** rotates the elements of **list** one position to the left while **RotateLeft[list,n]** cycles the elements **n** positions to the left. If a negative integer is used, then rotation occurs to the right. This function can be applied to successive levels of a list. **RotateLeft[list,{n1,n2,...}]** rotates through **ni** positions on successive levels.

RotateRight   130, 132, 860
                                  See Also: **Reverse**

RotateRight is used to rotate the elements of a list. **RotateRight[list]** rotates the elements of **list** one position to the right while **RotateRight[list,n]** cycles the elements **n** positions to the right. If a negative integer is used, then rotation occurs to the left. This function can be applied to successive levels of a list. **RotateRight[list,{n1,n2,...}]** rotates through **ni** positions on successive levels.

Round   49, 550, 860
                                  See Also: **Ceiling, Chop, Floor**

Round[x] rounds **x** to the closest integer where .5 is rounded down to 0.

Example:

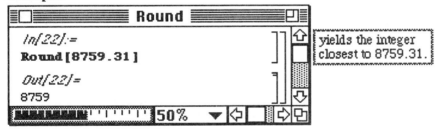

Row   356
                                  See Also: **TableForm, TableDirections**

Row is a **TableDirections** setting used with **TableForm** to indicate that dimensions are interpreted as rows.

RowReduce   660, 662, 860
                                  See Also: **LatticeReduce, NullSpace**

RowReduce[m] yields the row reduced form of the matrix **m** which is obtained by taking linear combinations of the rows of **m**. This command has the option **Modulus**. The setting **Modulus->p** causes the reduction to be modulo p. RowReduce also has the option **ZeroTest** which is used to determine if the elements of **m** are zero.

Example:

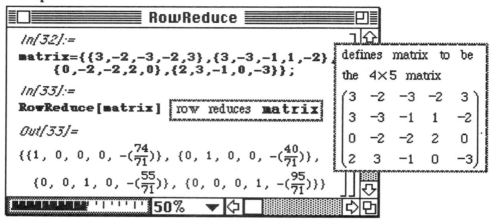

Rule(->)   243, 258, 283, 737, 860
See 6, 37, 163, 253,   See Also: **RuleDelayed**, **Replace**, **ReplaceAll**,
434, 435, 727   **Set**, **AlgebraicRules**

   Rule, symbolized by **->**, is used to represent a replacement rule. The rule **a->b** transforms **a** to **b**. Replace can be used to accomplish this as well. The assignment a=b indicates that the rule a->b should be used whenever it applies.

Example:

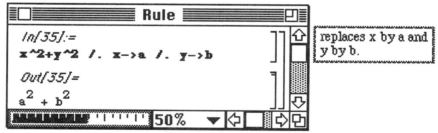

RuleCondition
   RuleCondition is an internal symbol.

RuleDelayed(:>)   243, 258, 283, 737, 860
See 99, 100   See Also: **Replace**, **Rule**, **SetDelayed**

   RuleDelayed is symbolized **:>**. The command **a:>b** is used to transform **a** into **b** where **b** is evaluated only when the rule is used. The definition **a:=b** indicates that **a:>b** be every instance it applies. The main difference between **Rule** and **RuleDelayed** is that **Rule** is used when an expression needs to be replaced with a particular value while **RuleDelayed** is used to state a command for finding that value.

Example:

In the following example, **RuleDelayed** is used to convert the algebraic expression
$\frac{1}{x-1} + \frac{1}{x+1}$ to a fraction with a single denominator; notice that using
Rule does not produce the same result.

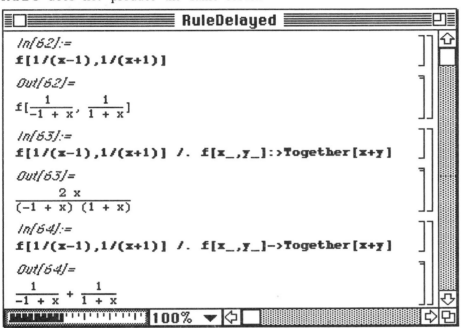

A similar example using $f(x)=x^2$ is shown below:

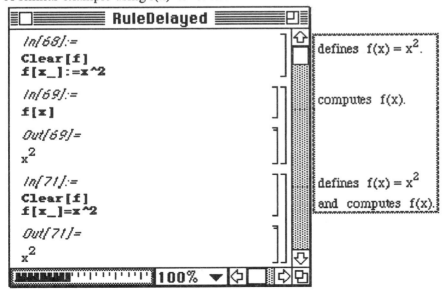

RuleForm

RuleForm is an internal symbol which is used for printing and formatting.

RuleTable

RuleTable is an internal symbol.

Run   482, 861

See Also: **Put**, **Splice**

  Run[expr1,expr2,...] prints **expr1**, **expr2**,... in **InputForm** by placing spaces between the expressions. It then runs it as an external command which does not receive input from *Mathematica*. Note that the place where the output is sent by the external program depends on the operating system. In most cases **Run** returns an integer value which represents the exit code given by the operating system. The command **!expression** also executes an external command. **Run** is not available on all operating systems.

RunThrough   483, 861

See Also: **Splice**, **Put**, **Get**, **Install**

  RunThrough["cmd",expression] offers the **InputForm** of **expression** as input and causes the external command **cmd** to be executed. It then reads the output obtained through the command and sends it back to *Mathematica*. Note that

RunThrough is not available on all operating systems.

S

SameQ (**===**)   228, 288, 861

See Also: **UnsameQ**, **Order**, **Equal**

SameQ[a,b] which is also symbolized as **a===b** yields a value of **True** if **a** and **b** are identical. It gives a value of **False** otherwise. More than two expressions may be considered with **expr1===expr2===expr3**. In this case, **True** results if all expressions are equivalent.

Example:

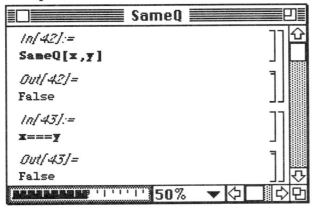

SameTest   201, 291, 861

See Also: **ZeroTest**

SameTest is an option used with **FixedPoint** to indicate the function used to determine if successive results are the same. This criteria is used to terminate the iterative algorithm of **FixedPoint**. The default setting of **SameTest** is **Equal**. Other settings for this option must be a function of two arguments which yields **True** or **False**.

SampleDepth   475, 861

See Also: **PlayRange**, **SampleRate**

SampleDepth is an option used with Play and ListPlay to indicate the number of bits to use for each amplitude level sample. *Mathematica* represents sound in the low-level form of a sequence of hexadecimal numbers. The default setting is SampleDepth->8. This setting leads to 256 amplitude levels which is enough in most cases. The **SampleDepth** option is used by placing the entry **{rate,depth}** in the argument for **SampleRate**.

SampledSoundFunction   475, 861

See Also: **Sound**, **Graphics**, **Graphics3D**, **Play**

SampledSoundFunction[func,n,r] is a sound primitive which represents the sound obtained by sampling the amplitude levels at a rate **r** where the amplitude levels are produced by applying the function **func** to **n** successive integers. If a list of functions is given for **func**, then sound is given on several channels. **Sound**, **Graphics**, and **Graphics3D** objects may all contain SampledSoundFunction primitives. **SampledSoundFunction** is generated by **Play**.

SampledSoundList   475, 862
                            See Also: **Sound, Graphics, Graphics3D,**
                            ListPlay

  SampledSoundList[{a1,a2,...},r] is a sound primitive which explicitly
lists the amplitude levels **{a1,a2,...}** which are sampled at a rate **r** to produce
sound. This primitive is generated by **ListPlay**, and may appear in **Sound**,
Graphics, and **Graphics3D** objects. Sound may be produced on several channels
by entering a list of amplitudes for each **ai** in the earlier command. These lists do not
have to be of the same length, since *Mathematica* automatically adds silence to the
shorter lists.

SampleRate   176, 862
                            See Also: **SampleDepth**

  SampleRate is an option used with sound primitives to indicate the number of
samples per second to produce for sound. A higher **SampleRate** setting leads to
clearer high-frequency sound components. If the setting is **SampleRate->r**, then
frequencies up to **r/2** are possible where frequencies are given in hertz. The default
setting is **SampleRate->8192**.

Save   178, 479, 862
                            See Also: **Get, Dump, PutAppend**

  Save is used to save the definitions of variables and functions in a *Mathematica* file.
This is done with the command **Save["filename",symbol1,symbol2,...]**.
Save also automatically saves those objects upon which **symbol1, symbol2**, ...
depend.

Scaled   413, 440, 862
                            See Also: **PlotRange**

  Scaled is used to indicate scaled coordinates between the values of 0 and 1. If the
original coordinates are **{x,y}**, then **Scaled[{x,y}]** yields the scaled coordinates
where each coordinate is between 0 and 1, and the origin is taken to be the lower
left-hand corner of the display region. In addition, the command
Scaled[{sx,sy},{x0,y0}] represents the position obtained by starting at the
point **{x0,y0}** and moving through the scaled units **{sx,sy}**. This command often
is used in two- and three-dimensional graphics primitives. Note that the definitions
which are given are easily extended to more than two dimensions.

Scan   207, 725, 862
                            See Also: **Map, Level, Apply**

  Scan is used to evaluate a function applied to certain parts of an expression without
building up a new expression. This command is useful when working with a function
that makes assignments or produces output. The command
Scan[func,expression] evaluates the function **func** to each element of
expression while **Scan[func,expression,level]** only evaluates **func**
applied to the levels of **expression** indicated by **level**. Note that the default value
of level is **{1}** which specifies the first level only. A value of **Infinity** for **level**
indicates that all levels be included. Also, a value of **n** specifies that levels 1 through **n**
be included.

Example:

In the following example, the function **f** is defined to **Print** the value of x^2. Notice that the result of **f[2]** is the printed expression 4 and the value of *Out[44]* is **Null**.

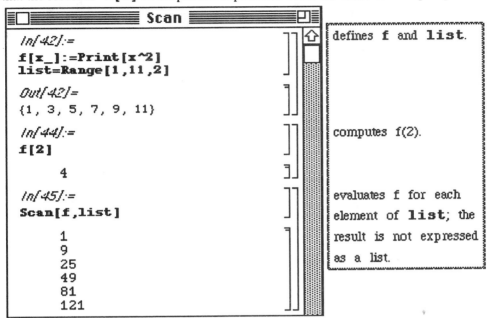

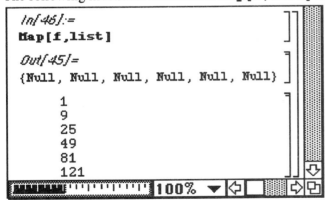

The following illustrates the result of **Map[f,list]** in this case.

SchurDecomposition   666, 862

See Also: **SingularValues, QRDecomposition**

SchurDecomposition[m] determines the Schur decomposition of the numerical matrix m. This produces the output {**q,t**} where q is an orthogonal matrix and t is block-upper triangular. Hence, the matrix m can be written as **m = q.t.Transpose[q]**. **SchurDecomposition** has the option **Pivoting**. With the setting **Pivoting->True**, the output {**q,t,d**} also includes the permuted diagonal matrix d where **m.d = d.q.t.Conjugate[Transpose[q]]**.

Example:

In the following example, **matrix** is defined to be the numerical matrix

$$\begin{bmatrix} -4. & 1. & 3. \\ 3. & 0. & -1. \\ 4. & 0. & -2 \end{bmatrix}.$$ Note that the same results would be obtained if

matrix were defined with the command

matrix={{-4.,1.,3.},{3.,0.,-1},{4.,0.,-2.}};. **sdm** represents the Schur decomposition of matrix.

```
═════════════ SchurDecomposition ═════════════
In[74]:=
matrix=N[{{-4,1,3},{3,0,-1},{4,0,-2}}];

In[75]:=
sdm=SchurDecomposition[matrix]

Out[75]=
{{{-0.716483, 0.676933, 0.168564},
   {0.39156, 0.590218, -0.70592},
   {0.57735, 0.439777, 0.687941}},
  {{-6.96394, 2.25037, -0.966268},
   {0, 1.20272, 0.0466579}, {0, 0, -0.238786}}}
```

sdm[[1]]//MatrixForm represents the first element of the list **sdm** and displays it in row-and-column form. **id=sdm[[1]].Transpose[sdm[[1]]]** computes

$$\begin{bmatrix} -0.716 & 0.676 & 0.168 \\ 0.391 & 0.590 & -0.705 \\ 0.577 & 0.439 & 0.687 \end{bmatrix} \cdot \begin{bmatrix} -0.716 & 0.676 & 0.168 \\ 0.391 & 0.590 & -0.705 \\ 0.577 & 0.439 & 0.687 \end{bmatrix}^{T}$$ and names the result

id.

```
In[76]:=
sdm[[1]]//MatrixForm

Out[76]//MatrixForm=
-0.716483    0.676933     0.168564
0.39156      0.590218    -0.70592
0.57735      0.439777     0.687941

In[77]:=
id=sdm[[1]].Transpose[sdm[[1]]]

Out[77]=
{{1., -1.35525 10^{-20}, 8.80914 10^{-20}},
  {-1.35525 10^{-20}, 1., -1.89735 10^{-19}},
  {8.80914 10^{-20}, -1.89735 10^{-19}, 1.}}
```

We use **Chop** to see that **id** represents the identity matrix.

sdm[[2]]//MatrixForm represents the second element of the list **sdm** and displays it in row-and-column form. **almost** represents the matrix

$$\begin{bmatrix} -0.716 & 0.676 & 0.168 \\ 0.391 & 0.590 & -0.705 \\ 0.577 & 0.439 & 0.687 \end{bmatrix} \cdot \begin{bmatrix} -6.963 & 2.250 & -0.966 \\ 0 & 1.202 & 0.046 \\ 0 & 0 & -0.238 \end{bmatrix} \cdot \begin{bmatrix} -0.716 & 0.676 & 0.168 \\ 0.391 & 0.590 & -0.705 \\ 0.577 & 0.439 & 0.687 \end{bmatrix}^T .$$

```
In[78]:=
Chop[id]

Out[78]=
{{1., 0, 0}, {0, 1., 0}, {0, 0, 1.}}

In[79]:=
sdm[[2]]//MatrixForm

Out[79]//MatrixForm=
-6.96394      2.25037      -0.966268
0             1.20272      0.0466579
0             0            -0.238786

In[80]:=
almost=sdm[[1]].sdm[[2]].Transpose[sdm[[1]]]

Out[80]=
{{-4., 1., 3.}, {3., 2.71051 10^-19, -1.},
   {4., 3.52366 10^-19, -2.}}
```

We use **Chop** to see that **almost** represents the matrix **matrix**.

```
In[81]:=
Chop[almost]

Out[81]=
{{-4., 1., 3.}, {3., 0, -1.}, {4., 0, -2.}}
```

ScientificForm   350, 863

See Also: **NumberForm, EngineeringForm**

ScientificForm[expression] prints all of the numbers in **expression** in scientific notation. The command can be entered as **ScientificForm[expression,d]** as well so that the scientific notation includes at most **d** digits. **ScientificForm** uses the same options as **NumberForm**, but the default setting for ExponentFunction which determines the value of the exponent for scientific notation is different from that used with **NumberForm**. With **NumberForm**, the setting **ExponentFunction->Null** indicates that scientific notation not be used. **ScientificForm[expression]** only affects the printing of **expression**. It does not alter any calculations involving **expression**.

Example:

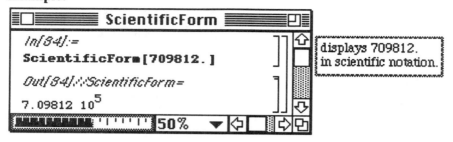

Sec   562, 863
                                See Also: **ArcSec**

Sec[z] represents the trigonometric function secant of z where $\sec(z) = \dfrac{1}{\cos(z)}$ and

z is given in radian measurement. Note that degree measurements can be converted to radians by multiplication with Degree. Exact values for **Sec[z]** are given when possible.

Example:

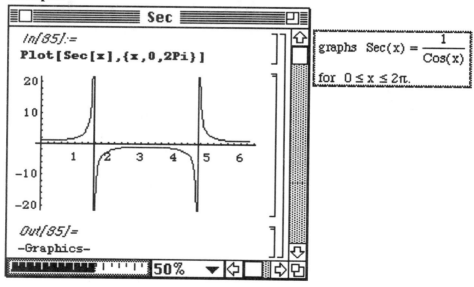

Sech   562, 863
                                See Also: **ArcSech**

Sech[z] represents the hyperbolic secant of z where $\mathrm{sech}(z) = \dfrac{1}{\cosh(z)}$

$$= \left(\frac{e^z + e^{-z}}{2} \right)^{-1} .$$

Example:
The following example defines f(x,y)=|sech(x+iy)| and then makes a **DensityPlot** of f(x,y) for −2 ≤ x ≤ 2 and −2 ≤ y ≤ 2 using 250 plot points. The resulting graphics object is displayed without a mesh and frame since the options **Frame->False** and **Mesh->False** are included.

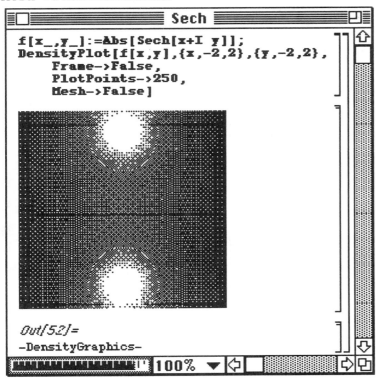

Second

See Also: **Timing**

Second represents the time unit of seconds used by such functions as **Timing** and **TimeConstrained**.

SeedRandom   552, 863

See Also: **Random**

SeedRandom is used to produce a pseudorandom number by supplying a specific seed. **SeedRandom[]** uses the time of day as a seed while **SeedRandom[sd]** uses the given seed **sd**. *Mathematica* uses the seed to begin the mathematical algorithm which generates the pseudorandom number. Giving the same seed assures that the same sequence of pseudorandom numbers will be obtained on different occasions.

Select   211, 221, 863
                                    See Also: **Drop**, **Take**, **Cases**

Select is used to determine the parts of expressions which possess a particular property. **Select[expression,func]** lists the elements of **expression** for which the function **func** is True. Also, **Select[expression,func,m]** finds the first **m** parts of **expression** with this quality. This is accomplished by applying **func** to the elements of **expression** and keeping only those parts where **func** yields True.

Example:

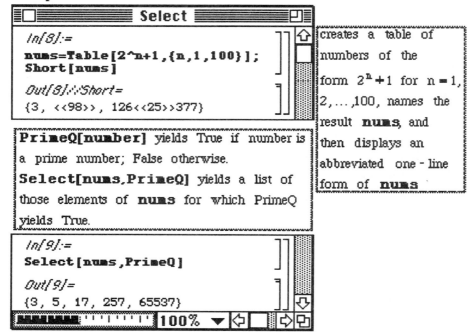

Sequence

Sequence[expr1,expr2,...] represents a sequence of arguments in an expression.

SequenceForm   349, 361, 863
                                    See Also: **TableForm**, **ColumnForm**

SequenceForm[expr1,expr2,...] prints the indicated sequence of expressions where these expressions are concatenated together. The baselines of these expressions are aligned.

Example:

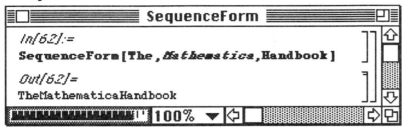

SequenceLimit
See 761

SequenceLimit[list] yields the approximation of the limit of the sequence whose first few terms are given in **list**. This approximation is found by the Wynn epsilon method. Note that this algorithm may yield a finite limit for a divergent sequence.

Series   100, 639, 863
See 414, 415, 595   See Also: **Normal**, **Limit**, **InverseSeries**,
                                                   Residue

Series is used to obtain power series expansions for functions of one and two variables. **Series[f[x],{x,a,n}]** yields the power series expansion for the function **f** about **x=a** to order $(x-a)^n$. Note that this power series is given by the

formula $\sum_{k=0}^{\infty} \frac{f^{(k)}(a)}{k!}(x-a)^n$. If f is a function of two variables, then

Series[f[x,y],{x,a,nx},{y,b,ny}] successively determines the power series of **f** with respect to y and then with respect to x.

Example:

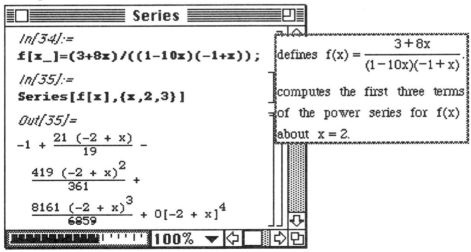

SeriesCoefficient

See Also: **Series**

SeriesCoefficient[ser,n] yields the coefficient of the term of order **n** in the series **ser**.

Example:

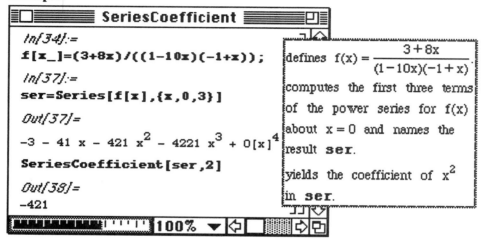

SeriesData

641, 864

See Also: **Series**

SeriesData[x,x0,{a0,a1,...},nmin,nmax,d] represents a power series expansion about **x = x0** where **a0, a1**, ... are the coefficients of the powers of (**x−x0**). These powers are given by **nmin/d**, **(nmin+1)/d**, ..., **nmax/d**. These objects are generated by **Series**. If a **SeriesData** object is printed, then a higher-order term of the form $O[x-x0]^n$ is included. **Normal** is used to remove these higher order terms. When operations such as differentiation and integration are performed on **SeriesData** objects, then a truncated expression is produced. The inverse of **SeriesData** objects can be determined with **InverseSeries**.

Example:

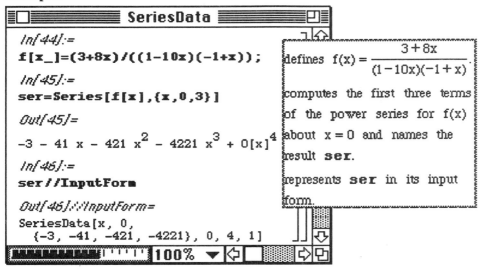

SessionTime   524, 743, 864
                               See Also: **Date**, **AbsoluteTime**, **TimeUsed**
  SessionTime[ ] yields the total amount of time (in seconds) that have elapsed since the beginning of the current *Mathematica* session. The error involved in this time is at least as much as the value of the global variable **$TimeUnit** which is about 1/60 of a second.

Example:

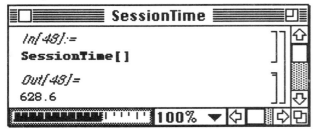

Set (=)   75, 251, 255, 258, 326, 735, 864
See 403   See Also: **Clear**, **DownValues**, **Literal**, **TagSet**,
                                Unset, **SetDelayed**
  Set, symbolized by **=**, is used to make definitions in *Mathematica*. In the case of **lhs=rhs**, *Mathematica* immediately evaluates **rhs** and assigns its value to **lhs**. The symbol **:=** is also used for definitions. However, the assignment made when using **:=** is delayed. The **Set** symbol, **=**, is used as **f[arguments]=rhs** to define functions if the assignment of the final value is desired. **HoldFirst** is an attribute of **Set**. New definitions of a particular symbol are usually placed in the order in which they are given. However, *Mathematica* places more specific definitions before already existing ones. Also, a sequence of assignments can be made with

`{left1,left2,...}={right1,right2,...}` where corresponding components are assigned. When the function **f** is defined in the form `f[x_]:=f[x]=...`, **f** remembers the values it computes: values of **f** computed are explicitly stored. Defining a function in this manner can be particulary useful when it is recursviely defined or when values are difficult to compute and will be used more than one time.

Example:

In the following example, **y=3** produces the same result as `Set[y,3]`; `Set[x,2]` produces the same result as **x=2**.

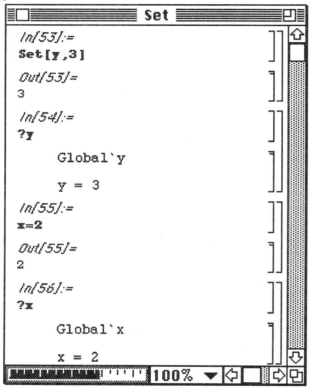

SetAccuracy   544, 865
                               See Also: **Accuracy**, **N**, **Precision**,
                               SetPrecision

 `SetAccuracy[expression,n]` yields a form of **expression** in which all numbers are given in **n**-digit accuracy. If additional digits are needed, then *Mathematica* adds numbers which are zero in base 2.

SetAttributes   230, 271, 865
See 263   See Also: **Attributes**, **ClearAttributes**,
                               Protect

 `SetAttributes[sym,attr]` adds the attribute of list of attributes given in attr to the attributes of the symbol sym. **SetAttributes** has the attribute **HoldFirst**.

SetDelayed(:=)   255, 258, 735, 865
See 7, 403   See Also: **Clear**, **Set**, **TagSetDelayed**, **Unset**,
                                    Rule, **RuleDelayed**

   SetDelayed, symbolized by **:=**, is used to define a delayed assignment. In the case
of **lhs:=rhs**, *Mathematica* evaluates **rhs** upon each request of **lhs** and leaves **rhs**
in an unevaluated form. This command is used as **f[args]:=rhs** in order to state
the command **rhs** for determining the value of the function for each argument value.
The assignment can be made with the statement **lhs:=rhs/;cond** where the
conditions for applying the rule **lhs:=rhs** are given in **cond**. When the function **f** is
defined in the form **f[x_]:=f[x]=...**, **f** remembers the values it computes: values
of **f** computed are explicitly stored.   **SetDelayed** has the attribute **HoldAll**.

Example:

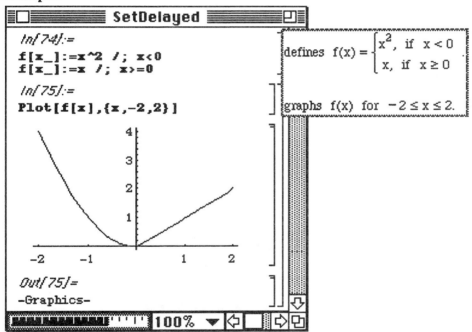

SetDirectory   180, 489, 865
                                    See Also: **Directory**, **ResetDirectory**, **$Path**
   SetDirectory["direct"] sets the current working directory to be **direct**
where **direct** can be any directory name recognized by the operating system. After
setting the directory, *Mathematica* returns the directory name. *Mathematica*
remembers the previous directories. It lists all of them with **DirectoryStack[]** and
gives the previous directory with **ResetDirectory[]**.

SetFileDate   492, 865
                                    See Also: **FileDate**
   SetFileDate["filename"] sets the modification date of the file **filename** to
be the current date. This command can be used as **SetFileDate["filename",d]**
in order to set the modification date of **filename** to be the indicated date **d** where **d** is
stated in the form **{year,month,day,hour,minute,second}**.

SetOptions   149, 517, 724, 865
See 574   See Also: **FullOptions**, **Options**

  SetOptions is used to set the default values for symbols. For the symbol **func**,
SetOptions[func,option1->val1,option2->val2,...] sets the default
values of the options **option1**, **option2**, ... to be **val1**, **val2**, ..., respectively. The
default values set with **SetOptions** remain until changed with another **SetOptions**
command. When used to specify the appearance of output, **SetOptions** includes the
options **SetOptions** and **TotalWidth** for the symbol **$Output**. The setting
PageWidth->n indicates that the output lines are broken so that they are at most **n**
characters long. Also, the setting **TotalWidth->n** indicates that **Short** is used in
such a way that each complete segment of output includes at most **n** characters. This
command can be used as **SetOptions[stream1,stream2,...]** or
SetOptions["name1","name2",...] to set the options for a stream or list of
streams.
Example:
The following example lists all options for the command **Plot**.

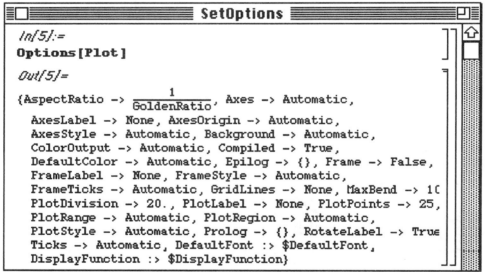

SetOptions[Plot,AspectRatio->1] causes the option
AspectRatio->1/GoldenRatio to be changed to **AspectRatio->1**. Options
for *Mathematica* commands can be permanently changed by modifying the **init.m**
file.

```
In[6]:=
SetOptions[Plot,AspectRatio->1]

Out[6]=
{AspectRatio -> 1, Axes -> Automatic, AxesLabel -> None,
  AxesOrigin -> Automatic, AxesStyle -> Automatic,
  Background -> Automatic, ColorOutput -> Automatic,
  Compiled -> True, DefaultColor -> Automatic, Epilog -> {}
  Frame -> False, FrameLabel -> None, FrameStyle -> Automat
  FrameTicks -> Automatic, GridLines -> None, MaxBend -> 1C
  PlotDivision -> 20., PlotLabel -> None, PlotPoints -> 25,
  PlotRange -> Automatic, PlotRegion -> Automatic,
  PlotStyle -> Automatic, Prolog -> {}, RotateLabel -> True
```

SetPrecision   544, 866

See Also: **Chop, N, Precision, SetAccuracy**

SetPrecision[expression,n] writes all numbers in **expression** so that they have precision of **n** digits. If **SetPrecision** increases the precision of a number, then zeros (given in base 2) are added to pad the number. **SetPrecision** only alters the appearance of **expression**. It does not affect the calculations involving **expression**.

Example:

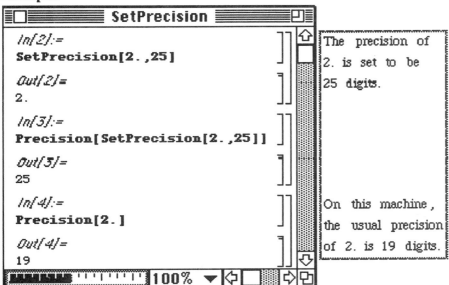

```
In[2]:=
SetPrecision[2.,25]

Out[2]=
2.

In[3]:=
Precision[SetPrecision[2.,25]]

Out[3]=
25

In[4]:=
Precision[2.]

Out[4]=
19
```

The precision of 2. is set to be 25 digits.

On this machine, the usual precision of 2. is 19 digits.

SetStreamPosition   503, 504, 866

See 432   See Also: **StreamPosition**

SetStreamPosition is used to set the integer-valued point in an open stream which is returned by **StreamPosition**. This value represents the number of bytes from the beginning of the string. **SetStreamPosition[stream,n]** sets the

position of stream to be **n**. Also, **SetStreamPosition[stream,0]** sets the current point to be the beginning of stream while
SetStreamPosition[stream,Infinity] sets the current point to be the end of stream.

Shading   156, 160, 162, 436, 452, 817, 866
See 123, 126, 131, 178,   See Also: **ClipFill**, **HiddenSurface**, **Lighting**,
196, 235, 236, 241, 243,   **ColorFunction**
254, 271, 397, 398, 422,
521, 576, 583

    Shading is a **SurfaceGraphics** function option which is used to indicate if the surface should be shaded or not. The setting **Shading->False** causes the surface to be left white. The mesh is still drawn if **Mesh->True** is included in the command as well. **Shading** is determined from height or from simulated illumination if **Lighting->True** is included.

Shallow   346, 517, 866
                                 See Also: **Short**

    Shallow[expression] gives a shortened skeleton form of **expression** where omitted parts are written as <<k>>. This command can be more specific with **Shallow[expression,n]** which gives all parts of **expression** below depth **n** in skeleton form. Also, **Shallow[expression,{n,length}]** places in skeleton form all parts of **expression** which are beyond depth **n** and longer than the given **length**. Finally, **Shallow[expression,{n,length},form]** gives all parts which match the pattern of **form** which are beyond depth **n** and longer than the given **length** as well in skeleton form. The default settings for **n** and **length** is 4.

Share   528, 866
                                 See Also: **ByteCount**, **MemoryInUse**

    Share is used to minimize the amount of memory used to store expressions. In many cases subexpressions are not stored in the same piece of computer memory. The command **Share[expression]** specifies that subexpressions of **expression** be shared in the same piece, and, thus, alters the manner in which **expression** is stored internally. **Share[]** attempts to minimize the amount of computer memory used to store all expressions. **Share** may also minimize the amount of time needed to obtain results.

Short   83, 346, 517, 867
See 139, 412, 431, 549   See Also: **Format**, **Shallow**

    Short is used to give output in a shortened form. **Short[expression,n]** prints **expression** on at most **n** lines while **Short[expression]** prints **expression** in its usual form minus one line. The omitted sequences of k elements of **expression** are given as <<k>>. If entire sequences are omitted, then they are represented as **Skeleton** objects. **Short** is not only useful with **OutputForm**. It can be used with **InputForm** as well. This function only affects the printing of expressions. It does not alter any calculations.

Example:

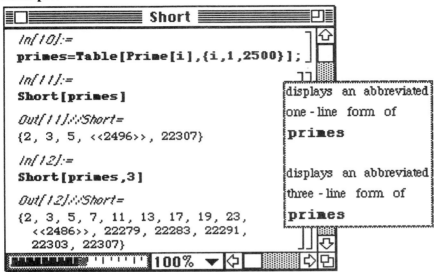

Show   139, 144, 156, 157, 395, 397, 867
See 127, 131, 165, 219,   See Also: **Graphics**, **GraphicsArray**,
312, 353, 354, 357, 381,   **Graphics3D**, **Plot**, **Plot3D**
525-534, 536-540, 547,
551, 553, 558, 559, 561,
562-565, 569, 570, 572,
573, 577, 578, 593, 596,
597, 691, 731, 732, 734

   Show is used to display two- and three-dimensional graphics objects. Therefore, it is useful with **ContourGraphics**, **DensityGraphics**, **Graphics**, **Graphics3D**, **GraphicsArray**, and **SurfaceGraphics**. The command **Show[graphics,options]** displays graphics using the indicated options. Several graphics objects can be shown at once with **Show[graphics1,graphics2,...]**. Note that all options included in the **Show** command override options used in the original graphics commands. The option **DisplayFunction** specifies whether graphs are to be shown or not. The setting **DisplayFunction->\$DisplayFunction** causes the graph to be shown while **DisplayFunction->Identity** causes the display to be suppressed. **Show** is automatically used with such functions as **Plot** and **Plot3D** to display graphics.
Example:

   In the following example, $f(x) = e^{-x^2 \cos^2(\pi x)}$. **plotone** is a graph of $f(x)$ for $-1 \le x \le 1$. **plottwo** is a graph of $f(x^2 - y^2)$ for $-2 \le x \le 2$ and $-2 \le y \le 2$. Neither graph is displayed since the option **DisplayFunction->Identity** is included within each command.

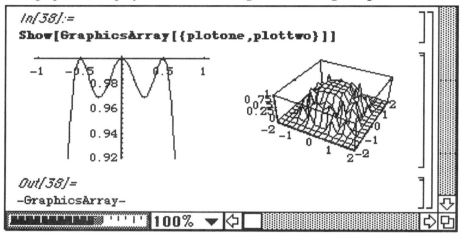

In[35]:=
`f[x_]=Exp[-x^2Cos[Pi x]^2];`

In[37]:=
```
plotone=Plot[f[x],{x,-1,1},
    DisplayFunction->Identity];
plottwo=Plot3D[f[x^2+y^2],{x,-2,2},{y,-2,2},
    DisplayFunction->Identity,
    Shading->False];
```

Both graphs are displayed below as a **Graphics Array** using the **Show** command.

In[38]:=
`Show[GraphicsArray[{plotone,plottwo}]]`

Out[38]=
`-GraphicsArray-`

`100%`

ShowAnimation   175
                       See Also: **Animation, Graphics`Animation`**

ShowAnimation is found in the package **Graphics`Animation`** and is used to animate selected graphics. The command is entered as **ShowAnimation[graphics1,graphics2,...]** to animate the listed sequence of graphics.

Sign   550, 604, 867
See 622, 623, 629   See Also: **Abs, Negative, NonNegative, Positive, TargetFunction**

Sign[x] yields a value of -1 if $x < 0$, 0 if $x = 0$, and 1 if $x > 0$. If **x** is a complex number, then **Sign[x]** is defined to be **x/Abs[x]**. **Sign[expression]** can be used to assign the property of **Positive** or **Negative** to **expression**. **Sign** is also a possible setting for the **ComplexExpand** option **TargetFunction**.

Example:

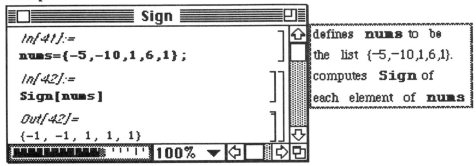

Signature   133, 558, 561, 671, 867
                                  See Also: **Order**, **Sort**, **Multinomial**

   Signature[{i1,i2,...}] yields the signature of the permutation needed to put
the list **{i1,i2,...}** in canonical order. The signature is equal to 1 if an even
number of transpositions is necessary to return to canonical order and is equal to −1 if
an odd number is required. If two members of **{i1,i2,...}** are equal, then a value
of 0 is returned.

Example:

The following example computes the signature of the permutation {2,5,1,4,3}.

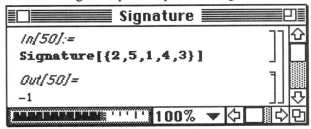

SignPadding   351, 867
                                  See Also: **NumberPadding**

   SignPadding is an option used with number formatting functions such as
NumberForm and **ScientificForm** to indicate whether or not padding should be
placed after the sign of a number. The setting **SignPadding->True** indicates that
necessary padding be placed between the sign and digits of the number while
SignPadding->False implies that the padding be inserted before the sign.

Simplify   77, 78, 868
See 113, 189, 201, 246,   See Also: **Expand**, **Factor**
247, 251, 252, 314, 315,
595, 597

   Simplify[expression] tries to determine the simplest form of **expression**
through a sequence of algebraic transformations. If **expression** is complicated, then
Mathematica can spend a great deal of time testing various transformations in an
attempt to determine the simplest form of **expression**. In this case, commands like
Expand and **Factor** are useful prior to application of **Simplify**. **Simplify** has

the option **Trig** where **Trig->False** does not apply trigonometric identities in the simplification process.

Example:

In the following example, **Simplify** is used to display the expression $\dfrac{-9-3x}{-2-7x}+\dfrac{-3-10x}{2+3x}$ as a fraction with a single denominator. The same result is obtained by using the commands **Together** and then **ExpandDenominator**.

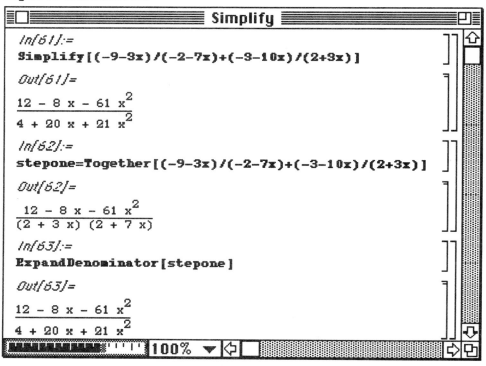

Sin   49, 562, 603, 868
See 28, 249, 263, 280,   See Also: **Csc**, **ArcSin**
478

    Sin[x] represents the trigonometric sine function of **x** where **x** is given in radian measurement. Multiplication by **Degree** converts degrees to radian measure.

Example:

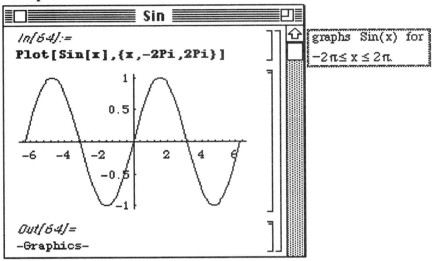

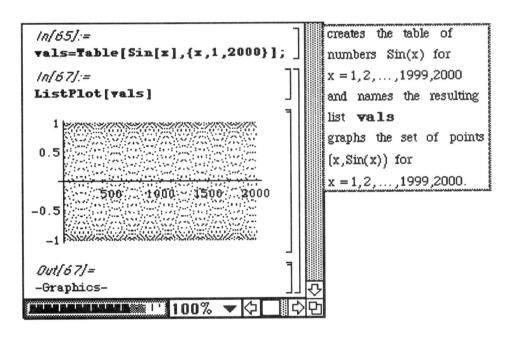

SingularityDepth   688
See Also: **NIntegrate**

SingularityDepth is an option used with **NIntegrate** to indicate the number of recursive subdivisions allowed before making a change of variable at the endpoints of the interval of integration. The default setting is **SingularityDepth->4**.

SingularValues   665, 868
                                  See Also: **PseudoInverse**, **QRDecomposition**,
                                  SchurDecomposition

SingularValues[m] computes the singular value decomposition of the matrix **m**.
Note that this decomposition yields the list {u,w,v} where u and v are row
orthogonal matrices and w is a list of the singular values of m such that
m = Transpose[u].DiagonalMatrix[w].v. **SingularValues** has the option
Tolerance->t which is used to indicate that singular values which are smaller than
t times the largest singular value should be omitted from the list w. The default setting
for this option is **Automatic** which represents $10^{(4-p)}$ where p is the numerical
precision of the input.
Example:
In the following example, notice that entering the command
matrix={{3.,2.,-5.},{-6.,-8.,-6.},{-5.,-5.,8.}}; defines matrix to
be the numerical matrix $\begin{pmatrix} 3 & 2 & -5 \\ -6 & -8 & -6 \\ -5 & -5 & 8 \end{pmatrix}$.

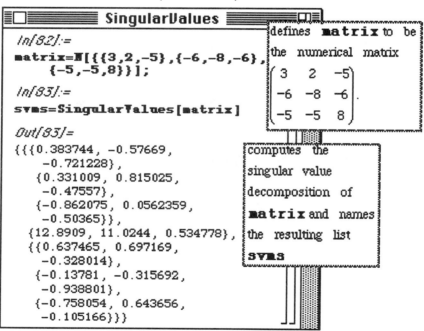

svms[[1]]//MatrixForm yields the first element of the list (of matrices) **svms**
and displays the result in row-and-column form; **svms[[2]]** yields the second
element of **svms**; and **svms[[3]]//MatrixForm** yields the third element of **svms**
and displays the result in row-and-column form.

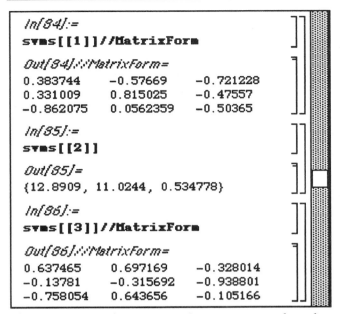

DiagonalMatrix[svms[[2]]] corresponds to the matrix

$$\begin{bmatrix} 12.89 & 0 & 0 \\ 0 & 11.02 & 0 \\ 0 & 0 & 0.53 \end{bmatrix}.$$ The following computation verifies that

$$\begin{bmatrix} 0.38 & -0.57 & -0.72 \\ 0.33 & 0.81 & -0.47 \\ -0.86 & 0.05 & -0.50 \end{bmatrix}^{T} \cdot \begin{bmatrix} 12.89 & 0 & 0 \\ 0 & 11.02 & 0 \\ 0 & 0 & 0.53 \end{bmatrix} \cdot \begin{bmatrix} 0.63 & 0.69 & -0.32 \\ -0.13 & -0.31 & -0.93 \\ -0.75 & 0.64 & -0.10 \end{bmatrix} \text{ is }$$

matrix.

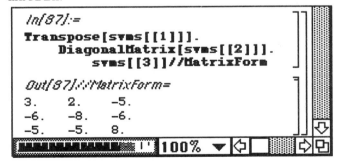

Sinh   562, 868

See Also: **Csch, ArcSinh**

Sinh[x] represents the hyperbolic sine function $\sinh(x) = \dfrac{e^{x} - e^{-x}}{2}$.

Example:

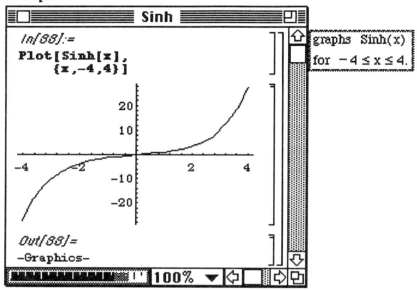

SinhIntegral

See Also: **CoshIntegral**

SinhIntegral[x] represents the hyperbolic sine integral which is given by the

formula $\int_0^x \dfrac{\sinh t}{t}\, dt$.

Example:

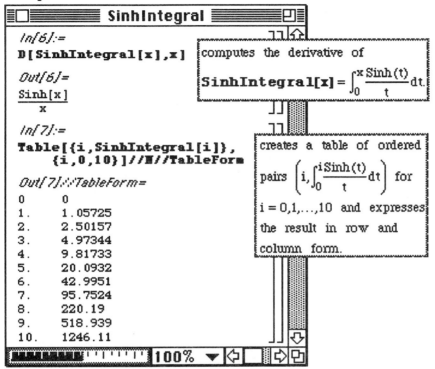

SinIntegral   571, 576, 868
See 468   See Also: **CosIntegral**, **ExpIntegralE**,
                                    ExpIntegralEi

SinIntegral[x] represents the sine integral function $Si(x) = \int_0^x \frac{\sin t}{t} dt$.

Example:

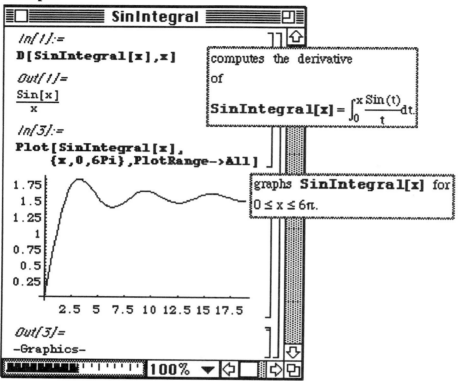

SixJSymbol   561, 868
See Also: **ClebschGordan**, **ThreeJSymbol**

SixJSymbol[{j1,j2,j3},{j4,j5,j6}] yields the couplings of three quantum mechanical angular momentum states. These can be integers, half-integers, or expressions. The results obtained with **SixJSymbol** are related to the Racah coefficients by a phase shift.

Skeleton   517, 868
See 412, 421   See Also: **Short**, **StringSkeleton**, **TotalWidth**,
                                 Shallow

Skeleton[k], the default value of which is **<<k>>**, represents a sequence of **k** terms omitted from an expression rendered with **Shallow** or **Short**.

Example:

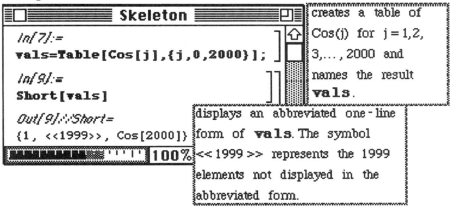

499, 503, 869
See Also: **Find, SetStreamPosition, Read**

Skip is used to move the current point past a sequence of objects of a particular form without reading these objects in the input stream. **Skip[stream,patt]** skips past an object of the form defined in **patt** while **Skip[stream,patt,n]** skips past **n** objects in the given form. **$Failed** is returned by **Skip** if it does not successfully skip over the indicated objects while **Null** is given if the **Skip** is successful.

Example:

The following shows the file **data**.

```
In[26]:=
!!data
    10   10   100 15    135 1.000
    4    5    72.5    9    90.5      0.670
    7    6.5 57.5    10   81   0.600
    10   5.5 78   14    107.5      0.796
    6.5  6.5 32.5    9    54.5      0.404
    7.5  6.5 60   10    84   0.622
    6.5  4.5 65    6    82   0.607
    3    5.5 73   15    96.5      0.715
    8    4    49.5    13   74.5      0.552
    5.5  5.5 60   12    83   0.615
    9    5.5 65    9    88.5      0.656
    6.5  2    71   13    92.5      0.685
    9    5    56.5    12   82.5      0.611
    10   4.5 60   13    87.5      0.648
    9    3    68   15    95   0.704
    6.5  3    42   15    66.5      0.493
    7    3    53.5    11   74.5      0.552
    7    5    50.5    6    68.5      0.507
    10   7.5 81   15    113.5      0.841
```

```
In[27]:=
grades=OpenRead["data"]

Out[27]=
InputStream[data, 9]

In[28]:=
Read[grades,Number]

Out[28]=
10

In[29]:=
Skip[grades,Number,5]

In[30]:=
StreamPosition[grades]

Out[30]=
22
```

prepares to read from the file **data** and names the resulting InputStream **grades**.

the first number of **grades** is 10.

skips the next five numbers of **grades**.

after skipping the next five numbers, the position of the current point is 22.

```
In[31]:=
Read[grades,Number]

Out[31]=
4

In[33]:=
SetStreamPosition[grades,100];
Read[grades,Number]

Out[33]=
32.5

In[35]:=
SetStreamPosition[grades,0];
Read[grades,Number]

Out[35]=
10

In[36]:=
Close[grades]

Out[36]=
data
```

reads the sixth number of **grades**.

sets the current point in **grades** at 100 and then reads the next number of **grades**.

sets the current point to the beginning of **grades** and reads the first number.

closes the stream **grades**.

100% ▼

Slot (#)   208, 869
                                      See Also: **SlotSequence**
   Slot, represented by the symbol **#**, stands for an argument in a pure function.   This
command yields the same results as **Slot[ ]** or **Slot[1]**. **#n** which is equivalent to
Slot[n] represents the **n**th argument of the function where **n** must be a non-negative
integer. The pure function itself is given with **#0**.

SlotSequence (##)   208, 869
                                      See Also: Slot
   SlotSequence, represented by the symbol **##**, stands for the argument sequence of
a pure function. This command yields the same results as **SlotSequence** or
SlotSequence[1]. **##n** which is equivalent to **SlotSequence[n]** represents the
sequence of arguments beginning with the **n**th argument of the function where **n** must
be a non-negative integer.

Socket
                                      See Also: **FileType**
   Socket is a possible outcome of such functions as **FileType**.

SolutionOf
   SolutionOf is an internal symbol.

Solve   95, 607, 612, 615, 617, 620, 646, 659, 683, 691, 869
See 115, 202, 273, 291,   See Also: **DSolve**, **Eliminate**, **FindRoot**,
472, 474   **LinearSolve**, **NSolve**, **Reduce**, **Roots**, **NRoots**
   Solve is used to solve equations or systems of equations where all equations must
include a double equals sign, **==**. Systems of equations may be entered in the form of a
list or be connected by the logical connective **&&**.
Solve[{lhs1==rhs1,lhs2==rhs2,..},{var1,var2,...}] solves the
given equations for the variables listed. The commands
Solve[{lhs1,lhs2,...}=={rhs1,rhs2,...},{var1,var2,...}] and
Solve[lhs1==rhs1&&lhs2==rhs2&&...,{var1,var2,...}] also yield the
same results.   The output of **Solve** is rendered in the form of the list
{{var1->a},...} if there are several variables or several solutions. The result
appears in the form **var1->a** if there is only one. *Mathematica* indicates the
multiplicity of roots by listing a repeated root the appropriate number of times.
Solve[eqn,var,elim] solves the given equation or system of equations for the
variable(s) given in **var** by eliminating the variable(s) given in **elim**. This allows for
certain variables to be given in terms of parameters. **Solve** has several options. One
of these options is **Mode**. **Mode->Modular** allows for a weaker form of equality in
which two integer expressions are equal modulo a fixed integer. This integer can be
explicitly given with **Modulus==p**. Otherwise, *Mathematica* tries to determine an
integer for which the given equations can be satisfied.   Another option is
InverseFunctions which indicates whether or not inverse functions should be used
in the solution process. The default setting for **InverseFunctions** is **Automatic**
which indicates that inverses are employed. If this is the case, a warning message is
printed in the output. If there are no solutions, then **Solve** yields the symbol **{}**.
Solve gives solutions which cannot be solved for explicitly in terms of **Roots**.
Solve is most useful when dealing with polynomial equations.

Example:

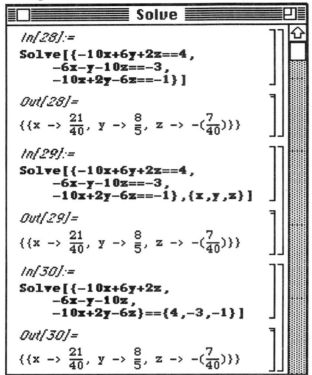

All three commands solve the system of equations
$$\begin{cases} -10x + 6y + 2z = 4 \\ -6x - y - 10z = -3 \\ -10x + 2y - 6z = -1 \end{cases}$$
for x, y, and z.

```
In[28]:=
Solve[{-10x+6y+2z==4,
    -6x-y-10z==-3,
    -10x+2y-6z==-1}]

Out[28]=
{{x -> 21/40, y -> 8/5, z -> -(7/40)}}

In[29]:=
Solve[{-10x+6y+2z==4,
    -6x-y-10z==-3,
    -10x+2y-6z==-1},{x,y,z}]

Out[29]=
{{x -> 21/40, y -> 8/5, z -> -(7/40)}}

In[30]:=
Solve[{-10x+6y+2z,
    -6x-y-10z,
    -10x+2y-6z}=={4,-3,-1}]

Out[30]=
{{x -> 21/40, y -> 8/5, z -> -(7/40)}}
```

Solve can also be used to solve literal equations.

```
In[31]:=
Solve[v==1/3 Pi r^2 h,r]

Out[31]=
         Sqrt[3/Pi] Sqrt[v]
{{r -> -------------------},
              Sqrt[h]

           Sqrt[3/Pi] Sqrt[v]
   {r -> -(-------------------)}}
                Sqrt[h]
```

solves $v = \dfrac{1}{3}\pi r^2 h$

for r.

`100%`

SolveAlways   620, 870
                              See Also: **AlgebraicRules**, **LogicalExpand**,
                              Reduce, **Solve**

   SolveAlways[equations,variables] yields parameter values for which the
given equation or system of equations which depend on a set of parameters is valid for
all variable values. As with **Solve**, systems of equations can be entered in the form of
a list or through the use of logical connectives **&&**. Note that equations must include a
double equals sign, **==**. The results of **SolveAlways** is given in the form of a list if
there is more than one parameter.
Solve[[!Eliminate[!equations,variables]] can be used to accomplish
the same results as **SolveAlways**. **SolveAlways** is most useful when dealing with
polynomial equations.
Example:
The following example finds the values of a, b, and c which make
$x^2+2x-1=(2a+2b+2c)x^2+(3a+2b-c)x-2a$ for all values of x.

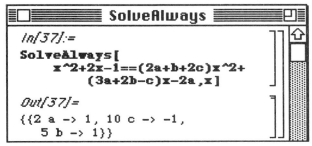

When the option Method->3 is included, the resulting values of a, b, and c are given.

Sort   130, 214, 379, 870
                              See Also: **Max**, **Min**, **Order**, **Orderless**,
                              OrderedQ, **$StringOrder**

   Sort[list] places **list** in canonical order where numbers are ordered according
to numerical value, strings are ordered by the character order given by
$StringOrder, and symbols are ordered according to the corresponding textual
names. An ordering function can be defined to be used by **Sort** in the command
Sort[list,func]. A possible definition of **func** is **(#2>#1)&** which places list
in increasing order. The default setting for func is **OrderedQ[{#1,#2}]&**.

Example:

The following example sorts the list of numbers {8,–8,–4,–10,–6} into the standard order.

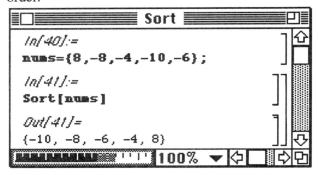

Sound   474, 870
                                        See Also: **SampledSoundFunction**,
                                        SampledSoundList

   Sound[{s1,s2,...}] represents a sound object made up of the sound primitives s1, s2, ... where sound objects are produced by **Play** and **ListPlay**. Possible sound primitives include **SampledSoundFunction** and **SampledSoundList**. **Sound** is played through the use of **Show**.

Space
   Space is string made up of a space.

SpaceForm
   SpaceForm[n] prints n spaces.

SpellingCorrection   384, 870
                                        See Also: **IgnoreCase**

   SpellingCorrection is an option used with **StringMatchQ** to indicate whether small segments of characters are allowed to differ in pattern matching. **SpellingCorrection->True** indicates that these small differences are allowed while the default setting of **SpellingCorrection->False** requires exact matches. The command **?sym** uses **SpellingCorrection->True** if *Mathematica* cannot find an exact match for the symbol **sym**. A warning message accompanies the output to indicate a possible spelling error.

SphericalHarmonicY   567, 870
See 462   See Also: **ClebschGordan**, **LegendreP**

   SphericalHarmonicY[l,m,theta,phi] represents the spherical harmonic

$Y_l^m(\theta, \phi)$. These functions are related to Legendre polynomials and satisfy the

orthogonality condition $\int Y_l^m(\theta, \phi)\, Y_{l'}^{m'}(\theta, \phi)\, d\Omega$ where $d\Omega$ represents integration

over the unit sphere.

SphericalRegion   175, 446, 871
See 521, 576   See Also: **PlotRegion**, **ViewPoint**

SphericalRegion is an option used with three-dimensional graphics functions to ensure that scaling in different plots do not vary. With the setting **SphericalRegion->True**, *Mathematica* places a sphere around the three-dimensional bounding box. The final image is then scaled so that the entire sphere fits inside of the display area. The center of the sphere and the center of the bounding box coincide. The radius of the sphere is chosen so that the bounding box fits just within the sphere. This option is particularly useful when animating sequences of plots which show an object from several different viewpoints.

SpinShow

SpinShow is a command found in the package **Graphics`Animation`**.

Splice   184, 871
                             See Also: **RunThrough**

Splice allows for the splicing of *Mathematica* output into external files. The command **Splice["filename"]** splices *Mathematica* output into the file **filename**. Information given within the symbols **<*** and ***>** is evaluated as *Mathematica* input, and this text is replaced by the output that results. An alternate form of this command is **Splice["inputfile","outputfile"]** so that *Mathematica* input is spliced into **inputfile** and the resulting output is sent to **outputfile**. Information which is not contained within **<*** and ***>** remains unchanged in the file. The options for **Splice** as well as their default values are **Delimiters->{"<*",{*>"}**, **FormatType->Automatic**, and **PageWidth->78**.

Sqrt   49, 871
See 12, 303, 453   See Also: **Power**, **PowerExpand**

Sqrt[x] yields the square root of x. **PowerExpand** can be used to convert **Sqrt[x^2]** to **x** and **Sqrt[x y]** to **Sqrt[x] Sqrt[y]**. These conversions are not automatically made with *Mathematica*.

Example:

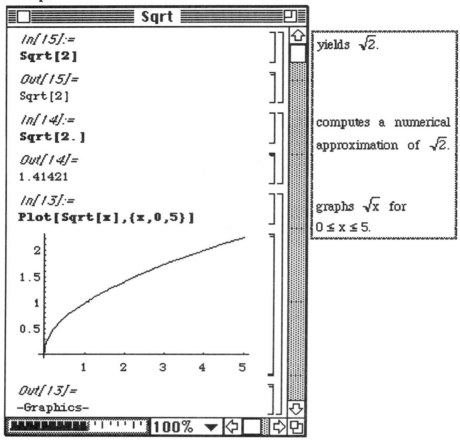

In[15]:= **Sqrt[2]**	yields $\sqrt{2}$.
Out[15]= Sqrt[2]	
In[14]:= **Sqrt[2.]**	computes a numerical approximation of $\sqrt{2}$.
Out[14]= 1.41421	
In[13]:= **Plot[Sqrt[x],{x,0,5}]**	graphs $\sqrt{x}$ for $0 \le x \le 5$.

Out[13]=
-Graphics-

Stack   306, 307, 732, 743, 871

See Also: **Trace**

  Stack[] lists the tags associated with current evaluations. **Stack[pattern]** lists
the expressions under current evaluation which match the given pattern. Also,
Stack[_] lists all expressions under current evaluation. **Stack** can be called from
within a **Dialog** and can be used during a calculation to determine the steps being
taken by *Mathematica* to determine the result. The value of **$RecursionLimit** is
the maximum length of **Stack[]**. **HoldFirst** is an attribute of **Stack**.

StackBegin   308, 872

See Also: **StackInhibit**

  StackBegin[expression] evaluates **expression** by first starting a fresh
evaluation stack. Hence, during the evaluation of **expression**, the stack includes
nothing outside of the **StackBegin**. This command is called by such functions as
TraceDialog[expression] so that only the evaluation of **expression** is shown
in the stack instead of the steps taken to call **TraceDialog**. **HoldFirst** is an
attribute of **StackBegin**.

StackComplete   308, 872
                                     See Also: **TraceAbove, TraceBackwards**
   StackComplete[expression] keeps the complete evaluation chain for each expression under current evaluation. The advantage of **StackComplete** is that previous forms of **expression** can be seen. The stack which results is the same as that found when the options **TraceBackwards->All** and **TraceAbove->All** are both used with **Trace**.

StackInhibit   307, 308, 872
                                     See Also: **StackBegin**
   StackInhibit[expression] evaluates **expression** without including it in the stack. **HoldFirst** is an attribute of **StackInhibit**.

StartingStepSize   700
                                     See Also: **NDSolve**
   StartingStepSize is an option used with **NDSolve** to state the initial step size to use for the independent variable.

StartProcess   obsolete in Version 2.0
                                     superseded by *MathLink* operations
   StartProcess[`command`] initiates an external process from which *Mathematica* commands can be called.

StirlingS1   558, 560, 872
                                     See Also: **PartitionsP, PartitionsQ,**
                                     StirlingS2
   StirlingS1[n,m] represents the Stirling number of the first kind $S_n^{(m)}$ where

$(-1)^{n-m}S_n^{(m)}$ yields the number of permutations of n elements which contain exactly

m cycles. Stirling numbers of the first kind satisfy the generating function relation

$$x\,(x-1)\cdots(x-n+1) = \sum_{m=0}^{n}S_n^{(m)}x^m.$$

Example:

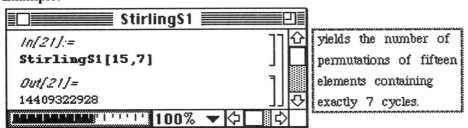

```
In[21]:=
StirlingS1[15,7]

Out[21]=
14409322928
```

yields the number of permutations of fifteen elements containing exactly 7 cycles.

StirlingS2   558, 560, 872
                                  See Also: **PartitionsP**, **PartitionsQ**,
                                  StirlingS1

StirlingS2[n,m] represents Stirling numbers of the second kind. These values yield the number of ways to partition a set of n elements into m non - empty subsets,

and they satisfy the relation $x^n = \sum_{m=0}^{n} S_n^{(m)} x(x-1)\cdots(x-m+1)$.

Example:

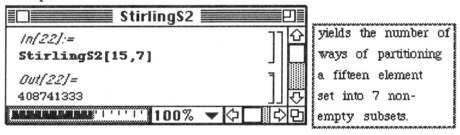

StreamPosition   503, 504, 872
See 432   See Also: **SetStreamPosition**

StreamPosition[stream] yields an integer which represents the current point in an open stream. In most computer systems, this integer is the number of bytes counted from the beginning of the stream to the current point.

Streams   489, 519, 743, 872
                                 See Also: **OpenRead**, **OpenWrite**, **Options**,
                                 SetOptions, **$Input**

Streams[] lists all of the input and output streams that are currently open. This list cannot be altered except indirectly through the use of functions such as **OpenRead**. Also, **Streams["streamname"]** lists only those streams with the name **streamname**.

String   365, 495, 712, 873
                                 See Also: **Characters**, **SyntaxQ**, **ToExpression**,
                                 ToString

String is the head of strings of text of the form **"text"** where a **String** contains a sequence of 8- or 16-bit characters. In standard **OutputForm**, the quotation marks are not printed with **text**. However, in **InputForm**, the quotation marks are included. In order to define a pattern which represents a string, **x_String** is used.

StringBreak   517, 873
                                 See Also: **Continuation**, **Indent**, **LineBreak**

StringBreak[n] is given at the end of the nth part of a string, number, or symbol name that is broken into several lines of output. Hence, **StringBreak** represents a hyphenation mark. In *Mathematica*, the default setting for **Format[StringBreak[n]]** is **"\"**, but other values can be indicated with **Format[StringBreak[n]]**.

StringByteCount   374, 873
                              See Also: **ByteCount, Characters,**
                              FileByteCount, ToCharacterCode
   StringByteCount["stringname"] yields the number of bytes necessary to
store the characters which make up the string **stringname**. This value is determined
by finding the integer code which corresponds to characters in **stringname** where
8-bit characters have integer codes from 0 to 255 and 16-bit characters have codes from
256 to 65791. If **stringname** is made up of 8-bit characters only, then the value of
StringByteCount["stringname"] is the same as that of
StringLength["stringname"].
Example:
The following example yields the number of bytes necessary to store the characters
which make up the string **The *Mathematica* Handbook**.

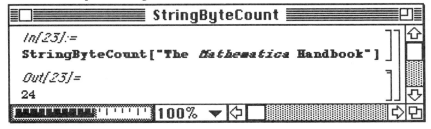

StringConversion   469, 487, 738, 873
                              See Also: **StringReplace**
   StringConversion is an output stream function option which is used to indicate
the manner in which strings that contain special characters should be displayed. With
StringConversion->func, the function func can be defined to replace special
characters in the output. Also, the default setting
StringConversion->Automatic indicates that \ sequences be used to display
special characters. The default setting
StringConversion:>$StringConversion which specifies that no replacement
be done on strings containing special characters.

StringDrop   376, 873
                              See Also: **Drop, StringPosition, StringTake**
   StringDrop is used to omit characters from a string.
StringDrop["stringname",n] deletes the first **n** characters from the string
stringname while **StringDrop["stringname",-n]** omits the last **n** characters
from **stringname**. Particular characters can be deleted with the command
StringDrop["stringname",{n}] which drops the **n**th character from
stringname and with **StringDrop["stringname",{m,n}]** which omits the
mth through the **n**th characters.

Example:
The following examples drop the first four characters, the last nine characters, and the fifth through sixteenth characters of the string **The *Mathematica* Handbook**.

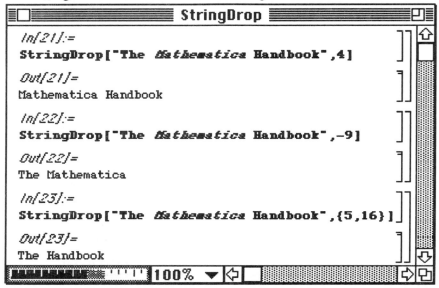

StringForm   348, 363, 381, 388, 874
                               See Also: **Message, SequenceForm, ToString**

StringForm is a format string command.
StringForm["ccc`` ccc",x1,x2,...]** replaces successive `` ` ` `` with successive **xi**. **StringForm[ "ccc`i`ccc,x1,x2,...]** replaces each `` `i` `` with the corresponding **xi. Also, **StringForm["ccc\`ccc,x1,x2,...]** replaces each \\` with the symbol `. This command is used to format output statements for programming languages.

StringInsert   376, 874
                               See Also: **Insert**

  StringInsert is used to insert a string into an already existing one.
StringInsert["ostring","nstring",n] inserts the new string **nstring** into the string **ostring** so that the first character of **nstring** is placed in position **n** in **ostring**. With the command **StringInsert["ostring","nstring",-n]** the last character of **nstring** becomes the **n**th position from the end of the string formed after insertion. In other words, **nstring** is inserted in the **n**th position counted from the end **ostring**.

Example:

In the following examples, the string *Mathematica* is first inserted in position five of the string **The Handbook** and then inserted in the tenth position from the right of **The Handbook.**

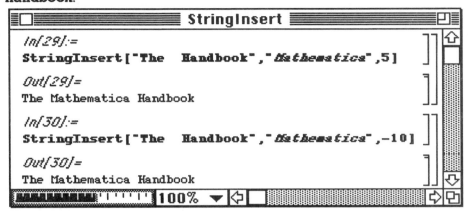

StringJoin(<>)   376, 378, 874

See Also: **Characters, Join**

   StringJoin is used to join several strings together. This can be accomplished in several different ways. Each of the following commands concatenates the indicated strings: **StringJoin["string1","string2",...]**, **"string1"<>"string2"<>...**, **StringJoin[{"string1","string2",...}]**. All arguments of StringJoin must be strings. If not, the output remains in symbolic form. **Flat** is an attribute of **StringJoin.**

Example:

The following example concatenates the strings **The**, *Mathematica*, and **Handbook**.

StringLength   376, 874

See Also: **Characters, Length, StringByteCount**

   StringLength["stringname"] yields the number of characters in the string **stringname** where **stringname** can be made up of both 8- and 16-bit characters.

Example:
The following example computes the length of the string **The** *Mathematica*
Handbook.

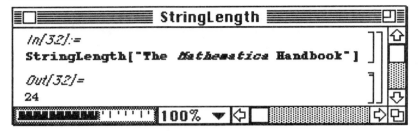

StringMatchQ   383, 874
                                    See Also: **Equal**, **MatchQ**, **Names**,
                                    StringPosition

    StringMatchQ is used for pattern matching.
StringMatchQ["string","patt"] yields a value of **True** if **string** is of the
pattern defined in **patt**. A value of **False** is returned otherwise. The definition of
patt can include metacharacters as well as literal characters.

StringPosition   376, 379, 875
                                    See Also: **Characters**, **FindList**, **Position**

    StringPosition determines the starting and terminal positions of particular
substrings contained in a string. This can be done in several ways.
StringPosition["string","sstring"] yields a list of the starting and ending
positions where the substring **sstring** appears in **string**. Note that **sstring** may
appear more than once in **string**. A limit can be placed on the number of positions
sought with **StringPosition["string","sstring",k]**. In this case, only the
first **k** appearances of **sstring** are considered. Also, more than one substring can be
considered with
StringPosition["string",{"sstring1","sstring2",...}].
StringPosition has several options. The setting **Overlaps->True** considers
substrings that overlap. The option setting **IgnoreCase->True** causes lower- and
upper-case letters to be treated equally. Strings that contain both 8- and 16-bit
characters can be used as arguments for **StringPosition**.
Example:
The string **Math** occurs at positions five through eight of the string **The**
Mathematica **Handbook**.

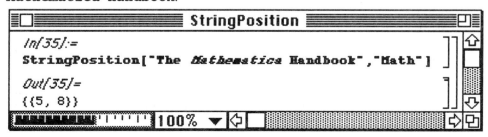

StringQ

StringQ[expression] yields a value of **True** if **expression** is a string and a value of **False** otherwise.

StringReplace   16, 376, 379, 514, 875
See Also: **Replace, StringPosition, ToLowerCase, ToUpperCase**

StringReplace["string","sstring"->"newsstring"] substitutes **newsstring** for **sstring** each time it occurs in **string**. Several replacements can be made with
StringReplace["string",{"sstring1"->"newsstring1", "sstring2"->"newsstring2",...}]. The option **IgnoreCase** can be used with **StringReplace** as it was with **StringPosition**. Also, **StringReplace** can be applied to strings that contain both 8- and 16-bit characters.

StringReverse   376, 875
See Also: **Reverse**

StringReverse["string"] places the characters of **string** in reverse order. Note that strings which contain both 8- and 16-bit characters can be considered with **StringReverse**.

Example:

The following example reverses the string **The _Mathematica_ Handbook**.

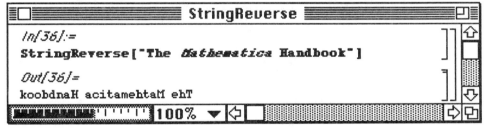

StringSkeleton   517, 875
See Also: **Short, Skeleton, TotalWidth**

StringSkeleton[n] is used with the output of **Short** to indicate **n** omitted characters in a string. The default setting is **. .** . However, this setting can be modified.

StringTake   376, 875
See Also: **StringDrop, StringPosition, Take**

StringTake selects a particular character or group of characters from a string.
StringTake["stringname",n] yields a new string which is made up of the first **n** characters in **stringname**. **StringTake["stringname",-n]** gives the string composed of the last **n** characters in **stringname**. Also,
StringTake["stringname",{n}] yields the nth character of **stringname** while **StringTake["stringname",{m,n}]** yields the characters in positions **m** through **n** from **stringname**. Strings that contain 8- as well as 16-bit characters can be used with **StringTake**.

Example:
The following yields the first three characters of the string **The Mathematica Handbook**.

The following yields the last eight characters of the string **The Mathematica Handbook**.

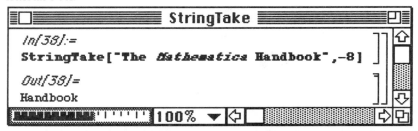

The following yields the fifth through fifteenth characters of the string **The Mathematica Handbook**.

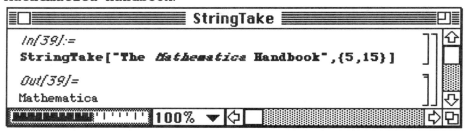

StringToStream   376, 382, 504, 876
                            See Also: **Characters**

    StringToStream["string"] changes **string** to an input stream so that it can be processed with the *Mathematica* functions **Read** and **Find**. This command is particularly useful when processing text and data from strings within *Mathematica* as opposed to those generated from external files. Streams created by **StringToStream** are closed with **Close**.

Stub   272, 342, 876
                            See Also: **DeclarePackage**

    Stub is an attribute assigned to the symbols created by **DeclarePackage**. This attribute indicates that the package which corresponds to the context of the symbol be automatically loaded whenever the symbol is encountered. In other words, **Needs** is called if the symbol is given explicitly in input. The package is loaded so that the definition of the symbol can be determined.

Subscript   361, 876
                                 See Also: **ColumnForm**, **Superscript**
   Subscript[expression] is used to create output forms where **expression** is printed as a subscript. This indicates that the top of **expression** is below the baseline.

Example:

Subscripted   360, 876
                                 See Also: **ColumnForm**
   Subscripted is used to indicate which arguments of a function should appear as subscripts and which should be given as superscripts.
Subscripted[f[x1,x2,...]] the listed arguments are given as subscripts. Also, **Subscripted[f[x1,x2,...],n]** indicates that the first **n** arguments appear as subscripts. This command can be modified with **-n** to specify the last **n** arguments or with **{m,n}** to indicate arguments **m** through **n**. Superscripts can be specified with the command **Subscripted[f[x1,x2,...],{sub1,sub2},{super1,super2}]** where arguments **sub1** through **sub2** appear as subscripts and those from **super1** to **super2** are given as superscripts. If only superscripts are desired, the command **Subscripted[f[x1,x2,...],{},supern]** can be used. Special care must be taken with **Subscripted** so that argument specifications do not overlap.

Subtract   47, 876
                                 See Also: **Decrement**, **Minus**
   Subtract represents the standard arithmetic operation. Hence, **a-b** is the same as **a+(-1*b)**.

Example:

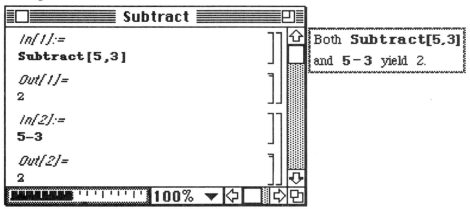

SubtractFrom(-=)   248, 876
See Also: **AddTo**, **TimesBy**, **Decrement**,
PreDecrement, **Set**

    SubtractFrom, symbolized **-=**, is used to subtract one value from another. Therefore, **i-=step** subtracts the value of **step** from that of **i**. This obtains the same result as the statement **i=i-step**. **HoldFirst** is an attribute of **SubtractFrom**.

Example:

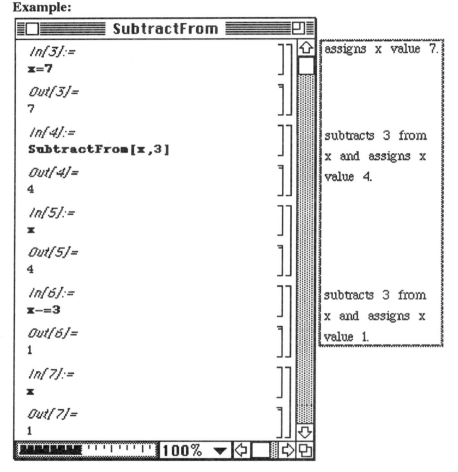

SubValues

See Also: **DownValues**, **UpValues**, **OwnValues**
    SubValues[f] lists the transformation rules which correspond to the values of **f[x,...][..]**, ..., the subvalues of **f**.

Sum   90, 285, 330, 683, 877
See 657, 660, 746-751, 769   See Also: **Do**, **NSum**, **Product**, **Table**
   Sum computes finite sums of single and multiple sums.
Sum[a[i],{i,imin,imax}] yields the value of
$$\sum_{i=imin}^{imax} a[i]$$ while a step size other than one unit is indicated with

Sum[a[i],{i,imin,imax,istep}]. The multiple sum $\sum_{i=imin}^{imax}\sum_{j=jmin}^{jmax} a[i,j]$

is computed with **Sum[a[i,j],{i,imin,imax},{j,jmin,jmax}]**. Note that
the order of summation is the same as that used with **Integrate** for multiple integrals
so the syntax for summation of more than a double sum is easily extended.

Example:

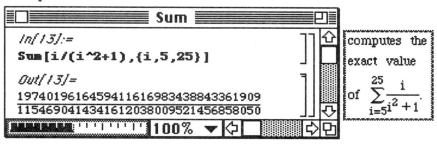

Superscript   361, 877
                                            See Also: **ColumnForm**, **Subscript**, **Subscripted**
   Superscript[expression] is used to create output forms where **expression**
is printed as a superscript. This indicates that the bottom of **expression** is at a
height of one character above the baseline.

SurfaceColor   457, 877
                                            See Also: **AmbientLight**, **Lighting**,
                                            LightSources, **RGBColor**
   SurfaceColor is a three-dimensional graphics directive which is used to indicate
the manner in which polygons reflect light. However, if no **SurfaceColor**
specification is stated, then *Mathematica* assumes that each polygon reflects any
incident color according to Lambert's law of reflection. That is, the intensity of the
reflected light is equal to $\cos(\beta)$ times the intensity of the incident light where β is the
angle between the normal vector to the surface and the direction of the incident light. If
β is greater than 90 degrees, then no light is reflected. **SurfaceColor** specifications
can be made with **SurfaceColor[GrayLevel[val]]** where the intensity of the
reflected light is equal to **val** times the intensity of the incident light times $\cos(\beta)$. The
reflected light is given in the same color. In the case of color,
SurfaceColor[RGBColor[r,g,b]] indicates that the red, green, and blue
components are determined by their respective products with the intensity of the
incident light times $\cos(\beta)$.   A second component in addition to those previously
mentioned can be included with **SurfaceColor** to indicate a specular reflection

component. This command is of the form **SurfaceColor[dir,spec]**. The specular reflection component, **spec**, is stated in terms of **GrayLevel**, **Hue**, or **RGBColor** and gives the fractions of each incident intensity color to be reflected in a specular manner by the polygons. A specular exponent, **n**, which indicates the reflection that should occur is included in **SurfaceColor[dir,spec,n]**. This exponent determines the rate at which the intensity of the specularly reflected light falls off. This rate is given by $\cos(\beta)^n$ as β increases. The specular exponent should be a number less than 10. Its default value is 1.

SurfaceGraphics   155, 156, 395, 447, 449, 450, 878
See 131, 196, 235, 236,   See Also: **ContourGraphics**, **DensityGraphics**,
350   **ListPlot3D**, **Plot3D**
   SurfaceGraphics[array] represents a three-dimensional graphics object where each element of **array** supplies a corresponding height for a point in the x,y-plane. **SurfaceGraphics** objects are displayed with **Show**. An array to specify shading can be included with **SurfaceGraphics[array,shadearray]**. The members of **shadearray** can be **GrayLevel**, **Hue**, or **RGBColor** directives as well as **SurfaceGraphics** objects. If **array** has the dimensions m × n, then **shadearray** must be (m−1) × (n−1). The options used with **Graphics3D** except **PolygonIntersections** and **RenderAll** are used with **SurfaceGraphics** with the addition of **ClipFill**, **ColorFunction**, **HiddenSurface**, **Mesh**, **MeshStyle**, and **MeshRange**. One difference occurs in the default setting for BoxRatios. With SurfaceGraphics, this setting is **BoxRatios->{1,1,0.4}**. **Plot3D** and **ListPlot3D** both produce **SurfaceGraphics** objects.

Switch   287, 878
                                    See Also: **Condition**, **If**, **Which**
   Switch[expression,patt1,val1,patt2,val2,...] evaluates **expression** and compares the outcome to the patterns defined by **patt1**, **patt2**, ... When the first match is found, then *Mathematica* returns the corresponding **val1**, **val2**, ... If no match is found, then the **Switch** command is returned unevaluated. If the last pattern listed is the symbol **_**, then the last **val** is returned if no match is found prior to reaching the last case.

Example:

In the following example, a is defined to have value 2. Since a does not have value 3 or 4, **Switch[a,3,x,4,y,2,z]** yields z.

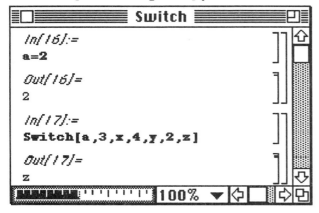

Symbol   224, 712, 878

See Also: **Head**, **Real**, **Integer**, **Complex**

Symbol represents the head associated with a symbol. The pattern used to stand for a symbol is **x_Symbol**.

Example:

Both **q** and the built-in constant **Pi** have **Head** Symbol. Note that **N[Pi]** has head **Real**.

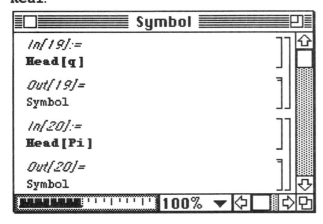

Syntax

Syntax is a system command with the attribute **Protected**.

SyntaxLength   381, 878

See Also: **$SyntaxHandler**

SyntaxLength["string"] yields the number of characters in **string** which were found to be syntactically correct. In other words, if a syntax error is encountered, then the position of the error is returned by **SyntaxLength**. This command is useful when the result of **SyntaxQ** is False.

SyntaxQ   381, 878
                                      See Also: **ToHeldExpression**, **$SyntaxHandler**
   SyntaxQ["string"] determines if there are any syntax errors in string. If no
errors exist, then **SyntaxQ** returns True. Otherwise, a value of False is returned.
The location of the error can be found with **SyntaxLength**.

SystemStub
   SystemStub is a system command defined as
```
SystemStub[f_,filename_]:=
Block[{arguments},Unprotect[f];
f[arguments___]:=AutoLoad[f,filename,{arguments}];
SetAttributes[f,{Protected,ReadProtected}]].
```

T
Tab

Tab represents a string made up of a tab character.

Table

See 122, 127, 131, 139, 162, 213, 239, 242, 244, 247, 249, 251, 253, 306, 328, 355, 356, 358, 371, 379, 381, 384, 399, 412, 421, 425, 429, 431, 527, 528, 530, 532, 533, 542, 549, 568, 592, 615-617, 666, 667, 670, 671, 673, 707-710, 712, 718, 720, 731, 749, 757, 766, 767, 770, 772

8, 116, 118, 122, 251, 285, 330, 649, 668, 879

See Also: **Array**, **DiagonalMatrix**, **Do**, **IdentityMatrix**, **Product**, **Range**, **Sum**

Table is used in several forms to create tables. **Table[expression,{i}]** generates n copies of expression. **Table[expression,{i,imax}]** creates a list of the values of expression from $i = 1$ to $i = imax$. A minimum value of i other than 1 is indicated with **Table[expression,{i,imin,imax}]** while a step size other than one unit is defined with **Table[expression,{i,imin,imax,istep}]**. Finally, **Table[expression,{i,imax,imax},{j,jmin,jmax},...]** creates a nested list where the outermost list is associated with i. Matrices, vectors, and tensors are all represented as tables in *Mathematica*.

Example:

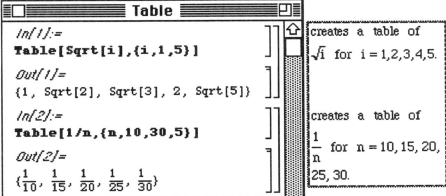

The following example creates a table of values of i+j for j=2, 4, 6 and i=1, 2, 3, 4.

```
In[3]:=
Table[i+j,{i,1,4},{j,2,6,2}]

Out[3]=
{{3, 5, 7}, {4, 6, 8}, {5, 7, 9}, {6, 8, 10}}
```

TableAlignments   357, 879
                             See Also: **TableDirections**

   TableAlignments is an option used with **TableForm** or **MatrixForm** to indicate the alignment of entries in each dimension of a nested list. In the case of columns, the settings are **Left**, **Center**, and **Right**. For rows, these are **Top**, **Center**, and **Bottom**. The default setting **TableAlignments->Automatic** specifies the settings of **Bottom** for row alignment and **Left** for column alignment. Also, the setting **TableAlignments->Center** indicates that all entries be centered both vertically and horizontally.

TableDepth   357, 879
                            See Also: **Length**, **TensorRank**

   TableDepth is a **TableForm** and **MatrixForm** option which indicates the maximum number of rows to include in the table or matrix. The default setting is **TableDepth->Infinity** which specifies that all possible rows are included. However, if the setting **TableDepth->n** is used, then the rows beyond level **n** are written as lists.

TableDirections   356, 357, 879
                            See Also: **TableSpacing**

   TableDirections is an option used with **TableForm** and **MatrixForm** to indicate if the dimensions should be given as rows or columns. The default setting is **TableDirections->{Column,Row,Column,Row,...}** which is also given by **TableDirections->Column**. The setting **TableDirections->Row** yields a similar alternating list with the first entry being **Row**. In addition, the setting can be made in the form **TableDirections->{direction1,direction2,...}** where each **directioni** can be either **Row** or **Column**.

TableForm   119, 354, 880
See 20, 306, 371, 399,   See Also: **ColumnForm**, **GraphicsArray**,
429, 456, 474, 770   **MatrixForm**

   TableForm[list] prints **list** in the form of a rectangular array of cells. Note that the size of the elements of **list** are not required to be the same as they are with **MatrixForm**. The width of each column and the height of each row is determined by the size of the largest element in the respective row or column. The options used with **TableForm** are **TableAlignments**, **TableDepth**, **TableDirections**, **TableHeadings**, and **TableSpacing**. **TableForm** only affects the appearance of **list**. It does not change later calculations involving **list**.

Example:

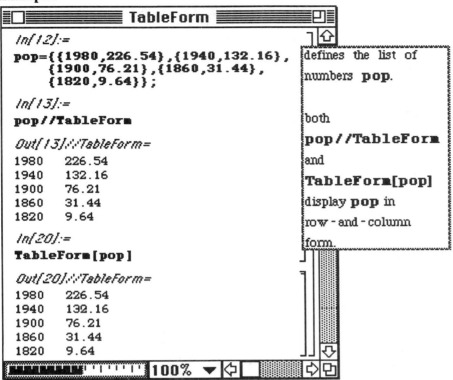

TableHeadings   357, 358, 880
                    See Also: **TableForm**

   TableHeadings is a **TableForm** and **MatrixForm** option which is used to indicate the manner in which table columns and rows should be labeled. The default setting for this option is **TableHeadings->{None,None,...}** which specifies that no labels be included. The setting **TableHeadings->Automatic** yields successive integer labels in each of the dimensions. Also, the setting can be made with **TableHeadings->{label1,label2,...}** to enter desired labels.

Example:

In the following example, the table **pop** is defined and then displayed in **TableForm**. The rows are not labeled; the columns are labeled "Year" and "Population (in millions)".

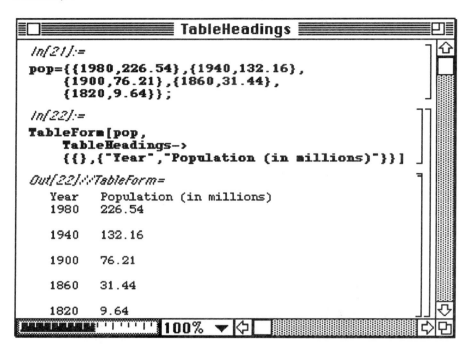

```
TableHeadings

In[21]:=
pop={{1980,226.54},{1940,132.16},
    {1900,76.21},{1860,31.44},
    {1820,9.64}};

In[22]:=
TableForm[pop,
    TableHeadings->
    {{},{"Year","Population (in millions)"}}]

Out[22]//TableForm=
    Year    Population (in millions)
    1980    226.54

    1940    132.16

    1900    76.21

    1860    31.44

    1820    9.64
```

100% ▼

TableSpacing   357, 880

See Also: **GraphicsSpacing**

TableSpacing is an option used with **TableForm** and **MatrixForm** to indicate the spacing to occur between adjacent rows and columns. This spacing is determined in terms of spaces for columns and blank lines for rows. The default setting **TableSpacing->Automatic** uses the spacing **{1,3,0,1,0,1,...}**. However, a particular sequence of spacing can be entered with **TableSpacing->{spacing1,spacing2,...}**.

TagSet   262, 735, 880

See Also: **Set, SetDelayed, UpSet**

TagSet is used to define upvalues and downvalues. The **TagSet** command, **f/:lhs=rhs**, causes **lhs** to be assigned the value of **rhs**. In addition, the symbol **f** is associated with this assignment as long as **f** is the head of **lhs**, the head of the head of **lhs**, or the head of one of the symbols. If **f** does not appear at one of these levels, it cannot be associated with the definition and a warning message results. In the case where **f** appears more than once in **lhs**, then the assignment is associated upon each occurrence.

TagSetDelayed   262, 880
                                  See Also: **Set**, **TagSet**, **SetDelayed**

TagSetDelayed, symbolized by **f/:lhs:=rhs**, yields a delayed assignment of the value of **rhs** to **lhs**. It also associates this assignment with the symbol **f**. **TagSetDelayed** is included in the warning message given with **TagSet** when **f** is too deep in **lhs** for association with the assignment.

TagUnset   718, 736, 881
                                  See Also: **Clear**, **Unset**

TagUnset, given by **f:lhs=.**, removes all assignments associated with **f** defined for lhs. Note that an assignment is removed only if **lhs** is identical to the left-hand side of the assignment and if the right-hand side **Condition** tests are also identical.

Take   125, 196, 881
                                  See Also: **Cases**, **Drop**, **First**, **Last**, **Part**,
                                  Select, **StringTake**, **Rest**

Take is used to select particular sequences from a list or expression. **Take[list,n]** yields the first **n** elements of **list**. **Take[list,-n]** returns the last **n** members of **list**. Also, **Take[list,{m,n}]** selects the terms from position **m** through position **n** from **list**.
Example:
In the following example, the list **pop** is defined. **Take[pop,2]** yields the first two elements of **pop**, **Take[pop,-2]** yields the last two elements of **pop**, and **Take[pop,{2,4}]** yields the second through fourth elements of **pop**.

```
≡≡≡≡≡≡≡≡≡≡≡≡≡≡≡ Take ≡≡≡≡≡≡≡≡≡≡≡≡≡

In[27]:=
pop={{1980,226.54},{1940,132.16},
    {1900,76.21},{1860,31.44},
    {1820,9.64}};

In[28]:=
Take[pop,2]

Out[28]=
{{1980, 226.54}, {1940, 132.16}}

In[29]:=
Take[pop,-2]

Out[29]=
{{1860, 31.44}, {1820, 9.64}}

In[30]:=
Take[pop,{2,4}]

Out[30]=
{{1940, 132.16}, {1900, 76.21}, {1860, 31.44}}

100%  ▼
```

Tan   49, 562, 881
                                   See Also: **ArcTan**, **Cot**

   Tan [x] represents the trigonometric function tangent of x where $\tan(x) = \dfrac{\sin(x)}{\cos(x)}$.

The argument of this function is given in radian measure. Note that multiplication

by **Degree** converts degrees to radians.

Example:

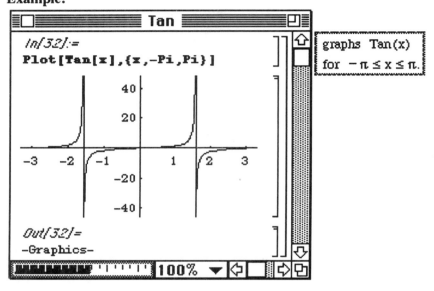

Tanh   562, 881
                                   See Also: **ArcTanh**, **Coth**

   Tanh [x] represents the hyperbolic trigonometric function $\tanh(x) = \dfrac{\sinh(x)}{\cosh(x)}$

$$= \dfrac{e^{x} - e^{-x}}{e^{x} + e^{-x}}.$$

Example:

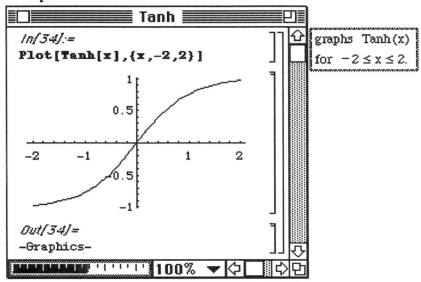

TargetFunctions   604
See Also: **ComplexExpand**

TargetFunctions is an option used with **ComplexExpand** to list the functions which should appear in the result. Possible functions include **Abs**, **Arg**, **Conjugate**, **Im**, **Re**, and **Sign**. The setting is made in the form **TargetFunctions->{functionlist}** where the members of **functionlist** include some or all of the functions listed above.

Example:

In the first calculation, ComplexExpand is used to expand e^{x+iy} assuming both x and y are real. In the second calculation, the option **TargetFunctions->{Arg,Abs}** is used to expand e^x in terms of $\mathtt{Arg[x]}$ and $\mathtt{Abs[x]}$.

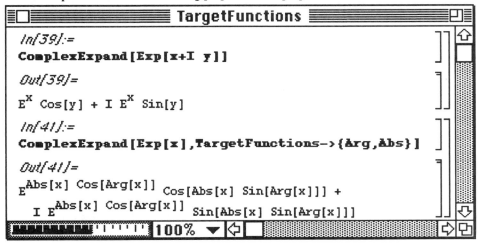

Temporary   272, 323, 881
                    See Also: **Module**, **Unique**
   Temporary is an attribute assigned to local variables which are removed from the
system when no longer in use. Symbols created by **Module** and **Unique** have this
attribute.
Example:

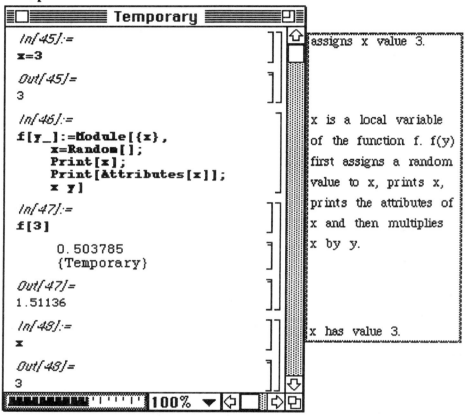

TensorRank   668, 881
                    See Also: **Depth**, **Dimensions**, **MatrixQ**, **VectorQ**
   TensorRank[expression] determines the depth to which the members of
expression are lists of the same length. If **expression** is a tensor, then
TensorRank[expression] yields the rank of the tensor. **TensorRank[list]**
is equivalent to **Length[Dimensions[list]]**.

Example:

In the following examples **TensorRank** is used to compute the **TensorRank** of the lists **{{-5,-8,-1},{1,4},{-1}}**, **{{-5,-8,-1},{1,4},{-1,-8,10}}**, and **{{-5,-8,-1},{1,4,5},{-1,-8,10}}**.

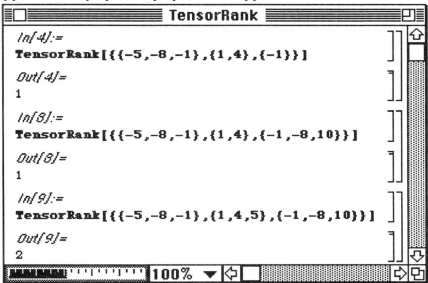

TeXForm   16, 183, 344, 739, 881

                                See Also: **InputForm**

   TeXForm[expression] places the output from **expression** in a form suitable for input to TEX. Multiple character names are given in Roman font while single characters appear in italics. **TeXForm** only affects the printing of expression. It does not change any calculations involving it.

Text   400, 430, 469, 882

See 512, 519, 531, 532   See Also: **AxesLabel**, **PlotLabel**

   Text is a graphics primitive which can be used with any two- or three-dimensional graphics command. **Text[expression,point]** yields text centered at the coordinates of **point**. A third component can be included in this command as well to indicate a relative position to **point**. This form of the command is **Text[expression,point,relpos]**. The setting of **relpos** may be one of the following: **{0,0}** which indicates that the text is centered at point, **{-1,0}** which means that the text be printed to the left of point, **{1,0}** which causes the text to be printed at the right-hand end of point, **{0,-1}** specifies that the text be printed above point, and **{0,1}** which indicates that it be printed below point. A fourth component can be included in the **Text** command to indicate a direction vector to determine the orientation of the text. The possible entries for this component are **{1,0}** for regular horizontal text, **{0,1}** for vertical text read from bottom to top, **{0,-1}** for vertical text read from top to bottom, and **{-1,0}** for horizontal upside-down text. Color specifications can be made with **Hue**, **GrayLevel**, **RGBColor**, or **CMYKColor**. Fonts are specified with **FontForm**.

TextForm   739, 882
                                          See Also: **OutputForm**
   TextForm[expression] prints **expression** in textual form. The results of
TextForm are given in **OutputForm**.

TextRendering   obsolete in Version 2.0
   TextRendering is an option used with functions such as **OpenWrite** to indicate
how text is rendered in an output file.

Thickness   409, 434, 882
See 558, 563, 709   See Also: **AbsoluteThickness**, **Dashing**,
                                          PointSize
   Thickness[t] is a graphics directive used with two- and three-dimensional
graphics functions which causes lines to be drawn with a thickness **t** which is a fraction
of the total width of the graph. The default value in two dimensions is
Thickness[0.004] while it is **Thickness[0.001]** in three.
Example:

The following example defines $f(x)$ to be the real part of $Y_2^1\left(\frac{\pi}{6}, x\right)$ and

$g(x)$ to be the imaginary part of $Y_3^1\left(\frac{\pi}{6}, x\right)$. Both are graphed for

$0 < x < 2\pi$. The graph of f is displayed in gray; the graph of g is dashed.

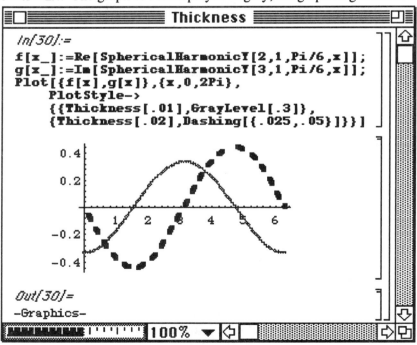

Thread   216, 883
                    See Also: **Distribute, Inner, Map, MapThread**
   Thread is used to thread a function over particular arguments. It can be entered in several different forms. **Thread[f[arguments]]** threads **f** over the lists that appear in **arguments**. **Thread[f[arguments],g]** threads **f** over the elements of **arguments** with head **g**. **Thread[f[arguments],g,n]** threads **f** over the elements in **arguments** with head **g** which occur in the first **n** positions. If the entry **−n** is used, then the positions are counted from the end of **arguments**. In the cases listed above, the elements with head **g** must be of the same length in order for **Thread** to be successful.

Example:

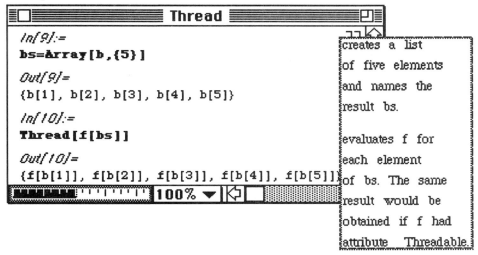

▣▢▦▦▦▦▦▦▦ **Thread** ▦▦▦▦▦▦▦▤▥

```
In[9]:=
bs=Array[b,{5}]

Out[9]=
{b[1], b[2], b[3], b[4], b[5]}

In[10]:=
Thread[f[bs]]

Out[10]=
{f[b[1]], f[b[2]], f[b[3]], f[b[4]], f[b[5]]}
```

creates a list of five elements and names the result bs.

evaluates f for each element of bs. The same result would be obtained if f had attribute Threadable.

ThreeJSymbol   561, 883
                    See Also: **ClebschGordan, SixJSymbol,**
                    SphericalHarmonicY
   ThreeJSymbol[{j1,m1},{j2,m2},{j3,m3}] yields the 3 - j symbol

given by $C^{j_1 j_2 j_3}_{m_1 m_2 m_3} = (-1)^{m_3 + j_1 - j_2} \sqrt{2(j_3) + 1} \begin{pmatrix} j_1 & j_2 & j_3 \\ m_1 & m_2 & -m_3 \end{pmatrix}$. These coefficients

are also called Wigner coefficients and are zero unless $m_1 + m_2 + m_3 = 0$.

Example:

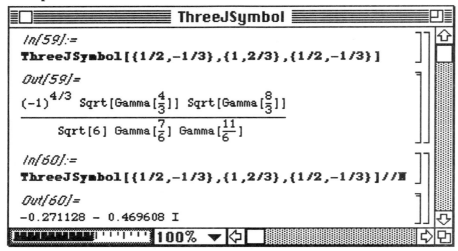

Through   213, 214, 883

See Also: **Map**, **Operate**

Through is used to distribute operators. **Through[p[f1,f2][x]]** yields **p[f1[x],f2[x]]** while **Through[expression,g]** distributes indicated operators when **g** is the head of **expression**.

Example:

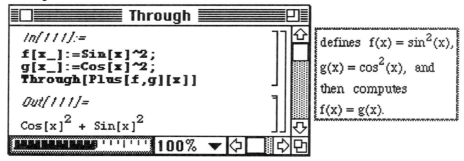

Throw   293, 883

See Also: **Catch**, **Goto**, **Return**

Throw[expression] is a control flow function which yields expression for the value of the enclosing **Catch** that is nearest.

Ticks   139, 420, 463, 884
See 127, 514, 522, 550,   See Also: **Axes**, **AxesLabel**, **FrameTicks**,
553, 582   **GridLines**, **MeshRange**

   Ticks is a two- and three-dimensional graphics function option which indicates how tick marks should be placed on axes. **Ticks** can be specified in several ways. **Ticks->None** implies that no marks be drawn, **Ticks->Automatic** displays tick marks automatically by placing the marks at points whose coordinates have the fewest number of decimal digits, and **Ticks->{xaxis,yaxis,...}** which states tick marks for each axis. In specifying individual axes specifications, many settings for **xaxis**, **yaxis**, ... are possible. These include **None** and **Automatic** which were previously described as well as **{m1,m2,...}** which lists the tick mark positions, **{{m1,label1},{m2,label2},...}** which lists the mark positions and corresponding label, **{{m1,label1,length1},...}** which also indicates a scaled length for each mark, **{{m1,length1,{poslength1,neglength1}},...}** which states lengths in the positive and negative directions, and **{{m1,length1,length1,style1},...}** which gives a specified style to use to draw the tick marks as well. These styles are indicated with such directives as **Thickness**, **GrayLevel**, and **RGBColor**. Labels which accompany tick marks appear in **OutputForm**.

TimeConstrained   525, 884
                                    See Also: **MemoryConstrained**, **Pause**, **Timing**,
                                    $IterationLimit, **$RecursionLimit**

   TimeConstrained[expression,t] attempts to evaluate **expression** within the time constraint of **t** seconds. The calculation is aborted if not completed in **t** seconds. A specified warning message can be entered as well with **TimeConstrained[expression,t,message]**. If a warning message is not indicated, then *Mathematica* yields **$Aborted**. Hence, it can be overruled with **AbortProtect**. **HoldFirst** is an attribute of **TimeConstrained**. The time limit is only accurate to within a value greater than **$TimeUnit** seconds.

Times (*)   47, 230, 234, 884
                                    See Also: **Divide**, **Dot**,
                                    NonCommutativeMultiply, **TimesBy**

   Times, symbolized with * or a space, is used to indicate the product of terms. Thus, **x*y** and **x y** both represent the product of **x** and **y**. **Flat**, **OneIdentity**, and **Orderless** are all attributes of **Times**. **Times[x]** yields **x** while **Times[]** yields **1**.

Example:

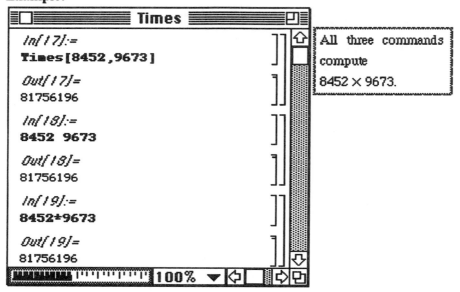

TimesBy (***=**)   248, 884

See Also: **AddTo**, **DivideBy**, **Set**, **SubtractFrom**

   TimesBy, symbolized by ***=**, is used to modify values. **x*=c** is equivalent to the statement **x=x*=c**. In other words, **x*=c** multiplies **x** by **c** and yields the new value of **x**.

Example:

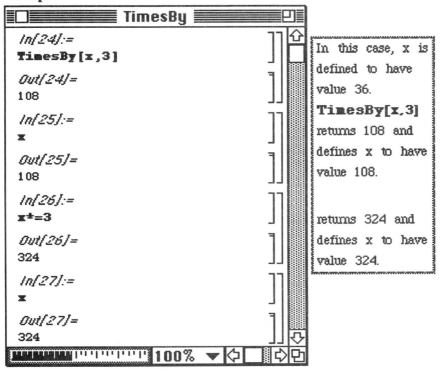

TimeUsed   524, 743, 885

See Also: **SessionTime**, **Timing**

TimeUsed[ ] yields the total number of seconds of CPU time used during the current *Mathematica* session. The error associated with **TimeUsed** is at least the value of **$TimeUnit** which is around 1/60 of a second. The time given by **TimeUsed** does not include the time used by external processes nor does it include time consumed during pauses due to **Pause**.

Example:

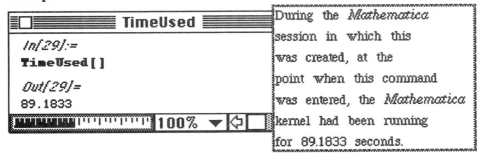

TimeZone   523, 743, 885
                                 See Also: **AbsoluteTime**, **Date**

TimeZone[] yields the number of hours which must be added to Greenwich mean time (GMT) to determine the correct local time assumed by the computer system. Daylight saving time corrections must be included in the **TimeZone** value.

Timing   525, 885
                                 See Also: **AbsoluteTime**, **TimeConstrained**,
                                 TimeUsed, **SessionTime**

Timing[expression] evaluates **expression** and returns its value along with the amount of time needed to perform the calculation. The output is of the form {**time,result**}. The value of **time** depends not only on the computer system but also on the precise state of the *Mathematica* session when the **Timing** command is called. **HoldAll** is an attribute of **Timing**. The error in the time obtained with **Timing** is at least as great as **$TimeUnit** which is approximately 1/60 of a second.
Example:
In the following example, **di** is defined to be the unevaluated command
Integrate[Cos[x y],{y,0,Pi/2},{x,0,y}] which corresponds to the iterated integral $\int_0^{\pi/2}\int_0^y \cos(xy)\,dx\,dy$.

value=Timing[ReleaseHold[di]] evaluates **di**, returns the result as a list where the first element of the list corresponds to the time (in seconds) necessary to perform the calculation, and names the resulting list **value**. Since **value[[2]]** corresponds to the exact value of the iterated integral, an approximation of its value is obtained with **N[value[[2]]]**.

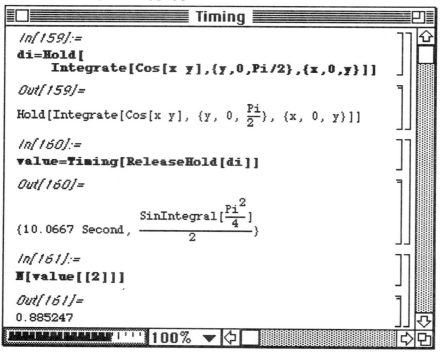

ToASCII   obsolete in Version 2.0
                                     superseded by **ToCharacterCode**

ToCharacterCode   366, 885
                                     See Also: **Characters**, **DigitQ**,
                                     FromCharacterCode, **LetterQ**
  ToCharacterCode["characters"] yields the integer code which corresponds
to the string **characters**.
Example:

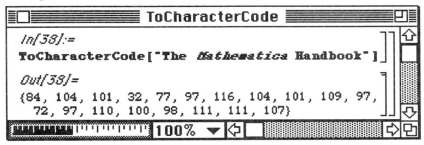

ToColor
  ToColor[color,form] causes **color** to be converted to **form** if **form** is
CMYKColor, **GrayLevel**, or **RGBColor**. Otherwise, **form[color]** is evaluated to
yield the expected graphics color directive.

ToDate   524, 885
                                     See Also: **FromDate**
  ToDate[time] converts the absolute time given in time which is the number of
seconds from January 1, 1990, to a date given in the form
{year,month,day,hour,minute,second}.
Example:

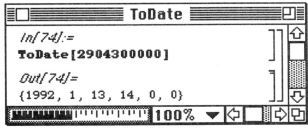

ToExpression   380, 885
                                     See Also: **Read**, **SyntaxLength**, **SyntaxQ**,
                                     ToHeldExpression, **ToString**
  ToExpression["string"] converts **string** to an expression and also
evaluates the resulting expression immediately. If there is a syntax error in **string**,
then *Mathematica* yields an error message and **$Failed**. Several strings can be
concatenated into a single expression with
ToExpression[{string1","string2",...}].

Example:

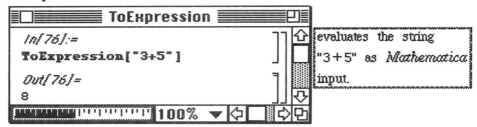

Together   78, 596, 886
See 403, 424   See Also: **Cancel**, **Collect**, **Expand**, **ExpandAll**,
                                ExpandDenominator, **ExpandNumerator**,
                                Factor, **Simplify**

   Together[expression] combines the terms of **expression** by adding them over a common denominator and simplifying the result. **Trig** is an option used with **Together**. The setting **Trig->True** causes trigonometric functions to be interpreted as rational functions of exponentials.

Example:

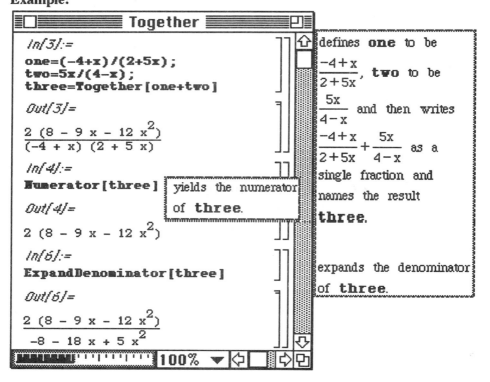

ToHeldExpression   381, 886
                                See Also: **ToExpression**
   ToHeldExpression["string"] converts string to an expression wrapped by **Hold**.

TokenWords   496, 886
                                        See Also: **WordSeparators**

TokenWords is an option used with such functions as **ReadList** to list "token words" to be used as delimiters for words to be read in the text. The specified token words are listed in the output.

Tolerance   666
                                        See Also: **SingularValues**

Tolerance is a **SingularValues** option which indicates the tolerance to use when removing small singular values. *Mathematica* removes those singular values which are smaller than the setting of **Tolerance** multiplied by the largest singular value.

ToLowerCase   378, 886
                                        See Also: **IgnoreCase, LowerCase,**
                                        StringReplace, ToUpperCase

ToLowerCase["string"] gives a string in which all characters are lower case. Hence, upper case characters are converted to lower case. The command **$Letters** lists all characters. If two are grouped in this list as {"char1","char2"}, then char1 is taken to be the lower case character while char2 is the upper case. This information is useful when working with extended or international character sets.
Example:
The following example converts the string **The *Mathematica* Handbook** to a string consisting of all lower case characters.

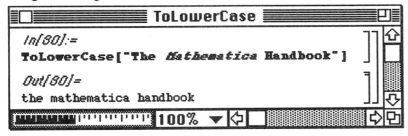

TooBig
See 176, 294

TooBig is an internal symbol.

Top   357
                                        See Also: **TableAlignments**

Top is a possible setting for the **TableAlignments** option used with **TableForm** and **MatrixForm**.

ToRules   607, 886
                                        See Also: **Roots, Reduce, Solve**

ToRules[expression] converts the logical statement **expression** to a list of transformation rules. **ToRules** objects are returned by **Solve** when an explicit solution cannot be found.

Example:

The following example defines **poly** to be the fifth degree polynomial $-1+9x+4x^2+3x^3-6x^4+x^5$. **Solve[poly==0]** attempts to solve the polynomial equation $-1+9x+4x^2+3x^3-6x^4+x^5=0$ for x. Since **Solve** cannot compute the exact solutions, a ToRules object is returned. In this case, approximations of the solutions could be obtained with **NRoots** or **FindRoot**.

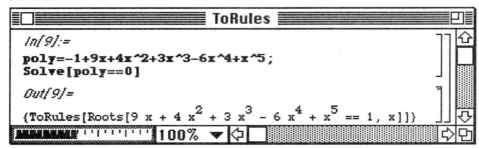

ToString   380, 886

                                     See Also: **HoldForm, ToExpression, WriteString**

   ToString[expression] yields the form of **expression** which would appear as text. By default **ToString** yields the string in standard output form given with **OutputForm**. However, **InputForm** can be specified. **ToString** has several options. These options (the same as those for **ToString**) along with their default settings include **FormatType->OutputForm, PageWidth->Infinity, StringConversion->Identity**, and **TotalWidth->Infinity**.

TotalHeight   886

                                     See Also: **PageWidth, Short, Skeleton**

   TotalHeight is an option used with output streams to indicate the maximum number of lines allowed to be printed in each output expression. If the limit is exceeded, then *Mathematica* uses **Short** to print the output. In order to set the value of **TotalHeight**, the command

SetOptions[outputstream,TotalHeight->n] is used. A setting of **TotalHeight->Infinity** indicates that expressions of all lengths be printed without the use of **Short**.

TotalWidth   517, 738, 887

                                     See Also: **PageWidth, Short, Skeleton**

   TotalWidth is an option used with output streams to indicate the maximum number of characters of text allowed to be printed for each output expression. If the limit is exceeded, then *Mathematica* uses **Short** to print the output. In order to set the value of **TotalWidth**, the command **SetOptions[outputstream,TotalWidth->n]** is used. A setting of **TotalWidth->Infinity** indicates that expressions of all lengths be printed without the use of **Short**.

ToUpperCase   378, 887
                                         See Also: **IgnoreCase, StringReplace,**
                                         ToLowerCase, UpperCaseQ

UpperCase["string"] converts all characters in **string** to upper case. The command **$Letters** lists all characters. If two are grouped in this list as {"char1","char2"}, then char1 is taken to be the lower case character while char2 is the upper case. This information is useful when working with extended or international character sets.

Example:
The following example converts the characters of the string **The Mathematica Handbook** to upper case characters.

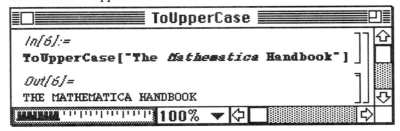

Trace   11, 276, 295, 732, 887
                                         See Also: **TraceDialog, TracePrint, TraceScan**

Trace allows for the "tracing" of evaluation processes. The command **Trace[expression]** yields a nested list of the subexpressions created during the evaluation of **expression**. Particular types of subexpressions can be sought with **Trace[expression,patt]** In this case, *Mathematica* only lists subexpressions which match the pattern defined in **patt**. Also, a particular symbol may be specified with **Trace[expression,symbol]** so that only those subexpressions involving transformation rules associated with **symbol** are listed. **Trace** has several available options. These options and their default settings are **MatchLocalNames->True, TraceAbove->False, TraceBackward->False, TraceDepth->Infinity, TraceForward->False, TraceOff->None, TraceOn**, and **TraceOriginal->False**.

Example:

The following examples yield lists of the subexpressions created during the evaluation of the commands **Solve[1-7x-2x^2==0]** and **NRoots[3-7x-4x^2==0,x]**. In the second case, the resulting list of expressions is displayed in **TableForm**.

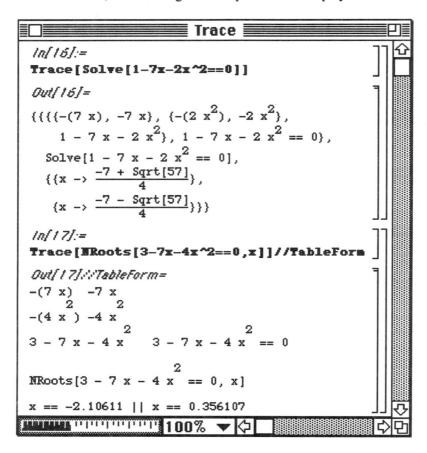

TraceAbove   302, 308, 887

See Also: **StackComplete**

TraceAbove is a **Trace** option which makes possible the observation of evaluation chains within which a particular evaluation chain occurs. The setting **TraceAbove->True** causes the first and last expressions in each relevant evaluation chain to be listed with Trace. The setting **TraceAbove->All** causes all expressions in these evaluation chains to be listed. Also, the setting **TraceAbove->{backexpr,forwardexpr}** causes *Mathematica* to search for expressions of the form **backexpr** in the backward direction and **forwardexpr** in the forward direction.

TraceAction

TraceAction is an option used with the functions **TraceDialog** and **TracePrint** to indicate the function to apply to each traced expression.

TraceBackward   302, 308, 888
                                  See Also: **StackComplete**
  TraceBackward is an option used with **Trace** to cause *Mathematica* to determine
the expressions which preceded a particular expression in an evaluation chain. The
setting **TraceBackwards->True** lists the first expression in the chain containing the
expression of interest. Also, **TraceBackwards->All** lists the entire chain of
expressions preceding the particular expression.

TraceDepth   301, 888
                                  See Also: **TraceOff**
  TraceDepth is a **Trace** option which specifies a level so that **Trace** ignores steps
which result in nested lists greater than the indicated level in depth. This makes the
function more efficient.

TraceDialog   305, 308, 888
                                  See Also: **Trace**
  TraceDialog[expression] traces the evaluation of **expression** and calls the
function **Dialog** when **expression** is encountered. The function can be used in
other forms as well. **TraceDialog[expression,patt]** calls **Dialog** only when
expressions match the pattern defined in **patt** while
TraceDialog[expression,symbol] only calls **Dialog** for expressions whose
evaluation uses a transformation rule associated with **symbol**. After the dialog is
initiated, expressions can be seen by using **%**. With **TraceDialog**, intermediate
values of expressions can be determined and reset.

TraceForward   302, 888
                                  See Also: **Trace**
  TraceForward is an option used with **Trace[expression,patt]** to trace the
expressions located by **Trace** which match the form of **patt**.
TraceForward->True causes **Trace** to include the final expression in the chain
containing matching expressions. **TraceForward->All** causes **Trace** to list all
expressions which occur in the chain after the matching expression.

TraceInternal
  TraceInternal is an option used with functions like **Trace** to indicate whether
internally generated expressions should be traced. The setting for this option is **True**
or **False**.

TraceLevel
  TraceLevel[] yields the level of output being filled during the evaluation of
functions such as **Trace**.

TraceOff   300, 888
                                  See Also: **TraceDepth, TraceOn**
  TraceOff is option used with **Trace[expression,patt]** in the form
TraceOff->offpatt in order to cease tracing within any expression matching the
form of **offpatt**. The setting **TraceOff->None** causes tracing in all expressions.
The value of **TraceOff** is modified during the evaluation of **Trace** by resetting the
value of **$TraceOff** which is a global variable.

TraceOn   300, 889

See Also: **TraceOff**

TraceOn is an option used with **Trace[expression,patt]** in the form
TraceOn->onpatt in order to cease tracing within any expression matching the
form of **onpatt**. The value of **TraceOn** is modified during the evaluation of **Trace**
by resetting the value of **$TraceOn** which is a global variable.

TraceOriginal   303, 889

See Also: **Trace**

TraceOriginal is an option used with **Trace** to indicate that every expression in
the evaluation chain, including the ones that evaluate to themselves, is considered by
Trace. The setting **TraceOriginal->True** causes the trivial chains to be included
in the **Trace**. The default is **TraceOriginal->False** since these trivial chains are
normally skipped.

TracePrint   305, 889

See Also: **Trace**

TracePrint[expression] is similar to **Trace[expression]** in that it traces
expression. However, instead of giving the output in the form of a list,
TracePrint prints expressions as they are encountered. The output of **TracePrint**
is indented to correspond to the nesting in the output of **Trace**. Since **TracePrint**
performs a task similar to that of **Trace**, it can appear in the same forms as **Trace**.
TracePrint[expression,patt] prints only those expressions which match the
pattern defined by **patt** while **TracePrint[expression,symbol]** considers
only those evaluations which rely on transformation rules associated with **symbol**.
TracePrint uses the same options as **Trace** except for **TraceBackward** and the
setting for **TraceOriginal** is always **True**. Hence, desired settings can be made for
TraceOn, **TraceOff**, **TraceAbove** and **TraceForward**. Note that the setting
TraceAbove->All leads to the printing of output in the forward direction only with
TracePrint.

TraceScan   305, 889

See Also: **Trace**

TraceScan is used to apply a function to expressions which appear in the evaluation
chain of an expression. **TraceScan[f,expression]** applies the function **f** to each
expression encountered during the evaluation of **expression**.
TraceScan[f,expression,patt] considers only the expressions which match
the pattern defined in **patt**. Also, **TraceScan[f,expression,symbol]**
considers only the evaluations which involve transformation rules associated with
symbol. In each of these three cases of **TraceScan**, the function **f** is applied to
expressions in unevaluated form. Finally, **TraceScan[f,expression,patt,g]**
applies **f** before evaluation and **g** after evaluation.

Transpose   123, 132, 651, 657, 669, 890
See 376, 408, 409, 427   See Also: **Flatten**

    Transpose is used to transpose both matrices and tensors. **Tranpose[m]**
transposes the matrix **m** by interchanging the rows and columns of m. Also,
Tensor[t,{k1,k2,...}] yields the tensor **t′** such that the **i**-th index becomes
the **ki**-th.
Example:

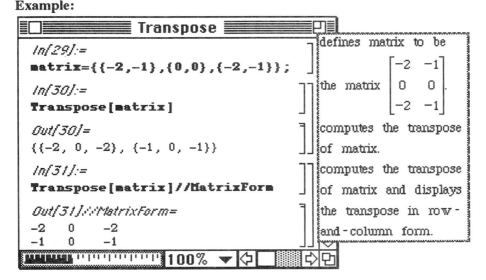

Trapezoidal
               See Also: **NIntegrate**
    Trapezoidal is a setting for the **Method** option used with **NIntegrate**. If
Method->Trapezoidal is selected, then *Mathematica* uses a trapezoidal algorithm
to approximate a single definite integral. A Cartesian product of one dimensional
trapezoidal rules is used if the integral is multi-dimensional.
Example:
In the following example, $f(x) = \sin(\sin(\sin(x)))$. Both the commands

NIntegrate[f[x],{x,0,2Pi}] and

NIntegrate[f[x],{x,0,2Pi},Method->Trapezoidal] are used

to approximate $\int_0^{2\pi} f(x)\,dx$. Note that the command

Chop[NIntegrate[f[x],{x,0,2Pi}]] would produce zero and the error

message resulting from the command **NIntegrate[f[x],{x,0,2Pi}]** is

not completely displayed.

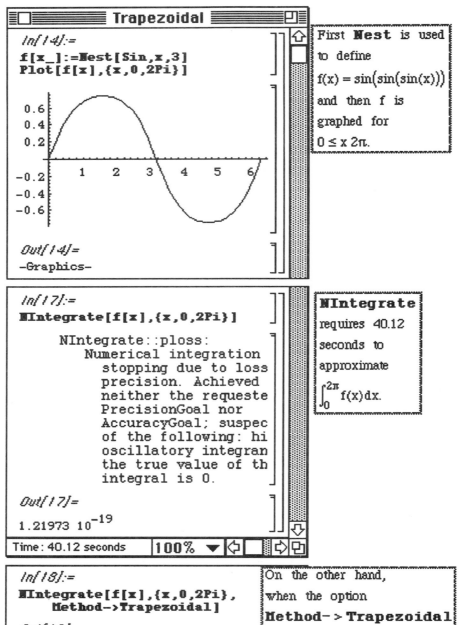

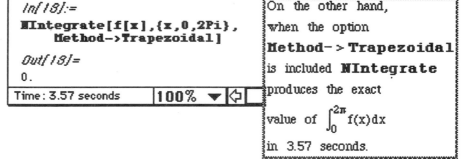

TreeForm   197, 344, 890
See 250   See Also: **FullForm**, **MatrixForm**

   TreeForm[expression] prints **expression** so that its tree structure is displayed. In other words, the various levels of **expression** are shown at different depths.

Example:

The following example defines **alg** to be the fraction

$\dfrac{4-2x}{-1-4x+x^2}$ and then expresses **alg** in **TreeForm**.

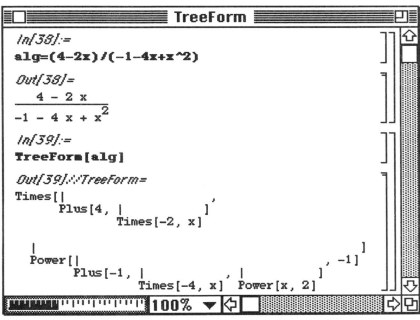

Trig   81, 603, 890
See 142, 143, 145, 151,   See Also: **ComplexExpand**
155

   Trig is an option used with functions such as **Expand** and **Factor** to indicate whether or not to consider trigonometric functions as rational functions of exponentials. **Trig->False** is the default setting of all functions except **Simplify**. With this setting, *Mathematica* treats trigonometric functions as indivisible objects. With the setting **Trig->True**, these functions are converted to exponential rational functions so that they can be manipulated.

True   93, 141, 287, 890
See 142, 143, 145, 151,   See Also: **All**, **Automatic**, **False**, **TrueQ**, **None**
153, 155, 259, 268, 514,
636

   True is used to represent the Boolean algebra value of true. It is also used as a setting for many options to indicate that the particular option should be performed.

TrueQ   288, 890

See Also: **Condition**, **If**, **SameQ**

TrueQ[expression] tests the logical statement given in **expression**. If **expression** is true, then True is given. Otherwise, False is the result.

Example:

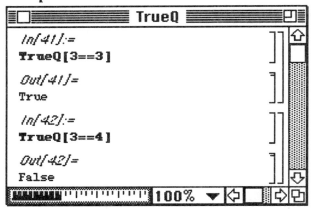

U

UnAlias

UnAlias is a system command with the attributes **HoldAll** and **Protected**.

Underflow

Underflow[] results when a numerical calculation is too small to represent.

Unequal (**!=**)   94, 890
See Also: **Equal, Order, UnsameQ**

Unequal, symbolized by **!=**, is used to determine if two values or expressions are unequal. Hence, **lhs!=rhs** yields True if **lhs** and **rhs** are unequal and False if they are identical. When working with approximate real numbers, *Mathematica* considers them unequal if they differ in the last two decimal places. If several expressions are considered with **expr1!=expr2!=...**, a value of True is given only when none of the **expri** are equal.

Example:

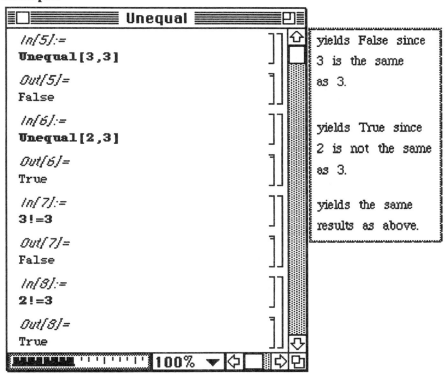

In[5]:= **Unequal[3,3]** *Out[5]=* False	yields False since 3 is the same as 3.
In[6]:= **Unequal[2,3]** *Out[6]=* True	yields True since 2 is not the same as 3.
In[7]:= **3!=3** *Out[7]=* False	yields the same results as above.
In[8]:= **2!=3** *Out[8]=* True	

Unevaluated   282, 732, 890
See Also: **Hold, HoldFirst, ReplaceHeldPart**

Unevaluated[expression] is used as an argument for functions so that **expression** remains unevaluated as the argument of a function. Hence, **f[Unevaluated[expression]]** temporarily assigns an attribute so that **f** does not immediately evaluate its argument.

Example:

In the following example, f and g are defined so that $f(x) = 0$,

$$f(\{x, y\}) = \left\{\frac{1}{2}(x + y), \frac{1}{2}(x - y)\right\}, \text{ and } g(x, y) = \{x + y, x - y\}.$$

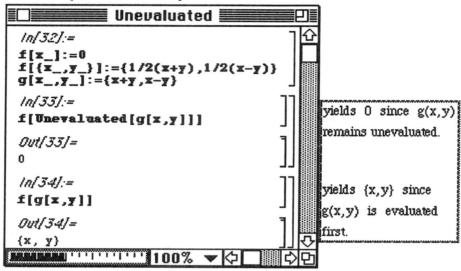

Uninstall   186, 509, 891

See Also: **Close, Install**

Uninstall[link] is used to terminate an external program called from within *Mathematica* with Install. In the process, **Uninstall** closes *MathLink* connections and discards *Mathematica* function definitions.

Union   129, 130, 891

See Also: **Complement, Intersection, Join, Sort**

Union[list] removes the repeated members of **list** and sorts the resulting list. Similarly, **Union[list1,list2,...]** joins the given lists, removes repeated elements, and sorts the result. In this case, **Union** yields the set of elements contained in the union of the **listi**.

Example:

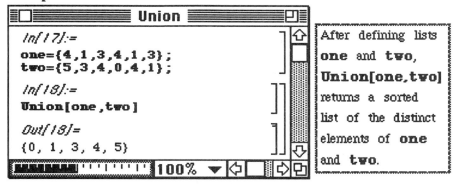

Unique   323, 891

See Also: **C, Module, Names, ToExpression**

Unique generates new symbols with unique names. **Unique[]** creates a new symbol $nnn where n is integer-valued while **Unique[x]** generates a unique symbol which begins with **x** of the form **x$nnn**. Several symbols are created with the command **Unique[{x,y,z,...}]**. **Unique** uses **$ModuleNumber** to generate new symbol names and increments its value each time it is used.

Example:

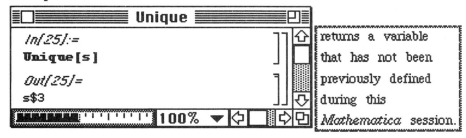

Unprotect   264, 273, 728, 891

See Also: **Locked, Protect, SetOptions**

Unprotect is used to remove the attribute Protected. **Unprotect[s]** removes **Protected** from the symbol **s** while **Unprotect[{symbol1,symbol2,...}]** removes **Protected** from each of the listed symbols. Also, **Union["pattern1","pattern2",...]** removes **Protected** from all symbols which match any of the listed patterns.

UnsameQ (=!=)   228, 288, 891

See Also: **Equal, Order**

Protected, symbolized by **=!=**, determines if values are not identical. Hence, **x=!=y** yields **True** if **x** and **y** are not identical and **False** otherwise.

Example:

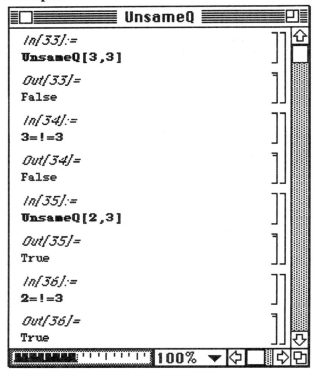

Unset(=.)   75, 247, 251, 736, 891
                                 See Also: **Clear**, **TagUnset**

   Unset, represented by **=.**, is used to remove values and definitions of symbols.
Therefore, **expression=.** clears the value of **expression**.

Update   310, 892
                                 See Also: **Condition**

   Update is used to avoid confusion caused when global variables occur in **/;**
conditions. **Update[sym]** causes *Mathematica* to update all expressions which
depend on the symbol **sym** To update all expressions, **Update[]** is used. Typically,
Update is rarely necessary.

UpperCaseQ   378, 892
                                 See Also: **LetterQ**, **LowerCaseQ**,
                                 ToCharacterCode, **ToUpperCase**

   UpperCaseQ["string"] tests the characters in **string** to determine if they are
all upper case. If so, a value of **True** is given. Otherwise, **False** results. These
upper case characters are given in the list generated by **$Letters** in which characters
appear in the pairs **{"char1","char2"}**. The second component is taken to be the
upper case character.

Example:
Since the string **The *Mathematica* Handbook** does not consist entirely of upper case characters, **UpperCaseQ["The Mathematica Handbook"]** returns False.

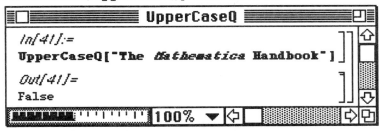

UpSet (^=)   261, 735, 892
                                     See Also: **TagSet, UpValues**

   UpSet, symbolized by **^=**, is used with assignments such as **lhs^=rhs** to assign the value of **rhs** to **lhs** and to associate this assignment to symbols in **lhs** which occur in the first level.   For example, instead of associating the assignment to **h**, **h[g[x]]^=rhs** associates it with **g**.

UpSetDelayed (^:=)   260, 261, 892
                                     See Also: **SetDelayed, UpSet**

   UpSetDelayed, represented with the symbols **^:=**, is used for delayed assignments. Hence, **lhs^:=rhs** assigns the delayed value of **lhs** to be **rhs**, and it associates this assignment with symbols in **lhs** at level one. In general,
h[g[arguments],...]^:=rhs assigns an upvalue for **g**.

UpValues   266, 736, 892
                                     See Also: **DownValues, Set**

   UpValues serves to determine the list of upvalues for a particular symbol as well as to assign upvalues to symbols. **UpValues[symbol]** lists the upvalues of **symbol** while **UpValues[symbol]=rhs** assigns the rules given in **rhs** as the upvalues of **symbol**.

Using   859
                                     See Also: **Roots**

   Using is an option used with **Roots** to indicate subsidiary equations to be used in the solution process.

V

ValueForm

   ValueForm is a symbol used internally by *Mathematica*.

ValueList

   ValueList is an internal symbol.

ValueQ   228, 892
                                      See Also: **Information**
   ValueQ[expression] determines if a value has been assigned to **expression**.
If an assignment has been made, then the result is True. Otherwise, False is given.
If the result of **ValueQ[expression]** is True, then **expression** would change if
it were given as *Mathematica* input.
Example:

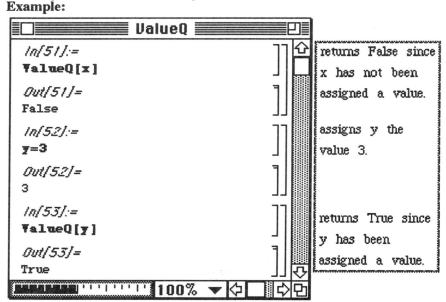

ValueTable

   ValueTable is a symbol used internally by *Mathematica*.

Variables   593, 892
                                      See Also: **Coefficient**
   Variables[polynomial] lists the independent variables in the given
polynomial.

Example:

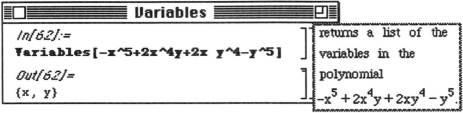

In the following example, the variables are **x**, **xy** and **y**. If the intention had been to define the polynomial of two variables $-x^5+2x^4y+2xy^4-y^5$ it should have been entered as either **-x^5+2x^4y+2x*y^4-y^5** or **-x^5+2x^4y+2x y^4-y^5**.

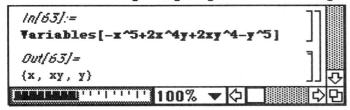

VectorQ   227, 652, 893
                                         See Also: **Dimensions**, **MatrixQ**, **NumberQ**,
                                         TensorRank

   VectorQ[expression] determines if **expression** is a vector by checking that **expression** is a list in which none of its elements are lists themselves. If **expression** is a vector, then **True** is given as the result. Another form of this command is **Vector[expression,test]** in which a condition **test** such as **NumberQ** is applied to each element of **expression**. A value of **True** results in this case only if **test** yields **True** for each element of **expression**.

Example:

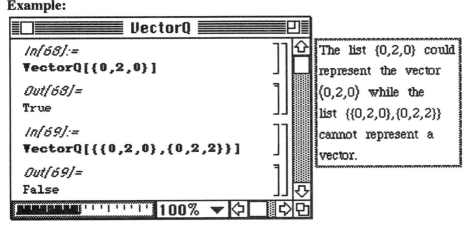

VerifyConvergence   832
                        See Also: **NProduct, NSum**

VerifyConvergence is an option used with functions such as **NSum** and
NProduct to indicate whether or not to explicitly check for convergence when
determining infinite sums or products. The setting **VerifyConvergence->True**
causes *Mathematica* to investigate the limit of the terms and the limit of the ratio of the
terms while the setting **VerifyConvergence->False** indicates that no testing for
convergence be done.

VerifySolutions
                        See Also: **Solve**

VerifySolutions is an option used with such functions as **Solve** to indicate if
solutions should be verified and extraneous solutions eliminated.

VerticalForm

VerticalForm is a symbol used internally by *Mathematica* for printing and
formatting purposes.

ViewCenter   443, 893
See 522, 576   See Also: **Graphics3D, SurfaceGraphics**

ViewCenter is an option used with **Graphics3D** and **SurfaceGraphics** to
indicate the point in scaled coordinates running from 0 to 1 which appears at the center
of the final display area. The default setting **ViewCenter->Automatic** causes
Mathematica to center the entire bounding box in the final display area. The setting
ViewCenter->{1/2,1/2,1/2} causes the center of the box to be centered in the
final image. The option setting **SphericalRegion->True** causes the
circumscribing sphere to be centered and, hence, overrides any setting of
ViewCenter.

ViewPoint   158, 442, 893
See 522, 573, 580, 582   See Also: **SphericalRegion, ViewCenter,**
                                       ViewVertical

ViewPoint is an option used with **Graphics3D** and **SurfaceGraphics** to
indicate the point from which the object is viewed. The coordinates for **ViewPoint**
are given in special scaled coordinates in which the longest side of the bounding box
has length 1 and the center of the box is **{0,0,0}**. The default setting is
{1.3,-2.4,2}. For a view directly from the front, **{0,-2,0}** is used. The point
{0,-2,-2} yields a view from the front and down. **{0,-2,2}** yields a view from
the front and up. For views from the left- and right-hand corners, respectively,
{-2,-2,0} and **{2,-2,0}** are entered. Finally, for a view directly above the object,
the point **{0,0,2}** is selected.

ViewVertical   443, 893
See 522, 569   See Also: **Graphics3D, SurfaceGraphics**

ViewVertical is an option used with **Graphics3D** and **SurfaceGraphics** to
indicate the direction in scaled coordinates to be given as vertical in the final display.
Hence, **ViewVertical** indicates the orientation of the object being viewed. The
default setting is **{0,0,1}** which specifies that the z direction in the original
coordinate system is vertical in the final image. The magnitude of the setting of
ViewVertical is not important. Only its direction affects the final image.

W

WeierstrassP   580, 584, 894
                    See Also: **WeierstrassPPrime**

WeierstrassP[u,g$_2$,g$_3$] represents the Weierstrass function $\rho(u;g_2,g_3)$

which yields the value of x such that $u = \int_{\infty}^{x} \left(4t^3 - g_2\,t - g_3\right)^{-1/2} dt$. Hence, it is the

inverse of an elliptic integral.

Example:

The following example approximates the value of x for which

$-1 = \int_{\infty}^{x}\left(4t^3 - t - 1\right)dt.$

```
In[6]:=
WeierstrassP[-1,1,1]

Out[6]=
1.08715
```

WeierstrassPPrime   580, 584, 894
                    See Also: **WeierstrassP**

WeierstrassPPrime[u,g$_2$,g$_3$] represents the derivative of the Weierstrass

function $\rho'(u;g_2,g_3)$ which is given by the formula $\rho'(u;g_2,g_3) = \dfrac{\partial}{\partial u}\,\rho(u;g_2,g_3).$

Example:

The following example computes the value of $\rho'(u;1,1)$ when $u=-1$.

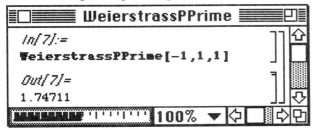

```
In[7]:=
WeierstrassPPrime[-1,1,1]

Out[7]=
1.74711
```

Which   287, 894
                    See Also: **Switch**

Which[test1,val1,test2,val2,..] evaluates the listed tests and returns the associated **vali** for the first **testi** which is found to be **True**. If all tests are **False**, then **Null** is returned by **Which**. However, the final **testi** can be entered as **True** so that a default value can be entered with the last **vali**.

Example:

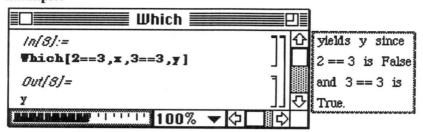

While   292, 894

See 530, 568   See Also: **Do**, **Fold**, **For**, **If**, **Nest**, **Select**

   While[test,body] repetitively evaluates **body** as long as **test** is True. When test is False, evaluation of **body** ceases. This command is similar to the while structure in programming languages, but the roles of the comma and semicolon are reversed from those in the language C. The **While** loop exits if **Break[]** is encountered during the evaluation of **body**. Also, if **Continue[]** is generated, it stops the evaluation of **body** but continues the loop.

Example:

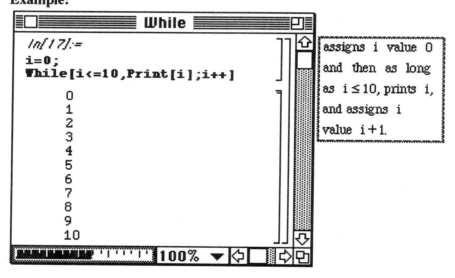

With   320, 321, 326, 894

                            See Also: **Block**, **Module**, **ReplaceAll**
   With is used to define local constants.

With[{a=a0,b=b0,...},expression] causes the variables **a**, **b**, ... which occur in expression to be replaced by **a0**, **b0**, ... However, the global values of these variables remain unchanged. Although **With** is similar to **Module**, **With** makes programming easier to understand. **HoldAll** is an attribute of **With**.

Example:

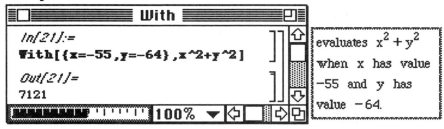

In[21]:=	evaluates $x^2 + y^2$
With[{x=-55,y=-64},x^2+y^2]	when x has value
Out[21]=	-55 and y has
7121	value -64.

Word   495, 894

                See Also: **Byte**, **Character**, **Expression**, **Hold**,
                Real, **Number**, **Record**, **String**

    Word represents a *Mathematica* object made up of a sequence of characters delimited by word separators. These words are read by such functions as **Read**, **ReadList**, and **Find**.

WordSearch   501, 894

                See Also: **AnchorSearch**, **Find**, **FindList**

    WordSearch is an option used with **Find** and **FindList** to indicate whether or not the word being sought must appear as a word. The default value is **WordSearch->False** which indicates that the word does not have to be given as a word separated by word or record separators.

WordSeparators   495, 501, 895

                See Also: **RecordSeparators**, **TokenWords**

    WordSeparators is an option used with functions like **Read**, **ReadList**, **Find**, and **FindList** to indicate words to be considered as delimiters for words. The default setting is **WordSeparators->{" ","\t"}**. More than one separator may occur between two words if the option **NullWords->False** is used. Also, different separators can be defined for the left- and right-hand sides of words. This is done with **WordSeparators->{{left1,left2,...},{right1,right2,...}}**.

WorkingPrecision   687, 688, 690, 695, 700, 895
See 760, 764, 765   See Also: **Accuracy**, **AccuracyGoal**, **N**,
                Precision, **NIntegrate**, **FindRoot**

    WorkingPrecision is an option used with numerical functions such as **NIntegrate** to indicate the number of digits to use in internal calculations. The default setting is **WorkingPrecision->$MachinePrecision**. Note that the final result often has fewer than the number of digits specified with **WorkingPrecision**.

Write   485, 895
                                   See Also: **Display**, **Message**, **Print**, **Read**

    Write[stream,{expression1,expression2,...}] writes the sequence of expressions one after the other with no breaks to the indicated stream. After all of the expressions are written, a new line is given to complete the **Write** command and the stream remains open. The commands **Message** and **Print** are based on **Write**. Expressions can be written to a list of streams with

WriteString[{stream1,stream2,...},expression1,
                            expression2,...].

WriteString   485, 895
                                   Se Also: **Write**

    WriteString[stream,{string1,string2,...}] writes the listed strings to the indicated stream without creating any new lines or extra characters. Strings can be written to a list of streams with

WriteString[{stream1,stream2,...},string1,string2,...].

WynnDegree
See 761

    WynnDegree is an option used with **SequenceLimit** to indicate the degree of the algorithm. A setting of **WynnDegree->1** causes **SequenceLimit** to use Aitken's delta-squared algorithm. **WynnDegree** can be used as an option for **NSum** and **NProduct** to be passed to **SequenceLimit** for use.

X

Xor   94, 730, 895

See Also: **And**, **If**, **LogicalExpand**, **Not**, **Or**

Xor represents the exclusive "or" function. Hence,
Xor[expression1,expression2,...] yields a value of False if there is an even number of expressions which are True and the rest are False. A value of True results if there is an odd number of True expressions with the rest False.

Example:

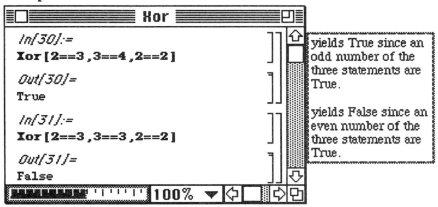

Z

ZeroTest   662, 896

See Also: **Modulus**, **SameTest**

ZeroTest is an option used with **Inverse**, **LinearSolve**, **NullSpace**, and **RowReduce** to indicate a function to apply to each combination of matrix elements to determine if the combinations are zero. This option is most useful with the setting **ZeroTest->(Expand[#]==0 &)** when working with matrices that are quite complicated symbolically. The default setting for this option is **ZeroTest->(Together[#]==0 &)**.

Zeta   2, 571, 574, 896

See Also: **LerchPhi**, **PolyLog**, **PrimePi**, **RiemannSiegelZ**

RiemannZeta[s] represents the Riemann zeta function $\zeta(s)$ which satisfies the

relation $\zeta(s) = \sum_{k=1}^{\infty} k^{-s}$, $s > 1$. The generalized Riemann zeta function or Hurwitz

zeta function $\zeta(s, a)$ is given by **RiemannZeta[s,a]** and is defined by

$\zeta(s, a) = \sum_{k=0}^{\infty} (k + a)^{-s}$, where all terms such that $k + a = 0$ are omitted.

Example:

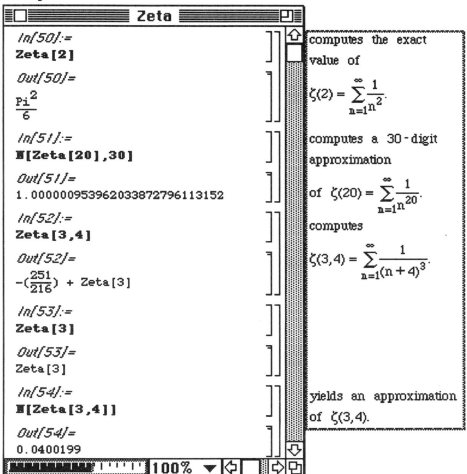

In[50]:= **Zeta[2]**	computes the exact value of $$\zeta(2) = \sum_{n=1}^{\infty} \frac{1}{n^2}.$$
Out[50]= $\dfrac{Pi^2}{6}$	
In[51]:= **N[Zeta[20],30]**	computes a 30-digit approximation of $\zeta(20) = \sum_{n=1}^{\infty} \frac{1}{n^{20}}.$
Out[51]= 1.000000953962033872796113152	
In[52]:= **Zeta[3,4]**	computes $$\zeta(3,4) = \sum_{n=1}^{\infty} \frac{1}{(n+4)^3}.$$
Out[52]= $-(\dfrac{251}{216})$ + Zeta[3]	
In[53]:= **Zeta[3]**	
Out[53]= Zeta[3]	
In[54]:= **N[Zeta[3,4]]**	yields an approximation of $\zeta(3,4)$.
Out[54]= 0.0400199	

$

$ 304, 322
                                                     See Also: **Trace**

$ appears in the names of variables returned by such functions as **Trace** and denotes a local variable.

$Aborted   311, 732, 896
                                                     See Also: **Abort, Interrupt**

$Aborted is returned when an expression encounters **Abort[]** during its evaluation.

Example:

In the following example, a command to compute

$\int_0^\pi \int_0^{5.45} J_0(r)\cos(r\,t)\,dr\,dt$ is entered and then aborted.

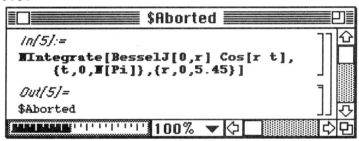

$AnimationDisplayFunction
                                                     See Also: **Animation**

$AnimationDisplayFunction is a system command defined by **Display[$Display,#1]&**.

$AnimationFunction
                                                     See Also: **Animation**

$AnimationFunction is a system command defined by **Null &**.

$BatchInput   529, 742, 896
                                                     See Also: **$BatchOuput, $IgnoreEOF, $Linked, $Notebooks**

$BatchInput is a global variable which indicates whether input is being given in batch mode. If **$BatchInput** is **True**, then input is being supplied to the *Mathematica* kernel in batch mode. This is the case when receiving input from a file.

$BatchOutput   529, 742, 896
                                                     See Also: **$BatchInput, $ComandLine, $Linked**

$BatchOutput is a global variable which indicates whether output should be given in batch mode. Therefore, if **$BatchOutput** is **True**, then *Mathematica* gives output in **InputForm** without *In[ ]* and *Out[ ]* labels and with the **PageWidth->Infinity**.

$CommandLine   529, 742, 747, 896
                 See Also: **Environment, In, $BatchInput,**
                 $BatchOutput, $Linked

    $CommandLine yields the original operating system command line which called *Mathematica*. The command line generated by **$CommandLine** is given in the form of a list of strings.

$ConditionHold
    $ConditionHold is a symbol which is used internally by *Mathematica*.

$Context   333, 711, 745, 896
                 See Also: **Context**

    $Context is a global variable which yields the context of the current *Mathematica* session. By default, the value of **$Context** is Global`. All results of this command are of the form contextname`.

Example:
The following example shows the current context in the *Mathematica* session in which the command was entered.

$ContextPath   334, 711, 745, 897
                 See Also: **Context, $Context**

    $ContextPath lists the context search path where each member of the list is of the form contextname`. This command is useful when working with a symbol that has the same name as a symbol in another context to ensure that the proper definition is used.

$CreationDate   529, 741, 897
                 See Also: **FileDate, $DumpDates,**
                 $ReleaseNumber, $VersionNumber

    $CreationDate is a global symbol which yields the date and time at which the version of *Mathematica* currently being used was released. Note that the date is given in **Date** format as {year,month,day,hour,minute,second}.

$DefaultFont   467, 745, 897
See 513, 520   See Also: **DefaultFont, FontForm**

    $DefaultFont is a global variable which yields the default font used to print text in graphics. If the value of **$DefaultFont** is changed, then it changes the font used for all plots. Therefore, if the setting should be changed only for one plot or a portion of a plot, the **DefaultFont** option used with *Mathematica* graphics functions or the **FontForm** directive should be used so that the changes are only applied locally. The value of **$DefaultFont** is of the form {"fontname",size}.

$Display   465, 518, 742, 897
                                      See Also: **$DisplayFunction**

$Display is a global variable which is used to indicate the stream to which
PostScript graphics objects are sent by functions such as **Plot** and **Show**. The value of
$Display is set during the initialization of the current *Mathematica* session.

$DisplayFunction   399, 742, 897
See 165, 513, 520, 579   See Also: **Display**, **DisplayFunction**, **Put**, **Run**,
                                      $SoundDisplayFunction

$DisplayFunction is the default setting for the graphics function option
DisplayFunction which controls the generation of graphical output. The setting of
$DisplayFunction is initially **Display[$Display,#1]&**. With the setting
DisplayFunction->$DisplayFunction, *Mathematica* displays the graphics
object.

$DumpDates   529, 741, 897
                                      See Also: **FileDate**, **$CreationDate**,
                                      $DumpSupported, **$ReleaseNumber**,
                                      $VersionNumber

$DumpDates is a global variable which lists the dates and times at which **Dump** was
used in creating the *Mathematica* system. Dates are given in **Date** format as
{year,month,day,hour,minute,second}. If **Dump** was not used, then {} is
returned. In this case, the value of **$DumpSupported** is **False**.

$DumpSupported   530, 741, 897
                                      See Also: **Dump**

$DumpSupported is a global variable which indicates whether or not **Dump** is
available on the *Mathematica* system. If so, then the value of **$DumpSupported** is
True. If **Dump** is not available, then its value is **False**.

$Echo   518, 742, 898

$Echo lists the files pipes to which input is echoed. Hence, **$Echo** yields an echo of
each line of input.

$Epilog   519, 522, 745, 898
See 513   See Also: **Dialog**, **Exit**, **Quit**

$Epilog is a global variable which indicates particular operations which should be
performed before terminating a *Mathematica* session or **Dialog**. For sessions, the
value of **$Epilog** is set to read in the file called **end.m**

$Failed   477, 898

$Failed is a symbol which is returned when operations fail to perform the task
asked of them.

Example:

Since *Mathematica* cannot open the file **doesnotexist**, $Failed is returned.

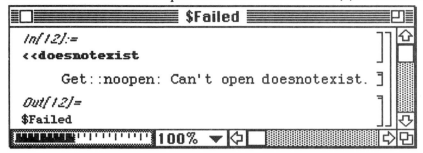

$$Failure2

  $$Failure2 is a symbol used internally by *Mathematica*.

$$Fonts

  $$Fonts is an internal symbol.

$IgnoreEOF 520, 521, 745, 748, 898
  See Also: **Exit**, **Quit**, **$BatchInput**

  $IgnoreEOF is a global variable which indicates whether end-of-file characters should be ignored. The setting **$IgnoreEOF = False**, the default value, causes *Mathematica* to recognize these special characters. The value of **$IgnoreEOF** is assumed **False** if *Mathematica* input is received from a file.

$Input 519, 743, 898
  See Also: **Get**, **Streams**, **$BatchInput**

  $Input is a global variable which yields the name of the current input stream. When reading in the file **"filename"** with the command **<<filename**, **$Input** is assigned the value of **"filename"**.

$Inspector 744, 898
  See Also: **Interrupt**

  $Inspector is a global variable which indicates the function used to determine the state of *Mathematica* during an interrupt. The default setting of **$Inspector** is **Dialog[]&**.

$IterationLimit 309, 732, 745, 898
  See Also: **$RecursionLimit**

  $IterationLimit is a global variable which indicates the limit for the maximum length of any evaluation chain encountered during a *Mathematica* session. Built-in functions such as **FixedPoint** and **Do** use the default setting of **$IterationLimit** for the option **IterationLimit**.

$Language   391, 519, 745, 899
                                             See Also: **MessageName**

$Language is used to set the language such as French in which messages should be given. This specification is made with the command **$Language="languagename"**. When a message is generated by a *Mathematica* function, a message of the form **s::t::language** where **language** is the setting of **$Language**. Different versions of *Mathematica* support different languages.

$Letters   379, 745, 899
                                             See Also: **$StringOrder**

$Letters lists the characters which are considered letters. This list contains sublists of the form **{"char1","char2"}** where **char1** is the lower case form and **char2** is the upper case form of a particular character. If a character does not have these two forms, it is given directly in the list instead of as a sublist.

Example:
In this case, the characters that are considered letters are the usual upper- and lower-case letters of the alphabet.

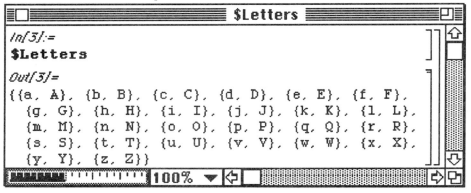

$Line   513, 521, 743, 899
                                            See Also: **In, Out**

$Line is a global variable which gives the line number of the current line of input. The number of the first input line in a **Dialog** is one larger than that of the previous line in the regular *Mathematica* session. However, when **Dialog** is exited, the value of **$Line** reverts back to its previous value in the *Mathematica* session.

$Linked   529, 741, 899
                                            See Also: **$BatchInput, $BatchOutput,**
                                            $CommandLine, $Notebooks

$Linked is a global variable which indicates whether the *Mathematica* kernel is being run through *MathLink*. If the value of **$Linked** is **True**, then the kernel is being run through *MathLink*. However, if this value is **False**, then it most likely is being run with a text-based interface.

$LinkedSupported   530, 741, 899
                              See Also: **$PipeSupported**

$LinkedSupported is a global variable which indicates whether or not *MathLink* is available to your version of *Mathematica* as well as the supporting computer system. A value of **True** specifies that *MathLink* can be used. On Unix-based systems, the value is **True** as it is on most systems that support multitasking.

$MachineEpsilon   546, 741, 899
                              See Also: **$MachinePrecision**,
                              $MaxMachineNumber, **$MinMachineNumber**

$MachineEpsilon is a parameter that measures the smallest number which can be added to **1.** to yield a distinct result. This quantity is important because when numbers are too close together, they are represented by identical bit patterns. Therefore, if the difference in two numbers is less than the value of **$MachineEpsilon**, the two cannot be distinguished. A typical setting of **$MachineEpsilon** is 2^{1-n}, where n is the number of binary bits used to internally represent machine-precision floating point numbers.

Example:

On a Macintosh IIci, the value of **$MachineEpsilon** is $1.0842 \ 10^{-19}$.

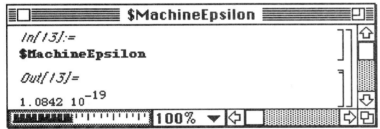

$MachineID   530, 741, 899
                              See Also: **$MachineName, $System**

$MachineID represents a unique identification code (if possible) for the computer system being used with *Mathematica*.

$MachineName   530, 741, 900
                              See Also: **$MachineID, $System**

$MachineName is the identifying name of the computer being used if this name has been defined. If it has not been assigned, then the value of **$MachineName** is " ".

$MachinePrecision   540, 546, 741, 900
                              See Also: **$MachineEpsilon**,
                              $MaxMachineNumber, $MinMachineNumber

$MachinePrecision represents the machine precision on the computer system. If an approximate real number is entered using fewer than **$MachinePrecision** digits, then *Mathematica* considers it to be a machine precision number. If more than **$MachinePrecision** digits are entered, then *Mathematica* treats the number as arbitrary precision. The value of **$MachinePrecision** is taken to be the default setting for the **WorkingPrecision** option used with numerical functions.

Example:
The **$MachinePrecision** of a Macintosh IIci is 19 digits.

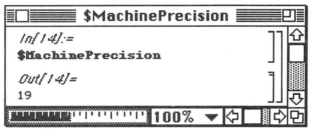

$MachineType   530, 741, 900
                                   See Also: **$OperatingSystem**, **$System**

$MachineType represents the type of the computer currently being used with *Mathematica*. These values include **"Macintosh"**, **"SPARC"**, **"IBM PC"**, and **"VAX"**.

Example:
In this case, the following command was entered on a Macintosh:

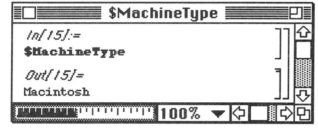

$MaxMachineNumber   546, 741, 900
                                   See Also: **$MachineEpsilon**,
                                   $MachinePrecision, **$MinMachineNumber**

$MaxMachineNumber is the largest positive machine-precision number which can be represented on the computer system. If a number greater than **$MaxMachineNumber** is entered, then *Mathematica* automatically changes it to arbitrary precision.

Example:
On a Macintosh IIci the value of **$MaxMachineNumber** is 1.18973×10^{4932}.

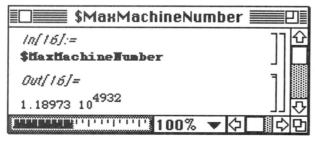

$MaxNumber

$MaxNumber is the largest number which can be represented with *Mathematica*.
Example:

In this case, the value of **$MaxNumber** is $1.44039712 \times 10^{323228010}$

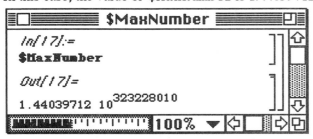

$$Media   obsolete in Version 2.0
                               superseded by **Streams[ ]**

$MessageList   389, 522, 743, 900
                               See Also: **Check**, **MessageList**

$MessageList yields the list of messages generated by a calculation. This list is
reset to **{}** after each line of output. To determine the list of messages associated with
a previous computation, the command **MessageList[n]** is used. This gives the list
for the **n**th output line.

$MessagePrePrint   388, 519, 744, 900
                               See Also: **$PrePrint**

$MessagePrePrint gives the function to apply to expressions before they are
given to **StringForm** for printing. The default value for **$MessagePrePrint** is
Short.

$Messages   518, 742, 900
                               See Also: **Message**

$Messages lists the files and pipes to which standard messages and output which
are produced by **Message** are sent.

$MinMachineNumber   546, 741, 901
                               See Also: **$MaxMachineNumber**

$MinMachineNumber represents the smallest positive machine-precision number
which can be used on the computer system. When numbers which are smaller than the
value of **$MinMachineNumber** are entered, they are automatically converted by
Mathematica to arbitrary-precision numbers.

Example:

In this case, the value of **$MinMachineNumber** is 1.0×10^{-4914}.

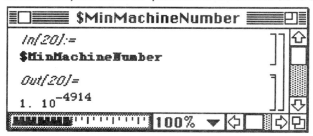

$MinNumber

   $MinNumber is the smallest number which can be represented on the computer system.
Example:

In this case, the value of **$MinNumber** is $1.05934595 \times 10^{-323228015}$.

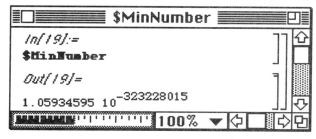

$ModuleNumber   322, 743, 901
                              See Also: **Temporary, $SessionID**

   $ModuleNumber is a global variable whose current value gives the unique serial number to be appended to the name of each local variable found within **Module**. These variables are of the form **name$nnn** where **name** is the local variable name given in Module and **$nnn** is the serial number. At the beginning of a *Mathematica* session, the value of **$ModuleNumber** is 1, and it is increased by one every time **Module** is called.

$NewMessage   390, 744, 901
                              See Also: **$NewSymbol**

   $NewMessage is a global variable which gives a function to be applied to the symbol and tag associated with a particular message that has not been defined. The value of **$NewMessage** is used by **Message** when the particular message name cannot be located explicitly nor the tag associated with the symbol **General**.

$NewSymbol   386, 711, 744, 901
                           See Also: **DeclarePackage, $NewMessage**

   $NewSymbol is used to define a function to apply to all new names and contexts which are encountered. This allows *Mathematica* to determine if there is a mistake in spelling or actually a new symbol name.

$Notebooks   529, 742, 901
                           See Also: **$BatchInput**, **$Linked**

   $Notebooks is a global variable which indicates whether or not a notebook-based interface is being used. If the value of **$Notebooks** is **True**, then the notebook-based interface is being used.

Example:
The notebook front end is supported on a Macintosh.

$NumberBits
   $NumberBits[x] lists the sign, the bits thought to be correct, the bits thought to be incorrect, and the binary exponent of the real number **x**.

$Off
   $Off is a symbol which is used to denote messages that have been turned off.

$OperatingSystem   530, 741, 901
                       See Also: **$MachineType**, **$System**

   $OperatingSystem is a global variable whose value specifies the operating system in use. Possible values of **$OperatingSystem** include **"MacOS"**, **"MS-DOS"**, **"Unix"**, and **"VMS"**.

Example:
Since this was created on a Macintosh, the operating system used was MacOS.

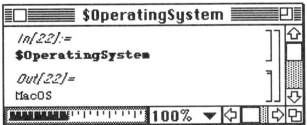

$Output   518, 742, 901
                       See Also: **Streams**

   $Output indicates the ouput channel to which standard output and text created by **Print** are sent.

$OutputForms   346, 516
   $OutputForms lists the formatting functions that are stripped when wrapped around the output.

$Packages   338, 745, 902
                                 See Also: **Contexts**, **DeclarePackage**,
                                 $ContextPath

$Packages lists the contexts associated with all packages loaded during a current *Mathematica* session. Execution of **EndPackage** causes **$Packages** to be updated.

$$ParenForm

$$ParenForm is a symbol which is used internally by *Mathematica*.

$Path   181, 490, 745, 747, 902
                                 See Also: **Directory**, **SetDirectory**

$Path lists the directories which are necessary for the search of files. On most computer systems, the special characters "**.**", "**..**", and "**~**" in directory names represent the current directory, the directory which is one level up in hierarchy, and the home directory, respectively.

$PathNameSeparator

$PathNameSeparator is a string that separates directory names and file names in the pathnames used by the current operating system.

$PipeSupported   530, 741, 902
                                 See Also: **$LinkSupported**

$PipeSupported is a global variable which specifies whether pipes are available for use on the computer system. A value of **True** indicates that pipes can be used with the particular version of *Mathematica*. On Unix-based systems and those which perform multi-tasking, the value of **$PipeSupported** is **True**.

$Post   514, 744, 902
                                 See Also: **$Pre, $PrePrint**

$Post is a global variable whose value is a function which is applied to each expression after evaluation.

$Pre   514, 744, 902
                                 See Also: **$Post**

$Pre is a global variable whose value is a function that is applied to all input before evaluation.

$PrePrint   514, 744, 902
                                 See Also: **$MessagePrePrint, $Post**

$PrePrint is a global variable whose value is a function that is applied after the result is placed in the form **Out[n]** but before it is printed.

$PreRead   514, 744, 903
                                 See Also: **StringReplace**, **ToExpression**

$PreRead is a global variable whose value represents a function to apply to each string of text before it is processed by *Mathematica*. Hence, **$PreRead** is applied before text is placed in the form **InString[n]**.

$PrintForms

$PrintForms lists the basic print forms and updates the list whenever **Format** definitions involving new printforms are entered.

Example:

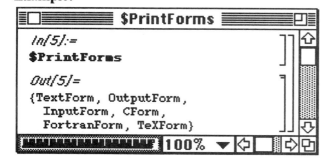

$PrintLiteral

$PrintLiteral is a symbol that is used internally by *Mathematica*.

$RasterFunction

$RasterFunction is a system function defined by
$RasterFunction=$AnimationDisplayFunction[#1];Null)&.

$RecursionLimit   308, 309, 330, 528, 732, 745, 903
                                   See Also: **MemoryConstrained**,
                                   $IterationLimit

$RecursionLimit is a global variable which indicates the maximum depth of the evaluation stack or the maximum depth of nesting that occurs in the list structure generated by **Trace**. Setting a value of **$RecursionLimit** other than **Infinity** causes *Mathematica* to avoid infinite loops and possible crashes.

Example:

In this case the value of **$RecursionLimit** is 256.

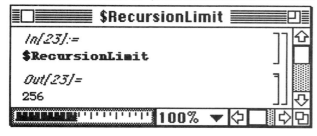

$ReleaseNumber   529, 741, 903
                                   See Also: **$VersionNumber**

$ReleaseNumber is a global variable which indicates the integer-valued release number on the version of the *Mathematica* kernel in use.

Example:

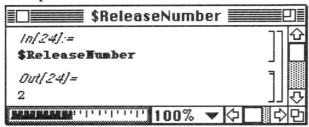

$Remote

$Remote specifies whether *Mathematica* is being used with a front end or in remote mode. A value of **True** indicates remote mode while False indicates use with a front end.

Example:

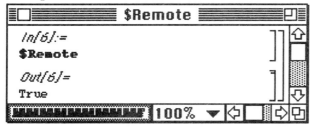

$SessionID   324, 530, 742, 903
See Also: **$ModuleNumber**

$SessionID is a global variable which represents a unique number for each *Mathematica* session on a particular computer. The value of **$SessionID** is based on the ID of the computer as well as the absolute date and time. When appropriate, this value may depend on the ID of a particular *Mathematica* process.

Example:

$SoundDisplay   518
See Also: **$SoundDisplayFunction**

$SoundDisplay represents the output channel to which sound output created by the default **$SoundDisplayFunction** is sent.

$SoundDisplayFunction
>476, 742, 903
>See Also: **ListPlay**, **Play**, **Show**,
>**$DisplayFunction**

$SoundDisplayFunction is a global variable which is the default setting for the **DisplayFunction** option for the functions **ListPlay** and **Play**. It is initially set to be the function **Display[$SoundDisplay,#]&**.

$StringConversion
>371, 744, 903
>See Also: **$DisplayFunction**

$StringConversion is the default setting for the **StringConversion** option of output functions such as **OpenWrite**. The initial setting of **$StringConversion** is **None** which causes all special characters to be output directly. A setting of **Automatic** indicates that special characters be converted to \ sequences. Also, a function to apply to all complete strings can be specified as the **$StringConversion** setting.

$StringOrder
>379, 745, 904
>See Also: **$LetterQ**

$StringOrder lists the order of characters by which strings and symbol names are sorted by functions such as **Sort** and **Order**. The default setting of **$StringOrder** is
{{"a","A"},{"b","B"},{"c","C"},..,{"z","Z"},"0","1",..,"9"}.
The comparison is first based on the ordering of the first level. Also, characters within sublists are considered equal and characters not appearing in the list are ignored. After the first level, if strings are still considered equal, then character order within sublists is considered. Then, if needed, characters not included in **$StringOrder** are considered and ordered according to their integer codes.

$SuppressInputFormHead

$SuppressInputFormHeads lists the heads of expressions whose InputForm should not be sent to a front end automatically.
Example:

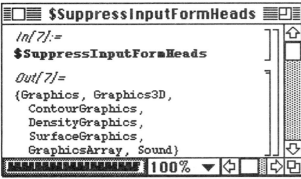

$SyntaxHandler   514, 515, 744, 904
                                 See Also: **SyntaxLength**, **SyntaxQ**

  $SyntaxHandler is a global variable whose value is a function which is applied to input that contains a syntax error. The function specified has two arguments, the input string and the character position of the syntax error. If **$SyntaxHandler** returns a string, then it is used as *Mathematica* input. However, if **$SyntaxHandler** returns **$Failed**, then the input is abandoned.

$System   530, 741, 904
                                 See Also: **$MachineType**, **$OperatingSystem**,
                                 $Version

  $System is a global variable which indicates the type of computer system being used. The same compiled external files can be run on computers which have the same value of **$System**.

$TemporaryPrefix

  $TemporaryPrefix represents the first part of the filenames given by **OpenTemporary[]**.

$Throw

  $Throw is a symbol used internally by *Mathematica*.

$TimeUnit   524, 525, 741, 904
                                 See Also: **Date**, **Timing**

  $TimeUnit represents the smallest interval of time that can be recorded on the computer system. This value is approximately 1/60 of a second.
Example:

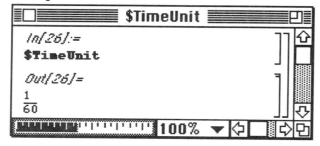

```
In[26]:=
$TimeUnit

Out[26]=
 1
---
 60
```

$TraceOff

  $TraceOff represents the value of currently active **TraceOff** option used with functions like **Trace**. The value of **$TraceOff** can be changed during the trace to alter the expressions which should not be traced.

$TraceOn

  $TraceOn represents the value of currently active **TraceOn** option used with functions like **Trace**. The value of **$TraceOn** can be changed during the trace to alter the expressions which are traced.

$TracePattern

$TracePattern represents the pattern argument that is currently active with such functions as **$TracePattern**. During the trace, its value can be changed to determine recorded and printed expressions.

$TracePostAction

$TracePostAction represents the currently active fourth argument of such functions as **TraceScan**. Its value can be changed during the trace to modify action taken after the evaluation of intercepted expressions.

$TracePreAction

$TracePreAction represents the currently active first argument of such functions as **TraceScan**. Its value can be changed during the trace to modify action taken before the evaluation of intercepted expressions.

$Unset

$Unset is a symbol which used internally by *Mathematica*.

$Urgent   518, 742, 904
                                 See Also: **$Display, $DisplayFunction, $Echo**

$Urgent is a global variable that indicates streams to send urgent output such as the results of the **?** command as well as input prompts.

$Version   529, 904
                                 See Also: **$System**

$Version represents the version of *Mathematica* which is being used.

Example:

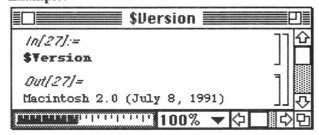

$VersionNumber   529, 905
                                 See Also: **$ReleaseNumber**

$VersionNumber represents the kernel version number of *Mathematica* which is being used. This value is given as a real number such as 1.2 or 2.0.

Example:

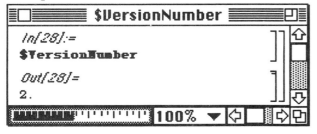

Graphics

This chapter contains a listing of all two- and three-dimensional graphics commands and options. All examples contained in this chapter appear numbered at the end of the chapter. In each case, the command or option is briefly described, other pages within The *Mathematica* Handbook containing descriptions or examples are listed, and any examples which illustrate the command are indicated. The page on which each command is first described is highlighted in bold if it is not the first page listed.

Two-Dimensional Graphics

Two-dimensional graphical images are objects of type **Graphics**, **ContourGraphics**, or **DensityGraphics**.

Graphics objects can be constructed with the commands **ListPlot**, **ParametricPlot**, and **Plot** or with graphics primitives; **ContourGraphics** are created with the commands **ContourPlot** and **ListContourPlot**; and **DensityGraphics** are created with the commands **DensityPlot** and **ListDensityPlot**. In general, all graphical images may be displayed using the command **Show** and displayed in different forms by taking advantage of the commands **GraphicsArray** and **Rectangle**.

Two-dimensional graphics primitives are:

Circle
See 44, 525
See **Example 1**

Disk
See pages 103, 526
See **Example 2**

Line
See 260, 519, 527, 558, 563
See **Example 3**

Point
See 165, 219, **352**, 354
See **Examples 4**, **31**

Polygon
See 356, 519, 529, 565
See **Example 5**

PostScript
See 364

Raster
See 380, 530
See **Example 6**

RasterArray
See 381

Rectangle
See 387, 531
See **Example 7**

Text
See 461, 519, 531, 532
See **Example 8**

Graphics
See 165, **183**, 219, 353, 354, 357, 381, 387, 525-533
Graphics options and their default values are:

AspectRatio->GoldenRatio^(-1)
See 20, 515, 516, 519, 525, 526, 534, 543-546, 548, 552, 553
The ratio of the height to the width of the display region is automatically set as the reciprocal of the golden mean.
See **Examples 9**, **18**, **20**, **23**, **24**

Axes->False
See 21, 517-519, 522, 523, 547, 555, 569, 570, 579
Axes are not included in the plot unless otherwise stated.
See **Examples 19, 27**

AxesLabel->None
See 22, 519, 555, 581
The axes are not labeled.
See **Example 28**

AxesOrigin->Automatic
See 22, 550, 554, 556
An internal algorithm is used to determine the point at which the axes cross. This
point is chosen to be the origin if (0,0) is in or near the plotting area.
See **Examples 25, 29**

AxesStyle->Automatic
See 22, 520
The axes are rendered without using additional graphics primitives such as
Dashing, Hue, and **Thickness.**

Background->Automatic
See 23, 520, 548, 556, 572
A white background is given.
See **Examples 20, 30**

ColorOutput->Automatic
See 51, 520
The color output is given by using any specified color directives.

DefaultColor->Automatic
See 83, 520
The color is selected so that it is complementary to the background.

DefaultFont:>$DefaultFont
See 84, 520, 537, 574
The value of **$DefaultFont** is initially **{"Courier",10}.**

DisplayFunction:>$DisplayFunction
See 103, 127, 131, 165, 312, 520, 534, 536-540, 547, 551, 553, 559, 561
The setting for **$DisplayFunction** is initially **Display[$Display,#]&.**
See **Examples 9, 11, 12, 13, 14, 15, 19, 24, 34, 36**

Epilog->{}
See 135
No additional graphics primitives are rendered after the main portion of the
graphics is given.
See **Example 32**

Frame->False
See 170, 411
The plot is not framed unless indicated with **Frame->True.**
See **Examples 18, 24**

FrameLabel->None
See 171
When a frame is requested, it is not labeled unless a specific label is included in the
FrameLabel option.

FrameStyle->Automatic
See 171, 544
The frame is rendered uniformly without the aid of additional graphics directives
such as **Dashing**, **GrayLevel**, or **Hue**.
See **Example 18**

FrameTicks->Automatic
See 171, 544
Tick marks are placed around the frame automatically.
See **Example 18**

GridLines->None
See 185, 545, 546, 559
Grid lines are not included in the plot unless they are indicated in the **GridLines**
option.
See **Examples 33, 18**

PlotLabel->None
See 348, 521, 574, 582
The plot is not labeled if a specific label is not indicated with **PlotLabel**.

PlotRange->Automatic
See 220, 308, 316, 318, **349**, 430, 521, 532, 533, 549, 550, 559, 569, 576, 579, 582
After the distribution of the coordinates is determined, those points which are
outlying are eliminated.
See **Examples 8, 21, 34**

PlotRegion->Automatic
See 349, 521
The default setting indicates that the plot fill the display region. This setting is
{{0,1},{0,1}}.

Prolog->{}
See 373, 521, 550, 558
No graphics primitives are rendered before the major part of the graphics is
rendered.
See **Examples 21, 32**

RotateLabel->True
See 400
Vertical labels on frame axes are read from bottom to top.

Ticks->Automatic
See 127, **465**, 522, 550, 553, 582
Tick marks are placed on the axes automatically.
See **Examples 21, 24**

ContourPlot
See 69, 130, 133, 197, 198, 232, 238, 534-539
See **Examples 9-14**
In addition to the above **Graphics** options and defaults, the command **ContourPlot** has the following options and default values:

AspectRatio->1
See 20, 512, 516, 519, 525, 526, 534, 543-546, 548, 552, 553
The ratio of the height to the width is one.
See **Example 9**

Compiled->True
See 54, 310, 311, 516-518, 523, 557
Mathematica automatically generates compiled functions.

ContourLines->True
See 69, 535
Contour lines are included in the contour plot.
See **Example 10**

Contours->10
See 69, 238, 536
Ten equally spaced contours are included in the contour plot.
See **Example 11**

ContourShading->True
See 69, 133, 238, 265, 536, 538
Regions are colored according to the setting of **ColorFunction**. By default, these regions are colored in shades of gray where the level of shading goes from black to white as the height increases.
See **Examples 11**, **13**

ContourSmoothing->None
See 69, 537
Contour lines are made up of line segments between consecutive grid lines.
See **Example 12**

ContourStyle->Automatic
See 69, 538
Contour lines are produced without using additional directives such as **Dashing**, **Hue**, or **Thickness**.
See **Example 13**

Frame->True
See 170, 411, 516, 539, 541, 543, 544, 553
Contour plots are enclosed in the frame unless otherwise requested.
See **Example 14**

PlotPoints->15
See 123, 124, 126, 131, 136, 137, 178, 196, 231, 235-238, 241-243, 248, 254, 271, **349**, 397, 398, 411, 516-518, 523, 524, 541, 576, 578, 582, 583
Fifteen sample points in the x and y directions are used to create the plot.

DensityPlot
See 90, 124, 237, 242, 411, 540, 541
See **Examples 15, 16**
In addition to the above **Graphics** options and defaults, the command
DensityPlot has the following options and default values:

AspectRatio->1
See 20, 512, 515, 519, 525, 526, 534, 543-546, 548, 552, 553
The ratio of the height to the width is one.

ColorFunction->Automatic
See 51, 522, 523
The default setting represents a range of gray levels.

Compiled->True
See 54, 310, 311, 515, 517, 518, 523, 557
Mathematica automatically generates compiled functions.

Frame->True
See 170, 411, 513, 515, 539, 541, 543, 544, 553
The density plot is automatically enclosed in a frame.
See **Example 16**

Mesh->True
See 292, 411, 522, 524, 540, 541, 569, 576, 582
A mesh is automatically drawn.
See **Examples 15, 16**

MeshStyle->Automatic
See 292, 523, 524, 569, 583
The mesh is rendered without using additional graphics directives such as
Dashing, **GrayLevel**, **Hue**, **RGBColor**, or **Thickness**.

PlotPoints->15
See 123, 124, 126, 131, 136, 137, 178, 196, 231, 235-238, 241-243, 248, 254, 271,
349, 397, 398, 411, 515, 517, 518, 523, 524, 541, 576, 578, 582, 583
Fifteen sample points in the x and y directions are used to create the plot.
See **Example 16**

ListContourPlot
See 263
ListContourPlot has the same options as **ContourPlot** except for
Compiled->True and **PlotPoints->15**.

ListDensityPlot
See 265
ListDensityPlot has the same options as **DensityPlot** except for
Compiled->True and **PlotPoints->15**.

ListPlot
See 139, 249, **267**, 425, 543-550
See **Examples 17-22**

In addition to the above **Graphics** options and defaults, the command **ListPlot** has the following options and default values:

Axes->Automatic
See 21, 513, 516, 518, 519, 522, 523, 547, 555, 569, 570, 579
Axes are automatically included in the plot.
See **Example 19**

PlotJoined->False
See 348, 543-546, 548
Points that are plotted are not joined with line segments.
See **Examples 18, 20**

PlotStyle->Automatic
See 240, 248, 318, **349**, 356, 358, 387, 462, 518, 548, 557, 560
Lines and points are printed according to the default settings for the corresponding graphics directives.
See **Example 20**

ParametricPlot
See 309-311, **338**
See **Examples 23-25**
In addition to the above **Graphics** options and defaults, the command **ParametricPlot** has the following options and default values:

Axes->Automatic
See 21, 513, 516, 518, 519, 522, 523, 547, 555, 569, 570, 579
Axes are automatically included in the plot.

Compiled->True
See 54, 310, 311, 515-516, 518, 523, 557
Mathematica automatically generates compiled functions.

MaxBend->10
See 288, 518
The plot is generated using an algorithm that limits the bend angle between successive segments to be less than 10.

PlotDivision->20
See 348, 518
The maximum factor by which to subdivide the sampling function is 20.

PlotPoints->25
See 123, 124, 126, 131, 136, 137, 178, 196, 231, 232, 235-238, 241-243, 248, 254, 271, **349**, 397, 398, 411, 515-517, 523, 524, 541, 576, 578, 582, 583
The function is sampled at 25 points.

PlotStyle->Automatic
See 240, 248, 318, **349**, 356, 358, 387, 462, 517, 548, 557, 560
Lines and points are printed according to the default settings for the corresponding
graphics directives.

Plot
See 121, 124, 127, 128, 129, 141, 146, 147, 160, 161, 165, 176, 180, 189, 193, 195,
200, 218, 220, 231, 233, 234, 236, 240, 256, 275, 294, 304, 307, 308, 316, 318, 331,
347, 355, 356, 358, 387, 410, 422, 425, 428, 430, 438, 458, 459, 462, 478, 554-557,
559, 560
See **Examples 26-35**
In addition to the above **Graphics** options and defaults, the command **Plot** has the
following options and default values:

Axes->Automatic
See 21, 513, 517- 519, 522, 523, 547, 555, 569, 570, 579
Axes are automatically included in the plot.
See **Example 27**

Compiled->True
See 54, 310, 311, 515-517, 523, 557
Mathematica automatically generates compiled functions.
See **Example 31**

MaxBend->10
See 288, 517
The plot is generated using an algorithm that limits the bend angle between
successive segments to be less than 10.

PlotDivision->20
See 348, 517
The maximum factor by which to subdivide the sampling function is 20.

PlotPoints->25
See 123, 124, 126, 131, 136, 137, 178, 196, 231, 232, 235-238, 241-243, 248, 254,
271, **349**, 397, 398, 411, 515-517, 523, 524, 541, 576, 578, 582, 583
The function is sampled at 25 points.

PlotStyle->Automatic
See 240, 248, 318, **349**, 356, 358, 387, 462, 517, 548, 557, 560
Lines and points are printed according to the default settings for the corresponding
graphics directives.
See **Examples 32, 35**

Three-Dimensional Graphics

Three-dimensional graphical images are objects of type **Graphics3D** or
SurfaceGraphics. **Graphics3D** objects can be constructed with the command
ParametricPlot3D or with graphics primitives. **SurfaceGraphics** objects can
be constructed with the commands **ListPlot3D** and **ParametricPlot3D**,
Plot3D or with three-dimensional graphics primitives. In general, all graphical
images may be displayed using the command **Show** and displayed in different forms by
taking advantage of the commands **GraphicsArray** and **Rectangle**.

Three-dimensional graphics primitives are:

Cuboid
See 7, 562
See **Example 37**

Polygon
See 356, 512, 529, 565
See **Example 40**

Line
See 260, 512, 527, 558, 563
See **Example 38**

Text
See 461, 512, 531, 532

Point
See 165, 219, **352**, 354, 512, 528,
558, 564
See **Example 39**

Graphics3D
See 184, 562-565

Graphics3D options and their default values are:

AmbientLight->GrayLevel[0.]
See 7
Simulated ambient light is given as **GrayLevel[0.]**.

AspectRatio->Automatic
See 20, 512, 515, 516, 525, 526, 534, 543-546, 548, 552, 553
The aspect ratio is determined from the original coordinate system so that the object
appears in its natural form.

Axes->False
See 21, 513, 517, 518, 522, 523, 547, 555, 569, 570, 579
No axes are displayed.
See **Examples 43, 49, 52**

AxesEdge->Automatic
See 21
Mathematica automatically chooses the edges on which the bounding box is drawn.

AxesLabel->None
See 22, 513, 555, 581
The axes are not labeled.
See **Example 49**

AxesStyle->Automatic
See 22, 513
The axes are rendered without using additional graphics primitives such as
Dashing, **Hue**, and **Thickness**.

Background->Automatic
See 23, 513, 548, 556, 572
A white background is given.
See **Example 44**

Boxed->True
See 34, 570, 579, 581
The edges are drawn on the bounding box.
See **Examples 43**, **49**, **50**

BoxRatios->Automatic
See 34, 570
This setting represents the side-length ratios.
See **Example 43**

BoxStyle->Automatic
See 34
The bounding box is rendered without using such graphics directives as **Dashing**,
GrayLevel, **RGBColor**, and **Thickness**.

ColorOutput->Automatic
See 51, 513
The color output is given by using any specified color directives.

DefaultColor->Automatic
See 83, 513
The color is selected so that it is complementary to the background.

DefaultFont:>$DefaultFont
See 84, 513, 574
The value of **$DefaultFont** is initially **{"Courier",10}**.
See **Example 12**, **46**

DisplayFunction:>$DisplayFunction
See 103, 127, 131, 165, 312, 569, 570, 572, 573, 576-579
The setting for **$DisplayFunction** is initially **Display[$Display,#]&**.
See **Examples 42-45**, **48**, **49**

Epilog->{}
See 135, 513, 558
No additional graphics primitives are rendered after the main portion of the
graphics is given.

FaceGrids->None
See 150, 583
Grid lines are not placed on the faces of the bounding box.
See **Example 52**

Lighting->True
See 258, 569
Simulated illumination is included in the plot.
See **Example 42**

LightSources ->{{{1., 0., 1.}, RGBColor[1, 0, 0]},
**   {{1., 1., 1.},RGBColor[0, 1, 0]},**
**   {{0., 1., 1.},RGBColor[0, 0, 1]}}**
See 258, 581
This setting gives the positions and intensities of the light sources used for
simulated illumination.
See **Example 50**

PlotLabel->None
See 348, 514, 574, 582
The plot is not labeled.
See **Examples 46, 51**

PlotRange->Automatic
See 220, 308, 316, 318, **349**, 430, 514, 532, 533, 549, 550, 569, 576, 579, 582
After the distribution of the coordinates is determined, those points which are
outlying are eliminated.
See **Examples 42, 49, 51**

PlotRegion->Automatic
See 349, 514
The default setting indicates that the plot fill the display region. This setting is
{{0,1},{0,1}}.

PolygonIntersections->True
See 357
Intersecting polygons are displayed.

Prolog->{}
See 373, 514, 550, 558
No graphics primitives are rendered before the major part of the graphics is
rendered.

RenderAll->True
See 391
PostScript is rendered for all polygons.

Shading->True
See 123, 126, 131, 178, 196, 235, 236, 241, 243, 254, 271, 397, 398, **420**, 422, 576,
583
Shading is used according to height or from simulated illumination if the option
setting **Lighting->True** is used.
See **Examples 48, 52**

SphericalRegion->False
See 437, 576
The three-dimensional object is scaled to fit in a circumscribing sphere.
See **Example 48**

Ticks->Automatic
See 127, **465**, 514, 550, 553, 582
Tick marks are placed automatically on the axes.
See **Example 51**

ViewCenter->Automatic
See 488, 576
The entire bounding box is centered in the display region.

ViewPoint->{1.3,-2.4,2.}
See 488, 573, 580, 582

Objects are viewed from the point (1.3,–2.4,2.0).
See **Examples 45**, **49**, **51**

ViewVertical->{0., 0., 1.}
See 488, 569
The z-axis in the original coordinate system is vertical in the final image.
See **Example 42**

ListPlot3D
See 268, 542, 567, 569
See **Examples 41**, **42**
Although **ListPlot3D** does not have the options **PolygonIntersections** and
RenderAll, in addition to the above **Graphics3D** options and default values,
ListPlot3D has the following options and default values:

Axes->True
See 21, 513, 517-519, 523, 547, 555, 569, 570, 579
The x-, y-, and z-axes are drawn automatically on the edges of the bounding box.
See **Example 42**

ClipFill->Automatic
See 46, 523, 569, 576, 582
Clipped areas of the surface are displayed like the rest of the surface.
See **Example 42**

ColorFunction->Automatic
See 51, 516, 523
The default setting represents a range of gray levels.

HiddenSurface->True
See 190, 524
Hidden surfaces are eliminated.

Mesh->True
See 292, 411, 516, 524, 540, 541, 569, 576, 582
A mesh is automatically drawn.
See **Example 42**

MeshRange->Automatic
See 292, 524
Specifies the range of x and y coordinates that correspond to the array of z values.

MeshStyle->Automatic
See 292, 516, 524, 569, 583
The mesh is rendered without using additional graphics directives such as
Dashing, GrayLevel, Hue, RGBColor, or **Thickness.**
See **Example 42**

ParametricPlot3D
See 339
See **Examples 43-46**
In addition to the above **Graphics3D** options and default values,
ParametricPlot3D has the following options and their default values are:

Axes->True
See 21, 513, 517-519, 522, 547, 555, 569, 570, 579
Both the x- and y-axes are drawn automatically.
See **Example 43**

Compiled->True
See 54, 310, 311, 515-518, 557
Mathematica automatically generates compiled functions.

PlotPoints->Automatic
See 123, 124, 126, 131, 136, 137, 178, 196, 235-238, 241-243, 248, 254, 271, **349,**
397, 398, 411, 515-518, 524, 541, 576, 578, 582, 583
This setting is **75** for curves and **{15,15}** for surfaces.

Plot3D
See 97, 123, 178, 235, 236, 243, 254, 271, **350,** 397, 398, 422, 575, 576, 578, 581-583
See **Examples 47-52**
Although **Plot3D** does not have the options **PolygonIntersections** and
RenderAll, in addition to the above **Graphics3D** options and default values,
Plot3D has the following options and default values:

Axes->True
See 21, 513, 517-519, 522, 547, 555, 569, 570, 579
The x-, y-, and z-axes are drawn automatically on the edges of the bounding box.
See **Examples 49, 52**

ClipFill->Automatic
See 46, 522, 569, 576, 582
Clipped areas of the surface are displayed like the rest of the surface.
See **Examples 48, 51**

ColorFunction->Automatic
See 51, 516, 522
The default setting represents a range of gray levels.

Compiled->True
See 54, 310, 311, 515-518, 557
Mathematica automatically generates compiled functions.

HiddenSurface->True
See 190, 522
Hidden surfaces are eliminated.

Mesh->True
See 292, 411, 516, 522, 540, 541, 569, 576, 582
A mesh is automatically drawn.
See **Examples 48, 51**

MeshRange->Automatic
See 292, 522
Specifies the range of x and y coordinates that correspond to the array of z values.

MeshStyle->Automatic
See 292, 516, 523, 569, 583
The mesh is rendered without using additional graphics directives such as
Dashing, GrayLevel, Hue, RGBColor, or **Thickness**.
See **Example 52**

PlotPoints->15
See 123, 124, 126, 131, 136, 137, 178, 196, 235-238, 241-243, 248, 254, 271, **349**, 397, 398, 411, 515-518, 523, 541, 576, 578, 582, 583
Fifteen sample points are used in the x and y directions.
See **Examples 48, 49, 51, 52**

Example 1:

one is a graphics object corresponding to the graph of the circle with equation $x^2 + y^2 = 1$; **two** is a graphics object corresponding to the graph of the ellipse with equation $(x-3)^2 + \dfrac{(y-2)^2}{4} = 1$; and **three** is a graphics object corresponding to the graph of the semi-circle with parametric equation

$$\begin{cases} x(t) = -2 + \dfrac{1}{2}\mathrm{Cos}(t) \\ y(t) = -3 + \dfrac{1}{2}\mathrm{Sin}(t) \end{cases},$$

$\pi \le t \le 2\pi$. All three graphics objects are displayed with the **Show** command.

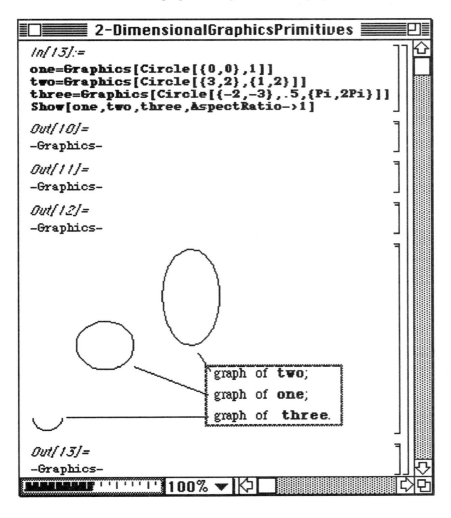

```
In[13]:=
one=Graphics[Circle[{0,0},1]]
two=Graphics[Circle[{3,2},{1,2}]]
three=Graphics[Circle[{-2,-3},.5,{Pi,2Pi}]]
Show[one,two,three,AspectRatio->1]

Out[10]=
-Graphics-

Out[11]=
-Graphics-

Out[12]=
-Graphics-
```

graph of **two**;
graph of **one**;
graph of **three**.

```
Out[13]=
-Graphics-
```

Example 2:

one is a graphics object corresponding to the graph of the disk with equation $x^2 + y^2 = 1$; **two** is a graphics object corresponding to the graph of the filled ellipse with equation $(x-3)^2 + \dfrac{(y-2)^2}{4} = 1$; and **three** is a graphics object corresponding to the graph of the filled semi–circle with parametric equation

$$\begin{cases} x(t) = -2 + \dfrac{1}{2}\mathrm{Cos}(t) \\ y(t) = -3 + \dfrac{1}{2}\mathrm{Sin}(t) \end{cases},$$

$\pi \le t \le 2\pi$. All three graphics objects are displayed with the **Show** command.

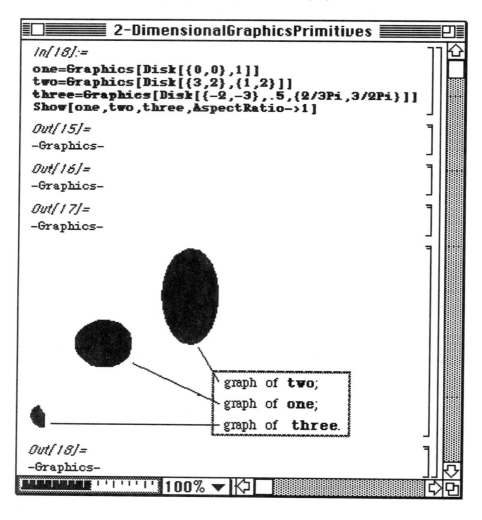

Example 3:

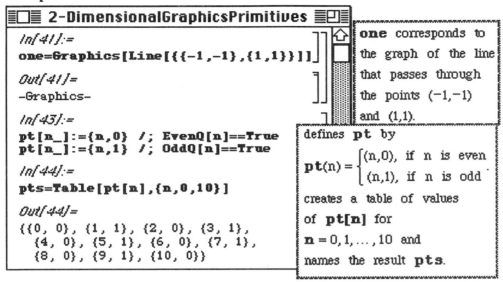

Line is used to connect consecutive elements of the set of ordered pairs **pts** with line segments. The resulting graphics object is named **two**. Both **one** and **two** are displayed in a graphics array.

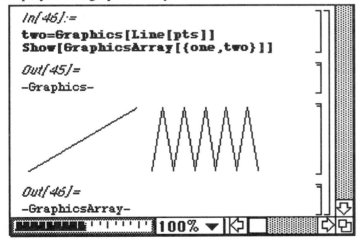

Example 4:

In the following example, **one** corresponds to a graphics object representing a point with coordinates $(-2,0)$; **two** corresponds to a slightly larger point with coordinates $(-1,0)$.

```
▛▀▛□▀▀▀    2-DimensionalGraphicsPrimitives    ▀▀▀▛□▛
In[74]:=
one=Graphics[Point[{-2,0}]]
two=Graphics[{PointSize[.5],Point[{-1,0}]}]
Out[73]=
-Graphics-
Out[74]=
-Graphics-
```

A table of points named **pairs** is created using the function **pt** where

$$\mathbf{pt}(n) = \begin{cases} \{n,0\}, & \text{if } n \text{ is even} \\ \{n,1\}, & \text{if } n \text{ is odd} \end{cases}.$$ A table of values of **pt**(n) is created for

n = 0, 1, ... , 9, 10.   The resulting ordered pairs are declared to represent points using the commands **Map** and **Point**; the resulting list of points is named **pnts**.

```
In[77]:=
pt[n_]:={n,0} /; EvenQ[n]==True
pt[n_]:={n,1} /; OddQ[n]==True
pairs=Table[pt[n],{n,0,10}];
In[78]:=
pnts=Map[Point,pairs]
Out[78]=
{Point[{0, 0}], Point[{1, 1}], Point[{2, 0}],
   Point[{3, 1}], Point[{4, 0}], Point[{5, 1}],
   Point[{6, 0}], Point[{7, 1}], Point[{8, 0}],
   Point[{9, 1}], Point[{10, 0}]}
```

Finally, **one**, **two** and **pnts** are displayed as a graphics array.

```
In[79]:=
Show[GraphicsArray[
    {one,two,
        Graphics[{PointSize[.05],pnts}]}
    ]]
```

```
Out[79]=
-GraphicsArray-
```

`100% ▼`

Example 5:

In the following example, **Polygon** and **GrayLevel[.3]** are used to create a polygon called.**polyone** which represents the triangle with vertices $(-3,-1)$, $(-4,-3)$, and $(2,2)$. The result is a triangle shaded slightly lighter than black.

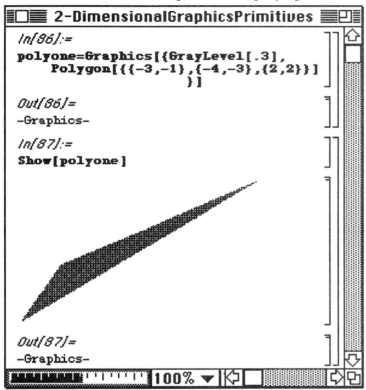

Example 6:

In the following example, c is defined to be a random complex number. **man[x,y,c,max]** is a function which first defines $f(z)=z^2+c$, sets $z=x+i\,y$, and then sets n=0. Then, as long as $\| f(z) \| < 2$ and $n < $ **max** (which has default value 15), z is set to be $f(z)$, and then n is increased by one. **man[x,y,c,max]** returns the value **(max-n)/max**. Thus, **man[x,y,c,max]** returns either the first value of n for which $\|$ **Nest[f,x+I y,n]** $\| < 2$ or **max**. Note that the variables **f**, **z**, and **n** are declared to be local to the module **man**.

```
≣□≣══════════════ Raster ═══════════════≣□≣
In[8]:=
c=Random[Complex,{0,1/2+1/2I}]

Out[8]=
0.340151 + 0.251893 I

In[12]:=
man[x_,y_,c_,max_:15]:=Module[{f,z,n},
    f[z_]:=z^2+c;
    z=x+I y;
    n=0;
    While[And[Abs[z]<2,n<max],
        PreIncrement[n];
        z=f[z]
        ];
    Return[(max-n)/max];
        ]
```

An array of numbers values is computed with the function **man** and the **Table** command. Observe that **man** always returns a number between 0 and 1. **Raster** is used to display the resulting table in various shades of gray.

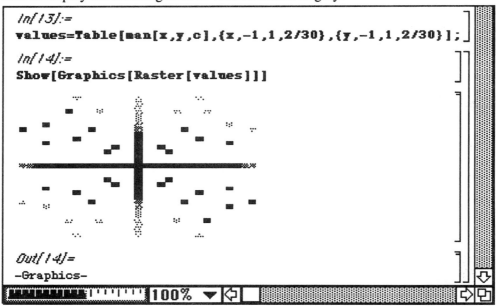

```
In[13]:=
values=Table[man[x,y,c],{x,-1,1,2/30},{y,-1,1,2/30}];

In[14]:=
Show[Graphics[Raster[values]]]
```

```
Out[14]=
-Graphics-
```

```
100% ▼
```

Example 7:

In the following example, **rec** is a gray rectangle with vertices $(-4,-7)$, $(5,-7)$, $(5,6)$, and $(-4,6)$.

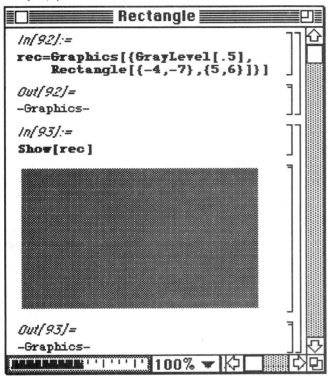

```
════════════ Rectangle ════════════
In[92]:=
rec=Graphics[{GrayLevel[.5],
    Rectangle[{-4,-7},{5,6}]}]

Out[92]=
-Graphics-

In[93]:=
Show[rec]




Out[93]=
-Graphics-
════════════ 100% ▼ ════════════
```

Example 8:

In the following example, different orientations of text are created and displayed.

```
═══════════════════ Text ═══════════════════
In[53]:=
f[x_]=Exp[3x]/x;
t[1]=Text[f[x],{0,0}];
t[2]=Text["f[x]",{0,1}];
t[3]=Text["The Mathematica Handbook",{5,0}];
t[4]=Text["The Mathematica Handbook",{5,1},{-1,0}];
t[5]=Text["The Mathematica Handbook",{5,2},{1,0}];
t[6]=Text["The Mathematica Handbook",{5,3},{0,-1}];
t[7]=Text["The Mathematica Handbook",{5,4},{0,1}];
```

```
Show[Graphics[Table[t[i],{i,1,7}]],
    PlotRange->{{-5,20},{-2,7}}]
```

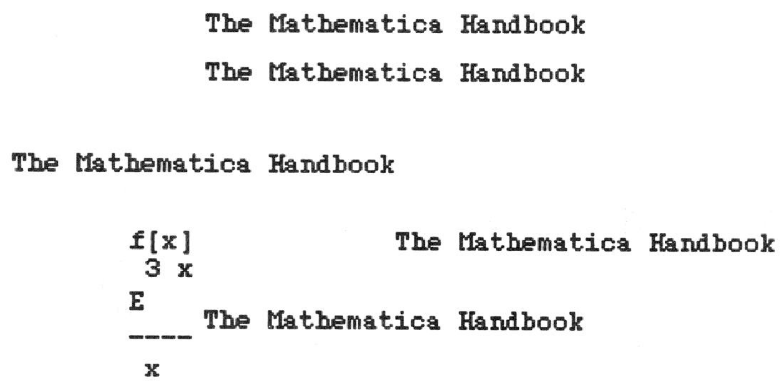

                    The Mathematica Handbook

                    The Mathematica Handbook

        The Mathematica Handbook

            f[x]   The Mathematica Handbook
             3 x
            E
            ____   The Mathematica Handbook
             x

Out[58]=
-Graphics-

100% ▼

In addition to displaying text, a variety of fonts and font sizes may also be displayed
with the setting **{"font"},size**:

In[129]:=
```
t[8]=Text[FontForm["The Mathematica Handbook",
  {"Dorovar",18}],{0,0}];
t[9]=Text[FontForm["The Mathematica Handbook",
  {"Venice",14}],{2,2},{0,0},{1,0}];
t[10]=Text[FontForm["The Mathematica Handbook",
  {"London",20}],{6,4},{0,0},{0,1}];
t[11]=Text[FontForm["The Mathematica Handbook",
  {"Palatino",12}],{8,4},{0,0},{0,-1}];
t[12]=Text[FontForm["The Mathematica Handbook",
  {"Symbol",24}],{0,4},{0,0},{-1,0}];
```

```
In[130]:=
Show[Graphics[Table[t[i],{i,8,12}]],
    PlotRange->{{-5,10},{-1,10}}]
```

$$\varsigma o o \beta \delta \nu \alpha\, H \alpha \lambda\, \tau\, \alpha \mu \varepsilon\, \pi\, \alpha\; M \varepsilon\, \eta T$$

The Mathematica Handbook

The Mathematica Handbook

```
Out[130]=
-Graphics-
```

Example 9:

The following example compares two contour graphs of $f(x,y)=2x^2-2y^2-4$ for

$-1 \leq x \leq 1$ and $-2 \leq y \leq 2$ created with **ContourPlot** using the default value of **AspectRatio** as well as **AspectRatio->2** and displaying the results as a graphics array with a similar result obtained with the command **ImplicitPlot** which is contained in the package **ImplicitPlot.m**, located in the **Graphics** folder (or directory). **ImplicitPlot[equation,{x,xmin,xmax},{y,ymin,ymax}]** graphs **equation** in the same manner as **ContourPlot** creates contour graphs of functions and has the same options as **ContourPlot**. Some equations can be graphed with the command **ImplicitPlot[equation,{x,xmin,xmax}]**, which has the same options as **Plot**. As with the **Plot** command,
several equations can be graphed simultaneously with the command
ImplicitPlot[{equation1,equation2,...},...].

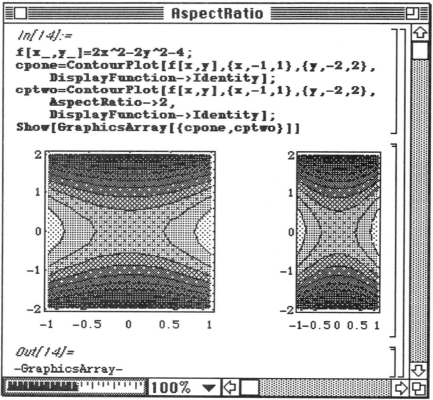

```
In[14]:=
f[x_,y_]=2x^2-2y^2-4;
cpone=ContourPlot[f[x,y],{x,-1,1},{y,-2,2},
    DisplayFunction->Identity];
cptwo=ContourPlot[f[x,y],{x,-1,1},{y,-2,2},
    AspectRatio->2,
    DisplayFunction->Identity];
Show[GraphicsArray[{cpone,cptwo}]]
```

```
Out[14]=
-GraphicsArray-
```

Before using a command contained in a package, be sure to load the package first. See the Preface for a brief discussion of loading packages.

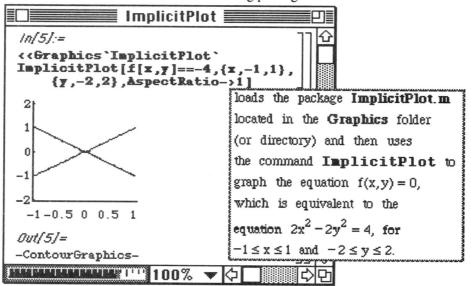

```
In[5]:=
<<Graphics`ImplicitPlot`
ImplicitPlot[f[x,y]==-4,{x,-1,1},
    {y,-2,2},AspectRatio->1]
```

loads the package **ImplicitPlot.m** located in the **Graphics** folder (or directory) and then uses the command **ImplicitPlot** to graph the equation $f(x,y) = 0$, which is equivalent to the equation $2x^2 - 2y^2 = 4$, for $-1 \leq x \leq 1$ and $-2 \leq y \leq 2$.

```
Out[5]=
-ContourGraphics-
```

Example 10:

The following example defines $f(x,y)=L_3(x+iy)$ and then creates a contour graph of the real part of $f(x,y)$ for $-4 \le x \le 4$ and $-4 \le y \le 4$. Since the option **ContourLines->False** is included, no contour lines are displayed.

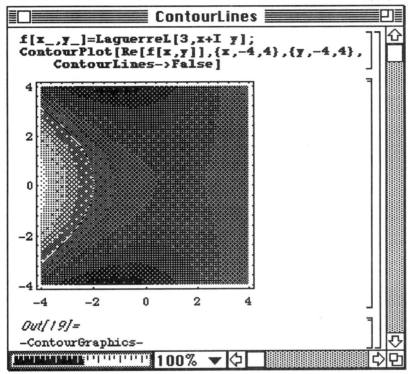

Example 11:

In the following example, contour graphs of $-4x^2+3y^2$ are shown using 10 contour levels, contour levels at -10, -5, 0, 10, and at 1 for $-2 \le x \le 2$ and $-2 \le y \le 2$. In the second example, the resulting contours correspond to graphs of the equations $-4x^2+3y^2=10$, $-4x^2+3y^2=-5$, $-4x^2+3y^2=0$, $-4x^2+3y^2=5$, and $-4x^2+3y^2=10$. In the third case, the option **ContourShading->False** is included so that the displayed graph corresponds to the graph of $-4x^2+3y^2=1$. Note that the option **Contours->n** specifies that **n** contours be displayed; the option **Contours->{list of numbers}** specifies that the contours corresponding to **list of numbers** be displayed.

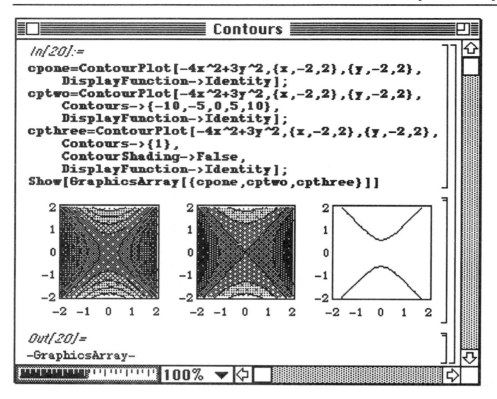

Example 12:
In the following examples, two contour graphs of

$$\text{erf}\left(x^2 - y^2\right) = \frac{2}{\sqrt{\pi}}\int_0^{x^2-y^2} e^{-t^2}\, dt \quad \text{are created for} \quad -2 \le x \le 2 \quad \text{and}$$

$-2 \le y \le 2$ and one for $-2 \le x \le 2$ and $-1 \le y < 1$. In the first case, no smoothing algorithm is applied to the resulting contours; in the second case, the option **ContourSmoothing->Automatic** instructs *Mathematica* to apply a smoothing algorithm to each contour. The resulting graphics objects are displayed as a graphics array to illustrate the slight difference between the results. In the third case, the default font is changed from Courier size 10 to Times size 10. Consequently, the numbering of the tick marks in the third contour graph are displayed in Times size 10.

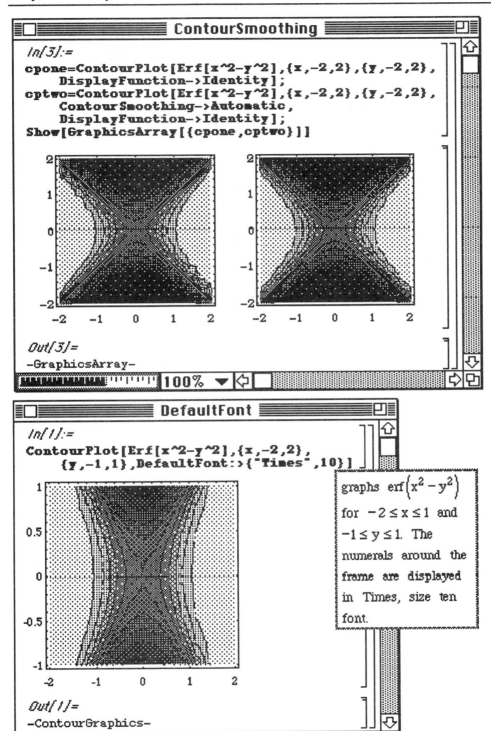

ContourSmoothing

In[3]:=
```
cpone=ContourPlot[Erf[x^2-y^2],{x,-2,2},{y,-2,2},
    DisplayFunction->Identity];
cptwo=ContourPlot[Erf[x^2-y^2],{x,-2,2},{y,-2,2},
    ContourSmoothing->Automatic,
    DisplayFunction->Identity];
Show[GraphicsArray[{cpone,cptwo}]]
```

Out[3]=
-GraphicsArray-

100%

DefaultFont

In[1]:=
```
ContourPlot[Erf[x^2-y^2],{x,-2,2},
    {y,-1,1},DefaultFont:>{"Times",10}]
```

graphs $\mathrm{erf}\left(x^2-y^2\right)$ for $-2 \leq x \leq 1$ and $-1 \leq y \leq 1$. The numerals around the frame are displayed in Times, size ten font.

Out[1]=
-ContourGraphics-

100%

Example 13:

The following example shows two contour graphs of $f(x,y) = (x^2 - 3)y^2$

for $-3 < x < 3$ and $-1 < y < 1$. In the second case, the space between contours is not shaded since the option **ContourShading->False** is included and the resulting contour lines are displayed in a shade of gray since the option **ContourStyle->GrayLevel[.3]** is included.

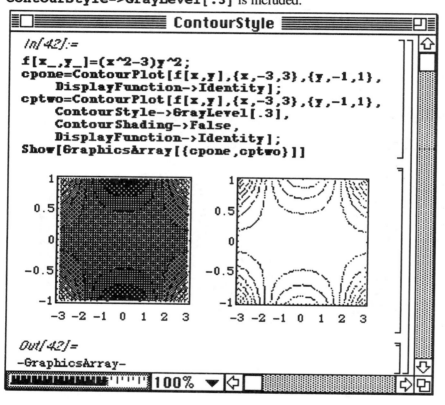

Example 14:

The following example compares the contour graphs of $f(x, y) = \sin(x + \cos(y))$

for $0 \leq x \leq 2\pi$ and $-\pi \leq y \leq \pi$ when the option **Frame->False** is included.

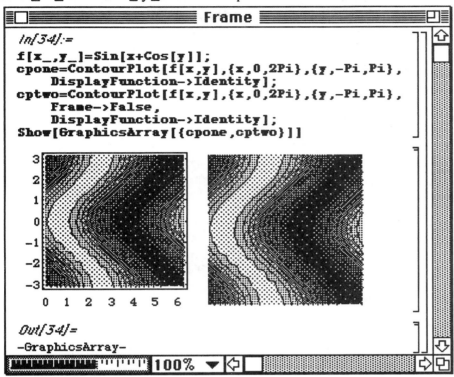

Example 15:

The following example shows two density graphs of

$f(x, y) = \sin(\cos(x) + \sin(y))$ for $0 \leq x \leq 4\pi$ and $-2\pi \leq y \leq 2\pi$.   In the

second case, the option **Mesh->False** causes the resulting graph to not have a mesh.

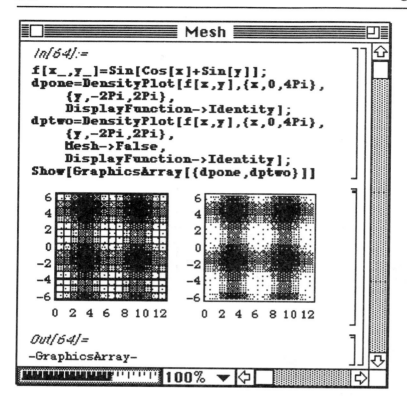

```
In[64]:=
f[x_,y_]=Sin[Cos[x]+Sin[y]];
dpone=DensityPlot[f[x,y],{x,0,4Pi},
    {y,-2Pi,2Pi},
    DisplayFunction->Identity];
dptwo=DensityPlot[f[x,y],{x,0,4Pi},
    {y,-2Pi,2Pi},
    Mesh->False,
    DisplayFunction->Identity];
Show[GraphicsArray[{dpone,dptwo}]]
```

```
Out[64]=
-GraphicsArray-
```

Example 16:

In the following example, all prior definitions of **c**, **f**, **g**, and **h** are cleared with the command **Clear** and then **c** is defined to be a random complex number. $f(z)=z^2+c$, and g(z) is defined to be the composition of f ten times with itself using the command **Nest**. Finally, h(z) is defined to be the minimum of the absolute value of g(z) and 30.

Then a density graph of h is created for $-1 \le x \le 1$ and $-1 \le y \le 1$ in which 150 plotpoints are used, the resulting graph is displayed without a mesh since the option **Mesh->False** is included and no frame is placed around the result since the option **Frame->False** is included.

DensityPlotOptions

```
In[2]:=
Clear[c,f,g,h]
c=Random[Complex]

Out[2]=
0.387824 + 0.348198 I

In[6]:=
f[z_]:=z^2+c;
g[z_]:=Nest[f,z,10];
h[z_]:=Min[Abs[g[z]],30];
DensityPlot[h[x+I y],{x,-1,1},
    {y,-1,1},Mesh->False,Frame->False,
    PlotPoints->150]
```

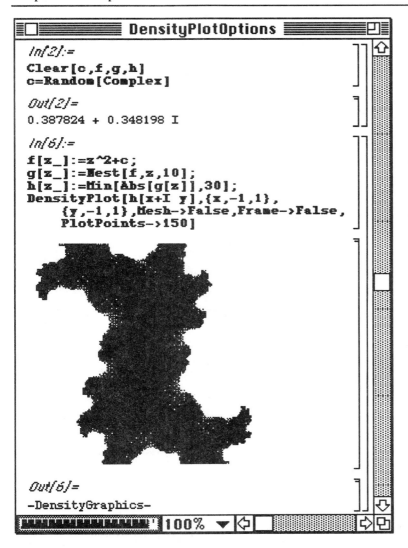

```
Out[6]=
-DensityGraphics-
```

100%

Example 17:

In the following example, a table of values for the vector-valued function f(t) is created and named **vals**. **vals** is used in several subsequent examples that illustrate some of the various **ListPlot** options.

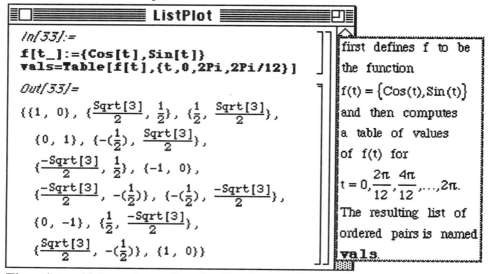

The points which result are plotted with **ListPlot**.

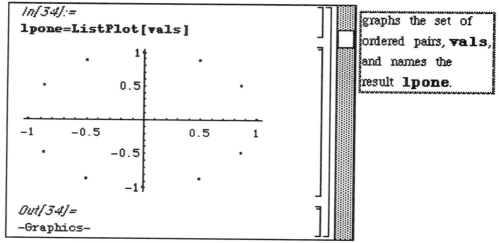

Example 18:

ListPlot can be used to graph both sets of points and sets of numbers. The following examples illustrate how to use **ListPlot** to plot both sets of points and sets of numbers and demonstrate several of **ListPlot**'s options. In the following example, the points in **lptwo** are connected with line segments with the setting **PlotJoined->True**. Also, the ratio of the lengths of the x- and y-axes is 1 because of the setting **AspectRatio->1**. Finally, the plot is framed as a result of the setting **Frame->True**.

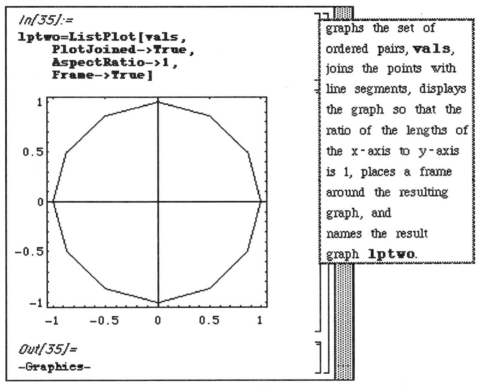

In[35]:=
```
lptwo=ListPlot[vals,
    PlotJoined->True,
    AspectRatio->1,
    Frame->True]
```

graphs the set of ordered pairs, **vals**, joins the points with line segments, displays the graph so that the ratio of the lengths of the x-axis to y-axis is 1, places a frame around the resulting graph, and names the result graph **lptwo**.

Out[35]=
-Graphics-

In **lpthree** below, the option setting **FrameTicks->None** causes the tick marks to be removed from the frame. Also, the setting **FrameStyle->GrayLevel[.3]** causes the frame to be plotted in gray.

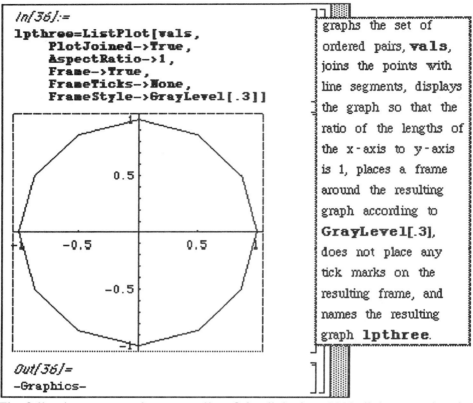

In[36]:=
```
lpthree=ListPlot[vals,
    PlotJoined->True,
    AspectRatio->1,
    Frame->True,
    FrameTicks->None,
    FrameStyle->GrayLevel[.3]]
```

graphs the set of ordered pairs, **vals**, joins the points with line segments, displays the graph so that the ratio of the lengths of the x-axis to y-axis is 1, places a frame around the resulting graph according to **GrayLevel[.3]**, does not place any tick marks on the resulting frame, and names the resulting graph **lpthree**.

Out[36]=
```
-Graphics-
```

The following command creates a list of the digits in a 2000-digit approximation of π and then uses **ListPlot** to graph the result.

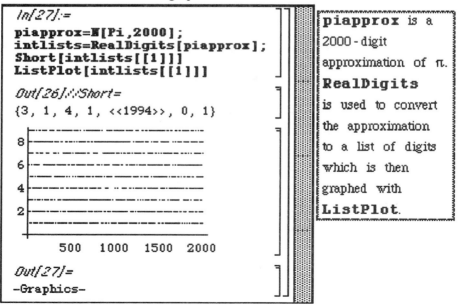

In[27]:=
```
piapprox=N[Pi,2000];
intlists=RealDigits[piapprox];
Short[intlists[[1]]]
ListPlot[intlists[[1]]]
```

piapprox is a 2000-digit approximation of π. **RealDigits** is used to convert the approximation to a list of digits which is then graphed with **ListPlot**.

Out[26]//Short=
```
{3, 1, 4, 1, <<1994>>, 0, 1}
```

Out[27]=
```
-Graphics-
```

The **GridLines** option is illustrated below in **lpfour**. With the setting **GridLines->Automatic**, *Mathematica* automatically places vertical and horizontal gridlines on the graph.

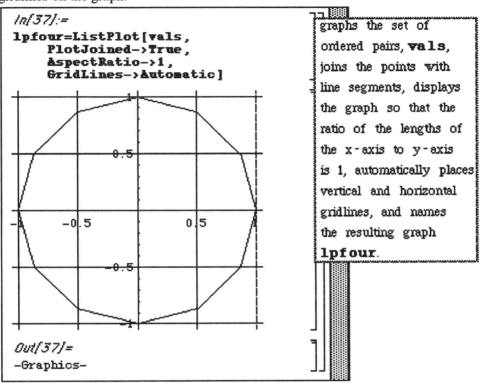

In[37]:=
```
lpfour=ListPlot[vals,
    PlotJoined->True,
    AspectRatio->1,
    GridLines->Automatic]
```

graphs the set of ordered pairs, **vals**, joins the points with line segments, displays the graph so that the ratio of the lengths of the x‑axis to y‑axis is 1, automatically places vertical and horizontal gridlines, and names the resulting graph **lpfour**.

Out[37]=
-Graphics-

Below in **lpfive**, particular settings for the **GridLines** option are made with
GridLines->{{-.75,-.25},{.25,.75}}. In this case, vertical gridlines are
placed at x = −.75 and x = −.25 while horizontal gridlines are placed at y = .25 and
y = .75.

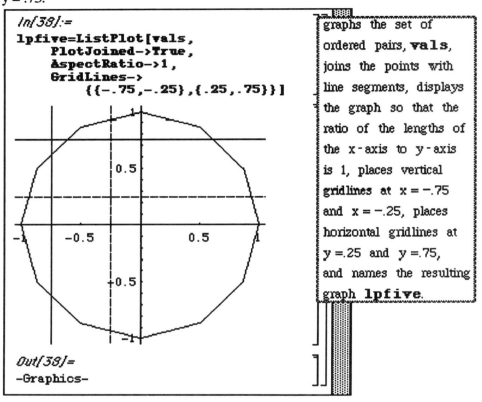

In[38]:=

```
lpfive=ListPlot[vals,
    PlotJoined->True,
    AspectRatio->1,
    GridLines->
        {{-.75,-.25},{.25,.75}}]
```

graphs the set of
ordered pairs, **vals**,
joins the points with
line segments, displays
the graph so that the
ratio of the lengths of
the x‑axis to y‑axis
is 1, places vertical
gridlines at x = −.75
and x = −.25, places
horizontal gridlines at
y = .25 and y = .75,
and names the resulting
graph **lpfive**.

Out[38]=
-Graphics-

Example 19:

To illustrate the **Axes** option, the function

$$f(n) = \frac{1}{n \sin(n)}$$ is defined below.   The list of values of $\left\{ \dfrac{1}{n \sin(n)} \right\}_{n=1}^{2500}$ is

calculated with **Table** and the result is named tfn.   **ListPlot** is then
used to plot this collection of function values in two ways. First, it is plotted with the
default setting of **Axes**. Then it is generated with the setting **Axes->None**. These
graphics are suppressed initially because the **DisplayFunction->Identity**
option is used. They are displayed together in a graphics array to note that no axes are
included in the second plot.

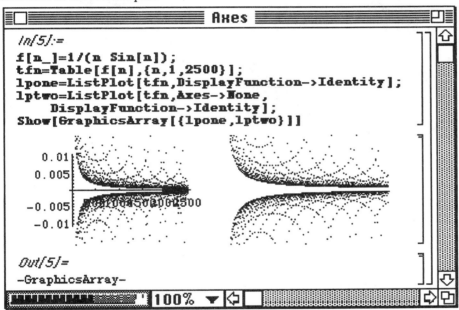

Example 20:

In **lpsix** below the list of numbers vals is used to illustrate the option **Background**.
The background is displayed with **GrayLevel[0]** (black) while the line segments
which join the points are rendered according to **GrayLevel[1]** (white). In the
second, case, the list of numbers, **tp**, is first defined and then graphed with **ListPlot**.
The options **PlotStyle**, **Background**, and **GrayLevel** are used to display the
graphs in white and the backgrounds in black.

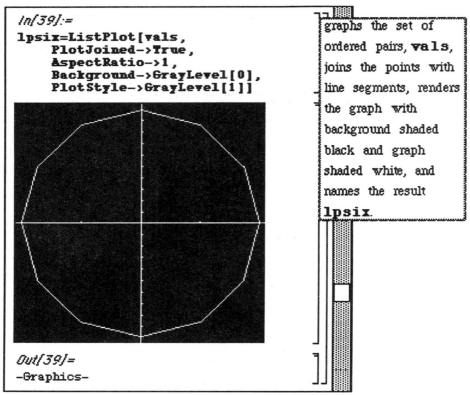

```
In[39]:=
lpsix=ListPlot[vals,
    PlotJoined->True,
    AspectRatio->1,
    Background->GrayLevel[0],
    PlotStyle->GrayLevel[1]]
```

graphs the set of
ordered pairs, **vals**,
joins the points with
line segments, renders
the graph with
background shaded
black and graph
shaded white, and
names the result
lpsix.

```
Out[39]=
-Graphics-
```

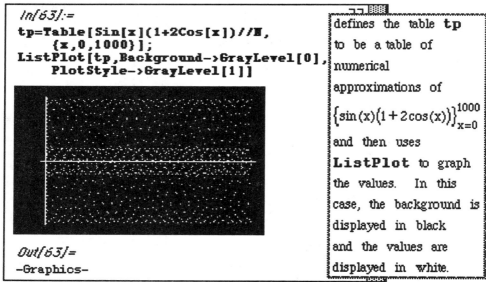

```
In[63]:=
tp=Table[Sin[x](1+2Cos[x])//N,
    {x,0,1000}];
ListPlot[tp,Background->GrayLevel[0],
    PlotStyle->GrayLevel[1]]
```

defines the table **tp**
to be a table of
numerical
approximations of
$\{\sin(x)(1+2\cos(x))\}_{x=0}^{1000}$
and then uses
ListPlot to graph
the values. In this
case, the background is
displayed in black
and the values are
displayed in white.

```
Out[63]=
-Graphics-
```

Example 21:

In the following example, a random complex number with real and imaginary parts between $-1/2$ and $1/2$ is found and called **c**. A function **f** is then defined as z^2+c.

This function is composed with itself 12 times, and the function which results is called **g**. A function **h** which collects the real and imaginary parts of **g** is then defined. Finally, a list of ordered pairs called **pairs** is created which represents the real and imaginary parts of **g** evaluated at complex numbers with real and imaginary parts between −1 and 1 using increments of 2/50. A shortened list of **pairs** is requested.

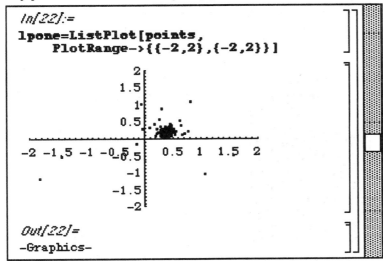

In[4]:=
```
c=Random[Complex,{-1/2-1/2I,1/2+1/2I}]
```

Out[4]=
```
0.269352 + 0.0393867 I
```

In[12]:=
```
f[z_]:=z^2+c;
g[z_]:=Nest[f,z,12];
h[z_]:={Re[g[z]],Im[g[z]]};
```

In[15]:=
```
pairs=Table[h[x+I y],{x,-1,1,2/50},
    {y,-1,1,2/50}];
Short[pairs]
```

Out[15]//Short=
```
{<<51>>}
```

pairs is then plotted with **ListPlot** using the **PlotRange** option. In this case, only points with real and imaginary parts between −2 and 2 are plotted in **lpone**.

In[22]:=
```
lpone=ListPlot[points,
    PlotRange->{{-2,2},{-2,2}}]
```

Out[22]=
```
-Graphics-
```

Below, **lptwo** demonstrates the **Ticks** and **Prolog** options. With the setting **Ticks->None**, no tick marks appear on the axes. Also, the points are printed according to **GrayLevel[.4]** since **Prolog->{GrayLevel[.4]}** is used. Note that the **PlotRange** in this case is different from that in **lpone** above.

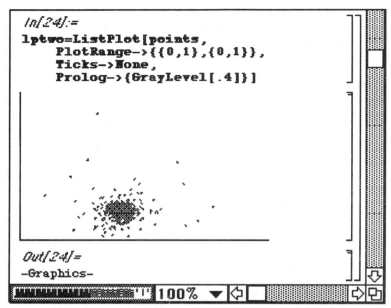

```
In[24]:=
lptwo=ListPlot[points,
    PlotRange->{{0,1},{0,1}},
    Ticks->None,
    Prolog->{GrayLevel[.4]}]
```

```
Out[24]=
-Graphics-
```

The package **Graphics** contained in the **Graphics** folder contains the command **BarChart** which produces bar charts of lists. After defining the list **dowaverage**, the following compares the results obtained with **ListPlot** and **BarChart**.

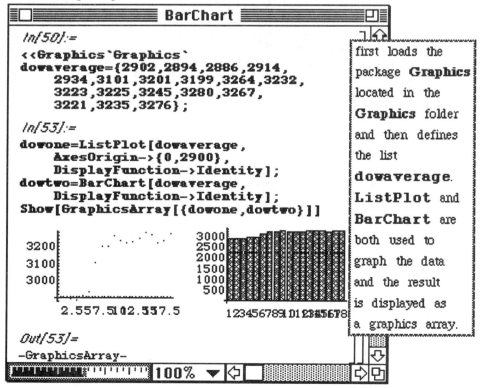

BarChart

```
In[50]:=
<<Graphics`Graphics`
dowaverage={2902,2894,2886,2914,
    2934,3101,3201,3199,3264,3232,
    3223,3225,3245,3280,3267,
    3221,3235,3276};
```

first loads the package **Graphics** located in the **Graphics** folder and then defines the list **dowaverage**. **ListPlot** and **BarChart** are both used to graph the data and the result is displayed as a graphics array.

```
In[53]:=
dowone=ListPlot[dowaverage,
    AxesOrigin->{0,2900},
    DisplayFunction->Identity];
dowtwo=BarChart[dowaverage,
    DisplayFunction->Identity];
Show[GraphicsArray[{dowone,dowtwo}]]
```

```
Out[53]=
-GraphicsArray-
```

Example 22:

The following example illustrates the use of **GraphicsArray** with some of the graphics generated by **ListPlot** in the previous examples. In this case, the plots **lpone**, **lptwo**, **lpthree**, **lpfour**, **lpfive**, and **lpsix** are displayed in the pairs indicated in the command below.

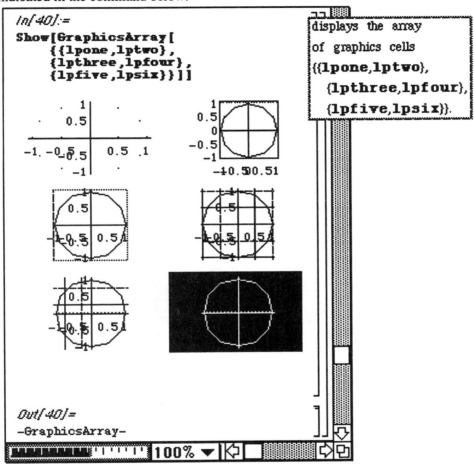

Example 23:

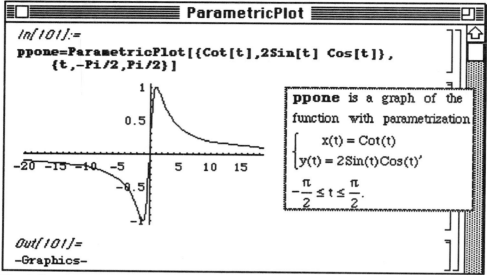

In[101]:=
```
ppone=ParametricPlot[{Cot[t],2Sin[t] Cos[t]},
    {t,-Pi/2,Pi/2}]
```

ppone is a graph of the function with parametrization

$$\begin{cases} x(t) = Cot(t) \\ y(t) = 2Sin(t)Cos(t)' \end{cases}$$

$$-\frac{\pi}{2} \le t \le \frac{\pi}{2}.$$

Out[101]=
-Graphics-

The following example shows the effect that **AspectRatio** has on the plot shown in **ppone** above. In this case, the setting **AspectRatio->1/4** is used. Therefore, the ratio of the lengths of the x-axis to the y-axis is 4 to 1.

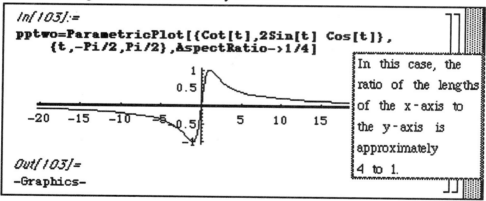

In[103]:=
```
pptwo=ParametricPlot[{Cot[t],2Sin[t] Cos[t]},
    {t,-Pi/2,Pi/2},AspectRatio->1/4]
```

In this case, the ratio of the lengths of the x-axis to the y-axis is approximately 4 to 1.

Out[103]=
-Graphics-

Example 24:

In the following example, x(t)=4cos(t)−cos(4t) and y(t)=4sin(t)−sin(4t). **ppone** is a parametric plot of {x(t),y(t)} for $0 \leq t \leq 2\pi$; **pptwo** is a parametric plot of {x(t),y(t)} for $0 \leq t \leq 2\pi$ in which the option **AspectRatio->1** is included; and **ppthree** is a parametric plot of {x(t),y(t)} for $0 \leq t \leq 2\pi$ in which the options **AspectRatio->1** and **Ticks->None** are included.

```
≡ AspectRatioandTicks ≡
In[14]:=
x[t_]=4Cos[t]-Cos[4t];
y[t_]=4Sin[t]-Sin[4t];
ppone=ParametricPlot[{x[t],y[t]},{t,0,2Pi},
     DisplayFunction->Identity];
pptwo=ParametricPlot[{x[t],y[t]},{t,0,2Pi},
     AspectRatio->1,
     DisplayFunction->Identity];
ppthree=ParametricPlot[{x[t],y[t]},{t,0,2Pi},
     AspectRatio->1,
     Ticks->None,
     DisplayFunction->Identity];
ppfour=ParametricPlot[{x[t],y[t]},{t,0,2Pi},
     AspectRatio->1,
     Ticks->None,
     Frame->True,
     DisplayFunction->Identity];
Show[GraphicsArray[{{ppone,pptwo},
     {ppthree,ppfour}}]]
```

The four graphics objects are finally displayed as a graphics array.

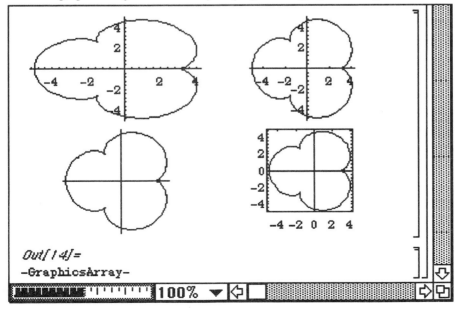

Out[14]=

-GraphicsArray-

Example 25:

AxesOrigin is demonstrated below with the plot generated in **ppone** above. However, in this case, **AxesOrigin->{-20,0}** causes the axes to meet at the point (−20,0) instead of the origin.

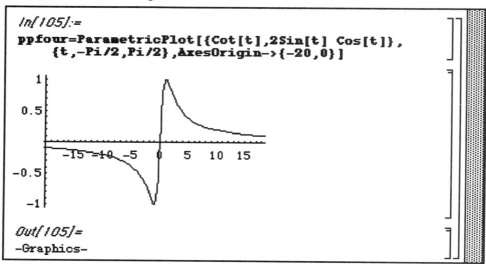

Example 26:

The function $f(x) = Sin(x^2)$ is plotted below with a basic **Plot** command with no additional options.

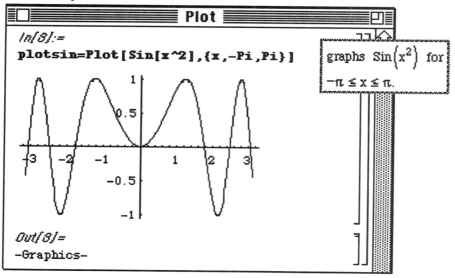

Example 27:

The **Axes** option is demonstrated below. The inclusion of **Axes->None** in the **Plot** command causes no axes to be included in the graph.

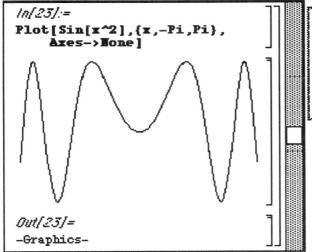

graphs $\mathrm{Sin}\left(x^2\right)$ for $-\pi \leq x \leq \pi$ and then displays the resulting graph without any axes.

Example 28:

The following example illustrates the **AxesLabel** option. In this case, the x- and y-axes are labeled.

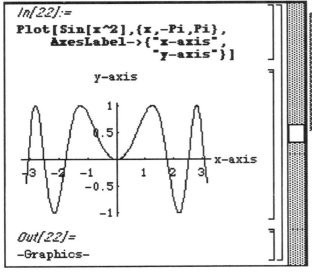

graphs $\mathrm{Sin}\left(x^2\right)$ for $-\pi \leq x \leq \pi$ and then labels the x-axis "x-axis" and the y-axis "y-axis."

Example 29:

The example below shows how the **AxesOrigin** affects the graph. Here, the axes meet at the point $(-\pi, 0)$ as opposed to $(0,0)$.

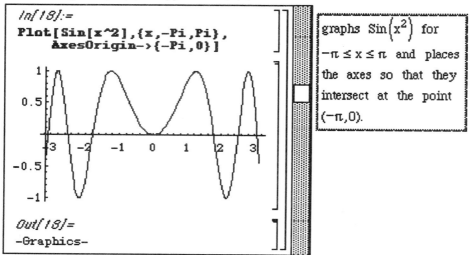

graphs $\text{Sin}\left(x^2\right)$ for $-\pi \le x \le \pi$ and places the axes so that they intersect at the point $(-\pi, 0)$.

Example 30:

Below, the **BackGround** option is demonstrated. In this case, the background of the plot is shaded according to the setting **GrayLevel[.8]**.

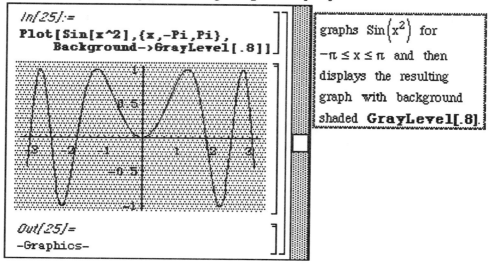

graphs $\text{Sin}\left(x^2\right)$ for $-\pi \le x \le \pi$ and then displays the resulting graph with background shaded **GrayLevel[.8]**.

Example 31:

The **Compiled** option is included in the following command. In this case, the function is not compiled before it is graphed. The computation time is shown below for comparison.

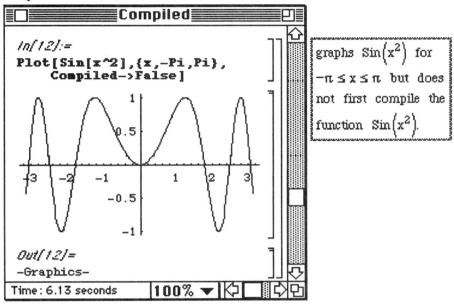

Example 32:

In the example below, the function f(x) = x Sin (x) is plotted according to the setting **GrayLevel[.2]**.

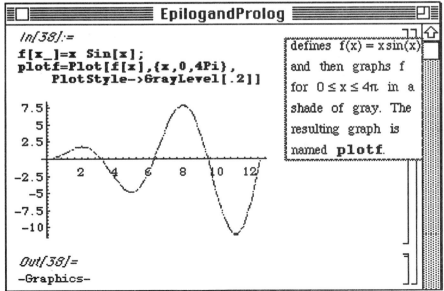

In **plottwo**, the plot called **plotf** generated above is again displayed. However, in this case, the tangent line to the curve at the point $(2\pi,0)$ is included after **plotf** is rendered using the directives included in the **Epilog** option.

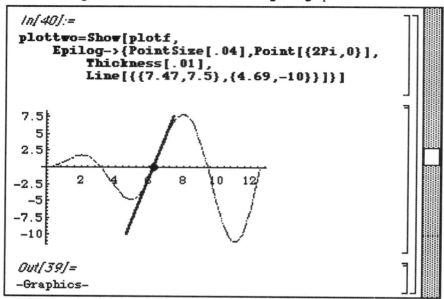

Next, in **plotthree**, the directives included in the **Prolog** option are used to generate **plotf** as well as the tangent line.

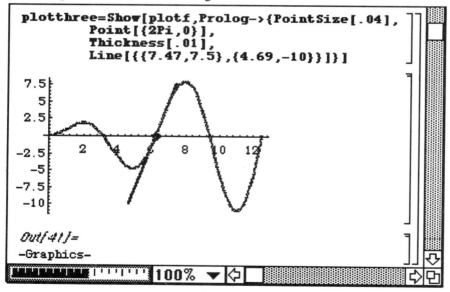

Example 33:

The following example illustrates how *Mathematica* places gridlines automatically with the option setting **GridLines->Automatic**.

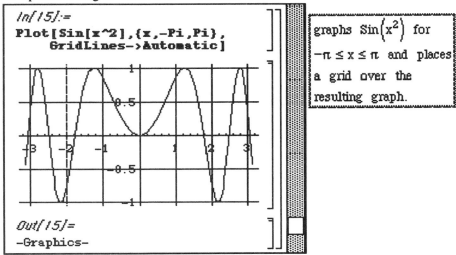

```
In[15]:=
Plot[Sin[x^2],{x,-Pi,Pi},
    GridLines->Automatic]
```

graphs $Sin\left(x^2\right)$ for $-\pi \le x \le \pi$ and places a grid over the resulting graph.

```
Out[15]=
-Graphics-
```

Example 34:

In the following example, f(x)=x sin(x). In both cases, f is graphed for $0 \le x \le \pi$. In the second case, the option **PlotRange->{0,1/2}** causes the set of numbers to be displayed on the vertical axis to correspond to the interval [0,1/2].

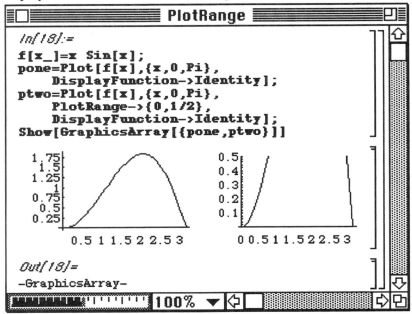

```
PlotRange

In[18]:=
f[x_]=x Sin[x];
pone=Plot[f[x],{x,0,Pi},
    DisplayFunction->Identity];
ptwo=Plot[f[x],{x,0,Pi},
    PlotRange->{0,1/2},
    DisplayFunction->Identity];
Show[GraphicsArray[{pone,ptwo}]]

Out[18]=
-GraphicsArray-
```

Example 35:

The **PlotStyle** option setting of **GrayLevel[.3]** is illustrated below. This setting causes the curve to be printed as gray instead of black.

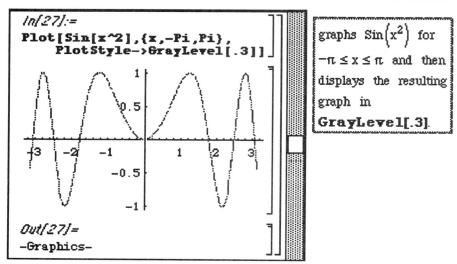

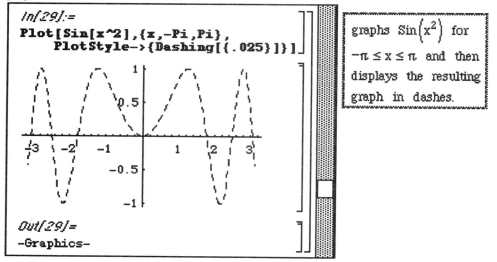

The **Dashing** setting for **PlotStyle** is demonstrated in the following example. In this case, the length of each segment of the dashed line is .025 of the total width of the graph.

Example 36:

The **DisplayFunction** option is illustrated below. In the first example, a set of six graphs of **Nest[Sin,x,n]** for $0 \leq x \leq 2\pi$ and n=1, 3, ...,11 are created with the command **plot**, which is defined to remember the values it computes, and then partitioned into an array. The graphs are not displayed since the option **DisplayFunction->Identity** is included in the definition of **plot**. The graphs are displayed as a graphics array using the commands **Show** and **GraphicsArray**. In the second plot called **pgone**, the setting **Identity** is used. This causes the graph to be suppressed initially. The setting of **$DisplayFunction** causes the plot to be displayed.

```
═══ DisplayFunction ═══
In[71]:=
plot[n_]:=plot[n]=Plot[Nest[Sin,x,n],
    {x,0,2Pi},DisplayFunction->
                Identity]
array=Partition[
    Table[plot[n],{n,1,11,2}],3]
Out[71]=
{{-Graphics-, -Graphics-, -Graphics-},
  {-Graphics-, -Graphics-, -Graphics-}}
```

```
In[72]:=
Show[GraphicsArray[array]]
```

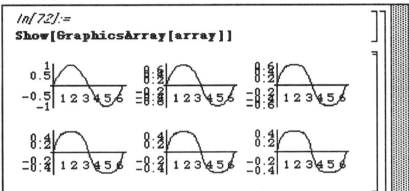

```
In[9]:=
pgone=Plot[Sin[x^2],{x,-Pi,Pi},
    DisplayFunction->Identity]
Out[9]=
-Graphics-

In[10]:=
Show[pgone,
    DisplayFunction->$DisplayFunction]
```

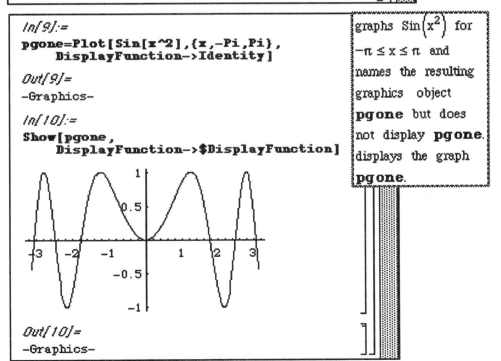

```
Out[10]=
-Graphics-
```

graphs $\mathrm{Sin}\left(x^2\right)$ for $-\pi \le x \le \pi$ and names the resulting graphics object **pgone** but does not display **pgone**. displays the graph **pgone**.

Example 37:

The following example illustrates the use of the **Cuboid** graphics primitive. **cubeone** represents the unit cube with opposite corners at (0,0,0) and (1,1,1). Also, **cubetwo** represents the cuboid with opposite corners at (2,4,5) and (3,7,8). Both cuboids are displayed within the same graphics cell.

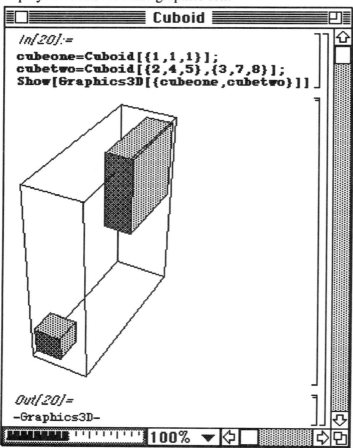

Example 38:

The **Line** graphics primitive is illustrated in several different forms below. **lineone** represents the line through the points (−4,4,2) and (−1,−3,−2). **linetwo** represents the line segments passing through the three points (−5,−1,1), (0,0,3), and (−3,3,1) and is printed according to the directive **Thickness[.02]**. Since the default value for the **Thickness** index is **.001** for three-dimensional graphics, **linetwo** appears thicker than the other two lines. Finally, **linethree** represents the line segments connecting the points (−1,−5,0), (0,4,5), (1,−1,0), and (−4,0,3). In addition to the **Thickness[.01]** graphics primitive, **linethree** is printed as a dashed line according to the directive **Dashing[{.01,.02}]**. This causes the line to be dashed with consecutive line segments of lengths .01 and .02 (which are repeated cyclically) of the total width of the graph.

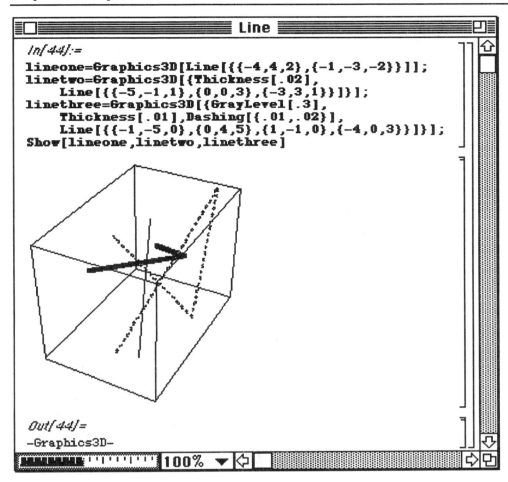

```
In[44]:=
lineone=Graphics3D[Line[{{-4,4,2},{-1,-3,-2}}]];
linetwo=Graphics3D[{Thickness[.02],
    Line[{{-5,-1,1},{0,0,3},{-3,3,1}}]}];
linethree=Graphics3D[{GrayLevel[.3],
    Thickness[.01],Dashing[{.01,.02}],
    Line[{{-1,-5,0},{0,4,5},{1,-1,0},{-4,0,3}}]}];
Show[lineone,linetwo,linethree]
```

```
Out[44]=
-Graphics3D-
```

Example 39:
In the example below, the **Point** graphics primitive is demonstrated. The point at (0,0,0) is represented with **pointone**. Since the default value of the **PointSize** directive is **.01** for three-dimensional graphics, the point represented by **pointone** is the smallest point displayed. The index of **PointSize** is increased to **.05** in **pointtwo**. Hence, the point at (1,1,1) is larger than the one at (0,0,0). The index for **PointSize** is increased to **.075** in **pointthree**, so the point at (2,2,2) is the largest of the three points. In addition, the **GrayLevel[.3]** directive is used, so **pointthree** is shaded as well.

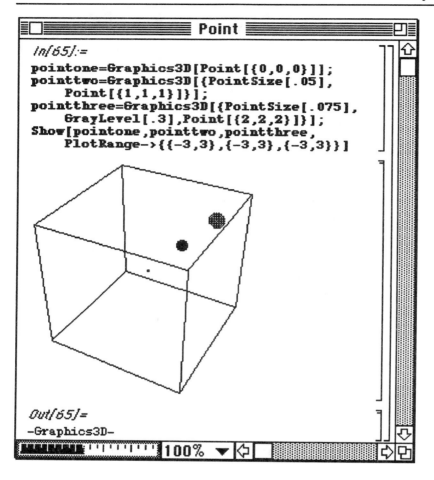

```
In[65]:=
pointone=Graphics3D[Point[{0,0,0}]];
pointtwo=Graphics3D[{PointSize[.05],
    Point[{1,1,1}]}];
pointthree=Graphics3D[{PointSize[.075],
    GrayLevel[.3],Point[{2,2,2}]}];
Show[pointone,pointtwo,pointthree,
    PlotRange->{{-3,3},{-3,3},{-3,3}}]
```

```
Out[65]=
-Graphics3D-
```

Example 40:

In the following example, the **Polygon** graphics primitive is illustrated. First, in **polyone**, the triangle with corners at (–7,–8,7), (4,10,–6), and (–9,–2,7) is created.

Next, in **polytwo**, the shaded triangle with corners (–1,7,5), (3,9,2), and (–7,–10,–5) is created using the **GrayLevel[.5]** directive. Hence, **polytwo** appears in the lighter print.

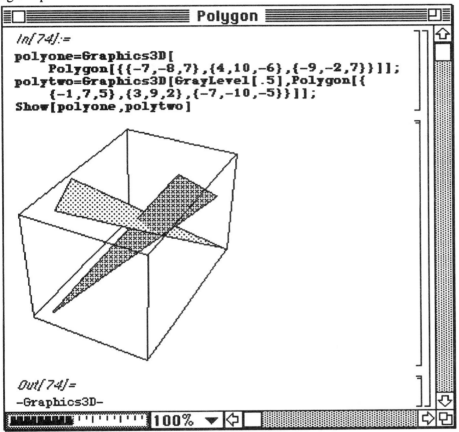

Example 41:

The following example illustrates the use of **ListPlot3D**. In this case, a list of three-dimensional points is given in **wcf**. A function **f** is then defined which drops the last two elements of any list to which **f** is applied. Finally, this function is applied to the elements of **wcf**, and **Flatten** is applied to the result. The list which is obtained is named **first**, because it contains the first coordinate of each point in **wcf**.

```
========================= ListPlot3D ===========================

In[31]:=
wcf={{35,5,33},{35,15,16},{35,25,8},
    {35,35,4},{35,45,2},{25,5,21},{25,15,2},
    {25,25,-7},{25,35,-12},{25,45,-14},
    {15,5,12},{15,15,-11},{15,25,-22},
    {15,35,-27},{15,45,-30},{5,5,0},
    {5,15,-25},{5,25,-36},{5,35,-43},
    {5,45,-46},{-5,5,-10},{-5,15,-38},
    {-5,25,-51},{-5,35,-58},{-5,45,-62},
    {-15,5,-21},{-15,15,-51},{-15,25,-66},
    {-15,35,-74},{-15,45,-78},{-25,5,-31},
    {-25,15,-65},{-25,25,-81},{-25,35,-89},
    {-25,45,-93}};
f[a_]:=Drop[a,2]
first=Map[f,wcf]//Flatten

Out[31]=
{33, 16, 8, 4, 2, 21, 2, -7, -12, -14, 12, -11,
  -22, -27, -30, 0, -25, -36, -43, -46, -10, -38,
  -51, -58, -62, -21, -51, -66, -74, -78, -31,
  -65, -81, -89, -93}
```

Since the list **first** is not an array, the command **Partition** is used to partition **first** into five element subsets. The resulting array is named **second**.

```
In[32]:=
second=Partition[first,5]

Out[32]=
{{33, 16, 8, 4, 2}, {21, 2, -7, -12, -14},
  {12, -11, -22, -27, -30},
  {0, -25, -36, -43, -46},
  {-10, -38, -51, -58, -62},
  {-21, -51, -66, -74, -78},
  {-31, -65, -81, -89, -93}}
```

Finally, **ListPlot3D** is used to graph **second**.

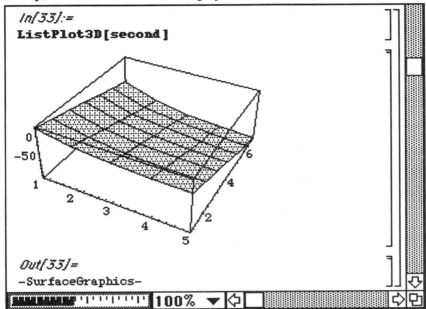

Example 42:

The example below illustrates how *Mathematica* can be used to produce fractals. The function **man** has real arguments **x** and **y**, complex argument **c**, and integer argument **max**. The **While** loop serves to nest the function **f**. After **man** is defined, a random complex number **c** is found to use as the argument of **man**. A table of **man** function values is created in **one** and saved as **datafile**.

```
 Graphics3DOptions

In[19]:=
man[x_,y_,c_,max_:12]:=Module[{f,z,n},
    f[z_]:=z^2+c;
    z=x+I y;
    n=0;
    While[And[Abs[z]<2,n<max],
        PreIncrement[n];
        z=f[z]
        ];
    Return[n/max];
                                    ]

In[27]:=
c=Random[Complex,{-1/3-1/3 I,1/3+1/3I}]

Out[27]=
0.238465 + 0.258619 I

In[29]:=
Clear[one]

In[31]:=
one=Table[man[x,y,c],{x,-1,1,2/30},{y,-1,1,2/30}];
one>>datafile
```

The file **datafile** is assigned the name **numbers** for later use.

```
In[2]:=
numbers=<<datafile;
```

Below, **ListPlot** is used to plot the data points found in **numbers**. **lpone** produces the graphics with the basic **ListPlot** command. The mesh and axes are removed in **lptwo**. The **ViewVertical** option is illustrated in **lpthree**. **lpfour** demonstrates the options **PlotRange**, **ClipFill**, and **MeshStyle**. In **lpfive**, the **MeshStyle** and **Lighting** options are applied to the graphics in **lpthree**.

```
In[28]:=
lpone=ListPlot3D[numbers,
    DisplayFunction->Identity];
lptwo=Show[lpone,Mesh->False,
    Axes->False];
lpthree=Show[lpone,MeshStyle->{GrayLevel[.8]},
    ViewVertical->{1,0,0}];
lpfour=Show[lpone,PlotRange->{0,.75},
    ClipFill->None,MeshStyle->{GrayLevel[.8]}];
lpfive=Show[lpthree,
    MeshStyle->{GrayLevel[.8]},
    Lighting->False];
Show[GraphicsArray[{{lptwo,lpthree},
    {lpfour,lpfive}}]]
```

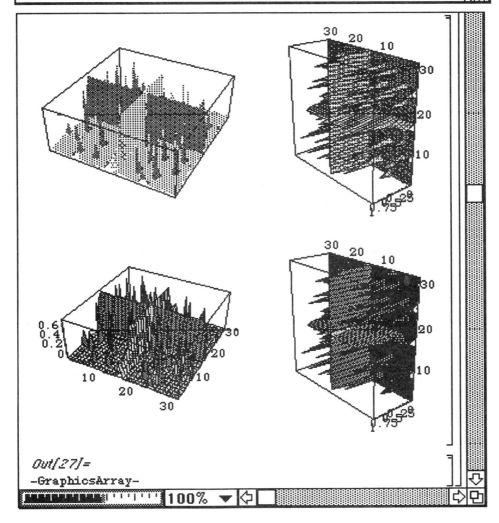

```
Out[27]=
-GraphicsArray-
```

Example 43:

Several **ParametricPlot3D** options are demonstrated in the following example.
ppone represents the parametric plot of the three-dimensional function defined by
x(t)= 3 cos(4t + 1), y(t) = cos(2t + 1), z(t) = 4 cos(2t + 5). In **pptwo**, the box which
normally accompanies a **ParametricPlot3D** object is eliminated with the option
setting **Boxed->False**. In addition to this option, **ppthree** includes
Axes->False, so the axes are also omitted in this plot. Finally, the option setting
BoxRatios->{1,1,1} is added to the list of options, so the ratio of the side lengths
of the bounding box (which is not displayed) in **ppfour** is 1:1:1. Note that in each
case, the option **DisplayFunction->Identity** is used to initially suppress the
display of these graphs. All four are then shown with the last command by using
DisplayFunction->$DisplayFunction with **Show**.

```
In[63]:=
x[t_]=3Cos[4t+1];
y[t_]=Cos[2t+3];
z[t_]=4Cos[2t+5];
ppone=ParametricPlot3D[
    {x[t],y[t],z[t]},{t,0,Pi},
    DisplayFunction->Identity];
pptwo=ParametricPlot3D[
    {x[t],y[t],z[t]},{t,0,Pi},
    Boxed->False,
    DisplayFunction->Identity];
ppthree=ParametricPlot3D[
    {x[t],y[t],z[t]},{t,0,Pi},
    Boxed->False,
    Axes->False,
    DisplayFunction->Identity];
ppfour=ParametricPlot3D[
    {x[t],y[t],z[t]},{t,0,Pi},
    Boxed->False,
    Axes->False,
    BoxRatios->{1,1,1},
    DisplayFunction->Identity];
Show[GraphicsArray[{{ppone,pptwo},
    {ppthree,ppfour}}]];
```

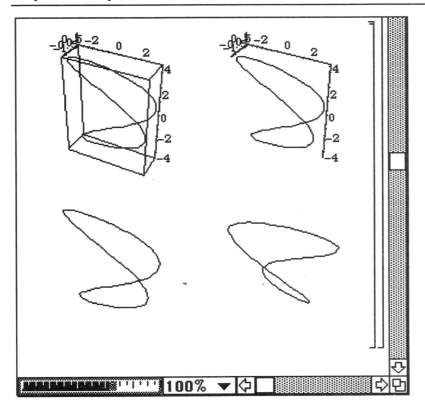

Example 44:
The following example illustrates how **ParametricPlot3D** can be used to produce a solid of revolution. In this case, the function f(x) = x sin(x) is rotated about the x-axis. In order to use **ParametricPlot3D**, appropriate functions for x, y, and z must be defined. Making use of polar coordinates, these functions become x(r,t) = r, y(r,t) = f(r) cos(t), and z(t) = f(r) sin(t). Notice that these parametric equations depend on two independent variables. In **ppone** below, the solid of revolution is produced using only the option **DisplayFunction->Identity** to suppress the display. In **pptwo**, however, the option setting **Background->GrayLevel[.7]** is used, so the background in this plot is shaded. Finally, both of these plots are displayed in a **GraphicsArray** to note their differences.

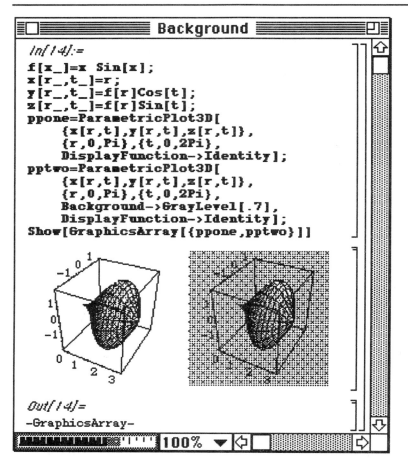

Example 45:

The following example illustrates the use of several **ParametricPlot3D** options. In this case, a solid of revolution is produced with **ParametricPlot3D** by revolving a function f(x) = sin(2x) about the y-axis. Therefore, with the aid of polar coordinates, the appropriate functions for x, y, and z are x(r,t) = r cos(t), y(r,t) = r sin(t), and z(r,t) = f(r). After defining these functions, the solid of revolution created with only the use of **DisplayFunction->Identity** is given in **ppone**. Then, in **pptwo**, the option setting **ViewPoint->{-0.010,-0.390,1.330}** is used. When these two plots are displayed in the **GraphicsArray** below, the difference in the viewpoint used in each is obvious.

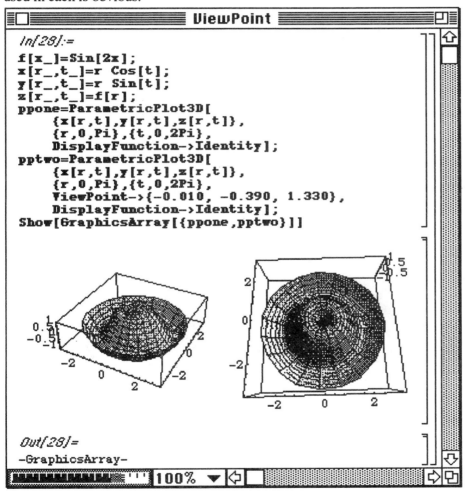

```
In[28]:=
f[x_]=Sin[2x];
x[r_,t_]=r Cos[t];
y[r_,t_]=r Sin[t];
z[r_,t_]=f[r];
ppone=ParametricPlot3D[
    {x[r,t],y[r,t],z[r,t]},
    {r,0,Pi},{t,0,2Pi},
    DisplayFunction->Identity];
pptwo=ParametricPlot3D[
    {x[r,t],y[r,t],z[r,t]},
    {r,0,Pi},{t,0,2Pi},
    ViewPoint->{-0.010, -0.390, 1.330},
    DisplayFunction->Identity];
Show[GraphicsArray[{ppone,pptwo}]]
```

```
Out[28]=
-GraphicsArray-
```

Example 46:

In the following example, x(s,t)=sin(t)cos(s), y(s,t)=sin(t)sin(s), and z(s,t)=cos(s). The command **SetOptions** is used to set the default font for the command **ParametricPlot3D** to be 10-point Times.

```
≡□□≡≡≡≡≡≡≡≡≡≡ Graphics3DOptions ≡≡≡≡≡≡≡≡≡□⌐≡

 In[36]:=
 x[s_,t_]:=Sin[t]Cos[s];
 y[s_,t_]:=Sin[t]Sin[s];
 z[s_,t_]:=Cos[t];

 In[38]:=
 SetOptions[ParametricPlot3D,
     DefaultFont:>{"Times",10}];
```

The command **ParametricPlot3D** is used to graph x(s,t)=sin(t)cos(s), y(s,t)=sin(t)sin(s), and z(s,t)=cos(s) for $0 \leq s \leq 2\pi$ and $0 \leq t \leq 2\pi$. The option **PlotLabel->"Unit Sphere"** causes the resulting graphics object to be labeled "Unit Sphere". Observe that all characters printed in the final graphics object are 10-point Times.

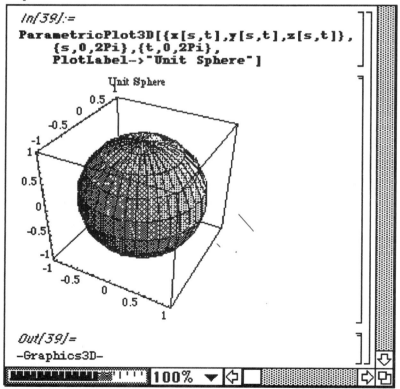

```
 In[39]:=
 ParametricPlot3D[{x[s,t],y[s,t],z[s,t]},
     {s,0,2Pi},{t,0,2Pi},
     PlotLabel->"Unit Sphere"]
```

```
 Out[39]=
 -Graphics3D-
```

Although not discussed in this book, the folder (or directory) **Graphics** contains several packages containing a variety of built-in commands for constructing various graphics objects. In particular, the package **Shapes** contains many familiar three-dimensional shapes like the sphere, Moebius strip, torus, and helix.

Example 47:
This example illustrates a basic **Plot3D** command. In this case, the function of two variables f(x,y) = cos(sin(x) + cos(y)) is plotted over the rectangular region for values of x between 0 and 2π and values of y between $-\pi$ and π. Note that no options are employed.

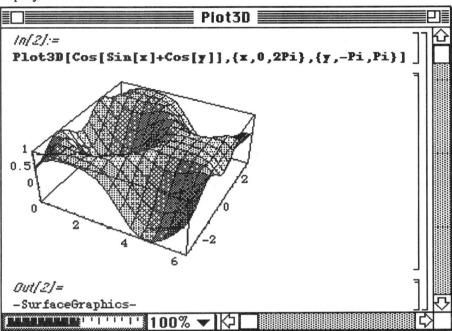

```
In[2]:=
Plot3D[Cos[Sin[x]+Cos[y]],{x,0,2Pi},{y,-Pi,Pi}]
```

```
Out[2]=
-SurfaceGraphics-
```

Example 48:
The example below illustrates the several **Plot3D** options. First the piece-wise defined function

$$f(x,y) = \begin{cases} x^2 + y^2; x, y < 0, \ x, y > 0 \\ -\left(x^2 + y^2\right); \ x \le 0 \text{ and } y \ge 0, \ x > 0 \text{ and } y < 0 \end{cases}$$

is defined. In **plotfone**, the options **Shading->False** is used which eliminates shading. Also, **PlotPoints->25** yields a smoother plot since the default setting is 15. In **plotftwo**, **Mesh->False** causes the mesh to be removed, and **SphericalRegion->True** causes the region to be scaled in such a way that a sphere drawn around the bounding box fits the specified display region. In **plotfthree**, the options **ClipFill->None** and **ViewCenter->{-2,-2,-2}** are included. The setting of **ViewCenter** represents the scaled coordinates of the point which appears at the center of the display region. In **plotffour**, the option settings **ClipFill->None** and **PlotRange->{-18,18}** cause holes to be placed in the surface where it is clipped. Note that **DisplayFunction->Identity** is used in each command to suppress the display.

```
═══════════════════════ ClipFill ═══════════════════════

In[2]:=
f[x_,y_]:=x^2+y^2  /;  x<=0  &&  y<=0  ||  x>0  &&  y>=0
f[x_,y_]:=-(x^2+y^2)  /;  x<=0  &&  y>=0  ||  x>0  &&  y<=0

In[6]:=
plotfone=Plot3D[f[x,y],{x,-3,3},{y,-3,3},
    Shading->False,
    PlotPoints->25,DisplayFunction->Identity];
plotftwo=Plot3D[f[x,y],{x,-3,3},{y,-3,3},
    Mesh->False,
    SphericalRegion->True,
    PlotPoints->25,DisplayFunction->Identity];
plotfthree=Plot3D[f[x,y],{x,-3,3},{y,-3,3},
    ClipFill->None,
    ViewCenter->{-2,-2,-2},
    SphericalRegion->True,
    PlotPoints->25,DisplayFunction->Identity];
plotffour=Plot3D[f[x,y],{x,-4,4},{y,-4,4},
    ClipFill->None,
    PlotRange->{-18,18},
    SphericalRegion->True,
    PlotPoints->25,DisplayFunction->Identity];
```

The four plots are displayed in pairs below in a **GraphicsArray**.

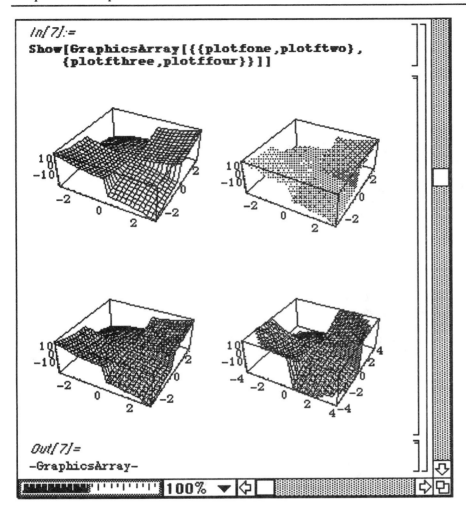

In[7]:=
```
Show[GraphicsArray[{{plotfone,plotftwo},
    {plotfthree,plotffour}}]]
```

Out[7]=
-GraphicsArray-

Example 49:
The following example illustrates how **Plot3D** is used to plot the tangent plane to a surface at a particular point. In this case, the surface is given by

$$f(x,y) = \cos(x^2 + y^2)e^{-(x^2+y^2)/10}.$$

This surface is plotted in pone with **PlotPoints->25** to generate a smoother plot than with the default setting of **PlotPoints->15**. The tangent plane to the surface at the point $(-2,1)$ is then determined by evaluating the first order partial derivatives of f at $(-2,1)$ in **dfx** and **dfy**. The tangent plane is then defined by z and plotted in **tan** using **PlotPoints->20**. Finally, the surface and tangent plane are displayed together in a **GraphicsArray**.

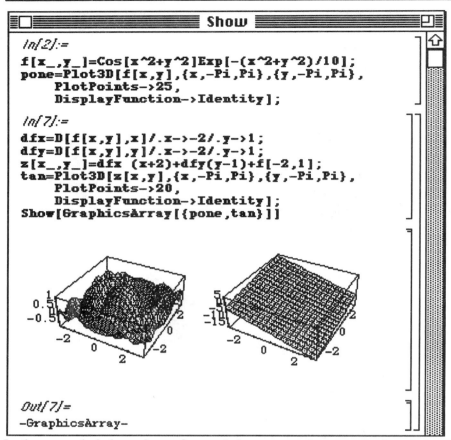

```
≡□≡≡≡≡≡≡≡≡≡≡≡≡≡≡ Show ≡≡≡≡≡≡≡≡≡≡≡≡□≡

In[2]:=

f[x_,y_]=Cos[x^2+y^2]Exp[-(x^2+y^2)/10];
pone=Plot3D[f[x,y],{x,-Pi,Pi},{y,-Pi,Pi},
     PlotPoints->25,
     DisplayFunction->Identity];

In[7]:=

dfx=D[f[x,y],x]/.x->-2/.y->1;
dfy=D[f[x,y],y]/.x->-2/.y->1;
z[x_,y_]=dfx (x+2)+dfy(y-1)+f[-2,1];
tan=Plot3D[z[x,y],{x,-Pi,Pi},{y,-Pi,Pi},
     PlotPoints->20,
     DisplayFunction->Identity];
Show[GraphicsArray[{pone,tan}]]
```

```
Out[7]=
-GraphicsArray-
```

In the example below, the surface and the tangent plane are displayed simultaneously. Because the option settings **Boxed->False** and **Axes->None** are used, the bounding box and axes are eliminated from the plot. Also, **PlotRange->{-1,1}** allows only points which yield z-values on this interval to be included in the plot.

```
In[8]:=
bothone=Show[pone,tan,
    Boxed->False,Axes->None,
    PlotRange->{-1,1},
    DisplayFunction->$DisplayFunction]
```

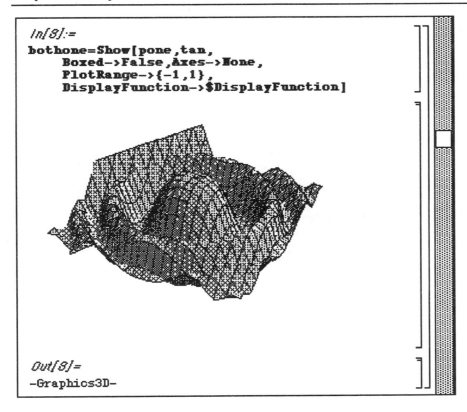

```
Out[8]=
-Graphics3D-
```

This example shows how the **ViewPoint** option can be used to improve the view of the plot. In this case, the view point is defined as (.553,– 1.225,–3.318) so that the tangent plane can be seen from below the surface.

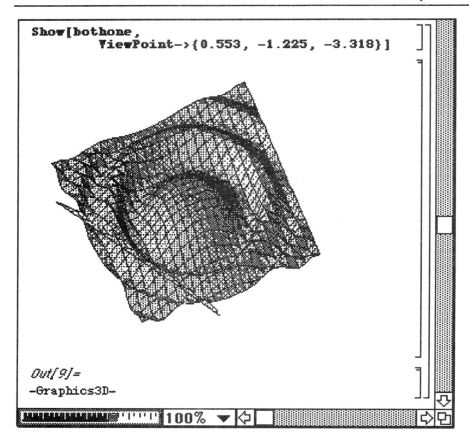

```
Show[bothone,
      ViewPoint->{0.553, -1.225, -3.318}]
```

Out[9]=
-Graphics3D-

100% ▼

Example 50:
The following two examples illustrate the **AxesLabel** and **LightSources** options.

The first example graphs the function $x^2y^2e^{-x^2-y^2}$. The option
AxesLabel->{"x-axis","y-axis","z-axis"} causes the axes to be labeled
x-axis, y-axis, and z-axis, respectively. The option **Boxed->False** causes the final
object to be displayed without a surrounding box. The second example illustrates the
LightSources option by graphing $J_y(x)$ for $0 \le x \le 25$ and $0 \le y \le 4$ where $J_y(x)$
denotes the Bessel function of the first kind of order y. Note that in situations where
color is desired, **GrayLevel** may be replaced by **RGBColor** or **Hue**.

Graphics3DOptions

In[40]:=

```
Plot3D[x^2y^2Exp[-x^2-y^2],
    {x,-3/2,3/2},{y,-3/2,3/2},
    AxesLabel->{"x-axis","y-axis",
        "z-axis"},Boxed->False]
```

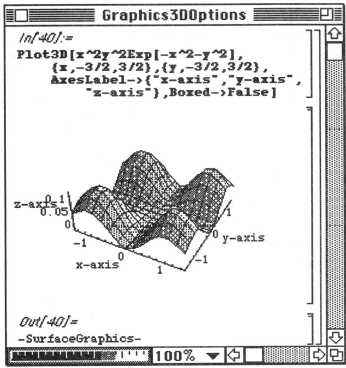

Out[40]=
-SurfaceGraphics-

100% ▼

LightSources

In[56]:=

```
Plot3D[BesselJ[y,x],{x,0,25},
    {y,0,4},LightSources->
    {{{25/2,2,2},GrayLevel[1]},
        {{25/2,2,-2},GrayLevel[1]}}]
```

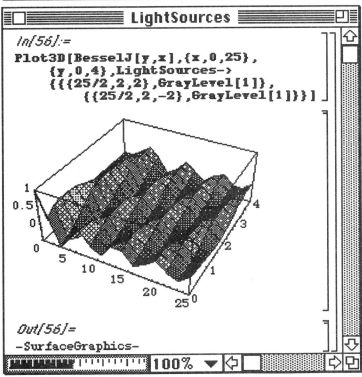

Out[56]=
-SurfaceGraphics-

100% ▼

Example 51:

The example below, illustrates several **Plot3D** options. The **Ticks** option causes tick marks to be placed only on the z-axis where they are placed automatically. The function is given as the label of the graph with **PlotLabel** option. Fifty sample points are used in the x and y directions with the setting of **PlotPoints**. This produces a smoother graph than that given with the default setting of **PlotPoints**. The mesh is removed from the surface of the plot with the setting of **Mesh**. The point $(-0.010, -1.090, 1.610)$ is used as the setting of **Viewpoint**. The range is limited to values of z on the interval $[0, .05]$ with the **PlotRange** setting. Also, the **ClipFill** option is demonstrated.

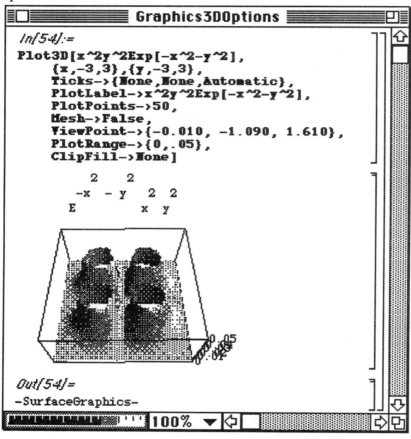

Example 52:
Several **Plot3D** options are illustrated in the graph below. No axes or shading are included since the options **Axes->False** and **Shading->False** are used. In addition, forty sample points are taken in both of the x and y directions with the setting **PlotPoints->40**. Grid lines are placed on the faces of the bounding box because of the option setting **FaceGrids->All**. Finally, **GrayLevel[.7]** is used to render the mesh because of the option **MeshStyle->GrayLevel[.7]**.

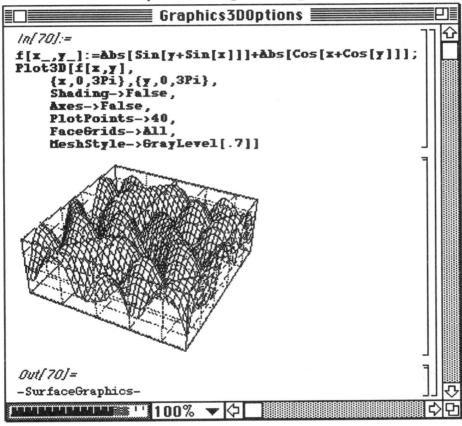

```
▤□▦▦▦▦▦▦▦▦▦▦ Graphics3DOptions ▦▦▦▦▦▦▦▦▦▦▥▦
 In[70]:=
 f[x_,y_]:=Abs[Sin[y+Sin[x]]]+Abs[Cos[x+Cos[y]]];
 Plot3D[f[x,y],
     {x,0,3Pi},{y,0,3Pi},
     Shading->False,
     Axes->False,
     PlotPoints->40,
     FaceGrids->All,
     MeshStyle->GrayLevel[.7]]
```

```
 Out[70]=
 -SurfaceGraphics-
```

Calculus Packages

The packages contained in the folder (or directory) **Calculus** are
FourierTransform, **LaplaceTransform**, **Pade**, and **VectorAnalysis**.

FourierTransform.m

The commands in the package **FourierTransform.m** are used to compute the
Fourier transform and Fourier series of functions. Use the built-in commands
Fourier and **InverseFourier** to compute discrete Fourier transforms of lists of
data. The commands **FourierTransform**, **FourierCosTransform**,
FourierSinTransform, **FourierExpSeries**, **FourierTrigSeries**,
FourierExpSeriesCoefficient, **FourierCosSeriesCoefficient**, and
FourierSinSeriesCoefficient can be used when *Mathematica* can compute
the required definite integrals. Otherwise, the numerical analogs (those commands
preceded with **N**) of these commands should be employed. In general, the numerical
commands are much faster than the others.

FourierTransform   Package: **FourierTransform.m**
FourierTransform[expression,t,w] yields the Fourier transform of
expression which is considered a function of t. Hence, the Fourier transform is
given in terms of w. This transform, $F(\omega)$, is determined with the formula

$$F(\omega) = A\int_{-\infty}^{\infty} f(t)e^{Bi\,\omega\,t} \, dt$$ where the values of A and B can be changed with the

settings of **$OverallFourierConstant** and
$FourierFrequencyConstant, respectively. The defaults for these
values are A = 1 and B = 1.

InverseFourierTransform
                           Package: **FourierTransform.m**
InverseFourierTransform[expression,w,t] yields the inverse
Fourier transform of **expression** which is considered a function of w. Therefore,
the inverse Fourier transform is given as a function of t and is based on the formula

$$f(t) = \frac{B}{2A\pi}\int_{-\infty}^{\infty} F(\omega)e^{-Bi\,\omega\,t} d\omega$$ where the values of A and B can be changed with

the settings of **$OverallFourierConstant** and
$FourierFrequencyConstant, respectively. The defaults for these values
are A = 1 and B = 1.

Delta   Package: **FourierTransform.m**,
                                 LaplaceTransform.m
Delta[t] represents Dirac's delta function with maximum value at $t = 0$ while

Delta[a+bt] yields the delta function with maximum at $t = -\dfrac{a}{b}$.

$OverallFourierConstant
                    Package: **FourierTransform.m**
  $OverallFourierConstant is used to set the value of A found in the formulas for the Fourier and inverse Fourier transforms. The default setting is A = 1.

$FourierFrequencyConstant
                    Package: **FourierTransform.m**
  $FourierFrequencyConstant is used to set the value of B found in the formulas for the Fourier and inverse Fourier transforms. The default setting is B = 1.

FourierCosTransform Package: **FourierTransform.m**
  FourierCosTransform[expression,t,w] yields the Fourier transform of **expression** which is considered a function of t. Hence, the Fourier cosine transform defined by $A \int_0^\infty f(t) \cos(Bi\,\omega t)\, dt$ is given as a function of w. The values of A and B are set with **$OverallFourierConstant** and **$FourierFrequencyConstant**, respectively. The defaults for these values are A = 1 and B = 1.

FourierSinTransform Package: **FourierTransform.m**
  FourierSinTransform[expression,t,w] yields the Fourier transform of **expression** which is considered a function of t. Hence, the Fourier cosine transform defined by $A \int_0^\infty f(t) \sin(Bi\omega t)\, dt$ is given as a function of w. The values of A and B are set with **$OverallFourierConstant** and **$FourierFrequencyConstant**, respectively. The defaults for these values are A = 1 and B = 1.

FourierExpSeries   Package: **FourierTransform.m**
  FourierExpSeries[f,{x,x0,x1},n] yields the nth order exponential Fourier series expansion for the function **f** which is periodic on the interval **(x0,x1)**. This series is represented by $\sum_{n=-\infty}^{\infty} f_n \exp\left(\frac{2\pi i n x}{x1 - x0}\right)$ where f_n represents the Fourier coefficients.
Example:
In the following example, f(x)=x. **FourierExpSeries** is used to compute the fourth order exponential Fourier series expansion for f on the interval (−1,1); the result is named **fes**.

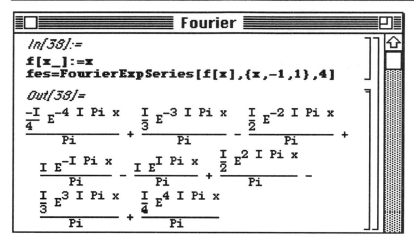

ComplexExpand is used to simplify **fes**.

To see that **fes** is an approximation of the periodic extension of f, prior definitions of f are first cleared, f is redefined to be periodic of period 2, and then the **Plot** command is used to graph both **fes** and f on the interval [0,4]. The graph of f appears dashed. Even though *Mathematica* produces an error message, which is not completely displayed, the resulting graph is correct.

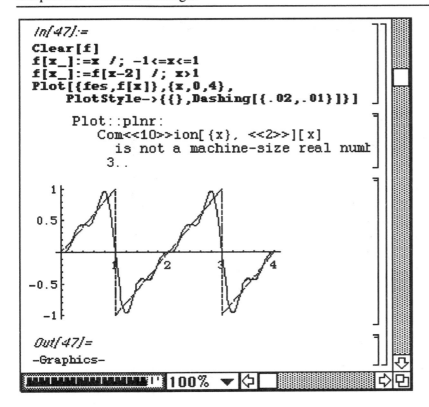

```
In[47]:=
Clear[f]
f[x_]:=x  /;  -1<=x<=1
f[x_]:=f[x-2] /;  x>1
Plot[{fes,f[x]},{x,0,4},
    PlotStyle->{{},Dashing[{.02,.01}]}]
```

```
Plot::plnr:
    Com<<10>>ion[{x}, <<2>>][x]
        is not a machine-size real numk
    3..
```

```
Out[47]=
-Graphics-
```

FourierTrigSeries   Package: FourierTransform.m

FourierTrigSeries[f,{x,x0,x1,n}] yields the nth order trigonometric Fourier series expansion for the function **f** which is periodic on the interval (**x0,x1**).

This series is represented by $\frac{1}{2}a_0 + \sum_{n=1}^{\infty}\left(a_n\cos\left(\frac{2n\pi x}{x1-x0}\right) + b_n\sin\left(\frac{2n\pi x}{x1-x0}\right)\right)$. The

coefficients a_n and b_n are given by $a_n = \frac{2}{x1-x0}\int_{x0}^{x1}f(x)\cos\left(\frac{2n\pi x}{x1-x0}\right) dx$,

$n = 0, 1, 2, ...$, and $b_n = \frac{2}{x1-x0}\int_{x0}^{x1}f(x)\sin\left(\frac{2n\pi x}{x1-x0}\right) dx$, $n = 0, 1, 2, ...$.

Example:

In the following example, $f(x)=x^2-x+1$. **FourierTrigSeries** is used to compute the first five terms of the periodic extension of f on the interval $[-1,1]$; the result is named **fts**.

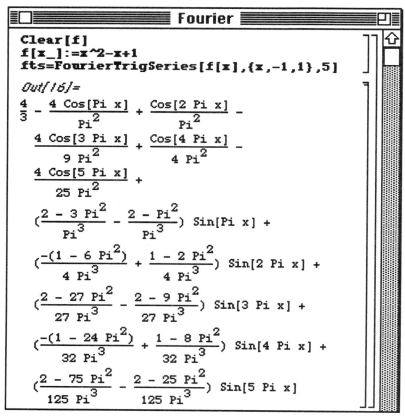

```
Clear[f]
f[x_]:=x^2-x+1
fts=FourierTrigSeries[f[x],{x,-1,1},5]
```

Out[16]=

$$\frac{4}{3} - \frac{4\,Cos[Pi\ x]}{Pi^2} + \frac{Cos[2\ Pi\ x]}{Pi^2} -$$

$$\frac{4\,Cos[3\ Pi\ x]}{9\ Pi^2} + \frac{Cos[4\ Pi\ x]}{4\ Pi^2} -$$

$$\frac{4\,Cos[5\ Pi\ x]}{25\ Pi^2} +$$

$$(\frac{2 - 3\ Pi^2}{Pi^3} - \frac{2 - Pi^2}{Pi^3})\ Sin[Pi\ x] +$$

$$(\frac{-(1 - 6\ Pi^2)}{4\ Pi^3} + \frac{1 - 2\ Pi^2}{4\ Pi^3})\ Sin[2\ Pi\ x] +$$

$$(\frac{2 - 27\ Pi^2}{27\ Pi^3} - \frac{2 - 9\ Pi^2}{27\ Pi^3})\ Sin[3\ Pi\ x] +$$

$$(\frac{-(1 - 24\ Pi^2)}{32\ Pi^3} + \frac{1 - 8\ Pi^2}{32\ Pi^3})\ Sin[4\ Pi\ x] +$$

$$(\frac{2 - 75\ Pi^2}{125\ Pi^3} - \frac{2 - 25\ Pi^2}{125\ Pi^3})\ Sin[5\ Pi\ x]$$

To see that **fts** is an approximation of the periodic extension of f, prior definitions of f are first cleared, f is redefined to be periodic of period 2, and then the **Plot** command is used to graph both **fts** and f on the interval [0,4]. The graph of f appears dashed.

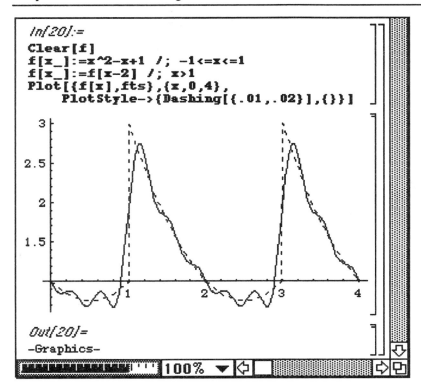

```
In[20]:=
Clear[f]
f[x_]:=x^2-x+1 /; -1<=x<=1
f[x_]:=f[x-2] /; x>1
Plot[{f[x],fts},{x,0,4},
    PlotStyle->{Dashing[{.01,.02}],{}}]
```

```
Out[20]=
-Graphics-
```

FourierCosSeriesCoefficient

Package: **FourierTransform.m**

FourierCosSeriesCoefficient[f,{x,x0,x1},n] yields the nth coefficient of the Fourier trigonometric series expansion for the function f which is even on the interval (**x0,x1**). This coefficient is

$$a_n = \frac{2}{x1 - x0} \int_{x0}^{x1} f(x)\cos\left(\frac{2n\pi x}{x1 - x0}\right) dx, \ n = 0, 1, 2, \dots .$$

FourierExpSeriesCoefficient

Package: **FourierTransform.m**

FourierExpSeriesCoefficient[f,{x,x0,x1},n] yields the nth coefficient of the Fourier exponential series expansion for the function f which is periodic on the interval (**x0,x1**). This coefficient is

$$f_n = \frac{1}{x1 - x0} \int_{x0}^{x1} f(x)\exp\left(\frac{2n\pi ix}{x1 - x0}\right) dx.$$

FourierSinSeriesCoefficient
Package: **FourierTransform.m**

FourierSinSeriesCoefficient[f,{x,x0,x1},n] yields the nth coefficient of the Fourier trigonometric series expansion for the function f which is odd on the interval (**x0,x1**). This coefficient is

$$b_n = \frac{2}{x1 - x0} \int_{x0}^{x1} f(x) \sin\left(\frac{2n\pi x}{x1 - x0}\right) dx.$$

Example:

In the following example, a_4, b_4, and f_4 are computed for $f(x) = x^2 - x + 1$, $-1 \le x \le 1$.

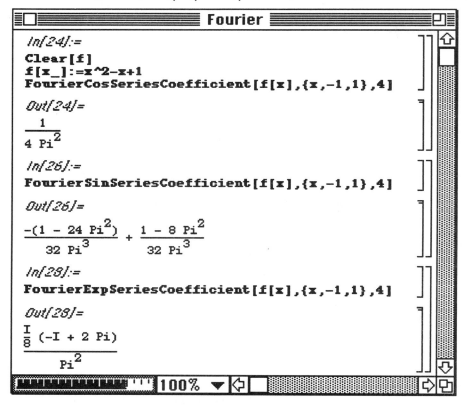

```
In[24]:=
Clear[f]
f[x_]:=x^2-x+1
FourierCosSeriesCoefficient[f[x],{x,-1,1},4]

Out[24]=
   1
 -----
      2
 4 Pi

In[26]:=
FourierSinSeriesCoefficient[f[x],{x,-1,1},4]

Out[26]=
         2              2
 -(1 - 24 Pi )   1 - 8 Pi
 ------------- + ---------
         3              3
   32 Pi          32 Pi

In[28]:=
FourierExpSeriesCoefficient[f[x],{x,-1,1},4]

Out[28]=
 I
 - (-I + 2 Pi)
 8
 -------------
          2
      Pi
```

NFourierTransform   Package: **FourierTransform.m**

NFourierTransform[f,t,w] yields the numerical value of the Fourier integral of **f**, a function of **t**, at **w**.

NFourierExpSeries   Package: **FourierTransform.m**

NFourierExpSeries[f,{x,x0,x1},n] yields the numerical approximation of the nth order exponential series expansion of **f** which is considered a periodic function of the variable x on the interval (x0,x1).

Example:

In the following example, $f(x) = \begin{cases} 1 & \text{if } 0 \le x \le 1 \\ 0 & \text{if } 1 < x \le 2 \end{cases}$. The command

f[x_]= f[x − 2] /; x > 2 defines f(x) for x ≥ 0 to be the

periodic extension of $f(x) = \begin{cases} 1 & \text{if } 0 \le x \le 1 \\ 0 & \text{if } 1 < x \le 2 \end{cases}$. f is then graphed

for $0 \le x \le 4$ and the resulting graph is named **plotf** for later

use.

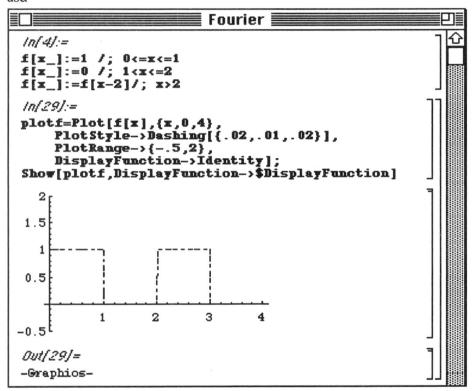

The commands **Table** and **NFourierExpSeries** are then used to create a table of
approximations of the nth order exponential series expansion of f which is considered a
periodic function of the variable x on the interval (0,2) for n=1, 2, 3, 4. The resulting
table is named **approxes** and displayed as a column with the command
ColumnForm. In this case, the result is rather long so the entire result is not displayed.

```
In[8]:=
approxes=Table[NFourierExpSeries[f[x],{x,0,2},n],
    {n,1,4}];
ColumnForm[approxes]

Out[8]=
                          -20                 -I Pi x
0.5 + 0. I + (2.12317 10     + 0.31831 I) E          +

            -20            I Pi x
  (2.12317 10    - 0.31831 I) E
                          -20           -21    -2 I Pi x
0.5 + 0. I + (-1.90582 10    + 5.0822 10    I) E

            -20              -I Pi x            -20
  (2.12317 10    + 0.31831 I) E        + (2.12317 10    -

            -20         -21    2 I Pi x
  (-1.90582 10    - 5.0822 10    I) E
                          -20         -3 I Pi x
0.5 + 0. I + (9.14796 10    + 0.106103 I) E          +

            -20           -21    -2 I Pi x
  (-1.90582 10    + 5.0822 10    I) E          +

            -20              -I Pi x            -20
  (2.12317 10    + 0.31831 I) E        + (2.12317 10    -

            -20         -21    2 I Pi x
  (-1.90582 10    - 5.0822 10    I) E
```

Finally, the resulting approximations are graphed on the interval [0,4] and displayed on the same axes as f. The resulting set of four graphics objects are displayed as a graphics array.

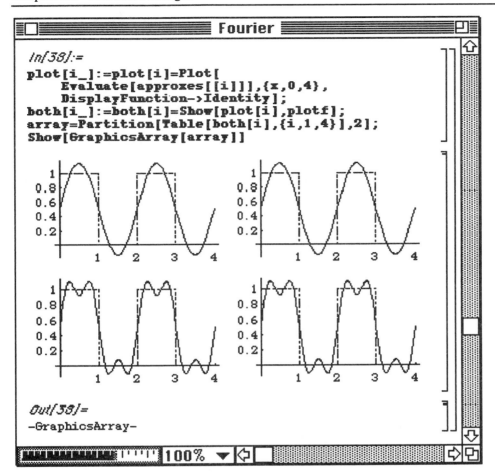

```
In[38]:=
plot[i_]:=plot[i]=Plot[
     Evaluate[approxes[[i]]],{x,0,4},
     DisplayFunction->Identity];
both[i_]:=both[i]=Show[plot[i],plotf];
array=Partition[Table[both[i],{i,1,4}],2];
Show[GraphicsArray[array]]
```

```
Out[38]=
-GraphicsArray-
```

NFourierTrigSeries   Package: **FourierTransform.m**
  NFourierTrigSeries[f,{x,x0,x1},n] numerically approximates the Fourier trigonometric series expansion to order **n** of the function **f** which is periodic on the interval (x0,x1).

NFourierExpSeriesCoefficient
                    Package: **FourierTransform.m**
  NFourierExpSeriesCoefficient[f,{x,x0,x1},n] numerically approximates the nth coefficient in the exponential series expansion of **f** where **f** is periodic on the interval (x0,x1).

NFourierSinSeriesCoefficient
                    Package: **FourierTransform.m**
  NFourierSinSeriesCoefficient[f,{x,x0,x1},n] numerically approximates the value of the nth coefficient in the sine series expansion of **f** where **f** is an odd function on the interval (x0,x1).

NFourierCosSeriesCoefficient

Package: **FourierTransform.m**

NFourierCosSeriesCoefficient[f,{x,x0,x1},n] numerically approximates the value of the nth coefficient in the cosine series expansion of **f** where **f** is an even function on the interval (**x0,x1**).

LaplaceTransform.m

The commands in the package **LaplaceTransform.m** can be used to compute Laplace transforms and inverse Laplace transforms of many familiar functions.

LaplaceTransform   Package: **LaplaceTransform.m**

LaplaceTransform[f,t,s] yields the Laplace transform of f(t). This value is determined by evaluating $\int_0^\infty f(t)e^{-st}dt$ and is, hence, a function of s.

InverseLaplaceTransform

Package: **LaplaceTransform.m**

InverseLaplaceTransform[g, s, t] yields the inverse Laplace transform $\mathscr{L}^{-1}\{g(s)\}$.

Example:

The following two examples first use the command **LaplaceTransform** to compute the Laplace transform of $t^4 e^{-t}$ and then the command **InverseLaplaceTransform** to compute the inverse Laplace transform of $\dfrac{s^2}{s^4 - 1}$.

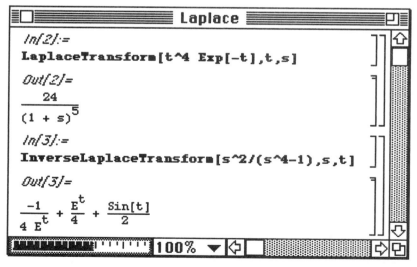

Pade.m

Pade Package: **Pade.m**
See Also: **LogicalExpand, Series, Solve**

Pade[f,{x,x0,m,n}] yields the Pade approximation of degree (m,n) centered at

x0 of the function **f** This approximation is of the from $\dfrac{p(x)}{q(x)}$ where the polynomials

p(x) and q(x) are of degree m and n, respectively, and the power series of

f(x)q(x) – p(x) about x = **x0** has leading term x^{m+n+1}.

Example:

In the following example, the Pade approximation with numerator and denominator of

degree 4 centered at x = 0 is computed for the indicated function.

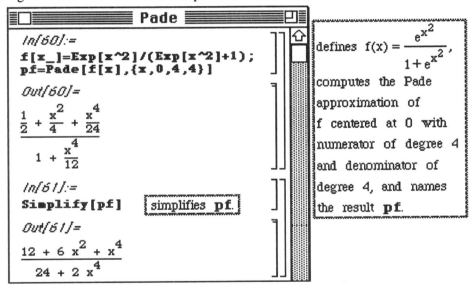

In this case, the commands **Series** and **Normal** are then used to compute the

Maclaurin polynomial of degree six for f; the result is named **sf**.

In[65]:=
sf=Series[f[x],{x,0,6}]//Normal

Out[65]=

$$\frac{1}{2} + \frac{x^2}{4} - \frac{x^6}{48}$$

Then **pf** and f and **sf** and f are both graphed on the same axes. The resulting graphics
objects are displayed as a graphics array. Observe that resulting Pade approximation is
much better than the Maclaurin polynomial approximation.

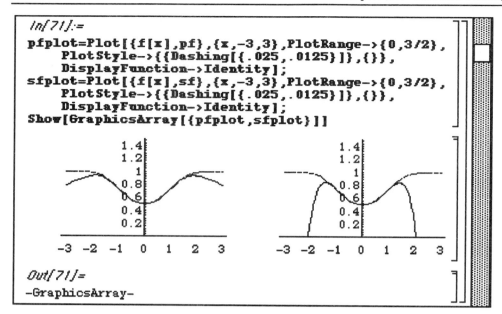

```
In[71]:=
pfplot=Plot[{f[x],pf},{x,-3,3},PlotRange->{0,3/2},
    PlotStyle->{{Dashing[{.025,.0125}]},{}},
    DisplayFunction->Identity];
sfplot=Plot[{f[x],sf},{x,-3,3},PlotRange->{0,3/2},
    PlotStyle->{{Dashing[{.025,.0125}]},{}},
    DisplayFunction->Identity];
Show[GraphicsArray[{pfplot,sfplot}]]
```

```
Out[71]=
-GraphicsArray-
```

EconomizedRationalApproximation

Package: **LaplaceTransform.m**

See Also: **LogicalExpand, Series, Solve**

EconomizedRationalApproximation[f,{x,{x1,x2},m,n] yields a
rational approximation of f that is good on the interval (x1,x2) which has degree (m,n).
This approximation is obtained by starting with the Padé approximation and perturbing
it with a Chebyshev polynomial. This decreases the error away from the center of the
interval, but it may slightly increase the error near the center.

Example:

As in the previous example, $f(x) = \dfrac{e^{x^2}}{1 + e^{x^2}}$. Then,

EconomizedRationalApproximation is used to compute a rational
approximation of f on the interval (−3,3); the result is named **eraf**.

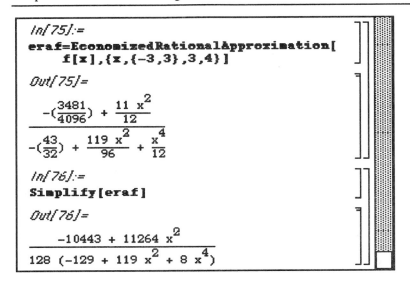

In[75]:=
eraf=EconomizedRationalApproximation[
f[x],{x,{-3,3},3,4}]

Out[75]=

$$\frac{-(\frac{3481}{4096}) + \frac{11 \, x^2}{12}}{-(\frac{43}{32}) + \frac{119 \, x^2}{96} + \frac{x^4}{12}}$$

In[76]:=
Simplify[eraf]

Out[76]=

$$\frac{-10443 + 11264 \, x^2}{128 \, (-129 + 119 \, x^2 + 8 \, x^4)}$$

Both the Pade approximation and the economized rational approximation are graphed for $-3 < x < 3$, the results are displayed as a graphics array. In this case, it appears as though the Pade approximation yields a much better approximation of f than the economized rational approximation.

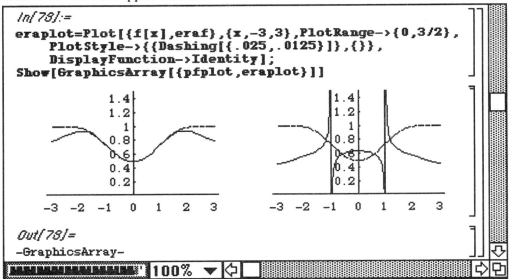

In[78]:=
eraplot=Plot[{f[x],eraf},{x,-3,3},PlotRange->{0,3/2},
PlotStyle->{{Dashing[{.025,.0125}]},{}},
DisplayFunction->Identity];
Show[GraphicsArray[{pfplot,eraplot}]]

Out[78]=
-GraphicsArray-

100%

VectorAnalysis.m

VectorAnalysis.m provides a variety of commands for performing calculus in various three-dimensional coordinate systems.

CoordinateSystem   Package: **VectorAnalysis.m**
   CoordinateSystem represents the default setting of the coordinate system. This setting is initially **Cartesian**.

Coordinates   Package: **VectorAnalysis.m**
   Coordinates[] lists the default names of the variables in the default coordinate system. **Coordinates[sys]** yields the default names of the variables in the coordinate system **sys**.
Example:

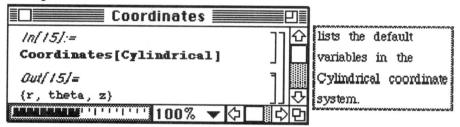

Bipolar   Package: **VectorAnalysis.m**
   Bipolar[u,v,z,a] represents the bipolar coordinate system which is based on two foci which are separated by a distance of 2**a**. If **u** is fixed, then a family of circles which pass through the foci is generated. If **v** is fixed, then a family of degenerate ellipses about one focus is produced. The **z**-coordinate determines the distance along the common foci. The default value of the parameter **a** is 1.

Bispherical   Package: **VectorAnalysis.m**
   Bispherical[u,v,phi,a] is similar to the bipolar system. However, the coordinate **phi** measures the azimuthal angle.

Cartesian   Package: **VectorAnalysis.m**
   Cartesian[x,y,z] represents the Cartesian coordinate system and is the default setting of **CoordinateSystem.**
Example:

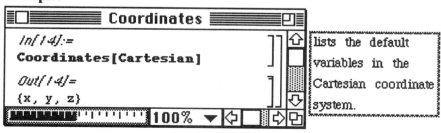

ConfocalEllipsoidal Package: **VectorAnalysis.m**
    ConfocalEllipsoidal[lambda,mu,nu,a,b,c] represents the canonical ellipsoidal coordinate system. Ellipsoids are produced if **lambda** is constant, hyperboloids of one sheet are generated with fixed **mu**, and hyperboloids of two sheets are given with constant **nu**. The defaults for the parameters **a**, **b**, and **c** are 3, 2, and 1, respectively.

ConfocalParaboloidal Package: **VectorAnalysis.m**
    ConfocalParaboloidal[lambda,mu,nu,a,b] represents the confocal paraboloidal coordinate system. In this system, elliptic paraboloids are generated which extend in the negative z direction for fixed **lambda**, hyperbolic paraboloids are produced with fixed **mu**, and elliptic paraboloids which extend in the positive z direction are given fixed **nu**. The default values of the parameters **a** and **b** are 2 and 1, respectively.

Conical   Package: **VectorAnalysis.m**
    Conical[lambda,mu,nu,a,b] represents the conical coordinate system. If **lambda** is fixed, then a sphere is generated while cones with the z-axis as axes and apexes at the origin is produced if **mu** is held constant. However, if **nu** is fixed, then the cones produced have the y-axis as axes. The default values for the parameters **a** and **b** are 1 and 2, respectively.

Cylindrical   Package: **VectorAnalysis.m**
    Cylindrical[r,theta,z] represents the cylindrical coordinate system where the polar coordinates **r** and **theta** are used in the x,y-plane and **z** represents the height above the xy-plane.

EllipticCylindrical Package: **VectorAnalysis.m**
    EllipticCylindrical[u,v,z,a] represents the elliptic cylindrical coordinate system which depends on two foci that are separated by a distance of 2**a**. A family of confocal ellipses results when **u** is fixed with **v** and **z** varied. Also, a family of confocal hyperbolas is produced when **v** is held constant. Distances along the axis of common focus is determined by the **z**-coordinate. The default value of **a** is 1.

OblateSpherical   Package: **VectorAnalysis.m**
    OblateSpherical[xi,eta,phi,a] represents the oblate spherical coordinate system in which elliptic cylindrical coordinates are rotated about an axis which is perpendicular to the axis that joins the two foci. The default value of **a** is 1.

ParabolicCylindrical Package: **VectorAnalysis.m**
    ParabolicCylindrical[u,v,z] represents the parabolic cylindrical coordinate system. Parabolas which are in opposite directions are generated when **z** is fixed and one of the remaining variables is varied. The **z**-coordinate indicates the distance along the axis of common focus.

Paraboidal   Package: **VectorAnalysis.m**
    Paraboidal[u,v,phi] represents the paraboidal coordinate system. Parabolas which are in opposite directions are generated when **phi** is fixed and one of the remaining variables is varied. The **phi** coordinate indicates the rotation about their common bisectors.

Example:

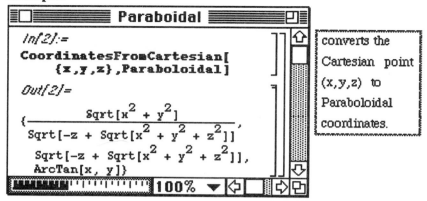

ProlateSpheroidal   Package: **VectorAnalysis.m**

  ProlateSpheroidal[xi,eta,phi,a] represents the prolate spheroidal coordinate system. This system is obtained through a rotation of the elliptic cylindrical coordinate system about the axis joining the two foci. The **phi** coordinate specifies the rotation. The default of the parameter **a** is 1.

Example:

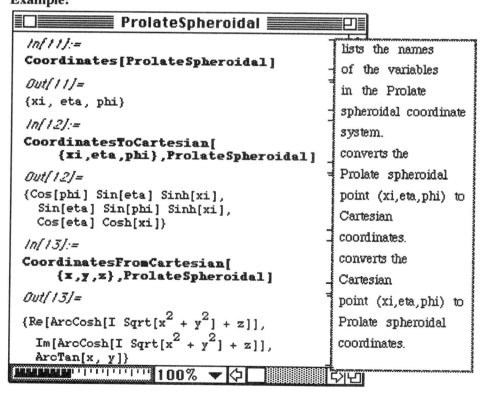

Spherical   Package: **VectorAnalysis.m**

  Spherical[r,theta,phi] represents the spherical coordinate system where **r** is the distance from the origin, **theta** is the angle measured from the positive z-axis, and **phi** is the angle in the xy-plane measured from the positive x-axis.

Example:

The following example displays the default variable names in spherical coordinates.

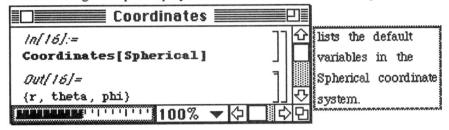

In[16]:=
Coordinates[Spherical]

Out[16]=
{r, theta, phi}

lists the default variables in the Spherical coordinate system.

Toroidal   Package: **VectorAnalysis.m**

  Toroidal[u,v,phi,a] represents the toroidal coordinate system. This system is obtained by rotating the bipolar coordinate system about an axis which is perpendicular to the axis joining the two foci. The rotation is determined by the value of **phi**. The default value for **a** is 1.

Example:

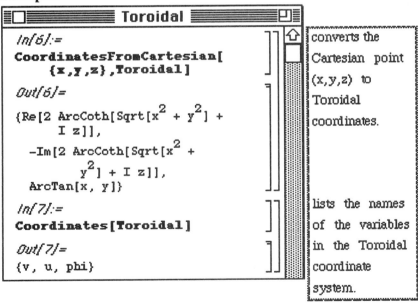

In[6]:=
**CoordinatesFromCartesian[
    {x,y,z},Toroidal]**

Out[6]=
{Re[2 ArcCoth[Sqrt[x^2 + y^2] +
      I z]],
  -Im[2 ArcCoth[Sqrt[x^2 +
        y^2] + I z]],
  ArcTan[x, y]}

In[7]:=
Coordinates[Toroidal]

Out[7]=
{v, u, phi}

converts the Cartesian point (x,y,z) to Toroidal coordinates.

lists the names of the variables in the Toroidal coordinate system.

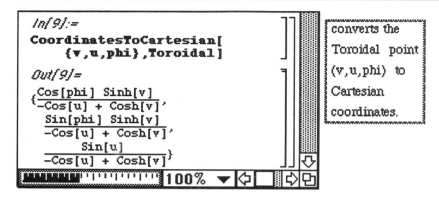

SetCoordinates   Package: **VectorAnalysis.m**
   SetCoordinates[sys] sets the default coordinate system to be **sys**. The names
of the variables are taken as the default values. In order to change these names, the
command **SetCoordinates[sys[vnames]]** is used where **vnames** is a list of
variable names in the coordinate system **sys**. Parameter names can be indicated as
well with **SetCoordinates[sys[vnames,pnames]]** where **pnames** is a list of
parameter names.

CoordinateRanges   Package: **VectorAnalysis.m**
   CoordinateRanges[] yields the range for each coordinate in the default
coordinate system. Also, **CoordinateRanges[sys]** yields the range for each
coordinate in the coordinate system **sys**.

Parameters   Package: **VectorAnalysis.m**
   Parameters[] lists the default parameters of the default coordinate system while
Parameters[sys] lists the default parameters of the coordinate system **sys**.

ParameterRanges   Package: **VectorAnalysis.m**
   ParameterRanges[] lists the range for each of the parameters of the default
coordinate system. In addition, **ParameterRanges[sys]** lists the range for each of
the parameters of the coordinate system **sys**.

CoordinatesToCartesian
                                Package: **VectorAnalysis.m**
   CoordinatesToCartesian[p] converts the point **p** in the default coordinate
system to Cartesian coordinates. **CoordinatesToCartesian[p,sys]** converts
the point **p** in the coordinate system **sys** to Cartesian coordinates.
Example:

The point $(5,\pi/6,\pi/4)$ in spherical coordinates is converted to Cartesian coordinates in
the example below.

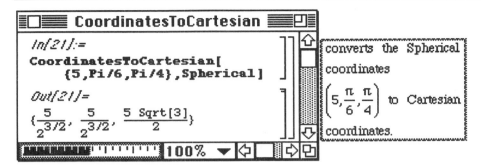

CoordinatesFromCartesian

Package: **VectorAnalysis.m**

CoordinatesFromCartesian[p] converts the point **p** in Cartesian coordinates to the default coordinate system. **CoordinatesFromCartesian[p,sys]** converts the point **p** in Cartesian coordinates to the coordinate system **sys**.

Example:

In the example below, the point $(-5,5,6)$ in Cartesian coordinates is given in cylindrical coordinates.

DotProduct   Package: **VectorAnalysis.m**
                             See Also: **Dot, Inner, Outer,**
                             NonCommutativeMultiply

DotProduct[u,v] computes the dot (scalar) product of the 3-dimensional vectors **u** and **v** which are given in the default coordinate system. These vectors are converted to the Cartesian coordinate system before the dot product is determined. Also, **DotProduct[u,v,sys]** computes the dot product of **u** and **v** which are given in the coordinate system **sys**.

Example:

In the following example, the dot product of the two vectors in spherical coordinates is calculated.

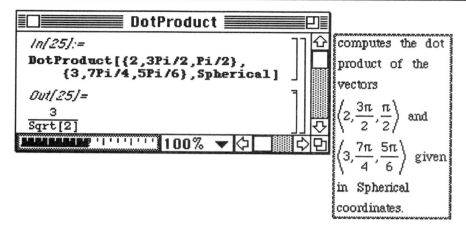

CrossProduct   Package: **VectorAnalysis.m**

CrossProduct[u,v] computes the cross product of the 3-dimensional vectors **u** and **v** which are given in the default coordinate system. These vectors are converted to the Cartesian coordinate system before the cross product is determined. Also, **DotProduct[u,v,sys]** computes the cross product of **u** and **v** which are given in the coordinate system **sys**.

Example:

In the example below, the cross product of the vectors in spherical coordinates $(2,3\pi/2,\pi/2)$ and $(3,7\pi/4,5\pi/6)$ is computed. The result is given in rectangular coordinates.

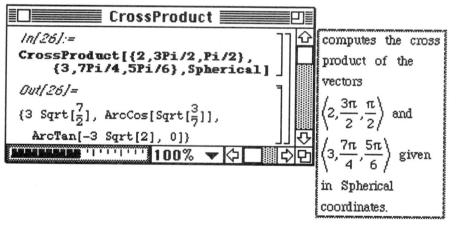

ArcLengthFactor   Package: **VectorAnalysis.m**

ArcLengthFactor[{f1,f2,f3},t] computes the derivative of the arc length along the 3-dimensional curve **{f1,f2,f3}** where each component is a function of **t**. This computation is performed in terms of the default coordinate system. In order to compute **ArcLengthFactor** in another coordinate system, the command **ArcLengthFactor[{f1,f2,f3},t,sys]** should be used.

Example:

The following examples illustrate the use of **ArcLengthFactor**. In the first example, the factor of the indicated vector-valued function is computed in Cartesian coordinates. In the second example, the factor is computed in terms of cylindrical coordinates.

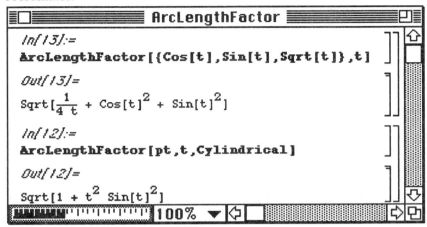

JacobianDeterminant   Package: **VectorAnalysis.m**

JacobianDeterminant[] computes the determinant of the Jacobian matrix which represents the transformation from the default coordinate system to Cartesian coordinates. This determinant is evaluated at a particular point **p** with the command **JacobianDeterminant[p]**. In order to compute the determinant of the transformation matrix from the coordinate system **sys**, different from he default system, the command **JacobianDeterminant[sys]** is used, and this determinant can be calculated for a particular point **p** with **JacobianDeterminant[p,sys]**.

Example:

In the examples below, the determinant of the transformation matrices which convert cylindrical and spherical coordinates to Cartesian coordinates, respectively, are computed. The corresponding transformation matrices are shown in the example following the description of **JacobianMatrix**.

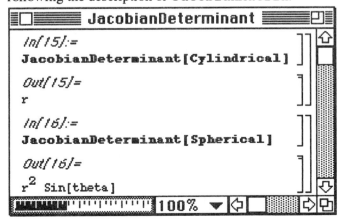

Below, the variable names in spherical coordinates are given as {r,p,t}. Hence the result involves these variables.

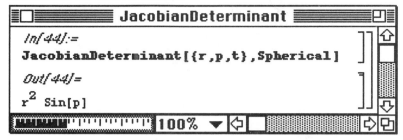

JacobianMatrix   Package: **VectorAnalysis.m**

JacobianMatrix[] yields the derivative matrix of the transformation from the default coordinate system to the Cartesian coordinate system. To evaluate this matrix at a particular point **p**, the command **JacobianMatrix[p]** is used. The Jacobian matrix from the coordinate system **sys** other than the default system to the Cartesian coordinate system is determined with **JacobianMatrix[sys]**, and this matrix is evaluated at a certain point with **JacobianMatrix[p,sys]**.

Example:
The example below illustrates the use of **JacobianMatrix**. In the first example, the Jacobian matrix which transforms spherical coordinates to Cartesian coordinates is determined and evaluated at (r,p,t). In the second example, similar calculations are performed for the matrix which transforms cylindrical to Cartesian coordinates.

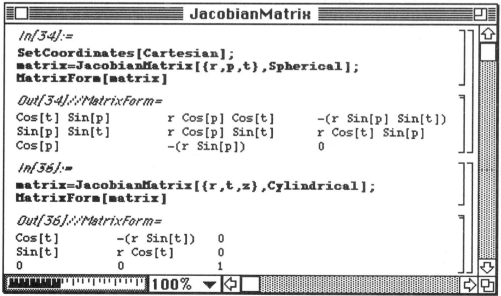

Curl   Package: **VectorAnalysis.m**

Curl[f] computes the curl of the vector field **f** in terms of the default coordinate system. In order to compute the curl in another coordinate system, the command **Curl[f,sys]** is used.

Example:

In the example below, the curl of the indicated (vector-valued) function of three variables $f(x, y, z) = \left\{ x^4 y^3 z^2, 4yz^2 + x^5, x^5 y^3 z \right\}$ is determined.

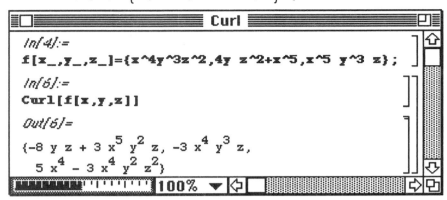

ScalarTripleProduct Package: **VectorAnalysis.m**

    ScalarTripleProduct[u,v,w] computes the triple scalar product of the 3-dimensional vectors **u**, **v**, and **w** which are given in the default coordinate system. These vectors are converted to the Cartesian coordinate system before the triple scalar product is determined. Also, **ScalarTripleProduct[u,v,w,sys]** computes the triple scalar product of **u**, **v**, and **w** which are given in the coordinate system **sys**.

Example:

The following example illustrates how **ScalarTripleProduct** is used to calculate the triple scalar product of the vectors

$\langle 5, -9, 4 \rangle$, $\langle 0, 8, -7 \rangle$, and $\langle 2, -4, 7 \rangle$ given in Cartesian coordinates.

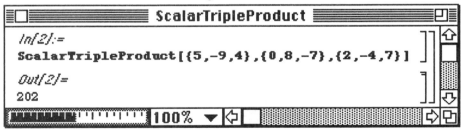

Grad Package: **VectorAnalysis.m**

    Grad[f] computes the gradient of the scalar function **f** in terms of the default coordinate system. In order to compute the gradient in another coordinate system, the command **Grad[f,sys]** is used.

Example:

The following example demonstrates how the gradient of the function of three variables $f(x, y, z) = x^5 y^3 + 4z^2 + 4x^3 y^3 z^2$ is computed with **Grad**.

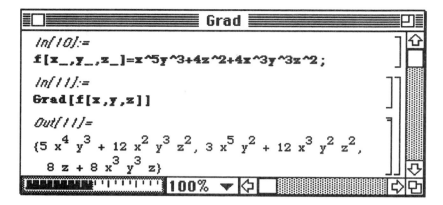

Div   Package: **VectorAnalysis.m**

Div[f] computes the divergence of the vector field **f** in terms of the default coordinate system. In order to compute the divergence in another coordinate system, the command **Div[f,sys]** is used.

Example:

The divergence of the function of three variables

$$f(x,y,z) = \left\{x^4 y^3 z^2, 4yz^2 + x^5, x^5 y^3 z\right\} \text{ is determined below.}$$

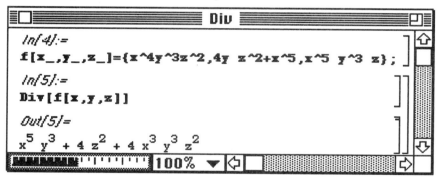

Laplacian

Package: **VectorAnalysis.m**

Laplacian[f] computes the Laplacian of the scalar function **f** in terms of the default coordinate system. In order to compute the Laplacian in another coordinate system, the command **Laplacian[f,sys]** is used.

Biharmonic   Package: **VectorAnalysis.m**

Biharmonic[f] computes the Laplacian of the Laplacian of the scalar function **f** in terms of the default coordinate system. In order to compute the Laplacian of the Laplacian in another coordinate system, the command **Biharmonic[f,sys]** is used.

Example:

The Laplacian and biharmonic of a general function of three variables are computed below. The symbol $g^{(i,j,k)}$ represents the function obtained by differentiating g i times with respect to the first argument, j times with respect to the second argument, and k times with respect to the third argument. See **Derivative**.

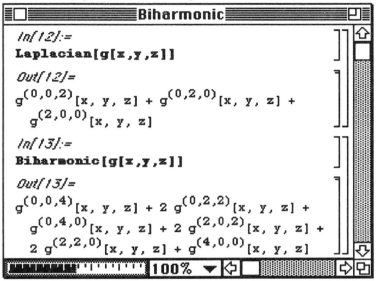

```
In[12]:=
Laplacian[g[x,y,z]]

Out[12]=
 (0,0,2)              (0,2,0)
g       [x, y, z] + g       [x, y, z] +
    (2,0,0)
   g       [x, y, z]

In[13]:=
Biharmonic[g[x,y,z]]

Out[13]=
 (0,0,4)                (0,2,2)
g       [x, y, z] + 2 g       [x, y, z] +
    (0,4,0)                (2,0,2)
   g       [x, y, z] + 2 g       [x, y, z] +
      (2,2,0)              (4,0,0)
   2 g       [x, y, z] + g       [x, y, z]
```

100%

Statistics Packages

The folder (or directory) **Statistics** contains the packages **ConfidenceIntervals**, **Continuous Distributions**, **DataManipulation**, **DescriptiveStatistics**, **DiscreteDistributions**, **HypothesisTests**, **InverseStatisticalFunctions**, **LinearRegression**, **MovingAverage**, and **NormalDistribution**.

ConfidenceIntervals.m

MeanCI   Package: **ConfidenceIntervals.m**

MeanCI[datalist,options] gives the confidence interval given in the form {**min,max**} for the population mean of the data indicated in **datalist**. This command has the options **ConfidenceLevel**, **KnownStandardDeviation**, and **KnownVariance** with default settings **.95**, **None**, and **None**, respectively.

Example:

A group of 100 college students who live off campus were asked to measure the distance in miles that they live from a certain point on campus. Their measurements are listed in **miles** below and the 95% confidence interval as well as the 90% confidence interval are calculated using this data.

```
================================ MeanCI ================================
In[2]:=
miles={7.76,14.61,2.83,5.95,4.06,3.25,
       1.64,7.93,4.4,12.18,1.62,14.53,2.38,
       13.26,12.23,2.2,7.17,1.22,8.49,11.79,
       5.54,12.13,14.92,7.85,6.28,2.94,13.52,
       9.91,1.08,8.83,8.59,12.22,2.38,8.89,
       10.72,13.47,9.08,7.21,5.56,1.85,6.74,
       5.31,9.31,2.47,13.77,2.01,4.19,10.66,
       6.53,8.19,12.41,4.42,2.77,3.91,13.26,
       7.72,13.32,10.59,9.73,1.37,5.23,12.18,
       4.48,1.05,11.16,13.93,10.66,6.76,11.24,
       11.89,4.46,14.55,9.99,7.99,13.13,5.72,
       3.46,13.43,8.49,9.02,9.14,2.16,7.86,8.48,
       10.53,3.94,4.09,4.41,6.9,12.9,3.21,
       4.38,9.2,2.72,9.46,13.59,1.57,3.76,
       10.27,12.9};
```

```
In[3]:=
MeanCI[miles]//N          The result means that 95% of the
                          students live between 6.8 and 8.5
Out[3]=                   miles from campus.
{6.89451, 8.53429}

In[4]:=
MeanCI[miles,ConfidenceLevel->.90]//N

Out[4]=                   The result means that 90% of the
{7.02832, 8.40048}        students live between 7.02 and 8.40
                     100% miles from campus.
```

MeanDifferenceCI Package: **ConfidenceIntervals.m**

  MeanDifferenceCI[data1,data2,options] yields the confidence interval of the difference **Mean[data1]-Mean[data2]** using the sample populations given in **data1** and **data2**. This interval is of the form {min,max}. The possible options used with **MeanDifferenceCI** are **ConfidenceLevel**, **KnownStandardDeviation**, **KnownVariance**, and **EqualVariances**. The default settings for these options are **.95**, **None**, **None**, and **False**, respectively.

Example:

Sports science studies indicate that women long-distance runners peak at the age of 27. Female participants of a 5-kilometer race were sampled with the times of those runners who were 27 years old given in **time27** and those of the other runners listed in **time**. **MeanDifferenceCI** is then used to find the 95% confidence interval that the population means are the same.

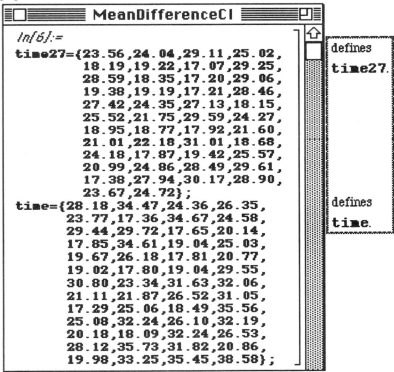

In the following calculation, **MeanDifference** is used to show that it is 95% certain that the difference in the means is between –4.71386 and and −.405234.

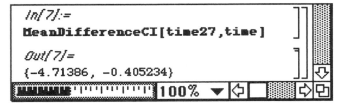

VarianceCI   Package: **ConfidenceIntervals.m**

   VarianceCI[datalist] uses the sample population given in **datalist** to determine the confidence interval for the variance of the population. This interval is given as **{min,max}**. **VarianceCI** has the option **ConfidenceLevel** with default setting **.95**.

Example:

A college mathematics department gives a 100 point standardized college algebra final examination. The scores of 100 students for a particular quarter are listed in **scores** below. **VarianceCI** is then used to determine the 95% confidence interval for the variance of the grades. The result means that it is 95% certain that the variance is between 373.73 and 643.583. In other words, the standard deviation is between 19.32 and 25.37.

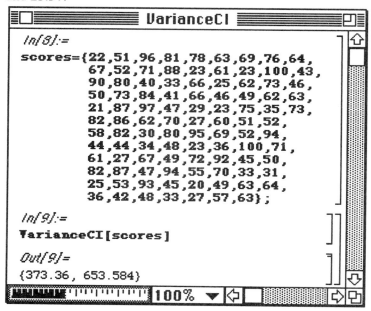

VarianceRatioCI   Package: **ConfidenceIntervals.m**

   VarianceRatioCI[data1,data2,options] yields the confidence interval of the ratio **Variance[data1]/Variance[data2]** for the sample populations indicated in **data1** and **data2**.

Example:

A sample of 75 scores from the standardized test administered the quarter following those considered in **scores** (given above in **VarianceCI**) are listed below in **scores2**. **VarianceRatioCI** is used to determine the confidence level of the ratio of the variance of the sample scores from both quarters listed in **scores** and **scores2**.

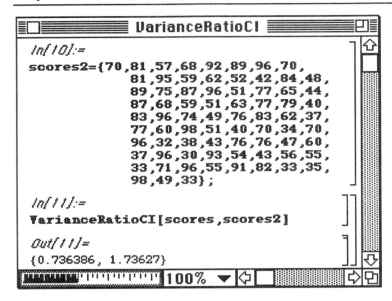

```
In[10]:=
scores2={70,81,57,68,92,89,96,70,
        81,95,59,62,52,42,84,48,
        89,75,87,96,51,77,65,44,
        87,68,59,51,63,77,79,40,
        83,96,74,49,76,83,62,37,
        77,60,98,51,40,70,34,70,
        96,32,38,43,76,76,47,60,
        37,96,30,93,54,43,56,55,
        33,71,96,55,91,82,33,35,
        98,49,33};

In[11]:=
VarianceRatioCI[scores,scores2]

Out[11]=
{0.736386, 1.73627}
```

ContinuousDistributions.m

NoncentralChiSquareDistribution
Package: **ContinuousDistributions.m**

NoncentralChiSquareDistribution[df,lbda] is the non-central chi-square distribution with **df** degrees of freedom and parameter of non-centrality **lbda**.

NoncentralFRatioSquareDistribution
Package: **ContinuousDistributions.m**

NoncentralFRatioSquareDistribution[ndf,ddf,lbda] is the non-central F distribution with **ndf** numerator degrees of freedom, **ddf** denominator degrees of freedom, and parameter of non-centrality **lbda**.

NoncentralStudentTDistribution
Package: **ContinuousDistributions.m**

NoncentralStudentTDistribution[df,lbda] is the student t-distribution with **df** degrees of freedom and parameter of non-centrality **lbda**.

BetaDistribution   586
Package: **ContinuousDistributions.m**

BetaDistribution[a,b] represents the continuous beta distribution with parameters **a** and **b**.

Example:
The beta distribution with a = 4 and b = 2 is found below. This distribution is called **beta** and the cumulative distribution function for **beta** is plotted.

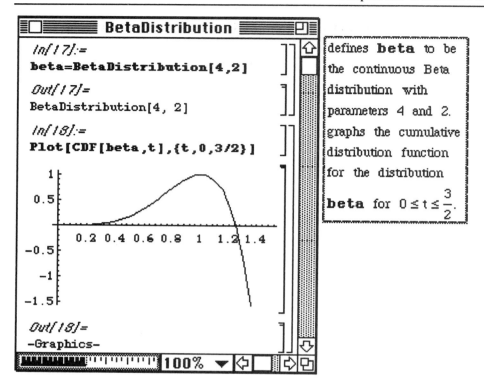

CauchyDistribution   586

Package: **ContinuousDistributions.m**

CauchyDistribution[a,b] is the Cauchy distribution where **a** represents the location parameter and **b** the scale parameter.

Example:

The Cauchy distribution with a = 5 and b = 2 is determined below and called **cauchy1**. The cumulative distribution of **cauchy1** is found and evaluated for certain values.

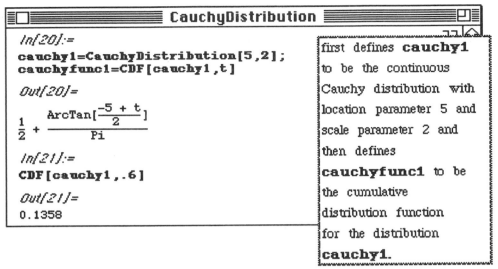

A table of three cumulative distribution functions is then computed in **cauchytable** and a table of three **GrayLevels** is computed and named **tablegray**.

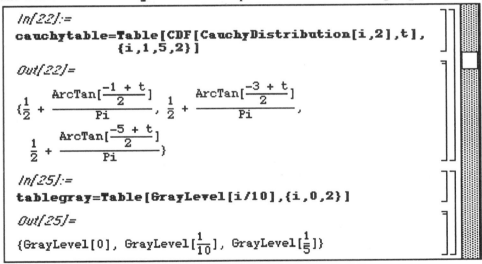

Finally, the three functions in **cauchytable** are graphed for $-5 \le t \le 9$ according to the shades of gray specified in **tablegray**.

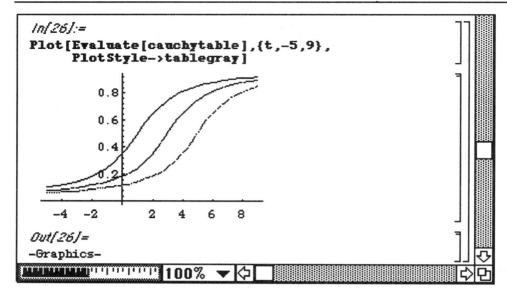

```
In[26]:=
Plot[Evaluate[cauchytable],{t,-5,9},
    PlotStyle->tablegray]
```

```
Out[26]=
-Graphics-
```

ChiDistribution   Package: **ContinuousDistributions.m**
  ChiDistribution[m] represents the chi distribution of **m** degrees of freedom.
Example:
A table of cumulative distribution functions for the chi distribution with m = 1, 3, and 5
is generated and called **chitable**.

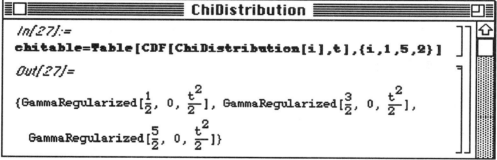

```
In[27]:=
chitable=Table[CDF[ChiDistribution[i],t],{i,1,5,2}]
```

$$\text{Out[27]=}$$

$$\{\text{GammaRegularized}[\tfrac{1}{2}, 0, \tfrac{t^2}{2}], \text{GammaRegularized}[\tfrac{3}{2}, 0, \tfrac{t^2}{2}],$$

$$\text{GammaRegularized}[\tfrac{5}{2}, 0, \tfrac{t^2}{2}]\}$$

This table is plotted using the same table of gray levels given above in **tablegray**
used in the beta distribution example above.

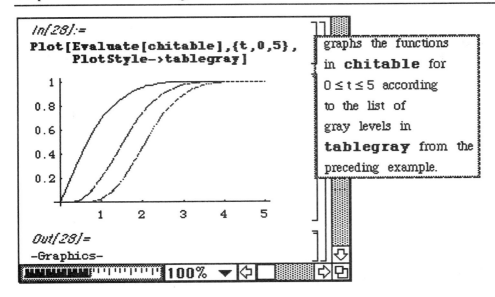

```
In[28]:=
Plot[Evaluate[chitable],{t,0,5},
      PlotStyle->tablegray]
```

graphs the functions in **chitable** for $0 \leq t \leq 5$ according to the list of gray levels in **tablegray** from the preceding example.

```
Out[28]=
-Graphics-
```

ExponentialDistribution
                          586
                    Package: **ContinuousDistributions.m**
   ExponentialDistribution[a] is the exponential distribution with parameter **a**.

Example:
A table of cumulative distribution functions for the exponential distribution with a = 1, 3, and 5 is generated below and called **exptable**. This table is plotted using the same table of gray levels used above.

ExponentialDistribution

```
In[29]:=
exptable=Table[CDF[ExponentialDistribution[i],t],
          {i,1,5,2}]

Out[29]=
{1 - E^{-t}, 1 - E^{-3 t}, 1 - E^{-5 t}}
```

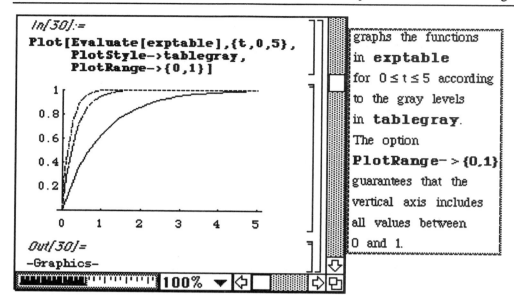

```
In[30]:=
Plot[Evaluate[exptable],{t,0,5},
    PlotStyle->tablegray,
    PlotRange->{0,1}]
```

```
Out[30]=
-Graphics-
```

graphs the functions in `exptable` for $0 \leq t \leq 5$ according to the gray levels in `tablegray`. The option `PlotRange->{0,1}` guarantees that the vertical axis includes all values between 0 and 1.

ExtremeValueDistribution
586, 587

Package: **ContinuousDistributions.m**

ExtremeValueDistribution[a,b] represents the Fisher-Tippett extreme value distribution.

Example:

A table of cumulative distribution functions for the extreme value distribution with $a = 1, 3, 5$ and $b = 2$ is generated and called **evdtable**. This table is plotted using the same table of gray levels used above and with the **PlotRange** option. This table of gray levels is created in the beta distribution example.

```
ExtremeValueDistribution

In[31]:=
evdtable=Table[CDF[ExtremeValueDistribution[i,2],t],
    {i,1,5,2}]

Out[31]=
{E^-E^-(-1 + t)/2,  E^-E^-(-3 + t)/2,
    E^-E^-(-5 + t)/2  }
```

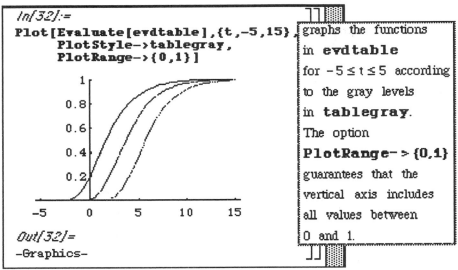

Another table is produced with a = 2, b = 1, 3, and 5. This table is called **evdtable2** and is plotted in a similar manner as **evdtable**.

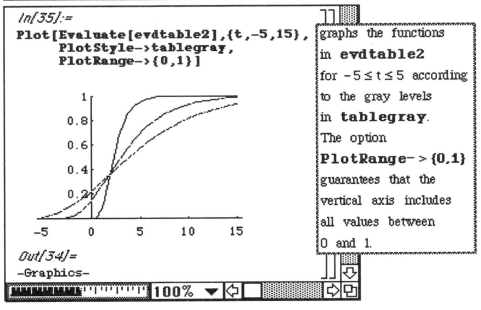

GammaDistribution   586
Package: ContinuousDistributions.m

GammaDistribution[a,b] is the gamma distribution where **a** is the shape parameter and **b** is the scale parameter.

Example:

A table of cumulative distribution functions for the gamma distribution is found below in **gammatable** with a =1, 2, 3 and b = 3. This table of functions is then plotted in the three levels of gray defined in **tablegray**. This table of gray levels is created in the beta distribution example.

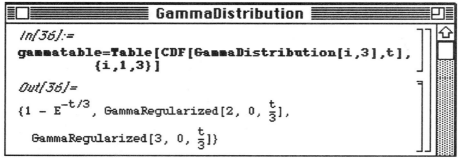

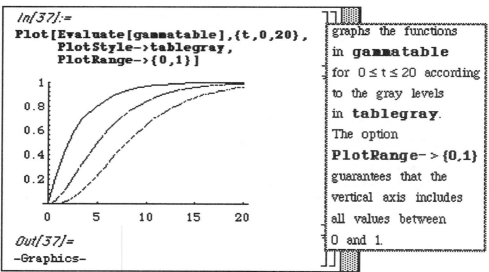

Also, a table of cumulative distribution functions for the gamma distribution with a = 3 and b = 1, 2, 3. This table is called **gammatable2** and plotted in the same manner as **gammatable**.

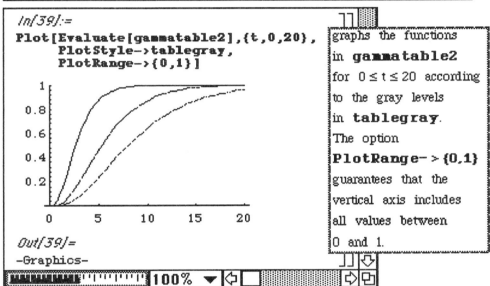

In[38]:=
```
gammatable2=Table[CDF[GammaDistribution[3,i],t],
        {i,1,3}]
```

Out[38]=
```
{GammaRegularized[3, 0, t],

   GammaRegularized[3, 0, t/2],

   GammaRegularized[3, 0, t/3]}
```

In[39]:=
```
Plot[Evaluate[gammatable2],{t,0,20},
    PlotStyle->tablegray,
    PlotRange->{0,1}]
```

graphs the functions in **gammatable2** for $0 \le t \le 20$ according to the gray levels in **tablegray**. The option **PlotRange->{0,1}** guarantees that the vertical axis includes all values between 0 and 1.

Out[39]=
-Graphics-

100%

HalfNormalDistribution

Package: ContinuousDistributions.m

HalfNormalDistribution[t] represents the half-normal distribution where **t** is the variance parameter.

Example:

A table of cumulative distribution functions for the half normal distribution is found below for the parameter t = 1, 2, 3. This table is named **hntable** and is plotted in three levels of gray given in **tablegray** where this table of gray levels is created in the beta distribution example. The **PlotRange** option is also employed.

╔══════════════ HalfNormalDistribution ══════════════╗

In[40]:=
```
hntable=Table[CDF[HalfNormalDistribution[i],t],
        {i,1,3}]
```

Out[40]=
$$\{Erf[\frac{t}{Sqrt[Pi]}], Erf[\frac{2\,t}{Sqrt[Pi]}], Erf[\frac{3\,t}{Sqrt[Pi]}]\}$$

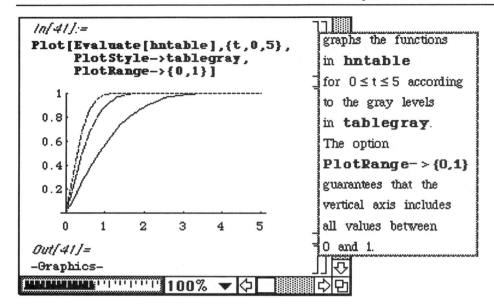

In[41]:=
```
Plot[Evaluate[hntable],{t,0,5},
     PlotStyle->tablegray,
     PlotRange->{0,1}]
```

graphs the functions
in **hntable**
for $0 \le t \le 5$ according
to the gray levels
in **tablegray**.
The option
PlotRange- > {0,1}
guarantees that the
vertical axis includes
all values between
0 and 1.

Out[41]=
-Graphics-

100% ▼

LaplaceDistribution   Package: **ContinuousDistributions.m**
   LaplaceDistribution[m,b] is the double exponential Laplace distribution
where **m** is the mean and **b** the variance parameter.
Example:
A table of cumulative distribution functions for the Laplace distribution is found below
for the parameters m = 1, 2, 3, and b = 2. The built-in function **sign** is defined by

$$\text{sign}[t] = \begin{cases} +1 & \text{if } t > 0 \\ 0 & \text{if } t = 0 \\ -1 & \text{if } t < 0 \end{cases}$$ The resulting table is named **laptable**

and is plotted according to the levels of gray defined in **tablegray** and with
PlotRange->{0,1}. Note that this table of gray levels is defined in the example of
beta distribution.

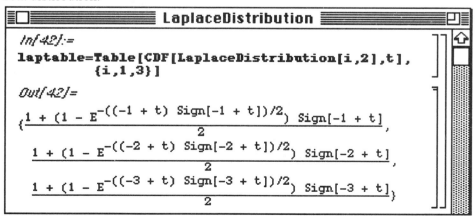

LaplaceDistribution

In[42]:=
```
laptable=Table[CDF[LaplaceDistribution[i,2],t],
     {i,1,3}]
```

Out[42]=
$$\{\frac{1 + (1 - E^{-((-1 + t)\ \text{Sign}[-1 + t])/2})\ \text{Sign}[-1 + t]}{2},$$

$$\frac{1 + (1 - E^{-((-2 + t)\ \text{Sign}[-2 + t])/2})\ \text{Sign}[-2 + t]}{2},$$

$$\frac{1 + (1 - E^{-((-3 + t)\ \text{Sign}[-3 + t])/2})\ \text{Sign}[-3 + t]}{2}\}$$

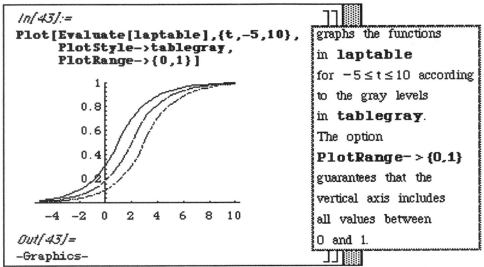

In[43]:=
```
Plot[Evaluate[laptable],{t,-5,10},
     PlotStyle->tablegray,
     PlotRange->{0,1}]
```

Out[43]=
-Graphics-

graphs the functions in **laptable** for $-5 \le t \le 10$ according to the gray levels in **tablegray**. The option **PlotRange->{0,1}** guarantees that the vertical axis includes all values between 0 and 1.

A second table is found with m = 2 and b = 1, 2, and 3. This table, named **laptable2**, is plotted in a similar manner.

In[44]:=
```
laptable2=Table[CDF[LaplaceDistribution[2,i],t],
        {i,1,3}]
```

Out[44]=
$$\{\frac{1 + (1 - E^{-((-2 + t)\ \text{Sign}[-2 + t])})\ \text{Sign}[-2 + t]}{2},$$
$$\frac{1 + (1 - E^{-((-2 + t)\ \text{Sign}[-2 + t])/2})\ \text{Sign}[-2 + t]}{2},$$
$$\frac{1 + (1 - E^{-((-2 + t)\ \text{Sign}[-2 + t])/3})\ \text{Sign}[-2 + t]}{2}\}$$

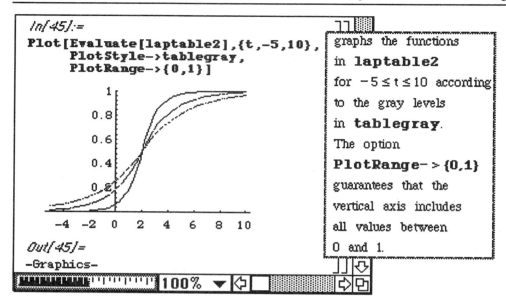

```
In[45]:=
Plot[Evaluate[laptable2],{t,-5,10},
    PlotStyle->tablegray,
    PlotRange->{0,1}]
```

graphs the functions in **laptable2** for $-5 \le t \le 10$ according to the gray levels in **tablegray**. The option **PlotRange-> {0,1}** guarantees that the vertical axis includes all values between 0 and 1.

```
Out[45]=
-Graphics-
```

LogNormalDistribution

586, 587

Package: **ContinuousDistributions.m**

LogNormalDistribution[m,s] represents the lognormal distribution. The mean parameter is **m** while the variance parameter is **s**.

Example:

A table named **lgntable** of cumulative distribution functions for the lognormal distribution is found below for the parameters m = 1, 2, 3, and s = 2. This table is plotted using the levels of gray given in **tablegray** as well as the **PlotRange** option. This table of gray levels is generated in the beta distribution example.

LogNormalDistribution

```
In[46]:=
lgntable=Table[CDF[LogNormalDistribution[i,2],t],
    {i,1,3}]

Out[46]=
```
$$\left\{\frac{1 + \text{Erf}[\frac{-1 + \text{Log}[t]}{2^{3/2}}]}{2}, \frac{1 + \text{Erf}[\frac{-2 + \text{Log}[t]}{2^{3/2}}]}{2}, \right.$$
$$\left.\frac{1 + \text{Erf}[\frac{-3 + \text{Log}[t]}{2^{3/2}}]}{2}\right\}$$

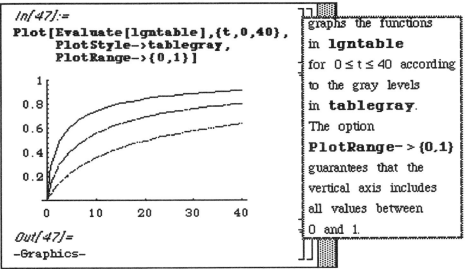

In[47]:=
```
Plot[Evaluate[lgntable],{t,0,40},
    PlotStyle->tablegray,
    PlotRange->{0,1}]
```

graphs the functions in **lgntable** for $0 \le t \le 40$ according to the gray levels in **tablegray**. The option **PlotRange- > {0,1}** guarantees that the vertical axis includes all values between 0 and 1.

Out[47]=
-Graphics-

Another table containing the cumulative distribution functions for the distributions with m = 2, s = 1, 2, and 3 is created. This table, named **lgntable2**, is plotted in a similar manner.

In[48]:=
```
lgntable2=Table[CDF[LogNormalDistribution[2,i],t],
        {i,1,3}]
```

Out[48]=

$$\{\frac{1 + Erf[\frac{-2 + Log[t]}{Sqrt[2]}]}{2}, \frac{1 + Erf[\frac{-2 + Log[t]}{2^{3/2}}]}{2},$$

$$\frac{1 + Erf[\frac{-2 + Log[t]}{3\ Sqrt[2]}]}{2}\}$$

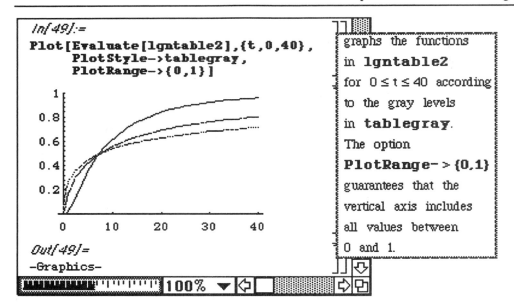

In[49]:=
```
Plot[Evaluate[lgntable2],{t,0,40},
    PlotStyle->tablegray,
    PlotRange->{0,1}]
```

graphs the functions in **lgntable2** for $0 \le t \le 40$ according to the gray levels in **tablegray**. The option **PlotRange-> {0,1}** guarantees that the vertical axis includes all values between 0 and 1.

Out[49]=
-Graphics-

LogisticDistribution 586

Package: **ContinuousDistributions.m**

LogisticDistribution[m,b] is the logistic distribution where **m** is the mean and **b** is variance parameter.

Example:

A table of cumulative distribution functions for the logistic distribution is found below with the parameters m = 1, 2, 3 and b = 2. This table is called **logistable** and is plotted using the settings for **GrayLevel** given in **tablegray** along with the **PlotRange** option. Note that **tablegray** was introduced in the beta distribution example.

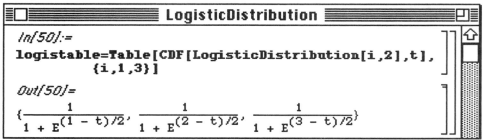

LogisticDistribution

In[50]:=
```
logistable=Table[CDF[LogisticDistribution[i,2],t],
    {i,1,3}]
```

Out[50]=

$$\{\frac{1}{1 + E^{(1 - t)/2}}, \frac{1}{1 + E^{(2 - t)/2}}, \frac{1}{1 + E^{(3 - t)/2}}\}$$

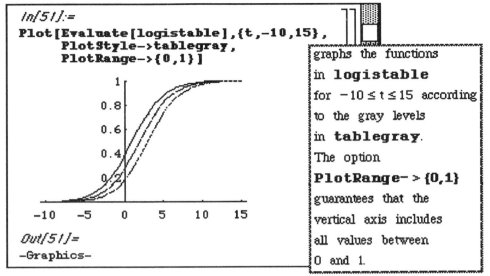

In[51]:=
```
Plot[Evaluate[logistable],{t,-10,15},
     PlotStyle->tablegray,
     PlotRange->{0,1}]
```

graphs the functions in **logistable** for $-10 \le t \le 15$ according to the gray levels in **tablegray**. The option **PlotRange- > {0,1}** guarantees that the vertical axis includes all values between 0 and 1.

Out[51]=
-Graphics-

A second table, named **logistable2**, is generated for m = 2 and b = 1, 2, 3 and plotted in a similar manner.

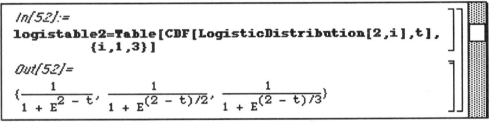

In[52]:=
```
logistable2=Table[CDF[LogisticDistribution[2,i],t],
          {i,1,3}]
```

Out[52]=

$$\{\frac{1}{1 + E^{2 - t}}, \frac{1}{1 + E^{(2 - t)/2}}, \frac{1}{1 + E^{(2 - t)/3}}\}$$

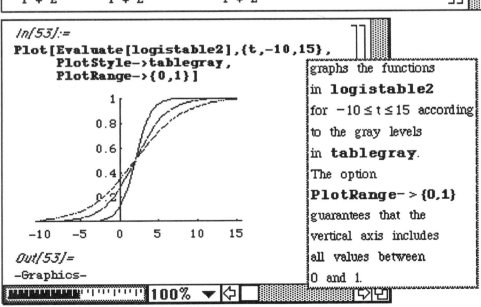

In[53]:=
```
Plot[Evaluate[logistable2],{t,-10,15},
     PlotStyle->tablegray,
     PlotRange->{0,1}]
```

graphs the functions in **logistable2** for $-10 \le t \le 15$ according to the gray levels in **tablegray**. The option **PlotRange- > {0,1}** guarantees that the vertical axis includes all values between 0 and 1.

Out[53]=
-Graphics-

100% ▼

RayleighDistribution 586

Package: **ContinuousDistributions.m**

RayleighDistribution[s] represents the Rayleigh distribution.

Example:

A table of cumulative distribution functions for the logistic distribution is found below with the parameters s = 1, 2, 3. This table is called **rdtable** and is plotted using three levels of gray defined in **tablegray** (created in the beta distribution example) as well as the **PlotRange** option.

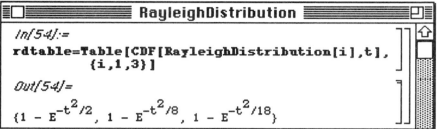

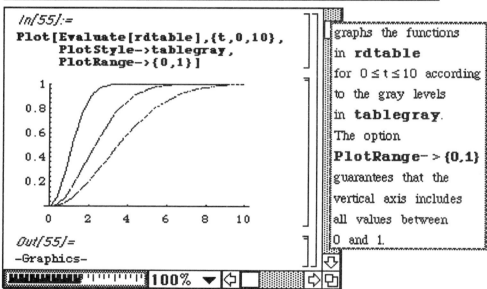

UniformDistribution 586

Package: **ContinuousDistributions.m**

UniformDistribution[a,b] yields the uniform distribution on the interval {a,b}.

Example:

A table of cumulative distribution functions for the uniform distribution is found below over the interval [0,i] where i = 1, 2, 3. The functions in **uniftable** are plotted according to the levels of gray given in **tablegray** which was introduced in the beta distribution example as well the **PlotRange** option.

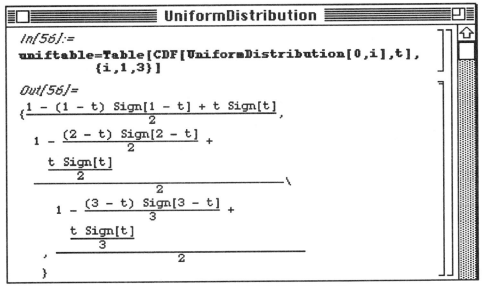

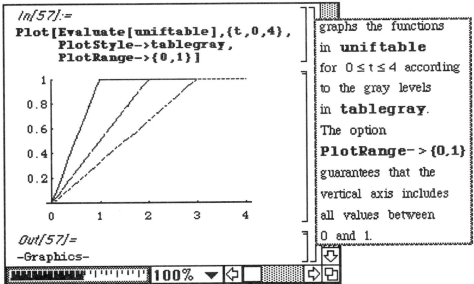

WeibullDistribution   586

Package: **ContinuousDistributions.m**

  WeibullDistribution[a,b] represents the Weibull distribution.

Example:

A table of cumulative distribution functions for the Weibull distribution is found below for a = 1, 2, 3 and b = 2. This table, named **wbtable**, is plotted using the levels of gray indicated in **tablegray** along with the setting **PlotRange->{0,1}**. Note that **tablegray** is created in the example for the beta distribution.

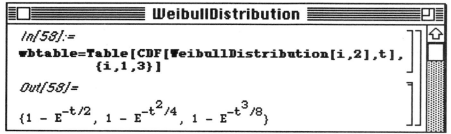

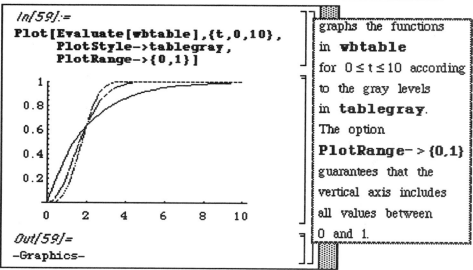

Another table, named **wbtable2**, is generated for a = 2 and b = 1, 2, 3. This table is plotted in a similar manner.

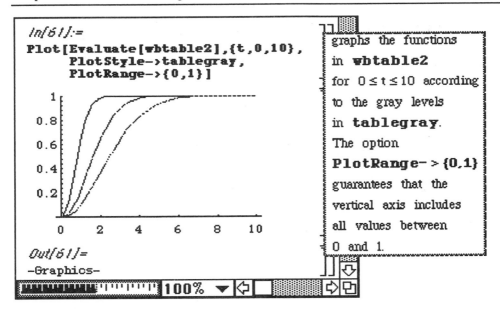

In[61]:=
```
Plot[Evaluate[wbtable2],{t,0,10},
    PlotStyle->tablegray,
    PlotRange->{0,1}]
```

graphs the functions in **wbtable2** for $0 \le t \le 10$ according to the gray levels in **tablegray**. The option **PlotRange- > {0,1}** guarantees that the vertical axis includes all values between 0 and 1.

Out[61]=
-Graphics-

DataManipulation.m

Column   Package: **DataManipulation.m**
   Column[datalist,n] yields the the nth column in the array **datalist** while
Column[datalist,{n1,n2,...}] lists the columns **n1,n2,...**.
Example:
A list of values called **dlist** is entered and placed in **MatrixForm**. The command
Column[dlist,2] extracts the second column of **dlist**. This result is displayed as
a column with **ColumnForm**.

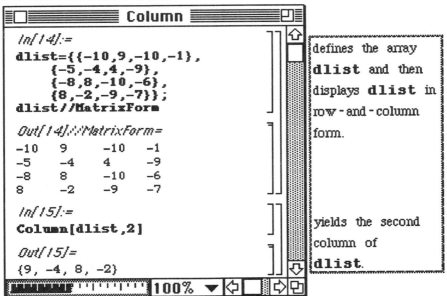

```
          Column
```

In[14]:=
```
dlist={{-10,9,-10,-1},
    {-5,-4,4,-9},
    {-8,8,-10,-6},
    {8,-2,-9,-7}};
dlist//MatrixForm
```

defines the array **dlist** and then displays **dlist** in row - and - column form.

Out[14]//MatrixForm=
```
-10    9      -10    -1
-5     -4     4      -9
-8     8      -10    -6
8      -2     -9     -7
```

In[15]:=
```
Column[dlist,2]
```

yields the second column of **dlist**.

Out[15]=
```
{9, -4, 8, -2}
```

ColumnTake   Package: **DataManipulation.m**

  ColumnTake[datalist,{n}] extracts the **n**th column of **datalist** while
ColumnTake[datalist,{m,n}] takes the **m**th through the **n**th columns from
datalist. This command can be entered as **ColumnTake[datalist,{-n}]** to
extract the **n**th column of **datalist** counting from the end of **datalist**.
Example:

A list of values called **dlist** which was entered in the **Column** example is considered
again below. The command **ColumnTake[dlist,{2}]** yields the second column
of **dlist**. The first two columns are extracted using the command
ColumnTake[dlist,{1,2}]. Also, the third column results with
ColumnTake[dlist,{-1}]. Results are more easily viewed in **MatrixForm**.

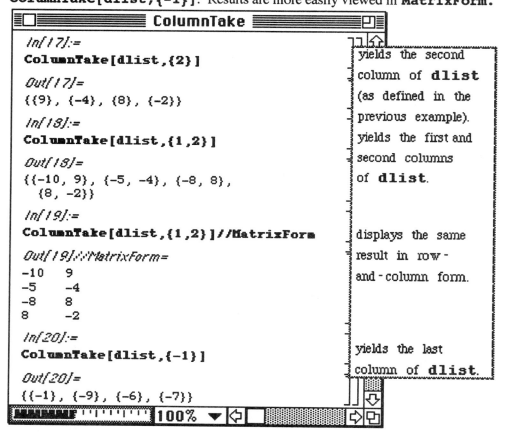

ColumnDrop   Package: **DataManipulation.m**

  ColumnDrop[datalist,{n}] removes the **n**th column from **datalist** while
ColumnDrop[datalist,{m,n}] removes the **m**th through the **n**th columns from
datalist. This command can be entered as **ColumnDrop[datalist,{-n}]** to
remove the **n**th column counting from the end of **datalist**.
Example:

The list of values called **dlist** which was entered in the **Column** example is
considered again below. The second column of **dlist** is eliminated by the command
ColumnDrop[dlist,{2}].

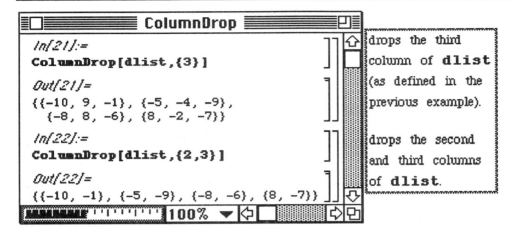

In[21]:=
ColumnDrop[dlist,{3}]

Out[21]=
{{-10, 9, -1}, {-5, -4, -9},
  {-8, 8, -6}, {8, -2, -7}}

In[22]:=
ColumnDrop[dlist,{2,3}]

Out[22]=
{{-10, -1}, {-5, -9}, {-8, -6}, {8, -7}}

drops the third column of **dlist** (as defined in the previous example).

drops the second and third columns of **dlist**.

ColumnJoin   Package: **DataManipulation.m**
    ColumnJoin[datalist1,datalist2,...] joins the columns of the lists of data. Note that the number of columns of each list must be equal.
Example:
Two lists of values called **listone** and **listtwo** are entered below.

In[25]:=
**listone={{1,-2,7},{10,3,0},
    {-9,2,0}};
listtwo={{1,-8,8},{-4,1,8}};**

The columns of these two lists are joined with **ColumnJoin[listone,listtwo]** and the result is viewed in **MatrixForm**. Note that the sublists of **listone** and **listtwo** have the same length.

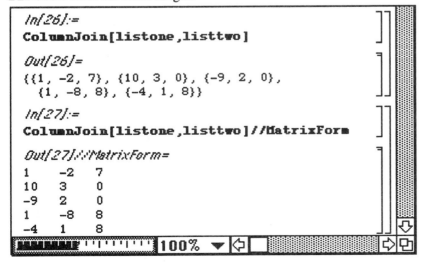

In[26]:=
ColumnJoin[listone,listtwo]

Out[26]=
{{1, -2, 7}, {10, 3, 0}, {-9, 2, 0},
  {1, -8, 8}, {-4, 1, 8}}

In[27]:=
ColumnJoin[listone,listtwo]//MatrixForm

Out[27]//MatrixForm=
1	-2	7
10	3	0
-9	2	0
1	-8	8
-4	1	8

RowJoin   Package: **DataManipulation.m**

RowJoin[datalist1,datalist2,...] joins the rows of the lists of data. Note that the number of rows of each list must be equal.

Example:

The list of values, called **listone**, used in the **ColumnJoin** example is used again below. Another list called **listthree** is entered as well.

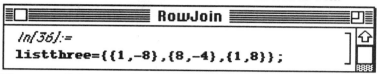

The rows of these two lists are joined with the command **RowJoin[listone,listthree]**. The result is then given in **MatrixForm**. Note that these lists have the same number of sublists.

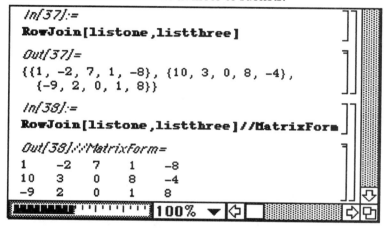

DropNonNumeric   Package: **DataManipulation.m**

DropNonNumeric[datalist] eliminates the non-numerical elements of **datalist** while **DropNonNumeric[dataarray]** removes the rows of **dataarray** which have non-numerical elements.

Example:

A list of values, called **clist**, is entered below. The command **DropNonNumeric[clist]** eliminates the elements of **clist** which are not numerical. A 3 × 3 array which contains only one non-numerical element which is located in the second row and column is then considered. **DropNonNumeric** causes the element of this array (the second row since elements are entered as rows) to be eliminated.

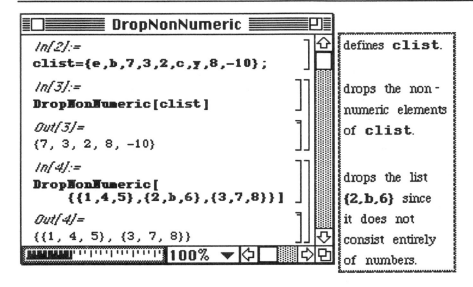

In[2]:= `clist={e,b,7,3,2,c,y,8,-10};`	defines **clist**.

In[3]:=
`DropNonNumeric[clist]`
Out[3]=
`{7, 3, 2, 8, -10}`
	drops the non-numeric elements of **clist**.

In[4]:=
`DropNonNumeric[`
`    {{1,4,5},{2,b,6},{3,7,8}}]`
Out[4]=
`{{1, 4, 5}, {3, 7, 8}}`
	drops the list {2,b,6} since it does not consist entirely of numbers.

DropNonNumericColumn Package: **DataManipulation.m**

   DropNonNumericColumn[dataarray] eliminates the columns of **dataarray** which have non-numerical elements.

Example:

A list of values, called **col**, is entered below and viewed in **MatrixForm** to see that the third column of col is non-numerical. The command **DropNonNumericColumn[col]** eliminates this column of **col**.

```
In[6]:=
col={{1,2,a},{3,4,b},{5,6,c}};
col//MatrixForm

Out[6]//MatrixForm=
1   2   a
3   4   b
5   6   c

In[7]:=
DropNonNumericColumn[col]//MatrixForm

Out[7]//MatrixForm=
1   2
3   4
5   6
```

A second array is then entered and viewed in **MatrixForm** to reveal that it contains one non-numeric element in the second column. Hence, **DropNonNumericColumn** removes the second column from this array.

```
In[8]:=
{{1,4,5},{2,b,6},{3,7,8}}//MatrixForm

Out[8]//MatrixForm=
1   4   5
2   b   6
3   7   8

In[9]:=
DropNonNumericColumn[{{1,4,5},
{2,b,6},{3,7,8}}]//MatrixForm

Out[9]//MatrixForm=
1   5
2   6
3   8
```

BooleanSelect   Package: **DataManipulation.m**

BooleanSelect[datalist,boolean] allows the elements of **datalist** for which the value of the corresponding member of **boolean** is True to remain in the list.

Example:

The following example indicates how **BooleanSelect** is used to return elements with corresponding True boolean values. Since the number **1** corresponds to True in the second list, the result of **BooleanSelect** is {1}.

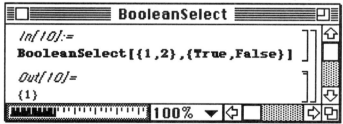

```
BooleanSelect

In[10]:=
BooleanSelect[{1,2},{True,False}]

Out[10]=
{1}
```

TakeWhile   Package: **DataManipulation.m**

TakeWhile[datalist,test] lists the elements of **datalist** while the value of **test** is True.

Example:

The following example illustrates the **TakeWhile** command. In this case, the elements of the given list are taken until an element for which the value of the test function **OddQ** is False.

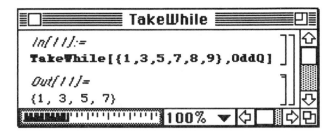

LengthWhile   Package: **DataManipulation.m**

  LengthWhile[datalist,test] yields the length of the list given by
TakeWhile[datalist,test]. In other words, **LengthWhile** gives the number
of adjoining elements of **datalist** from the beginning of the list for which **test** is
True. Possible settings for test include **IntegerQ**, **EvenQ**, **OddQ**, and **NumberQ**.
Example:
The following example yields the length of the list which results from the command
TakeWhile[{1,3,5,7,8,9},OddQ] which is considered in the **TakeWhile**
example. This list is **{1,2,5,7}** and has length 4 as indicated by the output below.

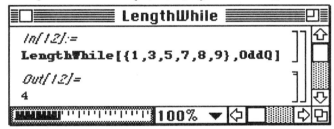

Frequencies   Package: **DataManipulation.m**

  Frequencies[datalist] yields a list of the elements of **datalist** with the
corresponding frequency of each. Hence, each member of the output list of
Frequencies is of the form **{freq,element}**.
Example:
In the example below, a list of integers, called **digits**, is entered which represents the
digits of 100! (also obtained with the command **Factorial[100]**).

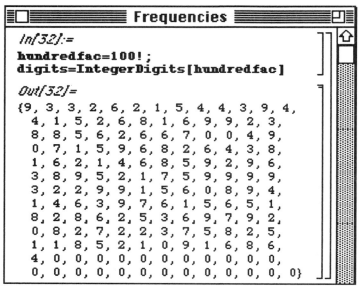

The frequencies of these digits are then determined. The results mean that 100! has thirty zeros, fifteen ones, nineteen twos, and so on.

```
In[33]:=
Frequencies[digits]

Out[33]=
{{30, 0}, {15, 1}, {19, 2}, {10, 3},
  {10, 4}, {14, 5}, {19, 6}, {7, 7},
  {14, 8}, {20, 9}}
```

QuantileForm   Package: **DataManipulation.m**

  QuantileForm[datalist] sorts the elements of **datalist** and prints these elements with the corresponding quantile position for each. The members of the output list have the form {quantile,element}.

Example:

In the example below, a list of integers, called **numbers**, is entered. The list of quantile numbers for each element of **numbers** is given with **QuantileForm[numbers]**.

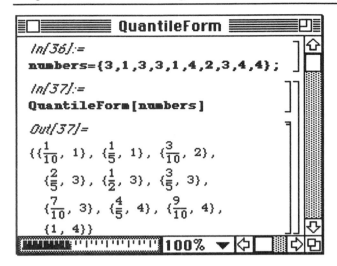

CumulativeSums   Package: **DataManipulation.m**

  CumulativeSums[datalist] lists the cumulative sums corresponding to the elements of **datalist**.

Example:

A list of integers, called **numbers**, is entered in the example below. The list of cumulative sums for **numbers**, 17, 17+(−13), 17+(−13)+(−13), 17+(−13)+(−13)+11, and so on, is then determined.

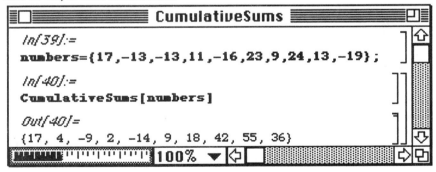

BinCounts   Package: **DataManipulation.m**

  BinCounts[numberlist,{a,b,step}] yields the number of elements of **numberlist** which lie on the intervals from **a** to **b** using increments of **step**.

Example:

A list of 50 integers, called **dlist**, is entered in the example below. The number of integers from this list which falls in the intervals 0-5, 6-10, 11-15, 16-20, and 21-25 is then found with **BinCounts**.

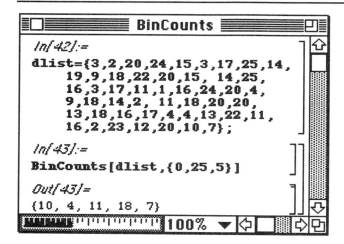

RangeCounts   Package: **DataManipulation.m**
    RangeCounts[numberlist,{cut1,cut2,...}] yields the number of the
elements of **numberlist** which lie on the intervals determined by the cut-off values
indicated in **{cut1,cut2,...}**.
Example:
A list of 50 integers, called **dlist**, which was entered in the **BinCounts** example is
considered again below. The number of integers from this list which fall in the
intervals less than 1, 1-3, 4-9, 10-17, 18-24, and 25 or greater is then found with
RangeCounts.

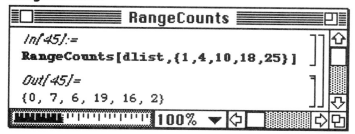

CategoryCounts   Package: **DataManipulation.m**
    CategoryCounts[datalist,{list1,list2,...}] yields the number of the
elements of **datalist** which match any of the elements of **list1, list2,** ... .
Example:
The list of 50 integers, called **dlist**, used in the **BinCounts** example above is
considered in the example below. The number of elements of **dlist** which match the
elements of **{1,5,10,15,20,25}** is found. In the same manner, **CategoryCount**
is used to count the number of zeros in the list **digits** which was defined in the
example for **Frequencies**.

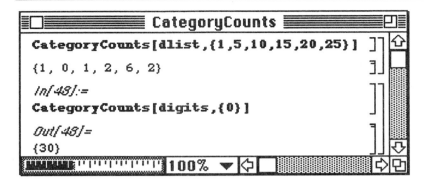

BinLists   Package: **DataManipulation.m**

  BinLists[numberlist,{a,b,step}] lists the elements of **numberlist** which lie in the intervals from **a** to **b** using increments of **step**. Elements of **numberlist** which match the upper limit of a subdivision of the interval from **a** to **b** are included in that interval.

Example:

Again, the list of 50 integers, called **dlist**, which is entered in the BinCounts example is considered below. The elements of **dlist** which fall in the bins defined by **BinCounts[dlist,{0,25,5}]** are listed according to the intervals in which they fall. The number of elements in each interval correspond to the results of **BinCounts[dlist,{0,25,5}]**.

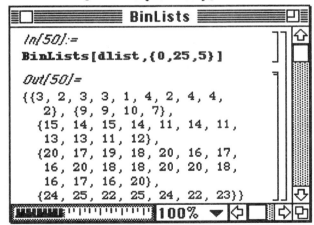

RangeLists   Package: **DataManipulation.m**

  RangeLists[numberlist,{cut1,cut2,...}] yields a list of the elements of **numberlist** which lie on the intervals determined by the cut-off values indicated in **{cut1,cut2,...}**.

Example:

The list of 50 integers, called **dlist**, which is introduced in the **BinCounts** example is considered in the example below. The elements of **dlist** which fall in the intervals defined in **RangeCounts[dlist,{1,4,10,18,25}]** are then given. The number in each interval corresponds to the results of **RangeCounts[dlist,{1,4,10,18,25}]**.

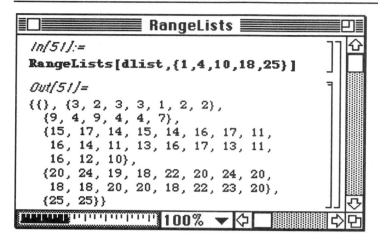

CategoryLists   Package: **DataManipulation.m**
  CategoryLists[datalist,{list1,list2,...}] yields a list of the
elements of **datalist** which match any of the elements of **list1, list2,** ... .
Example:
A list of 50 integers, called **dlist**, is entered in the example below. First, the
elements of **dlist** which match the elements in **{1,5,10,15,20,25}** are given
with **CategoryLists[dlist,{1,5,10,15,20,25}]**. The number of elements
which match each term of **{1,5,10,15,20,25}** match the results of
CategoryCounts[dlist,{1,5,10,15,20,25}]. Second, the elements of
dlist which match any of the elements of the sublists {8}, {1,5,10}, and {9,15,20,25}
are given.

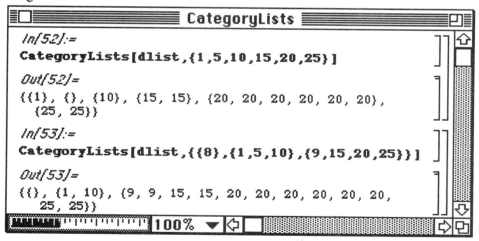

DescriptiveStatistics.m

Mean   Package: **DescriptiveStatistics.m**
Mean[datalist] yields the mean of the list **datalist** of n values given by

the formula $\sum_{i=1}^{n} x_i$ where x_i represents the ith element of **datalist**. **Mean** can be

used to determine the mean of the distributions included in the package

DiscreteDistributions.m.
Example:
A list of integers representing the grades of 50 students is given in **grades** below. The
mean of these grades is then determined. Since the result is given as a fraction, a
numerical approximation is requested.

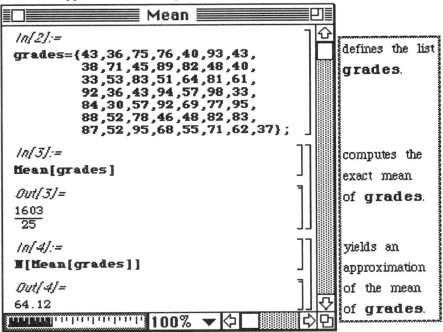

Median   Package: **DescriptiveStatistics.m**
   Median[datalist] yields the median of the list of values given in **datalist**
where the median is the middle term if **datalist** has an odd number of elements and
the mean of the two middle terms if **datalist** has an even number of elements.
Example:
The list of integers, called **grades**, which represents the grades of 50 students which is
considered in the example below. The median grade is found below.

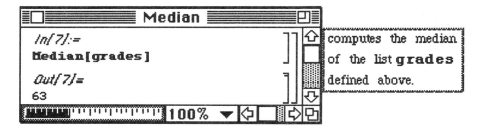

Mode

Mode[datalist] yields the mode of **datalist**. Hence, it gives the element or elements of **datalist** which occur most frequently.

Example:

The list of integers representing the grades of 50 students is introduced in the **Mean** example above. The mode of **grades** is found below.

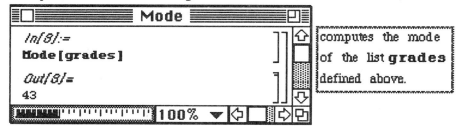

GeometricMean

GeometricMean[datalist] yields the geometric mean of the list

datalist of n values given by the formula $\prod_{i=1}^{n} x_i^{1/n}$ where x_i represents

the ith element of **datalist**.

Example:

A list of integers representing the grades of 50 students, called **grades**, is again considered below. In this case, the geometric mean of this list of grades is found. Since the exact value is given, a numerical approximation is determined.

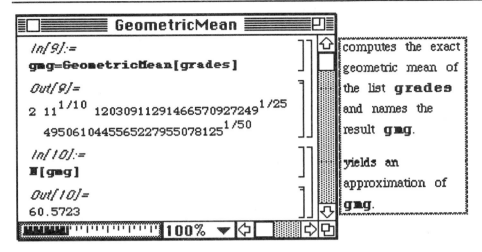

HarmonicMean

HarmonicMean[datalist] yields the harmonic mean of **datalist**.

This value is determined by the formula $\dfrac{n}{\displaystyle\sum_{k=1}^{n} \dfrac{1}{x_k}}$ where x_k represents the kth

element of **datalist**.

Example:

A list of integers representing the grades of 50 students is considered below. This list, called **grades**, is introduced in the **Mean** example above. In the following example, the harmonic mean of this list is found. Since the result is given as a fraction, a numerical approximation is determined.

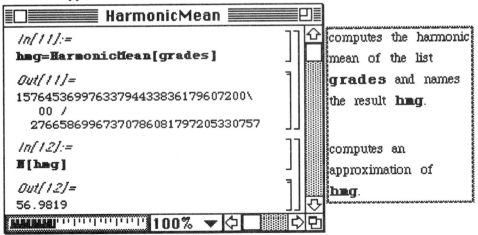

RootMeanSquare   Package: **DescriptiveStatistics.m**
  RootMeanSquare[datalist] computes the root mean square of the

elements of **datalist**. This value is given by $\sqrt{\dfrac{1}{n}\displaystyle\sum_{i=1}^{n}\dfrac{1}{x_i}}$ where x_i represents

the ith element of **datalist**.
Example:
The list of integers, called **grades**, representing the grades of 50 students is introduced
in the **Mean** example above. In the example below, the root mean square of this list of
grades is found. Since the exact value is given, a numerical approximation is
determined.

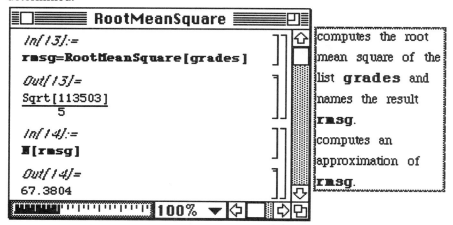

TrimmedMean   Package: **DescriptiveStatistics.m**
  TrimmedMean[datalist,frac] yields the mean of the elements of **datalist**
which are left after the fraction **frac** is removed from each end of the sorted list
corresponding to **datalist**. This command is entered as
TrimmedMean[datalist,{frac1,frac2}] to compute the mean of the
remaining elements after fractions **frac1** and **frac2** of the sorted list are removed
from the beginning and end of **datalist**, respectively.
Example:
The list of integers representing the grades of 50 students is considered in **grades**
below. This list is introduced in the **Mean** example above. The trimmed mean of this
list of grades is then found using **frac** = 1/10. Since the result is given as a fraction, a
numerical approximation is determined. The trimmed mean with
frac1 = **frac2** = 1/10 is found to show that the same result is obtained. To illustrate
that different fractions can be removed from each end of the list, the command
TrimmedMean[grades,2/10,1/10] is used.

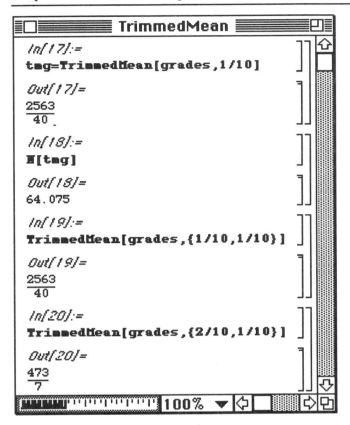

Quantile Package: **DescriptiveStatistics.m**

Quantile[datalist,p] yields the **p**th quantile of **datalist**. The value q which results corresponds to the number such that $P(x_i < q) \le p$ and $P(x_i > q) \ge p$. **Quantile** can be used with the distributions included in **DiscreteDistributions.m** as well.

Example:

The list of integers, called **grades**, representing the grades of 50 students is introduced in the **Mean** example above. In this example, the quartiles of this list of data is found by using **Quantiles**. The command **Quantiles[grades,.25]** gives the grade such that 25% of the grades fall below, **Quantiles[grades,.5]** gives the grade such that 50% of the grades fall below, and **Quantiles[grades,.75]** gives the grade such that 75% of the grades fall below. These values would be yielded by **Quantiles[datalist]** as well.

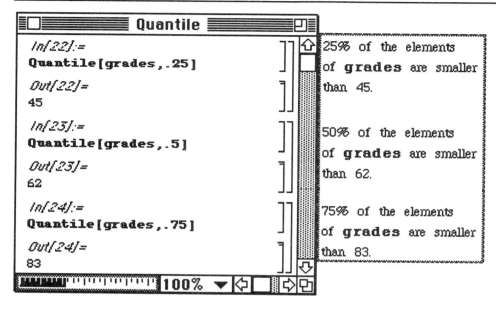

InterpolatedQuantile Package: **DescriptiveStatistics.m**

   InterpolatedQuantile[datalist,p] gives the pth quantile of the distribution obtained through linear interpolation of the elements of **datalist**.

Example:

The list of integers representing the grades of 50 students is considered in **grades** below. This list is introduced in the **Mean** example above. The quartiles of the distribution gained through linear interpolation of the grades is found by using **InterpolatedQuantiles**. Similar values of **p** are used below for comparison with those given under **Quantiles**.

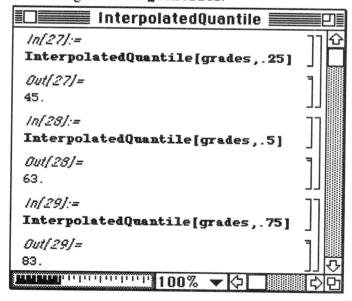

Quartiles Package: **DescriptiveStatistics.m**

Quartiles[datalist] yields the quartiles of **datalist**. These three values are also obtained with **Quantiles[datalist,p]** for **p** = **.25**, **.5**, and **.75**.

Example:

The list of integers, called **grades**, representing the grades of 50 students is introduced in the **Mean** example above. In the example below, the quartiles of the data listed in **grades** is found by using **Quartiles**.

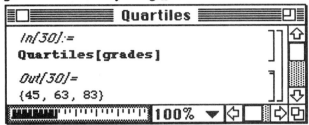

```
In[30]:=
Quartiles[grades]

Out[30]=
{45, 63, 83}
```

LocationReport Package: **DescriptiveStatistics.m**

LocationReport[datalist] lists the values of **Mean**, **HarmonicMean**, and **Median** for the elements given in **datalist**. The output appears in the form {Mean->mean,HarmonicMean->hmean,Median->median}.

Example:

The list of integers representing the grades of 50 students is considered in **grades** below. This list is introduced in the **Mean** example above. The list of values corresponding to the mean, harmonic mean, and median for the data in grades is determined with **LocationReport**. A numerical approximation of this result is then obtained.

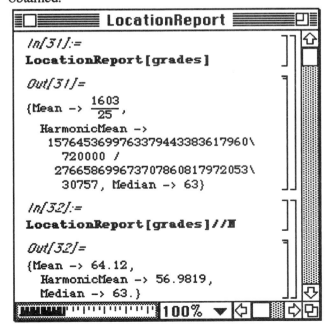

```
In[31]:=
LocationReport[grades]

Out[31]=
         1603
{Mean -> ----,
          25

  HarmonicMean ->
    15764536997633794433836179600\
    720000 /
    27665869967370786081797972053\
    30757, Median -> 63}

In[32]:=
LocationReport[grades]//N

Out[32]=
{Mean -> 64.12,
  HarmonicMean -> 56.9819,
  Median -> 63.}
```

SampleRange   Package: **DescriptiveStatistics.m**
  SampleRange[datalist] yields the range of the information in **datalist**. This value equals the difference between the largest and smallest elements of **datalist**.
Example:
A list of data which represents the monthly power bills of 30 households is entered below and called **price**.

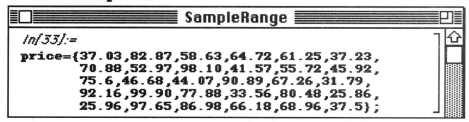

The sample range is then determined with **SampleRange**. This value is verified by taking the difference between the maximum and minimum values in the list of data.

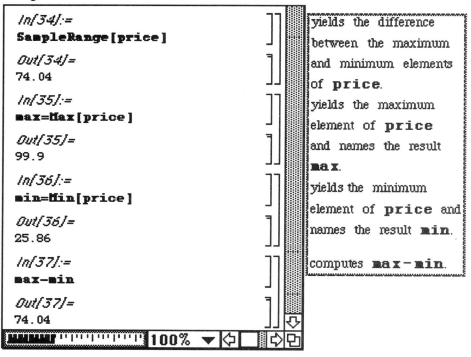

Variance   Package: **DescriptiveStatistics.m**
  Variance[datalist] yields the variance of **datalist** which is determined

by the formula $\dfrac{1}{n-1}\displaystyle\sum_{i=1}^{n}(x_i - \bar{x})^2$ where x_i represents the ith element of **datalist**,

$\bar{x}$ is the mean of **datalist**, and **datalist** has n elements. **Variance** can be

used with the discrete distributions defined in the package

DiscreteDistributions.m.
Example:
A list of data which represents the monthly power bills of 30 households is considered
below and called **price**. This list of data is introduced in the **SampleRange** example
above. In the following example, the variance of this data is determined with
Variance.

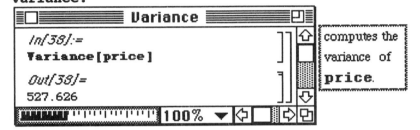

VarianceMLE   Package: **DescriptiveStatistics.m**
  VarianceMLE[datalist] yields the maximum likelihood approximation of

the variance of **datalist** which is determined by the formula $\dfrac{1}{n}\displaystyle\sum_{i=1}^{n}(x_i - \bar{x})^2$

where x_i represents the ith element of **datalist**, $\bar{x}$ is the mean of **datalist**,

and **datalist** has n elements.
Example:
A list of data, called **price**, which represents the monthly power bills of 30
households is considered below. This list of data is introduced in the **SampleRange**
example above. In this case, the maximum likelihood approximation of the variance of
this data is determined with **VarianceMLE.**

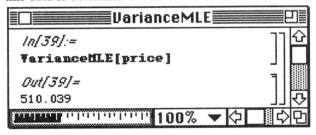

VarianceOfSampleMean Package: **DescriptiveStatistics.m**
  VarianceOfSampleMean[datalist] yields the variance of the sample

mean of **datalist** which is given by $\frac{1}{n-1}$ **Variance[datalist]**.

Example:
A list of data is defined below and named **data**. The variance of the sample mean of this data is determined with **VarianceOfSampleMean.**

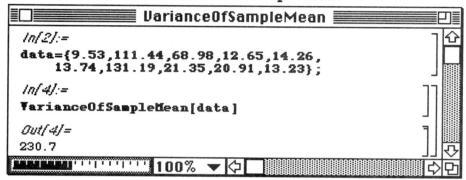

StandardDeviation   Package: **DescriptiveStatistics.m**
  StandardDeviation[datalist] gives the standard deviation of **datalist** which is equal to the square root of **Variance[datalist]**.
StandardDeviation can be used to compute the standard deviation of the discrete distributions given in the package **DiscreteDistributions.m**
Example:
A list of data which represents the monthly power bills of 30 households is considered below and called **price**. This list of data is introduced in the **SampleRange** example above. The standard deviation of this data is determined with **StandardDeviation** in the following example.

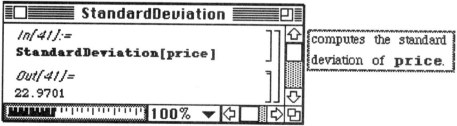

StandardDeviationMLE Package: **DescriptiveStatistics.m**
  StandardDeviation[datalist] yields the maximum likelihood approximation of the standard deviation of **datalist** which is equal to the square root of the value obtained with **VarianceMLE[datalist]**.
Example:
A list of data, called **price**, which represents the monthly power bills of 30 households is considered below. This list of data is introduced in the **SampleRange** example above. The maximum likelihood approximation of the standard deviation of this data is determined below with **StandardDeviationMLE.**

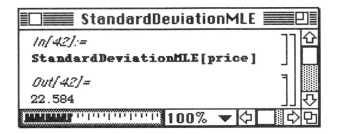

StandardErrorOfSampleMean
Package: **DescriptiveStatistics.m**
  StandardErrorOfSampleMean[datalist] yields the standard deviation of
the sample mean.
Example:
A list of data which represents the monthly power bills of 30 households is considered
below and called **price**. This list of data is introduced in the **SampleRange** example
above. The standard deviation of the data given in **price** is calculated with
StandardErrorOfSampleMean.

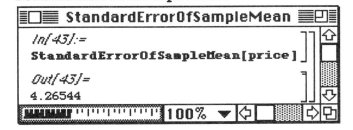

MeanDeviation   Package: **DescriptiveStatistics.m**
  MeanDeviation[datalist] yields the mean absolute deviation which is

determined by the formula $\dfrac{1}{n}\sum\limits_{i=1}^{n}\left|x_i - \bar{x}\right|$ where x_i represents the ith element of the list

datalist of length n and $\bar{x}$ is the mean of **datalist**.
Example:
A list of data, called **price**, which represents the monthly power bills of 30
households is considered below. This list of data is introduced in the **SampleRange**
example above. In this case, the mean absolute deviation of the data given in **price** is
computed with **MeanDeviation**.

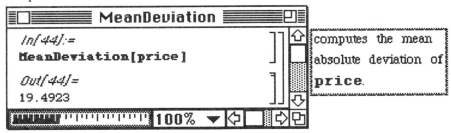

MedianDeviation   Package: **DescriptiveStatistics.m**

MedianDeviation[datalist] yields the median absolute deviation which is

the median of the values $|x_i - x_{med}|$ where x_i represents the ith element of the list

datalist of length n and x_{med} is the median of **datalist**.

Example:

A list of data which represents the monthly power bills of 30 households is considered below and called **price**. This list of data is introduced in the **SampleRange** example above. The median absolute deviation of the data given in **price** is determined with **MedianDeviation**.

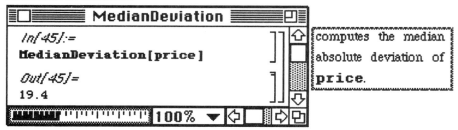

InterquartileRange   Package: **DescriptiveStatistics.m**

InterquartileRange[datalist] yields the value of the difference **Quantile[datalist,.75]-Quantile[datalist,.25]**.

Example:

A list of data, called **price**, which represents the monthly power bills of 30 households is considered below. This list of data is introduced in the **SampleRange** example above. In the following example, the interquartile range of the data given in **price** is determined with **InterquartileRange**. This calculation is then verified.

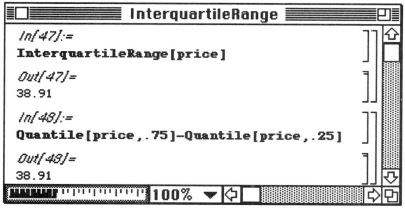

QuartileDeviation

QuartileDeviation[datalist] gives the quartile deviation of **datalist**.

Example:

A list of data which represents the monthly power bills of 30 households is considered below and called **price**. This list of data is introduced in the **SampleRange** example above. The quartile deviation of the data given in **price** is computed with **QuartileDeviation**.

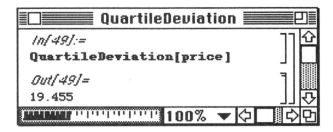

DispersionReport

DispersionReport[datalist] lists the values of variance, standard deviation, sample range, mean deviation, median deviation, and quartile deviation for the data listed in **datalist**. The result of **DispersionReport** is of the form of the list {Variance->var,StandardDeviation->sd,SampleRange->sr, MeanDeviation->md,QuartileDeviation->qd}.

Example:
A list of data, called **price**, which represents the monthly power bills of 30 households is considered below. This list of data is introduced in the **SampleRange** example above. The dispersion report of the data given in **price** is computed below with **DispersionReport**.

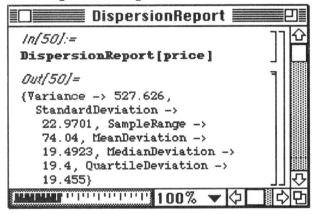

CentralMoment   Package: **DescriptiveStatistics.m**

CentralMoment[datalist,j] yields the jth central moment of

datalist. This value is found with the formula $\dfrac{1}{n}\sum_{i=1}^{n}(x_i - \bar{x})^j$ where x_i

represents the ith element of **datalist**, $\bar{x}$ is the mean of **datalist**, and

datalist has n elements.

Example:
A list of data which represents the monthly power bills of 30 households is considered below and called **price**. This list of data is introduced in the **SampleRange** example above. The first, second, and third central moments are calculated for the data given with **price**.

Skewness   Package: **DescriptiveStatistics.m**
   Skewness[datalist] gives the skewness coefficient of **datalist**. This

value is determined by the formula $\dfrac{1}{\sigma^3 n}\sum\limits_{i=1}^{n}(x_i - \bar{x})^3$ where x_i represents the ith element

of the list **datalist** of n elements, $\bar{x}$ is the mean of **datalist**, and σ is the

standard deviation of **datalist**. **Skewness** can be used to determine the

skewness of the discrete distributions found in **DiscreteDistributions.m**.
Example:

A list of data, called **price**, which represents the monthly power bills of 30 households is considered below. This list of data is introduced in the **SampleRange** example above. In the following example, the skewness is calculated for the data given with **price**. The computation is verified using the indicated formula following the determination of the standard deviation of **price**.

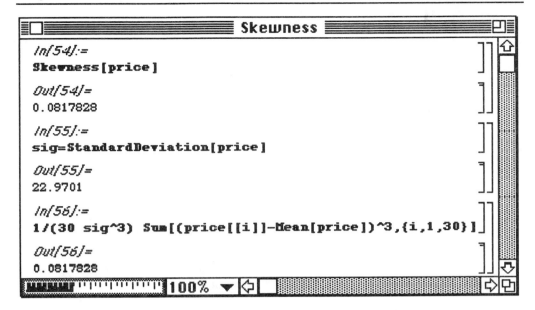

In[54]:=
Skewness[price]

Out[54]=
0.0817828

In[55]:=
sig=StandardDeviation[price]

Out[55]=
22.9701

In[56]:=
1/(30 sig^3) Sum[(price[[i]]-Mean[price])^3,{i,1,30}]

Out[56]=
0.0817828

PearsonSkewness1   Package: **DescriptiveStatistics.m**

  PearsonSkewness1[datalist] determines Pearson's first coefficient of

skewness for **datalist**. This value is determined by $\dfrac{3}{\sigma}(\bar{x} - x_{mode})$ where $\bar{x}$ and

x_{mode} represent the mean and mode of **datalist**, respectively, and σ is the

standard deviation of **datalist**.

Example:
A list of data which represents the monthly power bills of 30 households is considered
below and called **price**. This list of data is introduced in the **SampleRange** example
above. The determination of Pearson's first coefficient is attempted. However, since
no element of price is repeated, the mode of price does not exist.

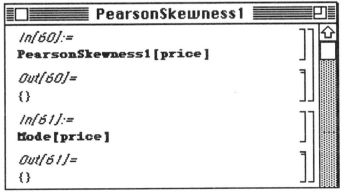

In[60]:=
PearsonSkewness1[price]

Out[60]=
{}

In[61]:=
Mode[price]

Out[61]=
{}

To illustrate the use of **PearsonSkewness1**, a list of 50 grades, called **grades**, is
entered. Then, Pearson's first coefficient is found.

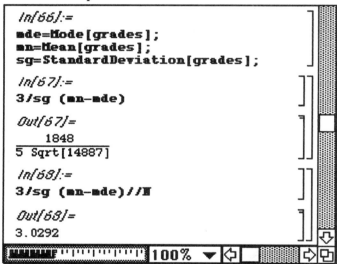

This result is verified using the stated formula above, and a numerical approximation of the result is requested.

PearsonSkewness2   Package: **DescriptiveStatistics.m**

PearsonSkewness2[datalist] determines Pearson's second coefficient of skewness for **datalist**. This value is determined by $\frac{3}{\sigma}(\bar{x} - x_{med})$ where $\bar{x}$ and x_{med} represent the mean and median of **datalist**, respectively, and σ is the standard deviation of **datalist**.

Example:

A list of data, called **price**, which represents the monthly power bills of 30 households is considered below. This list of data is introduced in the **SampleRange** example above. The determination of Pearson's second coefficient is performed below. This calculation is verified using the formula stated above.

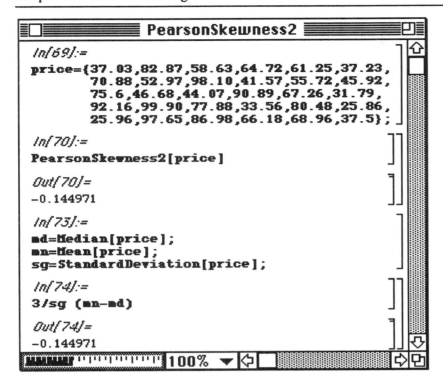

```
In[69]:=
price={37.03,82.87,58.63,64.72,61.25,37.23,
       70.88,52.97,98.10,41.57,55.72,45.92,
       75.6,46.68,44.07,90.89,67.26,31.79,
       92.16,99.90,77.88,33.56,80.48,25.86,
       25.96,97.65,86.98,66.18,68.96,37.5};

In[70]:=
PearsonSkewness2[price]

Out[70]=
-0.144971

In[73]:=
md=Median[price];
mn=Mean[price];
sg=StandardDeviation[price];

In[74]:=
3/sg (mn-md)

Out[74]=
-0.144971
```

QuartileSkewness   Package: **DescriptiveStatistics.m**

  QuartileSkewness[datalist] yields the quartile coefficient of skewness of **datalist**. This value measures the asymmetry between the first and third quantiles.

Example:

A list of data which represents the monthly power bills of 30 households is considered below and called **price**. This list of data is introduced in the **SampleRange** example above. The coefficient of skewness is computed in this example with **QuartileSkewness**.

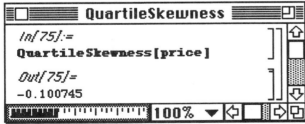

```
In[75]:=
QuartileSkewness[price]

Out[75]=
-0.100745
```

Kurtosis   Package: **DescriptiveStatistics.m**
Kurtosis[datalist] gives the kurtosis coefficient of **datalist**. This

value is determined by the formula $\dfrac{1}{\sigma^4 n}\sum\limits_{i=1}^{n}(x_i - \bar{x})^4$ where x_i represents the ith

element of the list **datalist** of n elements, $\bar{x}$ is the mean of **datalist**,

and σ is the standard deviation of **datalist**. **Kurtosis** can be used with the

discrete distributions given in **DiscreteDistributions.m**.
Example:
A list of data, called **price**, which represents the monthly power bills of 30
households is considered below. This list of data is introduced in the **SampleRange**
example above. The determination of the kurtosis coefficient is performed. This
calculation is then verified using the formula stated above.

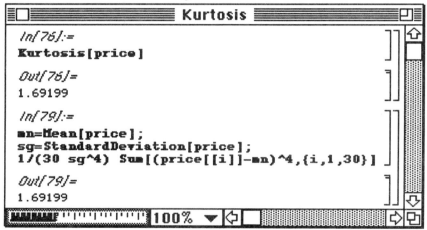

```
In[78]:=
Kurtosis[price]

Out[78]=
1.69199

In[79]:=
mn=Mean[price];
sg=StandardDeviation[price];
1/(30 sg^4) Sum[(price[[i]]-mn)^4,{i,1,30}]

Out[79]=
1.69199
```

KurtosisExcess   Package: **DescriptiveStatistics.m**
KurtosisExcess[datalist] gives the kurtosis excess of **datalist**.
Example:
A list of data which represents the monthly power bills of 30 households is considered
below and called **price**. This list of data is introduced in the **SampleRange** example
above. The determination of the kurtosis excess of the data listed in **price** is
performed below with **KurtosisExcess**.

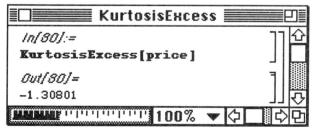

```
In[80]:=
KurtosisExcess[price]

Out[80]=
-1.30801
```

ShapeReport   Package: **DescriptiveStatistics.m**
  ShapeReport[datalist] lists the values of **Skewness**, **QuartileSkewness**,
and **KurtosisExcess** for datalist. These values appear in the form
{Skewness->skew,QuartileSkewness->qskew,
          KurtosisExcess->kexcess}.
Example:
A list of data, called **price**, which represents the monthly power bills of 30
households is considered below. This list of data is introduced in the **SampleRange**
example above. The determination of the shape report of the data listed in **price** is
performed with **ShapeReport** below.

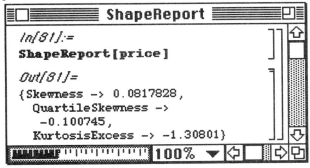

DiscreteDistributions.m

BernoulliDistribution
                    589
                    Package: **DiscreteDistributions.m**
  BernoulliDistribution[p] represents the Bernoulli distribution of mean **p**.
This is the probability distribution for one trial where success occurs with probability **p**
and failure with probability (**1-p**). Success and failure correspond to the values of 1
and 0, respectively.
Example:
The Bernoulli distribution with **p** = 0.4 is determined below and called **bd**. The mean
and variance for this case is then found.

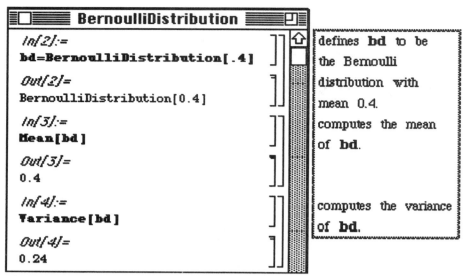

Also, the mean and variance for the Bernoulli distribution for any value of **p** is determined. The characteristic function for **bd** is calculated as well.

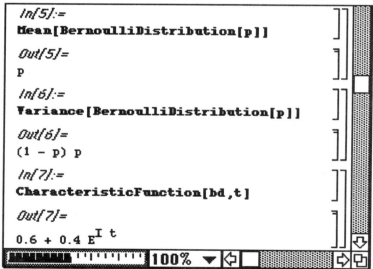

BinomialDistribution 589

Package: **DiscreteDistributions.m**

BinomialDistribution[n,p] yields the distribution $\binom{n}{m} p^n (1-p)^{n-m}$.

Thus, the number of successes in n trials in which success occurs with probability p and failure with probability (1-p).

Example:
The binomial distribution with **n** = 50 and **p** = 0.2 is determined below and called **bin**. The mean for this particular case of the binomial distribution is then determined. The mean as well as the variance are computed for the general form of the binomial distribution.

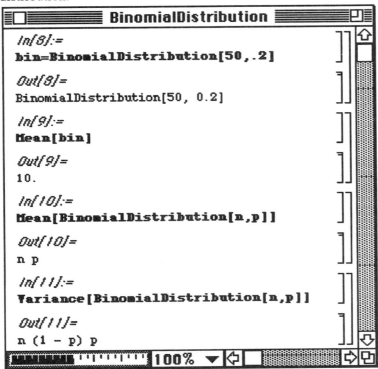

```
In[8]:=
bin=BinomialDistribution[50,.2]

Out[8]=
BinomialDistribution[50, 0.2]

In[9]:=
Mean[bin]

Out[9]=
10.

In[10]:=
Mean[BinomialDistribution[n,p]]

Out[10]=
n p

In[11]:=
Variance[BinomialDistribution[n,p]]

Out[11]=
n (1 - p) p
```

DiscreteUniformDistribution
589, 590
Package: **DiscreteDistributions.m**

  DiscreteUniformDistribution[ns] represents the discrete uniform distribution where there are **ns** states or outcomes. Each outcome occurs with equal probability.

Example:
The discrete distribution with **ns** = 7 is determined below and called **du**. The mean, standard deviation, variance, and characteristic function for this particular case of the distribution are then determined.

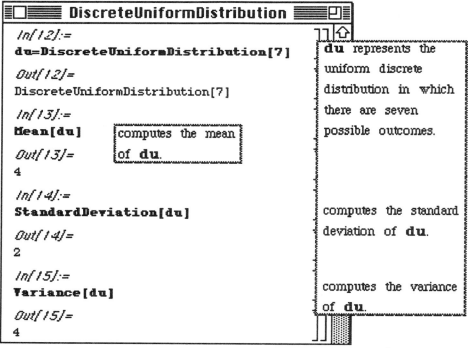

CharacteristicFunction is used to compute $\int p(x) e^{i\,tx}\,dx$, where p(x) is the probability density for **du**, the discrete uniform distribution in which there are seven possible outcomes.

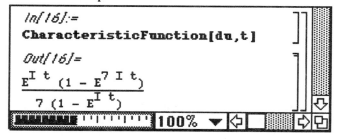

GeometricDistribution
589, 590
Package: **DiscreteDistributions.m**

GeometricDistribution[p] yields the geometric distribution. This represents the distribution of the number of trials before the first success in a sequence of trials in which the probability of success is **p** for each trial.

Example:

The geometric distribution is determined below and called **gd**. The mean and variance for the geometric distribution with parameter **p** is then determined.

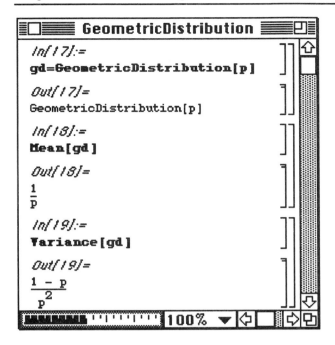

HypergeometricDistribution
589, 590
Package: **DiscreteDistributions.m**

HypergeometricDistribution[n,ns,ntot] yields the hypergeometric distribution using **n** trials with **ns** total successes in a population of **ntot** in size. This distribution is used instead of the binomial distribution when sampling without replacement is employed and has probability function

$$f(x) = \frac{\binom{ns}{x}\binom{ntot-ns}{n-x}}{\binom{ntot}{n}}.$$

Example:

The hypergeometric distribution is determined below and called **hgd**. The mean and variance for this distribution with parameters n, total, and success is then determined. The cumulative distribution function is found for **n** = 10, **ns** = 15, and **ntot** = 20 in **table1**.

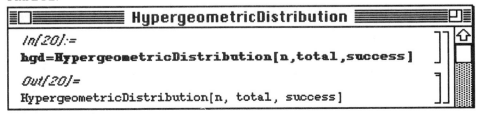

In[21]:=
Mean[hgd]

Out[21]=
$\dfrac{\text{n total}}{\text{success}}$

In[22]:=
Variance[hgd]

Out[22]=
$\dfrac{\text{n (-n + success) total } (1 - \frac{\text{total}}{\text{success}})}{(-1 + \text{success}) \text{ success}}$

In[23]:=
**table1=Table[CDF[HypergeometricDistribution[10,15,20],x],
       {x,1,10}]**

Out[23]=
$\{0, 0, 0, 0, \dfrac{21}{1292}, \dfrac{49}{323}, \dfrac{1}{2}, \dfrac{274}{323}, \dfrac{1271}{1292}, 1\}$

The values in **table1** are then plotted with **ListPlot**.

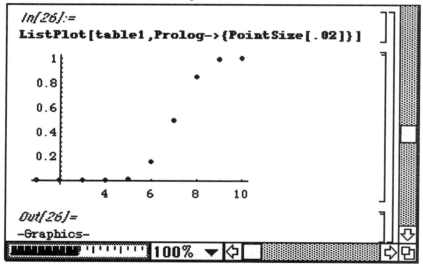

In[26]:=
ListPlot[table1,Prolog->{PointSize[.02]}]

Out[26]=
-Graphics-

100%

LogSeriesDistribution

Package: **DiscreteDistributions.m**

LogSeriesDistribution[t] yields the logarithmic series distribution with parameter **t**.

Example:

The logarithmic distribution with parameter **theta** is determined below and called **log**. The mean of this distribution is then computed as is the mean of the logarithmic distribution with **theta** = 0.8.

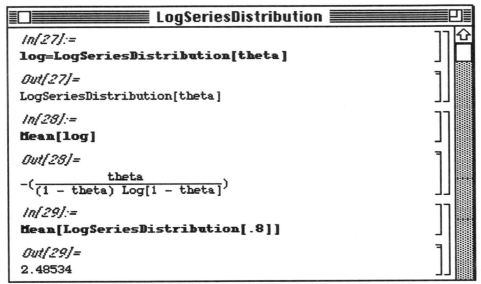

The cumulative distribution function for x-values on the interval from x = 1 to x = 30 using increments of 1 is created in **lgtable**.

```
In[30]:=
lgtable=Table[CDF[LogSeriesDistribution[.8],x],
        {x,1,30}]

Out[30]=
{1.8, 2.12, 2.29067, 2.39307, 2.4586, 2.50229,
   2.53225, 2.55322, 2.56814, 2.57887, 2.58668,
   2.59241, 2.59664, 2.59978, 2.60213, 2.60389,
   2.60521, 2.60621, 2.60697, 2.60755, 2.60799,
   2.60832, 2.60858, 2.60877, 2.60893, 2.60904,
   2.60913, 2.6092, 2.60925, 2.60929}
```

This table is then plotted with **ListPlot**.

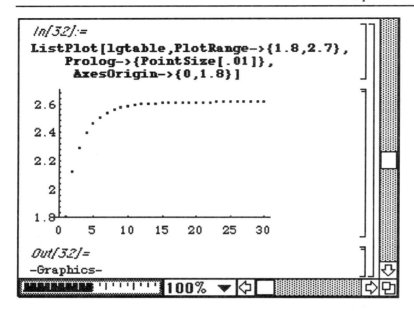

NegativeBinomialDistribution
589, 590

Package: **DiscreteDistributions.m**

NegativeBinomialDistribution[n,p] represents the distribution of the number of failures that happen in a sequence of trials before **n** successes occur assuming that the probability of success is **p**.

Example:

The negative binomial distribution with parameters **nf** and **p** is determined below and called **nbd**. The mean and variance of this distribution is then calculated. The characteristic function for this distribution is also found. The last example illustrates how commands from the package **DescriptiveStatistics** can be used with the distributions in **DiscreteDistributions**.

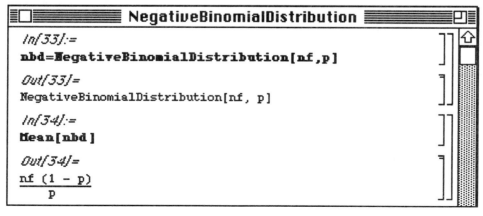

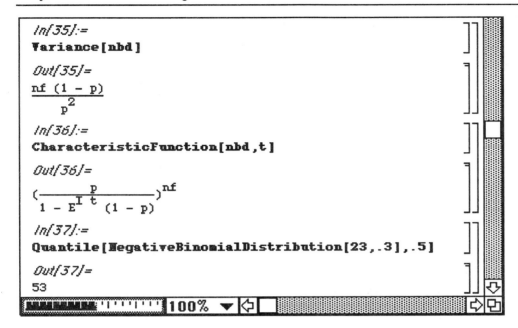

In[35]:=
Variance[nbd]

Out[35]=
$$\frac{nf\ (1\ -\ p)}{p^2}$$

In[36]:=
CharacteristicFunction[nbd,t]

Out[36]=
$$(\frac{p}{1\ -\ E^{I\ t}\ (1\ -\ p)})^{nf}$$

In[37]:=
Quantile[NegativeBinomialDistribution[23,.3],.5]

Out[37]=
53

100% ▼

PoissonDistribution 589
                    Package: **DiscreteDistributions.m**

The Poisson distribution has probablilty function $f(x) = \dfrac{\mu^x}{x!}e^{-\mu}$, mean μ,

and variance $\sigma^2 = \mu$. **PoissonDistribution[m]** gives the Poisson distribution of mean **m**.

Example:
The Poisson distribution with parameter **m** is determined below and called **pd**. The mean and variance of this distribution is then calculated. The .75-th quantile is determined to demonstrate that commands from the **DescriptiveStatistics** package can be used with the distributions in **DiscreteDistributions**.

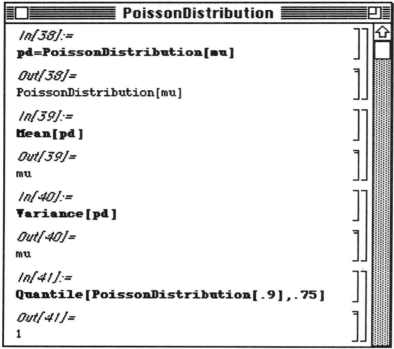

The cumulative distribution function is calculated in **pdtable** for values of x on the interval from x = 0 to x = 10.

```
In[42]:=
pdtable=Table[CDF[PoissonDistribution[.9],x],
        {x,0,10}]
Out[42]=
{0.40657, 0.772482, 0.937143, 0.986541, 0.997656,
  0.999657, 0.999957, 0.999995, 1., 1., 1.}
```

This table is then plotted with **ListPlot**.

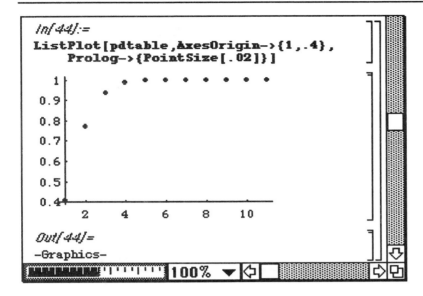

```
In[44]:=
ListPlot[pdtable,AxesOrigin->{1,.4},
     Prolog->{PointSize[.02]}]
```

```
Out[44]=
-Graphics-
```

PDF   588
                              Package: **DiscreteDistributions.m**
  PDF[d,x] yields the probability density function at x of the distribution **d**.
Example:
In the example below, the probability density function of the geometric distribution
with p = 0.3 is determined at x = 1. A table of function values is created in **pdf** and the
points are plotted with **ListPlot** to illustrate the probability density function in this
case.

```
In[45]:=
PDF[GeometricDistribution[.3],1]

Out[45]=
0.3

In[46]:=
pdf=Table[PDF[GeometricDistribution[.3],x],
     {x,0,15}]

Out[46]=
{0, 0.3, 0.21, 0.147, 0.1029, 0.07203, 0.050421,
  0.0352947, 0.0247063, 0.0172944, 0.0121061,
  0.00847426, 0.00593198, 0.00415239, 0.00290667,
  0.00203467}
```

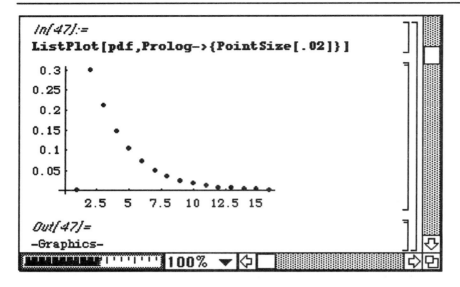

In[47]:=
ListPlot[pdf,Prolog->{PointSize[.02]}]

Out[47]=
-Graphics-

CDF   588
                               Package: **DiscreteDistributions.m**
   CDF[d,x] yields the cumulative density function at x of the distribution **d**.
Example:
In the example below, the cumulative density function of the geometric distribution
with p = 0.3 is determined. A table of function values is created in **gtable** and the
points are plotted with **ListPlot** to illustrate the cumulative density function in this
case.

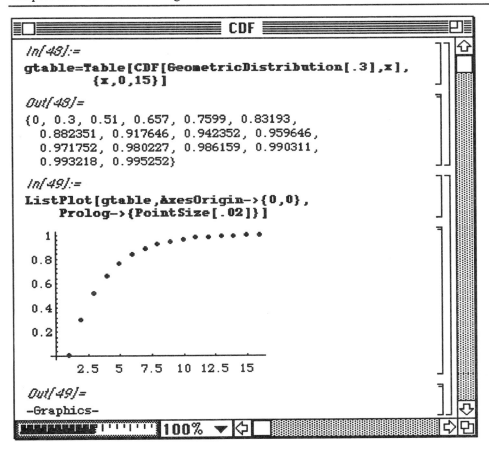

```
In[48]:=
gtable=Table[CDF[GeometricDistribution[.3],x],
       {x,0,15}]

Out[48]=
{0, 0.3, 0.51, 0.657, 0.7599, 0.83193,
   0.882351, 0.917646, 0.942352, 0.959646,
   0.971752, 0.980227, 0.986159, 0.990311,
   0.993218, 0.995252}

In[49]:=
ListPlot[gtable,AxesOrigin->{0,0},
       Prolog->{PointSize[.02]}]
```

Domain   Package: **DiscreteDistributions.m**

Domain[d] yields the variable values which can be used with the distribution **d**.

Example:

The use of the **Domain** command is illustrated for several distributions below. These include the Poisson distribution, the geometric distribution, and the binomial distribution.

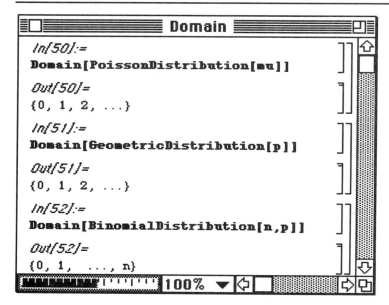

CharacteristicFunction
588

Package: **DiscreteDistributions.m**

CharacteristicFunction[d,t] gives the characteristic function (in the variable **t**) of the distribution **d**.

Example:

The characteristic function is determined for several distributions below. First, the characteristic function is found for the geometric distribution with p = 0.3, and then it is calculated for the geometric distribution with parameter p.

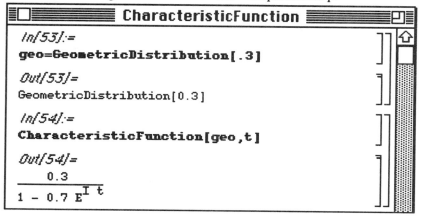

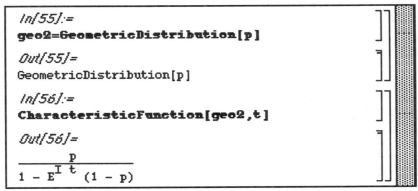

The characteristic function is determined for the discrete uniform distribution as well.

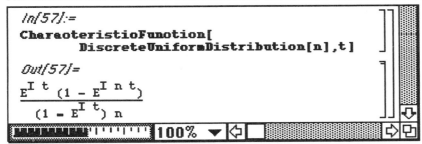

HypothesisTests.m

MeanTest

Package: **HypothesisTests.m**

MeanTest[datalist,m] yields the p-value associated with the test that the mean of the population given in **datalist** is equal to **m**. The p-value is obtained from the Student's t-distribution. **MeanTest** has the option **KnownVariance** in which case the p-value based on the normal distribution results. **MeanTest** also has the options **TwoSided**, **SignificanceLevel**, and **FullReport**.

Example:

In the following example, the list named **chol** represents the cholesterol level of 40 people. **MeanTest** is used to test the null hypothesis that the mean level is 220. If a .05 significance level is used, then the p-value given indicates that the null hypothesis is not rejected. The options **KnownVariance**, **SignificanceLevel**, **TwoSided**, and **FullReport** are also demonstrated.

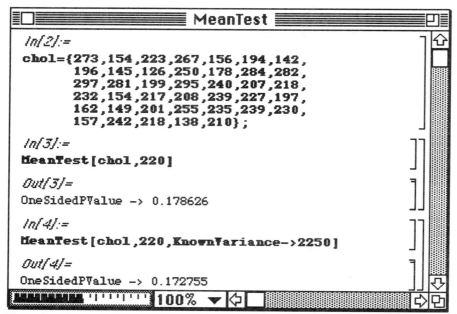

The **SignificanceLevel** option is illustrated below.

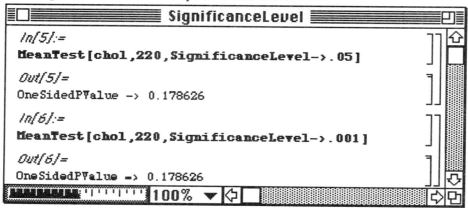

The options **TwoSided** and **FullReport** are shown below.

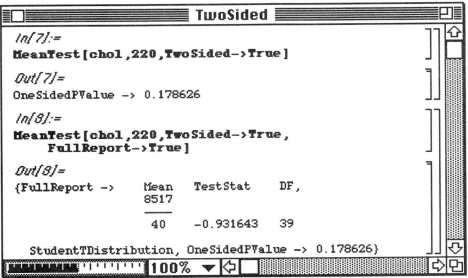

Notice in the first report below that the test statistic is obtained through the Student's t-distribution. However, with the setting **KnownVariance->2250** in the second command, the test statistic is obtained from the normal distribution as shown below.

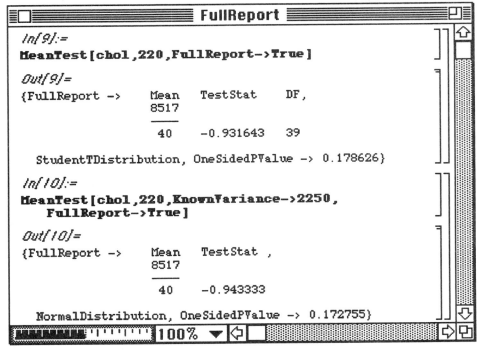

MeanDifferenceTest   Package: **HypothesisTests.m**
  MeanDifferenceTest[datalist1,datalist2,diff] yields the p-value for
the test that the difference between the two population means (for which **datalist1**
and **datalist2** are samples) is equal to **diff**. In this case, the p-value is based on
Welch's approximate t-test. If the option **EqualVariances->True** is employed,
then the p-value given is based on the Student's t-distribution.
MeanDifferenceTest has the options **KnownVariance** and
KnownStandardDeviation in which, if used, the p-value based on the Normal
distribution results. **MeanDifferenceTest** also has the options **TwoSided**,
SignificanceLevel, and **FullReport**.
Example:
In the following example, the lists **chol** and **chol2** represent the cholesterol level of
40 and 25 people, respectively. The list chol is introduced in the **MeanTest** example
above. **MeanDifferenceTest** is used to test the null hypothesis that the means of
the two populations are equal. If a .05 significance level is used, then the p-value given
indicates that the null hypothesis is not rejected. The options **KnownVariance**,
KnownStandardDeviation, **SignificanceLevel**,
TwoSided, and **FullReport** are also demonstrated.

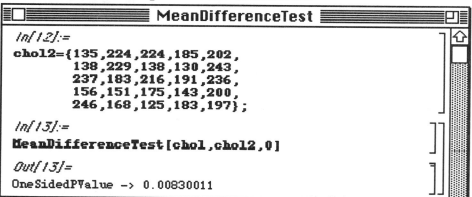

In the next two examples, note that the test statistics are obtained from the normal
distribution. This is the case when the **KnownVariance** or
KnownStandardDeviation option is used.

```
In[14]:=
MeanDifferenceTest[chol,chol2,0,
  KnownVariance->{2250,1530},
  SignificanceLevel->.05,
  FullReport->True]

Out[14]=
{FullReport ->      MeanDiff   TestStat,
                    26.725     2.46599

  NormalDistribution, OneSidedPValue -> 0.00683177}
```

In[15]:=
```
MeanDifferenceTest[chol,chol2,0,
  KnownStandardDeviation->{47.4,39.11},
  SignificanceLevel->.05,
  FullReport->True]
```

Out[15]=
```
{FullReport ->        MeanDiff    TestStat,
                      26.725      2.46701

   NormalDistribution, OneSidedPValue -> 0.0068123}
```

Without the use of either the **KnownVariance** or **KnownStandardDeviation** option, the test statistic is obtained from the Student's t-distribution as indicated below.

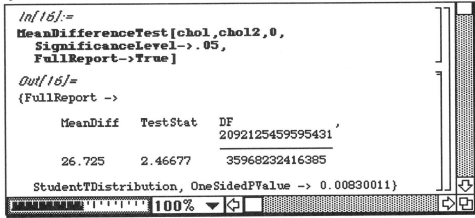

In[16]:=
```
MeanDifferenceTest[chol,chol2,0,
  SignificanceLevel->.05,
  FullReport->True]
```

Out[16]=
```
{FullReport ->

     MeanDiff    TestStat    DF                  ,
                             2092125459595431
                             ─────────────────
     26.725      2.46677     35968232416385

   StudentTDistribution, OneSidedPValue -> 0.00830011}
```
100% ▼

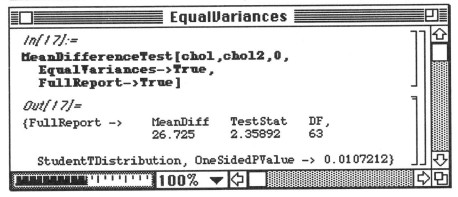

≡≡≡≡≡≡≡≡≡≡≡ **EqualVariances** ≡≡≡≡≡≡≡≡≡≡≡

In[17]:=
```
MeanDifferenceTest[chol,chol2,0,
  EqualVariances->True,
  FullReport->True]
```

Out[17]=
```
{FullReport ->        MeanDiff    TestStat    DF,
                      26.725      2.35892     63

   StudentTDistribution, OneSidedPValue -> 0.0107212}
```
100% ▼

VarianceTest   Package: **HypothesisTests.m**
   VarianceTest[datalist,var] yields the p-value for the test that the variance of the population with sample given in **datalist** is equal to **var**. This p-value is based on the chi-square distribution. **VarianceTest** has the options **FullReport**, **SignificanceLevel**, and **TwoSided**.

Example:

In the following example, the list named **chol** represents the cholesterol level of 40 people. **VarianceTest** is used to test the null hypothesis that the variance of the levels is 2250. If a .05 significance level is used, then the p-value given indicates that the null hypothesis is not rejected. The option **FullReport** is also demonstrated.

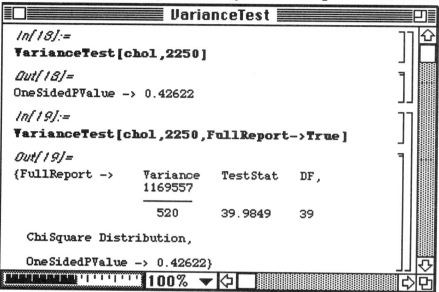

VarianceRatioTest   Package: **HypothesisTests.m**

   VarianceRatioTest[datalist1,datalist2,r] yields the p-value for the test to determine if the ratio of the population variances of samples **datalist1** and **datalist2** is equal to **r**. This p-value is based on the F-ratio distribution. **VarianceRatioTest** has the options **FullReport**, **SignificanceLevel**, and **TwoSided**.

Example:

In the following example, the lists **chol** and **chol2** represent the cholesterol level of 40 and 25 people, respectively. **VarianceRatioTest** is used to test the null hypothesis that the variances of the two populations is equal. If a .05 significance level is used, then the p-value given indicates that the null hypothesis is not rejected. The option **FullReport** is also demonstrated.

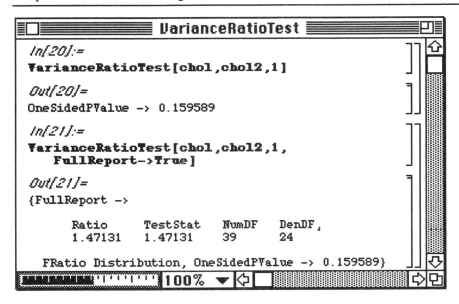

NormalPValue   Package: **HypothesisTests.m**

  NormalPValue[tstat] yields the p-value based on the normal distribution with mean zero and variance one for the test statistic **tstat**.

Example:

In the following example, the p-value based on the normal distribution is calculated for **tstat** = −1.96 and **tstat** = 1.96. The **TwoSided** option is also illustrated.

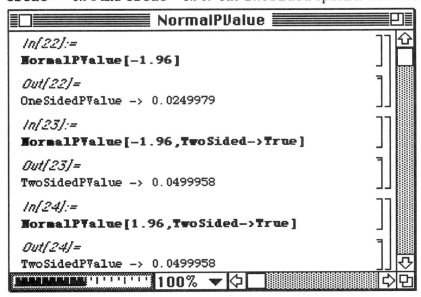

StudentTPValue   Package: **HypothesisTests.m**

StudentTPValue[tstat,df] provides the p-value based on the Student's t-distribution with **df** degrees of freedom for the test statistic **tstat**.

Example:

In the following example, the p-value based on the Student's t-distribution is calculated for **tstat** = 6.314 and **df** = 1 as well as for **tstat** = 1.311 and **df** = 29. The **TwoSided** option is also illustrated.

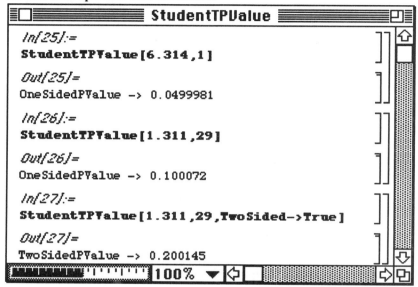

ChiSquarePValue   Package: **HypothesisTests.m**

ChiSquarePValue[tstat,df] provides the p-value based on the chi-square distribution with **df** degrees of freedom for the test statistic **tstat**.

Example:

In the following example, the p-value based on the chi-square distribution is calculated for **tstat** = 7.897 and **df** = 1. The **TwoSided** option is also illustrated.

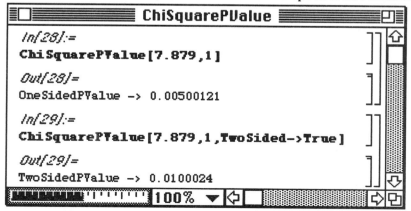

FRatioPValue   Package: **HypothesisTests.m**
   FRatioPValue[tstat,ndf,ddf] provides the p-value based on the F-ratio distribution with **ndf** and **ddf** degrees of freedom in the numerator and denominator, respectively, for the test statistic **tstat**.
Example:
In the following example, the p-value based on the F-ratio distribution is calculated for **tstat** = 3.26, **ndf** = 4, and **ddf** = 1. The **TwoSided** option is also illustrated in this case. The p-value is also obtained for **tstat** = 6.18, **ndf** = 7, and **ddf** = 8.

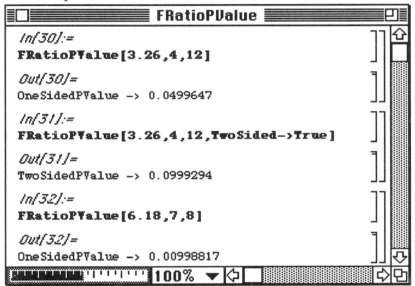

InverseStatisticalFunctions.m

InverseErf
                          Package: **InverseStatisticalFunctions.m**
   InverseErf[p] yields the value of **x** such that **p** = **Erf[x]** where **Erf[x]** is a built-in *Mathematica* function. This command can be entered as
InverseErf[x0,p] to determine the value of **x** such that **p** = **Erf[x0,x]** and as
InverseErf[x0,-p] to determine the value of **x** such that **p** = **Erf[x0,x]**. Notice that the arguments in each of these functions are real numbers, and the value of **p** is between **Erf[x0,-Infinity]** and **Erf[x0,Infinity]**.
Example:
In the following example, **InverseErf[p]** is plotted for **p** on the interval from **a1** to **b1** which are calculated below. Also, **InverseErf[1.0]** is computed. To verify the relationship between **InverseErf** and **Erf**, two examples follow.

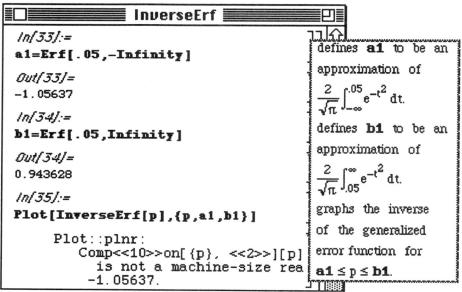

```
In[33]:=
a1=Erf[.05,-Infinity]

Out[33]=
-1.05637

In[34]:=
b1=Erf[.05,Infinity]

Out[34]=
0.943628

In[35]:=
Plot[InverseErf[p],{p,a1,b1}]

    Plot::plnr:
       Comp<<10>>on[{p}, <<2>>][p]
         is not a machine-size rea
         -1.05637.
```

defines **a1** to be an approximation of $\frac{2}{\sqrt{\pi}}\int_{-\infty}^{.05}e^{-t^2}\,dt$.

defines **b1** to be an approximation of $\frac{2}{\sqrt{\pi}}\int_{.05}^{\infty}e^{-t^2}\,dt$.

graphs the inverse of the generalized error function for **a1** $\le p \le$ **b1**.

In spite of the error message *Mathematica* generates, which is not completely displayed, the correct graph is displayed:

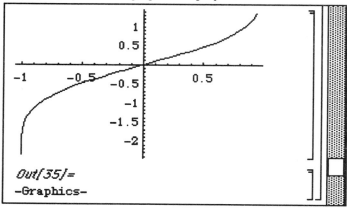

```
Out[35]=
-Graphics-
```

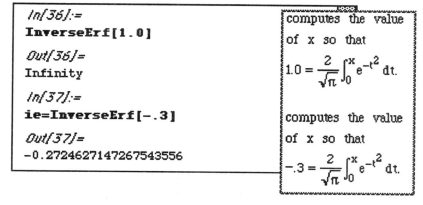

```
In[36]:=
InverseErf[1.0]

Out[36]=
Infinity

In[37]:=
ie=InverseErf[-.3]

Out[37]=
-0.2724627147267543556
```

computes the value of x so that $1.0 = \frac{2}{\sqrt{\pi}}\int_0^x e^{-t^2}\,dt$.

computes the value of x so that $-.3 = \frac{2}{\sqrt{\pi}}\int_0^x e^{-t^2}\,dt$.

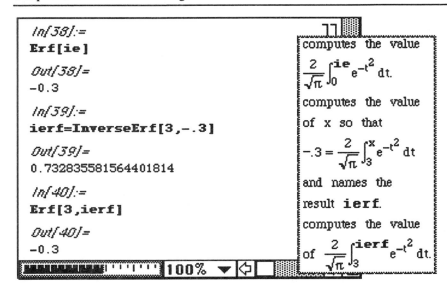

In[38]:=
Erf[ie]

Out[38]=
-0.3

In[39]:=
ierf=InverseErf[3,-.3]

Out[39]=
0.732835581564401814

In[40]:=
Erf[3,ierf]

Out[40]=
-0.3

computes the value

$$\frac{2}{\sqrt{\pi}} \int_0^{ie} e^{-t^2} dt.$$

computes the value of x so that

$$-.3 = \frac{2}{\sqrt{\pi}} \int_3^x e^{-t^2} dt$$

and names the result **ierf**.

computes the value of $\frac{2}{\sqrt{\pi}} \int_3^{ierf} e^{-t^2} dt.$

InverseErfc   Package: **InverseStatisticalFunctions.m**
  InverseErfc[p] yields the value of **x** such that **p=Erfc[x]** for $0 \le p \le 2$

The argument of **InverseErf** must be a real number.

Example:
In the following example, relationship between **InverseErfc** and **Erfc** is verified.

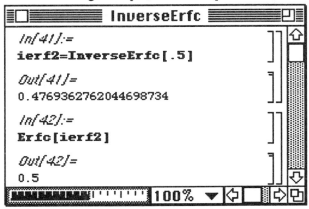

InverseErfc

In[41]:=
ierf2=InverseErfc[.5]

Out[41]=
0.476936276044698734

In[42]:=
Erfc[ierf2]

Out[42]=
0.5

InverseGammaRegularized
                Package: **InverseStatisticalFunctions.m**
  InverseGammaRegularized[a,x0,p] yields the value of **x** that satisfies
p=GammaRegularized[a,x0,x] where **a>0** and $0 \le x \le \infty$. All arguments are
real and the value of **p** must lie on the interval given by
GammaRegularized[a,x,0]$\le$p$\le$GammaRegularized[a,x,Infinity].
This command can be entered as **InverseGammaRegularized[a,x0,-p]** to
determine the value of **x** such that **p=GammaRegularized[a,x,x0]**.

Example:

In the first example below, the relationship between **InverseGammaRegularized** and **GammaRegularized** is verified. The values of **c** and **d** are determined so that **InverseGammaRegularized[4,1,p]** can be plotted on the interval [**c**,**d**]. A negative value of **p** is then considered to illustrate the earlier stated property.

The following command generates several error messages corresponding to the values of **p** for which **InverseGammaRegularized[4,1,p]** is not defined. Note that not all error messages are actually displayed in this case.

```
In[47]:=
Plot[InverseGammaRegularized[4,1,p],{p,c,d}]

    Plot::plnr:
        CompiledFunction[{p}, <<1>>, -Co<<8>>d
            is not a machine-size real number at
```

Nevertheless, the resulting graph is displayed correctly.

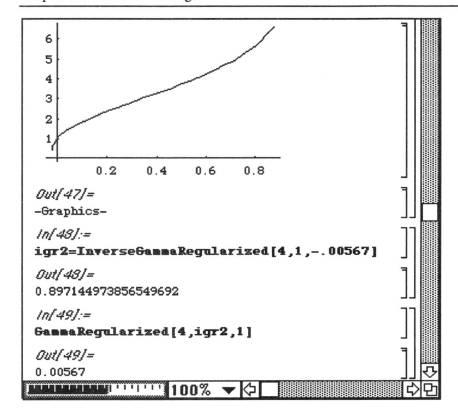

Out[47]=
-Graphics-

In[48]:=
igr2=InverseGammaRegularized[4,1,-.00567]

Out[48]=
0.897144973856549692

In[49]:=
GammaRegularized[4,igr2,1]

Out[49]=
0.00567

InverseBetaRegularized
Package: **InverseStatisticalFunctions.m**
InverseBetaRegularized[x0,p,a,b] gives the value of **x** that satisfies
p = BetaRegularized[x0,x,a,b] where **a** > 0, **b** > 0 and 0 ≤ x ≤ 1. All
arguments are real and the value of **p** must lie on the interval given by
BetaRegularized[x0,0,a,b] ≤ **p** ≤ **BetaRegularized[x0,1,a,b]**.
This command can be entered as **InverseBetaRegularized[x0,-p,a,b]** to
determine the value of **x** such that **p = BetaRegularized[x,x0,a,b]**.
Example:
In the first example below, the relationship between **InverseBetaRegularized**
and **BetaRegularized** is verified. The values of **c1** and **d1** are determined so that
InverseBetaRegularized[.1,p,2,1] can be plotted on the interval [**c1,d1**].
A negative value of **p** is then considered to illustrate the earlier stated property.

```
≣□□▭▭▭▭▭▭▭  InverseBetaRegularized  ▭▭▭▭▭▭▭□▤≣
In[50]:=
ibr=InverseBetaRegularized[.1,.5,2,1]

Out[50]=
0.714143

In[51]:=
BetaRegularized[.1,ibr,2,1]

Out[51]=
0.5

In[52]:=
c1=BetaRegularized[2,0,1,6]

Out[52]=
0

In[53]:=
d1=BetaRegularized[2,1,1,6]

Out[53]=
1
```

The following command generates several error messages corresponding to the values of **p** for which **InverseBetaRegularized[.1,p,2,1]** is not defined. Note that not all error messages are actually displayed in this case.

```
In[54]:=
Plot[InverseBetaRegularized[.1,p,2,1],{p,c1,d1}]

    Plot::plnr:
        Comp<<10>>on[{p}, <<2>>][p]
            is not a machine-size real number at p =
            1..
    Plot::plnr:
        Comp<<10>>on[{p}, <<2>>][p]
            is not a machine-size real number at p =
            0.994792.
```

Nevertheless, the resulting graph is displayed correctly.

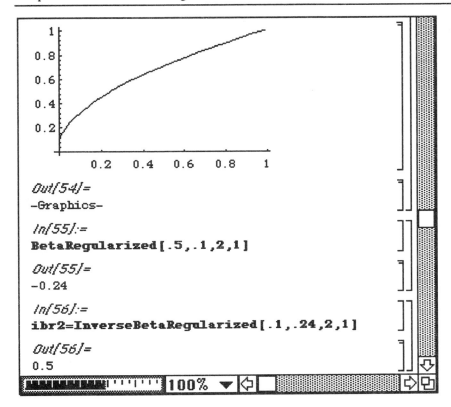

Out[54]=
-Graphics-

In[55]:=
BetaRegularized[.5,.1,2,1]

Out[55]=
-0.24

In[56]:=
ibr2=InverseBetaRegularized[.1,.24,2,1]

Out[56]=
0.5

100% ▼

LinearRegression.m

Regress

Package: **LinearRegression.m**

Regress[datalist,basisfunctionlist,vars] performs a regression analysis on the data given in **datalist**. The arguments of datalist are the same as those of **Fit** where the data is approximated using the functions indicated in **basisfunctionlist** and the variables in **vars**. When using linear regression, a linear combination of basis functions that yields least-squares fit is determined by **Regress**. **BasisNames**, **IncludeConstant**, **OutputList**, **OutputControl**, and **Weights** are all options used with **Regress**.

Example:

In the following example, the list **heart** which represents the age and peak heart rate of 10 individuals is entered. This data is plotted with **ListPlot**, and a quadratic regression is performed on **heart**. The least squares polynomial fit produced by **Regress** is also given with **Fit**. This polynomial as well as the data are shown together.

```
▤▢▰▰▰▰▰▰▰▰▰▰▰▰▰▰▰▰▰  Regress  ▰▰▰▰▰▰▰▰▰▰▰▰▰▰▰▰▰▱▤
```

In[61]:=

```
heart={{30,186},{38,183},{41,172},
       {38,177},{29,191},{39,175},
       {46,175},{41,176},{42,171},
       {24,201}};
```

In[62]:=

```
Regress[heart,{1,x,x^2},x]
```

Out[62]=

{ParameterTable ->

	Estimate	SE	TStat	PValue
1	292.242	28.8337	10.1354	0.0000195772
x	-5.13377	1.70498	-3.01104	0.0196333
x^2	0.0553981	0.0244893	2.26213	0.0581482

RSquared -> 0.921036, AdjustedRSquared -> 0.898475,

EstimatedVariance -> 9.27374,

ANOVATable ->

Model

Error   }

Total

	DoF	SoS	MeanSS	FRatio	PValue
	2	757.184	378.592	40.8241	0.000138356
	7	64.9162	9.27374		
	9	822.1			

In[63]:=

```
f=Fit[heart,{1,x,x^2},x]
```

Out[63]=

$292.242 - 5.13377 \, x + 0.0553981 \, x^2$

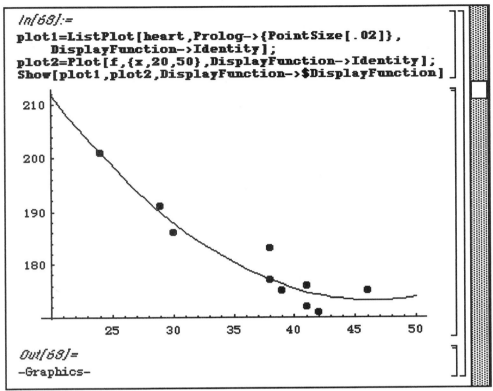

```
In[68]:=
plot1=ListPlot[heart,Prolog->{PointSize[.02]},
    DisplayFunction->Identity];
plot2=Plot[f,{x,20,50},DisplayFunction->Identity];
Show[plot1,plot2,DisplayFunction->$DisplayFunction]
```

```
Out[68]=
-Graphics-
```

A second list of data, called **heart2**, which represents the age, peak heart rate, and percent body fat of the 10 individuals is entered. A regression of this data is then performed using the basis vectors {1,**x**,**y**,**x y**}.

```
In[64]:=
heart2={{30,186,21.2},{38,183,24.1},{41,172,26.7},
        {38,177,25.3},{29,191,18.5},{39,175,25.2},
        {46,175,25.6},{41,176,20.4},{42,171,27.3},
        {24,201,15.8}};
```

```
In[65]:=
Regress[heart2,{1,x,y,x y},{x,y}]

Out[65]=
{ParameterTable ->

            Estimate      SE            TStat         PValue
      1     92.6363       84.6264       1.09465       0.315655

      x     -0.203246     2.49525       -0.0814531    0.937731

      y     -0.388125     0.446721      -0.86883      0.418333

      x y   0.00121114    0.0139357     0.086909      0.933572

   RSquared -> 0.811278, AdjustedRSquared -> 0.716917,

   EstimatedVariance -> 4.16349,

   ANOVATable ->

            DoF   SoS       MeanSS     FRatio     PValue }
      Model 3     107.388   35.796     8.59761    0.01362

      Error 6     24.9809   4.16349

      Total 9     132.369
```

BasisNames   Package: **LinearRegression.m**

   BasisNames is an option used with **Regress** and **DesignedRegress** in order to specify labels to be used in the output of these functions. The default setting of **BasisNames** is **Automatic**. Other settings are made in the form

BasisNames->{"label1","label2",...}.

Example:

The following example illustrates the **BasisNames** option of **Regress**. Notice that in the output of the **Regress** command entered below, the basis functions have the indicated labels "constant" and "linear term".

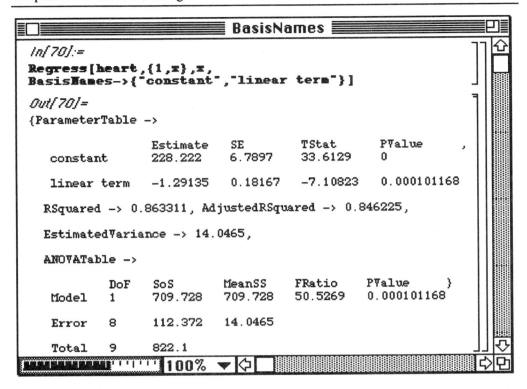

```
                                          BasisNames

In[70]:=
Regress[heart,{1,x},x,
BasisNames->{"constant","linear term"}]

Out[70]=
{ParameterTable ->

                    Estimate    SE         TStat       PValue         ,
         constant   228.222     6.7897     33.6129     0

         linear term  -1.29135  0.18167    -7.10823    0.000101168

      RSquared -> 0.863311, AdjustedRSquared -> 0.846225,

      EstimatedVariance -> 14.0465,

      ANOVATable ->

              DoF   SoS        MeanSS      FRatio      PValue         }
      Model   1     709.728    709.728     50.5269     0.000101168

      Error   8     112.372    14.0465

      Total   9     822.1
```

IncludeConstant   Package: **LinearRegression.m**

  IncludeConstant is an option used with **Regress** to specify whether or not the constant term is included in the approximating polynomial. Unless the setting **IncludeConstant->False** is made, **Regress** automatically includes a constant term in the polynomial even if a constant is not included in the list of basis functions.

Example:

The following example illustrates the use of the **IncludeConstant** option of **Regress**. Notice that in the first **Regress** command entered below, the constant term is included in the polynomial even though a constant is not entered as a basis function.

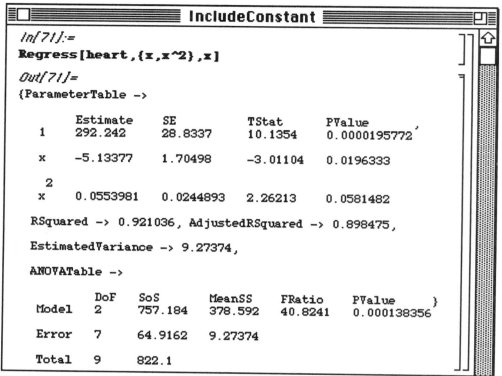

The following command includes the option setting **IncludeConstant->False** so that the constant is omitted.

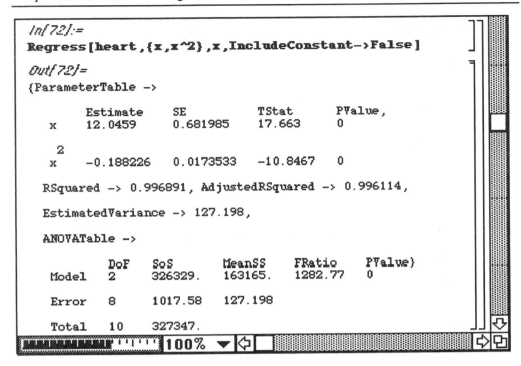

```
In[72]:=
Regress[heart,{x,x^2},x,IncludeConstant->False]

Out[72]=
{ParameterTable ->

        Estimate    SE          TStat       PValue,
   x    12.0459     0.681985    17.663      0

    2
   x    -0.188226   0.0173533   -10.8467    0

 RSquared -> 0.996891, AdjustedRSquared -> 0.996114,

 EstimatedVariance -> 127.198,

 ANOVATable ->

          DoF   SoS        MeanSS      FRatio      PValue}
   Model  2     326329.    163165.     1282.77     0

   Error  8     1017.58    127.198

   Total  10    327347.
```

OutputControl   Package: **LinearRegression.m**

   OutputControl is an option used with **Regress** and **DesignedRegress** to indicate whether or not the standard regression output is given. If the setting **OutputControl->NoPrint** is used, then no output is rendered. Hence, **OutputList** is used in conjunction with **OutputControl** to specify the statistics to be included in the output list. The default setting of **OutputControl** is **Automatic** which leads to standard output.

Example:

The example below illustrates the use of the **OutputControl** option of **Regress**. The setting **NoPrint** causes the output list to be suppressed.

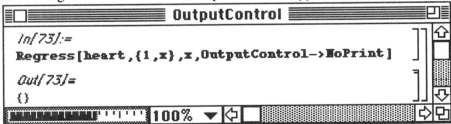

```
OutputControl

In[73]:=
Regress[heart,{1,x},x,OutputControl->NoPrint]

Out[73]=
{}
```

OutputList   Package: **LinearRegression.m**

   OutputList is an option used with **Regress** and **DesignedRegress** to indicate
the information to include in the list of output for these functions. Possible settings for
this option include **BestFit**, **BestFitCoefficients**, **ANOVATable**,
ConfidenceIntervalTable, **CovarianceMatrix**, **CorrelationMatrix**,
EstimatedVariance, **FitResiduals**, **ParameterTable**,
PredictedResponse, **RSquared**, and **AdjustedRSquared**. The setting of
OutputList is made in the form **OutputList->{comp1,comp2,...}** where
each component of the setting is one of the possibilities listed earlier.

Example:

The following example demonstrates the **OutputList** option of **Regress**. In this
case, instead of printing the entire output list of **Regress**, the combination of
OutputControl->NoPrint and **OutputList->{RSquared}** causes only the
value of **RSquared** to be printed. The list, called **heart** below, is introduced in the
Regress example above.

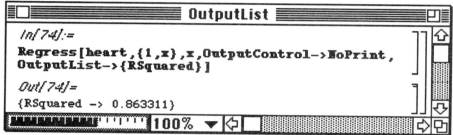

```
OutputList
In[74]:=
Regress[heart,{1,x},x,OutputControl->NoPrint,
OutputList->{RSquared}]

Out[74]=
{RSquared -> 0.863311}
                                        100%
```

Weights   Package: **LinearRegression.m**

   Weights is an option used with **Regress** and **DesignedRegress** to
specify a vector of weights for the error variances. This causes a weighted least squares

to be performed. The errors are assumed to have unequal variances of $\dfrac{\sigma^2}{w_j}$ where the

weight corresponding to the jth response is w_j.

Example:

The **Weights** option setting of **Regress** is demonstrated in the following example.
The list of weights **{1,1,1,1,14,4,4,9,16}** is used in the weighted least squares
procedure of the list of data **heart** which is introduced in the **Regress** example
above. The value of **RSquared** which results is different from that obtained in the
OutputList option above.

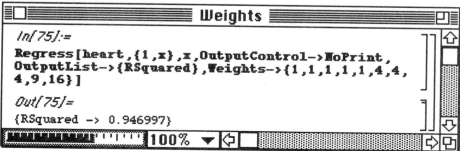

```
Weights
In[75]:=
Regress[heart,{1,x},x,OutputControl->NoPrint,
OutputList->{RSquared},Weights->{1,1,1,1,1,4,4,
4,9,16}]

Out[75]=
{RSquared -> 0.946997}
                                        100%
```

BestFit   Package: **LinearRegression.m**

   BestFit is a possible entry in **OutputList** which leads to the least squares polynomial to be included in the list of output of the functions **Regress** and **DesignedRegress**.

Example:

The **BestFit** option setting is illustrated in the example below. The least squares linear fit of the data given in the list **heart** is obtained. This list is introduced in the **Regress** example above.

```
In[76]:=
Regress[heart,{1,x},x,OutputControl->NoPrint,
OutputList->{BestFit}]

Out[76]=
{BestFit -> 228.222 - 1.29135 x}
```

BestFitCoefficients   Package: **LinearRegression.m**

   BestFitCoefficients is a possible entry in **OutputList** which leads to the coefficients of the least squares polynomial to be included in the list of output of the functions **Regress** and **DesignedRegress**.

Example:

In the following example, the **BestFitCoefficients** option setting is illustrated. The coefficients of the least squares linear fit of the data given in the list **heart** are obtained. This list is introduced in the **Regress** example above.

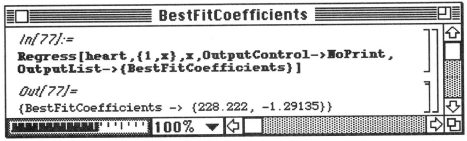

```
In[77]:=
Regress[heart,{1,x},x,OutputControl->NoPrint,
OutputList->{BestFitCoefficients}]

Out[77]=
{BestFitCoefficients -> {228.222, -1.29135}}
```

ANOVATable   Package: **LinearRegression.m**

   ANOVATable is a possible entry in **OutputList** which leads to the table of the analysis of variance to be included in the list of output of the functions **Regress** and **DesignedRegress**. This table is computed for a smaller model by assuming independent samples, normal populations, and equal population standard deviations. It includes the degrees of freedom, the sum of the squares, and the mean squares due to the model and the residuals. It also includes the F-statistic which compares the two models and the p-value. If the p-value is large, then the null hypothesis is rejected.

Example:

In the following example, the **ANOVATable** option setting is illustrated. With the indicated settings, only **ANOVATable** is given as output of **Regress**.

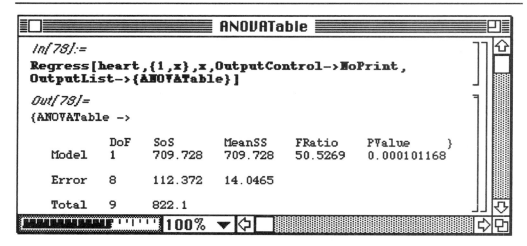

ConfidenceIntervalTable

Package: **LinearRegression.m**

ConfidenceIntervalTable is a possible entry for **OutputList** which causes a table of confidence intervals for the best fit coefficients to be included in the list of output for the functions **Regress** and **DesignedRegress**. The confidence intervals are based on the t distribution.

Example:

In the example below, the **ConfidenceIntervalTable** option setting is illustrated. With the indicated settings, only **ConfidenceIntervalTable** is given as output of **Regress**. Note that the data given in **heart** is introduced in the **Regress** example above.

CovarianceMatrix   Package: **LinearRegression.m**

   CovarianceMatrix is a possible entry in **OutputList** which causes the covariance matrix for the best fit coefficients to be included in the list of output for the functions **Regress** and **DesignedRegress**.

Example:

In the following example, the **CovarianceMatrix** option setting is illustrated. With the indicated settings, the covariance matrix of the data given in **heart** is given as the only output of **Regress**. This list of data is introduced in the **Regress** example above.

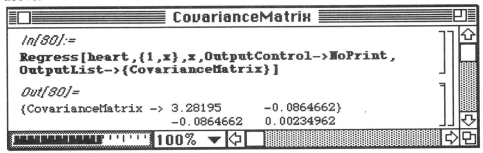

CorrelationMatrix   Package: **LinearRegression.m**

   CorrelationMatrix is a possible entry in **OutputList** which causes the correlation matrix for the best fit coefficients to be included in the list of output for the functions **Regress** and **DesignedRegress**.

Example:

The **CorrelationMatrix** option setting is illustrated in the following example. With the indicated settings, the only output of **Regress** is the correlation matrix of the data given in **heart**. Note that this list is introduced in the **Regress** example above.

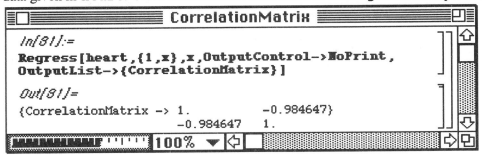

EstimatedVariance   Package: **LinearRegression.m**

   EstimatedVariance is a possible entry in **OutputList** which causes the value of the residual mean square to be given in the list of output for the functions **Regress** and **DesignedRegress**. The value of **EstimatedVariance** is found by dividing the residual sum of squares (RSS) by the degrees of freedom associated with it.

Example:

In the example below, the **EstimatedVariance** option setting is illustrated with **Regress**. With the indicated settings, the only output of **Regress** is the estimated variance of the data given in the list **heart**. Note that this list is introduced in the **Regress** example above.

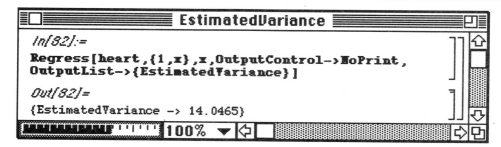

FitResiduals   Package: **LinearRegression.m**
   FitResiduals is a possible entry in **OutputList** which causes the differences
between the observed responses and the predicted responses to be included in the list of
output for the functions **Regress** and **DesignedRegress**.
Example:
In the example below, the **FitResiduals** option setting is illustrated with **Regress**.
With the indicated settings, the output list of **Regress** includes only the fit residuals of
the data given in the list **heart** which is introduced in the **Regress** example above.

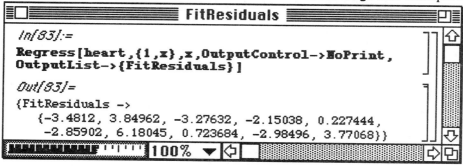

ParameterTable   Package: **LinearRegression.m**
   ParameterTable is a possible entry in **OutputList** which causes information
concerning the coefficient estimates to be given in the output list for the functions
Regress and **DesignedRegress**. This table includes the estimates, the standard
errors, and the t-statistics associated with testing if each parameter is 0. Assuming that
the number of predictors is p and the sample size is n, then the p-value is obtained by
comparing the resulting statistic to the t-distribution having (n-p) degrees of freedom.
Example:
In the following example, the **ParameterTable** option setting is illustrated. With
the indicated settings, only **ParameterTable** is given as output of **Regress** for the
data in the list **heart**. Note that this list is introduced in the **Regress** example above.

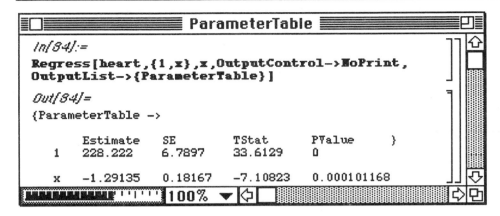

In[84]:=

**Regress[heart,{1,x},x,OutputControl->NoPrint,
OutputList->{ParameterTable}]**

Out[84]=

{ParameterTable ->

	Estimate	SE	TStat	PValue	}
1	228.222	6.7897	33.6129	0	
x	-1.29135	0.18167	-7.10823	0.000101168	

PredictedResponse   Package: **LinearRegression.m**

   PredictedResponse is a possible entry in **OutputList** which causes the values obtained by substitution in the best fit function to be given in the output list for the functions **Regress** and **DesignedRegress**.

Example:

The following example illustrates the use of the **PredictedResponse** option setting with **Regress**. With the indicated settings, the only values included in the output list for the data in **heart** are the predicted response values. Note that this list is introduced in the **Regress** example above.

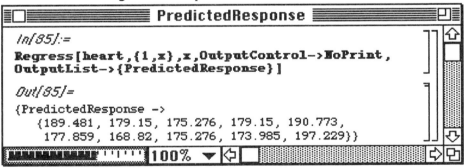

In[85]:=

**Regress[heart,{1,x},x,OutputControl->NoPrint,
OutputList->{PredictedResponse}]**

Out[85]=

{PredictedResponse ->
   {189.481, 179.15, 175.276, 179.15, 190.773,
    177.859, 168.82, 175.276, 173.985, 197.229}}

RSquared

Package: **LinearRegression.m**

   RSquared is a possible entry in **OutputList** which includes the coefficient of determination in the output list for the functions **Regress** and **DesignedRegress**. This quantity is determined by dividing the model sum of squares by the total sum of squares.

Example:

In the following example, the **RSquared** option setting is illustrated. With the indicated settings, only **RSquared** is given as output of **Regress** for the data in the list **heart** which is introduced in the **Regress** example above.

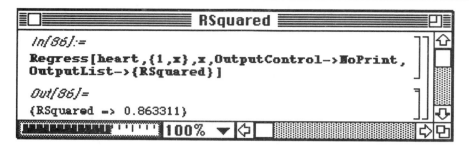

AdjustedRSquared   Package: **LinearRegression.m**

AdjustedRSquared is a possible entry in the **OutputList** option for the
functions **Regress** and **DesignedRegress**. If included in **OutputList**,
the value of **AdjustedRSquared** is included in the output. The value of

AdjustedRSquared is found from the formula $1 - \left(\dfrac{n-1}{n-p}\right)\left(1 - R^2\right)$ where n is the

sample size, p is the number of predictors, and R^2 is the coefficient of determination.
Example:
In the following example, the **AdjustedRSquared** option setting is illustrated. With
the indicated settings, only **AdjustedRSquared** is given as output of **Regress** for
the data in the list **heart**. Note that this list is introduced in the **Regress** example
above.

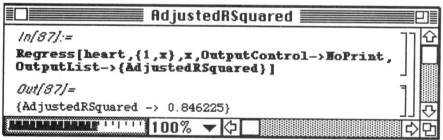

DesignMatrix   Package: **LinearRegression.m**

DesignMatrix[datalist,basisfunctionlist,vars] computes the
design matrix for the data given in **datalist** using the functions in
basisfunctionlist which depend on the variables listed in **vars**. The result of
DesignMatrix can be used as the **dmatrix** argument of **DesignMatrix**.
Example:
In the example below, the design matrix which corresponds to the data in **heart** is
determined using the indicated basis functions. This matrix is assigned the name dm
and has the function **Last** applied to it to obtain the observed responses. (Note that the
list **heart** is introduced in the **Regress** example above.)

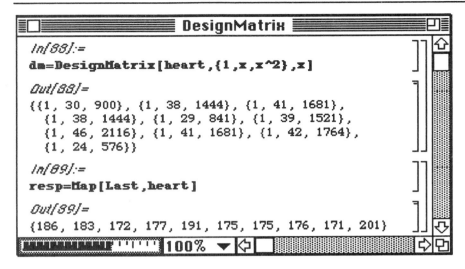

```
          ≡ DesignMatrix ≡
 In[88]:=
 dm=DesignMatrix[heart,{1,x,x^2},x]

 Out[88]=
 {{1, 30, 900}, {1, 38, 1444}, {1, 41, 1681},
   {1, 38, 1444}, {1, 29, 841}, {1, 39, 1521},
   {1, 46, 2116}, {1, 41, 1681}, {1, 42, 1764},
   {1, 24, 576}}
 In[89]:=
 resp=Map[Last,heart]

 Out[89]=
 {186, 183, 172, 177, 191, 175, 175, 176, 171, 201}
                      100%  ▼
```

DesignedRegress   Package: **LinearRegression.m**
  DesignedRegress[dmatrix,rdata] applies linear regression to the design
matrix given in **dmatrix** using the responses listed in the vector **rdata** of response
data. The output of **DesignedRegress** is identical to that of **Regress**. Also,
DesignedRegress has the options **BasisNames**, **OutputList**,
OutputControl, and **Weights**.
Example:
The following example demonstrates how the command **DesignedRegress** is used
with a design matrix to obtain the same output list as **Regress**. In this example, the
design matrix obtained for the data in **heart** is considered for comparison with earlier
results. Note that this list is first introduced in the **Regress** example above.

```
          ≡ DesignedRegress ≡
 In[90]:=
 dm=DesignMatrix[heart,{1,x,x^2},x]

 Out[90]=
 {{1, 30, 900}, {1, 38, 1444}, {1, 41, 1681},
   {1, 38, 1444}, {1, 29, 841}, {1, 39, 1521},
   {1, 46, 2116}, {1, 41, 1681}, {1, 42, 1764},
   {1, 24, 576}}
```

```
In[91]:=
DesignedRegress[dm,resp]

Out[91]=
{ParameterTable ->

        Estimate      SE           TStat       PValue
    1   292.242       28.8337      10.1354     0.0000195772    ,

    2   -5.13377      1.70498      -3.01104    0.0196333

    3   0.0553981     0.0244893    2.26213     0.0581482

RSquared -> 0.921036, AdjustedRSquared -> 0.898475,

EstimatedVariance -> 9.27374,

ANOVATable ->


    Model
                                                                }
    Error

    Total

        DoF   SoS         MeanSS      FRatio      PValue
        2     757.184     378.592     40.8241     0.000138356

        7     64.9162     9.27374

        9     822.1
```

MovingAverage.m

MovingAverage   Package: **MovingAverage.m**

MovingAverage[datalist,r] lists the **r**th moving averages of **datalist** where the **r**th moving average is a list of the n-**r** averages calculated with **r**+1 elements of **datalist** of length n. Also, **MovingAverage[dataarray,r]** lists the **r**th moving averages using the columns of **dataarray**.

Example:

The first, second, third, and fourth moving averages for the list {a1,a2,a3,a4,a5} are computed below.

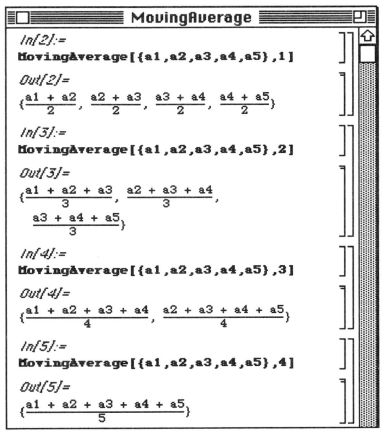

In addition, the moving averages for the indicated array are calculated.

In[6]:=

```
array={{a1,a2,a3,a4},{b1,b2,b3,b4},
       {c1,c2,c3,c4},{d1,d2,d3,d4}};
```

In[7]:=

```
MovingAverage[array,1]
```

Out[7]=

$$\{\{\frac{a1 + b1}{2},\ \frac{a2 + b2}{2},\ \frac{a3 + b3}{2},\ \frac{a4 + b4}{2}\},$$
$$\{\frac{b1 + c1}{2},\ \frac{b2 + c2}{2},\ \frac{b3 + c3}{2},\ \frac{b4 + c4}{2}\},$$
$$\{\frac{c1 + d1}{2},\ \frac{c2 + d2}{2},\ \frac{c3 + d3}{2},\ \frac{c4 + d4}{2}\}\}$$

In[8]:=

```
MovingAverage[array,2]
```

Out[8]=

$$\{\{\frac{a1 + b1 + c1}{3},\ \frac{a2 + b2 + c2}{3},$$
$$\frac{a3 + b3 + c3}{3},\ \frac{a4 + b4 + c4}{3}\},$$
$$\{\frac{b1 + c1 + d1}{3},\ \frac{b2 + c2 + d2}{3},$$
$$\frac{b3 + c3 + d3}{3},\ \frac{b4 + c4 + d4}{3}\}\}$$

In[9]:=

```
MovingAverage[array,3]
```

Out[9]=

$$\{\{\frac{a1 + b1 + c1 + d1}{4},\ \frac{a2 + b2 + c2 + d2}{4},$$
$$\frac{a3 + b3 + c3 + d3}{4},\ \frac{a4 + b4 + c4 + d4}{4}\}\}$$

In[10]:=

```
MovingAverage[array,4]
```

Out[10]=

```
{}
```

100% ▼

NormalDistributions.m

NormalDistribution   586
                     Package: **NormalDistributions.m**,
                     ContinuousDistributions.m

NormalDistribution[m,s] yields the normal distribution having mean **m** and standard deviation **s**. The normal distribution has density function

$$f(x) = \frac{1}{\sigma\sqrt{2\pi}}\, e^{\frac{-1}{2}\left(\frac{x-\mu}{\sigma}\right)^2}$$, where μ is the mean and σ is the standard deviation.

The normal distribution has many applications. Numerous physical measurements have distributions which are bell-shaped. Hence, the normal distribution as the distribution of a random variable. Also, the normal distribution is used to make inferences concerning characteristics of a population.

Example:

In the example below, a table of probability density functions which correspond to the normal distribution is created. This is done by, first, generating the table **nt** of the normal distribution with mean 0 and **sigma** = 1, 2, and 3. The probability density function for each of these distributions is determined in **pdftable**.

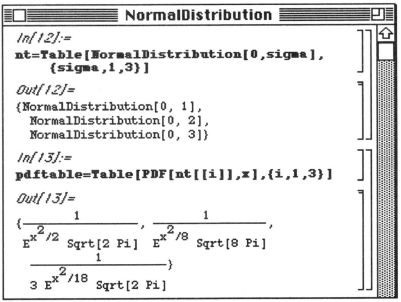

A table for three levels of gray is given in **gray**. Finally, the three probability density functions are plotted simultaneously using the levels of gray in **gray**.

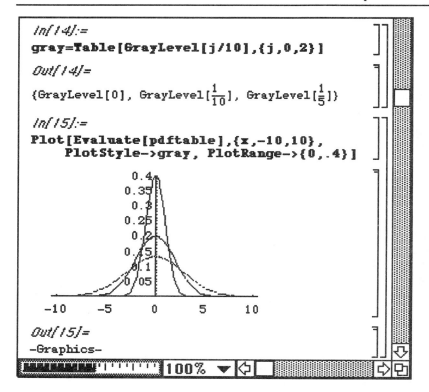

ChiSquareDistribution

587
Package: **NormalDistributions.m,
ContinuousDistributions.m**

   ChiSquareDistribution[df] yields the chi-square distribution with **df**
degrees of freedom. The chi-square distribution has distribution function

$$f(x) = c_m \int_0^x e^{-t/2} t^{(m-2)/2} \, dt, \quad \text{if} \quad x \geq 0, \quad \text{where} \quad c_m = \frac{1}{2^{m/2} \Gamma\left(\frac{m}{2}\right)}.$$

This distribution is used when testing percentage distribution of a population,
determining if two characteristics of a population are statistically dependent, and testing
the inferences for the standard deviation of a population.

Example:
In the example below, a table of probability density functions which correspond to the
chi-square distribution is created. This is done by, first, generating the table **chi** of
the chi-square distribution with **df** = 1, 8, and 15. The probability density function for
each of these distributions is determined in **pdftable**.

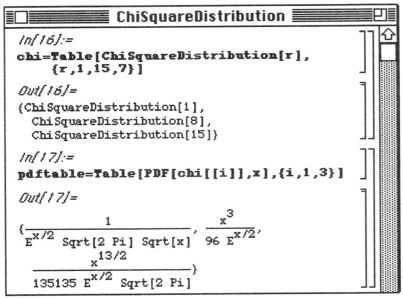

A table for three levels of line thickness is given in **thick**. Finally, the three probability density functions are plotted simultaneously for $0 \le x \le 10$ using the levels of **Thickness** in **thick**.

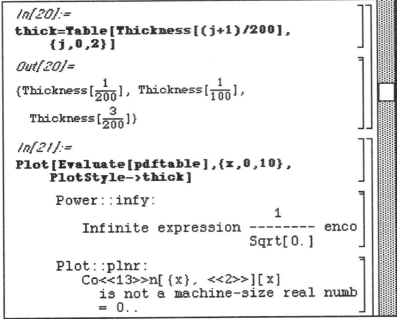

Even though an error message is generated, which is not completely displayed, when the first element of **pdftable**,

$$\frac{1}{e^{x/2} \sqrt{2 \pi x}},$$ is evaluated for $x = 0$, the resulting displayed graph is correct:

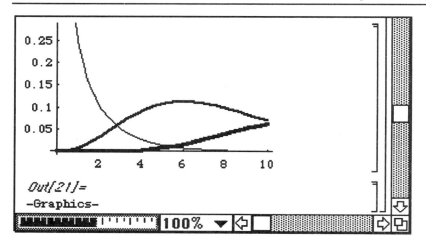

Out[21]=
-Graphics-

FRatioDistribution   586, 587
Package: **NormalDistributions.m**,
ContinuousDistributions.m

FRatioDistribution[ndf,ddf] represents the F-ratio distribution with **ndf** degrees of freedom in the numerator and **ddf** degrees of freedom in the denominator. This distribution is used for analysis of variance.

Example:

In the example below, a table of probability density functions which correspond to the F-ratio distribution is created. This is done by, first, generating the table **chi** of the chi-square distribution with **ndf** = 1, 2, 3 and **ddf** = 3, 4, 5. The probability density function for each of these distributions is determined in **pdftable**.

▤▢▤▤▤▤▤▤▤ FRatioDistribution ▤▤▤▤▤▤▢▤

In[29]:=
**ft=Table[FRatioDistribution[i,i+2],
         {i,1,3}]**

Out[29]=
{FRatioDistribution[1, 3],
  FRatioDistribution[2, 4],
  FRatioDistribution[3, 5]}

In[30]:=
pdftable=Table[PDF[ft[[i]],x],{i,1,3}]

Out[30]=

$$\{\frac{2\ 3^{3/2}}{\text{Pi Sqrt[x] (3 + x)}^2},\ \frac{64}{(4 + 2\ x)^3},$$

$$\frac{16\ \text{Sqrt[84375] Sqrt[x]}}{\text{Pi (5 + 3 x)}^4}\}$$

A table for three levels of gray is given in **gray**. Finally, the three probability density functions are plotted simultaneously for $0 \le x \le 5$ using the levels of gray in **gray**.

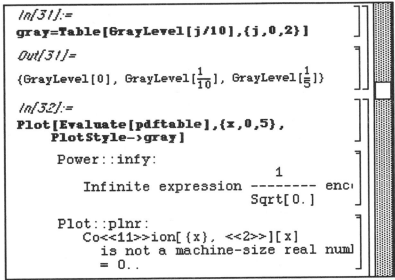

Even though an error message is generated, which is not completely displayed, when the first element of **pdftable**,

$$\frac{2 \cdot 3^{3/2}}{\pi (3 + x)^2 \sqrt{x}},$$ is evaluated for $x = 0$, the resulting displayed graph is correct:

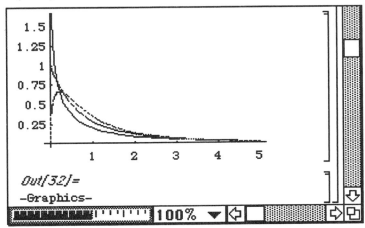

StudentTDistribution 586, 587

Package: **NormalDistributions.m**,
ContinuousDistributions.m

StudentTDistribution[df] represents the Student's t distribution with **df** degrees of freedom.

This distribution is the distribution of the random variable $\frac{\overline{x} - \mu}{s / \sqrt{n}}$ where $\overline{x}$ is a random variable, μ is the population mean, and $s / \sqrt{n}$ is the sample standard deviation.

Example:

In the example below, a table of probability density functions which correspond to the Student's t-distribution is created. This is done by, first, generating the table **sttable** of the Student's t-distribution with **df** = 1, 2, and 3. The probability density function for each of these distributions is determined in **pdfsttable**. A table for three levels of dashing is given in **dash**.

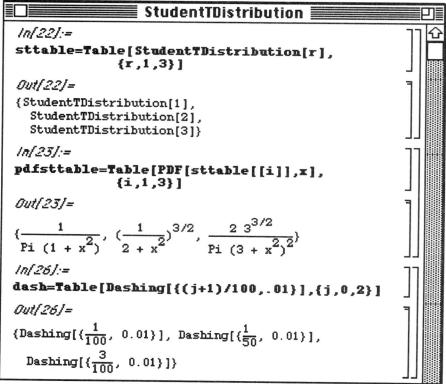

Finally, the three probability density functions are plotted simultaneously for $-5 \leq x \leq 5$ using the table **dash**.

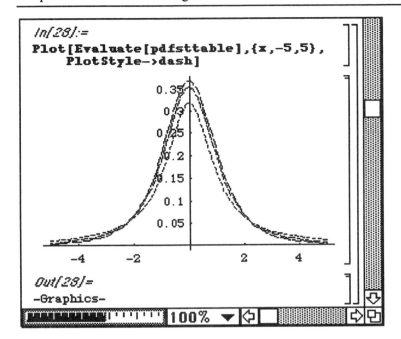

```
In[28]:=
Plot[Evaluate[pdfsttable],{x,-5,5},
     PlotStyle->dash]
```

```
Out[28]=
-Graphics-
```

Numerical Math Packages

Packages contained in the **Numerical Math** folder (or directory) include **Approximations, Butcher, CauchyPrincipalValue, ComputerArithmetic, GaussianQuadrature, IntervalArithmetic, ListIntegrate, NLimit, NewtonCotes**, and **PolynomialFit**.

Approximations.m

RationalInterpolation
                    Package: **Approximations.m**
  RationalInterpolation[func,{x,m,k},xlist}] yields the rational interpolant of degree **m** in the numerator and **k** in the denominator of the function **func** using values of the independent variable given in **xlist**. *Mathematica* automatically selects x-values on the interval **{a,b}** with the command **RationalInterpolation[func,{x,m,k},{x,a,b}]**.
RationalInterpolation has the options **Bias** and **WorkingPrecision**.
Example:
In the example below, the rational interpolant of numerator degree 2 and denominator degree 3 is determined for sin(x) and called **rinterp23**.

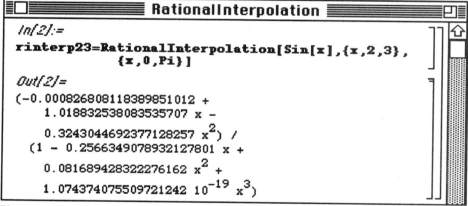

The error function **error23** is then calculated and plotted for $0 \le x \le \pi$.

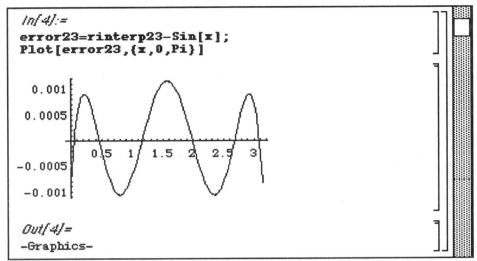

In[4]:=
```
error23=rinterp23-Sin[x];
Plot[error23,{x,0,Pi}]
```

Out[4]=
`-Graphics-`

Similar computations are performed for the interpolant with numerator degree 2 and denominator degree 5. The interpolating function and corresponding error function are called **rinter25** and **error25**, respectively.

In[5]:=
```
rinterp25=RationalInterpolation[Sin[x],{x,2,5},
          {x,0,Pi}]
```

Out[5]=
$$
\begin{aligned}
&(-0.0000265876092486271\,0663 + \\
&\quad 1.001079223865458152\ x - \\
&\quad 0.3186534138095714865\ x^2)\ / \\
&(1 - 0.3115783933518010029\ x + \\
&\quad 0.1493725647835072937\ x^2 - \\
&\quad 0.03195454496687344417\ x^3 + \\
&\quad 0.005085723785730154006\ x^4 - \\
&\quad 1.247943981366164143\ 10^{-19}\ x^5)
\end{aligned}
$$

The error function, **error25**, is determined and plotted below for $0 \le x \le \pi$.

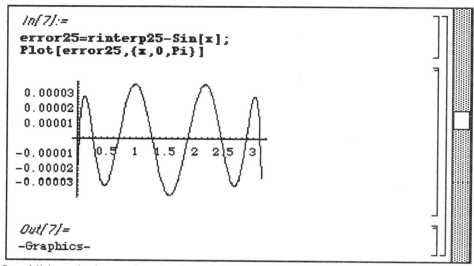

In addition, the interpolant is plotted simultaneously with sin(x) for comparison.

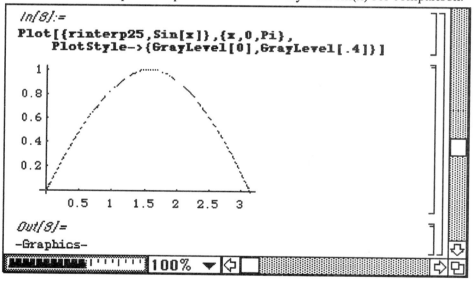

Bias   Package: **Approximations.m**
   Bias is an option used with **RationalInterpolation**,
MiniMaxApproximation, **GeneralRationalInterpolation**, and
GeneralMiniMaxApproximation which indicates a bias to the left or right for
selection of interpolation points. The setting for **Bias** is a value between −1 and 1.
Negative values indicate a bias to the left while positive values cause a bias to the right.
The default setting of **Bias** is **0**.

Example:
In the following example, the **Bias** option is illustrated. First, a bias to the right is considered.

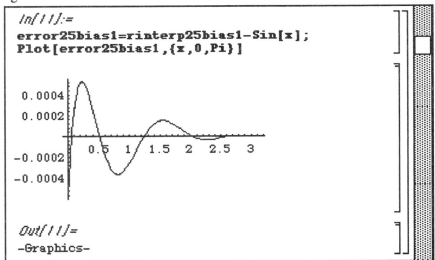

```
≣□≣▬▬▬▬▬▬▬▬▬▬▬▬▬▬▬ Bias ▬▬▬▬▬▬▬▬▬▬▬▬▬□≣
In[9]:=
rinterp25bias1=RationalInterpolation[Sin[x],
    {x,2,5},{x,0,Pi},Bias->.5]

Out[9]=
(-0.0005715003253790 74555 + 1.011975474371291464 x -

    0.322063893110556 8927 x² ) /
(1 - 0.27730579949360 3737 x +

    0.101287017384303 3989 x² -

    0.00187438672011883 0107 x³ -

    0.00360336382292901 9129 x⁴ +

    0.000954985290622585 689 x⁵)
```

The interpolant obtained is called **rinterp25bias1** and the corresponding error function **error25bias1** is plotted to show that the approximation is better to the right.

```
In[11]:=
error25bias1=rinterp25bias1-Sin[x];
Plot[error25bias1,{x,0,Pi}]
```

```
   0.0004
   0.0002

        0.5  1  1.5  2  2.5  3
  -0.0002
  -0.0004
```

```
Out[11]=
-Graphics-
```

Second, similar computations are performed to show a bias to the left. In this case, the interpolant is named **rinterp25bias2** and the error function **error25bias2**.

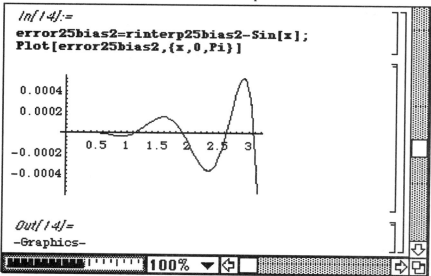

In[12]:=
```
rinterp25bias2=RationalInterpolation[Sin[x],
    {x,2,5},{x,0,Pi},Bias->-.5]
```

Out[12]=

$(-1.28845361241853899 \ 10^{-9} + 1.000004514625318691 \ x \cdot$

$0.3183685637952541821 \ x^2) \ /$

$(1 - 0.3181221276236717954 \ x +$

$0.1644354521188549509 \ x^2 -$

$0.04655728418435750326 \ x^3 +$

$0.01126673613852770751 \ x^4 -$

$0.0009440278836744448597 \ x^5)$

The error function is determined below and plotted.

In[14]:=
```
error25bias2=rinterp25bias2-Sin[x];
Plot[error25bias2,{x,0,Pi}]
```

Out[14]=
-Graphics-

Different forms of interpolation points can be considered. A table of eight random real numbers on the interval [0,1] is generated in **points** below to be used with **RationalInterpolation**.

EquallySpacedInterpolationPoint

In[7]:=
```
points=Table[Random[Real,{0,1}],{8}]
```

Out[7]=
```
{0.680302, 0.975964, 0.0180222, 0.595258,
  0.549447, 0.626906, 0.549913, 0.500042}
```

The x-values in **points** are then used to find the rational interpolant **rinterp25data**.

```
In[8]:=
rinterp25data=RationalInterpolation[Sin[x],
             {x,2,5},points]

Out[8]=

(-2.547377487175728553 10^-7 +
    1.000017039965622315 x -
    0.3559351618074943999 x^2) /
  (1 - 0.3557598491905566376 x +
    0.1658462198483981691 x^2 -
    0.05714029023160168875 x^3 +
    0.01593664366578483533 x^4 -
    0.003459226311079707273 x^5)
```

The corresponding error function is found and plotted below.

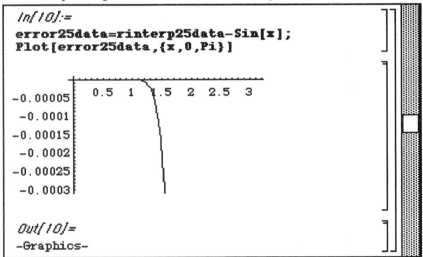

```
In[10]:=
error25data=rinterp25data-Sin[x];
Plot[error25data,{x,0,Pi}]
```

```
Out[10]=
-Graphics-
```

The interpolant is plotted simultaneously with sin(x) below.

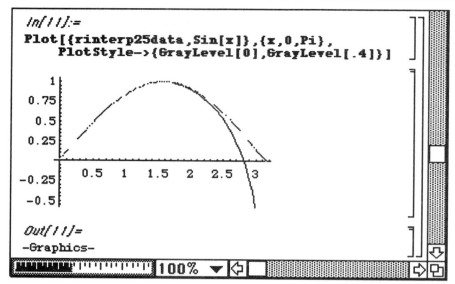

```
In[11]:=
Plot[{rinterp25data,Sin[x]},{x,0,Pi},
    PlotStyle->{GrayLevel[0],GrayLevel[.4]}]
```

```
Out[11]=
-Graphics-
```

Chebyshev interpolation points on the interval $[0,\pi]$ are determined with the function **cheby** below. The numerical approximation of eight interpolation points are then determined in **clist**.

Chebyshev Interpolation Points

```
In[12]:=
cheby[n_]:=Table[Pi/2(1+Cos[Pi(i-1)/(n-1)]),{i,1,n}];
```

```
In[13]:=
clist=cheby[8]//N
```

```
Out[13]=
{3.14159, 2.98603, 2.55017, 1.92033, 1.22126, 0.591421,
    0.155558, 0}
```

These Chebyshev points are then used to determine the rational interpolant in **rinterp25cheb**.

```
In[14]:=
rinterp25cheb=RationalInterpolation[Sin[x],
{x,2,5},clist]
```

```
Out[14]=
```

$$(2.16840434497100886\,8 \cdot 10^{-19} + 1.00048861803676485\,1\; x -$$
$$0.318465418135460638\,6\; x^2)\; /$$
$$(1 - 0.313407409153140580\,9\; x + 0.151626206410243950\,9\; x^2 -$$
$$0.033018621694500113\,52\; x^3 + 0.005255076856760988\,43\; x^4 -$$
$$5.10322089625480768\,5 \cdot 10^{-19}\; x^5)$$

The error function which corresponds to this interpolant is found and plotted below.

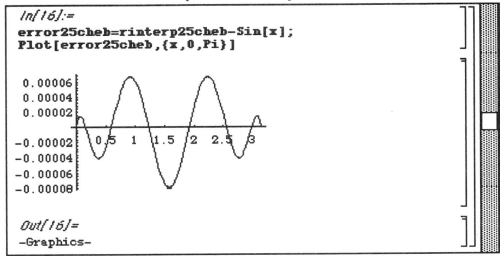

The interpolant and sin(x) are plotted simultaneously below.

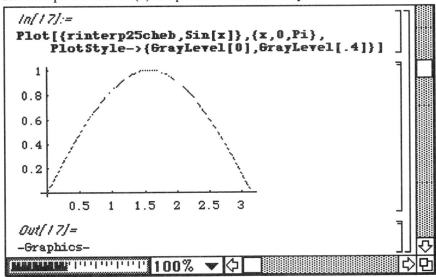

MiniMaxApproximation Package: **Approximations.m**

    MiniMaxApproximation[func,{x,{a,b},m,k}] yields a rational approximation of degree **m** in the numerator and **k** in the denominator of **func** which minimizes the maximum relative error between the approximation and **func**. The output list of **MiniMaxApproximation** consists of the values where the maximum error occurs, the approximation, and the maximum value of the relative error. Options for **MiniMaxApproximation** include **Bias**, **Brake**, **Derivatives**, **MaxIterations**, **PrintFlag**, **PlotFlag**, and **WorkingPrecision**. When **MiniMaxApproximation** fails to converge within the number of iterations specified with **MaxIterations**, then the approximation **app** which results can be used in

MiniMaxApproximation[func,app,{x,{a,b},m,k}] to attempt to determine an approximation which converges.

Example:

The minimax approximation is determined for e^x for various values of numerator and denominator degree on the interval [−1,1]. Below, **minmax1** represents the minimax approximation with numerator degree 2 and denominator degree 3.

```
═══════════════════ MinMaxApproximation ═══════════════════

In[18]:=
minmax1=MiniMaxApproximation[Exp[x],{x,{-1,1},2,3}]

Out[18]=
{{-1., -0.860402760875332968, -0.4810351102401415355,
    0.0287298291102361 4568, 0.523725530267565657,
    0.874375843962975761, 1.},
  {(0.999995728516493743 + 0.3993830531208874124 x +
      0.04939143775689999048 x^2) /
   (1 - 0.600610844359395323 x +
      0.1499285892068277471 x^2 -
      0.01634727648701311535 x^3),
    -4.334829627305958967 10^-6}}
```

minmax2 represents that of numerator degree 1 and denominator degree 3.

```
In[19]:=
minmax2=MiniMaxApproximation[Exp[x],{x,{-1,1},1,3}]

Out[19]=
{{-1., -0.780540149958884633, -0.2332526721189575157,
    0.384063278114427091 4, 0.837086888321999226, 1.},
  {(0.999947805166326063 + 0.2473761003323639972 x) /
   (1 - 0.753195764107918263 x +
      0.2523858470690285367 x^2 -
      0.04038448782337085886 x^3),
    0.000129087738962510761 9}}
```

minmax3 represents that with numerator degree 3 and denominator degree 3. Notice that the approximation associated with **minmax3** is smaller than that associated with the other two approximations.

```
In[20]:=
minmax3=MiniMaxApproximation[Exp[x],{x,{-1,1},3,3}]

Out[20]=
{{-1., -0.90190410762029585, -0.625608716127296433,
    -0.2237048620248246551, 0.2237048620248587361,
    0.625608716127312778, 0.901904107620303571, 1.},
  {(0.999999999999987987 + 0.4999994605028999588 x +

    0.0997835474734712475 x^2 + 0.0082294530908184275 8 x^3

    ) / (1 - 0.4999994605029049857 x +

    0.0997835474734719567 x^2 - 0.0082294530908184468 3 x^3

    ), 1.550057343484853228 10^{-7}}}
```

Brake   Package: **Approximations.m**

Brake is an option used with **MiniMaxApproximation** and **GeneralMiniMaxApproximation** which serves to monitor changes which occur in the value of extrema from one iteration to the next. The setting for **Brake** is of the form **{integer1,integer2}** where **integer1** specifies the number of iterations affected by braking and **integer2** indicates the magnitude of the braking applied on the first iteration. This option is more useful when considering an approximation of high degree.

Example:

The following example illustrates how the **Brake** option is used to cause **MiniMaxApproximations** to terminate when convergence is not achieved within 20 iterations, the default setting of **MaxIterations**.

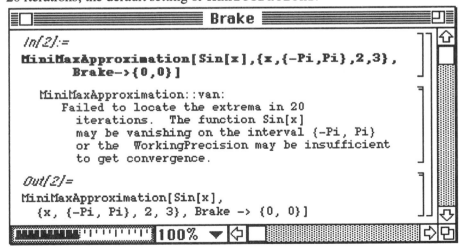
```
Brake

In[2]:=
MiniMaxApproximation[Sin[x],{x,{-Pi,Pi},2,3},
    Brake->{0,0}]

    MiniMaxApproximation::van:
        Failed to locate the extrema in 20
        iterations.  The function Sin[x]
        may be vanishing on the interval {-Pi, Pi}
        or the  WorkingPrecision may be insufficient
        to get convergence.

Out[2]=
MiniMaxApproximation[Sin[x],
    {x, {-Pi, Pi}, 2, 3}, Brake -> {0, 0}]
```

MaxIterations   Package: **Approximations.m**

MaxIterations is an option used with **MiniMaxApproximation** and
GeneralMiniMaxApproximation to specify the number of iterations to follow
when braking has ceased. The default setting of **MaxIterations** is **20**. When
convergence is not completed before the limit of MaxIterations is reached, then
Mathematica returns a warning message and the approximation obtained to that point.
The approximation which results can then be used as an argument of
MiniMaxApproximation to obtain a more accurate approximation.

Example:

The following example illustrates how **MaxIterations** is used to obtain an
approximation which can, in turn, be used as an initial approximation. Since the first
command yields insufficient results, the option **MaxIterations->2** causes an
interpolant which does not converge to be given. This approximation, called **app**, is
then used in the following **MiniMaxApproximation** command as an initial
approximation.

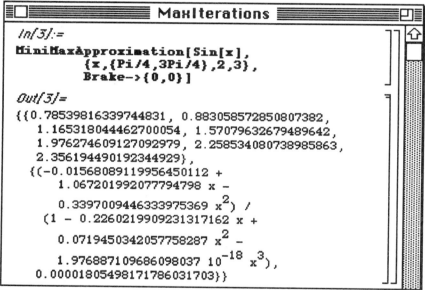

The interpolant found in **app2** is then used as the initial approximation for
MiniMaxApproximation to obtain an interpolant in **app3** which converges. The
function sin(x) is then plotted with this approximation.

```
In[4]:=
app=MiniMaxApproximation[Sin[x],
      {x,{Pi/100,99Pi/100},2,3},
      MaxIterations->2,Brake->{0,0}]
```

MiniMaxApproximation::conv:
   Warning: convergence was not complete.

```
Out[4]=
{{0.03141592653589793235, 0.115183388780219788,
   0.596585447636070416, 1.570796326794896625,
   2.545007205953722838, 3.026409264809573473,
   3.110176727053895306},
  {(-0.0004052983136386396521 +
      1.011942441957427201 x -

      0.3221112835240158501 x ) /
   (1 - 0.2645465221819906363 x +

      0.0842077733660670933 x +
                                   -19   3
      1.246169491743161992 10    x ),
   0.00270976817360663 7237}}
```

```
In[5]:=
app2=MiniMaxApproximation[Sin[x],app,
      {x,{Pi/100,99Pi/100},2,3},
      MaxIterations->2,Brake->{0,0}]
```

MiniMaxApproximation::conv:
   Warning: convergence was not complete.

```
Out[5]=
{{0.03141592653589793235, 0.0981337470354841348,
   0.58939870200399186, 1.570796326794896615,
   2.552193951585801388, 3.043458906554309082,
   3.110176727053895306},
  {(-0.0003985922569903155994 +
      1.0116304452498677 x -

      0.3220119718875428681 x ) /
   (1 - 0.2649336943824229662 x +

      0.0843310141051202364 x -
                                   -20   3
      1.478200919495768367 10    x ),
   0.00279388587090342 5319}}
```

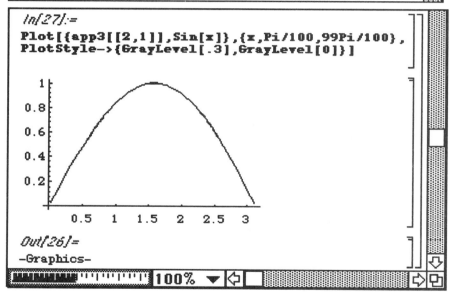

```
In[5]:=
app3=MiniMaxApproximation[Sin[x],app2,
      {x,{Pi/100,99Pi/100},2,3},
      MaxIterations->2,Brake->{0,0}]

Out[5]=
{{0.03141592653589793235, 0.098133745460573852 6,
  0.589398683113655497, 1.570796326794896556,
  2.552193970476137614, 3.043458908129219387,
  3.110176727053895306},
 {(-0.0003985922571779507238 +
    1.011630445093340366 x -

    0.3220119718377186701 x^2) /
  (1 - 0.264933694688033545 x +

    0.0843310142023991084 x^2 -

    1.31934326275845408 10^{-18} x^3),
  0.0027938860237846 80061}}
```

```
In[27]:=
Plot[{app3[[2,1]],Sin[x]},{x,Pi/100,99Pi/100},
PlotStyle->{GrayLevel[.3],GrayLevel[0]}]
```

```
Out[26]=
-Graphics-
```

Derivatives   Package: **Approximations.m**

Derivatives is an option used with **MiniMaxApproximation** and
GeneralMiniMaxApproximation to specify functions used for determining the
first two derivatives of the function being approximated. This option is particularly
useful when considering a function with derivatives that are complicated or if
Mathematica cannot compute them analytically. The function setting for
Derivative must be able to act on lists.

Example:
In the following example, the **Derivatives** option is illustrated. In this case, the function sin(x) and its first two derivatives are indicated as the vector-valued function **dlist**. This function is then incorporated into the **Derivatives** option of **MiniMaxApproximation**.

PrintFlag   Package: **Approximations.m**
  PrintFlag is an option used with **MiniMaxApproximation** and **GeneralMiniMaxApproximation** which causes the relative error information to be printed for each step in the iteration. This information consists of changes in the abscissae approximations as well as a list of ordered pairs made up of the abscissae of the extrema of the relative error and the value of the relative error at those abscissae. The default setting for this option is **False**.

Example:

A shortened output list of the results obtained with the option setting
PrintFlag->True are displayed below.

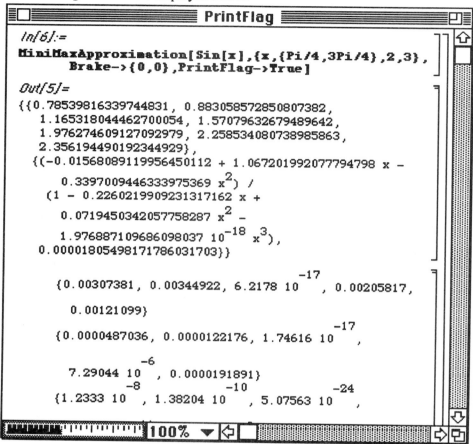

PlotFlag   Package: **Approximations.m**

PlotFlag is an option used with **MiniMaxApproximation** and
GeneralMiniMaxApproximation which causes the relative error to be plotted at
each step in the iteration. The default setting of this option is **False**. This option is
used to observe the changes which occur from one iteration to the next. Large
variances imply that braking should be employed.

Example:

The plots which result with the option setting **PlotFlag->True** are displayed below.

This is done for the function sin(x) on the interval $[\pi/4, 3\pi/4]$.

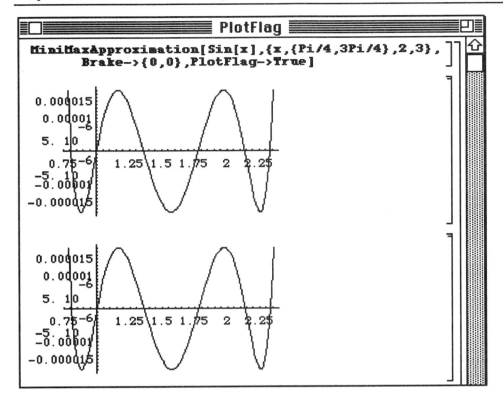

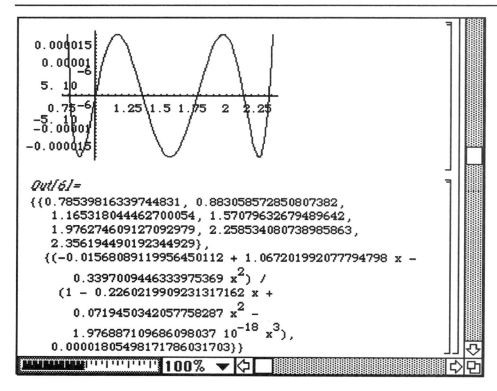

Out[6]=
{{0.78539816339744831, 0.883058572850807382,
  1.165318044462700054, 1.57079632679489642,
  1.976274609127092979, 2.258534080738985863,
  2.356194490192344929},
 {(-0.01568089119956450112 + 1.067201992077794798 x -

    0.3397009446333975369 x^2) /

  (1 - 0.2260219909231317162 x +

    0.0719450342057758287 x^2 -

    1.976887109686098037 10^{-18} x^3),

  0.00001805498171786031703}}

100% ▼

GeneralRationalInterpolation
Package: **Approximations.m**
   GeneralRationalInterpolation[{fxt,fyt},{t,m,k},x,tlist]
yields the rational interpolation of degree **m** in the numerator and **k** in the denominator for the curve defined by the parametric equations **{fxt,fyt}** using the values in **tlist** as interpolation points. The interpolation points are selected automatically from the interval **{t1,t2}** by
GeneralRationalInterpolation[{fxt,fyt},{t,m,k},x,{t,t1,t2}].
GeneralRationalInterpolation has the options **Bias** and
WorkingPrecision.
Example:
The following example illustrates the use of **GeneralRationalInterpolation** to approximate the function {t−sin(t),1−cos(t)}. The approximation procedure uses the interpolation points given in **xtable**.

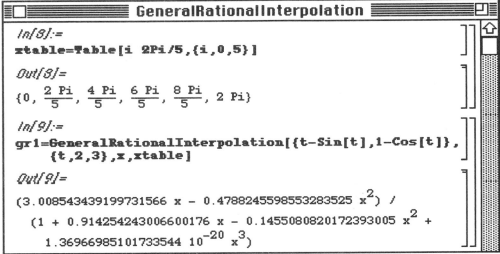

Plots for the interpolant and the function sin(x) are determined below where the output was suppressed initially with the **DisplayFunction->Identity** setting.

```
In[10]:=
plot1=Plot[gr1,{x,0,2Pi},
    PlotStyle->GrayLevel[.3],
    DisplayFunction->Identity];
In[11]:=
plot2=ParametricPlot[{t-Sin[t],1-Cos[t]},
    {t,0,2Pi},DisplayFunction->Identity];
```

The interpolant given in **gr1** is then plotted simultaneously with sin(x) on the interval $[0,2\pi]$.

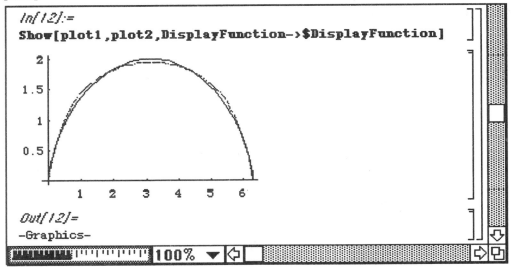

Equally spaced interpolation points are then considered with
GeneralRationalInterpolant below. This interpolant is found in **gr2** below,
and its plot in **plot3**.

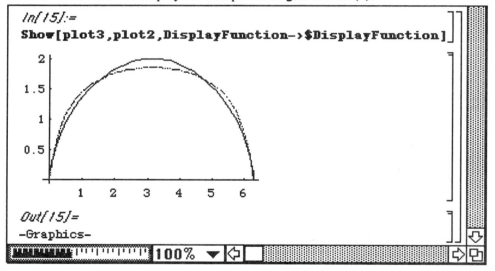

Show is used below to display the interpolant in **gr2** and sin(x).

GeneralMiniMaxApproximation
Package: **Approximations.m**

GeneralMiniMaxApproximation[{fxt,fyt},{t,{t1,t2},m,k},x}]
determines the rational approximation of degree **m** in the numerator and **k** in the
denominator (which minimizes the relative error) of the curve given by the parametric
equations **{fxt,fyt}**. If **GeneralMiniMaxApproximation** fails to converge,
then the approximation which results, app, can be used as an initial approximation in
the command
GeneralMiniMaxApproximation[{fxt,fyt},app,
        {t,{t1,t2},m,k},x}]

to find an approximation which converges. An error function other than relative error can be specified by
`GeneralMiniMaxApproximation[{fxt,fyt,g},{t,{t1,t2},m,k},x}]`.
The error function is defined by `(fyt-h(fxt))/g(t)` where `h(t)` is the minimax rational approximation. Hence, the default value of `g` is `fyt` which causes the relative error to be used. Using `1` for `g` leads to the absolute error being considered.
`GeneralMiniMaxApproximation` has the same options as
`MiniMaxApproximation`.
Example:
The use of `GeneralMiniMaxApproximation` is demonstrated below. In this example, `GeneralMiniMaxApproximation` is used to approximate
$\{1-\sin(t),1-\cos(t)\}$ on the interval $[\pi/4,7\pi/4]$. This interval can be divided into subintervals and the approximation performed over each subinterval to reduce the error associated with each approximation.

```
═□═════ GeneralMiniMaxInterpolation ════□═

In[19]:=

gminmax1=GeneralMiniMaxApproximation[
       {t-Sin[t],1-Cos[t]},
       {t,{Pi/4,7Pi/4},2,3},x]

Out[19]=
{{0.78539816339744831, 1.024132392247282465,
   1.807065254333024441, 3.141592653589793239,
   4.476120052846562041, 5.259052914932304017,
   5.497787143782138167},
 {(0.1364890574675249197 +
      2.282755262438005628 x -
     0.3633117838860453882 x²) /
   (1 + 0.576120283353523439 x -
     0.0916923909112166383 x² -
     6.42708282994128814 10⁻²⁰ x³),
  -0.02301944924693362737}}
```

The interpolant found in **gminmax1** is then plotted simultaneously with sin(x).

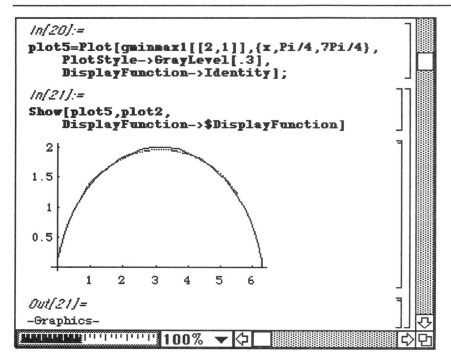

```
In[20]:=
plot5=Plot[qminmax1[[2,1]],{x,Pi/4,7Pi/4},
    PlotStyle->GrayLevel[.3],
    DisplayFunction->Identity];
In[21]:=
Show[plot5,plot2,
    DisplayFunction->$DisplayFunction]
```

```
Out[21]=
-Graphics-
```

Butcher.m

RungeKuttaOrderConditions

Package: **Butcher.m**

RungeKuttaOrderConditions[n,s] yields the order conditions

required by all s - stage Runge - Kutta methods of order n. This list includes

conditions for a[i,j], b[j], and c[i]   where $Y_i(x) = y(x_0) + (x - x_0) \sum_{j=1}^{s} a[i,j]\, f(Y_i(x))$,

$i = 1, 2, ..., s$, $Y(x) = y(x_0) + (x - x_0) \sum_{j=1}^{s} b[i]\, f(Y_i(x))$,   and $c[i] = \sum_{j=1}^{s} a[i,j]$.

Example:

Several examples of **RungeKuttaConditions** are given below. First, the conditions needed for 2-stage Runge-Kutta methods of order one are listed. Next, those of a 3-stage method of order two are given.

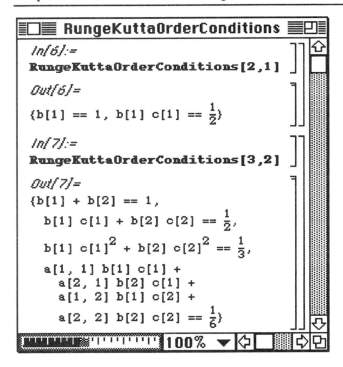

CauchyPrincipalValue.m

CauchyPrincipalValue Package: **CauchyPrincipalValue.m**
  CauchyPrincipalValue is used to compute the Cauchy principal value
of integrals.   This command can be entered in several forms.

CauchyPrincipalValue[f,a,{x,{sing},c}] computes the Cauchy

principal value of $\int_a^c f(x)dx$ where f has a singularity at x = **sing**. If more than one
singularity is encountered, then the command is entered as

CauchyPrincipalValue[f,{x,a,{sing1},{sing2},...,c}]. To take
advantage of symmetry properties,

CauchyPrincipalValue[f,{x,a,{b,eps},c}] determines the value of

$$\int_a^{b-eps} f(x)dx + \int_0^{eps} \left(f(b+t) + f(b-t)\right) dt + \int_{b+eps}^c f(x)dx \,.$$

CauchyPrincipalValue has the same options as **NIntegrate** since it
uses **NIntegrate** to evaluate these integrals.

Example:

In the examples below, the Cauchy principal value of $\int_0^2 \frac{1}{1-x^2}\,dx$, $\int_{-2}^2 \frac{1}{1-x^2}\,dx$, and

that of $\int_{-1/2}^1 \frac{1}{x+x^2}\,dx$ are computed.

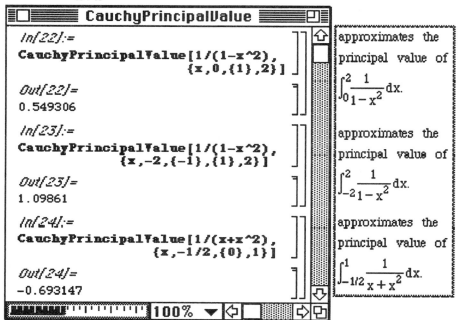

ComputerArithmetic.m

ComputerNumber   Package: **ComputerArithmetic.m**

ComputerNumber[num] changes the number **num** to a computer number using the current arithmetic. The arithmetic includes the number digits required for the mantissa and exponent as well as the settings of **RoundingRule**, **ExponentRange**, **MixedMode**, and **IdealDivide**. This command can be entered as **ComputerNumber[s,man,exp]** to create the computer number using sign **s** which is **1** or **-1**, mantissa **man**, and exponent **exp**. Note that settings according to the values listed in **Arithmetic[]** must be used for **man** and **exp**. Also, the complete computer number specification for **num** is given by **ComputerNumber[s,man,exp,val,num]** and can be viewed with **InputForm**.
Example:
The computer number representations of **E** and **EulerGamma** are computed below. These values are then added. **InputForm** is used to display the associated values of sign, mantissa, and exponent for **sum**.

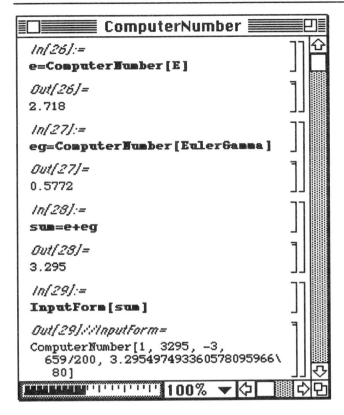

NaN   Package: **ComputerArithmetic.m**

NaN is the result when a number cannot be represented as a computer number under the current arithmetic.

Example:

The following example shows that **NaN** results when the incorrect number of digits appears in the mantissa. Only three are used below when the current arithmetic (the default value) calls for four. The computer number can be generated by altering the number of digits in the mantissa with **SetArithmetic**.

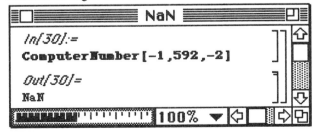

SetArithmetic   Package: **ComputerArithmetic.m**

   SetArithmetic is used to set arithmetic parameters. This setting can be made in several forms. **SetArithmetic[n]** sets the number of digits in base 10 to **n** while **SetArithmetic[n,b]** sets the number of digits to **n** and the base to **b**.
SetArithmetic has several options. These include **RoundingRule** with default value **RoundToEven**, **ExponentRange** with default setting **{-50,50}**, **MixedMode** with default **False**, and **IdealDivide** with default **False**.
Example:
In the first example below, the number which is considered in the **NaN** example above is computed using four digits in the mantissa which is the default setting. This computer number is also found by changing the number of digits required for the mantissa to three. This leads to the computation of the computer number which failed in the earlier example of **NaN**.

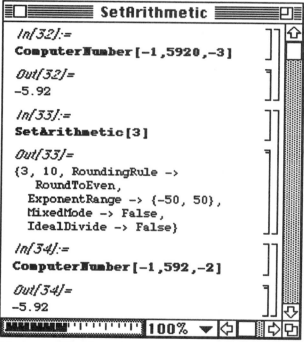

Also, modification of the base is performed in the following example which leads to numbers in base 9 using 4 digits in the mantissa.

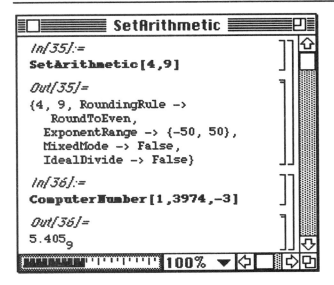

Arithmetic   Package: **ComputerArithmetic.m**
  Arithmetic[] lists the current values of the arithmetic parameters. These include
the settings of mantissa digits, base, **RoundingRule**, **ExponentRange**,
MixedMode, and **IdealDivide**. Changes in these values are made with
SetArithmetic.
Example:
The default settings are displayed below with **Arithmetic[]**.

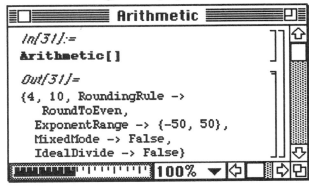

ExponentRange   Package: **ComputerArithmetic.m**
  ExponentRange is a **SetArithmetic** option used to indicate the values which
can be entered for the exponent within the **ComputerNumber** command. The default
setting of **ExponentRange** is **{-50,50}**, but this is changed with the setting
ExponentRange->{expmin,expmax}.
Example:
In the first command below, the default setting of **ExponentRange** is indicated in the
output list of **SetArithmetic[4,9]**. Then a computer number is generated using
this arithmetic.

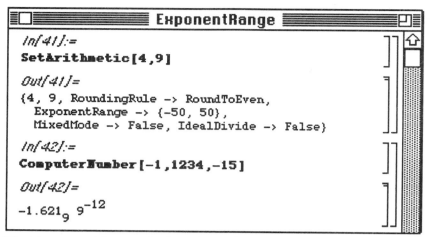

The **ExponentRange** is then changed to **{-10,10}** so that the indicated computer number cannot be generated due to the fact that the exponent is not in the range.

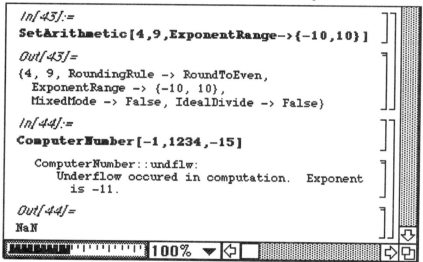

IdealDivide   Package: **ComputerArithmetic.m**

IdealDivide is an option used with **SetArithmetic** to indicate whether or not correctly rounded division is to be used when working with computer numbers. With the setting **IdealDivide->True**, *Mathematica* changes the quotient **a/b** to **a~IdealDivide~b** before changing it to **a b^(-1)**. Otherwise, with default setting **IdealDivide->False**, the quotient is automatically converted to **a b^(-1)** before it is considered by the **ComputerArithmetic** package.

Example:

The following example illustrates how **IdealDivide** is used to avoid errors in computer arithmetic.

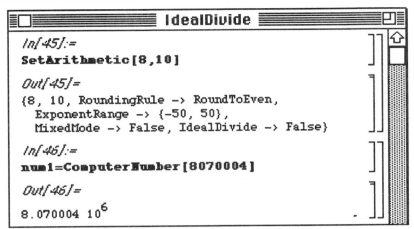

The reciprocal of 80700004 is determined and called **num2**. Then, the reciprocal of **num2** is found. Notice that the original number is not obtained.

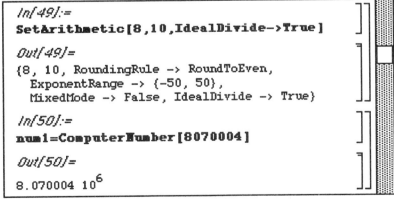

With the setting **IdealDivide->True**, this is not the case as shown below. Again, **num1** represents the computer number formulation of 8070004.

```
In[49]:=
SetArithmetic[8,10,IdealDivide->True]

Out[49]=
{8, 10, RoundingRule -> RoundToEven,
  ExponentRange -> {-50, 50},
  MixedMode -> False, IdealDivide -> True}

In[50]:=
num1=ComputerNumber[8070004]

Out[50]=
8.070004 10^6
```

num2 is the reciprocal of **num1**, and **num3** the reciprocal of **num2**.

In[51]:=
num2=1/num1

Out[51]=

IdealDivide[1, 8.070004 10^6]

In[52]:=
num3=1/num2

Out[52]=

IdealDivide[1, IdealDivide[1, 8.070004 10^6]]

InputForm is then used to view that the value of **num3** is 8070004.

In[53]:=
ComputerNumber[3]/num1

Out[53]=

3.7174703 10^{-7}

In[54]:=
IdealDivide[ComputerNumber[3],num1]

Out[54]=

3.7174703 10^{-7}

In[55]:=
ComputerNumber[1,3579,2]

Out[55]=
NaN

In[56]:=
SetArithmetic[4,9,IdealDivide->True]

Out[56]=
{4, 9, RoundingRule -> RoundToEven,
  ExponentRange -> {-50, 50},
  MixedMode -> False, IdealDivide -> True}

In[57]:=
ComputerNumber[1,3579,2]/ComputerNumber[1,2468,2]

Out[57]=
1.404$_9$

100% ▼

MixedMode   Package: **ComputerArithmetic.m**

    MixedMode is a **SetArithmetic** option which indicates whether arithmetic operations between computer numbers and non-computer numbers can be performed. The default setting of **MixedMode** is **False**, so these operations are not allowed unless the setting

MixedMode->True is made within **SetArithmetic**.

Example:

In the example below, the numbers **4** and **ComputerNumber[1,3974,-3]** cannot be added until the option **MixedMode->True** is used in **SetArithmetic**.

```
In[58]:=
SetArithmetic[4,8]

Out[58]=
{4, 8, RoundingRule -> RoundToEven,
  ExponentRange -> {-50, 50}, MixedMode -> False,
  IdealDivide -> False}

In[59]:=
4+ComputerNumber[1,3974,-3]

Out[59]=
4 + 7.606
         8

In[60]:=
SetArithmetic[4,8,MixedMode->True]

Out[60]=
{4, 8, RoundingRule -> RoundToEven,
  ExponentRange -> {-50, 50}, MixedMode -> True,
  IdealDivide -> False}

In[61]:=
4+ComputerNumber[1,3974,-3]

Out[61]=
13.61
     8
```

RoundingRule   Package: **ComputerArithmetic.m**

    RoundingRule is an option used with **SetArithmetic** to specify the type of rounding to be performed. Settings for **RoundingRule** include the default setting **RoundToEven**, **RoundToInfinity**, and **Truncation**. **RoundToEven** indicates that rounding be to the nearest representable computer number. If there is a tie, then the number is rounded to the computer number with an even mantissa. The setting **RoundToInfinity** implies that rounding be to the nearest representable computer number while, in the case of a tie, rounding is away from zero. The setting of **Truncation** causes excess digits to be dropped.

Example:

In the first two examples below, the **RoundingRule->RoundToEven** setting is illustrated.

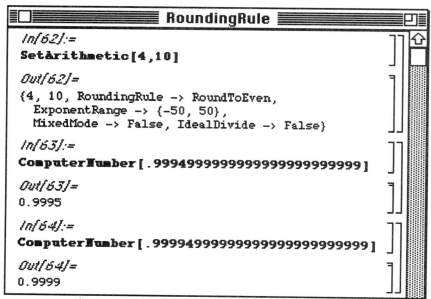

Then, the setting **RoundingRule->Truncation** is made in **SetArithmetic**, and two examples follow.

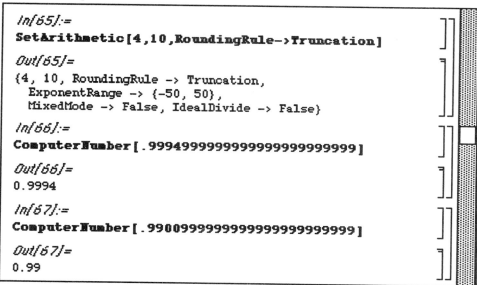

Finally, **RoundingRule->RoundToInfinity** is used.

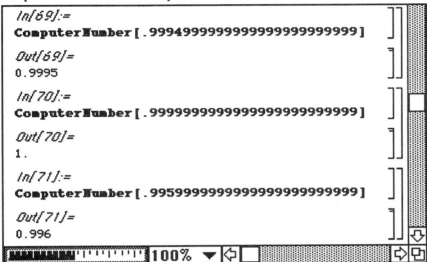

In[68]:=
SetArithmetic[4,10,RoundingRule->RoundToInfinity]

Out[68]=
{4, 10, RoundingRule -> RoundToInfinity,
   ExponentRange -> {-50, 50},
   MixedMode -> False, IdealDivide -> False}

The last three examples employ this rule for rounding. These results should be compared to the earlier examples.

In[69]:=
ComputerNumber[.9994999999999999999999999]

Out[69]=
0.9995

In[70]:=
ComputerNumber[.9999999999999999999999999]

Out[70]=
1.

In[71]:=
ComputerNumber[.9959999999999999999999999]

Out[71]=
0.996

`100%`

GaussianQuadrature.m

GaussianQuadratureWeights
Package: **GaussianQuadrature.m**

GaussianQuadratureWeights[n,a,b] yields the Gaussian quadrature weights and nodes for numerical integration. The method of Gaussian quadrature is

based on the Lagrange interpolation formula $p(x) = \sum_{i=1}^{n} f(x_i) \, \ell_i(x)$ where

$\ell_i(x) = \prod_{\substack{j=1 \\ j \neq i}}^{n} \left(\frac{x - x_j}{x_i - x_j} \right).$ If this formula provides a good approximation of f, then the

integral of p supplies a good approximation of the integral of f. Hence,

$$\int_a^b f(x)dx = \int_a^b p(x)dx = \sum_{i=1}^{n} f(x_i) \int_a^b \ell_i(x)dx = \sum_{i=1}^{n} A_i f(x_i)$$ where A_i represents the

weights and x_i the nodes for i = 1, 2, ..., n.

Example:

In the first example below, the four Gaussian quadrature weights and corresponding nodes are determined on the interval $[-1,1]$. The values in **gauss** are then used to derive the formula given in **approx** which is used to approximate the integral of the function f over $[-1,1]$.

GaussianQuadratureWeights

In[2]:=

```
gauss=GaussianQuadratureWeights[4,-1,1]
```

Out[2]=

```
{{-0.861136, 0.347855}, {-0.339981, 0.652145},
  {0.339981, 0.652145}, {0.861136, 0.347855}}
```

In[3]:=

```
approx=Sum[gauss[[i,2]] f[gauss[[i,1]]],
          {i,1,4}]
```

Out[3]=

```
0.347855 f[-0.861136] + 0.652145 f[-0.339981] +
  0.652145 f[0.339981] + 0.347855 f[0.861136]
```

In the following example, $f(x) = \sqrt{1-x^2}$ is defined so that an approximation of $\int_{-1}^{1} \sqrt{1-x^2}\,dx$ can be determined.

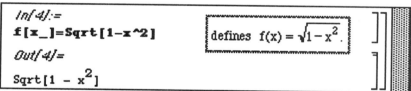

In[4]:=

```
f[x_]=Sqrt[1-x^2]
```
defines $f(x) = \sqrt{1-x^2}$.

Out[4]=

```
Sqrt[1 - x^2]
```

After defining the function above, this integral is approximated to obtain a value of 1.5828. The number of nodes is then increased to eight in **gauss2** and a similar calculation is performed to obtain an approximate integral value of 1.5708.

In[5]:=
approx

Out[5]=
1.58028

> computes the value of **approx** when $f(x) = \sqrt{1-x^2}$.

In[6]:=
gauss2=GaussianQuadratureWeights[8,-1,1]

Out[6]=
{{-0.96029, 0.101229}, {-0.796666, 0.222381},
  {-0.525532, 0.313707}, {-0.183435, 0.362684},
  {0.183435, 0.362684}, {0.525532, 0.313707},
  {0.796666, 0.222381}, {0.96029, 0.101229}}

In[7]:=
**approx2=Sum[gauss2[[i,2]] f[gauss2[[i,1]]],
          {i,1,8}]**

Out[7]=
1.57216

The next example shows how Gaussian quadrature can be used in cases where **NIntegrate** fails. This is accomplished by considering the function $\dfrac{\sqrt[3]{x^2 - 1}}{\sqrt{\sin\left(e^x - 1\right)}}$. **NIntegrate** does not yield an approximation of the integral of this function on the interval [0,1]. However, Gaussian quadrature can be used to obtain this value.

In[12]:=
Clear[f,approx2,gauss2]
gauss2=GaussianQuadratureWeights[8,0,1];
f[x_]=(x^2-1)^(1/3) (Sin[Exp[x]-1])^(-1/2);
**approx2=Sum[gauss2[[i,2]] f[gauss2[[i,1]]],
          {i,1,8}]**

Out[12]=
0.81527 + 1.41209 I

However, in this case **NIntegrate** does not yield an approximation of

$$\int_0^1 \frac{\sqrt[3]{x^2 - 1}}{\sqrt{\sin\left(e^x - 1\right)}}\, dx.$$

```
In[13]:=
NIntegrate[(x^2-1)^(1/3) (Sin[Exp[x]-1])^(-1/2),
          {x,0,1}]

    Power::infy:
                              1
         Infinite expression -------- encountered.
                            Sqrt[0.]

    NIntegrate::inum:
         Integrand ComplexInfinity is not numerical at {x}
                              -56
            = {4.48942 10    }.

Out[13]=
                    2      1/3
               (x  - 1)
NIntegrate[--------------------, {x, 0, 1}]
                            1/2
           Sin[Exp[x] - 1]
```

The next example illustrates how Gaussian quadrature is used to approximate the value of iterated integrals. A list of ten Gaussian quadrature weights and nodes on the interval [0,1] is determined in **gauss10** below.

```
In[15]:=
gauss10=GaussianQuadratureWeights[10,0,1]

Out[15]=
{{0.0130467, 0.0333357}, {0.0674683, 0.0747257},
  {0.160295, 0.109543}, {0.283302, 0.134633},
  {0.425563, 0.147762}, {0.574437, 0.147762},
  {0.716698, 0.134633}, {0.839705, 0.109543},
  {0.932532, 0.0747257}, {0.986953, 0.0333357}}
```

A function $f(r,\theta) = \left(1-r^2\right)\sin\left(1-\theta\pi\right)$ is defined below, and the integral of this function over the region $[0,1] \times [0,1]$ is approximated with the method of Gaussian quadrature.

```
In[17]:=
f[r_,theta_]:=(1-r^2) Sin[(1-theta)Pi]
Sum[gauss10[[i,2]] gauss10[[j,2]]*
          N[f[gauss10[[i,1]],
          gauss10[[j,1]]]],
          {i,1,10},{j,1,10}]

Out[17]=
0.424413
```

The result of using **NIntegrate** to approximate the value of
$$\int_0^1\int_0^1\left(1-r^2\right)\sin\left(1-\theta\pi\right)d\theta dr$$ is shown below.

```
In[18]:=
█Integrate[(1-r^2) Sin[(1-theta)Pi],
             {r,0,1},{theta,0,1}]
Out[18]=
0.424413
```

A table of the first four zeros of the Bessel function of order 0 are determined in **roots**
with **FindRoot** and the list of initial approximations {2.5, 5.5, 8.5, and 11.5}.

```
In[14]:=
roots=Table[FindRoot[BesselJ[0,r]==0,{r,start}],
       {start,2.5,11.5,3}]
Out[14]=
{{r -> 2.40483}, {r -> 5.52008}, {r -> 8.65373},
  {r -> 11.7915}}
```

Below, a function similar to those which appear in the solution of the wave equation on
a circular membrane is considered. This calculation depends on the roots of the Bessel
function of order 0 which are given in **roots** above. First,

$f(r,\theta) = r\left(1-r^2\right)J_0(\textbf{roots[[1,1,2]]}\ r)\sin\left((1-\theta)\pi\right)$, where $J_0(x)$ denotes the

Bessel function of the first kind of order zero and **roots[[1,1,2]]**
is the number 2.40483, is defined and then **Sum** and **gauss10** are used to approximate

the integral $\int_0^1\int_0^1 f(r,\theta)\,d\theta\,dr$:

```
In[21]:=
Clear[f];
f[r_,theta_]=r (1-r^2) BesselJ[0,roots[[1,1,2]] r]±
             Sin[(1-theta)Pi];
Sum[gauss10[[i,2]] gauss10[[j,2]]±
            █[f[gauss10[[i,1]],
            gauss10[[j,1]]]],
            {i,1,10},{j,1,10}]
Out[21]=
0.0950561
```

In the following example, first

$f(r,\theta,k) = r\left(1-r^2\right)J_0(\textbf{roots[[k,1,2]]}\ r)\sin\left((1-\theta)\pi\right)$, where $J_0(x)$ denotes

the Bessel function of the first kind of order zero and **roots[[k,1,2]]**
denotes 2.40483 when k=1, 5.52008 when k=2, 8.65373 when k=3, and 11.7915 when
k=4, is defined, then a_k is defined to be an approximation of

the integral $\int_0^1\int_0^1 f(r,\theta,k)\cos\left(k\pi\theta\right)d\theta\,dr$, and finally coefficients **a[1]**, **a[2]**,

a[3] are computed.

```
In[24]:=
Clear[f];
f[r_,theta_,k_]:=r (1-r^2)±
        BesselJ[0,roots[[k,1,2]] r]±
        Sin[(1-theta)Pi];
a[k_]:=Sum[gauss10[[i,2]] gauss10[[j,2]]±
        N[f[gauss10[[i,1]],
        gauss10[[j,1]],k]]±
        N[Cos[k Pi gauss10[[j,1]]]]],
    {i,1,10},{j,1,10}]
In[25]:=
a[1]
Out[25]=
8.04758 10^-20
In[26]:=
a[2]
Out[26]=
0.00171712
In[27]:=
a[3]
Out[27]=
9.26235 10^-22
```

Next, a function for the computation of coefficients **b[k]** is created by defining

$$g(r,\theta,k) = r\left(1-r^2\right)J_0(\mathbf{roots[[k,1,2]]}\,r)\sin\left((1-\theta)\pi\right),\ \text{where}\ J_0(x)\ \text{denotes}$$

the Bessel function of the first kind of order zero and **roots[[k,1,2]]** denotes 2.40483 when k=1, 5.52008 when k=2, 8.65373 when k=3, and 11.7915 when k=4, is defined, then b_k is defined to be an approximation of

the integral $\int_0^1\!\!\int_0^1 f(r,\theta,k)\sin\left(k\,\pi\,\theta\right)d\theta\,dr.$

Notice that both **a[k]** and **b[k]** are defined for k=1, 2, 3, and 4 since **roots** only contains four numbers. Additional terms could have been defined by creating additional approximations of the zeros of $J_0(x)$.

Finally **uj**(r,θ,t,m) is defined by

$$\mathbf{uj}(r,\theta,t,m) = a_m J_0(\mathbf{roots[[m,1,2]]}\,r)\cos(2\mathbf{roots[[m,1,2]]}\,t)\cos(\pi\theta\,m) +$$

$$b_m J_0(\mathbf{roots[[m,1,2]]}\,r)\cos(2\mathbf{roots[[m,1,2]]}\,t)\sin(\pi\theta\,m),\ \text{where}$$

a_m corresponds to **a[m]** and b_m corresponds to **b[m]**.

```
In[31]:=
Clear[g];
g[r_,theta_,k_]:=r (1-r^2) BesselJ[0,roots[[k,1,2]] r]*
  Sin[(1-theta)Pi];
b[k_]:=Sum[gauss10[[i,2]] gauss10[[j,2]]*
            N[f[gauss10[[i,1]],
            gauss10[[j,1]],k]]*
            N[Sin[k Pi gauss10[[j,1]]]]],
  {i,1,10},{j,1,10}]
```

```
In[32]:=
uj[r_,theta_,t_,m_]:=
    a[m]*BesselJ[0,roots[[m,1,2]] r]*
    Cos[2 roots[[m,1,2]] t]*Cos[Pi theta m]+
    b[m]*BesselJ[0,roots[[m,1,2]] r]*
    Cos[2 roots[[m,1,2]] t]*Sin[Pi theta m]
```

```
In[33]:=
uj[r,theta,t,4]
```

```
Out[33]=
0.0000240706 BesselJ[0, 11.7915 r] Cos[23.5831 t]

   Cos[4 Pi theta] - 4.71493 10^-22
   BesselJ[0, 11.7915 r] Cos[23.5831 t] Sin[4 Pi theta]
```

The sum of the first four terms is determined below by defining

$$\texttt{uapprox}(r,\theta,t) = \sum_{m=1}^{4} \texttt{u j}(r,\theta,t,m).$$

```
In[35]:=
Clear[uapprox]
uapprox[r_,theta_,t_]=Sum[uj[r,theta,t,m],{m,1,4}]
```

```
Out[35]=
8.04758 10^-20 BesselJ[0, 2.40483 r] Cos[4.80965 t]
   Cos[Pi theta] + 0.00171712 BesselJ[0, 5.52008 r]
   Cos[11.0402 t] Cos[2 Pi theta] +

   9.26235 10^-22 BesselJ[0, 8.65373 r] Cos[17.3075 t]
   Cos[3 Pi theta] + 0.0000240706 BesselJ[0, 11.7915 r]
   Cos[23.5831 t] Cos[4 Pi theta] +
   0.0746569 BesselJ[0, 2.40483 r] Cos[4.80965 t]

   Sin[Pi theta] - 2.20113 10^-21 BesselJ[0, 5.52008 r]
   Cos[11.0402 t] Sin[2 Pi theta] +

   2.94743 10^-12 BesselJ[0, 8.65373 r] Cos[17.3075 t]

   Sin[3 Pi theta] - 4.71493 10^-22
   BesselJ[0, 11.7915 r] Cos[23.5831 t] Sin[4 Pi theta]
```

This function is plotted with **ParametricPlot3D** below.

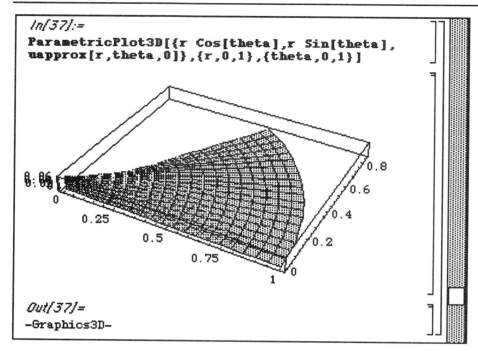

```
In[37]:=
ParametricPlot3D[{r Cos[theta],r Sin[theta],
uapprox[r,theta,0]},{r,0,1},{theta,0,1}]
```

```
Out[37]=
-Graphics3D-
```

GaussianQuadratureError
Package: GaussianQuadrature.m

GaussianQuadratureError[n,f,a,b] determines the error of the associated Gaussian quadrature formula.

Example:

The application of **GaussianQuadratureError** is illustrated below with n =4 on the interval [−1,1] for a function g. This yields an expression which involves the eighth derivative of g. With n = 8, this expression depends on the sixteenth derivative of g. For an interval of length a beginning at x = −1, the error term involves a. Hence, the error decreases with a.

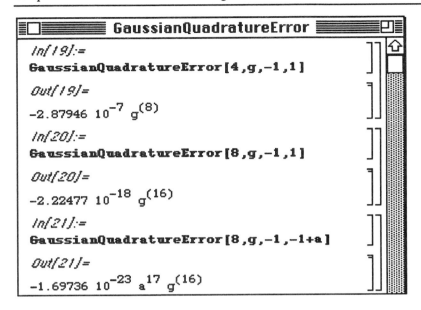

IntervalArithmetic.m

Interval   Package: **IntervalArithmetic.m**
   Interval[x] places the number **x** in the form of an interval. The output of this function is **Interval[x1,x,x2]**. Another form of this command is
Interval[a,b] which forms an interval with bounds **a** and **b**. Also, the interval can be directly entered as **Interval[a,x,b]**. Basic algebraic properties can be used with Interval objects.
Example:
Several examples of **Interval** are given below. First, the number 1 is placed in the form of an interval and called **d**. This is followed by a similar command to place −1 in interval notation. This expression is called **f**, and difference is computed. Another algebraic operation is then calculated.

```
┌─────────────────────────────────────────┐
│ ▤□▤▤▤▤▤▤▤▤▤▤ Interval ▤▤▤▤▤▤▤▤ ▣▤ │
│ In[21]:=                              ⬆  │
│ d=Interval[1]                            │
│                                          │
│ Out[21]=                                 │
│ Interval[ 999999 ,  1,  1000001 ]        │
│           1000000       1000000          │
│                                          │
│ In[22]:=                                 │
│ f=Interval[-1]                           │
│                                          │
│ Out[22]=                                 │
│ Interval[-( 1000001 ),  -1,              │
│            1000000                       │
│   -( 999999 )]                           │
│      1000000                             │
│                                          │
│ In[23]:=                                 │
│ d-f                                      │
│                                          │
│ Out[23]=                                 │
│ Interval[ 999999 ,  2,  1000001 ]        │
│           500000        500000           │
│                                          │
│ In[24]:=                                 │
│ 3 d+f                                    │
│                                          │
│ Out[24]=                                 │
│ Interval[ 499999 ,  2,  500001 ]         │
│           250000       250000            │
└─────────────────────────────────────────┘
```

The well known constant **E** is then written as an interval. To see that the result is indeed an interval, **InputForm** is employed. Intervals can be defined in different ways as shown below.

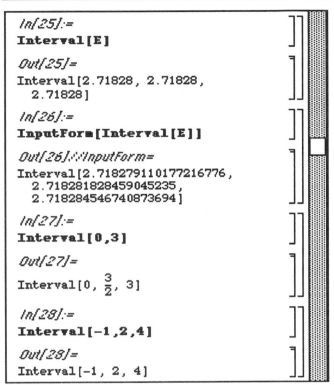

```
In[25]:=
Interval[E]

Out[25]=
Interval[2.71828, 2.71828,
  2.71828]

In[26]:=
InputForm[Interval[E]]

Out[26]//InputForm=
Interval[2.718279110177216776,
  2.718281828459045235,
  2.718284546740873694]

In[27]:=
Interval[0,3]

Out[27]=
Interval[0, 3/2, 3]

In[28]:=
Interval[-1,2,4]

Out[28]=
Interval[-1, 2, 4]
```

However, the results of these commands can be used in algebraic operations together as indicated below.

```
In[29]:=
Interval[0,3]+Interval[-1,2,4]

Out[29]=
Interval[-1, 7/2, 7]
```

SetEpsilon   Package: **IntervalArithmetic.m**

SetEpsilon[n] is used to set the value of **eps** which is used to form the bounds for **Interval[x]**. The bounds are set with **Interval[x-eps,x,x+eps]** where $eps = 10^{-n}$.

Example:

The value of epsilon is set to be 10^{-4}. This new value of epsilon is then used to write **E** in interval notation. Notice the difference between this result and that obtained in the example above for **Interval**.

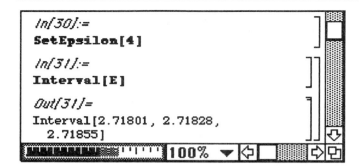

ListIntegrate.m

ListIntegrate   Package: **ListIntegrate.m**
   ListIntegrate approximates the integral of the function which has the values
given in a list of data. This command can have several forms.
ListIntegrate[{val1,val2,...},h] computes the approximation for
function values listed in **{val1,val2,...}** using the constant step-size **h** in the
independent variable. This command can be entered as
ListIntegrate[{val1,val2,...},h,k] to approximate the integral using the
nearest **k** points for each subinterval. Also,
ListIntegrate[{{x1,y1},{x2,y2},...},k] approximates the integral of the
function defined for the points listed in **{{x1,y1},{x2,y2},...}** using the nearest
k points for each subinterval. In this case, variable step-size is employed.
Example:
In the first example below, a list of data is entered in **vals**. These values are then used
with **ListIntegrate** to approximate the integral using a step size of 2. A third
component which indicates that the nearest 4 points on each subinterval be employed in
the approximation is then used to yield the same result.

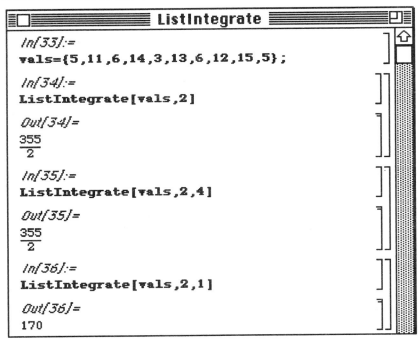

Next, a list of function values for the function f(x) = 2x–1 is generated in **table**. **ListIntegrate** is then used to approximate the integral of this function on the interval [0,10]. **Integrate** is also used to show that the approximation produced with **ListIntegrate** is accurate.

```
In[37]:=
table=Table[2 x-1,{x,0,10,1}]

Out[37]=
{-1, 1, 3, 5, 7, 9, 11, 13, 15, 17, 19}

In[38]:=
ListIntegrate[table,1]

Out[38]=
90

In[39]:=
Integrate[2x-1,{x,0,10}]

Out[39]=
90
```

Ordered pairs can be used as data. This is illustrated below with the points listed in **datalist**. **ListIntegrate** is used to approximate the integral using these data points.

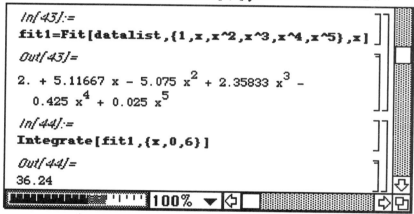

Then, a fifth degree polynomial which approximates the data is computed in **fit1**. The integral of **fit1** on the interval [0,6] yields a value of 36.24.

```
In[43]:=
fit1=Fit[datalist,{1,x,x^2,x^3,x^4,x^5},x]

Out[43]=
2. + 5.11667 x - 5.075 x^2 + 2.35833 x^3 -
    0.425 x^4 + 0.025 x^5

In[44]:=
Integrate[fit1,{x,0,6}]

Out[44]=
36.24
```

NLimit.m

NLimit   Package: **NLimit.m**
   NLimit[expression,x->x0] yields the numerical approximation of
expression as **x** approaches **x0**. Note that the value of **x0** may be finite or
Infinity. **NLimit** is based on Wynn's ε algorithm or a generalized Euler
transformation. Options of **NLimit** include **Method** which can be set as either
EulerSum or **SequenceLimit** (**EulerSum** is the default setting), **Scale** which has
default value **1**, **Terms** which has default setting **7**, **WorkingPrecision** which has
default setting **$MachinePrecision**, and **WynnDegree** which has default value **1**.
Example:
The use of **NLimit** is illustrated below in the computation of
$\lim\limits_{x\to\infty} \dfrac{x!}{e^x}$.   In this case, **NLimit** is successful in determining this limit
while **Limit** is not.

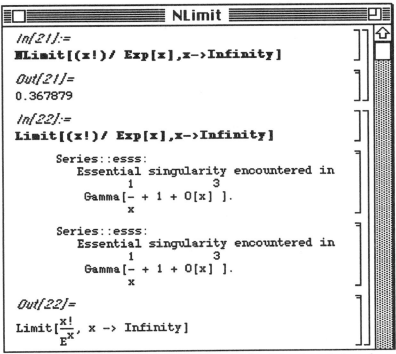

The numerical approximation of this exact limit is given below for comparison with the result obtained above with **NLimit**.

The **Scale** option is then demonstrated with the computation of another limit,

$$\mathrm{Lim}_{n \to \infty} \frac{\left(\frac{n}{e}\right)^n \sqrt{n}}{n!},$$ which is useful in the derivation of Stirling's formula.

The option setting **WorkingPrecision->30** is used as well to illustrate the affects of the **Scale** settings.

```
In[25]:=
NLimit[((n/E)^n)Sqrt[n]/n!,n->Infinity,
WorkingPrecision->30]

Out[25]=
0.39894228317027

In[26]:=
NLimit[((n/E)^n)Sqrt[n]/n!,n->Infinity,Scale->2,
WorkingPrecision->30]

Out[26]=
0.3989422809589

In[27]:=
NLimit[((n/E)^n)Sqrt[n]/n!,n->Infinity,Scale->3,
WorkingPrecision->30]

Out[27]=
0.398942280621
```

Below, the limit which arises in Stirling's formula is computed. This is followed by a limit, $\displaystyle \lim_{x \to \infty} \frac{Ln(x)}{Ln(x) - 1}$, which cannot be computed with **NLimit**.

```
In[30]:=
NLimit[((n/E)^n)Sqrt[2Pi n]/n!,n->Infinity]

Out[30]=
1.

In[31]:=
NLimit[Log[x]/(Log[x]-1),x->Infinity]

Out[31]=
              Log[x]
NLimit[ ───────────── , x -> Infinity]
           -1 + Log[x]
```

Next, the **Method** option is employed with **NLimit**. This option allows for the computation of the limit, $\displaystyle \lim_{x \to \infty} \frac{Ln(x)}{Ln(x) - 1}$, which was not determined above without the setting **Method->SequenceLimit**. The **WynnDegree** option is also used to investigate this limit.

```
In[32]:=
NLimit[Log[x]/(Log[x]-1),x->Infinity,
Method->SequenceLimit]

Out[32]=
1.06934

In[33]:=
NLimit[Log[x]/(Log[x]-1),x->Infinity,
Method->SequenceLimit,WynnDegree->2]

Out[33]=
1.09246
```

Below, **Infinity** is used as the setting of **WynnDegree**, and the number of terms is increased with **Terms** to improve the approximation given by **NLimit**.

```
In[34]:=
NLimit[Log[x]/(Log[x]-1),x->Infinity,
Method->SequenceLimit,WynnDegree->Infinity]

Out[34]=
1.09246

In[35]:=
NLimit[Log[x]/(Log[x]-1),x->Infinity,
Method->SequenceLimit,WynnDegree->Infinity,
Terms->200]

Out[35]=
1.0004
```

The number of terms is increased to 300 below to further improve the approximation of the limit with **NLimit**.

```
In[36]:=
NLimit[Log[x]/(Log[x]-1),x->Infinity,
Method->SequenceLimit,WynnDegree->Infinity,
Terms->300]

Out[36]=
1.00019
```

EulerSum   Package: **NLimit.m**

EulerSum[f,{i,i0,Infinity}] approximates the infinite sum $\sum\limits_{i0}^{\infty} f$ by making use of Euler's transformation. **EulerSum** has the options **EulerRatio**, **ExtraTerms**, **Terms**, and **WorkingPrecision**.

Example:

The sum of each of the well-known series $\sum_{n=0}^{\infty} \frac{(-1)^n}{2n+1}$ and $\sum_{n=0}^{\infty} \frac{(-1)^n}{(2n+1)^n}$ are approximated below with **EulerSum**. The exact sum of the former series is $\frac{\pi}{4}$. The numerical approximation of this value is given below for comparison.

```
In[37]:=
EulerSum[(-1)^i 1/(2i+1),{i,0,Infinity}]

Out[37]=
0.785398

In[38]:=
N[Pi/4]

Out[38]=
0.785398

In[39]:=
EulerSum[(-1)^i 1/(2i+1)^2,{i,0,Infinity}]

Out[39]=
0.915966
```

A combination of the **Terms** and **EulerRatio** options are illustrated below. The **EulerRatio** setting of .9 improves the approximation in this case. The approximate sum obtained with **EulerSum** can be compared to the numerical approximation of the exact sum of this series which is $\frac{\pi^2}{6}$.

```
In[44]:=
EulerSum[ 1/(i^2),{i,1,Infinity},Terms->100,
EulerRatio->.9]

Out[44]=
1.6392

In[45]:=
EulerSum[ 1/(i^2),{i,1,Infinity},Terms->1000,
EulerRatio->.9]

Out[45]=
1.644

In[46]:=
EulerSum[ 1/(i^2),{i,1,Infinity},Terms->1000]

Out[46]=
1.65015

In[47]:=
N[Pi^2/6]

Out[47]=
1.64493
```

The series $\sum_{n=0}^{\infty} \dfrac{1}{(2n+1)^n}$ is considered below. First, the option settings

Terms->5000 and **WorkingPrecision->30** are employed. The numerical

approximation of the exact sum $\dfrac{\pi^2}{8}$ is computed for comparison. In an

attempt to improve the approximation, the option **ExtraTerms** is used.

```
In[54]:=
EulerSum[ 1/((2i+1)^2),{i,0,Infinity},
    Terms->5000,WorkingPrecision->30]

Out[54]=
1.233957824812

In[55]:=
N[Pi^2/8]

Out[55]=
1.2337

In[56]:=
EulerSum[ 1/((2i+1)^2),{i,0,Infinity},
    Terms->5000,WorkingPrecision->30,
    ExtraTerms->8]

Out[56]=
1.23262001

In[57]:=
EulerSum[ 1/((2i+1)^2),{i,0,Infinity},
    Terms->5000,WorkingPrecision->30,
    ExtraTerms->9]

Out[57]=
1.2385
```

Scale   Package: **NLimit.m**
   Scale is an option used with **NLimit** to specify the initial step-size used in approximating the limit. The default setting for **Scale** is **1**.
Example:
See **NLimit**.

Terms   Package: **NLimit.m**
   Terms is an option used with **NLimit** and **EulerSum** which indicates the number of terms generated before the initiation of extrapolation. The default setting of **Terms** is **7** when used with **NLimit** and **5** when used with **EulerSum**.
Example:
See **NLimit** and **EulerSum**.

ExtraTerms   Package: **NLimit.m**
   ExtraTerms is an option used with **EulerSum** to indicate the number of terms used in extrapolation. The default setting of **ExtraTerms** is **7**.
Example:
See **EulerSum**.

EulerRatio Package: **NLimit.m**

EulerRatio is an option used with **EulerSum** to indicate the ratio used in the transformation.

Example:
See **EulerSum**

ND Package: **NLimit.m**

ND[f,x,x0] numerically approximates the value of $\dfrac{\partial f}{\partial x}$ at $x = \mathbf{x0}$. The command

ND[f,{x,n},x0] approximates the nth derivative. **ND** has the options **Scale**,

Terms, and **WorkingPrecision** with default settings of 1, 7, and

$MachinePrecision, respectively.
Example:
ND is used to approximate the derivative of x! in the example below. This derivative is evaluated at $x = 1$. Several options are then illustrated.

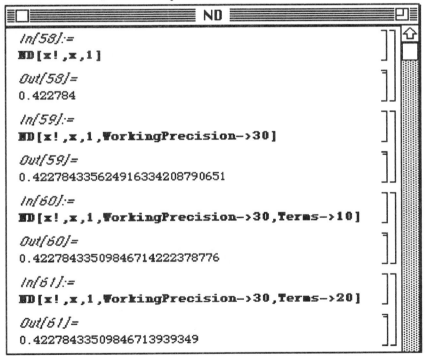

```
In[58]:=
ND[x!,x,1]

Out[58]=
0.422784

In[59]:=
ND[x!,x,1,WorkingPrecision->30]

Out[59]=
0.422784335624916334208790651

In[60]:=
ND[x!,x,1,WorkingPrecision->30,Terms->10]

Out[60]=
0.422784335098467142223378776

In[61]:=
ND[x!,x,1,WorkingPrecision->30,Terms->20]

Out[61]=
0.422784335098467139349
```

The value obtained with **ND** can be compared to the numerical approximation of the derivative of the gamma function at $x = 2$.

```
In[62]:=
N[D[Gamma[x+1],x]/.x->1,30]
Out[62]=
0.422784335098467139393487909992
In[63]:=
N[%]
Out[63]=
0.422784
```

A table of abscissa and derivative values on the interval [0,6] using increments of .25 are generated in **deriv**. These points are plotted then with **ListPlot**.

```
In[65]:=
deriv=Table[{a,ND[x!,x,a]},{a,0,6,.25}];
In[69]:=
ListPlot[Evaluate[deriv],PlotJoined->True]
```

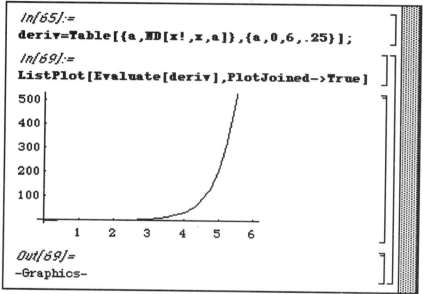

```
Out[69]=
-Graphics-
```

The function sin(x!) is considered below. The derivative of this function is approximated on the interval [0,5] in the table **ndsine** and these values are plotted with **ListPlot**.

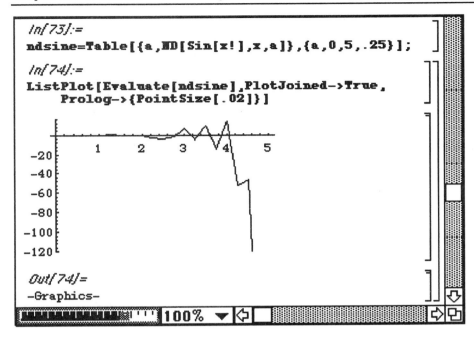

In[73]:=
```
ndsine=Table[{a,ND[Sin[x!],x,a]},{a,0,5,.25}];
```

In[74]:=
```
ListPlot[Evaluate[ndsine],PlotJoined->True,
    Prolog->{PointSize[.02]}]
```

Out[74]=
-Graphics-

NewtonCotes.m

NewtonCotesWeights   Package: **NewtonCotes.m**

   NewtonCotesWeights[n,a,b] lists the values of the nodes and weights used for the Newton-Cotes method of numerical integration over the interval from **a** to **b**. This method unlike Gaussian Quadrature estimates the integral at n equally spaced points. The output of **NewtonCotesWeights** is a list of expressions of the form {weighti,xi}. **NewtonCotesWeights** has the option **Type** which can be set to **Closed** or **Open** to indicate if the endpoints are included in the sum. A setting of **Open** specifies that they are not.

Example:

The Newton-Cotes nodes and weights are determined below for the interval [−4,4] with n = 2, 4, and 8.

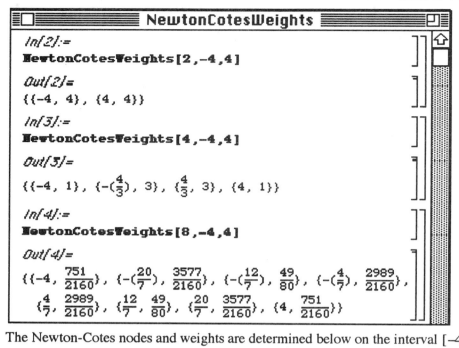

The Newton-Cotes nodes and weights are determined below on the interval [−4,4] and
n = 8. Notice that with the option setting **Type->Open**, the values x = −4 and x = 4
are not included as they are in the previous example for **NewtonCotesWeights**.

```
In[5]:=
NewtonCotesWeights[8,-4,4,Type->Open]
Out[5]=
{{-(7/2), 295627/241920}, {-(5/2), 71329/241920}, {-(3/2), 17473/8960},
   {-(1/2), 128953/241920}, {1/2, 128953/241920}, {3/2, 17473/8960},
   {5/2, 71329/241920}, {7/2, 295627/241920}}
```

A user-defined function **ncotes** is then defined to compute these values given a value
of n and an interval [a,b]. Elements of the output list given by **ncotes** are extracted
with the techniques illustrated below.

```
In[6]:=
ncotes[n_,a_,b_]:=NewtonCotesWeights[n,a,b]

In[7]:=
ncotes[8,-4,4]
```

$$Out[7]=$$

$$\{\{-4, \tfrac{751}{2160}\}, \{-(\tfrac{20}{7}), \tfrac{3577}{2160}\}, \{-(\tfrac{12}{7}), \tfrac{49}{80}\}, \{-(\tfrac{4}{7}), \tfrac{2989}{2160}\},$$

$$\{\tfrac{4}{7}, \tfrac{2989}{2160}\}, \{\tfrac{12}{7}, \tfrac{49}{80}\}, \{\tfrac{20}{7}, \tfrac{3577}{2160}\}, \{4, \tfrac{751}{2160}\}\}$$

```
In[8]:=
ncotes[8,-4,4][[1,1]]
```

$$Out[8]=$$
$$-4$$

```
In[9]:=
ncotes[8,-4,4][[1,2]]
```

$$Out[9]=$$
$$\frac{751}{2160}$$

This function is then used within the function **approx** to approximate the value of the integral of f on the interval [a,b] using the Newton-Cotes method with n nodes.

```
In[10]:=
approx[n_,a_,b_]:=
Sum[ncotes[n,a,b][[i,2]]*f[ncotes[n,a,b][[i,1]]],
    {i,1,n}]
```

The general formula for Newton-Cotes numerical integration with n = 8 is given below.

```
In[11]:=
approx[8,-4,4]
```

$$Out[11]=$$

$$\frac{751\ f[-4]}{2160} + \frac{3577\ f[-(\tfrac{20}{7})]}{2160} + \frac{49\ f[-(\tfrac{12}{7})]}{80} +$$

$$\frac{2989\ f[-(\tfrac{4}{7})]}{2160} + \frac{2989\ f[\tfrac{4}{7}]}{2160} + \frac{49\ f[\tfrac{12}{7}]}{80} + \frac{3577\ f[\tfrac{20}{7}]}{2160} +$$

$$\frac{751\ f[4]}{2160}$$

This approximation technique is demonstrated by producing a table of approximations of the function $f(x) = \dfrac{1}{1+x^2}$ on the interval $[-4, 4]$ for $n = 2, 4, 6, 8, 10.$

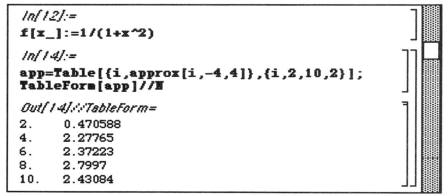

Most numerical analysis texts include commonly used Newton-Cotes formulas for n=1, 2, 3, and 4. The formula for n = 4 is entered below as **fourrule**. This formula is then used to approximate $\int_{-4}^{4}\dfrac{dx}{1+x^2}$ as above. The result obtained with **fourrule** is identical to that given for n = 4 in the table **app** above.

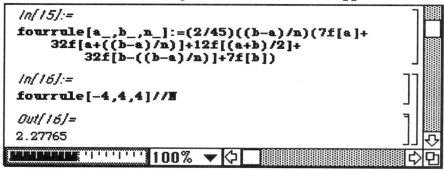

NewtonCotesError   Package: **NewtonCotes.m**

   NewtonCotesError[n,f,a,b] yields the error formula for the Newton-Cotes numerical approximation of the integral of f on the interval [a,b] using n equally spaced points.

Example:

NewtonCotesError is demonstrated below in general for a function f on the interval [−4,4] using four equally spaced points. The **Type->Open** option setting is then used to yield a different error.

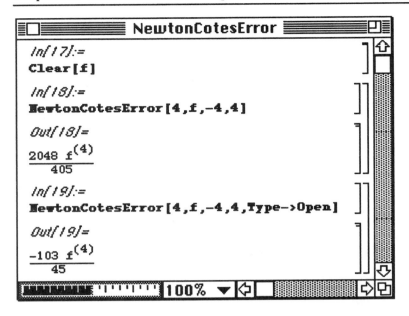

Type   Package: **NewtonCotes.m**

Type is an option used with **NewtonCotesWeights** and **NewtonCotesError** to indicate the type of quadrature which should be employed. The default setting is **Closed** which specifies that the endpoints of the interval are used. In order to exclude the use of endpoints, the setting **Type->Open** must be made.
Example:
See **NewtonCotesWeights** and **NewtonCotesError**.

PolynomialFit.m

PolynomialFit   See Also: **Fit, InterpolatingFunction**
                           Package: **PolynomialFit.m**

PolynomialFit[datalist,n] yields the least squares polynomial fit of degree **n** for the data listed in **datalist**. The result of **PolynomialFit** is given as a pure function.
Example:
In the example below, a list of y-values is given in **data**. A fourth degree polynomial least squares fit is then determined and called **poly**. This polynomial can be evaluated at x-values as evidenced below by **poly[20]**. To reveal the formula for this polynomial, **Expand** is used. A table of values of **poly** on the interval [1,10] is created for comparison with the values in **data**.

```
≡□≡≡≡≡≡≡≡≡ PolynomialFit ≡≡≡≡≡≡≡  □

In[2]:=
data={13,3,14,7,1,16,11,16,2,16};

In[3]:=
poly=PolynomialFit[data,4]

Out[3]=
FittingPolynomial[<>, 4]

In[4]:=
poly[20]

Out[4]=
1435.11

In[5]:=
Expand[poly[x]]

Out[5]=
                                          2
27.6667 - 21.2418 x + 7.01661 x  -
                 3              4
    0.885198 x  + 0.0381702 x

In[6]:=
Table[poly[i],{i,1,10}]

Out[6]=
{12.5944, 6.77855, 6.28205, 8.08392,
   10.0793, 11.0793, 10.8112, 9.91841,
   9.96037, 13.4126}
```

100%

Additional References

Abell, Martha L. and Braselton, James P., *Mathematica by Example*, Academic Press (1992);

Boyland, Philip, Technical Report: Guide to Standard *Mathematica* Packages, Wolfram Research, Inc. (1991);

Crandall, Richard E., *Mathematica* for the Sciences, Addison-Wesley (1990);

Gray, Theodore and Glynn, Jerry, Exploring Mathematics with *Mathematica*, Addison-Wesley (1990);

Maeder, Roman, Programming in *Mathematica*, Second Edition, Addison-Wesley (1991);

Wagon, Stan, *Mathematica* in Action, W. H. Freeman and Co. (1991);

Withoff, David, Technical Report: *Mathematica* Warning Messages, Wolfram Research, Inc. (1991);

Wolfram Research, Inc., *Mathematica*: A System for Doing Mathematics by Computer, User's Guide; and

Wolfram, Stephen, *Mathematica*: A System for Doing Mathematics by Computer, Second Edition, Addison-Wesley (1991).

In addition to the Technical Reports listed above, Wolfram Research, Inc. also publishes the following:
> Installation Manual;
> Release Notes;
> The 3-Script File Format;
> *MathLink* External Communication in *Mathematica*;
> PostScript Generated by *Mathematica*;
> The *Mathematica* Compiler;
> Upgrading Packages to *Mathematica* 2.0; and
> Major New Features in Version 2.0.

For purchasing information, contact Wolfram Research, Inc. at 100 Trade Center Drive, Champaign, IL 61820-7237.

Mathematica-related journals currently available include:
> The *Mathematica* Journal, published quarterly by the Advanced Book Program, Addison-Wesley Publishing Company; and

> *Mathematica* in Education, published quarterly. Contact Paul Wellin, Editor, Department of Mathematics, Sonoma State University, 1801 East Cotati Avenue, Rohnert Park, CA, 94928.

Index

The index provides a comprehensive listing of all objects included in both sections of <u>The</u> <u>Mathematica</u> Handbook.

If the description of the object does not occur on the first page listed, bold numerals are used to indicate the page on which it is discussed. For example, the built-in constant **GoldenRatio** has index entry:

GoldenRatio, 20, **182**, 303, 512

which means that **GoldenRatio** is described on page 182 although it is referred to on pages 20, 303, and 512. On the other hand, the command **ComplexExpand** has index entry:

ComplexExpand, 58, 113, 202, 459, 586

which means that **ComplexExpand** is discussed on page 58; additional examples are given on pages 113, 202, 459, and 586.

In addition, if the object has an abbreviated form, the abbreviation is listed in parentheses. For example, the object **SetDelayed** has index entry:

SetDelayed (:=), 7, 403, **417**

which means that **SetDelayed** has the abbreviated form :=, is described on page 417, and additional examples are given on pages 7 and 403.

A

Abort, 1, 44
$Aborted, 496
AbortProtect, 1
Above, 1
Abs, 1, 66, 123, 126, 130, 131, 133, 235,
    237, 238, 240, 241, 242, 411, 541, 568,
    583
AbsoluteDashing, 2
AbsolutePointSize, 2
AbsoluteThickness, 2
AbsoluteTime, 2
AccountingForm, 2
Accumulate, 3
Accuracy, 3
AccuracyGoal, 3
AddTo (+=), 4
AdjustedRSquared, 690, 692-695, **702**,
    704
AiryAi, 4
AiryAiPrime, 5
AiryBi, 5
AiryBiPrime, 6
AlgebraicRules, 6
AlgebraicRulesData, 6
Alias, 6
All, 7
Alternatives (|), 7
AmbientLight, 7, 519
Analytic, 7, 259
AnchoredSearch, 7
And (&&), 8, 277, 389, 530, 568, 576
Animate, 8
$AnimationDisplayFunction, 496
$AnimationFunction, 496
ANOVATable, 690, 692-695, **697**, 704
Apart, 8
ApartSquareFree, 9
Append, 9
AppendTo, 9
Apply (@@), 10, 351
ArcCos, 11, 71
ArcCosh, 12
ArcCot, 13, 74
ArcCoth, 14
ArcCsc, 14
ArcCsch, 14
ArcLengthFactor, 604
ArcSec, 15
ArcSech, 15
ArcSin, 16, 215
ArcSinh, 16
ArcTan, 17, 615

ArcTanh, 17
Arg, 18
Args, 18
Args$, 19
Arithmetic, 739
ArithmeticGeometricMean, 19
Array, 19, 341, 463
AspectRatio, 20, 512, 515, 516, 519, 525,
    526, 534, 543-546, 548, 552, 553
AtomQ, 20
Attributes, 21
AutoLoad, 21
Automatic, 21, 127, 513, 514
Auxiliary, 21
Axes, 21, 513, 517-519, 522, 523, 547,
    555, 569, 570, 579
AxesEdge, 21, 519
AxesLabel, 22, 513, 519, 555, 581
AxesOrigin, 22, 513, 550, 554, 556, 668,
    671, 673
AxesStyle, 22, 513, 520

B

Background, 23, 513, 520, 548, 556, 572
BarChart, 550
BaseForm, 23
BasisNames, 692
$BatchInput, 496
$BatchOutput, 496
Begin, 23
BeginPackage, 23
Below, 24
BernoulliB, 24
BernoulliDistribution, 661
BesselI, 25
BesselJ, 26, 581, 749-751
BesselK, 27
BesselY, 28
BestFit, 697
BestFitCoefficients, 697
Beta, 28
BetaDistribution, 613
BetaRegularized, 29, 688, 689
Bias, 716
Biharmonic, 608, 609
BinCounts, 639
BinLists, 641
Binomial, 30
BinomialDistribution, 662, 674
Bipolar, 598
Bispherical, 598
Blank (_), 31, 32
BlankForm, 31

BlankNullSequence (___), 31
BlankSequence (__), 33
Block, 33
BooleanSelect, 636
Bottom, 34
Boxed, 34, 520, 570, 579, 581
BoxRatios, 34, 520, 570
BoxStyle, 34, 520
Brake, 723, 725-729
Break, 34
Byte, 34
ByteCount, 35

C

C, 36, 112
CallProcess, 36
Cancel, 36
Cartesian, 598
Cases, 37
Catalan, 38, 39
Catch, 38
CategoryCounts, 640
CategoryLists, 642
CauchyDistribution, 614
CauchyPrincipalValue, 735
CDF, 614-631, 666, 667, 670, **672**
Ceiling, 39
CellArray, 39
Center, 39, 53
CentralMoment, 655
CForm, 39
Character, 40
CharacteristicFunction, 662, 664, 669,
    674
CharacteristicPolynomial, 40
Characters, 41
ChebyshevT, 41
ChebyshevU, 42
Check, 42
CheckAbort, 43
ChiDistribution, 616
ChiSquareDistribution, 708
ChiSquarePValue, 682
Chop, 44, 163, 170, 224-230, 322, 376,
    409
Circle, 44, 512, 525
Clear, 45, 568
ClearAll, 45
ClearAttributes, 45, 263
ClebschGordan, 45
ClipFill, 46, 522, 523, 569, 576, 582
Close, 46, 432
CMYKColor, 46

Coefficient, 46
CoefficientList, 48
Collect, 50
ColonForm, 51
ColorFunction, 51, 516, 522, 523
ColorOutput, 51, 513, 520
Column, 52, 631
ColumnDrop, 632
ColumnForm, 52, 122, 592
ColumnJoin, 633
ColumnTake, 632
$CommandLine, 497
Compile, 54
Compiled, 54, 310, 311, 515-518, 523,
    557
CompiledFunction, 54
Complement, 56
Complex, 57, 253, 379, 530, 541, 549
ComplexExpand, 58, 113, 202, 459, 586
ComplexInfinity, 59, 122, 271
Compose, 60
ComposeList, 60
ComposeSeries, 61
Composition, 62
CompoundExpression (;), 63, 299
ComputerNumber, 736, 738-745
Condition (/;), 64, 417, 527, 528, 576,
    587, 589, 591
$ConditionHold, 497
ConfidenceIntervalTable, 698
ConfidenceLevel, 610
ConfocalEllipsoidal, 599
ConfocalParaboloidal, 599
Conical, 599
Conjugate, 65
Constant, 66
Constants, 66
ConstrainedMax, 66
ConstrainedMin, 67
$Context, 497
Context, 68
$ContextPath, 497
Contexts, 68
ContextToFilename, 68
Continuation, 68
Continue, 68
ContourGraphics, 69, 130, 197, 232, 238
ContourLevels, 69
ContourLines, 69, 515, 535
ContourPlot, 69, 130, 133, 197, 198, 232,
    238, 515, 534-539
Contours, 69, 238, 515, 536

ContourShading, 69, 133, 238, 265, 515, 536, 538
ContourSmoothing, 69, 515, 537
ContourSpacing, 69
ContourStyle, 69, 515, 538
CoordinateRanges, 602
Coordinates, 598, 600, 601
CoordinatesFromCartesian, 600, 601, **603**
CoordinatesToCartesian, 600, **602**, 603
CoordinateSystem, 598
CopyDirectory, 69
CopyFile, 70
CorrelationMatrix, 699
Cos, 26, **70**, 431
Cosh, 25, **71**,
CoshIntegral, 72
CosIntegral, 72
Cot, 73
Coth, 73
Count, 75
CovarianceMatrix, 699
CreateDirectory, 75
$CreationDate, 497
CrossProduct, 604
Csc, 76
Csch, 76
Cubics, 77
Cuboid, 77, 519, 562
CumulativeSums, 639
Curl, 606
Cyclotomic, 77, 79
Cylindrical, 599, 603, 605, 606

D
D, 72, 73, **79**, 189, 275, 429, 430
DampingFactor, 80
Dashing, 22, 80, 462, 560, 563, 587, 589, 591, 596, 597, 712
Date, 81
Debug, 81
DeclarePackage, 81
Decompose, 81
Decrement (--), 82
Default, 32, **83**,
DefaultColor, 83, 513, 520
$DefaultFont, 497, 513, 520
DefaultFont, 84, 513, 520, 537, 574
DefaultValues, 84
Definition, 45, 64, **84**,
Degree, 85
Delete, 85
DeleteCases, 87

DeleteContents, 87
DeleteDirectory, 88
DeleteFile, 88
Delimiters, 89
Delta, 584
Denominator, 89
DensityGraphics, 90, 124, 237, 242
DensityPlot, 90, 124, 237, 242, 411, 516, 540, 541
Depth, 90
Derivative ('), 91
Derivatives, 726
DesignedRegress, 703
DesignMatrix, 702
Det, 93
DiagonalMatrix, 95, 427
Dialog, 96
DialogIndent, 98
DialogProlog, 98
DialogSymbols, 99
DigitBlock, 100
DigitQ, 101
Digits, 101
Dimensions, 101
DirectedInfinity, 102
Direction, 102
Directory, 102
DirectoryStack, 102
DiscreteUniformDistribution, 663, 675
Disk, 103, 512, 526
Dispatch, 103
DispersionReport, 655
$Display, 498
Display, 103
$DisplayFunction, 165, **498**, 513, 520, 579, 731, 734, 691
DisplayFunction, 103, 127, 131, 165, 312, 513, 520, 534, 536-540, 547, 550, 551, 553, 559, 561, 569, 570, 572, 573, 576-579, 591, 593, 596, 597, 731, 732, 691
Distribute, 103
Div, 608
Divide (/), 104
DivideBy (/=), 104
Divisors, 105
DivisorSigma, 106
Do, 107
Domain, 673
Dot (.), 108, 287, 376, 408, 409
DotProduct, 603
DoubleExponential, 109
DoublyInfinite, 109

DownValues, 110
Drop, 110, 566
DropNonNumeric, 634
DropNonNumericColumn, 635
DSolve, 111
DSolveConstants, 114
Dt, 114
$DumpDates, 498
$DumpSupported, 498

E

E, 27, **116**, 270, 303, 737
$Echo, 498
EconomizedRationalApproximation, 596
EdgeForm, 116
Eigensystem, 116
Eigenvalues, 117
Eigenvectors, 118
Eliminate, 119
EllipticCylindrical, 599
EllipticE, 120
EllipticExp, 121
EllipticExpPrime, 122
EllipticF, 122
EllipticK, 123, 232, 235
EllipticLog, 124
EllipticNomeQ, 124
EllipticPi, 125
EllipticTheta, 126
EllipticThetaC, 128
EllipticThetaD, 128
EllipticThetaN, 129
EllipticThetaPrime, 130
EllipticThetaS, 132
Encode, 133
End, 133
EndAdd, 133
EndOfFile, 134
EndPackage, 134
EndProcess, 134
EngineeringForm, 134
Environment, 134
$Epilog, 498
Epilog, 135, 513, 520, 558
Equal (==), 8, 120, **135**, 277, 291, 307-309, 322, 333, 389, 434, 435, 527, 528
EqualVariance, 679
EquatedTo, 135
Erf, 136, 216, 621, 624, 625, 684, 685
Erfc, 137, 685
Erfi, 137
EstimatedVariance, 690, 692-695, **699**, 704

EulerE, 138
EulerGamma, 72, **138**, 737
EulerPhi, 139
EulerRatio, 763, **765**
EulerSum, 761
Evaluate, 139, 240, 248, 356, 358, 593, 616-631, 708, 709, 711, 713, 766, 767
EvenQ, 140, 527, 528
Exit, 140
Exp, 141
Expand, 141, 202, 211, 287, 365, 772
ExpandAll, 142
ExpandDenominator, 144, 424, 470
ExpandNumerator, 144
ExpIntegralE, 145
ExpIntegralEi, 146
Exponent, 147
ExponentFunction, 148
ExponentialDistribution, 617
ExponentRange, 739
ExponentStep, 148
Expression, 148
ExtendedGCD, 149
ExtraTerms, 764
ExtremeValueDistribution, 618

F

FaceForm, 150
FaceGrids, 150, 520, 583
Factor, 150, 377
FactorComplete, 152
Factorial (!), 20, **152**
Factorial2 (!!), 152
FactorInteger, 153, 301
FactorList, 153
FactorSquareFree, 155
FactorSquareFreeList, 155
FactorTerms, 155
FactorTermsList, 156
Fail, 156
$Failed, 498
$$Failure2, 499
False, 123, 126, 131, 133, **156**, 178, 235, 236, 238, 241, 243, 254, 265, 271, 310, 311, 377, 397, 398, 411, 513, 636
File, 156
FileByteCount, 157
FileDate, 157
FileInformation, 158
FileNames, 158
FileType, 159
Find, 159
FindList, 159

FindMinimum, 159
FindRoot, 161, 749
First, 162
Fit, 163, 690, 758
FitResiduals, 700
FittingPolynomial, 772
FixedPoint, 165
FixedPointList, 165
Flat, 166
Flatten, 166, 566
FlattenAt, 166
Floor, 167
Fn, 167
Fold, 167
FoldList, 168
Font, 168
FontForm, 168, 532
$$Fonts, 499
For, 168
Format, 169
FormatType, 169
FormatValues, 169
FortranForm, 169
Fourier, 170
FourierCosSeriesCoefficient, 589, 590
FourierCosTransform, 585
FourierExpSeries, 585
FourierExpSeriesCoefficient, 585, 590
$FourierFrequencyConstant, 585
$FourierOverallConstant, 585
FourierSinSeriesCoefficient, 590
FourierSinTransform, 585
FourierTransform, 584
FourierTrigSeries, 587
Frame, 170, 411, 513, 515, 516, 539, 541, 543, 544, 553
Framed, 170
FrameLabel, 171, 514
FrameStyle, 171, 514, 544
FrameTicks, 171, 514, 544
FRatioDistribution, 710
FRatioPValue, 683
FreeQ, 171
Frequencies, 637
FresnelC, 172, 216
FresnelS, 172
FromASCII, 172
FromCharacterCode, 173
FromDate, 173
FullAxes, 173
FullDefinition, 173
FullForm, 173
FullGraphics, 174

FullOptions, 174
FullReport, 677-681
Function (&), 174

G
Gamma, 5, **176**, 766
GammaDistribution, 620
GammaRegularized, 177, 616, 620, 621, 686
GaussianIntegers, 151, 153, **178**
GaussianQuadratureError, 752
GaussianQuadratureWeights, 745
GaussKronrod, 179
GaussPoints, 179
GCD, 179
GegenbauerC, 179
General, 181, 296, 328
GeneralMiniMaxApproximation, 732
GeneralRationalInterpolation, 730, 732
Generic, 181
GeometricDistribution, 664, 671, 673-675
GeometricMean, 644
Get (<<), 181, 499, 568
GetContext, 182
GoldenRatio, 20, **182**, 303, 512
Goto, 182
Grad, 607
Gradient, 183
Graphics, 165, **183**, 219, 353, 354, 357, 381, 387, 525-533
GraphicsArray, 127, 131, **183**, 312, 527, 528, 534, 536-540, 547, 550, 551, 553, 559, 561, 569, 570, 572, 573, 576-578, 593, 596, 597
GraphicsSpacing, 183
Graphics3D, 184, 519, 562-565
GrayLevel, 184, 240, 248, 318, 356, 358, 462, 519, 529, 531, 548, 550, 556, 557, 560, 563-565, 569, 583, 615, 708, 716, 720, 721, 726, 731, 732, 734
Greater (>), 184
GreaterEqual (>=), 185, 417
GridLines, 185, 514, 545, 546, 559
GroebnerBasis, 186

H
HalfNormalDistribution, 621
HarmonicMean, 645
Hash, 187
HashTable, 187

Head, 7, 58, **187**, 204, 213, 262, 381, 385, 451
HeadCompose, 187
Headers, 188
Heads, 188
HeldPart, 188
HermiteH, 188
HiddenSurface, 190, 522, 524
Hold, 190, 468
HoldAll, 190
HoldFirst, 190
HoldForm, 191
HoldRest, 191
HomeDirectory, 191
HorizontalForm, 192
Hue, 192
HypergeometricDistribution, 665
HypergeometricPFQ, 192
HypergeometricPFQRegularized, 194
HypergeometricU, 196
Hypergeometric0F1, 197
Hypergeometric0F1Regularized, 197
Hypergeometric1F1, 198
Hypergeometric1F1Regularized, 199
Hypergeometric2F1, 200
Hypergeometric2F1Regularized, 201

I

I, 13, 18, 58, **202**
IdealDivide, 740
Identity, 127, 131, 165, **203**, 312, 387
IdentityMatrix, 94, **203**, 286
If, 203
IgnoreCase, 205
$IgnoreEOF, 499
Im, 196-198, **205**, 254, 271, 398, 462, 549
ImplicitPlot, 534
Implies, 206
In, 206
IncludeConstant, 694
IncludeSingularTerm
Increment (++), 169, **206**, 490
Indent, 207
Indeterminate, 208
Inequality, 208
Infinity, 15, **209**, 216, 367, 684, 686
Infix, 209
Information (??), 209
Inner, 210
$Input, 499
Input, 204, **210**
InputForm, 210, 415, 737

InputStream, 211, 432
InputString, 211
Insert, 212
$Inspector, 499
Install, 212
InString, 212
Integer, 7, 37, 87, 204, **213**, 379, 385
IntegerDigits, 214, 255, 638
IntegerQ, 214
Integrate, 72, 73, 181, 189, 191, **215**, 275, 468, 757, 758
InterpolatedQuantile, 648
InterpolatingFunction, 217, 307-311
InterpolatingPolynomial, 219
Interpolation, 221
InterpolationOrder, 221
InterquartileRange, 654
Interrupt, 221
Intersection, 221
Inverse, 222, 246
InverseBetaRegularized, 687
InverseErf, 683
InverseErfc, 685
InverseFourier, 223
InverseFourierTransform, 584
InverseGammaRegularized, 685
InverseLaplaceTransform, 594
InverseFunction, 224
InverseFunctions, 224
InverseJacobiCD, 224
InverseJacobiCN, 225
InverseJacobiCS, 225
InverseJacobiDC, 226
InverseJacobiDN, 226
InverseJacobiDS, 227
InverseJacobiNC, 227
InverseJacobiND, 228
InverseJacobiNS, 228
InverseJacobiSC, 229
InverseJacobiSD, 229
InverseJacobiSN, 230
InverseSeries, 230
InverseWeierstrassP, 230
Interval, 753, 756
$IterationLimit, 499

J

JacobiAmplitude, 231
Jacobian, 231
JacobianDeterminant, 605
JacobianMatrix, 606
JacobiCD, 231
JacobiCN, 231

JacobiCS, 232
JacobiDC, 233
JacobiDN, 234
JacobiDS, 235
JacobiNC, 236
JacobiND, 237
JacobiNS, 237
JacobiP, 238
JacobiSC, 240
JacobiSD, 241
JacobiSN, 241
JacobiSymbol, 242
JacobiZeta, 243
Join, 243
JordanForm, 244

K

KnownStandardDeviation, 679
KnownVariance, 676-678
Kurtosis, 660
KurtosisExcess, 660

L

Label, 247
LaguerreL, 247, 535
$Language, 500
LaplaceDistribution, 622
LaplaceTransform, 594
Laplacian, 608
Last, 248, 703
LatticeReduce, 249
LCM, 250
LeafCount, 250
Left, 53, **251**
LegendreP, 251, 253
LegendreQ, 252
LegendreType, 253
Length, 182, **255**, 306
LengthWhile, 637
LerchPhi, 255
Less (<), 256, 417
LessEqual (<=), 169, **257**, 490
LetterQ, 257
$Letters, 500
Level, 258, 290
Lighting, 258, 521, 569
LightSources, 258, 521, 581
Limit, 208, 209, **259**, 759
$Line, 500
Line, 260, 512, 519, 527, 558, 563
LinearProgramming, 260
LinearSolve, 261
LineBreak, 261

LineForm, 261
$Linked, 500
$LinkSupported, 501
List ({...}), 148, **262**,
Listable, 262, 280
ListContourPlot, 263, 516
ListDensityPlot, 265, 516
ListIntegrate, 756
ListPlay, 266
ListPlot, 139, 249, **267**, 425, 517, 543-
      550, 666, 671-673, 766, 767
ListPlot3D, 268, 522, 542, 567, 569
ListQ, 269
Literal, 269, 296
LocationReport, 649
Locked, 269
Log, 270
LogGamma, 270
LogicalExpand, 271
LogisticDistribution, 626
LogIntegral, 274
LogNormalDistribution, 624
LogSeriesDistribution, 666
LowerCaseQ, 275

M

$MachineEpsilon, 501
$MachineID, 501
MachineID, 276
$MachineName, 501
MachineName, 276
MachineNumberQ, 276
$MachinePrecision, 501
$MachineType, 502
MainSolve, 277
MakeRules, 278
MantissaExponent, 278
Map (/@), 165, 219, **279**, 353, 354, 407,
      528, 566, 703
MapAll (//@), 281
MapAt, 281
MapIndexed, 282
MapThread, 282
MatchBox, 283
MatchLocalNameQ, 283
MatchLocalNames, 283
MatchQ, 283
MatrixExp, 284
MatrixForm, 242, 245, **285**, 287, 408,
      409, 427, 477, 606, 631- 634, 635, 636
MatrixPower, 286
MatrixQ, 287
Max, 288, 650

MaxBend, 288, 517, 518
MaxIterations, 289
$MaxMachineNumber, 502
MaxMemoryUsed, 289
$MaxNumber, 503
MaxRecursion, 289
MaxSteps, 289
$$Media, 503
Mean, 643, 657-660, 662-665, 667, 668, 670
MeanCI, 610
MeanDeviation, 653
MeanDifferenceCI, 611
MeanDifferenceTest, 678
MeanTest, 675
Median, 644, 659
MedianDeviation, 654
MemberQ, 290
MemoryConstrained, 291
MemoryInUse, 291
Mesh, 292, 411, 516, 522, 524, 540, 541, 569, 576, 582
MeshRange, 292, 522, 524
MeshStyle, 292, 516, 523, 524, 569, 583
Message, 293
$MessageList, 503
MessageList, 293
MessageName (::), 43, **295**,
$MessagePrePrint, 503
$Messages, 503
Messages, 295
MetaCharacters, 296
Method, 278, **296**, 435, 761
Min, 297, 541, 650
MiniMaxApproximation, 721, 723-729
$MinMachineNumber, 503
$MinNumber, 504
Minors, 297
MinRecursion, 298
Minus (-), 298
MixedMode, 743
Mod, 298
Mode, 299, 644, 657, 658
Modular, 299
Module, 204, **299**, 460, 530, 568
$ModuleNumber, 504
Modulus, 151, 154, **300**
MoebiusMu, 280, **300**
MovingAverage, 704
MultiDimensional, 301
Multinomial, 302
Multiplicity, 302

N

N, 3, 38, 249, **303**, 345, 770
NameQ, 303
Names, 182, **304**
NaN, 737
NBernoulliB, 306
ND, 765
NDSolve, 306
Needs, 312
Negative, 312
NegativeBinomialDistribution, 668
Nest, 313, 478, 541, 549, 561
NestList, 314
$NewMessage, 504
$NewSymbol, 504
NewtonCotesError, 770
NewtonCotesWeights, 767
NFourierCosSeriesCoefficient, 594
NFourierExpSeries, 590
NFourierExpSeriesCoefficient, 593
NFourierSinSeriesCoefficient, 593
NFourierTransform, 590
NFourierTrigSeries, 593
NIntegrate, 302, **315**, 478, 748, 749
NLimit, 758
NonAssociative, 316
NonCommutativeMultiply (**), 316
NonConstants, 316
None, 317, 514
NonNegative, 317
NoPrint, 695-700, 702
Normal, 317, 595
NormalDistribution, 707
NormalPValue, 681
Not (!), 204, **319**
$Notebooks, 505
NProduct, 319
NProductExtraFactors, 320
NProductFactors, 320
NProtectedAll, 320
NProtectedFirst, 320
NProtectedRest, 320
NRoots, 193, 239, **320**, 474
NSolve, 321
NSum, 322
NSumExtraTerms, 323
NSumTerms, 323
Null, 323, 407
NullRecords, 324
NullSpace, 324
NullWords, 325
Number, 325, 384
$NumberBits, 505

NumberForm, 325
NumberFormat, 325
NumberPadding, 325
NumberPoint, 325
NumberQ, 326
NumberSeparator, 326
NumberSigns, 326
Numerator, 326, 470
NValues, 326

O

O, 62, 272, 318, **327**, 413-415
OblateSpherical, 599
OddQ, 327, 527, 528, 637
$Off, 505
Off, 328
On, 328
OneIdentity, 329
Open, 768, 771
OpenAppend, 329
OpenRead, 329, 432
OpenTemporary, 330
OpenWrite, 330
Operate, 330
$OperatingSystem, 505
Optional (:), 330
OptionQ, 331
Options, 331, 418
Or (||), 332, 576
Order, 333
OrderedQ, 334
Orderless, 334
Out (%), 334
Outer, 334
$Output, 505
OutputControl, 695-702
OutputForm, 335
$OutputForms, 505
OutputList, 696, 697
OutputStream, 336
Overflow, 336
Overlaps, 336
OwnValues, 336

P

$Packages, 506
PaddedForm, 337
Pade, 595
PageHeight, 337
PageWidth, 337
ParabolicCylindrical, 599
Paraboloidal, 599

ParameterRanges, 602
Parameters, 602
ParameterTable, 690, 692, 693, **700**, 704
ParametricPlot, 309-311, **338**, 517, 552-554 , 731
ParametricPlot3D, 339, 523, 570, 572-574, 752
$$ParenForm, 506
ParentDirectory, 341
Part ([[...]]), 91, 113, 162, 245, 246, 273, 308, **341**, 375, 376, 408, 409, 427, 468, 657, 660, 707, 709, 710, 712, 746-751, 769
Partition, 127, 131, **342**, 561, 566
PartitionsP, 342
PartitionsQ, 343
$Path, 506
$PathnameSeparator, 506
Pattern (:), 343
PatternTest (?), 344
Pause, 344
PDF, 671, 707, 709, 710, 712
PearsonSkewness1, 657
PearsonSkewness2, 658
Permutations, 344
Pi, 3, 303, **344**
$PipeSupported, 506
Pivoting, 345
Plain, 345
Play, 345
PlayRange, 346
Plot, 22, 121, 124, 127, 128, 129, 141, 146, 147, 160, 161, 165, 176, 180, 189, 193, 195, 200, 218, 220, 231, 233, 234, 236, 240, 256, 275, 294, 304, 307, 308, 316, 318, 331, **347**, 355, 356, 358, 387, 410, 422, 425, 428, 430, 438, 458, 459, 462, 478, 518, 554-557, 559, 560, 587, 589, 591, 593, 596, 597, 614, 615, 617-631, 684, 686, 688, 691, 708, 709, 711, 713, 715-721, 726, 731, 732, 734
PlotColor, 348
PlotDivision, 348, 517, 518
PlotFlag, 728
PlotJoined, 348, 517, 543-546, 548, 766, 767
PlotLabel, 348, 514, 521, 574, 582
PlotPoints, 123, 124, 126, 131, 136, 137, 178, 196, 231, 232, 235-238, 241-243, 248, 254, 271, **349**, 397, 398, 411, 515-518, 523, 524, 541, 576, 578, 582, 583

PlotRange, 220, 308, 316, 318, **349**, 430, 514, 521, 532, 533, 549, 550, 559, 569, 576, 579, 582, 591, 596, 597, 618-631, 668, 708
PlotRegion, 349, 514, 521
PlotStyle, 240, 248, 318, **349**, 356, 358, 387, 462, 517m 518, 548, 557, 560, 587, 589, 591, 596, 597, 615, 617-631, 708, 709, 711, 713, 716, 720, 721, 726, 731, 732, 734
Plot3D, 97, 123, 178, 235, 236, 243, 254, 271, **350**, 397, 398, 422, 523, 575, 576, 578, 581-583
Plot3Matrix, 350
Plus (+), 173, **351**, 464
Pochhammer, 351
Point, 165, 219, **352**, 354, 512, 519, 528, 558, 564
PointForm, 353
PointSize, 165, 219, **353**, 528, 558, 564, 666, 668, 671-673, 691
PoissonDistribution, 669, 674
PolyGamma, 354
Polygon, 356, 512, 519, 529, 565
PolygonIntersections, 357, 521
PolyLog, 216, **357**
PolynomialDivision, 358
PolynomialFit, 771
PolynomialGCD, 359
PolynomialLCM, 359
PolynomialMod, 360
PolynomialQ, 361
PolynomialQuotient, 361
PolynomialRemainder, 362
Position, 362
Positive, 363
$Post, 506
Postfix, 354
PostScript, 364, 512
Power (^), 173, 279, **364**
PowerExpand, 365
PowerMod, 366
$Pre, 506
PrecedenceForm, 366
Precision, 366, 419
PrecisionGoal, 367
PreDecrement (--), 367
PredictedResponse, 701
Prefix, 368
PreIncrement (++), 368, 530, 568
Prepend, 369
PrependTo, 370
$PrePrint, 506

$PreRead, 506
Prime, 162, 244, **370**, 421
PrimePi, 371
PrimeQ, 371, 412
Print, 44, 108, 169, 204, 299, **372**, 407, 460, 490
PrintFlag, 727
PrintForm, 372
$PrintForms, 507
$PrintLiteral, 507
Product, 372
ProlateSpheroidal, 600
Prolog, 373, 514, 521, 550, 558, 666, 668, 671-673, 691, 767
PromptForm, 373
Protect, 373
Protected, 373
PseudoInverse, 373
Put (>>), 374, 568
PutAppend (>>>), 374

Q
Quantile, 647, 654, 669, 670
QuantileForm, 638
QuartileDeviation, 654
Quartiles, 649
QuartileSkewness, 659
QRDecomposition, 375
Quartics, 376
Quit, 377
Quotient, 378

R
Random, 213, **379**, 460, 530, 541, 549, 718
Range, 379, 407
RangeCounts, 640
RangeLists, 641
Raster, 380, 512, 530
RasterArray, 381, 512
$RasterFunction, 507
Rational, 381
RationalInterpolation, 714, 717-720
Rationalize, 382
Raw, 382
RawMedium, 382
RayleighDistribution, 628
Re, 243, **382**, 397, 462, 549
Read, 383, 432
ReadList, 383
ReadProtected, 385
Real, 7, 379, **385**, 718

RealDigits, 385, 544
RealInterval, 386
Record, 386
RecordLists, 386
RecordSeparators, 386
Rectangle, 387, 512, 531
$RecursionLimit, 507
Reduce, 388
Regress, 689, 693-702
Release, 389
ReleaseHold, 190, 191, **389**, 468
$ReleaseNumber, 507
$Remote, 508
Remove, 389
Removed, 390
RenameDirectory, 390
RenameFile, 390
RenderAll, 391, 521
Repeated (..), 391
RepeatedNull (...), 391
RepeatedString, 391
Replace, 391
ReplaceAll (/.), 6, 163, 273, 307-311,
    392, 403, 727
ReplaceHeldPart, 393
ReplacePart, 393
ReplaceRepeated (//.), 394
ResetDirectory, 394
ResetMedium, 394
Residue, 394
Rest, 395
Resultant, 395
Resultant2, 396
Return, 97, 99, 100, **396**, 530, 568
Reverse, 396
RGBColor, 396
RiemannSiegelTheta, 396
RiemannSiegelZ, 398
Right, 53, **399**
RootMeanSquare, 646
Roots, 377, **399**
RotateLabel, 400, 514
RotateLeft, 401
RotateRight, 401
Round, 401
RoundingRule, 743
Row, 401
RowJoin, 634
RowReduce, 401
RSquared, 690, 692-696, **701**, 703
Rule (->), 6, 37, 163, 253, **402**, 434, 435,
    727
RuleCondition, 402

RuleDelayed (:>), 99, 100, **402**
RuleForm, 404
RuleTable, 404
Run, 404
RungeKuttaOrderConditions, 734
RunThrough, 404

S
SameQ (===), 405
SameTest, 405
SampleDepth, 405
SampledSoundFunction, 405
SampledSoundList, 406
SampleRange, 650
SampleRate, 406
Save, 406
ScalarTripleProduct, 607
Scale, 760, **764**
Scaled, 406
Scan, 406
SchurDecomposition, 407
ScientificForm, 409
Sec, 410
Sech, 410
Second, 411
SeedRandom, 411
Select, 412
Sequence, 412
SequenceForm, 412
SequenceLimit, 413, 761
Series, 413-415, 595
SeriesCoefficient, 414
SeriesData, 414
$SessionID, 508
SessionTime, 415
Set (=), 403, **415**
SetAccuracy, 416
SetArithmetic, 738, 740-745
SetAttributes, 263, **416**
SetCoordinates, 602, 606
SetDelayed (:=), 7, 403, **417**
SetDirectory, 417
SetEpsilon, 755
SetFileDate, 417
SetOptions, 418, 574
SetPrecision, 419
SetStreamPosition, 419, 432
Shading, 123, 126, 131, 178, 196, 235,
    236, 241, 243, 254, 271, 397, 398, **420**,
    422, 521, 576, 583
Shallow, 420
ShapeReport, 661
Share, 420

Short, 139, 412, **420**, 431, 549
Show, 127, 131, 165, 219, 312, 353, 354, 357, 381, 387, 388, **421**, 525-534, 536-540, 547, 550, 551, 553, 558, 559, 561, 562-565, 569, 570, 572, 573, 577, 578, 593, 596, 597, 691, 731, 732, 734
show file (!!), 383
ShowAnimation, 422
Sign, 422, 622, 623, 629
Signature, 423
SignificanceLevel, 676, 678, 679
SignPadding, 423
Simplify, 113, 189, 201, 246, 247, 251, 252, 314, 315, **423**, 595, 597
Sin, 28, 249, 263, 280, **424**, 478
SingularityDepth, 425
SingularValues, 426
Sinh, 427
SinhIntegral, 428
SinIntegral, 429, 468
SixJSymbol, 430
Skeleton (<<...>>), 412, 421, **430**
Skewness, 656
Skip, 431
Slot (#), 433
SlotSequence (##), 433
Socket, 433
SolutionOf, 433
Solve, 115, 202, 273, 291, **433**, 472, 474
SolveAlways, 435
Sort, 244, 435
Sound, 436
$SoundDisplay, 508
$SoundDisplayFunction, 509
Space, 436
SpaceForm, 436
SpellingCorrection, 436
Spherical, 601, 603-606
SphericalHarmonicY, 436, 462
SphericalRegion, 437, 521, 576
SpinShow, 437
Splice, 437
Sqrt, 12, 303, **437**, 453
Stack, 438
StackBegin, 438
StackComplete, 439
StackInhibit, 439
StandardDeviation, 652, 657-660, 664
StandardDeviationMLE, 652
StandardErrorOfSampleMean, 653
StartingStepSize, 439
StartProcess, 439
StirlingS1, 439

StirlingS2, 440
StreamPosition, 432, **440**
Streams, 440
String, 440
StringBreak, 440
StringByteCount, 441
$StringConversion, 509
StringConversion, 441
StringDrop, 441
StringForm, 442
StringInsert, 442
StringJoin (<>), 443
StringLength, 443
StringMatchQ, 444
$StringOrder, 509
StringPosition, 444
StringQ, 445
StringReplace, 445
StringReverse, 445
StringSkeleton, 445
StringTake, 445
StringToStream, 446
Stub, 446
StudentTDistribution, 711
StudentTPValue, 682
Subscript, 447
Subscripted, 447
Subtract (-), 447
SubtractFrom (-=), 448
SubValues, 448
Sum, 449, 657, 660, 746, 747-751, 769
Superscript, 449
$SuppressInputFormHeads, 509
SurfaceColor, 449
SurfaceGraphics, 131, 196, 235, 236, 350, **450**,
Switch, 450
Symbol, 451
Syntax, 451
$SyntaxHandler, 510
SyntaxLength, 451
SyntaxQ, 452
$System, 510
SystemStub, 452

T

Tab, 453
Table, 122, 127, 131, 139, 162, 213, 239, 242, 244, 247, 249, 251, 253, 306, 328, 355, 356, 358, 371, 379, 381, 384, 399, 412, 421, 425, 429, 431, **453**, 527, 528, 530, 532, 533, 542, 548, 549, 561, 568, 592, 615-617, 666, 667, 670, 671, 673, 707-710, 712, 718, 720, 731, 749, 757, 766, 767, 770, 772
TableAlignments, 454
TableDepth, 454
TableDirections, 454
TableForm, 20, 306, 371, 399, 429, **454**, 456, 474, 770
TableHeadings, 455
TableSpacing, 456
TagSet (/:...=), 456
TagSetDelayed (/:...:=), 457
TagUnset (/:...=.), 457
Take, 457
TakeWhile, 636
Tan, 458
Tanh, 458
TargetFunctions, 459
Temporary, 460
$TemporaryPrefix, 510
TensorRank, 460
Terms, 761, 763, **764**, 765
TeXForm, 461
Text, 461, 512, 519, 531, 532
TextForm, 462
TextRendering, 462
Thickness, 462, 558, 563, 709
Thread, 463
ThreeJSymbol, 463
Through, 464
$Throw, 510
Throw, 464
Ticks, 127, **465**, 514, 522, 550, 553, 582
TimeConstrained, 465
Times (*), 465
TimesBy (*=), 466
$TimeUnit, 510
TimeUsed, 467
TimeZone, 468
Timing, 468
ToASCII, 469
ToCharacterCode, 469
ToColor, 469
ToDate, 469
ToExpression, 469
Together, 403, 424, **470**

ToHeldExpression, 470
TokenWords, 471
Tolerance, 471
ToLowerCase, 471
TooBig, 176, 294, **471**
Top, 471
Toroidal, 601
ToRules, 471
ToString, 472
TotalHeight, 472
TotalWidth, 472
ToUpperCase, 473
Trace, 473
TraceAbove, 474
TraceAction, 474
TraceBackward, 475
TraceDepth, 475
TraceDialog, 475
TraceForward, 475
TraceInternal, 475
TraceLevel, 475
$TraceOff, 510
TraceOff, 475
$TraceOn, 510
TraceOn, 476
TraceOriginal, 476
$TracePattern, 511
$TracePostAction, 511
$TracePreAction, 511
TracePrint, 476
TraceScan, 476
Transpose, 376, 408, 409, 427, **477**
Trapezoidal, 477
TreeForm, 250, **477**
Trig, 142, 143, 145, 151, 155, **479**
TrimmedMean, 646
True, 142, 143, 145, 151, 153, 155, 259, 268, **479**, 514, 636
TrueQ, 480
TwoSided, 677, 681-683
Type, 768, **771**

U

UnAlias, 481
Underflow, 481
Unequal (!=), 481
Unevaluated, 481
UniformDistribution, 628
Uninstall, 482
Union, 483
Unique, 483
Unprotect, 483
UnsameQ (=!=), 483

$Unset, 511
Unset (=.), 484
Update, 484
UpperCaseQ, 484
UpSet (^=), 485
UpSetDelayed (^:=), 485
UpValues, 485
$Urgent, 511
Using, 485

V
ValueForm, 486
ValueList, 486
ValueQ, 486
ValueTable, 486
Variables, 486
Variance, 651, 662-666, 669, 670
VarianceCI, 612
VarianceMLE, 651
VarianceOfSampleMean, 652
VarianceRatioCI, 612
VarianceRatioTest, 680
VarianceTest, 679
VectorQ, 487
VerifyConvergence, 488
VerifySolutions, 488
$Version, 511
$VersionNumber, 511
VerticalForm, 488
ViewCenter, 488, 522, 576
ViewPoint, 488, 522, 573, 580, 582
ViewVertical, 488, 522, 569

W
WeibullDistribution, 629
Weights, 696
WeierstrassP, 489
WeierstrassPPrime, 489
Which, 489
While, 490, 530, 568
With, 490
Word, 491
WordSearch, 491
WordSeparators, 491
WorkingPrecision, 491, 760, 764, 765
Write, 492
WriteString, 492
WynnDegree, 492, 761

X
Xor, 493

Z
ZeroLimit,
ZeroTest, 494
Zeta, 494